T0322010

Transfer Learning

Transfer learning deals with how systems can quickly adapt themselves to new situations, new tasks and new environments. It gives machine learning systems the ability to leverage auxiliary data and models to help solve target problems when there is only a small amount of data available in the target domain. This makes such systems more reliable and robust, keeping the machine learning model faced with unforeseeable changes from deviating too much from expected performance. At an enterprise level, transfer learning allows knowledge to be reused so experience gained once can be repeatedly applied to the real world.

This self-contained, comprehensive reference text begins by describing the standard algorithms and then demonstrates how these are used in different transfer learning paradigms and applications. It offers a solid grounding for newcomers as well as new insights for seasoned researchers and developers.

QIANG YANG is the Head of AI at WeBank and a chair professor of computer science and engineering at Hong Kong University of Science and Technology. He is a fellow of the ACM, AAAI, IEEE, IAPR and AAAS, and has served on the AAAI Executive Council and as president of IJCAI. Awards include the 2004/2005 ACM KDDCUP Championship, the ACM SIGKDD Distinguished Service Award and AAAI Innovative AI Applications Award. His books include *Intelligent Planning, Crafting Your Research Future and Constraint-Based Design Recovery for Software Engineering.*

YU ZHANG is an associate professor in the Department of Computer Science and Engineering at Southern University of Science and Technology. He has published about sixty papers in top-tier AI and machine learning conferences and journals. He won the best paper awards at UAI 2010 and PAKDD 2019, and the best student paper award in the 2013 IEEE/WIC/ACM International Conference on Web Intelligence. He was awarded the Young National Distinguished Scholar in China.

WENYUAN DAI is the Founder and CEO of 4Paradigm Co., Ltd. He was a principal architect and senior scientist in Baidu, helping to develop one of China's largest machine learning systems, and a principal scientist in Huawei Noah's Ark Lab. He has published numerous papers in ICML, NIPS, AAAI, KDD and other conferences, primarily on transfer learning and AutoML. He won the ACM-ICPC World Final 2005 and the PKDD best student paper award in 2007, and in 2017 was named *MIT Technology Review* Innovators under 35 in China and Fortune 40 under 40 in China.

SINNO JIALIN PAN is Provost's Chair Associate Professor in the School of Computer Science and Engineering at Nanyang Technological University, Singapore and was formerly Lab Head of Text Analytics with the Data Analytics Department, Institute for Infocomm Research, Singapore. He was named AI 10 to Watch by *IEEE Intelligent Systems* in 2018.

Transfer Learning

QIANG YANG
Hong Kong University of Science and Technology

YU ZHANG
Southern University of Science and Technology

WENYUAN DAI
4Paradigm Co., Ltd.

SINNO JIALIN PAN
Nanyang Technological University

CAMBRIDGE
UNIVERSITY PRESS

CAMBRIDGE
UNIVERSITY PRESS

University Printing House, Cambridge CB2 8BS, United Kingdom

One Liberty Plaza, 20th Floor, New York, NY 10006, USA

477 Williamstown Road, Port Melbourne, VIC 3207, Australia

314–321, 3rd Floor, Plot 3, Splendor Forum, Jasola District Centre,
New Delhi – 110025, India

79 Anson Road, #06–04/06, Singapore 079906

Cambridge University Press is part of the University of Cambridge.

It furthers the University's mission by disseminating knowledge in the pursuit of
education, learning, and research at the highest international levels of excellence.

www.cambridge.org
Information on this title: www.cambridge.org/9781107016903
DOI: 10.1017/9781139061773

First published 2020

A catalogue record for this publication is available from the British Library.

ISBN 978-1-107-01690-3 Hardback

Contents

Preface

This book is about the foundations, methods, techniques and applications of transfer learning. Transfer learning deals with how learning systems can quickly adapt themselves to new situations, new tasks and new environments. Transfer learning is a particularly important area of machine learning, which we can understand from several angles. First, the ability to learn from small data seems to be a particularly strong aspect of human intelligence. For example, we observe that babies learn from only a few examples and can quickly and effectively generalize from the few examples to concepts. This ability to learn from small data can be partly explained by the ability of humans to leverage and adapt the previous experience and pretrained models to help solve future target problems. Adaptation is an innate ability of intelligent beings and artificially intelligent agents should certainly be endowed with transfer learning ability.

Second, in machine learning practice, we observe that we are often surrounded with lots of small-sized data sets, which are often isolated and fragmented. Many organizations do not have the ability to collect a huge amount of big data due to a number of constraints that range from resource limitations to organizations interests, and to regulations and concerns for user privacy. This *small-data challenge* is a serious problem faced by many organizations applying AI technology to their problems. Transfer learning is a suitable solution for addressing this challenge because it can leverage many auxiliary data and external models, and adapt them to solve the target problems.

Third, transfer learning can make AI and machine learning systems more reliable and robust. It is often the case that, when building a machine learning model, one cannot foresee all future situations. In machine learning, this problem is often addressed using a technique known as regularization, which leaves room for future changes by limiting the complexity of the models. Transfer learning takes this approach further, by allowing the model to be complex while being prepared for changes when they actually come.

In addition, when facing unforeseeable changes and taking a learned model across domain boundaries, transfer learning still makes sure that the model performance does not deviate from the expected performance too much. In this way, transfer learning allows knowledge to be reused so experience gained once can be repeatedly applied to the real world. From a software system's perspective, if a system is capable of adapting itself via transfer learning in new domains, it is said to be more robust and more reliable when the external environment changes. Such systems are often preferred in engineering practice.

If we continuously apply transfer learning in our machine learning practice, we can obtain a lifelong machine learning system that can draw knowledge from a succession of problem-solving experience, both in a long period of time and from a large variety of tasks. Transfer learning endows an intelligent system with the lifelong learning ability.

Last, but not least, a transfer learning system can be the backbone of a sound business model in which user privacy is taken into serious consideration, such that a pretrained model can be downloaded and adapted at the edge of a computer network without leaking user data accumulated at the edge or from the cloud. By moving the model one way from a server to a client, the privacy at the client side is effectively protected. In addition, by carefully structuring the transfer learning algorithms, private user information on the cloud side can also be protected.

Like AI in general and machine learning in particular, the concept of transfer learning has gone through decades of evolution. From AI's early years, researchers have considered the ability to transfer one's knowledge as one of the fundamental cornerstones of intelligence. Transfer learning is also given different names and explored under different guises, including learning by analogy, case-based reasoning, knowledge reuse and reengineering, lifelong machine learning, never-ending learning and domain adaption, to name a few. Outside of AI and Computer Science, the concept of transfer learning has also been invented under different terms. In the fields of educational theory and learning psychology, for example, the concept of *transfer of learning* has been an important subject in modeling what constitutes effective learning and teaching for educators; it is believed that the best teaching enables the student to learn "how to learn" and adapt the learned knowledge in future situations. Despite different names, their spirits are all similar: to be able to leverage one's past experience to help make more effective decisions in the future.

The study of transfer learning involves many areas of study in science and engineering, including AI, algorithmic theories, probability and statistics, to name a few. The field is also undergoing rapid changes as interests in AI grow, and many new areas contribute to the field. As the first book of its kind in the area, we hope to use it as a tool to help educate the newcomers of machine learning research and application field, as well as a reference book for seasoned machine learning researchers and application developers to use.

The book is partitioned into two parts. Part I presents the foundations of transfer learning. Chapter 1 gives an overview and introduction to transfer learning. Chapters 2–14 introduce various theoretical and algorithmic aspects of transfer learning. Part II, which includes Chapters 15–22, covers many application fields of transfer learning. We give concluding remarks in Chapter 23.

The book is an accumulation of hard research work by a group of researchers that spans over a decade, mainly consisting of Professor Qiang Yang's current and former graduate students, postdoctoral researchers and research associates. We have assigned each chapter to one or more students, and then the four main editors either wrote other chapters or went in depth in each chapter to help refine the content, or did both.

The following is a list of these authors.

- Chapter 1: Sinno Jialin Pan and Qiang Yang
- Chapter 2: Xiang Zhang
- Chapter 3: Xu Geng
- Chapter 4: Xueyang Wu
- Chapter 5: Han Tian
- Chapter 6: Ying Wei
- Chapter 7: Yinghua Zhang
- Chapter 8: Bo Liu
- Chapter 9: Yu Zhang
- Chapter 10: Yu Zhang
- Chapter 11: Ben Tan
- Chapter 12: Yu Zhang and Ying Wei
- Chapter 13: Jinliang Deng
- Chapter 14: Lianghao Li and Qiang Yang
- Chapter 15: Xiawei Guo, Yuqiang Chen, Weiwei Tu, and Wenyuan Dai
- Chapter 16: Yinghua Zhang and Weiyan Wang
- Chapter 17: Wenyi Xiao and Zheng Li
- Chapter 18: Kaixiang Mo
- Chapter 19: Weike Pan and Guangneng Hu
- Chapter 20: Qian Xu, Bo Liu and Qiang Yang
- Chapter 21: Vincent W. Zheng and Hao Hu
- Chapter 22: Leye Wang and Yexin Li

Finally, we wish to thank the managerial work of Yutao Deng, who helped keep the schedules and manage team works. To all, our sincere thanks! Without their tremendous effort, the book would have been impossible to complete.

We the editors wish to also thank our colleagues, organizations and collaborators over the years. We thank the support of Hong Kong University of Science and Technology, Hong Kong CERG Fund, Hong Kong Innovation and Technology Fund, the 4Paradigm Corp., Nanyang Technological University Singapore, Webank and many others for their generous support.

Finally, we wish to acknowledge the support of our families, whose patience and encouragement allowed us to finally complete the book.

PART I

FOUNDATIONS OF TRANSFER LEARNING

1
Introduction

1.1   AI, Machine Learning and Transfer Learning

AI was a vision initiated by Alan Turing when he asked the famous question: "Can machines think?" This question has motivated generations of researchers to explore ways to make machines behave intelligently. Throughout recent history, AI has experienced several ups and downs, much of which evolve around the central question of how machines can acquire knowledge from the outside world.

Attempts to make machines think like humans have gone a long way, from force-feeding rule-like knowledge bases to machine learning from data. Machine learning has thus grown from an obscure discipline to a major industrial and societal force in automating decisions that range from online commerce and advertising to education and health care. Machine learning is becoming a general enabling technology for the world due to its strong ability to endow machines with knowledge by letting them learn and adapt through labeled and unlabeled data. Machine learning produces prediction models from data, thus often requiring well-defined data as "teachers" to help tune statistical models. This ability in making accurate predictions of future events are based on observations and understanding of the task domains. The data samples in the training examples are often "labeled," which means that observations and outcomes of predictions in the training data are coupled and correlated. These examples are then used as "teachers" by a machine learning algorithm to "train" a model that can be applied to new data.

One can find many illustrative examples of machine learning in the real world. One example is in the area of face recognition in computer-based image analysis. Suppose that we have obtained a large pool of photos taken indoors. A machine learning system can then use these data to train a model that reports whether a new photo corresponds to a person appearing in the pool. An application of this model would be a gate security system for a building, where a task would be to ascertain whether a visitor is an employee in the organization.

Even though a machine learning model can be made to be of high quality, it can also make mistakes, especially when the model is applied to different scenarios from its training environments. For example, if a new photo is taken from an outdoor environment with different light intensities and levels of noise such as shadows, sunlight from different angels and occlusion by passersby, the recognition capability of the system may dramatically drop. This is because the model trained by the machine learning system is applied to a "different" scenario. This drop in performance shows that models can be outdated and needs updating when new situations occur. It is this need to update or **transfer** models from one scenario to another that lends importance to the topic of the book.

The need for transfer learning is not limited to image understanding. Another example is understanding Twitter text messages by natural language processing (NLP) techniques. Suppose we wish to classify Twitter messages into different user moods such as happy or sad by its content. When one model is built using a collection of Twitter messages and then applied to new data, the performance drops quite dramatically as a different community of people will very likely express their opinions differently. This happens when we have teenagers in one group and grown-ups in another.

As the previous examples demonstrate, a major challenge in practicing machine learning in many applications is that models do not work well in new task domains. The reason why they do not work well may be due to one of several reasons: lack of new training data due to the small data challenge, changes of circumstances and changes of tasks. For example, in a new situation, high-quality training data may be in short supply if not often impossible to obtain for model retraining, as in the case of medical diagnosis and medical imaging data. Machine learning models cannot do well without sufficient training data. Obtaining and labeling new data often takes much effort and resources in a new application domain, which is a major obstacle in realizing AI in the real world. Having well-designed AI systems without the needed training data is like having a sports car without an energy.

This discussion highlights a major roadblock in populating machine learning to the practical world: it would be impossible to collect large quantities of data in every domain before applying machine learning. Here we summarize some of the reasons to develop such a transfer learning methodology:

1) *Many applications only have small data*: the current success of machine learning relies on the availability of a large amount of labeled data. However, high-quality labeled data are often in short supply. Traditional machine learning methods often cannot generalize well to new scenarios, a phenomenon known as overfitting, and fail in many such cases.

2) *Machine learning models need to be robust*: traditional machine learning often makes an assumption that both the training and test data are drawn from the same distribution. However, this assumption is too strong to hold in many

practical scenarios. In many cases, the distribution varies according to time and space, and varies among situations, so we may never have access to new training data to go with the same test distribution. In situations that differ from the training data, the trained models need adaptation before they can be used.

3) *Personalization and specialization are important issues:* it is critical and profitable to offer personalized service for every user according to individual tastes and demands. In many real world applications, we can only collect very little personal data from an individual user. As a result, traditional machine learning methods suffer from the cold start problems when we try to adapt a general model to a specific situation.

4) *User privacy and data security are important issues:* often in our applications we must work with other organizations by leveraging multiple data sets. Often these data sets have different owners and cannot be revealed to each other for privacy or security concerns. When building a model together, it would be desirable for us to extract the "essence" of each data set and adapt them in building a new model. For example, if we can adapt a general model at the "edge" of a network of devices, then the data stored on the device need not to be uploaded to enhance the general model; thus, privacy of the edge device can be ensured.

These objectives for intelligent systems motivated the development of transfer learning. In a nutshell, *transfer learning* refers to the machine learning paradigm in which an algorithm extracts knowledge from one or more application scenarios to help boost the learning performance in a target scenario. Compared to traditional machine learning, which requires large amounts of well-defined training data as the input, transfer learning can be understood as a new learning paradigm, which the rest of the book will cover in detail. Transfer learning is also a motivation to solve the so-called data sparsity and cold start problems in many large-scale and online applications (e.g., labeled user rating data in online recommendation systems may be too few to allow these online systems to build a high-quality recommendation system).

Transfer learning can help promote AI in less-developed application areas, as well as less technically developed geographical areas, even when not much labeled data is available in such areas. For example, suppose we wish to build a book recommendation system in a new online shopping application. Suppose that the book domain is so new that we do not have many transactions recorded in this domain. If we follow the supervised learning methodology in building a prediction model in which we use the insufficient training data in the new domain, we cannot have a credible prediction model on users' next purchase. However, with transfer learning, one can look to a related, well-developed but different domain for help, such as an existing movie recommendation domain. Exploiting transfer learning techniques, one can find the similarity and differences between the book and the movie domains. For example, some authors also turn their books into movies, and movies and books can attract similar user groups. Noticing these similarities can allow one to focus on adapting the new parts for the book-recommendation task, which allows one to further exploit the underlying similarities between the data sets. Then, book domain classification and user preference learning models can be adapted from those of the movie domain.

Based on the transfer learning methodologies, once we obtain a well-developed model in one domain, we can bring this model to benefit other similar domains. Hence, having an accurate "distance" measure between any task domains is necessary in developing a sound transfer learning methodology. If the distance between two domains is large, then we may not wish to apply transfer learning as the learning might turn out to produce a negative effect. On the other hand, if two domains are "close by," transfer learning can be fruitfully applied.

In machine learning, the distance between domains can often be measured in terms of the features that are used to describe the data. In image analysis, features can be pixels or patches in an image pattern, such as the color or shape. In NLP, features can be words or phrases. Once we know that two domains are close to each other, we can ensure that AI models can be propagated from the well-developed domains to less-developed domains, making the application of AI less data dependent. And this can be a good sign for successful transfer learning applications.

Being able to transfer knowledge from one domain to another allows machine learning systems to extend their range of applicability beyond their original creation. This generalization ability helps make AI more accessible and more robust in many areas where AI talents or resources such as computing power, data and hardware might be scarce. In a way, transfer learning allows the promotion of AI as a more inclusive technology that serves everyone.

To give an intuitive example, we can use an analogy to highlight the key insights behind transfer learning. Consider driving in different countries in the world. In the USA and China, for example, the driver's seat is on the left of the car and drives on the right side of the road. In Britain, the driver sits on the right side of the car, and drives on the left side of the road. For a traveler who is used to driving in the USA to travel to drive in Britain, it is particularly hard to switch. Transfer learning, however, tells us to find the invariant in the two driving domains that is a common feature. On a closer observation, one can find that no matter where one drives, the driver's distance to the center of the road is the closest. Or, conversely, the driver sits farthest from the side of the road. This fact allows human drivers to smoothly "transfer" from one country to another. Thus, the insight behind transfer learning is to find the "invariant" between domains and tasks.

Transfer learning has been studied under different terminologies in AI, such as knowledge reuse and CBR, learning by analogy, domain adaptation, pre-training, fine-tuning, and so on. In the fields of education and learning psychology, transfer of learning has a similar notion as transfer learning in machine learning. In particular, transfer of learning refers to the process in which past experience acquired from previous source tasks can be used to influence future learning and performance in a target situation (Thorndike and S. Woodworth, 1901). Transfer of learning in the field of education shares a common goal as transfer learning in machine learning in that they both address the process of learning in one context and applying the learning in another. In both areas, the learned knowledge or model is taken to a future target task for use after some adaptation. When one delves into the literature of education theory and learning psychology (Ellis, 1965; Pugh and Bergin, 2006; Schunk, 1965; Cree and Macaulay, 2000), one can find that, despite the fact that transfer learning in machine learning aims to endow machines with the ability to adapt and transfer of learning in education tries to study how humans adapt in education, the processes or algorithms of transfer are similar.

A final note on the benefit of transfer learning is in simulation technology. Often in complex tasks, such as robotics and drug design, for example, it is too expensive to engage real world experiments. In robotics, a mobile robot or an autonomous vehicle needs to collect sufficient training data. For example, there may be many ways in which a car is involved in a car crash but to create car crashes is far too expensive in real life. Instead, researchers often build sophisticated simulators such that a trained model taught in the simulator environment is applied to the real world after adaptation via transfer learning. The transfer learning step is needed to account for many future situations that are not seen in the simulated environment and adapt the simulated prediction models, such as obstacle avoidance models in autonomous cars, to unforeseeable future situations.

1.2 Transfer Learning: A Definition

To start with, we define what "domain," "task" and "transfer learning" mean by following the notations introduced by Pan and Yang (2010). A *domain* $\mathbb{D}$ consists of two components: a feature space $\mathcal{X}$ and a marginal probability distribution $\mathbb{P}^X$, where each input instance $\mathbf{x} \in \mathcal{X}$. In general, if two domains are different, then they may have different feature spaces or different marginal probability distributions. Given a specific domain, $\mathbb{D} = \{\mathcal{X}, \mathbb{P}^X\}$, a *task* $\mathbb{T}$ consists of two components: a label space $\mathcal{Y}$ and a function $f(\cdot)$ (denoted by $\mathbb{T} = \{\mathcal{Y}, f(\cdot)\}$). The function $f(\cdot)$ is a predictive function that can be used to make predictions on unseen instances $\{\mathbf{x}^*\}$s. From a probabilistic viewpoint, $f(\mathbf{x})$ can be written as $P(y|\mathbf{x})$. In classification, labels can be binary, that is, $\mathcal{Y} = \{-1, +1\}$, or discrete values, that is, multiple classes. In regression, labels are of continuous values.

For simplicity, we now focus on the case where there are one source domain $\mathbb{D}_s$ and one target domain $\mathbb{D}_t$. The two-domain scenario is by far the most popular of the research works in the literature. In particular, we denote by $\mathcal{D}_s = \{(\mathbf{x}_{s_i}, y_{s_i})\}_{i=1}^{n_s}$ the *source domain labeled data*, where $\mathbf{x}_{s_i} \in \mathcal{X}_s$ is the data instance and $y_{s_i} \in \mathcal{Y}_s$ is the corresponding class label. Similarly, we denote by $\mathcal{D}_t = \{(\mathbf{x}_{t_i}, y_{t_i})\}_{i=1}^{n_t}$ the target domain labeled data, where the input $\mathbf{x}_{t_i}$ is in $\mathcal{X}_t$ and $y_{t_i} \in \mathcal{Y}_t$ is the corresponding

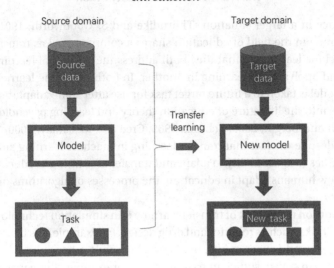

Figure 1.1 An illustration of a transfer learning process

output. In most cases, $0 \le n_t \ll n_s$. Based on these notations, transfer learning can be defined as follows (Pan and Yang, 2010).

Definition 1.1 (transfer learning)   Given a source domain $\mathbb{D}_s$ and learning task $\mathbb{T}_s$, a target domain $\mathbb{D}_t$ and learning task $\mathbb{T}_t$, *transfer learning* aims to help improve the learning of the target predictive function $f_t(\cdot)$ for the target domain using the knowledge in $\mathbb{D}_s$ and $\mathbb{T}_s$, where $\mathbb{D}_s \ne \mathbb{D}_t$ or $\mathbb{T}_s \ne \mathbb{T}_t$.

A transfer learning process is illustrated in Figure 1.1. The process on the left corresponds to a traditional machine learning process. The process on the right corresponds to a transfer learning process. As we can see, transfer learning makes use of not only the data in the target task domain as input to the learning algorithm, but also any of the learning process in the source domain, including the training data, models and task description. This figure shows a key concept of transfer learning: it counters the lack of training data problem in the target domain with more knowledge gained from the source domain.

As a domain contains two components, $\mathbb{D} = \{\mathcal{X}, \mathbb{P}^X\}$, the condition $\mathbb{D}_s \ne \mathbb{D}_t$ implies that either $\mathcal{X}_s \ne \mathcal{X}_t$ or $\mathbb{P}^{X_s} \ne \mathbb{P}^{X_T}$. Similarly, as a task is defined as a pair of components $\mathbb{T} = \{\mathcal{Y}, \mathbb{P}^{Y|X}\}$, the condition $\mathbb{T}_s \ne \mathbb{T}_t$ implies that either $\mathcal{Y}_s \ne \mathcal{Y}_t$ or $\mathbb{P}^{Y_s|X_s} \ne \mathbb{P}^{Y_t|X_t}$. When the target domain and the source domain are the same, that is, $\mathbb{D}_s = \mathbb{D}_t$, and their learning tasks are the same, that is, $\mathbb{T}_s = \mathbb{T}_t$, the learning problem becomes a traditional machine learning problem.

Based on this definition, we can formulate different ways to categorize existing transfer learning studies into different settings. For instance, based on the homogeneity of the feature spaces and/or label spaces, we can categorize transfer learning into two settings: (1) homogeneous transfer learning and (2) heterogeneous transfer learning, whose definitions are described as follows (Pan, 2014).[1]

Definition 1.2 (homogeneous transfer learning)   Given a source domain $\mathbb{D}_s$ and a learning task $\mathbb{T}_s$, a target domain $\mathbb{D}_t$ and a learning task $\mathbb{T}_t$, *homogeneous transfer learning* aims to help improve the learning of the target predictive function $f_t(\cdot)$ for $\mathbb{D}_t$ using the knowledge in $\mathbb{D}_s$ and $\mathbb{T}_s$, where $\mathcal{X}_s \cap \mathcal{X}_t \neq \emptyset$ and $\mathcal{Y}_s = \mathcal{Y}_t$, but $\mathbb{P}^{X_s} \neq \mathbb{P}^{X_t}$ or $\mathbb{P}^{Y_s|X_s} \neq \mathbb{P}^{Y_t|X_t}$.

Definition 1.3 (heterogeneous transfer learning)   Given a source domain $\mathbb{D}_s$ and a learning task $\mathbb{T}_s$, a target domain $\mathbb{D}_t$ and a learning task $\mathbb{T}_t$, *heterogeneous transfer learning* aims to help improve the learning of the target predictive function $f_t(\cdot)$ for $\mathbb{D}_t$ using the knowledge in $\mathbb{D}_s$ and $\mathbb{T}_s$, where $\mathcal{X}_s \cap \mathcal{X}_t = \emptyset$ or $\mathcal{Y}_s \neq \mathcal{Y}_t$.

Besides using the homogeneity of the feature spaces and label spaces, we can also categorize existing transfer learning studies into the following three settings by considering whether labeled data and unlabeled data are available in the target domain: supervised transfer learning, semi-supervised transfer learning and unsupervised transfer learning. In supervised transfer learning, only a few labeled data are available in the target domain for training, and we do not use the unlabeled data for training. For unsupervised transfer learning, there are only unlabeled data available in the target domain. In semi-supervised transfer learning, sufficient unlabeled data and a few labeled data are assumed to be available in the target domain.

To design a transfer learning algorithm, we need to consider the following three main research issues: (1) when to transfer, (2) what to transfer and (3) how to transfer.

When to transfer asks in which situations transferring skills should be done. Likewise, we are interested in knowing in which situations knowledge should **not** be transferred. In some situations, when the source domain and the target domain are not related to each other, brute-force transfer may be unsuccessful. In the worst case, it may even hurt the performance of learning in the target domain, a situation which is often referred to as *negative transfer*. Most of current studies on transfer learning focus on "what to transfer" and "how to transfer," by implicitly assuming that the source domain and the target domain are related to each other. However, how to avoid negative transfer is an important open issue that is attracting more and more attentions.

What to transfer determines which part of knowledge can be transferred across domains or tasks. Some knowledge is specific for individual domains or tasks, and some knowledge may be common between different domains such that they may help improve performance for the target domain or task. Note that the term

---

[1] In the rest of book, without explicit specification, the term "transfer learning" denotes homogeneous transfer learning.

"knowledge" is very general. Thus, in practice, it needs to be specified based on different context.

How to transfer specifies the form that a transfer learning method takes. Different answers to the question of "how to transfer" give a categorization for transfer learning algorithms:

(1) instance-based algorithms, where the knowledge transferred corresponds to the weights attached to source instances;
(2) feature-based algorithms, where the knowledge transferred corresponds to the subspace spanned by the features in the source and target domains;
(3) model-based algorithms, where the knowledge to be transferred is embedded in part of the source domain models and
(4) relation-based algorithms, where the knowledge to be transferred corresponds to rules specifying the relations between the entities in the source domain.

Each of these types of transfer learning corresponds to an emphasis on which part of the knowledge is being considered as a vehicle to facilitate the knowledge transfer. Specifically, a common motivation behind **instance-based transfer learning approaches** is that, although the source domain labeled data cannot be reused directly due to the domain difference, part of them can be reused for the target domain after reweighting or resampling. In this way, the source-domain labeled instances with large weights can be considered as "knowledge" to be transferred across domains. An implicit assumption behind the instance-based approaches is that the source domain and the target domain have a lot of overlapping features, which means that the domains share the same or similar support.

However, in many real world applications, only a portion of the feature spaces from the source and target domains overlap, which means that many features cannot be directly used as bridges for the knowledge transfer. As a result, some instance-based methods may fail to work effectively for knowledge transfer. **Feature-based transfer learning approaches** are more promising in this case. A common idea behind feature-based approaches is to learn a "good" feature representation for both the source domain and the target domain such that, by projecting data onto the new representation, the source domain labeled data can be reused to train a precise classifier for the target domain. In this way, the knowledge to be transferred across domains can be considered as the learned feature representation.

Model-based transfer learning approaches assume the source domain and the target domain share some parameters or hyperparameters of the learning models. A motivation of model-based approaches is that a well-trained source model has captured a lot of useful structure, which is general and can be transferred to learn a more precise target model. In this way, the knowledge to be transferred is the domain-invariant structure of the model parameters. A recently widely used pretraining technique for transfer learning based on deep learning is indeed a model-based approach. Specifically, the idea of pretraining is to first train a deep learning model using sufficient source data, which could be quite different from the target data. After the deep model is trained, a few target labeled data are used to fine-tune part of the parameters of the pretrained deep model, for example, to fine-tune parameters of several layers while fixing parameters of other layers.

Different from the three aforementioned categories of approaches, **relation-based transfer learning approaches** assume that some relationships between objects (i.e., instances) are similar across domains or tasks. Once these common relationships are extracted, then they can be used as knowledge for transfer learning. Note that, in this category, data in the source domain and the target domain are not required to be independent and identically distributed as the other three categories.

1.3 Relationship to Existing Machine Learning Paradigms

Transfer learning and machine learning are closely related. On one hand, the aim of transfer learning encompasses that of machine learning in that its key ingredient is "generalization." In other words, it explores how to develop general and robust machine learning models that can apply to not only the training data, but also unanticipated future data. Therefore, all machine learning models should have the ability to conduct transfer learning. On the other hand, transfer learning differs from other branches of machine learning in that transfer learning aims to generalize commonalities across different tasks or domains, which are "sets" of instances, while machine learning focuses on generalize commonalities across "instances." This difference makes the design of the learning algorithms quite different.

Specifically, machine learning algorithms such as semi-supervised learning, active learning and transfer learning can be used to partially address the labeled data sparsity issue for a target domain, but they have different assumptions. Semi-supervised learning aims to address the labeled data sparsity problem in the same domain by making use of a large amount of unlabeled data to discover an intrinsic data structure to effectively propagate label information. Common assumptions behind semi-supervised learning techniques are (1) the underlying intrinsic data structure is very useful to learn a precise model even without sufficient labeled data and (2) the training data, including labeled and unlabeled, and the unseen test data are still represented in the same feature space and drawn from the same data distribution.

Instead of exploring unlabeled data to train a precise model, active learning, which is another branch in machine learning for reducing the annotation effort of supervised learning, tries to design an active learner to pose queries, usually in the form of unlabeled data instances to be labeled by an oracle (e.g., a human annotator). The key motivation behind active learning is that a machine learning algorithm can achieve greater accuracy with fewer training labels if it is allowed

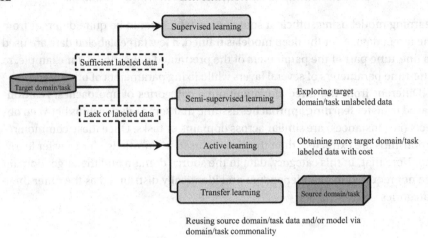

Figure 1.2 Relationship of transfer learning to other learning paradigms

to choose the data from which it learns. However, active learning assumes that there is a budget for the active learner to pose queries in the domain of interest. In some real world applications, the budget may be quite limited, which means that the labeled data queried by active learning may not be sufficient enough to learn an accurate classifier in the domain of interest.

Transfer learning, in contrast, allows the domains, tasks and distributions used in the training phase and the testing phase to be different. The main idea behind transfer learning is to borrow labeled data or extract knowledge from some related domains to help a machine learning algorithm to achieve greater performance in the domain of interest. Thus, transfer learning can be referred to as a different strategy for learning models with minimal human supervision, compared to semi-supervised and active learning.

One of the most related learning paradigms to transfer learning is multi-task learning. Although both transfer learning and multitask learning aim to generalize commonality across tasks, transfer learning is focused on learning on a target task, where some source task(s) is(are) used as auxiliary information, while multitask learning aims to learn a set of target tasks jointly to improve the generalization performance of each learning task without any source or auxiliary tasks. As most existing multitask learning methods consider all tasks to have the same importance, while transfer learning only takes the performance of the target task into consideration, some detailed designs of the learning algorithms are different. However, most existing multitask learning algorithms can be adapted to the transfer learning setting.

We summarize the relationships between transfer learning and other machine learning paradigms in Figure 1.2, and the difference between transfer learning and multitask learning in Figure 1.3.

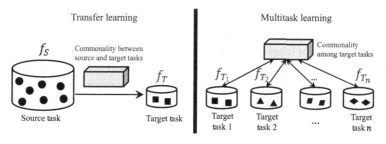

Figure 1.3 Relationship between transfer learning and multitask learning

1.4 Fundamental Research Issues in Transfer Learning

As we mentioned earlier, there are three research issues in transfer learning, namely, "what to transfer," "how to transfer" and "when to transfer." As the objective of transfer learning is to transfer knowledge across different domains, the first question is to ask what knowledge across domains can be transferred to boost the generalization performance of the target domain, which is referred to as the "what to transfer" issue. After identifying what knowledge to be transferred, a follow-up question is how to encode the knowledge into a learning algorithm to transfer, which corresponds to the "how to transfer" issue. The "when to transfer" issue is to ask in which situations transfer learning should be performed or can be performed safely. A fundamental research question behind these three issues is how to measure the "distance" between any pair of domains or tasks. With the distance measure between domains or tasks, one can identify what common knowledge between tasks can be used to reduce distance between domains or tasks, that is, what to transfer, and figure out how to reduce the distance between domains or tasks based on the identified common knowledge, that is, how to transfer. Moreover, with the distance measure between domains or tasks, one can logically decide "when to transfer": if the distance is very large, it is advised not to conduct transfer learning. Otherwise, it is "safe" to do so.

A subsequent question is thus: what form should such a notion of distance measure be in? Traditionally, there are various types of statistical measures for the distance between any two probability distributions. Typical measures among them include Kulback–Leibler divergence, A-distance (which measures the domain separation) and Maximum Mean Discrepancy (MMD), to name a few. Recall that a domain contains two components: a feature space and a marginal probability distribution, and a task also contains two components: a label space and a conditional probability distribution. Therefore, existing statistical measures for the distance between probability distributions could be used to measure the distance between domains or tasks by assuming the source domain (task) and the target domain (task) share the same feature (label) space. However, there are some limitations on using statistical distance measures for transfer learning. First, researchers have found that these general distribution-based distance measures are often too coarse to serve the purpose well in measuring the distance in the transferrability between two domains or tasks. Second, if the domains have different feature spaces and/or label spaces, one has to first project the data onto the same feature and/or label space, and then apply the statistical distance measures as a follow-up step. Therefore, more research needs to be done on a general notion of distances between two domains or tasks.

1.5   Applications of Transfer Learning

1.5.1   Image Understanding

Many image understanding tasks from object recognition to activity recognition have been considered. Typically, these computer vision tasks require a lot of labeled data to train a model, such as using the well-known ImageNet data set. However, when computer vision situations slightly change, such as changing from indoors to outdoors and from still cameras to moving cameras, the model needs to be adapted to account for new situations. Transfer learning is an often used technique to solve these adaptation problems.

In image analysis, many recent works combined deep learning architecture with transfer learning. For example, Long et al. (2015) explore a deep learning architecture in which domain distances are minimized between the source and target domains. In a paper published by Facebook (Mahajan et al., 2018), Mahajan et al. apply transfer learning to image classification. The approach involves first training a deep learning model based on a very large image data set. This pretrained model is then fine-tuned on specific tasks in a target domain, which involves relatively small amounts of labeled data. The model is a deep convolutional network trained for the task of classification based on hashtags assigned to billions of social media images, and the target tasks are object recognition or image classification. Their analysis shows that it is important to both increase the size of the pretraining data set as well as to select a closely related label space between source and target tasks. This observation suggests that transfer learning requires the design of "label-space engineering" approaches to match source and target learning tasks. Their work also suggests that improvements on target tasks may be obtained by increasing source model complexity and data set sizes.

Transfer learning also allows image analysis to play an important role in applications with a large societal impact. In the work by Xie et al. (2016), authors from Stanford University Earth Sciences apply transfer learning to predict poverty levels on earth based on satellite images. First, they used daytime images to predict the nighttime light images. The resulting model is then transferred to predicting poverty. This results in a very accurate prediction model that required much less human labeling effort to build compared to traditional survey-based methods.

1.5.2 Bioinformatics and Bio-imaging

In biology, many experiments are costly and data are very few. Examples include bio-imaging when doctors try to use computers to discover potential diseases, and when software models are used to scan complex DNA and protein sequences for patterns to point to a particular illness or cure. Transfer learning has been increasingly used to help leverage the knowledge from one domain to another to address the difficulty that labeled data in biology is costly to obtain. For example, Xu and Yang (2011) give an early survey of transfer learning and multitask learning in bioinformatics applications, and Xu et al. (2011) present a transfer learning process to identify protein cellular structures in a target domain where the labeled data is in short supply. In biomedical image analysis, a difficult problem is to collect enough training data to train a model for identifying image patterns that designate illnesses such as cancer. Such identification requires large amounts of training data. However, these data are often very expensive to obtain as they require costly human experts to label. Furthermore, the data for pretrained models and future models are often from different distributions. These problems inspire many research works to apply transfer learning to adapt the pretrained model in new tasks. For example, in the work by Shin et al. (2016), a pretrained model based on ImageNet data is used as the source domain model, which is then transferred for use in a medical image domain for thoraco-abdominal lymph node detection and interstitial lung disease classification, with great success.

1.5.3 Recommender Systems and Collaborative Filtering

It is often the case that an online product recommendation system is difficult to set up due to the cold start problem. This problem can be alleviated if we discover similarities between domains and adapt a recommendation model from a mature domain to the new domain. This often saves time and resources that make an otherwise impossible task successful. For example, Li et al. (2009b) and Pan et al. (2010b) give early accounts of applying transfer learning for online recommendation. In their applications, cross-domain recommendation systems transfer user preference models from an existing domain (say, a book recommendation domain) to a new domain (say, a movie recommendation domain). The scenario corresponds to the business case where an online commerce site opens a new line of business and wishes to quickly deploy a recommendation model for the operation in the new business line. In doing so, it must overcome the problem of a lack of transaction data in the new business line. Another line of work is in integrating reinforcement learning and recommendation systems to allow the items that are recommended to be both accurate according to past history of a user and potentially diverse to enrich users' interests. As an example, Liu et al. (2018) present a bandit algorithm that balances between recommendation accuracy and topic diversity, to allow a system to explore new topics as well as cater to users' recent choices. Relating to transfer learning, the work shows that the recommendation strategy in balancing exploration and exploitation can indeed be transferred between domains.

1.5.4 Robotics and Autonomous Cars

In designing robotics and autonomous cars, learning from simulations is a particularly useful approach. These are examples of hardware interactions, where it is costly to gather labeled data for training reinforcement learning and supervised learning models. Taylor and Stone (2007) described how transfer learning helps by allowing researchers to build a simulated model in a more or less ideal domain, the source domain, and then learn a policy to deal with the anticipated events in a target domain. The target domain model can handle more cases in the real world to further handle more unanticipated and noisy data. When the models adapt well, much labor and many resources can be saved from retraining the target domain model. In the work by Tai et al. (2017), a mapless motion planner was designed based on a ten-dimensional sparse range findings and trained in an end-to-end deep reinforcement learning algorithm. Then the learned planner is transferred to the real world by generalizing via real world samples.

1.5.5 NLP and Text Mining

Text mining is a good application for transfer learning algorithms. Text mining aims to discover useful structural knowledge from text and applies to other domains. Among all the problems in text mining, text classification aims to label new text documents with different class tags. A typical text classification problem is *sentiment classification*. On the Web, there are enormous user-generated contents at online sites such as online forums, blogs, social networks and so on. It is very important to be able to summarize opinions of consumers on products and services. Sentiment classification addresses this problem by classifying the reviews into positive and negative categories. However, on different domains, such as different types of products, different types of online sites and different sectors of business, users may express their opinions using different words. As a result, a sentiment classifier trained on one domain may perform poorly on other domains. In this case, transfer learning can help adapt a well-trained sentiment classifier across different domains.

Recently, work on pretraining gained new insights into the nature of transfer learning. Devlin et al. (2018) highlight one successful condition for transfer learning applications: having a sufficient amount of source domain training data. For example, Google's NLP system BERT (Bidirectional Encoder Representations from Transformers) applies transfer learning to a number of NLP tasks, showing that transfer learning with a powerful pretained model can solve a variety of traditionally difficult problems such as question answering problems (Devlin et al., 2018). It has accomplished surprising results by leading in many tasks in the open competition SQuAD 2.0 (Rajpurkar et al., 2016). The source domain consists of an extremely large collection of natural language text corpus, with which BERT trained a model that is based on the bidirectional transformers based on the attention mechanism. The pertained model is capable of making a variety of predictions in a language model more accurate than before, and the predictive power increases with increasing amounts of training data in the source domain. Then, the BERT model is applied to a specific task in a target domain by adding additional small layers to the source model in such tasks as Next Sentence classification, Question Answering and Named Entity Recognition (NER). The transfer learning approach corresponds to model-based transfer, where most hyperparameters stay the same but a selected few hyperparameters can be adapted with the new data in the target domain.

1.6   Historical Notes

Many human learning activities follow the style of transfer learning. We observe that people often apply the knowledge gained from previous learning tasks to help learn a new task. For example, a baby can be observed to first learn how to recognize its parents before using this knowledge to help it learn how to recognize other people.

Transfer learning has deep roots in AI, psychology, educational theory and cognitive science. In AI, there have been many forms of transfer learning. Learning by analogy is one of the fundamental insights of AI. Humans can draw on the past experience to solve current problems very well. In AI, there have been several early works on analogical reasoning such as dynamic memory (Schank, 1983). Using analogy in problem solving, Carbonell (1981) and Winston (1980) pointed out that analogical reasoning implies that the relationship between entities must be compared, not just the entity themselves, to allow effective recall of previous experiences. Forbus et al. (1998) have argued for high-level structural similarity as a basis of analogical reasoning. Holyoak and Thagard (1989) have developed a computational theory of analogical reasoning using this strategy, when abstraction rules that allow the two instances to be mapped to a unified representation are given as input.

Analogical problem solving is the cornerstone for case-based reasoning (CBR), where many systems have been developed. For example, HYPO (Ashley, 1991) retrieves similar past cases in a legal case base to argue in support of a claim or make counterarguments. PRODIGY (Carbonell et al., 1991) uses a collection of previous problem-solving cases as a case base, and retrieves the most similar cases for adaptation. Most operational systems of analogical reasoning such as CBR systems (Kolodner, 1993) have relied on an assumption that the past instances and the new target problem are in the same representational space.

Table 1.1 *Notations*

$\mathcal{D}$	A data set
$\mathcal{X}$	A feature space
$\mathcal{H}$	A hypothesis space
$\mathbb{P}$	A probability distribution
$\mathbb{E}_{\mathbb{P}}[\cdot]$	Expectation with respect to distribution $\mathbb{P}$
$tr(\mathbf{A})$	Trace of matrix $\mathbf{A}$
min	Minimization
max	Maximization
$\mathbf{I}_n$	An $n \times n$ identity matrix
$\mathbf{I}$	An identity matrix with the size depending on the context
$\mathbf{0}$	A zero vector or matrix with the size depending on the context
$\mathbf{1}$	A vector or matrix of all ones with the size depending on the context
$\|\cdot\|_p$	The ℓ_p norm of a vector where $0 \le p \le \infty$
$\|\cdot\|_1$	The ℓ_1 norm of a vector or matrix
$\|\cdot\|_F$	The Frobenius norm of a matrix
$\|\cdot\|_{S(p)}$	The Schatten p-norm norm of a matrix
$\mu_i(\cdot)$	The i-th largest eigenvalue or singular value of a matrix
$N(\mu, \sigma)$	A univariate or multivariate normal distribution with mean μ and variance σ
$\|\mathbf{A}\|_{p,q}$	The $\ell_{p,q}$ norm of a matrix, that is, $\|\mathbf{A}\|_{p,q} = \left\| (\|\mathbf{a}_1\|_p, \ldots, \|\mathbf{a}_n\|_p) \right\|_q$ where $\mathbf{a}_i$ is the ith row of $\mathbf{A}$.
$\mathbf{A}^{-1}$	The inverse of a nonsingular matrix $\mathbf{A}$
$\mathbf{A}^+$	The inverse of a nonsingular matrix $\mathbf{A}$ or the pseduo-inverse of a singular matrix

There have been some surveys on transfer learning in machine learning literature. Pan and Yang (2010) and Taylor and Stone (2009) give early surveys of the work on transfer learning, where the former focused on machine learning in classification and regression areas and the latter on reinforcement learning approaches. This book aims to give a comprehensive survey that cover both these areas, as well as the more recent advances of transfer learning with deep learning.

1.7 About This Book

This book mainly consists of two parts. The first part is to introduce the foundation of transfer learning in terms of representative methodologies and theoretical studies. The second part is to discuss some advanced topics in transfer learning and show some successful applications of transfer learning. The notations used in this book are summarized in Table 1.1.

The book is the effort of years of original research and survey of the research field by many former and current students of Professor Qiang Yang at Hong Kong University of Science and Technology and several other organizations. In chronological order of chapters, the composition of the book is outlined as follows:

Chapter 2 covers instance-based transfer learning. One of the most straightforward transfer learning methods is to identify instances or samples from the source domains and assign them weights. Then, these instances with sufficiently high weights are transferred to the target domain to help train a better machine learning model. In doing so, it is important to transfer only those instances that can contribute to the learning in the target domain and at the same time avoid "negative transfer." The instance-based transfer learning methods can also be useful when multiple source domains exist.

Chapter 3 covers feature-based transfer learning. Features constitute a major element of machine learning. They can be straightforward attributes in the input data, such as pixels in images or words and phrases in a text document, or they can be composite features composed by certain nonlinear transformations of input features. Together these features comprise a high-dimensional feature space. Feature-based transfer is to identify common subspaces of features between source and target domains, and allow transfer to happen in these subspaces. This style of transfer learning is particularly useful when no clear instances can be directly transferred, but some common "style" of learning can be transferred.

Chapter 4 discusses model-based transfer learning. Model-based transfer is when parts of a learning model can be transferred to a target domain from a source domain, where the learning in the target domain can be "finetuned" based on the transferred model. Model-based transfer learning is particularly useful when one has a fairly complete collection of data in a source domain, and the model in the source domain can be made very powerful in terms of coverage. Then learning in a target domain corresponds to adapting the general model from the source domain to a specific model in a target domain on the "edge" of a network of domains.

Chapter 5 explores relation-based transfer learning. This chapter is particularly useful when knowledge is coded in terms of a knowledge graph or in relational logic form. When some dictionary of translation can be instituted, and when knowledge exists in the form of some encoded rules, this type of transfer learning can be particularly useful.

Chapter 6 presents heterogeneous transfer learning. Sometimes, when we deal with transfer learning, the target domain may have a completely different feature representation from that of the source domain. For example, we may have collected labeled data about images, but the target task is to classify text documents. If there is some relationship between the images and the text documents, transfer learning can still happen at the semantic level, where the semantics of the common knowledge between the source and the target domains can be extracted as a "bridge" to enable the knowledge transfer.

Chapter 7 discusses adversarial transfer learning. Machine learning, especially deep learning, can be designed to generate data and at the same time classify data. This dual relationship in machine learning can be exploited to mimic the power of imitation and creation in humans. This learning process can be modeled as a game between multiple models, and is called adversarial learning. Adversarial learning can be very useful in empowering a transfer learning process, which is the subject of this chapter.

Chapter 8 discusses the use of transfer learning in reinforcement learning. Reinforcement learning allows rewards to be delayed, and introduces the concept of actions and states in a learning system. Learning a policy in a reinforcement learning problem requires a huge amount of training data, which is time consuming to prepare. Transfer learning alleviates this pain and is promising when the source and target domains and tasks can be closely aligned.

Chapter 9 discusses multitask learning. So far, transfer learning has been discussed along a time line: a source domain and a model have been well prepared before transfer learning can happen to a target domain in a later time point. Multitask learning aims to learn at the same time point, by allowing several tasks to benefit with common knowledge for each other. This is the style of learning when a student takes several courses in the same semester, when the student finds that some common contents or learning methodology can be commonly shared between the courses.

Chapter 10 discusses transfer learning theory. Learning theory tells the general capability of a learning system, by relating the number of samples with the generalization error bounds of a particular algorithm. This line of work generally follows the methodology of probably approximately correct learning, or PAC learning. When the bound is tight, the error bound can also be used to design new algorithms. The transfer learning theory, when properly done, can help give assurances for a learning system's capability.

Chapter 11 surveys transitive transfer learning. Transfer learning so far has been discussed in a source to target domain transfer model. When the source and target domains are "far" from each other, there is no directly relation between the two, transfer cannot directly happen between the two domains. Even though this poses difficulty for transfer learning, there are still opportunities for transfer learning when we can find some intermediate domains as "stepping-stones" for knowledge to "hop over" to target domains. For example, this might happen when we consider a student entering a university taking a calculus class; through several semesters' of knowledge transfer, they eventually they take some advanced physics or computing classes.

Chapter 12 presents learning to transfer as a way to achieve automated transfer learning. Just like a typical machine learning system, the engineering process can be very tedious, as there may be many parameters to tune. As a result, researchers introduced the concept of automatic machine learning (AutoML) to automate the parameter tuning process through automatic optimization. Likewise, transfer learning requires many engineering efforts, and, when sufficient transfer learning experience is gained, this experience can in turn become the training data for building a parameter-tuning model for automatic transfer learning (AutoTL).

Chapter 13 presents few-shot learning. Few-shot learning is when models have been built well enough in a source domain, there may be cases where only few training data, or even no training data, are required in the target domain before a target domain model is well trained.

Chapter 14 discusses lifelong machine learning. When transfer learning is engaged continuously along a time line, the system can draw knowledge from all previous experience in a lifelong manner. A challenge is to decide how to store the previous knowledge and how to select the previous experience to reuse when solving the next task in life.

Chapter 15 discusses privacy-preserving transfer learning. When transfer learning happens between two organizations, we wish to protect the sensitive and private information about users and the confidential data in the source domain. We wish to do this while transferring the knowledge itself. Thus, care should be taken not to allow the target domain to reverse engineer the sensitive data when transfer learning is applied. In this chapter, we discuss how differential privacy is integrated with transfer learning to protect the user privacy and ensure data confidentiality.

Chapter 16 discusses applications of transfer learning in computer vision, which is one of the most extensive application fields of transfer learning. We survey the work in this area, paying special attention to medical imaging and transfer learning.

Chapter 17 discusses applications of transfer learning in NLP. NLP is one of the main application areas of transfer learning, which requires special attention due to the language specific nature of NLP.

Chapter 18 discusses applications of transfer learning in dialogue systems. We particularly separated dialogue systems out of the general survey on NLP in the previous chapter because this is an increasingly important application area not only in its own right, but also as a human–computer interaction medium that will grow in the years to come.

Chapter 19 presents applications of transfer learning in recommendation systems. Recommendation systems is a machine learning technique and, at the same time, an important application area of machine learning. Transfer learning is particularly important in recommendation systems because this domain constantly suffers from the so-called "cold start" problem and data sparsity problem where not enough data and knowledge have been gained in a newly started area. Transfer learning has proven to be very useful in alleviating these problems.

Chapter 20 discusses applications of transfer learning in bioinformatics and bioimaging. Biological data are increasingly accumulated with advancement of genetic and biomedical technology. This gives application opportunities to machine learning. However, this is a domain where collecting high-quality samples is extremely difficult, expensive and time consuming. Thus, transfer learning can be very useful, especially when the genetics domain is full of data of very high dimensionality and low sample sizes. We give an overview of works in this area.

Chapter 21 presents applications of transfer learning in activity recognition based on sensors. Activity recognition refers to finding people's activities from sensor readings, which can be very useful for assisted living, security and a wide range of other applications. A challenge in this domain is the lack of labeled data, and this challenge is particularly fit for transfer learning to address.

Chapter 22 discusses applications of transfer learning in urban computing. There are many machine learning problems to address in urban computing, ranging from traffic prediction to pollution forecast. When data has been collected in one city, the model can be transferred to a newly considered city via transfer learning, especially when there is not sufficient high-quality data in these new cities.

Chapter 23 gives a summary of the whole book with an outlook for future works.

2
Instance-Based Transfer Learning

2.1 Introduction

Intuitively, instance-based transfer learning approaches aim to reuse labeled data from the source domain help to train a more precise model for a target learning task. If the source domain and the target domain are quite similar, we can directly merge the source domain data into the target domain. Then it becomes a standard machine learning problem in a single domain. However, in many cases, this "direct adoption" strategy of source domain instances cannot help to solve the target task.

A common motivation behind instance-based transfer learning approaches is that some source domain labeled data are still useful for learning a precise model for the target domain while some are useless or even may hurt the performance of the target model if used. We can use the bias-variance analysis to understand this motivation. When the target domain data set is small, the model may have a high variance level and thus the model's generalization error is large. By adding a part of the source domain data as an auxiliary data set, the model's variance can potentially be reduced. However, if the data distributions of the two domains are very different, the new learning model may have a high bias. Therefore, if we can single out those source domain instances that follow a similar distribution as those in the target domain, we can reuse them and have both the variance and bias of the target learning model reduced.

Briefly, there are two key issues to resolve in using instance-based transfer learning. The first issue is how to single out the source domain-labeled instances that are similar to the target domain ones, because these instances are useful to train the target domain model. The second issue is how to utilize the identified "similar" source domain-labeled instances in an algorithm to learn a more accurate target domain learning model.

Recall that a domain $\mathbb{D} = \{\mathcal{X}, \mathbb{P}^X\}$ has two components: a feature space $\mathcal{X}$ and a marginal probability distribution $\mathbb{P}^X$. Given $\mathbb{D}$, a task $\mathbb{T} = \{\mathcal{Y}, \mathbb{P}^{Y|X}\}$ has two components: the label space $\mathcal{Y}$ and the conditional probability distribution $\mathbb{P}^{Y|X}$. A common assumption behind most instance-based transfer learning approaches is that the input instances of the source domain and the target domain have the same or very similar support, which means that the features for most instances have a similar range of values. Furthermore, the output labels of the source and target tasks are the same. This assumption ensures that knowledge can be transferred across domains via instances. According the definitions of a domain and a task, this assumption implies that, in instance-based transfer learning, the difference between domains/tasks is only caused by the differences of the marginal distribution of the features (i.e., $\mathbb{P}_s^X \neq \mathbb{P}_t^X$) or conditional probabilities (i.e., $\mathbb{P}_s^{Y|X} \neq \mathbb{P}_t^{Y|X}$).

When $\mathbb{P}_s^X \neq \mathbb{P}_t^X$ but $\mathbb{P}_s^{Y|X} = \mathbb{P}_t^{Y|X}$, we refer to the problem setting as noninductive transfer learning.[1] For example, suppose a hospital, either private or public, aims to learn a prediction model for a specific disease from its own patients' electronic medical records. Here we consider each hospital as a different domain. As the populations of patients of different hospitals are different, the marginal probabilities $\mathbb{P}^X$s are different across different domains. However, as the reasons that cause the specific disease are the same, the conditional probabilities $\mathbb{P}^{Y|X}$ across different domains remain the same. When $\mathbb{P}_s^{Y|X} \neq \mathbb{P}_t^{Y|X}$, we refer to the problem setting as inductive transfer learning. For instance, consider avian influenza virus as the specific disease in the previous example. As avian influenza virus has been evolving, the reasons causing avian influenza virus may change across different subtypes of avian influenza virus, for example, H1N1 versus H5N8. Here we consider learning a prediction model for each subtype of avian influenza virus for a specific hospital as a different task. As the reasons that cause different subtypes of avian influenza virus are different, the conditional probabilities $\mathbb{P}^{Y|X}$ are different across different tasks. In noninductive transfer learning, as the conditional probabilities across domains are the same, that is, $\mathbb{P}_s^{Y|X} = \mathbb{P}_t^{Y|X}$, it can be theoretically proven that, even without any labeled data in the target domain, an optimal predictive model can be learned from the source domain-labeled data and the target domain-unlabeled data. While in the inductive transfer learning case, as the conditional probabilities are different across tasks, a few labeled data in the target domain would then be required to exist to help transfer the conditional probability or the discriminative function from the source task to the target task. Since the assumptions of noninductive transfer learning and inductive transfer learning are different, the designs of instance-based transfer learning approaches for these two settings are different. In the following, we will review the motivations, basic ideas and representative methods for noninductive and inductive transfer learning in detail.

---

[1] Note that here we do not adopt the term "transductive transfer learning" used by Pan and Yang (2010) because the term "transductive" has been widely used to distinguish whether a model has an out-of-sample generalization ability, which may cause some confusion if used to define transfer learning problem settings.

2.2 Instance-Based Noninductive Transfer Learning

As mentioned earlier, in noninductive transfer learning, the source task and the target task are assumed to be the same, and the supports of the input instances across domains are assumed to be the same or very similar, that is, $\mathcal{X}_s = \mathcal{X}_t$. The only difference between domains is caused by the marginal distribution of input instances, that is, $\mathbb{P}_s^X \neq \mathbb{P}_t^X$. Under this setting, we are given a set of source domain-labeled data $\mathcal{D}_s = \{(\mathbf{x}_{s_i}, y_{s_i})\}_{i=1}^{n_s}$, and a set of target domain-unlabeled data $\mathcal{D}_t = \{(\mathbf{x}_{t_i})\}_{i=1}^{n_t}$. The goal is to learn a precise predictive model for the target domain unseen data.

In the following, we show that, under the assumptions in noninductive transfer learning, one is still able to learn an optimal predictive model for the target domain even without any target domain-labeled data. Suppose our goal is to learn a predictive model in terms of parameters θ_t for the target domain, based on the learning framework of empirical risk minimization (Vapnik, 1998), the optimal solution of θ_t can be learned by solving the following optimization problem.

$$\theta_t^* = \arg\min_{\theta_t \in \Theta} \mathbb{E}_{(\mathbf{x},y) \in \mathbb{P}_t^{X,Y}} [\ell(\mathbf{x}, y, \theta)], \tag{2.1}$$

where $\ell(\mathbf{x}, y, \theta)$ is a loss function in terms of the parameters θ_t. Since there are no target domain-labeled data, one cannot optimize (2.1) directly. It has been proven by Pan (2014) that, by using the Bayes' rule and the definition of expectation, the optimization (2.1) can be rewritten as follows,

$$\theta_t^* = \arg\min_{\theta_t \in \Theta} \mathbb{E}_{(\mathbf{x},y) \sim \mathbb{P}_s^{X,Y}} \left[\frac{P_t(\mathbf{x}, y)}{P_s(\mathbf{x}, y)} \ell(\mathbf{x}, y, \theta_t) \right], \tag{2.2}$$

which aims to learn the optimal parameter θ_t^* by minimizing the weighted expected risk over source domain-labeled data. In noninductive transfer learning, as $\mathbb{P}_s^{Y|X} = \mathbb{P}_t^{Y|X}$, by decomposing the joint distribution $\mathbb{P}^{X,Y} = \mathbb{P}^{Y|X}\mathbb{P}^X$, we obtain $\frac{P_t(\mathbf{x},y)}{P_s(\mathbf{x},y)} = \frac{P_t(\mathbf{x})}{P_s(\mathbf{x})}$. Hence, (2.2) can be further rewritten as

$$\theta_t^* = \arg\min_{\theta_t \in \Theta} \mathbb{E}_{(\mathbf{x},y) \sim \mathbb{P}_s^{X,Y}} \left[\frac{P_t(\mathbf{x})}{P_s(\mathbf{x})} \ell(\mathbf{x}, y, \theta_t) \right], \tag{2.3}$$

where a weight of a source domain instance $\mathbf{x}$ is defined as the ratio of marginal distributions of input instances between the target domain and the source domain at the data point $\mathbf{x}$. Given a set of source domain-labeled data $\{(\mathbf{x}_{s_i}, y_{s_i})\}_{i=1}^{n_s}$, by defining $\beta(\mathbf{x}) = \frac{P_t(\mathbf{x})}{P_s(\mathbf{x})}$, an empirical approximation of (2.3) can be written as[2]

$$\theta_t^* = \arg\min_{\theta_t \in \Theta} \sum_{i=1}^{n_s} \beta(\mathbf{x}_{s_i}) \ell(\mathbf{x}_{s_i}, y_{s_i}, \theta_t), \tag{2.4}$$

Therefore, to properly reuse the source domain-labeled data to learn a target model, one needs to estimate the weight's $\{\beta(\mathbf{x}_{s_i})\}$. As shown in (2.4), to estimate $\{\beta(\mathbf{x}_{s_i})\}$,

---

[2] In practice, a regularization term is added to avoid model overfitting.

that is, density ratios, only input instances without labels from the source domain and the target domain are required. A simple solution to estimate $\{\beta(\mathbf{x}_{s_i})\}$ for each source domain instance is to first estimate $\mathbb{P}_t^X$ and $\mathbb{P}_s^X$, respectively, and then compute the ratio $\frac{P_t(\mathbf{x}_{s_i})}{P_s(\mathbf{x}_{s_i})}$ for each specific source domain instance $\mathbf{x}_{s_i}$. However, it is well known that density estimation itself is a difficult task (Tsuboi et al., 2009), especially when data are of high dimensions. In this way, the error caused by density estimation will be propagated to the density ratio estimation.

In the literature (Quionero-Candela et al., 2009), more promising solutions have been proposed to estimate $\frac{\mathbb{P}_t^X}{\mathbb{P}_s^X}$, directly bypassing the density estimation step. In the following sections, we introduce how to directly estimate the density ratio by reviewing several representative methods.

2.2.1 Discriminatively Distinguish Source and Target Data

One simple and effective approach to learn the weights is to transform the problem of estimating the marginal probability density ratio to the problem of distinguishing whether an instance is from the source domain or the target domain. This can be formulated as a binary classification problem with data instances from the source domain being labeled as 1 and those from the target domain being labeled as 0.

For example, Zadrozny (2004) proposes a rejection sampling-based method for correcting sample selection bias. The rejection sampling process is defined as follows. A binary random variable $\delta \in \{1, 0\}$, which is called selection variable, is introduced. An instance $\mathbf{x}$ is sampled from the target marginal distribution $\mathbb{P}_t^X$ with probability $P_t(\mathbf{x})$, that is, $P_t(\mathbf{x}) = P(\mathbf{x}|\delta = 0)$. Similarly, $P_s(\mathbf{x})$ can be rewritten as $P_s(\mathbf{x}) = P(\mathbf{x}|\delta = 1)$. $\mathbf{x}$ is accepted by the source domain with probability $P(\delta = 1|\mathbf{x})$ or rejected with probability $P(\delta = 0|\mathbf{x})$. In mathematics, with the new variable δ, the density ratio for each data instance $\mathbf{x}$ can be formulated as

$$\frac{P_t(\mathbf{x})}{P_s(\mathbf{x})} = \frac{P(\delta = 1)}{P(\delta = 0)} \frac{P(\delta = 0)}{P(\delta = 1)} \frac{P_t(\mathbf{x})}{P_s(\mathbf{x})}, \tag{2.5}$$

where $P(\delta)$ is the prior probability of δ in the union data set of the source domain and the target domain. By using the Bayes, rule and the equivalent forms of $P_s(\mathbf{x})$ and $P_t(\mathbf{x})$ in terms of δ, (2.5) can be further reformulated as

$$\frac{P_t(\mathbf{x})}{P_s(\mathbf{x})} = \frac{P(\delta = 1)}{P(\delta = 0)} \left(\frac{1}{P(\delta = 1|\mathbf{x})} - 1 \right).$$

Therefore, the density ratio for each source domain data instance can be estimated as $\frac{P_t(\mathbf{x})}{P_s(\mathbf{x})} \propto \frac{1}{P_{s,t}(\delta = 1|\mathbf{x})}$. To compute the probability $P(\delta = 1|\mathbf{x})$, we regard it as a binary classification problem and train a classifier to solve it. After calculating the ratio for each source data instance, a model can be trained by either reweighting each source data instance or performing importance sampling on the source data set.

Following the idea of Zadrozny (2004), Bickel et al. (2007) propose a framework to integrate the density ratio estimation step and the model training step with reweighted source data instances. Let $\mathbb{P}^X$ denote the probability density of $\mathbf{x}$ in the union data set of the source domain and the target domain. We can use any classifier to estimate the probability $P(\delta = 1|\mathbf{x})$. Suppose the classifier is parameterized by $\mathbf{v}$ and the parameters for the final learning model that is trained on the reweighted source domain data are denoted by $\mathbf{w}$. All the parameters can be optimized using the maximum a posterior (MAP) approach:

$$[\mathbf{w}, \mathbf{v}]_{MAP} = \underset{\mathbf{w}, \mathbf{v}}{\arg\max} P(\mathbf{w}, \mathbf{v}|\mathcal{D}_s, \mathcal{D}_t),$$

where $\mathcal{D}_s$ and $\mathcal{D}_t$ denote the source data set and the target data set, respectively. Note that $P(\mathbf{w}, \mathbf{v}|\mathcal{D}_s, \mathcal{D}_t)$ is proportional to $P(\mathcal{D}_s|\mathbf{w}, \mathbf{v})P(\mathcal{D}_s, \mathcal{D}_t|\mathbf{v})P(\mathbf{w})P(\mathbf{v})$. Therefore, the MAP solution can be found by maximizing $P(\mathcal{D}_s|\mathbf{w}, \mathbf{v})P(\mathcal{D}_s, \mathcal{D}_t|\mathbf{v})P(\mathbf{w})P(\mathbf{v})$.

2.2.2 Kernel Mean Matching

Another effective approach to estimate the density ratio is using the techniques of kernel embedding of distributions (Smola et al., 2007a). For instance, Huang et al. (2006) propose the Kernel Mean Matching (KMM) method to directly learn the density ratio by aligning the mean of source domain data instances to that of target domain data instances in a reproducing kernel Hilbert space (RKHS).

Specifically, we use β_i to denote $\frac{P_t(\mathbf{x}_i^s)}{P_s(\mathbf{x}_i^s)}$ for each source domain data instance $\mathbf{x}_i^s$ and define $\boldsymbol{\beta}$ as $\boldsymbol{\beta} = (\beta_1, \beta_2, \ldots, \beta_{n_s})$, where n_s is the size of the source domain data set. KMM makes use of the theory of Maximum Mean Discrepancy (MMD) (Gretton et al., 2007) between distributions. Given two samples, based on MMD, the distance between two sample distributions is simply the distance between the two mean elements in an RKHS. Therefore, KMM aims to learn the weights of source domain instances by matching the mean of the reweighted source domain instances to that of the target domain instances in an RKHS:

$$\min_{\boldsymbol{\beta}} \left\| \mu(\mathbb{P}_t^X) - \mathbb{E}_{\mathbb{P}_s^X}[\beta(\mathbf{x})\Phi(\mathbf{x})] \right\| \quad \text{s.t. } \beta(\mathbf{x}) \geq 0, \ \mathbb{E}_{\mathbb{P}_s^X}[\beta(\mathbf{x})\Phi(\mathbf{x})] = 1, \quad (2.6)$$

where Φ transforms each source domain data instance into the RKHS $\mathcal{F}$, and $\mu(\mathbb{P}_t^X)$ is the expectation of the target domain instances in the RKHS, that is, $\mu(\mathbb{P}_t^X) = \mathbb{E}_{\mathbb{P}_t^X}[\Phi(\mathbf{x})]$.

In practice, one can optimize the following empirical objective:

$$\min_{\boldsymbol{\beta}} \left\| \frac{1}{n_s} \sum_{i=1}^{n_s} \beta_i \Phi(\mathbf{x}_i^s) - \frac{1}{n_t} \sum_{i=1}^{n_t} \Phi(\mathbf{x}_i^t) \right\|^2 \quad \text{s.t. } \beta_i \geq 0, \ \left| \frac{1}{n_s} \sum_{i=1}^{n_s} \beta_i - 1 \right| \leq \epsilon, \quad (2.7)$$

where ϵ is a positive real number. After solving the optimal $\boldsymbol{\beta}$, that is, the weights, $\boldsymbol{\beta}$ can be incorporated into (2.4) with any specified loss function to learn a predictive model θ_t^* for the target domain.

2.2.3 Function Approximation

A third representative approach to estimate density ratio is to consider the density ratio as an unknown function, and learn a combination of a series of base functions to approximate it. This is also known as covariate shift methods (Sugiyama et al., 2008). To be specific, by defining $\frac{P_t(\mathbf{x})}{P_s(\mathbf{x})}$ as a function $\omega(\mathbf{x})$, one could assume $\omega(\mathbf{x})$ is a linear combination of several base functions as

$$\widetilde{\omega}(\mathbf{x}) = \sum_{l=1}^{b} \alpha_l \phi_l(\mathbf{x}),$$

where $\boldsymbol{\alpha} = (\alpha_1, \dots, \alpha_b)^T$ are coefficients to be learned and $\phi_l(\cdot)$ is the lth base function that can be linear or nonlinear. In this way, $P_t(\mathbf{x})$ can be approximated by $\widetilde{P}_t(\mathbf{x}) = \widetilde{\omega}(\mathbf{x}) P_s(\mathbf{x})$. The coefficients $\boldsymbol{\alpha}$ can be learned by minimizing a loss function between $P_t(\mathbf{x})$ and $\widetilde{P}_t(\mathbf{x})$. Different loss functions lead to different specific methods.

For instance, Sugiyama et al. (2008) propose to use Kullback–Leibler (KL) divergence as the loss function. The resultant method is known as KL Importance Estimation Procedure (KLIEP), whose objective is written as follows,

$$D_{\text{KL}}(\mathbb{P}_t^X, \widetilde{\mathbb{P}}_t^X) = \int_{\mathscr{X}_t} P_t(\mathbf{x}) \log \frac{P_t(\mathbf{x})}{\widetilde{\omega}(\mathbf{x}) P_s(\mathbf{x})} d\mathbf{x} \tag{2.8}$$

$$= \int_{\mathscr{X}_t} P_t(\mathbf{x}) \log \frac{P_t(\mathbf{x})}{P_s(\mathbf{x})} d\mathbf{x} - \int_{\mathscr{X}_t} P_t(\mathbf{x}) \log \widetilde{\omega}(\mathbf{x}) d\mathbf{x}. \tag{2.9}$$

Note that, in (2.9), the ground-truth marginal probability of the target domain data, $\mathbb{P}_t^X$, is used. However, it can shown that, empirically, minimizing the aforementioned KL divergence can be approximated by solving the following optimization problem, where the ground truth marginal probability of the target domain data is canceled out:

$$\max_{\boldsymbol{\alpha}} \frac{1}{n_t} \sum_{j=1}^{n_t} \log \left(\sum_{l=1}^{b} \alpha_l \phi_l(\mathbf{x}_j^t) \right) \quad \text{s.t.} \quad \frac{1}{n_s} \sum_{i=1}^{n_s} \sum_{l=1}^{b} \alpha_l \phi_l(\mathbf{x}_i^s) = 1, \quad \alpha_l \geq 0 \ \forall l \in \{1, \dots, b\}.$$

Another example of the loss function in discrepancy between $\omega(\mathbf{x})$ and $\widetilde{\omega}(\mathbf{x})$ is the squared loss (Kanamori et al., 2009). The resultant optimization problem can be written as follows,

$$\min_{\boldsymbol{\alpha}} \int_{\mathscr{X}_s \cup \mathscr{X}_t} (\widetilde{\omega}(\mathbf{x}) - \omega(\mathbf{x}))^2 P_s(\mathbf{x}) d\mathbf{x}.$$

Besides, using KL divergence and squared loss as the loss function, many other forms of loss functions can be used.

2.3 Instance-Based Inductive Transfer Learning

Different from noninductive transfer learning, in inductive transfer learning, the source task and the target task can be different in terms of conditional probabilities, that is, $\mathbb{P}_s^{Y|X} \neq \mathbb{P}_t^{Y|X}$. As the conditional probability is changed across different tasks, if there are no labeled data in the target domain, then it is very difficult if not impossible to adapt $\mathbb{P}_s^{Y|X}$ to construct a precise $\mathbb{P}_t^{Y|X}$. Therefore, in most instance-based inductive transfer learning approaches, besides a set of source domain-labeled data $\mathscr{D}_s = \{(\mathbf{x}_{s_i}, y_{s_i})\}_{i=1}^{n_s}$, a small set of target domain-labeled data $\mathscr{D}_t = \{(\mathbf{x}_{t_i}, y_{t_i})\}_{i=1}^{n_t}$ is also required as inputs.[3] The goal is still to learn a precise predictive model for the target domain unseen data.

2.3.1 Integration of Source and Target Loss

An intuitive solution to make use of both source domain-labeled data and target domain-labeled data to train a model for the target domain is to decompose the loss function into two parts: one is for the source domain-labeled data, and the other is for the target domain-labeled data. A trade-off parameter is usually introduced to balance the impact of the two losses.

As an early representative work, Wu and Dietterich (2004) propose an instance-based K-nearest-neighbor (KNN) classifier to optimize the classification accuracy on both the source domain and the target domain. Specifically, in a traditional KNN classifier, the hypothesis $h(\mathbf{x})$ is defined by k training data instances that are closest to each test instance $\mathbf{x}$. In the proposed KNN-based inductive transfer learning method, K_s nearest source domain instances and K_t nearest target domain instances are first identified for a target domain test data instance $\mathbf{x}_i^t$. Then, for each class label y, the overall vote on the instance $\mathbf{x}_i^t$, denoted by $V(y)$, is computed as $V(y) = \theta(\frac{V_t(y)}{K_t}) + (1-\theta)(\frac{V_s(y)}{K_s})$, where $V_t(y)$ and $V_s(y)$ are the numbers of votes on class y from the K_t and the K_s nearest instances from the target domain and the source domain, respectively, and θ is a trade-off parameter to control the relative importance of the source domain nearest neighbors and the target domain nearest neighbors.

Such an idea can be applied to other base classifier beyond KNN. Wu and Dietterich (2004) also propose a support vector machine (SVM) based approach (Smola and Schölkopf, 2004) for instance-based inductive transfer learning methods. Recall that the objective function of SVMs is

$$\min_j \sum_j \alpha_j + C\sum_j \epsilon_j \text{ s.t. } y_i\left(\sum_j y_j\alpha_j K(\mathbf{x}_j,\mathbf{x}_i) + b\right) \geq 1 - \epsilon_i \; \forall i, \; \alpha_j \geq 0 \; \forall j,$$

where α_js are the model parameters of a SVM, ϵ_js are slack variables to absorb errors and C is a parameter to control how much penalty is conducted the misclassified examples. In the inductive transfer learning setting, Wu and Dietterich (2004) proposed to modify the objective function and constraints by considering the source domain-labeled data and the target domain-labeled data differently. Suppose α_j^s and ϵ_j^s denote the model parameters and slack variables for the source

---

[3] In some approaches, a set of target-unlabeled data is assumed to be given as well.

domain instance $\mathbf{x}_j^s$ for $j \in \{1, \ldots, n_s\}$, respectively. Similarly, α_j^t and ϵ_j^t denote the parameter and slack variable for the target domain instance $\mathbf{x}_j^t$, respectively, for $j \in \{1, \ldots, n_t\}$. The parameters C_s and C_t are trade-off parameters. Then the revised objective function of SVMs is formulated as

$$\min \sum_{j=1}^{n_s} \alpha_j^s + \sum_{j=1}^{n_t} \alpha_j^t + C_s \sum_{j=1}^{n_s} \epsilon_j^s + C_t \sum_{j=1}^{n_t} \epsilon_j^t,$$

$$\text{s.t.} \quad y_i^t \left(\sum_{j=1}^{n_t} y_j^t \alpha_j^t K\left(\mathbf{x}_j^t, \mathbf{x}_i^t\right) + \sum_{j=1}^{n_s} y_j^s \alpha_j^s K\left(\mathbf{x}_j^s, \mathbf{x}_i^t\right) + b \right) \geq 1 - \epsilon_i^t \ i \in \{1, \ldots, n_t\},$$

$$y_i^s \left(\sum_{j=1}^{n_t} y_j^t \alpha_j^t K\left(\mathbf{x}_j^t, \mathbf{x}_i^s\right) + \sum_{j=1}^{n_s} y_j^s \alpha_j^s K\left(\mathbf{x}_j^s, \mathbf{x}_i^s\right) + b \right) \geq 1 - \epsilon_i^s \ i \in \{1, \ldots, n_s\},$$

$$\alpha_j^t \geq 0 \ j \in \{1, \ldots, n_t\}, \ \alpha_j^s \geq 0 \ j \in \{1, \ldots, n_s\}.$$

Generally speaking, the revised SVM jointly optimizes the losses on the labeled data of both the source domain and the target domain.

Liao et al. (2005) further extend this idea to logistic regression, and propose the "Migratory-Logit" algorithm. Migratory-Logit models the difference between two domains by introducing a new "auxiliary variable" μ_i for each source data instance $(\mathbf{x}_i^s, y_i^s)$. The parameter μ_i could be geometrically understood as a "intercept term" that makes $\mathbf{x}_i^s$ migrate toward class y_i^s in the target domain. It measures how mismatch the source data instance $\mathbf{x}_i^s$ is with respect to the target domain distribution $\mathbb{P}_t^X$ and thus controls the importance of source data instances. For a target domain data instance $(\mathbf{x}_i^t, y_i^t)$, the posterior probability of its label y_i^t is the same as the traditional logistic regression, that is, $P(y_i^t | \mathbf{x}_i^t; \mathbf{w}) = \delta(y_i^t \mathbf{w}^T \mathbf{x}_i^t)$, where $\mathbf{w}$ is the parameter vector and $\delta(a) = \frac{1}{1 + \exp(-a)}$ is the Sigmoid function. For a source domain instance $(\mathbf{x}_i^s, y_i^s)$, the posterior probability of y_i^s is defined as:

$$P(y_i^s | \mathbf{x}_i^s; \mathbf{w}, \mu_i) = \delta(y_i^s \mathbf{w}^T \mathbf{x}_i^s + y_i^s \mu_i).$$

By defining $\boldsymbol{\mu} = (\mu_1, \ldots, \mu_m)^T$, the log-likelihood is computed as

$$\mathcal{L}(\mathbf{w}, \boldsymbol{\mu}; \mathcal{D}_s \cup \mathcal{D}_t) = \sum_{i=1}^{n_t} \ln \delta(y_i^t \mathbf{w}^T \mathbf{x}_i^t) + \sum_{i=1}^{n_s} \ln \delta(y_i^s \mathbf{w}^T \mathbf{x}_i^s + y_i^s \mu_i).$$

Then, all the parameters can be learned by maximizing the log-likelihood with the optimization problem formulated as

$$\max_{\mathbf{w}, \boldsymbol{\mu}} \ L(\mathbf{w}, \boldsymbol{\mu}; \mathcal{D}_s \cup \mathcal{D}_t) \quad \text{s.t.} \quad \frac{1}{n_s} \sum_{i=1}^{n_s} y_i^s \mu_i \leq C, \ y_i^s \mu_i \geq 0, \ \forall i \in \{1, 2, \ldots, n_s\},$$

where C is a hyper parameter to control the overall importance of the source domain data set.

The aforementioned approaches assume that, in the target domain, only labeled data are available as inputs for transfer learning algorithms. In many scenarios, plenty of unlabeled data may be available in the target domain as well.

Jiang and Zhai (2007) propose a general semi-supervised framework for instance-based inductive transfer learning, where both labeled and unlabeled data in the target domain are utilized with the source domain labeled data to train a target predictive model.

In the work by Jiang and Zhai (2007), a parameter α_i is introduced for each source domain instance $(\mathbf{x}_i^s, y_i^s) \in \mathcal{D}_s$ to measure how $P_s(y_i^s|\mathbf{x}_i^s)$ is different from $P_t(y_i^s|\mathbf{x}_i^s)$. Another parameter β_i is introduced for each source domain instance $(\mathbf{x}_i^s, y_i^s) \in \mathcal{D}_s$ to approximate the density ratio $\frac{P_t(\mathbf{x}_i^s)}{P_s(\mathbf{x}_i^s)}$. Then, for each target domain unlabeled instance $\mathbf{x}_i^{t,u} \in \mathcal{D}_t$ and each possible label y, a parameter $\gamma_i(y)$ is used to measure how likely the true label of $\mathbf{x}_i^{t,u}$ is y. Let $\mathcal{D}_t = \mathcal{D}_l \cup \mathcal{D}_u$ where $\mathcal{D}_l = \{(\mathbf{x}_j^{t,l}, y_j^{t,l})\}_{j=1}^{n_{t,l}}$ represents the subset of target domain-labeled instances and $\mathcal{D}_u = \{(\mathbf{x}_k^{t,u})\}_{k=1}^{n_{t,u}}$ represents the subset of target domain-unlabeled instances. To find an optimal classifier in terms of parameters θ, Jiang and Zhai (2007) propose to solve the following optimization problem:

$$\theta = \underset{\theta}{\text{argmax}} \; \frac{\lambda_s}{C_s} \sum_{i=1}^{n_s} \alpha_i \beta_i \log P(y_i^s|\mathbf{x}_i^s; \theta) + \frac{\lambda_{t,l}}{C_{t,l}} \sum_{j=1}^{n_{t,l}} \log P(y_j^{t,l}|\mathbf{x}_j^{t,l}; \theta)$$

$$+ \frac{\lambda_{t,u}}{C_{t,u}} \sum_{k=1}^{n_{t,u}} \sum_{y \in \mathcal{Y}} \gamma_k(y) \log(P(y|\mathbf{x}_k^{t,u}; \theta)) + \log P(\theta),$$

where $C_s = \sum_{i=1}^{n_s} \alpha_i \beta_i$, $C_{t,l} = n_{t,l}$, and $C_{t,u} = \sum_{k=1}^{n_{t,u}} \sum_{y \in \mathcal{Y}} \gamma_k(y)$ are normalization factors, the regularization parameters λ_s, $\lambda_{t,l}$ and $\lambda_{t,u}$ control the relative importance of each part with the sum equal to 1, and the prior $P(\theta)$ encodes the normal prior for θ. In this way, the source domain-labeled data, the target domain-labeled data and the target domain-unlabeled data are fully utilized to learn the optimal solution of θ.

2.3.2 Boosting-Style Methods

Another group of methods of instance-based inductive transfer learning is based on the boosting algorithm, which aims to identify misleading source domain instances by iteratively updating their weights. For instance, the TrAdaBoost algorithm proposed by Dai et al. (2007b) is the first boosting-style algorithm for an instance-based inductive transfer learning setting.

TraAdaBoost adopts a similar instance reweighting strategy used in AdaBoost to find useful data instances from the source domain. Specifically, TrAdaBoost first trains a model h on the union of $\mathcal{D}_s$ and $\mathcal{D}_t$. Then it uses h to make predictions on the target domain data and calculates the mean loss on the target domain as $\epsilon = \frac{\sum_{i=1}^{n_t} w_i^t l(h(\mathbf{x}_i^t), y_i^t)}{\sum_{i=1}^{n_t} w_i^t}$, where w_i^t is the weight for $\mathbf{x}_i^t$ and $l(\cdot, \cdot)$ is the loss function. For each target domain instance, its weight is updated as $w_i^t = w_i^t \beta^{-l(h(\mathbf{x}_i^t), y_i^t)}$, where $\beta = \epsilon/(1 - \epsilon)$. This reweighting strategy is similar to AdaBoost in that, if a target domain data instance has a higher loss, its weight should be increased in the next iteration.

For each source domain instance, if it has a higher loss, it may not be helpful to the target task and so its loss will be decreased in the next iteration. The rule to update the weight for each source domain instance is $w_i^s = w_i^s \theta^{l(h(x_i^s), y_i^s)}$, where $\theta = 1/(1 + \sqrt{2\ln n_s/(n_s + n_t)})$.

With these update rules, TraAdaBoost iteratively reweights both the source domain-labeled data and the target domain-labeled data to reduce the impact of misleading data instances in the source domain, and learn a series of classifiers to construct an ensemble classifier for the target domain.

2.3.3 Instance Generation Methods

Instead of reusing source domain-labeled data for the target domain, an alternative approach is to develop generative models to generate new instances for the target domain to be used to learn a precise target domain predictive model. Such generative models usually require sufficient source domain data and a few target domain data as inputs.

Instance-based transfer learning can also be used to adapt the style of instances in the target domain based on the source domain instances. For instance, Gatys et al. (2016) transfer image styles with a deep generative model to create new target images by preserving the semantic content of target images while synthesizing its texture from a source image. Basically, the overall loss function to generate a new image consists of two losses: the content loss $\mathscr{L}_{content}$ and the style loss $\mathscr{L}_{style}$:

$$\mathscr{L} = \alpha \mathscr{L}_{content}(G, T) + \beta \mathscr{L}_{style}(G, S), \qquad (2.10)$$

where G is the output image, S is the source image providing style and T is the target image offering content. Here $\mathscr{L}_{content}$ is defined as

$$\mathscr{L}_{content}(G, T, l) = \frac{1}{2}\sum_{i,j}(G_{i,j}^l - T_{i,j}^l)^2, \qquad (2.11)$$

where l stands for the lth layer of deep learning model, i stands for the feature mapping of the ith filter in the layer and j stands for the jth element of the vectorized feature mapping. In addition, the style loss is formulated as

$$\mathscr{L}_{style}(G, S) = \sum_l^L w_l E_l = \sum_l^L w_l \sum_{i,j}\left(Gamm(G)_{i,j}^l - Gamm(S)_{i,j}^l\right)^2, \qquad (2.12)$$

where $Gamm(\cdot)_{i,j}^l$, the style representation, is defined as the inner product between the vectorized feature maps i and j in layer l, that is, $Gamm(G)_{i,j}^l = \sum_k F_{ik}^l F_{jk}^l$. Specifically, in the work by Gatys et al. (2016), a nineteen-layer Visual Geometry Group Network network is used as the base model and all of its max-pooling layers are replaced by the mean pooling layers. First, the style and content features are extracted from source images and target images. Then, a random white noise image G_0 is passed through the network and its style features G^l and content features F^l are computed. Gradients with respect to the pixel values can be computed using error back-propagation and is used to iteratively update the generated image G.

Although the task studied in Gatys et al.'s (2016) work is about style transfer for images, the idea of generating new instances in the target domain by capturing some important properties of the source domain can be applied to many other transfer learning applications. We will review more generative models for transfer learning later in Chapter 7.

3

Feature-Based Transfer Learning

3.1 Introduction

As discussed in the previous chapter, a common assumption behind instance-based approaches is that the source domain data and the target domain data have similar or the same support. However, the assumption may be too strong to be satisfied in many real world scenarios, where the source domain data and the target domain data have some nonoverlapping features. For example, consider sentiment classification on customers' reviews of different types of products. Here, each type of products can be referred to as a domain, where customers may use common as well as domain-specific words to express their opinions. For instance, the word "boring" may be used to express negative sentiment on the DVD domain, while it is never used to express opinions on the furniture domain. Therefore, some words or features are observed on some domain(s) but not observed on other domain(s). This means that some features are source (or target) domain specific, which do not have the support in the opposite domain. In this case, reweighting or resampling instances cannot help much to reduce the discrepancy between domains. To address this issue, in this chapter, we introduce another approach to transfer learning known as feature-based transfer learning, which allows transfer learning to operate in an abstracted "feature space" instead of the raw input space. In this chapter, we focus on introducing homogeneous feature-based transfer learning methods. Recall that, in homogeneous transfer learning, we assume that $\mathbf{X}_s \cap \mathbf{X}_t \neq \emptyset$ and $\mathbf{Y}_s = \mathbf{Y}_t$. Note that, in an extreme case, there may be no overlapping features across the source domain and the target domain, but there may exist some translators between the two spaces to enable successful transfer learning. This is referred to as heterogeneous transfer learning, which will be reviewed in Chapter 6.

A common idea behind feature-based transfer learning approaches is to learn a pair of mapping functions $\{\varphi_s(\cdot), \varphi_t(\cdot)\}$ to map data respectively from the source domain and the target domain to a common feature space, where the difference between domains can be reduced. After that, a target classifier is trained on the new feature space with the mapped source domain and target domain data. For testing on target domain unseen data, one first maps the data onto the new feature space, and then performs the trained target classifier to make predictions.

Detailed motivations and assumptions on learning the pair of feature mappings behind different feature-based approaches are different. In this chapter, we summarize some main existing feature-based transfer learning approaches and classify them into three categories. The first category of the approaches aims to learn transferable features across given target and source domains by minimizing the domain differences (known as domain discrepancy) explicitly. Another category of the approaches aims to learn universal features that are expected to be high-quality features across all domains. The third category of the approaches is based on "feature augmentation" across domains, which seek to extend the feature space by considering extra correlations learned from data.

3.2 Minimizing the Domain Discrepancy

In many real world applications, observed high-dimensional data instances are often controlled by a set of latent factors or components in the domain. These latent factors can be referred to as features. The difference between domains might be caused by a subset of the features. If one can identify the latent features that do not cause the difference between domains, and use them to represent the data instances across domains, then one is able to train an accurate classifier in the target domain from the source domain training data with the new feature representation. Therefore, how to learn such domain invariant features, or equivalently, how to learn feature mappings between domains, $\{\varphi_s(\cdot), \varphi_t(\cdot)\}$, to map different domain instances onto a common space spanned by the domain invariant features, is critical to feature-based transfer learning. A key research issue in learning such domain invariant features is how to measure "domain invariance." So far, several metric criteria have been proposed to measure domain invariance for learning features, which are reviewed in the following sections.

3.2.1 Maximum Mean Discrepancy

Maximum Mean Discrepancy (MMD) is a nonparametric criteria to measure distance between distributions based on kernel embedding in reproducing kernel Hilbert space (RKHS) (Gretton et al., 2005). Given two domain samples $\mathbf{X}_s$ (source) and $\mathbf{X}_t$ (target), drawn from two distributions, respectively, the MMD distance is estimated empirically as follows,

$$\text{MMD}(\mathbf{X}_s, \mathbf{X}_t) = \left\| \frac{1}{n_s} \sum_{i=1}^{n_s} \phi(x_i^s) - \frac{1}{n_t} \sum_{i=1}^{n_t} \phi(x_i^t) \right\|_{\mathscr{H}}, \tag{3.1}$$

where $\phi(x)$ maps each instance to the Hilbert space $\mathscr{H}$ associated with the kernel $k(x_i, x_j) = \phi(x_i)^T \phi(x_j)$, and n_s and n_t are the sample sizes of the source and the target domains, respectively. By using the kernel trick, the MMD distance in (3.1) can be simplified as

$$\text{MMD}(\mathbf{X}_s, \mathbf{X}_t) = \text{tr}(\mathbf{KL}), \tag{3.2}$$

where $\mathbf{K} = \begin{bmatrix} \mathbf{K}_{s,s} & \mathbf{K}_{s,t} \\ \mathbf{K}_{s,t}^T & \mathbf{K}_{t,t} \end{bmatrix} \in \mathbb{R}^{(n_S + n_T) \times (n_S + n_T)}$ is a composite kernel matrix, with $\mathbf{K}_{s,s}$, $\mathbf{K}_{t,t}$ and $\mathbf{K}_{s,t}$ being the kernel matrices in the source domain, the target domain and across domains, respectively, and $\mathbf{L}$ is a matrix with the (i, j)-th entry l_{ij} defined as $l_{ij} = \begin{cases} \frac{1}{n_s^2} & x_i, x_j \in X_s \\ \frac{1}{n_t^2} & x_i, x_j \in X_t \\ -\frac{1}{n_s n_t} & \text{otherwise.} \end{cases}$

MMD Embedding

With the MMD distance, Pan et al. (2008b) propose a dimensionality reduction algorithm, known as MMD embedding (MMDE), for transfer learning, whose high-level idea is formulated as follows,

$$\min_{\varphi} \text{MMD}(\varphi(\mathbf{X}_S), \varphi(\mathbf{X}_T)) + \lambda \Omega(\varphi) \tag{3.3}$$

$$\text{s.t. constraints on } \varphi(\mathbf{X}_S) \text{ and } \varphi(\mathbf{X}_T),$$

where φ is the mapping to be learned, which maps the original data to a low-dimensional space across domains. The first term in (3.3) aims to minimize the MMD distance in distributions between the source and the target domain data, $\Omega(\varphi)$ is a regularization term on the mapping φ, and the constraints are to ensure original data properties to be preserved.

Based on the definition of the MMD distance, (3.3) can be written as

$$\min_{\varphi} \text{tr}(\mathbf{KL}) + \lambda \Omega(\varphi) \tag{3.4}$$

$$\text{s.t. constraints on } \varphi(\mathbf{X}_S) \text{ and } \varphi(\mathbf{X}_T),$$

where $\mathbf{K}$ is the kernel matrix induced by the kernel function $k(\mathbf{x}_i, \mathbf{x}_j) = \psi(\mathbf{x}_i)^T \psi(\mathbf{x}_j)$, and $\psi(\cdot)$ is defined as $\psi(\mathbf{x}) = \phi(\varphi(\mathbf{x}))$ or $\psi = \phi \circ \varphi$.

In general, the optimization (3.4) is computationally intractable as the kernel function $k(\mathbf{x}_j, \mathbf{x}_j)$ can be highly nonlinear of the mapping $\varphi(\cdot)$, which is unknown and to be learned. To make it computationally solvable, Pan et al. (2008b) proposed to first transform the optimization (3.4) to a kernel matrix learning problem as follows,

$$\min_{\mathbf{K} \geq 0} \text{tr}(\mathbf{KL}) - \lambda \text{tr}(\mathbf{K})$$

$$\text{s.t. } \mathbf{K}_{ii} + \mathbf{K}_{jj} - 2\mathbf{K}_{ij} = d_{ij}^2, \ \mathbf{K1} = \mathbf{0}, \tag{3.5}$$

where λ is a regularization parameter. The first term in the objective function of (3.5) is to minimize the MMD distance between the projected source and target domain data, while the second term that maximizes the trace of $\mathbf{K}$ aims to preserve the variance in the new feature space as the colored maximum variance unfolding (MVU) (Weinberger et al., 2004) does. The first constraint preserves the pairwise distance and the second constraint guarantees that the embedded data are centered. After solving (3.5), principal component analysis (PCA) is applied on $\mathbf{K}$ to get the leading eigenvectors to reconstruct the desired future mapping for the source and the target domain data.

One disadvantage of MMDE that it is an transductive learning method, which cannot generalize to out-of-sample data. Moreover, the optimization problem in (3.5) is a semi-definite programming (SDP) problem, which is computationally expensive to be solved.

Transfer Component Analysis

To overcome the limitations of MMDE, transfer component analysis (TCA) is proposed by Pan et al. (2010) by using an empirical kernel rather than by learning a kernel matrix from scratch. Specifically, in TCA, the kernel matrix in MMDE is decomposed as $\mathbf{K} = \tilde{\mathbf{K}}\mathbf{W}\mathbf{W}^T\tilde{\mathbf{K}}$, where $\mathbf{K}$ is an empirical kernel, which is given, and $\mathbf{W} \in \mathbb{R}^{(n_S + n_T) \times m}$ with $m \ll n_S + n_T$, which is to be learned. The optimization problem is formulated as

$$\min_{\mathbf{W}} \ \mathrm{tr}(\tilde{\mathbf{K}}\mathbf{W}\mathbf{W}^T\tilde{\mathbf{K}}\mathbf{L}) + \lambda \mathrm{tr}(\mathbf{W}^T\mathbf{W})$$
$$\text{s.t. } \mathbf{W}^T\tilde{\mathbf{K}}\mathbf{H}\tilde{\mathbf{K}}\mathbf{W} = \mathbf{I} \tag{3.6}$$

where $\mathbf{H} = \mathbf{I}_{n_1 + n_2} - \frac{1}{n_1 + n_2}\mathbf{1}\mathbf{1}^T$ is the centering matrix. Similar to MMDE, the first term in the objective is to minimize the MMD distance between the mapped source domain and the target domain data. The second term is a regularization term on $\mathbf{W}$. The constraint is to maximize the data variance after projection. It is easy to show that the optimization (3.6) has a closed-form solution, that is, $\mathbf{W}$ contains the m leading eigenvectors of $(\tilde{\mathbf{K}}\mathbf{L}\tilde{\mathbf{K}} + \lambda\mathbf{I})^{-1}\tilde{\mathbf{K}}\mathbf{H}\tilde{\mathbf{K}}$.

Compared with MMDE, TCA avoids solving an SDP problem and thus it is more efficient. Moreover, TCA can easily handle out-of-sample data[1] directly. Besides, instead of the two-step nature of MMDE, which first learns the kernel matrix and then conducts PCA to obtain the transformed data, TCA can obtain the transformed data with the use of $\mathbf{W}$ in one stage.

Deep Architectures with MMD

In the context of deep learning, researchers have proposed to use a deep neural network to approximate the feature mapping $\phi(\cdot)$ induced by a kernel function. For instance, Tzeng et al. (2014) propose encoding MMD to measure the distance between hidden features learned in a convolutional neural network (CNN). In this way, the network automatically learns a cross-domain representation by jointly maximizing label dependence if available and minimizing domain invariance. The base deep architecture is illustrated in Figure 3.1, where the input data

---

[1] The out-of-sample data is referred to as the data that are not observed in training.

$x_S \in \mathcal{X}_S$ from the source domain and $x_T \in \mathcal{X}_T$ from the target domain are transformed by the first several layers of the CNN. The transformation with the first layers can be considered as an approximate of $\psi(\cdot)$ in MMDE.

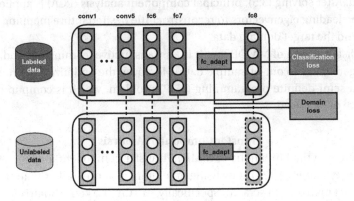

Figure 3.1 Deep CNN for both classification loss as well as domain invariance, where the dashed line means the weight sharing (adapted from Tzeng et al. [2014]).

As a follow-up work, Long et al. (2015) propose a multi-kernel MMD (MK-MMD) as an alternative to compute the MMD distance to measure the domain divergence for deep learning models. The basic idea is to use multiple positive semi-definite kernels to compute the MMD distance, which is supposed to be able to provide a more flexible and robust distance measure for neutral networks to learn cross-domain feature representation.

To take label information into account when measuring domain discrepancy, Long et al. (2017) propose joint distribution discrepancy (JDD) on joint distributions $P(X_s, Y_s)$ from the source domain and $P(X_t, Y_t)$ from the target domain. The architecture of the resulting joint adaptation networks (JANs) is shown in the Figure 3.2. As can be seen from the figure, not only the last hidden layer, but also all the fully connected layers and the output layer are involved in the computation of the JDD criteria in the JAN.

3.2.2 Bregman Divergence-Based Regularization

Besides using the MMD distance to measure domain invariance, Si et al. (2010) propose a transfer subspace learning method based on Bregman divergence regularization. The proposed high-level objective function is formulated as

$$\min_{\phi} F(\phi) + \lambda D_w(\phi(X_s)||\phi(X_t)), \tag{3.7}$$

where $F(\phi)$ defines a task-specific goal, for example, minimizing a classification error, and $D_w(\phi(X_s)||\phi(X_t))$ is the Bregman divergence between $\phi(X_s)$ and $\phi(X_t)$.

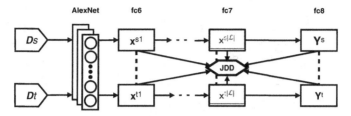

Figure 3.2 The architecture of the JAN (adapted from Long et al. [2017]) based on the AlexNet

Given a mapping function U, its first derivative U', and its inverse $\xi = (U')^{-1}$, the Bregman divergence is defined as

$$D_W(\phi(X_s)\|\phi(X_t)) = \int d(\xi(P_s^{\phi(x)}), \xi(P_t^{\phi(x)}))d\mu,$$

where

$$d(\xi(P_s^{\phi(x)}), \xi(P_t^{\phi(x)})) = (U(\xi(P_t^{\phi(x)})) - U(\xi(P_s^{\phi(x)}))) - P_s^{\phi(X_S)}(\xi(P_t^{\phi(x)}) - \xi(P_s^{\phi(x)})),$$

with $d\mu$ being the Lebesgue measure for $\phi(x)$, and the probability densities for the source and the target domains in the projected space are denoted by $P_s^{\phi(x)}$ and $P_t^{\phi(x)}$, respectively.

3.2.3 Measurement with Assumptions on Specific Distributions

By assuming that data follows a Gaussian distribution, Castrejon et al. (2016) investigate using statistics information of the feature activations to learn cross-modal scene representations in the transfer learning fashion. The proposed method regularizes cross-modal CNNs for images with different styles and multi-layer perceptron (MLP) for the language model so that they have a shared representation that is agnostic of the modality. Figure 3.3 shows how the high-level representation is shared across different domains of the image and the language model.

Moreover, the proposed method further introduces a regularization term over the activations to encourage them to have similar statistics across modalities in the intermediate hidden layers. Let $P_i(h)$ be a distribution over the hidden activations in the i-th layer. Then, the regularization term can be computed as $\mathcal{R}_i = -\ln P_i(h; \theta_i)$ by taking the negative logarithm, where θ_i denotes the hyperparameters. By instantiating P_i with a normal distribution as $P_i(h; \mu, \Sigma) \sim N(\mu, \Sigma)$, the regularization term $R_i(h)$ can be computed as

$$P_i(h; \mu_i, \Sigma_i) = \frac{1}{2}(h - \mu_i)^T \Sigma_i^{-1}(h - \mu_i)$$

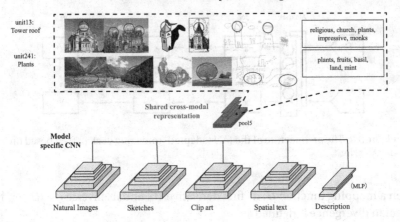

Figure 3.3 Low-level representations are specific for each modality (bottom elements) and a high-level representation is shared across all modalities (highlighted on the top) (adapted from Castrejon et al. [2016]).

Moreover, a mixture of Gaussian distributions can be used to define P_i, which is more flexible than a single Gaussian distribution.

3.2.4   Data-Dependant Domain Discrepancy Measurements

There is a variety of criteria to measure domain discrepancy. However, it is very difficult to design a universal measure that is proper for all application problems. To address this issue, researchers have studied to formulate the problem of evaluating domain invariance as a learning problem.

Tzeng et al. (2015) introduce the domain confusion loss to learn a domain-invariant representation, which could better utilize a classifier trained on the labeled source data. First, the proposed method simply performs binary classification using the domain labels. With a particular feature representation θ_{repr}, it futher evaluates the domain invariance by learning the best domain classifier. This learning procedure can be done by optimizing the following objective function

$$\mathcal{L}_D(x_S, x_T, \theta_{repr}; \theta_D) = -\sum_d 1[y_D = d]\ln(q_d), \qquad (3.8)$$

where $q = \text{softmax}(\theta_D^T f(x; \theta_{repr}))$ and y_D denotes the domain from which the example is drawn. For a particular domain classifier θ_D, the loss that seeks to "maximally confuse" the two domains by computing the cross entropy between the output predicted domain labels and a uniform distribution over domain labels is defined as

$$\mathcal{L}_D(x_S, x_T, \theta_{repr}; \theta_D) = -\sum_d \ln(q_d). \qquad (3.9)$$

(3.8) and (3.9) are updated alternatingly during training.

Note that, besides the work already mentioned, there exist many works to learn a classification model to distinguish the source and the target domain examples using the domain labels. Once learned, a domain classifier can play the role of a discriminator together with another neural network that generates domain-confusion examples as a generator to play a max-min game. These related works will be discussed in Chapter 7.

3.3 Learning Universal Features

Most of the works reviewed in the previous section aim to learn domain invariant features across a source domain and a target domain, which are given in advance. There exist another branch of feature learning approaches, which aims to learn a universal feature representation from several domains. Since the features apply to any domain in consideration, it is called "universal." This idea is partly inspired by the work of self-taught learning (Raina et al., 2007), which aims to learn a universal feature representation from plenty of unlabeled data whose ground-truth labels can be different from those of the target task. Self-taught learning was applied to image-classification problems. Most existing methods in this vain consist of three steps: (1) learn higher-level features from unlabeled data of source or auxiliary domains; (2) represent the target domain labeled data based on the learned higher-level features; and (3) train a classifier from the target domain labeled data with the new representation.

Note that, given multiple source or auxiliary domains, a universal feature representation can also be learned by adapting multitask feature learning methods (Argyriou et al., 2006; Zhang and Yang, 2017b). In multitask feature learning, common features are learned across different tasks. Such common features can be considered as universal features for other tasks. Various multitask learning methods will be reviewed in Chapter 9.

3.3.1 Learning Universal Codes

Raina et al. (2007) propose to apply sparse coding (Lee et al., 2007), which is an unsupervised feature construction method, to learn high-level universal features for any target task. The basic idea of this approach consists of two steps. At the first step, higher-level basis vectors, that is, a dictionary of codes, $\{\mathbf{b}_1, \ldots, \mathbf{b}_{n_s}\}$, are learned from plenty of unlabeled data, which can be from a number of source domains in the context of transfer learning, as follows:

$$\min_{\mathbf{A}, \mathbf{B}} \sum_i \|\mathbf{x}_i^s - \sum_j a_i^j \mathbf{b}_j\|_2^2 + \beta \|\mathbf{a}^i\|_1,$$
$$\text{s.t. } \|\mathbf{b}_j\|_2 \leq 1 \ \forall j \in 1, \ldots, n_s, \tag{3.10}$$

where $\mathbf{a}^i = (a_i^1, \ldots, a_i^{n_s})^T$ is a new representation on the basis matrix $\mathbf{B} = (\mathbf{b}_1, \ldots, \mathbf{b}_{n_s})$ for $\mathbf{x}_i^s$ and β is the regularization parameter. The objective function of (3.10) balances two goals: (i) the first goal is to reconstruct x_i^s as a weighted combination of bases $\{\mathbf{b}_1, \ldots, \mathbf{b}_{n_s}\}$ with the corresponding weights as a_i^j; and (ii) the second goal encourages $\mathbf{a}^i$ to be sparse. After learning $\mathbf{B}$, the second step aims to learn high-level features for target data, which is from the target domain in the context of transfer learning, by solving the following problem

$$\hat{\mathbf{a}}^i = \operatorname*{argmin}_{\mathbf{a}^i} \|\mathbf{x}_i^t - \sum_j a_j^i \mathbf{b}_j\|_2^2 + \beta \|\mathbf{a}^i\|_1. \tag{3.11}$$

Finally, we can learn a model based on the new representation $\{\hat{\mathbf{a}}^i\}$ for the target domain with the associated labels.

3.3.2 Deep Universal Features

Motivated by the use of sparse coding for learning universal features, Glorot et al. (2011) propose applying deep autoencoders to learn high-level features as universal features. Specifically, Given an input $\mathbf{x}$, a deep encoder $f(\cdot)$ maps it to a hidden code as $\mathbf{h} = f(\mathbf{x})$, and a deep decoder $g(\cdot)$ aims to reconstruct the input with the hidden code via $\hat{\mathbf{x}} = g(\mathbf{h})$. As the encoder and decoder are trained with various auxiliary domains, the output of the encoder, $\mathbf{h}$, is considered a universal feature representation for each input instance. Chen et al. (2012b) further propose a variant of autoencoders, namely marginalized stacked denoising autoencoders, to improve the efficiency and effectiveness for learning universal features across domains.

Besides using the reconstruction loss as used in sparse coding and antoencoders to learn universal features, some researchers proposed using clustering on auxiliary tasks to learn universal features. Compared with the reconstruction loss, clustering is lightweight unsupervised learning in terms of the complexity. It can also increase the interpretability of the learned representations. As shown in Figure 3.4, Liao et al. (2016) investigate several k-means styled loss functions as regularizations such as sample clustering, spatial clustering and co-clustering.

Assume that the representation of one layer in a neural network is to be a 4-D tensor $Y \in R^{N \times C \times H \times W}$, where N, C, H, and W are the size of a mini-batch, the number of hidden units, the height of the representation and the corresponding width, respectively. Specifically, by unfolding each data instance into a matrix $T^{\{N\} \times \{H,W,C\}}$, the loss for the sample clustering is defined as:

$$\mathcal{R}_{sample}(Y, \mu) = \frac{1}{2NCHW} \sum_{n=1}^N \|T^{\{N\} \times \{H,W,C\}}(Y)_n - \mu_{z_n}\|^2. \tag{3.12}$$

The representation of an example can be regarded as a C-channel "image." Pixels

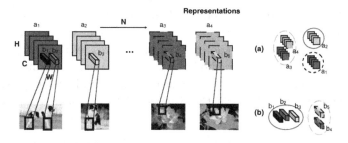

Figure 3.4 (a) Sample clustering; (b) spatial clustering (adapted from Liao et al. [2016]).

consisting of C channels can be clustered by spatial clustering as

$$\mathscr{R}_{spatial}(Y,\mu) = \frac{1}{2NCHW} \sum_{i=1}^{NHW} ||T^{\{N,H,W\}\times\{C\}}(Y)_i - \mu_{z_i}||^2. \quad (3.13)$$

Moreover, clustering can be performed on the channel by using the following loss

$$\mathscr{R}_{spatial}(Y,\mu) = \frac{1}{2NCHW} \sum_{i=1}^{NC} ||T^{\{N,C\}\times\{H,W\}}(Y)_i - \mu_{z_i}||^2. \quad (3.14)$$

In Liao et al. (2016), the authors focused on investigating whether the representation for clustering is applicable to unseen categories, which is a zero-shot learning problem. Given these features trained by the loss in (3.12), one can learn the output embedding E via a structured SVM without regularization as

$$\min_E \frac{1}{N} \sum_{n=1}^{N} \max_{y\in\mathscr{Y}}\{0, \Delta(y_n, y) + x_n^T E[\phi(y) - \phi(y_n)]\}, \quad (3.15)$$

where x_n and y_n are the feature and the class label of the n-th example, Δ is the 0-1 loss function, and ϕ is the class-attribute matrix provided by the Caltech–UCSD (University of California, San Diego) Birds data set with each entry indicating how likely one attribute is present in a given class.

3.4 Feature Augmentation

Daumé III (2007) proposes a simple approach for domain adaptation, which augments the feature vector for both the source and the target domains data using domain-specific information and treats them as new inputs to a learning algorithm.

Define $\mathscr{X}$ and $\mathscr{Y}$ as the input and output spaces, respectively. Suppose the original input space is denoted by $\mathscr{X} \in \mathbb{R}^F$. The proposed method augments the original input space to $\widetilde{X} \in \mathbb{R}^{3F}$. The mapping functions $\Phi^s, \Phi^t : \mathscr{X} \to \widetilde{\mathscr{X}}$ for the source and the target domains are defined as

$$\Phi^s(\mathbf{x}) = \langle \mathbf{x}, \mathbf{x}, \mathbf{0}\rangle, \quad \Phi^t(\mathbf{x}) = \langle \mathbf{x}, \mathbf{0}, \mathbf{x}\rangle, \quad (3.16)$$

where **0** denotes a zero vector in the F-dimensional space. The first part of the augmented feature represents the general feature, while the second and third parts represent the source and target domain specific features, respectively.

It's easy to generalize this method to a kernelized version. Assume that each data point x is projected to a RKHS with the corresponding kernel $k : \mathcal{X} \times \mathcal{X} \to \mathcal{R}$. k can be written as the dot product of two vectors $k(\mathbf{x}, \mathbf{x}') = \langle \Phi(\mathbf{x}), \Phi(\mathbf{x}') \rangle_{\mathcal{X}}$. We can define Φ^s and Φ^t in terms of Φ as

$$\Phi^s(\mathbf{x}) = \langle \Phi(\mathbf{x}), \Phi(\mathbf{x}), \mathbf{0} \rangle, \ \Phi^t(\mathbf{x}) = \langle \Phi(\mathbf{x}), \mathbf{0}, \Phi(\mathbf{x}) \rangle. \tag{3.17}$$

Denote the expanded kernel by $\tilde{k}(\mathbf{x}, \mathbf{x}')$. When $\mathbf{x}$ and $\mathbf{x}'$ are from the same domain, $\tilde{k}(\mathbf{x}, \mathbf{x}') = \langle \Phi(\mathbf{x}), \Phi(\mathbf{x}') \rangle_{\mathcal{X}} + \langle \Phi(\mathbf{x}), \Phi(\mathbf{x}') \rangle_{\mathcal{X}} = 2k(\mathbf{x}, \mathbf{x}')$. When $\mathbf{x}$ and $\mathbf{x}'$ are from different domains, $\tilde{k}(\mathbf{x}, \mathbf{x}') = \langle \Phi(\mathbf{x}), \Phi(\mathbf{x}') \rangle_{\mathcal{X}} = k(\mathbf{x}, \mathbf{x}')$.

Considering the kernel as a measurement for similarity, the kernelized formulation is intuitively pleasing in that data points from the same domain are inherently twice as large as cross-domain points. Consider testing on the target data, the training data in the target domain have twice as much influence as source points.

Note that this feature augmentation method decomposes a hypothesis into three sub-hypothesis as $h = \langle h_c, h_s, h_t \rangle$, which is equivalent to learning two domain-specific hypotheses $w_s = h_c + h_s$ and $w_t = h_c + h_t$. This method can be naturally extended to the semi-supervised learning setting by assuming that w_s and w_t make agreement on each unlabeled target domain example x_i as

$$w_s \cdot x_i \approx w_t \cdot x_i \iff \langle h_c, h_s, h_t \rangle \cdot \langle 0, x_i, -x_i \rangle \approx 0 \tag{3.18}$$

In this way, one can construct a feature map for unlabeled data as

$$\Phi^u(\mathbf{x}) = \langle \mathbf{0}, \mathbf{x}, -\mathbf{x} \rangle.$$

After that, any standard semi-supervised learning classifiers can be applied with the feature maps defined for source domain labeled data and labeled and unlabeled target domain data.

4

Model-Based Transfer Learning

4.1 Introduction

Model-based transfer learning, also known as parameter-based transfer learning, assumes that the source task and the target task share some common knowledge in the model level. That means the transferred knowledge is encoded into model parameters, priors or model architectures. Therefore, the goal of model-based transfer learning is to discover what part of the model learned in the source domain can help the learning of the model for target domain.

Similar to instance-based transfer learning and feature-based transfer learning, model-based transfer learning leverages the knowledge in the source domain. However, the most important difference is that model-based transfer learning leverages the model-level knowledge rather than the instance or feature level. Intuitively, reusing the model learned from the source domain is more efficient and able to integrally grasp the high-level knowledge of the source domain data, because one does not need to resample the training data or conduct relational inference on complicate data representations.

With the assumption that a well-trained source model θ_s has learned a lot of the structure from data, then, for another related target task, this structure can be transferred to learn a more precise target model θ_t with a few labeled data in the target domain. As shown in Figure 4.1(a), with only a few training samples from the target domain, we can only learn a simple model to prevent the risk of overfitting. However, with the help of a well-trained source model, a more powerful model can be obtained using only limited training examples in the target domain, as shown in Figure 4.1.

Most model-based transfer learning algorithms are proposed under the inductive transfer learning setting, where some labeled instances are assumed to be available in the target domain. Note that some existing model-based transfer learning methods are adapted from model-based multitask learning approaches. Recall that the difference between multitask learning and transfer learning is that multitask learning tries to optimize the performance on a lot of target tasks simultaneously, while transfer learning only focuses on improving the performance of one

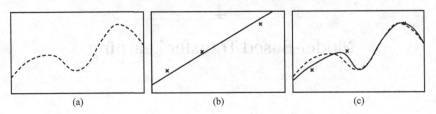

Figure 4.1 (a) Source model (the dash line). (b) Target model (the solid line) only with limited target data (the crosses). (c) The target model (the solid line) transferred with the source model (the dash line) as a prior.

target domain by exploiting knowledge from auxiliary task(s). For example, Evgeniou and Pontil (2004) propose a regularized multitask learning method based on support vector machines (SVMs), where the optimization objective is to equally minimize the loss over all tasks. Hence, the final learned model has a best overall performance balancing all the tasks. However, this result may not guarantee the optimal performance on the desired target task. In transfer learning setting, one only focuses on the performance of the target task. This difference can be eliminated by simply changing the weight assignment for difference tasks in the objective function in multitask learning. In the chapter, related multitask learning algorithms will be only briefly mentioned as they will be introduced more specifically in Chapter 9.

Based on specific assumptions in different model-based transfer learning methods, we classify these algorithms into two categories: transferring knowledge through shared model components (Section 4.2) and transferring knowledge through regularization (Section 4.3). The first category, transferring knowledge through shared model components, covers the transfer learning algorithms that establish the target model by reusing some components in the source model or reusing some hyperparameters of the source model (Li et al., 2006; Tommasi et al., 2010; Jie et al., 2011). Moreover, there are methods that learn both the source and target models simultaneously (Lawrence and Platt, 2004; Bonilla et al., 2007; Schwaighofer et al., 2005).

The second category aims to transfer knowledge through regularization. Regularization is a technique used to solve ill-posed machine learning problems and to prevent model overfitting by restricting model flexibility. In model-based transfer learning algorithms, the regularization is used to constrain parameters based on some prior hypotheses. The SVM has been a commonly used base model in this category because of its nice computational properties and good performance in many applications. With the introduction of deep models, some approaches have transferred model parameters in a pretrained deep learning model from auxiliary tasks, where the parameters are used to initialize target domain models.

4.2 Transfer through Shared Model Components

The prior, short for the prior probability distribution, is the probability distribution that entails beliefs about some uncertain events before seeing any evidence. For example, consider you are playing a coin toss game with your friend. If the toss result is heads, you win, and otherwise, you lose. Before the toss, you are supposed to bet on one side of the coin, that is, heads or tails. It is likely that you will arbitrarily choose one side, because you know that either side has equal probability to appear. However, if you have known that heads is more likely to happen, you will more likely bet on heads. In this example, the prior is the probability that the coin will turn land on heads.

The prior gives you better and more effective estimation before you make decision, so you do not have to toss the coin for many times to see which side is more likely to appear. Similarly, in real world applications, if we can apply such a prior to a new task, we may obtain a model of satisfactory performance even with limited training data in the target task. With this motivation, many model-based transfer-learning algorithms have been proposed (Lawrence and Platt, 2004; Schwaighofer et al., 2005; Li et al., 2006; Bonilla et al., 2007; Tommasi et al., 2010; Jie et al., 2011; Ma et al., 2014; Shu et al., 2015; Bousmalis et al., 2016; Chen et al., 2016a; Ghifary et al., 2016).

4.2.1 Transfer Learning via Gaussian Processes

First we give a brief introduction to Gaussian process (GP) and then introduce how the methods proposed in the work by Lawrence and Platt (2004), Schwaighofer et al. (2005), and Bonilla et al. (2007) utilize GP to share knowledge between tasks.

GP is a commonly used tool to model the data distribution with a Gaussian prior. A GP is a stochastic process such that every finite collection of random variables has a multivariate normal distribution. In supervised learning, it can be used to predict the label of unseen data based on the measure of the similarities between training data. Given labels as well as the data $\mathbf{X} = [\mathbf{x}_1, \mathbf{x}_2, \ldots, \mathbf{x}_N]^T$, by defining latent variables $\mathbf{z} = [z_1, z_2, \ldots, z_N]^T$, the prior distribution over the latent variables is given by a Gaussian prior as

$$p(\mathbf{z}|\mathbf{X}, \theta) = N(\mathbf{0}, \mathbf{K}), \tag{4.1}$$

where θ denotes the parameters and $\mathbf{K}$ is the covariance function, as known as the *kernel*, to depict a multivariate normal distribution. $\mathbf{K}$ can take different forms such as the linear kernel $\mathbf{K}(\mathbf{x}, \mathbf{x}') = \mathbf{x}^T \mathbf{x}'$ and the squared exponential kernel $\mathbf{K}(\mathbf{x}, \mathbf{x}')$ $= \sigma^2 \exp\left(-\frac{\|\mathbf{x} - \mathbf{x}'\|^2}{2\ell^2}\right)$, where ℓ and σ are included in θ to be estimated.

In a GP, variables $\mathbf{y}$ are independent of $\mathbf{X}$ given $\mathbf{z}$. The joint likelihood of overall data can be formulated as

$$p(\mathbf{y}, \mathbf{z}|\mathbf{X}, \theta) = p(\mathbf{z}|\mathbf{X}, \theta) \prod_{i=1}^{N} p(y_i|z_i), \tag{4.2}$$

where the conditional probability $p(y_i|z_i)$ gives the relationship between observations and the latent variables. (4.2) consists of two parts, the prior and the likelihood $p(y_i|z_i)$.

Suppose that we have M related but different tasks, each of which is modeled as a GP on the corresponding training data $\{(\mathbf{X}_m, \mathbf{y}_m)\}$. The probability distribution for $\mathbf{y} = (\mathbf{y}_1^T, \ldots, \mathbf{y}_M^T)^T$ is

$$p(\mathbf{y}|\mathbf{X}, \theta) = \prod_{m=1}^{M} p(\mathbf{y}_m|\mathbf{X}_m, \theta). \tag{4.3}$$

Note that θ is shared by different tasks.

Lawrence and Platt (2004) utilize (4.3) to define a multitask GP by constraining the covariance matrix K to be a block diagonal matrix as

$$\mathbf{K} = \begin{bmatrix} \mathbf{K}_1 & \mathbf{0} & \mathbf{0} & \mathbf{0} \\ \mathbf{0} & \mathbf{K}_2 & \mathbf{0} & \mathbf{0} \\ \mathbf{0} & \mathbf{0} & \ddots & \mathbf{0} \\ \mathbf{0} & \mathbf{0} & \mathbf{0} & \mathbf{K}_m \end{bmatrix},$$

and uses the informative vector machine (IVM) to find a sparse representation to reduce the computation and speedup the training.

Schwaighofer et al. (2005) combine the hierarchical Bayesian learning and GP together for multitask learning. In this algorithm, the hierarchical Bayesian modeling essentially learns the mean and covariance functions of the GP. The algorithm takes two steps:

(1) learn a common collaborative kernel matrix from the data via a simple and efficient expectation-maximization (EM) algorithm;
(2) generalize the covariance matrix by using a generalized Nyström method.

Bonilla et al. (2007) relaxed the constraints on covariance matrix in Lawrence and Platt (2004). It uses a shared covariance function on data and a free-form covariance matrix over different tasks to model the inter-task dependencies, so it allows a better flexibility.

4.2.2   Knowledge Transfer via Bayesian Models

The aforementioned methods learn the common prior based on GP, while the prior can be transferred from the source domains. Other Bayesian models can also be used for model-based transfer learning, which we review here in this section.

Li et al. (2006) propose an algorithm that transfers the priors from some source domains (more specifically, visual categories) to estimate the parameter distribution of some target domain objects in images based on a Bayesian method. By transferring the prior, the algorithm allows the learning of a new category using a single or a few examples. General information coming from previously learned unrelated categories is represented with a suitable prior probability distribution on the parameters of the probabilistic models.

Bayesian models have also been applied to applications in natural language processing (NLP). Dai et al. (2007a) propose a transfer learning algorithm based on the naive Bayes classifier for text classification. Prior knowledge is transferred as a probability distribution in two steps. First, one builds a traditional naive Bayes model based on data in the source domain. Second, an EM algorithm is used to find the model for the target domain based on the source model, where the Kulback–Leibler divergence is used to measure the difference between two domains. The EM algorithm gradually minimizes the differences between the newly learned model and the target domain distribution.

4.2.3   Model Transfer via Deep Models

With the development of deep learning, researchers have attempted to leverage the powerful expressive ability of deep learning to extract and transfer knowledge such as the relationships among categories. The knowledge distillation technique, which involves a teacher network and a student network, is a good example. Originally, knowledge distillation, also known as soft labeling, is proposed to do the model compression, in which we may regard the source domain as being identical to the target one.

In model-based transfer learning, one can distill a soft label l for the class category k by averaging over the softmax of all activations of source examples in the category k. We can denote this average as $l^{(k)}$. In case that the simple softmax produces a very peaked distribution, we can use a softmax with a high temperature τ so that the related classes can preserve enough information about the relationship among the classes.

Formally, the loss for the relational knowledge among the classes based on soft labels can be defined as

$$\mathscr{L}_{softlabel}(x_t, y_t; \theta_{repr}, \theta_c) = -\sum_i l^{(k)} \mathrm{softmax}(\theta_c^T f(x_T; \theta_{repr})/\tau). \qquad (4.4)$$

Consider Figure 4.2 as an example. The soft label $l^{(bottle)}$ is a K-dimensional vector, where each dimension indicates the similarity of bottles to each of the K categories. In this example, the soft label of a bottle will have a higher weight on the mug than the keyboard, since bottles and mugs are more visually similar. Thus, training with these soft labels enforces the relationship that bottles and mugs should be closer in the feature space than those between bottles and keyboards.

4.2.4   Other Strategies

Different from the Bayesian methods, Jie et al. (2011) propose a method that uses off-the-shelf models as priors to learn a new model. They defined a score

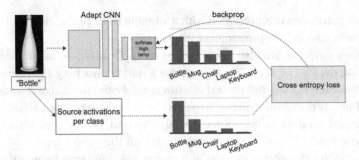

Figure 4.2 An illustration of the soft labeling method (adapted from Tzeng et al. [2014])

function $s(\mathbf{x}_i, y)$ to measure the probability that a sample $\mathbf{x}_i$ belongs to class y as

$$s(\mathbf{x}_i, y) = \bar{\mathbf{w}} \cdot \bar{\phi}(\mathbf{x}_i, y) = \mathbf{w}^{(0)} \cdot \phi^{(0)}(\mathbf{x}, y) + \sum_{z=1}^{F} \mathbf{w}^{(y,z)} \cdot \phi^{(y,z)}\left(s_p(\mathbf{x}, z), y\right),$$

where $\phi^{(\cdot)}$ is a feature-mapping function and $\mathbf{w}^{(\cdot)}$ is the parameter that separates the corresponding two classes by a hyperplane. The score of the new class y is calculated using the model trained on the target data as well as the prior knowledge from the source data.

4.3 Transfer through Regularization

Shared knowledge can also be transferred through the regularization. Many researches have explored ways to use the regularization to leverage the transferred knowledge between a source domain and a target domain.

The standard form of regularization in a model is as follows:

$$\tilde{J}(\theta; \mathbf{X}, \mathbf{y}) = J(\theta; \mathbf{X}, \mathbf{y}) + \alpha \Omega(\theta), \tag{4.5}$$

where J is the original objective function and $\tilde{J}$ is the regularized objective function with the regularization term $\Omega(\cdot)$ on parameter θ with a regularization weight α.

Evgeniou and Pontil (2004) propose that the model parameter can be decomposed into two parts, a task-specific part and a task-invariant part. The target and source model parameters can be modeled as

$$\boldsymbol{\theta}_s = \boldsymbol{\theta}_0 + \mathbf{v}_s \tag{4.6}$$

$$\boldsymbol{\theta}_t = \boldsymbol{\theta}_0 + \mathbf{v}_t. \tag{4.7}$$

$\boldsymbol{\theta}_0$, the task-invariant parameter, represents the invariant characteristics over tasks and is supposed to be transferred in model-based transfer learning. $\mathbf{v}_T$ and $\mathbf{v}_S$, the

Figure 4.3 Adapt the parameter θ to detect a new class "lions" $\tilde{\theta}$ using a regularizer $\Omega(\cdot)$

task-specific parameters, depict the specific characteristics of a certain task and can be learned from the data from the specific domain.

What we can leverage from source models is the task-invariant parameters, which are trained from sufficient data, so the generalization performance of the target model could be improved.

4.3.1 Support Vector Machine-Based Regularization

As mentioned earlier, SVMs are commonly used for regularized model-based transfer learning because they have some nice properties

(1) SVMs elegantly separate the data using a hyperplane and only a few data determine the boundary, which makes the model transfer intuitively easy and the computing cost relatively low.
(2) The objective function of SVMs is simple in that it is convenient to add constraints and regularizers.

We can show that (4.5) can be generalized to SVMs. A standard SVM has the following objective function as

$$\min_{\mathbf{w}} \frac{1}{2}\|\mathbf{w}\|^2 \quad \text{s.t. } y_i[\mathbf{w}\cdot\mathbf{x}_i + b] >= 1 \ \forall i. \tag{4.8}$$

Yang et al. (2007c) propose an adaptive SVM (A-SVM), which learns a new decision boundary that is close to the original decision boundary. In A-SVM, the target model is defined as $f_t(\mathbf{x}) = f_s(\mathbf{x}) + \Delta f(\mathbf{x})$, where $\Delta f(\mathbf{x})$ is the permutation function that shifts the source decision boundary to fit the target data.

Similar to Yang et al. (2007c), Jiang et al. (2008) propose a cross-domain SVM (CD-SVM) algorithm to transfer knowledge from an SVM trained from a source task to a new task. The motivation behind CD-SVM is that, if a support vector learned by a source SVM falls in the neighborhood of some target domain training data, then it tends to have a distribution similar to the source domain, and thus can be used to help train a new SVM for the target domain. Therefore, in CD, the target domain SVM can be optimized by adding neighborhood constraints of the support vectors learned in the source domain.

Aytar and Zisserman (2011) improve (Yang et al., 2007c) in the application of object category detection and propose a deformable adaptive SVM (DA-SVM). It utilizes the trained image detector of other categories as the regularization term to train on a new category using a minimum number of possible training samples in the current category. Duan et al. (2009) propose a domain transfer SVM (DT-SVM) for video concept detection. DT-SVM tries to decrease the mismatch across domain distributions, which are measured by MMD and, at the same time, learn a decision function for the target domain. In video-concept detection applications, the change of a key frame is very frequent, which makes the feature representations difficult to capture without a large amount of data. To address this problem, DT-SVM proposes a unified framework to simultaneously learn an optimal kernel function as well as a robust SVM classifier. Bruzzone and Marconcini (2010) propose a domain adaptation SVM that exploits a semi-supervised method to adapt the traditional SVM to a new domain while validating adapted classifier with noisy labels. Xu et al. (2014a) propose an adaptive structural SVM (A-SSVM) to adapt the classifier parameters between domains. This method introduces a data-dependent regularization term for source domain selection and integrates different feature extraction methods. By doing this, A-SSVM is able to capture the structural knowledge through feature space and trained parameters.

Tommasi et al. (2010) propose an SVM-based adaptation algorithm that exploits some prior knowledge to imitate the human ability on recognizing objects even from only one single view. This algorithm selects and adapts the weights of the prior knowledge from different categories by assuming that the new categories are similar to some of the existing categories. This method modifies the objective function in conventional least squares SVMs (LS-SVMs) by changing the regularization term where the modified objective function is formulated as

$$\min_{\mathbf{w}_t, b} \frac{1}{2} \|\mathbf{w}_t - \beta \mathbf{w}_s\|^2 + \frac{C}{2} \sum_{i=1}^{l} [y_i - \mathbf{w}_t \cdot \phi(\mathbf{x}_i) - b]^2,$$

where $\mathbf{w}_s$ and $\mathbf{w}_t$ are the parameter of the source and target models, respectively.

The regularization term constrains the target model parameter to be close to the source parameter with β, a scaling factor between 0 and 1, controlling the closeness measurement.

4.3.2 MKL-Based Transfer Learning

Formula (4.5) can be further generalized to the multi-kernel learning (MKL) setting when $J(\theta;\mathbf{X},\mathbf{y})$ is a combination of multiple kernels. MKL is used to directly constrain the form of kernels rather than using a prior for the kernel function. For instance, Duan et al. (2012a) propose a domain transfer MKL (DT-MKL) method, which enforces the decision boundary for the target task so that it is similar to the source decision boundary.

Schweikert et al. (2008) propose learning a linear combination of the source SVM classifiers. The decision function is defined as

$$f(\mathbf{x}) = \sum_{i=1}^{n} \alpha_i k(\mathbf{x}_i, \mathbf{x}) + b, \forall \mathbf{x}_i \in \mathscr{D}, \tag{4.9}$$

where $k(\cdot,\cdot)$ is a kernel function and α_i is a coefficient. Hence the overall objective function is defined as

$$[k,f] = \underset{k,f}{\arg\min} \ \Omega\big(\mathrm{DIST}_k^2(\mathscr{D}_s, \mathscr{D}_t^l)\big) + \theta R(k, f, \mathscr{D}_t^l). \tag{4.10}$$

This objective function consists of two terms. The first term minimizes a distributional distance $\mathrm{DIST}(\cdot,\cdot)$ between two domains. $\mathscr{D}_t^l$ is the set of labeled instances in the target domain. In the second term, function $R(\cdot)$ represents the structural risk of the classifier $f(\cdot)$ and kernel $k(\cdot)$, given the target data $\mathscr{D}_t^l$. Here the kernel function $k(\cdot)$ is assumed to be a linear combination of the base kernels $\{k_j\}$'s, that is,

$$k = \sum_{j=1}^{M} d_j k_j, \tag{4.11}$$

where M is the total number of source models. It is noteworthy that both this method and A-SVM (Yang et al., 2007c) do not utilize the abundant unlabeled data in the target domain.

Duan et al. (2012c) propose an adaptive MKL (A-MKL) method. This algorithm learns a kernel function and a classifier by optimizing both structural risk and distribution discrepancy between the source and target domain.

Besides exploring the input kernel, Guo and Wang (2013) propose a domain adaptive input-output kernel learning (DA-IOKL) algorithm that simultaneously learns both the input and the output kernels with a discriminative vector-valued decision function by reducing the data mismatch based on the MMD distance and minimizing the structural risk.

4.3.3 Fine-tuning Approaches for Deep Models

As deep learning becomes a popular machine learning technique to use in many applications, researchers have begun to endow deep models with transfer learning capabilities. Parameter fine-tuning is a simple and effective technique for knowledge transfer in terms of model parameters.

Greedy Layer-wise Pretraining and Fine-tuning

The idea of greedy layer-wise pretraining has been widely used in training deep belief networks and autoencoders. In this approach, the parameters trained using unsupervised learning are used to initialize specific classification tasks (Bengio, 2012). This approach assumes that unsupervised learning tasks such as instance reconstruction can reveal good representations. The parameters initialized with them should be in a good region for the downstream tasks. Such initialization strategy can be considered as a kind of regularization on the learned model parameters.

In the greedy layer-wise algorithms, the first stage is to use unsupervised learning to train each layer; this is known as the pretraining stage. Specifically, for the l-th layer, we train an unsupervised learning model by taking the training examples $h_{l-1}(x)$, which are the output of the $(l-1)$-th layer, to reproduce representations $h_l(x) = R_l(h_{l-1}(x))$ at the next level.

The second stage is fine-tuning with the supervised signals for the downstream tasks like classification. Several variants have been designed for the fine-tuning step. The most common one is to initialize a linear or nonlinear supervised predictor by taking $h_L(x)$ in the first stage as the input and then fine-tune the model parameters with respect to a supervised training loss.

Fine-tuning from Parameters Learned with Supervision

Greedy layer-wise pretraining was a popular method in the early history of deep learning, but later it was replaced by the dropout and batch normalization to train all layers in an end-to-end manner. With a more stable optimization method and a large amount of labeled data, one is able to directly train a supervised deep model from scratch. A critical issue is how to transfer the parameters learned with supervision across different supervised tasks.

Experiments have been conducted to evaluate transferrability of different layers of a pretrained convolutional neural network CNN model (Yosinski et al., 2014). Figure 4.4 illustrates the setup of the experiments. The ImageNet data set is split into two halves, namely A and B. The models in the first two rows are trained on A and B, respectively. They are used as base models. In the last two rows, the first several layers of the models are initialized by the learned values while other layers are randomly initialized. XnY stands for the first n layers that are copied from base model X and frozen to do transfer learning in Y. Meanwhile, XnY^+ stands for the transferred first n layers, which can be fine-tuned by Y.

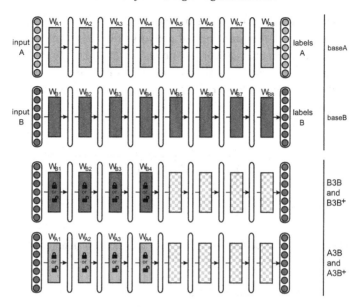

Figure 4.4 Overview of the experimental settings in CNN (adapted from Yosinski et al. [2014])

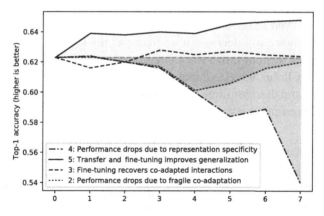

Figure 4.5 Experiment results of the transferability of the representations in CNN (adapted from Yosinski et al. [2014])

Figure 4.5 shows the results of different transfer-learning settings. Apparently, the setting of transfer and fine-tuning helps AnB^+ outperform the base model B. The AnB and BnB with the frozen transferred layers encounter a huge drop when n is large. It shows that the lower layers are more transferrable and the representations in the higher layers are more related to specific tasks.

Similarly, experiments have also been conducted to evaluate the transferrability of the parameters of recurrent neural networks (RNNs) for natural language classification tasks (Mou et al., 2016). As shown in Figure 4.6, the RNN model for natural language classification consists of three kinds of layers: (1) E: the embedding layer, (2) H: the hidden layer of RNNs that captures sequential patterns and (3) O: the output layer.

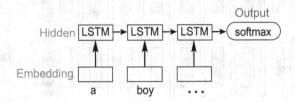

Figure 4.6 An LSTM model for natural language classification (adapted from Mou et al. [2016]). LSTM, long short-term memory network

To analyze the transferrability of each layer, several experiments were conducted in the work by Mou et al. (2016), including a large movie review data set, IMDb, a small movie review data set MR, and a small six-way question data set QC. The results under different transfer learning settings are tested, including frozen, fine-tuning and transferring between tasks. The results of RNNs are similar to those of CNN. The higher layers like the hidden and output layers are not so transferable. Even in the same semantic setting that transfers from IMDb to MR, the performance will decrease if we freeze all the layers. In the case of dissimilar tasks such as from IMDb to QC, freezing the hidden layer has resulted in a dramatic drop. If the model is initialized with the parameters learned from the source domain and then continue to fine-tune, the performance is usually higher than or at least competitive with the base model.

Fine-tuning from Different Modalities

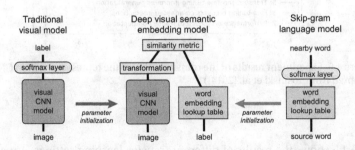

Figure 4.7 The DeViSE model (adapted from Frome et al. [2013])

Frome et al. (2013) learn semantic knowledge in the a text domain and transferred the knowledge to a visual object recognition domain. First, a skip-gram neural language model is pretrained for the distributed representations of words. In parallel, a state-of-the-art deep neural network for visual object recognition is trained by the LSVRC 2012 1K data set. Finally, a deep visual semantic model is built by combining the representation layers of the pretrained visual object recognition network and neural language model. The model will continue to fine-tune parameters. The model and the training process are shown in Figure 4.7.

5

Relation-Based Transfer Learning

5.1 Introduction

In previous chapters, we have reviewed instance-based, feature-based and model-based transfer learning methods, all of which implicitly assumed that data instances are independent and identically distributed. However, many real-world domains often contain some structures among the data instances, leading to relational structures in these domains. For example, a social network can be viewed as a relational graph where nodes represent persons and links are the relationships between people. In a relational domain, instances are related with multiple relations, which violates the independent assumption among data required by classical machine learning methods. Many models have been proposed that learn from data in relational domains.

However, similar to supervised learning, the problem of insufficient data also haunts the performance of learning models on relational domains. When the relational domain changes, the learned model usually performs poorly and has to be rebuilt from scratch. Beside the low quantities of high-quality data instances, the available relations may also be too scarce to learn an accurate model, especially when there are many kinds of relations. So transfer learning is suitable for relational learning to overcome the reliance on large quantities of high-quality data by leveraging useful information from other related domains, leading to relation-based transfer learning. In addition, relation-based transfer learning can speed up the learning process in the target domain and hence improve the efficiency.

In general, relation-based transfer learning aims to build the mapping of the relational knowledge between the source relational domain and the target relational domain. The transfer is based on the assumption that the relations among the data in the source domain and the target domain have common regularities. Thus, to some extent, the domain-independent relational knowledge can be transferred based on relational features. An illustrative example that shows how to transfer the relational knowledge from the academic domain to the movie domain is given in Figure 5.1.

To answer the query "how to transfer" for transfer learning, statistical relational

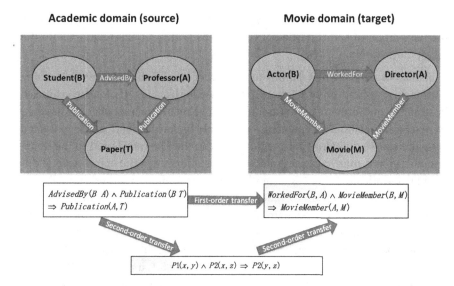

Figure 5.1 An example of relational transfer mechanisms (adapted from Davis and Domingos [2009])

learning gives a typical example of how to conduct relation-based transfer, with leading works such as Getoor and Taskar (2007) and Nickel et al. (2016). In this area, Markov logic networks (MLNs) (Richardson and Domingos, 2006) provide an ideal tool for representing structural relations. MLNs are a logic-probability mixed model, where relations are encoded as predicates and the regularities of relations are represented as formulas. Relation-based transfer learning methods based on MLNs exact weighted logic formulas from the source domain representing relations regularities. Then, based on the regularities, logic formulas with predicates from the target domain are created as candidates. These candidates are sifted, revised and reweighted in order to properly model the target domain.

There are two mechanisms of relation-based transfer learning, including first-order relation-based and second-order relation-based transfer learning. First-order relation-based transfer learning methods assume that, if two relational domains are related, they may share some similar relations among data instances that can be transferred across domains. For example, if a student who is unfamiliar with a certain "movie" problem domain is told that the relation $WorkedFor$ between an actor and a director is analogous to the relation $AdvisedBy$ between a student and a professor, and that the relation $MovieMember$ is similar to the relation $Publication$, then the student can predict some rules in the "movie" domain based on what he/she knows in the academic domain. Hence, given the knowledge of the student in the academic domain that a professor is a coauthor of papers written by his/her students, which is formulated as a first-order logic formula in Figure 5.1, the student may infer that a director is a member of movies his/her employed actors participate in by substituting similar relations into the target movie domain.

Instead of transferring relations in first-order relation-based transfer learning approaches, second-order relation-based transfer learning approaches can also be used. Second-order relations assume that two related relational domains share some similar relation-independent structural regularities that can be extracted from the source domain. These regularities can then be transferred to the target domain. In fact, many abstract rules about relations stay valid across several different real world domains. For example, the distributional hypothesis initially discovered in linguistics (Harris, 1954) finds that words with similar distributional characteristics tend to be semantically related. Recently, it was found that this distributional characteristics was valid for social networks (Mitzlaff et al., 2014). Likewise, papers' citation structures also tend to be semantically similar in citation networks (Ganguly and Pudi, 2017). In Figure 5.1, a relation-independent structural pattern is represented as a second-order logic formula with predicate variables, which is learned from a source domain. This second-order relation can be instantiated with relations in the target domain to obtain new rules, which is a form of transfer learning.

There also exist works that consider transferring across different networks (Ye et al., 2013; Fang et al., 2013, 2015), where the structural knowledge of the networks are assumed to be transferable. Ye et al. (2013) propose the construction of generalizable latent features through matrix factorization by considering both the source and the target networks, and then adoption of an AdaBoost-style algorithm with instance weighting to train a target classifier. Fang et al. (2013) constructed a label propagation matrix to capture the influence of the structural information to the labels of nodes in a network. The goal was to discover common signature subgraphs between two networks to construct new structural features for the target network. The relational knowledge contained in edges is then transferred across relational domains by discovering common latent structural features shared by the source and the target networks. For the co-extraction of sentiment and topic lexicons across domains with no labeled data in the target domain, Li et al. (2012) proposed a two-stage relation-based transfer learning framework by leveraging transferable syntactic relations between topical and sentimental words. In the first stage, a simple strategy is proposed to generate a few high-quality sentiment and topic seeds for the target domain and in the second stage, a novel relational adaptive bootstrapping method is applied to expand the seeds by exploiting the relations between topic and opinion words.

There has not been much research about "when to transfer" for relational domains. The weighted pseudo-log-likelihood (WPLL) could be used as a metric to measure the "degree" of a set of formulas being satisfied. Zhuo and Yang (2014) developed a score function based on WPLL to measure the similarity between source and target domains in order to capture the transferability between the source and target domains.

5.2 Markov Logic Networks

Markov networks (Koller and Friedman, 2009), also known as Markov random fields, are a graphical model to use a undirected graph to describe the joint probability of variables. MLNs (Richardson and Domingos, 2006) are a template language to define a Markov network that predicts the probability of relations between entities and it combines techniques in the statistics and logic to offer a simple way to represent uncertain knowledge logic.

For a first-order logic knowledge base, the hard constraints of formulas make it difficult for logic to represent uncertainty. Graphical models such as the Markov network provide a unifying structure for various probabilistic models but they can only represent distributions over the propositional logic, which is insufficient in expressing higher-order knowledge. By assigning each logic formula a real-valued weight to represent its credibility, an MLN softens the hard constraints and builds an interface between the first-order logic and graphical models.

An MLN consists of two parts, a first-order logic part and a numerical part for weights associated with each logic formula. A first-order logic formula defines the correlation between predicates and the associated weight embodies the credibility of the corresponding formula, making the set of formulas soft constraints. In this way, formulas in an MLN can tolerate uncertainty and allows even contradictory knowledge.

An MLN is constructed based on an intuition that the fewer formulas a world violated, the more probable it is. Similarly, the larger the weight of a formula, the more likely it is true. More precisely, the weight for every formula denotes the difference in the logarithm of the probability between a world that satisfies it and a world that does not satisfy it while fixing other entities. The interpretation of this intuition comes from the logic, while the implementation is based on the Markov networks.

With the aforementioned MLN, we can now use it as a representation language to express transferrable knowledge between two domains.

5.3 Relation-Based Transfer Learning Based on MLNs

Relation-based transfer learning using MLNs aims to extract common relations from the source domain and transfer the relational knowledge to the target domain. This fits the transfer learning motivation as we wish the framework to work with limited relational data. Research in this area is divided into two categories:

shallow transfer, where the source and the target domains share the same types of objects and relations, and *deep transfer*, where the types of objects and relations are different across domains (Davis and Domingos, 2009; Van Haaren et al., 2015). These two categories respectively use the first-order and second-order relation-based transfer learning techniques based on MLN.

In the first-order relation-based transfer learning approach, we aim to find an explicit mapping of predicates across domains to generate new formulas for the target domain. In the second-order approach, we extract the structural regularities from the source domain in the form of second-order logic and then transfer them to the target domain.

5.3.1   Shallow Transfer via First-Order Logic

Mihalkova et al. (2007) propose a transfer via automatic mapping and revision (TAMAR) algorithm that finds and adapts the mappings of predicates across domains. For example, with the mapping between entities in an academic scholar domain (e.g., professors, students and publications) and a movie domain (e.g., directors, actors and movies), rules that are applicable to one domain may be transferred to another after replacing some loic predicates according to the mapping. In the TAMAR algorithm, the source MLN is first mapped to the target domain and the clauses from the source domain can then be revised based on the mapping. The revised MLN can be used as a relational model for the inference or reasoning in the target domain. In the end, this mapping is evaluated by the WPLL score, which measures the performance of the mapped MLN on the target data.

The definition of WPLL is given below (Mihalkova et al., 2007):

$$\log \tilde{P}_w(X = x) = \sum_{r \in R} c_r \sum_{k=1}^{g_r} \ln P_w(X_{r,k} = x_{r,k} | MB_x(X_{r,k})), \qquad (5.1)$$

where R is the set of first-order predicates, g_r is the number of groundings of first-order predicate r and $x_{r,k}$ is the truth value of the k-th groundings of r. The WPLL score is different from the likelihood for a data set in that the likelihood is the multiplication of conditional probability of every ground fact given its Markov blanket but the pseudo probability in WPLL for each predicate is weighted by c_r. WPLL does not require inference over the model, and it can be learned by stochastic gradient descent algorithms.

TAMAR is built on WPLL: instead of evaluating all possible mappings to find the best one, TAMAR utilizes a greedy method. By finding the best mapping of each source clause individually, TAMAR constructs a *local mapping* for the predicates appearing in the source clause. To find the best local mapping for each source clause, TAMAR will exhaustively search through the space of all legal mappings, each of which maps a source predicate to a target predicate (or empty predicate) with consistent type-mapping constraints. These constraints ensure that, if the

Table 5.1 *An example of the predicate and clause mapping algorithm*

Source domain	Target domain
$Publication(title, person)$	$MovieMenber(movie, person)$
$Professor(person)$	$Director(person)$
$Student(person)$	$Actor(person)$
$AdvisedBy(person, person)$	$WorkedFor(person, person)$
$Publication(P, A) \wedge Publication(P, B) \wedge$ $Professor(A) \wedge Student(B)$ $\implies AdvisedBy(B, A)$	$MovieMenber(P, A) \wedge MovieMenber(P, B) \wedge$ $Director(A) \wedge Actor(B)$ $\implies WorkedFor(B, A)$

actor is mapped to the student, it cannot be mapped to other types. Two predicates are compatible if they have the same number of arguments and the types of arguments are compatible according to the current type constraints. With a new compatible mapping that has no conflicts with other mappings, the mapping and corresponding type-mapping constraints are updated.

After this construction, legal mappings are evaluated based on the WPLL score of the MLN model that consists of only the translated clauses. The best local predicate mapping is the one with the highest WPLL score. The process is iterated to find local mappings for all source clauses. Table 5.1 illustrates the output of the mapping algorithm. The mapped structure is then revised to fit the data in the target domain based on various criteria:

- Self-diagnosis: Each clause c in the transferred MLN is checked to test whether it should be shortened, lengthened or kept unchanged by considering every possible way to treat c as an implication, with only one literal as the conclusion and the remaining the antecedents. Thus, if a clause made the wrong conclusion, it is possible to lengthen it by adding more antecedents as constraints. For clauses that fail to draw the correct conclusion because of the failure of antecedents, it is possible to shorten the clause to reduce the conditions required.
- Structure update: Literals are removed from clauses marked as the "shortening" and added for clauses marked as the "lengthening" based on the WPLL score.
- New clause discovery: Techniques such as relational pathfinding (Richards and Mooney, 1992) are used to find new clauses in the target domain. Clauses that can improve the WPLL will be added into the set.

Mihalkova et al. (2007) conduct experiments on TAMAR under several transfer scenarios on several benchmark data sets. Empirical results demonstrate that TAMAR is able to reduce the amount of the training time and the size of the training data for learning an accurate MLN model in the target domain, when compared with learning a model from scratch in the target domain.

As an extension of the TAMAR algorithm, a short-range to long-range (SR2LR) algorithm is proposed by Mihalkova and Mooney (2008) to study the single-entity centered setting in transfer learning, where only one entity in the target domain is available. Two types of clauses are assumed to exist in SR2LR, including the short-range clauses concerning properties of one single entity and long-range clauses concerning properties of multiple entities. With only one entity available, the short-range clauses can still be used to construct the mapping between predicates in the source and target domains. These clauses can further be generalized to translate to long-range clauses. Similar to TAMAR, the mapping construction in SR2LR relies on an exhaustive search through the space consisting of all locally legal mappings. However, instead of using the WPLL score for evaluation, SR2LR simply checks whether the verifiable groundings of short-range clauses are satisfied on the target data because of the restricted nature of the available target data.

Kumaraswamy et al. (2015) propose a language-bias transfer learning (LTL) algorithm for cross-domain transfer learning. Different from TAMAR, the LTL algorithm performs the matching of type declarations in the source and target domains in a sequential way, where LTL incrementally constructs a search tree and stops the search in a path when there is a mismatch of the type constraints. This approach allows the LTL algorithm to learn more efficiently because the search tree needs not to be fully constructed and traversed in the target domain.

5.3.2 Deep Transfer via Second-Order Logic

In addition to the relation matching, some abstract rules about relationships keep valid across domains such as the transitivity property, distributional hypothesis and homophily. Homophily is the basic heuristic for latent methods that similar entities are likely to be related, and relations involving similar entities are likely to be related. Learning these high-level concepts and transferring them into new domains will lead to faster and more accurate relational learning. In MLN-based transfer learning, the structural regularities of relations in the source domain are represented in the form of a second-order logic. For the second-order logic, variables can range over relations (predicates) as well as objects (constants), making the representation of common rules among various relations possible. For example, the transitivity property can be represented as $r(z, y) \land r(x, z) \implies r(x, y)$, where r can be a variable representing predicates and x, y, z represent objects. In a social network, the formula can be instantiated as $Friends(z, y) \land Friends(x, z) \implies Friends(x, y)$, while, in the relational algebra, it can be instantiated as $Equal(z, y) \land Equal(x, z) \implies Equal(x, y)$.

Davis and Domingos (2009) propose a deep transfer via Markov logic (DTM) algorithm to transfer relational knowledge based on a form of the second-order Markov logic. The basic idea of the DTM algorithm is to discover structural regularities in the source domain in the form of Markov logic formulas with predicate variables and to instantiate these formulas with predicates from the target domain. The first-order Markov logic can be extended to the second-order Markov logic by considering grounding atoms with predicates as well as constant symbols. Because different formulas over the same predicates can capture the same regularity, DTM uses second-order cliques to cluster similar second-order structures and then transfers them based on the cliques.

We now consider DTM in more detail. A second-order clique defined in DTM is a set of literals with predicate variables with restrictions. Given a set of first-order formulas in the source domain, which can be obtained with any learner that can induce the first-order logic formulas from data, DTM converts each formula based on the second-order logic by replacing all predicate names with predicate variables. Then, the converted second-order formulas are grouped as cliques if they are over the same set of literals. Note that DTM requires that no cliques are the same modulo variable renaming, which means that, if two formulas can be renamed to share the same set of literals, they should be in the same clique. For example, two first-order formulas $Complex(z, y) \land Interacts(x, z) \implies Complex(x, y)$ and $Location(z, y) \land Interacts(x, z) \implies Location(x, y)$ in the source domain can be converted as $r(z, y) \land s(x, z) \implies r(x, y)$ and $s(z, y) \land r(x, z) \implies s(x, y)$. The two formulas are grouped as one clique $\{r(z, y), s(x, z), r(x, y)\}$ because they share the same set of literals after renaming variable r to s and s to r.

After grouping the clauses into second-order cliques, each clique that appears more than twice will be evaluated and transferred to the target domain. From the perspective of SRL, the literals in the same clique are dependent. The more correlated literals in a clique are, the more probable that some of the second-order formulas derived from that clique can express the regularities of relations in the source domain. In this way, DTM scores a clique by evaluating the correlation between literals in the clique. For each first-order instantiation of a second-order clique, DTM computes its Kulback–Leibler (KL) divergences for all possible sub-clique decompositions. For example, for $\{r(z, y), s(x, z), r(x, y)\}$ and its instantiation $\{Complex(z, y), Interacts(x, z), Complex(x, y)\}$, there are three pairs of sub-cliques:

$$\{Complex(z, y), Interacts(x, z)\} - \{Complex(x, y)\}$$
$$\{Complex(z, y), Complex(x, y)\} - \{Interacts(x, z)\}$$
$$\{Complex(z, y), Interacts(x, z)\} - \{Complex(x, y)\}.$$

The probability of each sub-clique is computed by the Dirichlet distribution. Each instantiation receives the minimum KL divergence over the set of its decompositions, and each second-order clique receives an average score of its top m first-order instantiations. Then, cliques with high scores will be transferred to the target domain.

The transfer-learning mechanism of DTM can be regarded as biasing the learner in the target domain to favor models containing previously discovered regularities in the source domain via the second-order cliques. A second-order clique gives rise to several second-order formulas with all possible ways to negate the literals, which are then transformed to the clause form according to MLN, in a clique. Every second-order clause represents a probabilistic way on how literals in the clique are correlated. For the cliques having at least one true grounding in the target domain, the legal instantiations can be directly picked, refined or as the seeds for the search of formulas in the target domain.

Different from DTM, which applies an auxiliary tool, that is, the second-order clique, to collect candidates of reliable second-order formulas, the two-order-deep transfer learning algorithm proposed by Van Haaren et al. (2015) directly computes the posterior distributions of all second-order formulas given the data in the source domain and then uses those posterior distributions as prior distributions over second-order formulas in the target domain to train the MLN in the target domain.

5.3.3 Transfer Learning by Structural Analogy

Wang and Yang (2011) present another approach to relation-based transfer learning across domains. By examining knowledge transfer in humans, we could find that human beings do not rely on such low-level relatedness to transfer knowledge across domains. In fact, humans are able to make analogy across different domains by resolving the *high* level (structural) similarities even when the learning tasks (domains) are seemingly irrelevant. For example, we can easily understand the analogy between debugging for computer viruses and diagnosing human diseases. Even though the computer viruses (harmful codes) themselves have nothing in common with bacteria or germs, and the computer systems are totally different from our bodies, we can still make the analogy based on the following *structural* similarities:

(1) Computer viruses cause malfunction of computers. Diseases cause disfunction of the human body.
(2) Computer viruses spread among computers through the networks. Infectious diseases spread among people through various interactions.
(3) System updates help computers avoid certain viruses. Vaccines help human beings avoid certain diseases.

Understanding these structural similarities helps us abstract away the details specific to the domains, and build a mapping between the abstractions (see Figure 5.2). The mapping builds on the high-level structural relatedness of the two domains, instead of their low-level "literal similarities." In other words, the attributes of the "computer" and the "human" themselves do not matter to the mapping, whereas their relationships to other entities in their own domains matter. Such a "structural similarity" can be determined if we can correctly identify *analogs* across completely different representation spaces.

To capture this intuition, Wang and Yang (2011) introduce an algorithm for transfer learning by structural analogy. This algorithm builds on functional space embedding of distributions (Smola et al., 2007b), and addresses transfer learning in a setting that the source domain and target domain are using completely

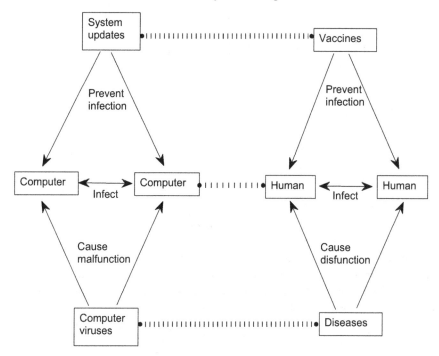

Figure 5.2 The analogy between debugging for computer viruses and diagnosing human diseases based on structural similarities. The dash lines bridge analogs across domains

different representation spaces. As we cannot directly compare features across domains, we extract the structural information of the features within each domain by mapping the features into the reproducing kernel Hilbert space, such that the "structural dependencies" of features across domains can be estimated by kernel matrices of the features within each domain (Smola et al., 2007b). Hence, the learning process is formulated as simultaneously selecting and associating features from both domains to maximize the dependencies between the selected features and response variables (labels), as well as between the selected features from both domains. With the learned cross-domain mapping, a structural similarity between the two domains can be readily computed, which can be used in place of simple similarity measures in computational analogy systems such as case-based reasoning. By treating the analogs from both domains as equivalent, we can transfer knowledge to achieve a better understanding of the domains, such as higher accuracy for classification tasks.

6

Heterogeneous Transfer Learning

6.1 Introduction

As reviewed in previous chapters, the majority of work done in the area of transfer learning focuses on cases where examples in a source domain and those in a target domain share the same representation structure but follow different probability distributions. In this chapter, we introduce *heterogeneous transfer learning*, which pushes the boundary further by allowing a source domain and a target domain to lie in incommensurable feature spaces or different label spaces.

Even though transfer learning is a powerful framework to apply in many situations, homogeneous transfer learning only focuses on generalization performance across the same domain representations. As such, homogeneous transfer learning is limited. As an example, consider the situation in Figure 6.1. In this example, increasing the annotated high-resolution photographs in a source domain offers little help in classifying the categories of sketch images, given that the categories of televisions and computer monitors are "visually" similar. This is partly due to the limitation of homogeneous transfer learning. In this case, however, *heterogeneous transfer learning*, which considers knowledge across domains with different feature and label spaces, can bring out similar knowledge in the two domains. Heterogeneous transfer learning enables different *perspectives or aspects of knowledge* to be transferred from a source to a target domain. In the example in Figure 6.1, text documents, lying in a completely different feature space from images, characterize televisions and computer monitors with more descriptive and discriminative abilities. Therefore, they can provide additional knowledge to further improve the classification of sketch images in the target domain. By borrowing the knowledge learned from classifying high-resolution photographs in those categories associated with televisions and computer monitors, say TV boxes and keyboards, heterogeneous transfer learning can search for more hints about the visual differences between televisions and monitors.

Besides, it may often be the case that a source domain in the same feature and label representation as a target domain is not easily accessible to users. Consider the task of human activity recognition using sensor data collected from cell-

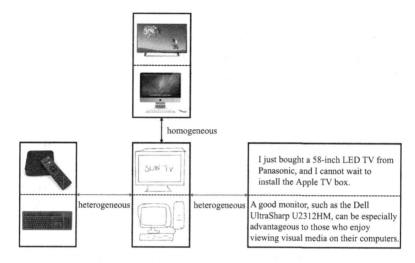

Figure 6.1 An illustration of homogeneous and heterogeneous transfer learning

phones. This task requires many sensor records to be annotated with activity names as labels. However, the annotation of such sensor data is especially laborious and expensive (Wei et al., 2016a). In this case, finding a source domain with sufficient labeled sensor records is as difficult, if not more, as building a model in the target domain. In contrast, heterogeneous transfer learning *offers greater flexibility for source domain selection* by allowing a source domain to be chosen from a different feature space or a different label space. For the activity recognition example, heterogeneous transfer learning algorithms can transfer knowledge from social media messages to sensor records, which may greatly help improve activity recognition performance.

Last, but not the least, heterogeneous transfer learning *gets closer to human intelligence where knowledge can be transferred between different types of signals easily*. This is evidenced by the multimodal sensory system of the brain. The multimodal sensory neural system of humans can integrate signals from different sensory modalities, such as visual stimuli, auditory stimuli, tactile stimuli and olfactory stiumli. When signals in some of the modalities are absent or insufficient, the system can leverage knowledge from other modalities to guarantee the effectiveness of perception (Recanzone, 2009). For example, we usually understand others' speech based on the auditory stimuli from sound bites. However, if some other people are whispering in a low voice that we cannot hear them clearly, the multimodal sensory system is capable of transferring knowledge from the visual stimuli, such as the shape of mouth, to improve speech understanding and so on.

The rest of this chapter is organized as follows. In Section 6.2, we first give a formal definition regarding heterogeneous transfer learning. Section 6.3 details existing solutions toward heterogeneous transfer learning, and discusses their advantages as well as disadvantages. In Section 6.4, we present some successful applications of heterogeneous transfer learning and an empirical comparison of different algorithms on several data sets. Finally, we conclude the chapter with some potentially influential proposals of future research.

6.2   The Heterogeneous Transfer Learning Problem

While *homogeneous transfer learning* algorithms assume that $\mathcal{X}_s = \mathcal{X}_t, \mathcal{Y}_s = \mathcal{Y}_t$, $\mathbb{P}_s^X \neq \mathbb{P}_t^X$ or $\mathbb{P}_s^{Y|X} \neq \mathbb{P}_t^{Y|X}$, *heterogeneous transfer learning* pushes the boundary further by relaxing the assumption in homogeneous transfer learning to allow the feature spaces of the two domains to be different, that is, $\mathcal{X}_s \neq \mathcal{X}_t$, or the label spaces to be different, that is, $\mathcal{Y}_s \neq \mathcal{Y}_t$. Given such a source domain $\mathcal{D}_s$ and a target domain $\mathcal{D}_t$, heterogeneous transfer learning have two goals: (1) to learn transferable knowledge from the source domain $\mathcal{D}^s$ to improve the learning of $P_t^{Y|X}$ in the target domain by reducing its generalization error on unseen data and (2) to reduce the number of labeled data used in training in the target domain; that is, n_t^l, to achieve the same level of generalizability with $P_t^{Y|X}$.

Provided with incommensurable representation or label structures, heterogeneous transfer learning algorithms have to rely on the correspondence annotated by human beings to bridge domains. For example, if knowledge is expected to be transferred from text documents, shown to the left of Figure 6.2, to improve image classification, shown to the right of Figure 6.2, annotators have to explicitly specify whether a document is semantically related with a picture, for example, the document describing a horse and the horse picture are related. We formally define the correspondence as follows.

Definition 6.1 (correspondence)   The correspondence is defined as $\mathscr{C} = \bigcup_i \bigcup_j c_{ij}$,

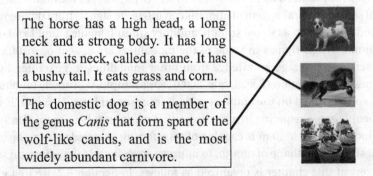

| The horse has a high head, a long neck and a strong body. It has long hair on its neck, called a mane. It has a bushy tail. It eats grass and corn. |
| The domestic dog is a member of the genus *Canis* that form spart of the wolf-like canids, and is the most widely abundant carnivore. |

Figure 6.2 An illustration of the correspondence annotated by human beings between a pair of heterogeneous domains, that is, text documents and images

where c_{ij} indicates the degree of semantic relatedness between the j-th example in a source domain $\mathbf{x}_s^j$ and the i-th example in a target domain $\mathbf{x}_t^i$.

Besides the annotated correspondence shown in the Figure 6.2, the correspondence set $\mathscr{C}$ can also be built by labels. If the label of a source instance, say "horse," and the label of a target instance, say "pony," are semantically close, we are also able to infer that the source instance and the target instance have correspondence. The correspondence is a prerequisite for heterogeneous transfer learning algorithms to build either instance or feature mappings, as homogeneous transfer learning algorithms do, to enable knowledge transfer.

6.3 Methodologies

Heterogeneous transfer learning can be categorized into two groups according to the type of "heterogeneity" that we refer to. The first branch addresses the problem caused by knowledge transfer under the feature-space mismatches, that is, $\mathscr{X}_s \neq \mathscr{X}_t$. The second branch enables knowledge transfer even if the label spaces from the two domains are different, that is, $\mathscr{Y}_s \neq \mathscr{Y}_t$.

6.3.1 Heterogeneous Feature Spaces

To the best of our knowledge, almost all current heterogeneous transfer learning works transfer knowledge across domains in different feature spaces. First of all, we summarize and categorize these methodologies as a hierarchical tree shown in Figure 6.3. The approaches are classified into two main streams. The first stream of approach, which we call single-level alignment, aligns heterogeneous domains by building a single level of mappings (either instance or feature mappings as we mentioned earlier). The second line, called multi-level alignment, however, performs multiple levels of mappings to make different domains align.

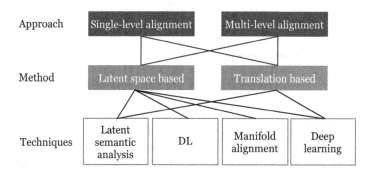

Figure 6.3 The hierarchical categorization of methodologies for heterogeneous transfer learning across domains in different feature spaces DL, dictionary learning

There have been two categories of alignment strategies according to the way mappings are built: (1) latent space-based methods that learn a latent space expanded by multiple latent factors shared across domains and (2) translation-based methods that directly translate from a source feature space to a target feature space. Figure 6.4 presents the general ideas of these two kinds of methods and differences between them. To be more specific, the latent space-based alignment

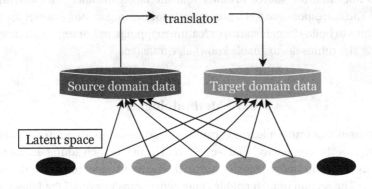

Common latent factors across domains

Figure 6.4 Overview of the two strategies for the alignment of domains in different feature spaces

strategy can be implemented by techniques including (1) latent semantic analysis, (2) DL, (3) manifold alignment and (4) deep learning. Before proceeding to introduce details of the techniques and their representative works, the explored research works so far are shown in Table 6.1.

Table 6.1 *The explored research works so far in heterogeneous transfer learning across domains in different feature spaces.*

Approach \ Techniques	Latent space based				Translation based
	Latent factor analysis	DL	Manifold alignment	Deep learning	
Single-level alignment	✓	✓	✓		✓
Multi-level alignment		✓		✓	✓

Latent Space-Based Single-Level Alignment
Latent Factor Analysis

Latent factor analysis is a statistical method that describes observed variables and their relationship in terms of a potentially fewer number of unobserved variables called latent factors. The general idea behind latent factor analysis for heterogeneous transfer learning is to extract latent factors shared by a source and a target domain, given observed feature representations of both domains. By projecting a target domain onto the latent space where the shared latent factors lie, the feature representation of the target domain is enriched with these shared latent factors that encode knowledge from one or multiple source domains, and improve the performance in kinds of tasks.

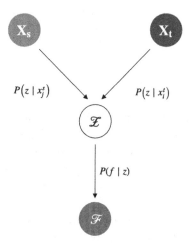

Figure 6.5 Overview of the annotation-based probabilistic latent semantic analysis model (adapted from Yang et al. [2009])

Yang et al. (2009) first propose and investigate heterogeneous transfer learning. This work leverages a large corpus of unlabeled text documents, the source domain, to help images as the target domain better cluster. The authors put forward a probabilistic approach named annotation-based probabilistic latent semantic analysis (aPLSA). The core of aPLSA lies in employing the image–text multiview data, which are tagged images on Flickr in the empirical studies of this work. Both images and their auxiliary tags are projected into a common semantic latent space where latent factors dictating the distribution of low-level features of images are finally output as clusters. Specifically, $\mathcal{Z} = \{z_i\}_{i=1}^{d_c}$, $\mathbf{X}_s$, $\mathbf{X}_t$, $\mathcal{F}$ denote the the latent variable set, tags, image instances, and low-level image features, respectively. $\{z_i\}_{i=1}^{d_c}$, meanwhile, are regarded as the clusters that are finally desired. Mathematically, the goal of this model is to cluster target images, that is, to assign a $z_i \in \mathcal{Z}$ with the highest probability for each specific target image $\mathbf{x}_i^t$ in a probabilistic fashion:

$$g(\mathbf{x}_i^t) = \arg\max_{z \in \mathcal{Z}} P(z|\mathbf{x}_i^t). \tag{6.1}$$

To extract $\mathcal{Z}$, aPLSA follows two chains, as Figure 6.5 shows. The first chain decides the low-level features $\mathcal{F}$ from images $\mathbf{X}_t$ passing though $\mathcal{Z}$:

$$P(f|\mathbf{x}_i^t) = \sum_{z \in \mathcal{Z}} P(f|z)P(z|\mathbf{x}_i^t). \tag{6.2}$$

The other chain is inferred from auxiliary tags, and characterizes the correlation between tags $\mathbf{X}_s$ and low-level features $\mathcal{F}$ though $\mathcal{Z}$:

$$P(f|\mathbf{x}_j^s) = \sum_{z \in \mathcal{Z}} P(f|z)P(z|\mathbf{x}_j^s). \tag{6.3}$$

Jointly considering both chains, aPLSA designs a log-likelihood objective function as shown in (6.4) and estimates the probabilities $P(f|z)$, $P(z|\mathbf{x}_j^s)$ and $P(z|\mathbf{x}_i^t)$ via the expectation-maximization (EM) algorithm:

$$\mathcal{L} = \sum_d [\lambda \sum_d \frac{A_{id}}{\sum_{d'} A_{id'}} log P(f_d|\mathbf{x}_i^t) + (1-\lambda) \sum_l \frac{B_{jd}}{\sum_{d'} B_{jd'}} log P(f_d|\mathbf{x}_j^s)], \tag{6.4}$$

where $A \in \mathbb{R}^{n_t \times d_t}$ is the correlation matrix between image instances and low-level image features, and $B \in \mathbb{R}^{n_s \times d_t}$ captures the correlation between tags and low-level image features. When finally the EM algorithm converges, the estimated $P(z|\mathbf{x}_i^t)$ is output to derive the final result, $\arg\max_{z \in \mathcal{Z}} P(z|\mathbf{x}_i^t)$.

Matrix factorization is widely known and adopted for its superiority toward extracting latent factors. Shi et al. (2010b) propose a model called heterogeneous spectral mapping (HeMap), which follows the idea of matrix factorization to learn a shared latent space. HeMap aims to learn the optimal projection of target examples $\mathbf{X}_t$ in the latent space, that is, $\mathbf{Z}_t$, and that of source examples $\mathbf{X}_s$, that is, $\mathbf{Z}_s$. The authors proposed the following optimization objective for HeMap:

$$\min_{\mathbf{Z}_s, \mathbf{Z}_t} \ell(\mathbf{Z}_s, \mathbf{X}_s) + \ell(\mathbf{Z}_t, \mathbf{X}_t) + \ell(\mathbf{Z}_s, \mathbf{Z}_t), \tag{6.5}$$

where the first loss term ensures that projections of source examples in the latent space preserve the original structure as much as possible. The same applies to the second loss, while the third term measures and lessens the difference between two projections. Specifically, $\ell(\mathbf{Z}_s, \mathbf{X}_s) = \|\mathbf{X}_s - \mathbf{Z}_s \mathbf{P}_s\|_F^2$ with $\mathbf{P}_s$ representing the projection matrix that maps $\mathbf{X}_s$ to $\mathbf{Z}_s$. Similarly, $\ell(\mathbf{Z}_t, \mathbf{X}_t) = \|\mathbf{X}_t - \mathbf{Z}_t \mathbf{P}_t\|_F^2$. As for $\ell(\mathbf{Z}_s, \mathbf{Z}_t)$, a strong hidden assumption is made that the source and target domain are semantically similar so that their projections should be semantically close. As a consequence, $\ell(\mathbf{Z}_s, \mathbf{Z}_t) = \frac{1}{2}(\|\mathbf{X}_s - \mathbf{Z}_t \mathbf{P}_s\|_F^2 + \|\mathbf{X}_t - \mathbf{Z}_s \mathbf{P}_t\|_F^2)$.

Clearly, HeMap does not require any correspondence data between a source and a target domain while aPLSA, as we mentioned earlier, does. The performance of HeMap highly relies on the data themselves. Only when a source and a target domain are semantically sufficiently close to each other is HeMap expected to learn an effective latent space that encodes the shared semantic knowledge from both domains.

Singh and Gordon (2008) first propose a collective matrix factorization (CMF) to extract shared factors (common interests of users) among multiple relations (multiple user-item relations) in the field of recommendation. Specifically, CMF simultaneously factorizes multiple matrices with correspondence in rows or columns while enforcing the factorized latent factors to be the same.

Subsequently, CMF and its variants have been extensively investigated for transfer learning (Gupta et al., 2010; Zhu et al., 2011; Wang et al., 2011; Long et al.,

2014). Zhu et al. (2011) is an example approach for tackling heterogeneous transfer learning problems. In this work, the proposed approach, known as heterogeneous transfer learning for image classification (HTLIC), conducts knowledge transfer from sufficient unlabeled text documents to images in a target domain. To bridge the gap between domains, the images $\mathbf{X}_t$ are treated as the target domain and the text corpora $\mathbf{X}_s$ as the source domain. It is assumed that the correspondence mapping between the two domains is not given. Thus, HTLIC must make full use of certain auxiliary tagged images from an online source (Flickr) $A = \{\mathbf{x}_i^{at}, \mathbf{x}_i^{as}\}_{i=1}^{l}$. In this equation, $\mathbf{x}_i^{at} \in \mathbb{R}^{d_t}$ has the same representational structure as $\mathbf{x}_i^t$, $\mathbf{x}_i^{as} \in \mathbb{R}^{d_s}$ is the corresponding d_s-dimensional tag vectors of images. Their approach then constructs two matrices with the columns aligned, which are further jointly factorized by following the operations of CMF. Based on this, on one hand, the authors built a matrix by characterizing the correlation between low-level image features and tags from $\mathbf{A}$. This correlation matrix is defined as:

$$\mathbf{G} = (\mathbf{X}_{at})^T \mathbf{X}_{as} \in \mathbb{R}^{d_s \times d_t}. \tag{6.6}$$

The other matrix captures the relationship between unlabeled documents and tags in $\mathbf{A}$. The matrix, denoted as $\mathbf{F} \in \mathbb{R}^{n_s \times d_t}$, can be inferred from $\mathbf{X}_s$ and $\mathbf{X}_{as}$. Clearly, the constructed matrices $\mathbf{G}$ and $\mathbf{F}$ are aligned in terms of the columns, both lying in the feature space of the source domain. Subsequently, HTLIC applies CMF to jointly factorize $\mathbf{G}$ and $\mathbf{F}$ and formulates the following objective function:

$$\min_{\mathbf{U},\mathbf{V},\mathbf{W}} \lambda \|\mathbf{G} - \mathbf{U}\mathbf{V}^T\|_F^2 + (1 - \lambda)\|\mathbf{F} - \mathbf{W}\mathbf{V}^T\|_F^2 + R(\mathbf{U}, \mathbf{V}, \mathbf{W}), \tag{6.7}$$

where $\mathbf{G}$ is decomposed into $\mathbf{U}$ – the correlation matrix between low-level image features and latent factors – and $\mathbf{V}$ – the correlation matrix between d_s tags and latent semantic factors. Similarly, $\mathbf{F}$ is factorized into $\mathbf{W}$ – the latent semantic representation of documents – and $\mathbf{V}$ too. The formulation enforces that the correlation matrices between tags and latent factors that are factorized from both sides are the same. When dealing with an out-of-sample target example $\mathbf{x}_*^t$, its semantic representation in the latent space is inferred by applying the learnt $\mathbf{U}$, that is, $\mathbf{x}_*^t \mathbf{U}$.

Although quite a few works similar to Yang et al. (2009), Shi et al. (2010b) and Zhu et al. (2011) have taken a significant step, they face the danger of negative transfer. If heterogeneous domains to be projected are wildly irrelevant, it is likely that projections in the shared latent subspace will perform badly in either classification or clustering. Duan et al. (2012b) alleviate the problem to some extent by (1) augmenting projections with original features instead of purely depending on projections and (2) learning the latent subspace with supervision taken into consideration. Figure 6.6 illustrates the overall idea of heterogeneous feature augmentation (HFA) proposed in the work by Duan et al. (2012b). HFA introduces a common latent subspace, and projects both heterogeneous domains onto this subspace, which is augmented by original features. On one hand, HFA

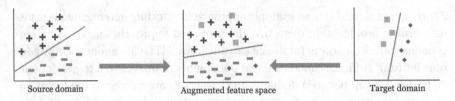

Source domain   Augmented feature space   Target domain

Figure 6.6 The overview of HFA (adapted from Duan et al. [2012b]). Examples from heterogeneous feature spaces are all transformed into the augmented feature space in the middle

incorporates original features in the common latent subspace so as to avoid negative transfer as much as possible. In fact, the idea of feature augmentation or feature replication on the basis of original features has been proved to be effective in homogeneous transfer learning (Daumé III, 2007). As Figure 6.6 shows, HFA defines two augmented feature maps, $\phi_s(\cdot)$ and $\phi_t(\cdot)$, to map a source and a target domain into the common latent space, respectively. First, the source and the target domain are projected onto a latent subspace in dimension d_c using two projection matrices $\mathbf{P} \in \mathbb{R}^{d_c \times d_s}$ and $\mathbf{Q} \in \mathbb{R}^{d_c \times d_t}$, respectively. Second, original features from the source domain are incorporated in $\phi_s(\cdot)$ while $\phi_t(\cdot)$ is padded with a zero vector $\mathbf{0}_{d_s}$. Third, original features from the target domain are incorporated in $\phi_t(\cdot)$ while $\phi_s(\cdot)$ is padded with a zero vector $\mathbf{0}_{d_t}$.

On the other hand, HFA learns the optimal $\mathbf{P}_s$ and $\mathbf{P}_t$ in a supervised fashion to maximize the classification performance. HFA achieves this goal by minimizing the structural risk functional of support vector machines (SVMs) to learn $\mathbf{P}_s$, $\mathbf{P}_t$ and parameter $\mathbf{w}$ simultaneously. The formulation is as follows:

$$\min_{\mathbf{P}_s, \mathbf{P}_t} \min_{\mathbf{w}, b, \xi_j^s, \xi_i^t} \frac{1}{2}\|\mathbf{w}\|^2 + C(\sum_{j=1}^{n_s} \xi_j^s + \sum_{i=1}^{n_t} \xi_i^t),$$

$$\text{s.t.} \quad y_j^s(\mathbf{w}^T \phi_s(\mathbf{x}_j^s) + b) \geq 1 - \xi_j^s, \quad \xi_j^s \geq 0$$

$$y_i^t(\mathbf{w}^T \phi_t(\mathbf{x}_i^t) + b) \geq 1 - \xi_i^t, \quad \xi_i^t \geq 0$$

$$\|\mathbf{P}_s\|_F^2 \leq \lambda_p, \quad \|\mathbf{P}_t\|_F^2 \leq \lambda_q, \tag{6.8}$$

where $C > 0$ is a trade-off parameter, and $\lambda_p, \lambda_q > 0$ are predetermined parameters to control the complexity of $\mathbf{P}_s$ and $\mathbf{P}_t$, respectively.

Clearly, a major limitation of HFA is that it can only learn with labeled examples. If only a few annotated examples are provided, it is very hard to apply HFA to achieve satisfactory performance. The ability to take full advantage of unlabeled examples is also in a desperate need. Li et al. (2014) enable the ability by pushing HFA further and propose a semi-supervised HFA (SHFA) method. SHFA is similar to HFA but trains in a semi-supervised manner. The semi-supervised formulation follows transductive SVM (Joachims, 1999) as follows:

$$\min_{\mathbf{P}_s, \mathbf{P}_t} \min_{\mathbf{y}_u, \mathbf{w}, b, \xi_j^s, \xi_i^t, \xi_i^u} \frac{1}{2}(\|\mathbf{w}\|^2 + b^2) - \rho + \frac{C}{2}(\sum_{i=1}^{n_s}(\xi_j^s)^2 + \sum_{i=1}^{n_t}(\xi_i^t)^2) + \frac{C_u}{2}\sum_{i=1}^{n_u}(\xi_i^u)^2,$$

$$\text{s.t.}\quad y_j^s(\mathbf{w}^T\phi_s(\mathbf{x}_j^s) + b) \geq \rho - \xi_j^s,$$

$$y_i^t(\mathbf{w}^T\phi_t(\mathbf{x}_i^t) + b) \geq \rho - \xi_i^t,$$

$$y_i^u(\mathbf{w}^T\phi_t(\mathbf{x}_i^u) + b) \geq \rho - \xi_i^u,$$

$$\mathbf{1}'\mathbf{y}_u = \delta, \quad \|\mathbf{P}_s\|_F^2 \leq \lambda_p, \quad \|\mathbf{P}_t\|_F^2 \leq \lambda_q. \tag{6.9}$$

In summary, SHFA is a preferred method among the algorithms introduced in this line of research work because: (1) it is capable of taking advantage of both labeled and unlabeled data; (2) it does not require auxiliary correspondence data and (3) it effectively augments latent representations with original features.

Dictionary Learning

Olshausen and Field (1997) first introduce the idea of learning an over-complete dictionary from data, rather than using the off-the-shelf bases, to sparsely code any signals in the data set. Learning robust dictionaries plays a key role in wide applications of DL and sparse coding. In heterogeneous transfer learning, some research works (Wang et al., 2012; Shekhar et al., 2013; Zhuang et al., 2013) learn a dictionary for each domain and enable the semantic meanings of the dictionaries to be coupled across domains. To couple the semantic meanings, this line of methods requires correspondence across domains.

Before proceeding to detail these works, we would first elaborate the definition of coupled dictionaries. Suppose that $\mathbf{d}_j^s$ is the j-th dictionary atom in a source domain's representational structure, and $\mathbf{d}_i^t$ is the i-th dictionary atom in a target domain's representation. If $\mathbf{d}_j^s$ represents a group of instances semantically relating to "sports" in the source domain and so does $\mathbf{d}_i^t$, we could say that $\mathbf{d}_j^s$ and $\mathbf{d}_i^t$ share a latent factor. Two dictionaries $\mathbf{D}_s$ and $\mathbf{D}_t$ are coupled, if and only if all dictionary atoms correspondingly share latent factors.

Early works couple dictionaries by enforcing the sparse codes of a pair of instances known to have correspondence across domains to be the same (Yang et al., 2010; Zhu et al., 2014). Wang et al. (2012) point out that such a strong assumption

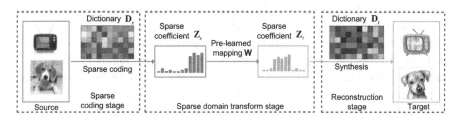

Figure 6.7 The overview of the semi-coupled DL method (adapted from Wang et al. [2012])

would impair the flexibility of representation. Instead, they relaxed this assumption by first learning two sets of sparse codes for two domains, respectively, and then bridging them with a stable transformation. Figure 6.7 provides a very intuitive overview of the proposed method called semi-coupled DL (SCDL). The formulation of the objective is:

$$\min_{\mathbf{Z}_s, \mathbf{D}_s, \mathbf{Z}_s, \mathbf{D}_t, \mathbf{W}} \|\mathbf{X}_s - \mathbf{D}_s \mathbf{Z}_s\|_F^2 + \|\mathbf{X}_t - \mathbf{D}_t \mathbf{Z}_t\|_F^2 + \gamma \|\mathbf{Z}_s - \mathbf{W} \mathbf{Z}_t\|_F^2$$
$$+ \lambda_s \|\mathbf{Z}_s\|_1 + \lambda_t \|\mathbf{Z}_t\|_1 + \lambda_W \|\mathbf{W}\|_F^2,$$
$$\text{s.t.} \ \|\mathbf{d}_i^s\|_2 \le 1, \quad \|\mathbf{d}_i^t\|_2 \le 1, \quad \forall i, \tag{6.10}$$

where λ_s, λ_t and λ_W are trade-off parameters. The third term of (6.10) models the linear transformation between sparse codes across domains. The ℓ_1 norm of $\mathbf{Z}_s$ and $\mathbf{Z}_t$ ensure the sparsity of sparse codes. The constraints imposed are to guarantee that each dictionary atom is well normalized. To facilitate classification, Zhuang et al. (2013) impose a structured sparsity constraint on the sparse codes based on (6.10). The structured sparsity constraint, achieved by ℓ_1/ℓ_2 norm, can produce more discriminative dictionaries, with each atom capturing the shared structures within the same class of each domain.

Furthermore, Jia et al. (2010) propose a model called factorized latent spaces with structured sparsity, which not only constrains sparse codes with structured sparsity, but also dictionaries. As a result, original examples in either domain can be represented by only a subset of dictionary atoms. A limitation may be that simply enforcing the sparse codes to be inter-translated or identical does not support that dictionary atoms from different domains lie in a common latent space. To address this limitation, Yu et al. (2014) propose formulating the coupled DL as a co-clustering problem with cluster centers as dictionaries. Each cluster, consisting of examples from heterogeneous domains, is regarded as a latent factor shared by all heterogeneous domains.

Another approach is proposed by Shekhar et al. (2013), who put forward a model called shared domain-adapted DL (SDDL), which projects both domains into a common low-dimensional space and then learns a shared discriminative dictionary in this latent space, which is illustrated in Figure 6.8. Different from previous models, SDDL does not require the existence of correspondence that is used to couple different domains. Instead, SDDL aims to learn a single shared dictionary that can optimally reconstruct both domains. In detail, the projection matrices and the shared discriminative dictionary are learned jointly in the model, which facilitates learning common internal structures from both domains according to Shekhar et al. (2013). The reasons for the pre-projections are given as follows: (1) heterogeneous feature spaces across different domains should be comparable; (2) irrelevant and noisy information is disregarded after projection and (3) the low-dimensional space is much more computationally efficient.

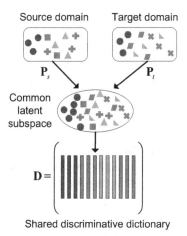

Figure 6.8 The overview of the proposed SDDL method (adapted from Shekhar et al. [2013])

Mathematically, the optimization problem in SDDL is shown as

$$\{\mathbf{D}^*, \tilde{\mathbf{P}}^*, \tilde{\mathbf{Z}}^*\} = \arg\min_{\mathbf{D}, \tilde{\mathbf{P}}, \tilde{\mathbf{Z}}} \mathscr{C}_1(\mathbf{D}, \tilde{\mathbf{P}}, \tilde{\mathbf{Z}}) + \lambda \mathscr{C}_2(\tilde{\mathbf{P}}),$$

$$\text{s.t. } \mathbf{P}_i \mathbf{P}_i^T = \mathbf{I}, \quad i = s, t \quad \text{and} \quad \|\tilde{\mathbf{z}}_j\|_0 \le T_0, \quad \forall j. \tag{6.11}$$

Clearly, the objective is composed of two parts: (1) $\mathscr{C}_1$ that minimizes the representation error in the low-dimensional projected space and (2) $\mathscr{C}_2$ that is the regularizer to preserve the variance in the original data as principal component analysis does. The definitions of $\mathscr{C}_1$ and $\mathscr{C}_2$ are given in (6.12) and (6.13), respectively,

$$\mathscr{C}_1(\mathbf{D}, \mathbf{P}_s, \mathbf{P}_t, \mathbf{Z}_s, \mathbf{Z}_t) = \|\mathbf{P}_s \mathbf{X}_s - \mathbf{D}\mathbf{Z}_s\|_F^2 + \|\mathbf{P}_t \mathbf{X}_t - \mathbf{D}\mathbf{Z}_t\|_F^2, \tag{6.12}$$

$$\mathscr{C}_2(\mathbf{P}_s, \mathbf{P}_t) = \|\mathbf{X}_s - \mathbf{P}_s^T \mathbf{P}_s \mathbf{X}_s\|_F^2 + \|\mathbf{X}_t - \mathbf{P}_t^T \mathbf{P}_t \mathbf{X}_t\|_F^2. \tag{6.13}$$

After mapping the original data with two projection matrices $\mathbf{P}_s \in \mathbb{R}^{d_c \times d_s}$ and $\mathbf{P}_t \in \mathbb{R}^{d_c \times d_t}$ into the d_c-dimensional latent space, SDDL learns a shared dictionary with K atoms, that is, $\mathbf{D} \in \mathbb{R}^{d_c \times K}$. Simultaneously, we infer the sparse representations $\mathbf{Z}_s$ and $\mathbf{Z}_t$ over the shared dictionary for the source and target domains, respectively. During the testing phase, a testing target example is first projected into the latent space with $\mathbf{P}_t$, as Figure 6.8 shows. In the following, its sparse representation over the shared dictionary $\mathbf{D}$ is inferred and passed further for classification or other tasks.

SDDL is effective only when two domains do not differ a lot. Otherwise a shared dictionary in the low-dimensional space may be incapable of reconstructing both domains. If the correspondence data across domains is accessible, coupled DL methods such as SCDL are more promising. Overall, this line of methods especially stands out in visual applications, given the fact that sparse coding has been proved to be the most effective in representing images.

Manifold Alignment

Manifold alignment, first introduced by Ham et al. (2003), is a class of machine learning algorithms that align underlying structures of different data sets. The assumption behind manifold alignment is that several data sets lie on a common manifold. As reviewed in the work by Pan and Yang (2010), manifold alignment algorithms have been successfully applied into transfer learning. There have also been several efforts toward addressing heterogeneous transfer learning using manifold alignment (Wang and Mahadevan, 2009, 2011; Mao et al., 2013). The key idea is to project domains into a low-dimensional space where the original topology of the common manifold is preserved.

The topology of the common manifold consists of two parts: (1) geometric structures between examples within the same domain and (2) geometric structures between examples across domains. The first kind of topology is easily obtained by directly comparing feature vectors of examples. The second type of topology to be preserved, however, relies on the annotated correspondence (Wang and Mahadevan, 2009) or the correspondence built from labels (Wang and Mahadevan, 2011), as we mentioned earlier.

In the work by Wang and Mahadevan (2011), m domains are provided, with $X_i \in \mathbb{R}^{d_i \times n_i}$ defined as the data in the i-th domain. d_i is the dimension of the i-th domain and n_i is the number of examples in it. The goal is to learn m projection functions $f_1, \cdots, f_m$ to map the m domains into a new d_c-dimensional latent space. The first kind of topology preservation is defined as:

$$C = \frac{1}{2}\mu \sum_{i=1}^{m} \sum_{j=1}^{n_i} \sum_{j'=1}^{n_i} \|f_i^T \mathbf{x}_j^i - f_i^T \mathbf{x}_{j'}^i\|^2 W_i(j, j'), \qquad (6.14)$$

where $W_i(j, j')$ is the similarity between the j-th example $\mathbf{x}_j^i$ and the j'-th instance $\mathbf{x}_{j'}^i$ in the i-th domain. The second type of topology is preserved via labels of examples in the work by Wang and Mahadevan (2011), that is, the examples across domains with the same label should be similar (minimizing (6.15)) and those with different labels should be separated (maximizing (6.16)),

$$A = \frac{1}{2} \sum_{a=1}^{m} \sum_{b=1}^{m} \sum_{j=1}^{n_a} \sum_{j'=1}^{n_b} \|f_a^T \mathbf{x}_j^a - f_b^T \mathbf{x}_{j'}^b\|^2 W_s^{a,b}(j, j'), \qquad (6.15)$$

$$B = \frac{1}{2} \sum_{a=1}^{m} \sum_{b=1}^{m} \sum_{j=1}^{n_a} \sum_{j'=1}^{n_b} \|f_a^T \mathbf{x}_j^a - f_b^T \mathbf{x}_{j'}^b\|^2 W_d^{a,b}(j, j'), \qquad (6.16)$$

where $W_s^{a,b}(j, j') = 1$ if $\mathbf{x}_j^a$ and $\mathbf{x}_{j'}^b$ carry the same label, otherwise $W_s^{a,b}(j, j') = 0$. $W_d^{a,b}(j, j')$ acts the opposite. Combining (6.14), (6.15) and (6.16), the final objective to minimize is $\mathcal{O} = (A + C)/B$.

When there exist few or no labeled data in the target domain, the alignment in Wang and Mahadevan's (2011) work tends to be ineffective. In this case, if annotated correspondence is provided, simply redefine $W_s^{a,b}(j, j')$ as the provided correlation between instances $\mathbf{x}_j^a$ and $\mathbf{x}_{j'}^b$, and finally minimize $A + C$ instead. In fact, the method proposed by Wang and Mahadevan (2009) can even handle the case where neither labels nor annotated correspondence is available. The proposed method considers local geometric structures around each example to be the bridge between examples across domains.

At the end of this section, we would like to compare different latent space-based methods, as shown in the Table 6.2. Latent factor analysis with flexible factor extraction techniques can cover a wide range of applications, while the latent space is learned by only maximizing the likelihood. If the applications to be addressed are within the visual domain, DL could outperform on top of sparse representations. However, the performance could be compromised by the high dimension. Manifold alignment specializes in preserving geometric structures of original data in a common latent space. It may fail if the manifold underlying the original data is not approximated accurately.

Translation-Based Single-Level Alignment

Dai et al. (2008) first propose a translation-based approach named translated learning via risk minimization (TLRisk) to transfer knowledge from text to images for image classification. The proposed model establishes a "feature level translator" via correspondence between images and text to translate text features into image features. Consequently, the feature-level translator can bridge a source domain (text documents) and a target domain (images). The key of TLRisk lies in two Markov chain assumptions presented here:

$$\theta_y \rightarrow c \rightarrow f^s \rightarrow f^t \rightarrow \mathbf{x}_i^t \rightarrow \theta_{\mathbf{x}_i^t}, \tag{6.17}$$

$$\theta_y \rightarrow c \rightarrow f^t \rightarrow \mathbf{x}_i^t \rightarrow \theta_{\mathbf{x}_i^t}, \tag{6.18}$$

where c, θ_y, f^s, f^t, $\mathbf{x}_i^t$ and $\theta_{\mathbf{x}_i^t}$ denote the c-th class label, the classifier associated with the c-th class, feature representations of an example belonging to the c-th class in a source domain, feature representations of an example belonging to the c-th class in a target domain, the example which is represented by f_t in the target domain, and the classifier associated with the example. The TLRisk classifies a target example $\mathbf{x}_i^t$ by directly evaluating the empirical risk $R(\mathbf{x}_i^t, c)$ and pinpointing the class c that minimizes this loss. According to Dai et al. (2008),

Table 6.2 *Comparison of latent space based methods.*

	Latent factor analysis	DL	Manifold alignment
Advantages	• A variety of applications • The way of extracting latent factors is flexible, linear or nonlinear	• Sparse representations make DL stand out in visual applications	• Latent space preserves geometric structures
Disadvantages	• Latent space is learned by only maximizing the likelihood	• Not scalable to large-scale applications with high dimension	• Assumption of the existence of a manifold

$R(\mathbf{x}_i^t, c) \propto \Delta(\theta_{\mathbf{x}_i^t}, \theta_y) \propto \text{KL}(p(f^t|\theta_y)\|p(f^t|\theta_{\mathbf{x}_i^t}))$. A source domain is translated and contributes to calculating $p(f^t|\theta_y)$,

$$p(f^t|\theta_y) = \int_{\mathcal{X}_s} \sum_{c \in \mathcal{Y}} p(f^t|f^s)p(f^s|c)p(c|\theta_y)df^s + \sum_{c \in \mathcal{Y}} p(f^t|c)p(c|\theta_y). \qquad (6.19)$$

$p(f_t|f_s)$ in (6.19) is the translator built from correspondence. Later on, Chen et al. (2010b) follow this work and first applied heterogeneous transfer learning on visual contextual advertising, which recommends advertisements for images without surrounding text.

By pointing out that the robustness of TLRisk highly relies on high-quality correspondence data, Kulis et al. (2011) propose a method, called asymmetric regularized cross-domain transformation (ARC-t), to leverage labels of both domains to learn a translator. The method imposes similarity and dissimilarity constraints – a pair of examples across domains carrying the same label should be as similar as possible after the translation, while a pair of examples with different labels is expected to be dissimilar after the translation. The objective function can be expressed as:

$$\min_{\mathbf{T}} \Omega(\mathbf{T}) + \lambda \sum_{i,j} c((\mathbf{x}_j^s)^T \mathbf{T} \mathbf{x}_i^t), \qquad (6.20)$$

where Ω regularizes the complexity of the translator $\mathbf{T}$. The function $c(\cdot)$ is defined as $c((\mathbf{x}_j^s)^T \mathbf{T} \mathbf{x}_i^t) = (\max(0, l - (\mathbf{x}_j^s)^T \mathbf{T} \mathbf{x}_i^t))^2$ if $\mathbf{x}_j^s$ and $\mathbf{x}_i^t$ are from the same category, and is formulated as $c((\mathbf{x}_j^s)^T \mathbf{T} \mathbf{x}_i^t) = (\max(0, (\mathbf{x}_j^s)^T \mathbf{T} \mathbf{x}_i^t - u))^2$ if they carry different labels. Translated source examples can, as a consequence, be trained together with target examples for kinds of tasks such as classification.

Hoffman et al. (2013) designed an end-to-end model called max-margin domain transforms (MMDT), which simultaneously learns a classifier and a translator using labeled examples from both domains. MMDT adopts a linear translation matrix bridging domains, and incorporates it into an SVM-style max-margin classifier. The overall objective is formulated as

$$\min_{\mathbf{T}, \mathbf{w}, b} \quad \frac{1}{2}\|\mathbf{T}\|_F^2 + \frac{1}{2}\|\mathbf{w}\|_2^2$$

$$\text{s.t.} \quad y_j^s\left(\begin{bmatrix} \mathbf{x}_j^s \\ 1 \end{bmatrix}^T \begin{bmatrix} \mathbf{w} \\ b \end{bmatrix}\right) \geq 1 \quad \forall i \in \mathcal{D}_s$$

$$y_i^t\left(\begin{bmatrix} \mathbf{x}_i^t \\ 1 \end{bmatrix}^T \mathbf{T}^T \begin{bmatrix} \mathbf{w} \\ b \end{bmatrix}\right) \geq 1 \quad \forall i \in \mathcal{D}_t, \qquad (6.21)$$

where $\mathbf{T} \in \mathbb{R}^{d_t \times d_s}$ is the translation matrix that translates every target example $\mathbf{x}^t \in \mathbb{R}^{d_t \times 1}$ into the source domain with d_s-dimension, and $\mathbf{w}$ and b are parameters of the max-margin classifier.

Obviously, both ARC-t and MMDT do not require the correspondence between domains. However, there is no free lunch. They work only when sufficient labeled examples in the target domain are available. To be more flexible, Qi et al. (2011a) propose a model called text-to-image (TTI), which is capable of learning a translator from not only correspondence, but also labels, if provided. Different from Dai et al. (2008) and Chen et al. (2010b), TTI classifies a target example by directly propagating labels of source examples. As Figure 6.9 shows, the final label of a tar-

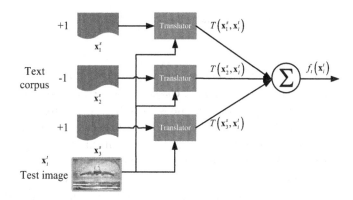

Figure 6.9 An illustration of the label propagation process from text to images (adapted from Qi et al. [2011a])

get example $\mathbf{x}_i^t$ is determined by a linear combination of labels of source examples. The coefficients are decided by the values of the translator function. The intuition behind this idea resembles the nearest neighbor classifier. Mathematically,

$$f_t(\mathbf{x}_i^t) = \sum_{i=1}^{n_s} y_j^s T(\mathbf{x}_j^s, \mathbf{x}_i^t),$$ (6.22)

where $T(\cdot, \cdot)$ is the translator function. The authors define the translator function as the inner product of a source example and a target example in a hypothetical topic space, that is,

$$T(\mathbf{x}_j^s, \mathbf{x}_i^t) = \langle \mathbf{P}^s \mathbf{x}_j^s, \mathbf{P}^t \mathbf{x}_i^t \rangle = (\mathbf{P}^s \mathbf{x}_j^s)^T \mathbf{P}^t \mathbf{x}_i^t = (\mathbf{x}_j^s)^T \mathbf{S} \mathbf{x}_i^t.$$ (6.23)

Therefore, TTI actually combines the ideas of both latent space and translation. To learn the translator function, TTI takes the collective power of labeled target examples and the correspondence between domains. Specifically, the optimization problem is formulated as

$$\min_{\mathbf{S}} \gamma \sum_{i=1}^{n_t} \ell(y_i^t \sum_{j=1}^{n_s} y_j^s (\mathbf{x}_j^s)^T \mathbf{S} \mathbf{x}_i^t) + \lambda \sum_{i,j} \chi(c_{i,j} \cdot (\mathbf{x}_j^s)^T \mathbf{S} \mathbf{x}_i^t) + \Omega(\mathbf{S}),$$ (6.24)

where the first term minimizes the losses of predicted labels of target examples, and the second term maximizes the consistency between the known correspondence $c_{i,j}$ and the translator function value. Note that the function $\chi(a)$ is small if a is large. The last term in (6.24) controls the complexity of $\mathbf{S}$.

Unlike the aforementioned works that learn a translator using data themselves,

Zhou et al. (2014b) borrow an idea from multitask learning and learn a translator based on source and target predictive models, that is, $\mathbf{w}^s$ and $\mathbf{w}^t$. Specifically, the problem is formulated as a non-negative least absolute shrinkage and selection operator problem:

$$\min_{\mathbf{T}} \frac{1}{n_c} \sum_{c=1}^{n_c} \|\mathbf{w}_t^c - \mathbf{T}\mathbf{w}_s^c\|_2^2 + \sum_{i=1}^{d_t} \lambda_i \|\mathbf{t}_i\|_1$$

$$\text{s.t. } \mathbf{t}_i \geq 0, \tag{6.25}$$

where λ_i is a regularization parameter. For a multi-class problem in either domain, the authors considered n_c binary classifiers $\{\mathbf{w}_*^1, \cdots, \mathbf{w}_*^{n_c}\}$ with $*$ denoting s or t. The first loss term, therefore, enforces the learned translator $\mathbf{T}$ to be class-invariant. The authors believed that the translator matrix $\mathbf{T}$ should be highly sparse – each source domain feature can be characterized with only a small subset of target domain features. That is the reason why the second term, the ℓ_1 regularization on rows in $\mathbf{T}$, is proposed to guarantee the sparsity on each row of the translator. The constraint imposed ensures the correlation between source and target predictive models to be non-negative.

The label for a testing target example $\mathbf{x}_*^t$ can be predicted by $y_*^t = F(\{(\mathbf{T}\mathbf{w}_s^c)^T \mathbf{x}_*^t\}_{c=1}^{n_c})$, where the function F combines the results from all n_c binary source classifiers to make a decision. The primary advantage of this method, called sparse heterogeneous feature representation (SHFR), is its efficiency. First, it avoids learning a dense translator that depends quadratically on the feature dimensions. Second, it is capable of learning a translator $\mathbf{T}$ without using source domain data. Once a set of binary classifiers, that is, $\{\mathbf{w}_s^c\}$, has been trained on a source domain, they can be directly applied in the SHFR model.

Compared to latent space-based methods, translation-based methods pursue more agreement between the final objective of a task, say classification accuracy, and the optimization objective with regard to a translator. Unfortunately, they are also in the risk of poor generalization ability. When the relationship between examples across domains is unseen during testing, the translation-based methods probably fail.

Multi-level Alignment

Over the years, researchers have realized that the single-level alignment approach has a strong assumption that only one level of operation is sufficient to align heterogeneous domains. In fact, the complex interrelationship between different domains could be characterized by a hierarchy, which calls for "deep alignment." Ideally, all the techniques we mentioned earlier including latent space and translation-based techniques can achieve multi-level alignment by sequentially repeating for multiple times. However, not all of them have been investigated so far for multi-level alignment. Here, we introduce DL and deep learning-based methods that have been explored.

Dictionary Learning

As a deep alignment version of the SDDL model (Shekhar et al., 2013), Nguyen et al. (2015) present so-called domain adaptation using a sparse and hierarchical network (DASH-N). DASH-N adopts a similar idea of projecting both domains into a common latent space in which a shared discriminative dictionary is learned as SDDL, while it makes a difference by projecting multiple times and learning multiple shared dictionaries in a hierarchical network. Figure 6.10 shows the carefully designed architecture of the hierarchical network. The authors tailor

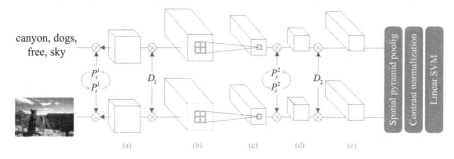

Figure 6.10 Overview of the DASH-N model (adapted from Nguyen et al. [2015])

DASH-N for visual applications. First of all, DASH-N performs dimension reduction and contrast normalization for input images from heterogeneous domains using corresponding projection matrices, that is, P_s^1 and P_t^1. Second, DASH-N obtains the sparse codes by applying a shared dictionary D_1 in the low-dimensional space. Third, DASH-N performs the max pooling. These three steps corresponding to procedures (a)–(c) in Figure 6.10 are repeated in the next layers. The times of repeating equals to the number of alignment levels. All the projections and shared dictionaries are learned jointly with the final classification performance as the supervision. Multiple levels of alignment as well as this end-to-end learning scheme ensure that the source domain can greatly benefit the target domain of interest.

Deep Learning

Deep neural networks have made tremendous success and achieved the state-of-the-art performance on computer vision as well as other machine learning tasks (Bengio, 2009). The success partly attributes to the capability of deep neural networks in learning extremely powerful hierarchical nonlinear representations of inputs. Motivated by recent advances on deep learning, several heterogeneous deep learning approaches (Zhou et al., 2014a; Shu et al., 2015; Wang et al., 2018a) have been proposed.

Zhou et al. (2014a) propose a hybrid heterogeneous transfer learning (HHTL) algorithm, which alternates between learning robust representations and learning translators in a layer-wise fashion. Inspired by the effectiveness of marginalized stacked denoized autoencoder (mSDA) (Chen et al., 2012b) in homogeneous transfer learning, the authors adopt mSDA to learn high-level feature representa-

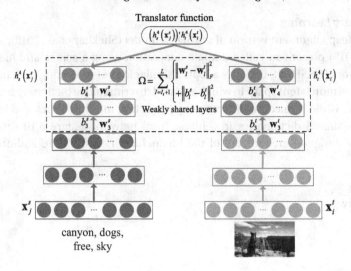

Figure 6.11 Overview of the weakly shared deep transfer network (adapted from Shu et al. [2015])

tions, which is formulated as

$$\min_{\mathbf{W}_*} \sum_{m=1}^{M} \|\mathbf{X}_* - \mathbf{W}_* \tilde{\mathbf{X}}_*^m\|_F^2, \tag{6.26}$$

where $*$ denotes s or t. Here $\tilde{\mathbf{X}}_*^m$ is the m-th corrupted version of $\mathbf{X}_*$. With the optimal learned $\mathbf{W}_*$, a high-level representation $\mathbf{H}_*^1 = \tanh(\mathbf{W}_* \mathbf{X}_*)$ can be obtained. Considering that the high-level representations $\mathbf{H}_s^1$ and $\mathbf{H}_t^1$ still lie in different feature spaces, the authors proposed learning a translator $\mathbf{T}^1$ by minimizing the following objective,

$$\|\mathbf{H}_{s(c)}^1 - \mathbf{T}\mathbf{H}_{t(c)}^1\|_F^2 + \lambda \|\mathbf{T}^1\|_F^2, \tag{6.27}$$

where λ balances between the alignment and the complexity of the translator $\mathbf{T}^1$. Note that $\mathbf{H}_{s(c)}^1$ and $\mathbf{H}_{t(c)}^1$ represent a subset of $\mathbf{H}_s^1$ and $\mathbf{H}_t^1$ that have the correspondence that is indispensable to align features across domains.

This process can be recursively carried out by replacing $\mathbf{X}_*$ in (6.26) with $\mathbf{H}_*^1$ and in the next layer replacing $\mathbf{H}_{*(c)}^1$ in (6.27) with $\mathbf{H}_{*(c)}^2$. As a consequence, a series of weight matrices $\{\mathbf{W}_*^l\}_{l=1}^L$, high-level representations $\{\mathbf{H}_*^l\}_{l=1}^L$ and translators $\{\mathbf{T}^l\}_{l=1}^L$ can be obtained. A classifier f is then trained on the augmented source domain data $\mathbf{H}_s = [\mathbf{H}_s^1, \cdots, \mathbf{H}_s^L]$. A testing target example $\mathbf{x}^t$ is first augmented as $\mathbf{h}^t = [\mathbf{T}\mathbf{h}^{t,1}, \cdots, \mathbf{T}\mathbf{h}^{t,L}]$, and its label is predicted by applying f, that is, $f(\mathbf{h}^t)$.

Unfortunately, the layer-wise training method with the alternative manner in Zhou et al.'s (2014a) work is highly inefficient. Shu et al. (2015) address this problem by designing a deep neural network architecture named as weakly shared deep transfer networks (WSDTNs), as shown in Figure 6.11. WSDTN learns

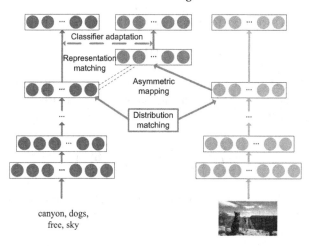

Figure 6.12 Overview of the deep asymmetric transfer network (adapted from Wang et al. [2018a])

hierarchical representations for each domain, while constrains parameters of top layers are weakly shared by both domains. It has been widely accepted that representations in deep neural networks range from low-level descriptors to high-level semantic factors as the layer increases. The discrepancy between heterogeneous domains is usually large in low-level descriptors, which is the reason why only parameters of top layers are constrained to be shared. This work can be regarded as an extension of the framework in TTI (Qi et al., 2011a) mentioned earlier, by replacing the translator function ((6.23)) in a bilinear form with a sufficiently effective and robust translator $(h_s^L(\mathbf{x}_j^s))^T h_t^L(\mathbf{x}_i^t)$, where $h_s^L(\mathbf{x}_j^s)$ is the hidden representation of the L-th layer for the j-th source example $\mathbf{x}_j^s$, and $h_t^L(\mathbf{x}_i^t)$ has a similar definition. The overall objective, therefore, follows (6.24), except that the constraints on parameters of top layers across domains are also incorporated, that is,

$$\Omega = \sum_{l=l_{\min}}^{L} \|\mathbf{w}_l^s - \mathbf{w}_l^t\|_F^2 + \|b_l^s - b_l^t\|_2^2,$$

where $l_{\min}$ denotes the index of the lowest layer from which the weakly shared constraints are imposed.

Both HHTL and WSDTN, however, are not end-to-end because they separate learning invariant representations across domains because they consist of two stages, that is, learning invariant representations across domains and training a classifier. Wang et al. (2018a) propose an end-to-end deep asymmetric transfer network (DATN) for unbalanced domain adaptation, as shown in Figure 6.12. DATN adopts a classical Siamese structure similar to WSDTN, but differs in the alignment of domains in top layers. The alignment are two-fold: (1) a translator is learned to bridge hidden representations of both domains and (2) the distributions of hidden representations across domains should be as close as possible.

The loss function to achieve the first alignment is shown as

$$\mathscr{L}_{pair} = \|\mathbf{H}_{s(c)}^L - \mathbf{T}\mathbf{H}_{s(c)}^L\|_F^2 + \lambda\|\mathbf{T}\|_F^2, \tag{6.28}$$

where the L-th layer is the topmost layer. The distribution discrepancy, which is minimized to guarantee the second type of alignment, is measured using MMD (Gretton et al., 2012) as

$$\mathscr{L}_{dist} = \left\|\frac{1}{n_s}\sum_{j=1}^{n_s}\mathbf{h}_j^{s,L} - \frac{1}{n_t}\sum_{i=1}^{n_t}\mathbf{h}_i^{t,L}\right\|_2^2. \tag{6.29}$$

With the translator $\mathbf{T}$, the high-level representation of both domains is aligned. In this case, the approach adapts the source domain classifier to classify target examples by using the following objective function

$$\mathscr{L}_{trans} = -\frac{1}{n_t^l}\sum_{i=1}^{n_t^l}\sum_{c=1}^{n_c} 1\{y_i^t = c\}\log\frac{e^{\mathbf{h}_i^{t,l,L}\mathbf{T}\mathbf{w}_{s,c}}}{\sum_{c'=1}^{n_c}e^{\mathbf{h}_i^{t,l,L}\mathbf{T}\mathbf{w}_{s,c'}}}, \tag{6.30}$$

where $1\{\cdot\}$ is a indicator function, $\mathbf{h}_i^{t,l,L}$ denotes the hidden representation of the ith labeled target example at the L-th layer, and $\mathbf{w}_{s,c}$ represents the softmax parameters trained on source examples for the c-th class. The overall objective is a linear combination of (6.28), (6.29) and (6.30).

Multi-level alignment is more powerful and flexible than the single-level alignment. However, if the groundtruth alignment between domains could be as simple as in the single level, single-level alignment is more preferred because of low computational cost and wide applications.

6.3.2   Heterogeneous Label Spaces

Compared to research in heterogeneous feature spaces, only a limited amount of work has been done to transfer knowledge between domains in heterogeneous label spaces. Existing work in this area can be categorized into two major areas, aligning labels and aligning features across domains.

Shen et al. (2006b) address the label mismatch problem by resorting to a label taxonomy to relate labels in different domains. Specifically, the proposed approach pre-generates a collection of classifiers, each of which is for one class in an auxiliary label taxonomy and adapts one of these classifiers to the target domain in real time. The label of the selected classifier is expected to have the smallest distance to the label of the target domain in the taxonomy. Rohrbach et al. (2010) propose a similar method, which, however, differs in automatically extracting the semantic relationship among labels from some linguistic data sets, such as WordNet, Wikipedia, Yahoo images and Flickr. With the help of the extracted semantic relationship of labels, the pre-trained classifiers in source domains could be reused by the target domain. Shi et al. (2013a) first propose a probabilistic translation method to align the label spaces without requiring explicit semantic relationship between labels. The key is a decision rule:

$$p(y^t|\mathbf{x}^t) = \sum_{y^s} p(y^s|\mathbf{x}^t)p(y^t|y^s), \qquad (6.31)$$

where the posterior probability $p(y^s|\mathbf{x}^t)$ can be obtained by applying the pretrained classifier on the source domain to target examples. The estimation of $p(y^t|y^s)$ follows

$$p(y^t|y^s) = \frac{1}{p(y^s)}p(y^t, y^s) = \frac{1}{\sum_{\mathbf{x}^s} p(\mathbf{x}^s)} \sum_{\mathbf{x}^s} p(y^t|\mathbf{x}^s)p(\mathbf{x}^s), \qquad (6.32)$$

where $\mathbf{x}^s$ denotes a source example with y^s as the label. $p(\mathbf{x}^s)$ can be estimated to be the proportion of $\mathbf{x}^s$ in all source examples. $p(y^t|\mathbf{x}^s)$, similar to $p(y^s|\mathbf{x}^t)$, can be obtained by applying the classifier trained on the target domain to source examples.

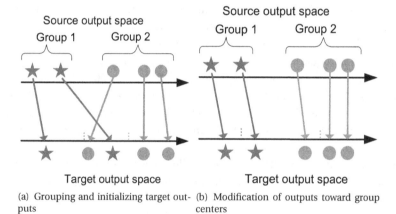

(a) Grouping and initializing target outputs (b) Modification of outputs toward group centers

Figure 6.13 The alignment of label spaces for regression problems (adapted from Shi et al. [2010a])

The aforementioned works are for classification problems where the label space is categorical and discrete. Shi et al. (2010a) first propose an heterogenous regression model to unify two label spaces for regression problems. The basic idea, as shown in Figure 6.13, is to assign source examples regression values in the label space of a target domain by preserving the similarity between them.

Qi et al. (2011b) claim that the aforementioned label alignment is disadvantageous, considering that the relationship between labels may vary across examples. Despite that, the label "mountain" seems irrelevant to the label "castle," a source image labeled as "mountain" and a target image that is labeled as "castle" but contains a castle built on a mountain are obviously correlated. Therefore, the authors propose aligning labels by building a feature-level translator similar to Qi et al.

(2011a). Besides, the feature-based transfer learning algorithms for homogeneous transfer learning, for example, transfer component analysis (Pan et al., 2011), can be adapted to achieve knowledge transfer between domains in the same feature space but different label spaces by training in an unsupervised manner.

6.4 Applications

Heterogeneous transfer learning techniques have been applied successfully in many real world applications. In applications to images, most works focus on improving the clustering or classification performance of images with the help of text documents (Yang et al., 2009; Qi et al., 2011a; Zhu et al., 2011). In addition, heterogeneous transfer learning is referred to as "heterogeneous domain adaptation" in the computer vision community (Duan et al., 2012b; Hoffman et al., 2013; Wu et al., 2013; Li et al., 2014). In this area, the goal is to enable knowledge transfer between images or videos in different feature representational structures. For example, Wu et al. (2013) address the video activity recognition in the target domain by transferring knowledge from a very related source domain. However, the valuable source domain should be best represented by optical flows that differ from the silhouettes features in the target domain. Yet another widely studied application is cross-language transfer learning (Dai et al., 2008; Ling et al., 2008; Zhang et al., 2010a; Huang et al., 2013; Gouws et al., 2015). For example, Ling et al. (2008) leverage labeled English web pages to help the classification of Chinese web pages. Li et al. (2014) propose a HFA method to solve the cross-lingual sentiment classification problem.

Human activity recognition enables a wide spectrum of machine learning applications. The success of human activity recognition relies on sufficient annotated sensor records, while annotating raw sensor readings either in real time or post hoc is particularly challenging. Fortunately, people nowadays proactively share happenings about and around them, as well as their whereabouts on social media platforms such as Twitter. Such platforms thus provide a huge and rich semantic repository of activities that people are performing at different times and locations. Wei et al. (2016a) first proposed the transfer of knowledge from social media messages oftentimes represented as bag-of-words to physical sensor records characterized as numerical values.

Several researchers have applied heterogeneous transfer learning to the recommendation problem. In the work by Li et al. (2009a), a method is put forward to transfer the rating knowledge from a source domain (movie recommendation) to a target domain (book recommendation domain), where a common shared subspace known as the codebook-based method links the source and target domains. This method works even when the two domains do not have overlap over items or products.

In Shi et al.'s (2012) work, the target task is to predict movie ratings in the Internet movie database (IMDB). Five different data sets are available in this approach to form the source domains: a genre database, a database of a sound technique, information about running times, an actor graph with two movies connected if they share common actors or actresses, and a director graph defined similarly. Shi et al. (2012) build a gradient boosting consensus model, which integrates all the five data sets in different feature spaces, to accurately predict ratings in the "out-of-sample" condition.

Several public data sets exist on which heterogeneous transfer learning techniques can be fairly compared.

Office[1]: The data set is a standard domain adaptation data set in computer vision. This data set contains 4,106 images in thirty-one categories collected from three sources: amazon (object images in Amazon), dslr (high-resolution images taken from a digital SLR camera) and webcam (low-resolution images taken from a web camera). amazon and webcam, as the source domains, are represented as 800 dimensional speeded up robust features (SURF) features (Bay et al., 2008), while dslr is represented as 600-dimensional SURF features.

IXMAS[2]: This data set consists of five views of actions, each of which is taken from a camera. The actions covers eleven classes, and each action is executed three times by twelve subjects. Each view is represented in both optimal flows and silhouettes. At each time, one of the views acts as the target domain, and the other views together act as the source domain. The target domain adopts the silhouettes representation while the source takes optimal flows.

Cross-lingual sentiment (CLS)[3]: This data set contains 800,000 product reviews in the four languages, English, German, French and Japanese. The reviews cover three categories: books, DVDs and music. For each category and each language, the data set is officially split into a training set, a test set and an unlabeled set. The training and test sets include 2,000 reviews, and the sizes of the unlabeled set vary from 9,000 to 170,000. The English is regarded as the source domain and each of the other three languages acts as the target domain, respectively.

Data sets providing the correspondence usually come from Flickr. Therefore, here we introduce a few heterogeneous data sets with the correspondence that could facilitate training heterogeneous transfer learning algorithms.

FLICKR30K[4]: Flickr30K contains 31,783 images, each of which is annotated with five descriptive sentences by workers on Amazon Mechanical Turk. Overall, there arc 158,915 crowd sourced captions.

MIRFLICKR[5]: The data set has two versions, MIRFLICKR-25000 and MIRFLICKR-1M. They consist of 25,000 and one million tagged images, respectively. Besides, the MIRFLICKR-25000 data set is fully labeled with thirty-nine tags.

---

[1] https://people.eecs.berkeley.edu/~jhoffman/domainadapt/
[2] http://4drepository.inrialpes.fr/public/viewgroup/6
[3] www.uni-weimar.de/en/media/chairs/webis/corpora/corpus-webis-cls-10/
[4] https://illinois.edu/fb/sec/229675
[5] http://press.liacs.nl/mirflickr/

NUS-WIDE[6]: The data set includes 269,648 images associated with tags from Flickr. Six types of low-level features are extracted, including 64-dimensional color histogram, 144-dimensional color correlogram, 73-dimensional edge direction histogram, 128-dimensional wavelet texture, 225-dimensional block-wise color moments and 500-dimensional bag of words based on scale-invariant feature transform descriptions. Moreover, all the images are labeled by eighty-one concepts for the sake of evaluation.

In Table 6.3, we show results from a few published papers on heterogeneous transfer learning. The table presents the performance comparison of different heterogeneous transfer learning algorithms and non-transfer methods. Qi et al. (2011a) crawl tagged images from Flickr and text documents from Wikipedia with the names of ten categories as keywords. For each category, the authors built a category/non-category binary classification task. We present the comparison result in the bird/non-bird task as an example in the first line of the table. According to Qi et al. (2011a), the translation-based method TTI outperforms HTLIC (Zhu et al., 2011), a latent space-based method, and TLRisk (Dai et al., 2008), another translation-based method. Note that SVM-t (SVM trained only on the target domain) does not transfer any knowledge and only trains on the target domain.

In addition, we also show comparison results on domain adaptation data sets in computer vision reported by Hoffman et al. (2013). Note that T-SVM denotes the transductive SVMs (Joachims, 1999), which does not transfer knowledge from the source domain, but takes full advantage of unlabeled examples in the target domain. Finally, we present results on the cross-view activity recognition data set and cross-lingual sentiment classification data set. Generally speaking, compared to the non-transfer methods SVM-t and T-SVM, heterogeneous transfer learning does contribute to target domains by borrowing knowledge from source domains.

Table 6.3 *Comparison of different heterogeneous transfer learning methods and non-transfer learning methods. DAMA, domain adaptation with manifold alignment*

Data set (reference)	Source → target	Baselines(%)		HTL methods(%)					
Flickr and Wikipedia (Qi et al., 2011a)		SVM-t		HTL	TLRisk	TTI			
	documents → images	67.07		62.07	71.83	72.62			
		SVM-t	T-SVM	HeMap	SDDL	DAMA	HFA	SHFA	MMDT
Office (Hoffman et al., 2013)	amazon → dslr	52.90	53.50	42.80	50.40	53.30	55.40	56.10	62.30
	webcam → dslr	52.90	53.50	42.20	49.40	53.20	54.30	55.10	63.30
				HeMap	DAMA	HFA			
	other → view 1			33.70	33.20	26.60			
	other → view 2			39.90	34.40	33.00			
IXMAS (Wu et al., 2013)	other → view 3			29.20	28.10	30.70			
	other → view 4			34.70	31.60	31.80			
	other → view 5			22.90	13.40	13.40			
		SVM-t	T-SVM	HeMap	DAMA	HFA	SHFA		
CLS (Li et al., 2014)	English → German	65.60	50.40	58.30	64.60	66.50	70.20		
	English → French	60.40	67.80	49.80	65.70	66.90	70.50		
	English → Japanese	57.40	63.90	51.30	64.40	64.20	67.80		

[6] http://lms.comp.nus.edu.sg/research/NUS-WIDE.htm

7

Adversarial Transfer Learning

7.1 Introduction

One way to apply transfer learning is to use generative modeling in machine learning. This leads to adversarial models. One approach is to use unsupervised generative modeling to reduce the dependency on labeled data. In a target domain, the labeled data are limited, but there may be abundant unlabeled data available in a source domain. In the natural language understanding area, for example, at the time when this book is written, there are around 6,000 tweets posted on Twitter every second, around 300 hours of video are uploaded to Youtube every minute and around one million images are shared on Flickr every day. Unsupervised feature learning can then be used to build representations from the unlabeled data, and generative models can be used to enable knowledge transfer to a target domain (Zhu, 2005; Bengio et al., 2013).

There are two types of generative models, *explicit* and *implicit* models. An explicit generative model has a specified density function with its parameters being estimated via the principle of maximum likelihood method. An implicit generative model does not require an explicit density function; instead, it acts like a simulator by generating samples to follow the underlying data distribution. Generative models, as the late physicist Richard Feynman said, "If I cannot create, I do not understand," can generate samples similar to a given training data when the resultant model captures the intrinsic structure of the data. However, generative modeling is challenging as well, due to the high dimensionality and multimodality of real world data.

Among generative models, generative adversarial networks (GANs) (Goodfellow et al., 2014) have emerged as implicit generative models that achieved great success in many applications. These applications include image super-resolution, image inpainting, video frame prediction and so on. Empirical results demonstrate that GANs can learn visual semantic representations and can generate visually realistic images in a specific type of transfer learning known as "style transfer." There is growing interest in GANs. Extensive theoretical analyses and various variants have also been developed for the GAN framework. In the next section, we give details on the operations of GANs.

Adversarial learning works naturally with transfer learning. As a generative model, GANs can generate and augment the target domain data, in a new type of transfer learning known as "data augmentation." This can be achieved by "translating" source domain samples to a target domain while retaining their label information at the same time. The learning-based data augmentation approach differs from traditional instance-based transfer learning models as it "creates" additional target domain data. In contrast, the traditional models such as TrAdaBoost and kernel mean matching learn the weights for the labeled source domain samples only. Adversarial learning can also be used to learn a shared latent feature space across domains by minimizing the task loss in the source domain and maximizing the domain confusion loss. Instead of learning domain invariant features as reviewed in Chapter 3, adversarial features for transfer learning are learned by solving a min-max game.

In this chapter, we first introduce GANs and then present adversarial transfer learning models.

7.2   Generative Adversarial Networks

GANs are originally proposed by Goodfellow et al. (2014). For clarity, we call it *vanilla GAN*. Given large amounts of unlabeled samples, GANs are trained to generate samples that follow the same underlying data distribution. When GANs are trained with digit or face images, they are able to generate realistic-looking samples. Since then, the GAN as a framework has been extensively studied. Various network architectures and training objectives are proposed to improve the training stability and generate realistic samples (Radford et al., 2015; Chen et al., 2016b; Nowozin et al., 2016). In addition to theoretical studies, adversarial learning has also been adopted in various applications to achieve state-of-the-art performance, including image super-resolution (Ledig et al., 2017), video frame prediction (Vondrick et al., 2016), sequence modeling (Yu et al., 2017) and so on.

The structure of a vanilla GAN is shown in Figure 7.1. It is composed of two sub-networks, a generator (G) and a discriminator (D). The generator learns the mapping from a prior distribution (usually the uniform or Gaussian distribution), denoted by p_z, to the true data distribution, denoted by p_{data}. The mapping characterized by the generator is denoted by p_G. The noise sampled from the prior distribution, the true data sample and the generated data sample are denoted by z, x and $\hat{x}$, respectively. The GAN introduces a discriminator to guide the generator. The discriminator is trained to perform a binary classification task where the true data samples and the generated samples are positive and negative samples, respectively. When a sample is fed into the discriminator, it outputs the probability that the input sample comes from the true data distribution.

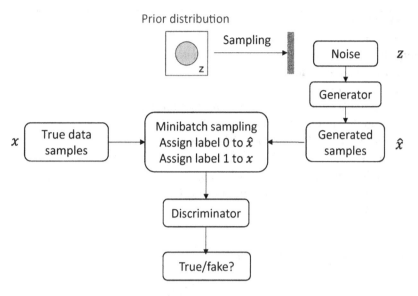

Figure 7.1 The GAN framework. Two sub-networks, a generator and a discriminator compete against each other. The generator maps a vector sampled from a prior distribution to the data space. The discriminator tries to distinguish true data samples from the generated samples while the generator aims to fool the discriminator

In a GAN, the relationship between the discriminator and the generator is like a police and a thief: the police try to discern the thief from ordinary people and the thief aims to fool the police, which forms an adversarial objective. The interaction between the generator and discriminator can be formulated as a two-player min-max game:

$$\min_G \max_D V(G, D),$$

where

$$V(G, D) = \mathbb{E}_{\mathbf{x} \sim p_{data}}[\log D(\mathbf{x})] + \mathbb{E}_{\mathbf{z} \sim p_{\mathbf{z}}}[\log(1 - D(G(\mathbf{z})))]. \tag{7.1}$$

Both the generator and discriminator are multi-layer perceptrons. The model can be trained with gradient descent algorithms in an alternating manner, as outlined in Algorithm 7.1. In each iteration of the optimization process, the discriminator is updated first with the generator fixed and then the generator is optimized by fixing the discriminator. This process repeats until the model reaches the convergence.

Theoretical analysis shows that, if there is infinite model capacity and training time, there is a global optimum such that $p_G = p_{data}$. If the generator is fixed and

---

Algorithm 7.1 Training the GAN

Input: Unlabeled data samples $\{\mathbf{x}_1, \ldots, \mathbf{x}_n\}$
Output: The generator G and the discriminator D
  while not converge **do**
    for k steps **do**
      Sample a mini-batch of data samples from p_{data}
      Sample a mini-batch of noises from $p_{\mathbf{z}}$
      Optimize the discriminator D by maximizing (7.1)
    end for
    Sample a mini-batch of noises from $p_{\mathbf{z}}$
    Optimize the generator G by minimizing (7.1)
  end while

---

the discriminator is trained to its optimality, there is

$$D_G^*(\mathbf{x}) = \frac{p_{data}(\mathbf{x})}{p_{data}(\mathbf{x}) + p_G(\mathbf{x})},$$

where $D_G^*(\mathbf{x})$ denotes the optimal discriminator with a fixed generator. Given a fixed optimal discriminator D_G^*, the objective in (7.1) becomes

$$\begin{aligned}
C(G) &= \min_G V(G, D_G^*) \\
&= \min_G -\log(4) + 2 \cdot JSD(p_{data}(\mathbf{x}) \| p_G(\mathbf{x})),
\end{aligned} \tag{7.2}$$

where $JSD(\cdot)$ denotes the Jenson-Shannon divergence. (7.2) shows that the objective for the generator is to minimize the Jensen–Shannon divergence between the generated distribution p_G and the true data distribution p_{data} and that the global optimum can be achieved when $p_G = p_{data}$. If both the generator and discriminator have enough capacity, p_G will converge to p_{data} as expected.

In practice, optimizing the objective as defined in (7.1) might cause gradient vanishing; that is, the gradient value used to update the network parameters during a learning process approaches zero when iterating through too many layers, which makes the learning stop. This is because, in the early stage of training, the generated samples are poor and the discriminator can easily distinguish the generated samples from the true data samples, and, as a result, the gradient of $\log(1 - D(G(\mathbf{z})))$ vanishes. To provide sufficient gradient values, the generator is trained to maximize $\log(D(G(\mathbf{z})))$ instead, which is referred to as non-saturating GAN (NS-GAN).

In spite of the strong learning capacity, GANs are notoriously difficult to train. Common problems include the following.

(1) Mode collapsing where the model fails to generate samples in certain regions.
(2) The min-max game fails to reach an equilibrium.
(3) Unrealistic samples.

A large body of research work addresses the aforementioned issues from various perspectives. Radford et al. (2015) propose a deep convolutional GANs (DCGANs), which adopts a CNN as the generator. CNNs have been successful in discriminative tasks and combining with the objective of GAN makes CNNs applicable for unsupervised representation learning. Salimans et al. (2016) propose two techniques to stabilize the training procedure of the GAN, namely *feature matching* and *minibatch discrimination*. Feature matching requires that the activations of the generated samples and the true data samples in intermediate layers of the discriminator are similar. Minibatch discrimination encourages the discriminator to consider multiple samples in combination instead of an individual sample. There are also attempts to extending GANs to other information theoretic measures such as total variance divergence (Zhao et al., 2016), f-divergence (Nowozin et al., 2016) and Wasserstein distance (Arjovsky and Bottou, 2017; Arjovsky et al., 2017). To improve the quality of generated samples, Denton et al. (2015) developed a LapGAN to integrate multiple conditional GANs within a Laplacian pyramid. At each level of the pyramid, a generative model that is trained with the objective of GAN upscales low-resolutional images to fine-grained ones.

7.3 Transfer Learning with Adversarial Models

As GANs as well as adversarial learning have emerged as a novel and powerful framework, researchers have attempted to develop transfer learning models based on the adversarial learning framework. Table 7.1 summarizes traditional and adversarial transfer learning models that are categorized by problem settings that they address and transfer approaches that they adopt.

We review two approaches in adversarial transfer learning. The first approach is instance-based transfer learning. As a generative model, GANs can generate target domain data. Adversarial learning can be used to "translate" a labeled source domain sample to a target domain sample while retaining its label. Adversarial learning can build correspondences between the source and target domain samples in a completely unsupervised manner.

Another type of adversarial transfer learning model takes a feature-based transfer learning approach, which finds a common feature space with an adversarial objective. The feature-based transfer learning with adversarial learning can be further decomposed into two categories based on problem settings. Adversarial domain adaptation learns a discriminative classifier with labeled source domain data and unlabeled target domain, while adversarial feature learning focuses on the self-taught learning setting where high-level representations are constructed with massive unlabeled source domain data and then a classifier is learned with limited labeled target data.

Table 7.1 *Traditional and adversarial transfer learning methods*

Approach/problem		Unlabeled 𝕋		Labeled 𝕋	
		Unlabeled 𝕊	Labeled 𝕊	Unlabeled 𝕊	Labeled 𝕊
Traditional transfer learning	Instance-based		Covariate shift		TrAdaBoost
	Feature-based	Unsupervised transfer learning	Domain adaptation	Self-taught learning	Multitask learning, fine-tuning
Adversarial transfer learning	Instance-based	Unsupervised cross-domain instance alignment (Kim et al., 2017; Zhu et al., 2017; Yi et al., 2017)	Generate target domain data (Shrivastava et al., 2017)		
	Feature-based		Adversarial domain adaptation (Ganin et al., 2016; Bousmalis et al., 2016; Tzeng et al., 2017)	Adversarial feature learning (Donahue et al., 2016)	

7.3.1 Generating Target Domain Data

In a target domain, labeled data are often difficult to obtain and costly to label. Generative models can create samples for the target domain. For example, labeled data can be collected in a simulated road-driving environment in autonomous driving. Using the simulated labeled data as a source domain and adapting the the source-domain model to the target domain allow us to train an autonomous driving system in a real world domain. As unlabeled data are easy to collect, it is possible to generate target domain data with adversarial learning.

There are two types of models that generate target domain data. The first type learns mapping from the source samples to the target samples and thus creates labeled target domain samples, while the other type learns bi-directional mapping between the samples of the two domains.

A typical model that translates source domain samples to the target domain is SimGAN (Shrivastava et al., 2017). In SimGAN, adversarial learning bridges the discrepancy between the source and target domains while retaining the label information simultaneously. SimGAN learns with unlabeled target domain data and uses the labeled simulated data as a source domain. The network architecture of SimGAN is shown in Figure 7.2. Synthetic images are first generated by a simulator and then they are modified by a generator. The outputs of the generator are denoted by refined images. A discriminator is introduced to discern unlabeled target domain images and refined images. The generator is trained with an adversarial objective to fool the discriminator. To retain the label of a synthetic image after the refinement, a self-regularization loss is adopted to train the generator and defined

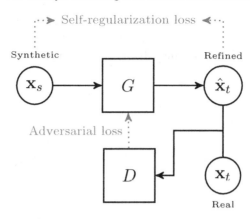

Figure 7.2 Overview of SimGAN. The generator refines synthetic images from a simulator to improve realism, as guided by the discriminator. In addition to the adversarial loss, a self-regularization loss is introduced to the annotations from the simulator after the refinement

as

$$\ell_{reg} = \|\psi(\mathbf{x}_s) - \psi(\hat{\mathbf{x}}_t)\|_1, \tag{7.3}$$

where ℓ_{reg} denotes the self-regularization loss, ψ denotes mapping from the image space to a new space, and $\mathbf{x}_s$ and $\hat{\mathbf{x}}_t$ denote the real and refined images, respectively. In practice, mapping ψ is usually identical mapping such that $\psi(\mathbf{x}) = \mathbf{x}$, and the self-regularization loss ℓ_{reg} is the per-pixel difference between the synthetic and refined images. Minimizing the the self-regularization loss encourages the refined image to reserve the simulated annotations.

In SimGAN, two additional modifications are made to the vanilla GAN in order to improve realism of refined images and stabilize training. The first modification is the local adversarial loss where the discriminator classifies local patches sampled from a refined image. This modification can avoid artifacts. The second modification is updating the discriminator with a history of refined images, which stabilizes the training procedure. The SimGAN is evaluated on the MPIIGaze data set for gaze estimation (Zhang et al., 2015b; Wood et al., 2016) and the hand pose estimation data set, the New York University (NYU) hand pose data set (Tompson et al., 2014). In quantitative evaluation, SimGAN outperforms state-of-the-art models on the MPIIGaze data set with a relative improvement of 21 percent. On the NYU hand pose data set, SimGAN, which does not require any label in the target domain, outperforms a model that is trained with real labeled images by 8.8 percent.

Another type of model builds bi-directional mapping between the source and target domains. It can be helpful for applications such as image editing. If the relationship between faces with black hair and those with blonde hair is known, one can imagine how he/she looks when he/she wants to change the hair color. Paired data are necessary to build such correspondences (Isola et al., 2017). However, with adversarial learning, models can discover cross-domain relations without paired data.

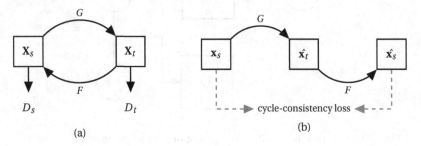

(a)   (b)

Figure 7.3 The network architecture of CycleGAN. (a) The bi-directional mappings G and F are learned simultaneously. (b) The cycle-consistency loss encourages the two mappings to inverses of each other

A typical model to address this setting is CycleGAN (Zhu et al., 2017), whose framework is shown in Figure 7.3. Let G denote the mapping from the source domain samples to the target domain samples. There are infinite possibilities to map the source domain samples to the target domain with the generated target samples following the target domain distribution. Learning the mapping G is an under-constrained problem.

To address the issue, an inverse mapping F is introduced to learn mapping from the target domain to the source domain. The two mappings G and F are learned simultaneously and they are bijections. To learn the mapping G, two losses are considered. The first loss is an *adversarial loss* that ensures that the translated sample $G(\mathbf{x}_s)$ is indistinguishable from target domain samples and defined as

$$\ell_{GAN}(G, D_t) = \mathbb{E}_{\mathbf{x}_t \sim p(\mathbf{X}_t)}[\log D_t(\mathbf{x}_t)] + \mathbb{E}_{\mathbf{x}_s \sim p(\mathbf{X}_s)}[\log(1 - D_t(G(\mathbf{x}_s)))], \qquad (7.4)$$

where D_t denotes the target domain discriminator that is introduced to distinguish true target domain samples and the translated samples from the source domain.

The network that characterizes the mapping G is trained to minimize $\ell_{GAN}(G, D_t)$. The target domain discriminator is trained to maximize $\ell_{GAN}(G, D_t)$, which formulates a two-player min-max game. A similar adversarial loss $\ell_{GAN}(F, D_s)$ can be defined for the mapping F and the source domain discriminator D_s. Another loss is a *cycle-consistent loss* that encourages G and F to be the inverse of each other, that is, $F(G(\mathbf{x}_s)) = \mathbf{x}_s$ and $G(F(\mathbf{x}_t)) = \mathbf{x}_t$, and defined as

$$\ell_{cyc}(G, F) = \mathbb{E}_{\mathbf{x}_s \sim p(\mathbf{X}_s)}[\|F(G(\mathbf{x}_s)) - \mathbf{x}_s\|_1] + \mathbb{E}_{\mathbf{x}_t \sim p(\mathbf{X}_t)}[\|G(F(\mathbf{x}_t)) - \mathbf{x}_t\|_1]. \qquad (7.5)$$

Putting (7.4) and (7.5) together, the full objective of the CycleGAN is formulated as

$$\ell(G, F, D_s, D_t) = \ell_{GAN}(G, D_t) + \ell_{GAN}(F, D_s) + \lambda\ell_{cyc}(G, F),$$

where λ balances the importance of the adversarial loss and the cycle-consistency loss. Qualitative analyses show that meaningful correspondences across domains can be established. "Real versus fake" perceptual studies on Amazon Mechanical Turk show that CycleGAN can fool human annotators on around 25 percent of trials. Yet their performance is still weaker than the model with strong paired supervision data. Also, failure cases are observed when there are geometric changes.

Researchers have proposed several models with similar characteristics (Kim et al., 2017; Yi et al., 2017; Zhu et al., 2017). These models differ from CycleGAN in implementation details. DiscoGAN (Kim et al., 2017) adopts a similar network architecture to DCGAN. CycleGAN adapts the architecture in Johnson et al. (2016a)'s work, which uses residual blocks and instance normalization in the generator and PatchGAN as the discriminator. Different from DCGAN, the discriminator in PatchGAN decides whether the input image is real or fake at the patch level. There are few parameters in the patch-level discriminator of PatchGAN and it can be applied to images with arbitrary sizes. DualGAN (Yi et al., 2017) uses PatchGAN as the discriminator as well and it adopts a U-shaped network proposed in the work by Isola et al. (2017) as the generator.

7.3.2 Learning Domain-Invariant Features via Adversarial Learning

The ability to learn common feature spaces is crucial to transfer learning. After projecting data from both the source and the target domains into a shared feature space, transfer-learning tasks can be performed with data from both domains.

Adversarial learning can learn a shared latent feature space across domains. When there are labeled data in the source domain and unlabeled data in the target domain, a common feature space satisfies the following two conditions:

(1) discriminative for source domain classification tasks,

(2) indistinguishable between the source and target domains.

Motivated by the two criteria, Ganin et al. (2016) propose a domain-adversarial neural network (DANN). The network architecture is shown in Figure 7.4. The network is composed of three sub-networks, a feature extractor shared across domains, a label predictor for classification in the source domain and a domain classifier. The three sub-networks are denoted by G, C and D, respectively. The feature extractor and the label predictor minimize the classification error ℓ_y in the source domain, which ensures the learned representations are discriminative. Meanwhile, the feature extractor maximizes the domain classification error ℓ_d, making the feature distributions domain-invariant. The feature extractor and the label predictor compete with the domain classifier.

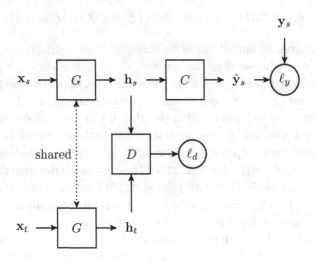

Figure 7.4 The DANN framework

Conceptually, the optimization process of a DANN formulates a min-max game with the objective as

$$\min_{G,C} \max_{D} V(G,C,D),$$

where

$$V(G,C,D) = \frac{1}{n_s} \sum_{i=1}^{n_s} \ell_y^i(G,C) - \lambda \left(\frac{1}{n_s} \sum_{i=1}^{n_s} \ell_d^i(G,D) + \frac{1}{n_t} \sum_{i=1}^{n_t} \ell_d^i(G,D) \right), \qquad (7.6)$$

where the hyperparameter λ balances the two terms. As G is minimized with respect to ℓ_y while it is maximized with respect to ℓ_d, a gradient reversal layer (GRL) is proposed. The gradient from the domain classifier D to the feature extractor G is multiplied by a negative constant during the back-propagation optimization.

Several models are developed on the basis of DANN. Bousmalis et al. (2016) assume that modeling domain-specific features helps extract domain-invariant features. They propose a domain separation network that decomposes feature representations into private and shared parts. Tzeng et al. (2017) unify existing domain adaptation models with adversarial learning in a framework. This unified framework considers various design choices and facilitates exploration of novel architectures.

Another model, known as joint adaptation networks, is proposed and it outperforms DANN on several image classification data sets (Long et al., 2017). This model considers how to match the joint distributions of the activations from both source and target domains in multiple layers by minimizing the joint maximum mean discrepancy (JMMD). The JMMD is parameterized by a multi-layer neural network and adversarial learning is applied to learn distinguishable features. In the work by Pei et al. (2018), a multi-adversarial domain adaptation approach is proposed to capture the multimodal structure of the data. For a K-category classification problem, K domain discriminators are introduced where each domain discriminator matches the source domain samples and target domain samples associated with the same category. A data sample is softly assigned to a category with the probability produced by the label predictor. When the label space of the target domain is a subspace of the source domain, which is referred to as partial domain adaptation, it is necessary to select a subset of source domain samples from a shared label space. Instance weighting is used in conjunction with adversarial feature learning in the works by Cao et al. (2017) and Zhang et al. (2018).

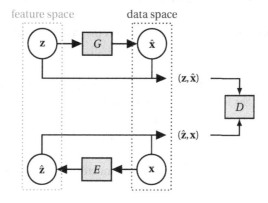

Figure 7.5 The network architecture of BiGAN, where a bi-directional mapping between the data space and the feature space is learned

Adversarial learning can learn common features in an unsupervised manner where both the source and target domains are unlabeled. Vanilla GANs learn to generate data from a hidden representation, but it has no feature learning ability. Two similar models (Donahue et al., 2016; Dumoulin et al., 2016) are developed independently to address the issue. Donahue et al. (2016) propose a bi-directional GAN (BiGAN), which learns the inverse mapping from data to latent feature space at the same time. The network architecture of BiGAN is shown in Figure 7.5. An encoder is introduced to learn the inverse mapping. The discriminator accepts $(\mathbf{x}, \mathbf{z})$ pairs as inputs, and a pair is labeled as 1 if $\mathbf{x}$ comes from the true data distribution and labeled as 0 otherwise. As a direct extension of the vanilla GAN, BiGAN defines an objective function as

$$\min_{G,E} \max_D V(D, E, G),$$

where

$$V(D, E, G) = \mathbb{E}_{\mathbf{x} \sim p_{data}} [\mathbb{E}_{\mathbf{z} \sim p_E(\cdot|\mathbf{x})} [\log D(\mathbf{x}, \mathbf{z})]] + \mathbb{E}_{\mathbf{z} \sim p_{\mathbf{z}}} [\mathbb{E}_{\mathbf{x} \sim p_G(\cdot|\mathbf{z})} [\log (1 - D(\mathbf{x}, \mathbf{z}))]].$$

The learned representations of the encoder are then applied to other supervised learning tasks and achieve competitive results with unsupervised and self-supervised feature learning models as shown by Donahue et al. (2016).

7.4 Discussion

Adversarial transfer learning models have great potential as they combine two prominent approaches for learning with limited data. It allows "translation" between two domains, which is helpful to artistic creation applications such as image/video editing. It also provides a learning-based data augmentation approach. For example, we can train a self-driving car with the images from computer games, which are refined by a GAN. In terms of discriminative feature learning, adversarial transfer learning measures the domain discrepancy with a parameterized network, which avoids hand-crafted statistical distances such as MMD and KL divergence.

Adversarial transfer learning is a fast-advancing approach and there are plentiful open challenges for future research, for example, how to incorporate target domain label information, and how to address heterogeneous transfer learning settings where either the feature spaces or the label spaces of the two domains are different. It is expected that the two lines of research works, generative adversarial learning and transfer learning, can be connected in a principled approach and novel ideas are exchanged between them.

8

Transfer Learning in Reinforcement Learning

8.1 Introduction

Reinforcement learning is a paradigm of machine learning when the learner interacts with an unknown environment. In reinforcement learning (Sutton and Barto, 1998), an agent can be modeled via a Markov decision process (MDP), where the agent sequentially takes actions and receives corresponding rewards. The rewards can be time delayed. Guided by this limited reward signal, reinforcement learning aims to acquire a policy that decides on how to take actions in different future situations. An optimal policy is defined to maximize the cumulative rewards.

We take the game playing in Figure 8.1 as an example, which is often adopted in reinforcement learning research works (Silver et al., 2016). In each step, an intelligent agent must decide on how to make a move, for example, fire or go left, according to the current state of the game. An intelligent agent should learn this policy from the delayed reward, that is, pass or fail at the end, to optimize the success rate.

Reinforcement learning significantly differs from supervised learning in several aspects. Supervised learning learns from labeled training samples provided by an oracle teacher and optimizes the generalization performance measured on unseen testing data. Unlike the limited reward signal in reinforcement learning settings, in supervised learning, the labels describe the correct action in various situations, for example, the correct move in each round of a game. Clearly, such high-quality and informative labeled samples are not available in many real world applications, which is the target application area of reinforcement learning.

A major challenge for reinforcement learning is the *exploitation-exploration trade-off*, which refers to the critical decision of agents when interacting with an environment. To maximize the cumulative rewards, an agent is suggested to exploit actions that are the best in the past observations. Since only the rewards corresponding to the selected actions are observed, the agent should also explore the unattempted actions as well. The short-term rewards may be sacrificed in pursuit of the long-term cumulative rewards. Theoretically, an optimal policy should never stop the exploration (Lai and Robbins, 1985). For example, to maximize the

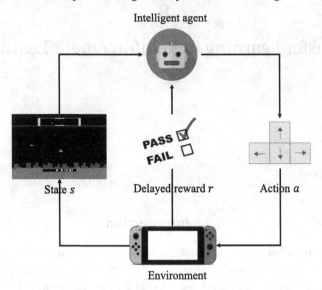

Figure 8.1 An example of game playing to illustrate reinforcement learning

happiness, one has to sequentially decide to go to the favorite restaurant (exploitation) or try a new restaurant (exploration). Different from reinforcement learning, most supervised learning algorithms ignore the exploration phase.

Reinforcement learning achieves great success in wide-range applications, including game playing (Mnih et al., 2013, 2015), the game Go (Silver et al., 2016), dialogue systems (Genevay and Laroche, 2016; Mo et al., 2018), natural language processing (Ranzato et al., 2015; Nguyen et al., 2017), recommender systems (Li et al., 2010; Zhao et al., 2018) and so on. Nevertheless, when a reinforcement learning agent faces a complex problem with large state and action spaces or it has to learn from scratch, the learning process requires a large amount of the interactions with the environment. Such interactions, unfortunately, are Resource-comsuming in most applications. For instance, each interaction with a user in a recommender system costs a certain amount of money.

A versatile, intelligent agent is supposed to solve a reinforcement learning problem more efficiently even when it faces a new domain where not much experience has been gained to train the agent from scratch. In this case, it is natural to apply transfer learning by leveraging the knowledge from related reinforcement learning domains. As discussed in previous chapters, transfer learning is broadly studied in the supervised learning and unsupervised learning settings. As attention on reinforcement learning gains speed, transfer learning for reinforcement learning also gains increasing interest from game playing to robotics. Knowledge transfer between reinforcement learning problems is proved to be effective both empirically and theoretically. In this chapter, we introduce several families of transfer learning algorithms tailored for reinforcement learning.

This chapter is organized as follows. First, we discuss the background knowledge of reinforcement learning, the key concepts of the transfer learning and the objective of transfer learning in reinforcement learning. Then, we categorize all related algorithms according to the problem setting and the type of the transferred knowledge.

8.2 Background

In this section, we introduce fundamental concepts of reinforcement learning. Then, we discuss essential components of transfer learning, including "what to transfer," "how to transfer" and "when to transfer" in the context of reinforcement learning. Finally, we introduce different objectives of transfer learning for reinforcement learning.

8.2.1 Reinforcement Learning

In this section, we formally define reinforcement learning problems.

First, an MDP M is defined as a tuple $< S_M, A_M, P_M, R_M, \gamma >$. S_M and A_M denote the state and action spaces, which could infinite. For continuous states, $S_M \in \mathbb{R}^d$ stands for the state variables. The state and action combined serve as the representation for an MDP. The transition function $P_M : S_M \times A_M \to S_M$ decides the next visited state given the current state and the action taken. The transition function P_M can be either deterministic or stochastic. Reinforcement learning algorithms that explicitly estimate the transition function P_M are called model-based learning. $R_M : S_M \to \mathbb{R}_M$ stands for the reward function that generates an instantaneous reward when arriving at a new state. γ denotes a discount factor. For the majority of reinforcement learning problems, the transition function P_M and the reward function R are unknown and require the exploration by interacting with the environment.

The solution to the MDP M is a policy $\pi_M : S_M \to A_M$, which adaptively and sequentially decides the actions in various states. In step n, the agent is aware of the current state $s_n \in S_M$ and selects an action $a_n = \pi_M(s_n) \in A_M$ according to the policy π_M. Then, the agent observes the corresponding reward r_n and transits to the next state $s_{n+1} \in S_M$. An optimal policy π_M^* aims to maximize the cumulative rewards, that is, $\sum_{n=0} r_n$, in an episodic MDP with discounted cumulative rewards, that is, $\sum_{n=0} \gamma^t r_n$, in a non-episodic MDP. Furthermore, searching for the optimal policy is equivalent to maximizing the value function, for example, the Q-function. As a result, we can get

$$Q^*(s_n, a_n) = Q^{\pi^*}(s_n, a_n) = \text{argmax}_\pi \, \mathbb{E}^\pi_{s_n, a_n} \left[\sum_{n' \geq 0} \gamma^{n'} r_{n'+n} \right]. \tag{8.1}$$

The optimal Q-function is also known to satisfy the Bellman equation, which is defined as

$$Q^*(s_n, a_n) = \mathbb{E} \left[R_M(s_{n+1}) + \gamma \max_{a_{n+1}} Q^*(s_{n+1}, a_{n+1}) \right]. \tag{8.2}$$

When the state or action space is very large or even continuous, we usually represent the value function with a functional approximation, where the feature functions are used as the representation of an MDP. Among traditional reinforcement learning methods, the linear function approximation plays a dominated role. In contrast, deep reinforcement learning methods exploit powerful deep neural networks, including multi-layer perceptrons, deep convolution neural networks (Mnih et al., 2013), deep recurrent networks (Hausknecht and Stone, 2015) and so on. Deep reinforcement learning learns useful representations for the value function by leveraging the representation learning ability of deep neural networks. Furthermore, deep reinforcement learning is capable of learning the value function and the policy in an end-to-end manner. As one of the representative deep reinforcement learning methods, deep Q-network (DQN) with experience replay improves the performance game playing significantly (Mnih et al., 2013) and it adopts the convolutional neural network to extract the representation directly from the raw frames of the game.

8.2.2   Transfer Learning for Reinforcement Learning Tasks

Transfer learning in reinforcement learning aims to improve the performance of a target-domain MDP M_t by leveraging the knowledge from one or multiple related but different source MDPs $\{M_s\}$. Without loss of generality, we mainly discuss the case with a single source domain in this section for clarity.

Here we take the mountain car learning task often used in illustrating reinforcement learning problems (Moore, 1991; Taylor et al., 2008a). We take this task as an example to illustrate different concepts in transfer learning for reinforcement learning. According to Figure 8.2, an agent drives an car toward the goal. In a two-dimensional mountain car version of the task, we treat the horizontal position and the velocity combined, that is, $(x, \dot{x})$, as the state. The agent should decide the action among {Left, Neutral, Right} in each time step. In a three-dimensional mountain car task version, the state concerns the two-dimensional space denoted by $(x, \dot{x}, y, \dot{y})$ and the action space contains five choices, that is, {Neutral, West, East, South, North}. To drive the car to the goal as fast as possible, the instantaneous reward for each time step is -1.

To introduce the transfer-learning setting, we first define concepts for "domain"

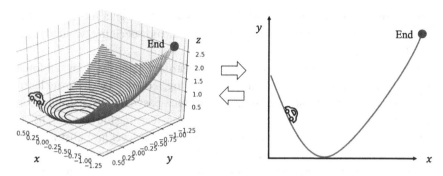

Figure 8.2 Illustration of the mountain car example. In both two-dimensional and three-dimensional example, the car agent must travel along the mountain toward the goal (adapted from Lazaric et al. [2008])

and "task" for an MDP M, respectively. The domain of an MDP M, that is, $\mathcal{D}_M$, includes the state space S and the action space A. In a continuous MDP, the domain mainly indicates the continuous state variables and action space. If two MDPs belong to different domains, either the state space or the action space is different. Transfer learning for MDPs with different domains depends on the handcrafted or learned inter-domain mapping between the source and target domains.

Given a domain M, the task describes the remaining components of an MDP, including the transition function P_M and the reward function R_M. The MDPs with different tasks have distinctive dynamics or reward functions. As we discussed earlier, P_M and R_M can be unknown to the agent and require the exploitation and exploration.

In the following, we illustrate different domains and different tasks based on the mountain car problem.

Different domains $S_{M_s} \neq S_{M_t}$**:** The source MDP solves the three-dimensional mountain car problem, while the target one is for the two-dimensional case.

Different domains $A_{M_s} \neq A_{M_t}$**:** The source and target MDPs are both in the two-dimensional space. In the target MDP, however, the "Neutral" action is forbidden.

Different tasks $P_{M_s} \neq P_{M_t}$**:** In the source MDP, the car owns a powerful engine, but the car of the target MDP has a under-powered engine. Therefore, the same action has different influences on the states in the source and target MDPs.

Different tasks $R_{M_s} \neq R_{M_t}$**:** In the source MDP, the car is only required to achieve the goal. However, in the target MDP, we require the car to arrive at the goal as soon as possible.

According to Pan and Yang (2010), essential issues to design a successful transfer learning algorithm for reinforcement learning include deciding "what to transfer," "how to transfer," and "when to transfer."

"What to transfer" categorizes the transfer learning algorithms for reinforcement learning into instance-based transfer learning, feature-based transfer learning and model-based transfer learning. The instance-based transfer learning identifies and reuses a subset of source experiences when learning the target MDP. The feature-based transfer learning algorithms extract high-level and abstract concepts from the source MDPs and accordingly change the state or action space of the target MDP that focuses more on promising regions in the state or action space or utilizes more powerful function approximator. The model-based transfer learning reuses the value function or the transition function learned from the source experiences in the target MDP.

"How to transfer" decides on which algorithm to discover and reuse the related knowledge. The method used by a knowledge-transfer algorithm heavily relies upon "what to transfer." In the context of instance-based transfer learning, how to transfer mainly indicates the criteria with which to identify related source experiences. In the context of feature-based transfer learning, "how to transfer" relates to how the representation of the source knowledge can be reused by the target domain. In the context of model-based transfer learning, how to transfer considers how to reuse the source experiences in the target domain.

"When to transfer" mainly indicates the timing of using transfer learning. Source MDPs are not guaranteed to be helpful in improving the performance of the target MDP. When facing dramatically different source and target MDPs, the brute-force knowledge transfer may jeopardize the target performance via the so-called negative transfer. When facing multiple source MDPs, when to transfer emphasizes the necessity of selective transfer by identifying the similarity between the source and target MDPs. When to transfer calls for a deeper and theoretical understanding of transfer learning including the similarity measurement of different MDPs, how to guarantee to avoid the negative transfer and so on.

8.2.3   The Objectives of Transfer Learning in Reinforcement Learning

In the supervised learning setting, the merits of transfer learning is verified by comparing the performance of transfer learning algorithms with that of algorithms without using knowledge transfer. Researchers anticipate the jump-start performance of transfer learning algorithms when the target training samples are insufficient, that is, the target domain suffers the so-called "cold-start" problem. The learning behavior as a function of the number of training samples is investigated to prove that transfer learning provides improved performance in cold-start situations.

Reinforcement learning aims to maximize the cumulative rewards within a time horizon by interacting with the environment. In the context of reinforcement learn-

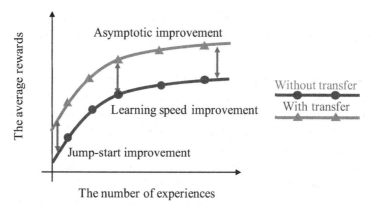

Figure 8.3 Three objectives of transfer learning algorithms in reinforcement learning

ing, transfer learning aims to improve the cumulative rewards in three circumstances including the jump-start improvement, asymptotic improvement and learning speed improvement (Lazaric, 2012). These three objectives can be used to measure the effectiveness of transfer learning algorithms. We separately discuss these objectives in the following. When a transfer learning algorithm returns a learned policy π_t for the target MDPs, to better understand the improvement, the gap between the action-value function of π_t and the optimal policy π^* can be decomposed as

$$\|Q^{\pi_t} - Q^*\| \leq \epsilon_{\text{approx}}\left(Q^{\pi_t}, Q^*\right) + \epsilon_{\text{est}}(N_t) + \epsilon_{\text{opt}}. \tag{8.3}$$

In (8.3), the approximation error, that is, $\epsilon_{\text{approx}}(Q^{\pi_t}, Q^*)$, denotes the asymptotic error caused by the bias of the function approximation. In an MDP with small state and action spaces, the agent can perfectly learn the optimal value function and suffer from no approximation error. The estimation error $\epsilon_{\text{est}}(N_t)$ is due to the estimation of the value function using finite experiences. As a result, the estimation error decreases and converges to stable values with the increasing target-domain experience. Finally, the optimization error, that is, ϵ_{opt}, is caused by the non-global optimum of optimizing the function approximation. The optimization error often occurs in deep reinforcement learning.

Jump-start improvement: The advantage of knowledge transfer Can be empirically measure by the performance improvement at the beginning of the learning process compared to algorithms without transfer learning. The intuitive idea to achieve knowledge transfer is To directly use the policies or value functions learned in the source MDPs to initialize the target one. If source and target MDPs are similar enough, the transferred policy or value function can achieve better performance compared to the random initialization, thereby leading to the jump-start improvement as shown in Figure 8.3. Jump-start improvement does not guarantee the asymptotic improvement and the learning speed improvement.

Asymptotic improvement: Asymptotic improvement measures the improvement of the final performance and discusses whether transfer learning can reduce the approximation error of the target MDP, that is, $\epsilon_{approx}(Q^{\pi_t}, Q^*)$ in (8.3). Clearly, for a target MDP with only small state and action spaces, the approximation error can be zero and hence it cannot be further reduced. When the function approximation is used, the approximation error depends on the hypothesis space of the function approximation. As a result, transferring the complementary state variables to the target function approximation can improve the final performance. In the mountain car learning problem, if the function approximation in the target MDP only considers the position, augmenting the hypothesis space by transferring the velocity could definitively reduce the approximation error.

Learning speed improvement: The critical motivation for applying transfer learning in reinforcement learning is to improve the efficiency of learning by reducing the required target-domain interactions with the environment. That is, transfer learning can learn more efficiently than the non-transfer cases. Thus, the learning speed improvement can be used to measure whether knowledge transfer can reduce the estimation error much faster as a function of the interactive experience, as shown in (8.3). Transfer learning achieves this improvement by guiding the exploitation and exploration more efficiently in the target MDP. Learning speed improvement can be achieved via any of the instance-based, model-based and feature-based transfer learning methods. In instance-based transfer learning, reusing the experiences in source MDPs is equivalent to interacting with related environments without cost. In the model-based transfer, the policy or the value function learned in the source MDP is used. In the feature-based transfer, the extracted high-level representation changes that of the target MDP. All the transferred source knowledge guides the agent to focus on the regions of the state and action that Are more likely to be optimal in source MDPs and speeds up the exploitation and exploration. The learning speed improvement can be measured empirically by *time to threshold* and *area ratio* and analyzed theoretically by *finite-sample analysis* (Taylor and Stone, 2009). Given a performance threshold, time to threshold compares the number of interactions with environment required by reinforcement learning algorithms with and without transfer learning in the target domain. Time to threshold, however, ignores the learning curve of the algorithms and selecting the performance threshold could be tricky as well. *Area ratio* quantifies the improvement of the area under the performance curve compared to algorithms without transfer learning. Besides the empirical measurement, theoretical analysis of the estimation error in (8.3) and "sample complexity" (Brunskill and Li, 2013) provide more solid verification.

Table 8.1 *The Taxonomy of transfer learning algorithms for reinforcement learning*

Problems/solutions		Inter-task transfer	Inter-domain transfer
Instance-based transfer		Lazaric et al. (2008); Genevay and Laroche (2016); Laroche and Barlier (2017)	Taylor et al. (2008a); Bou-Ammar et al. (2015); Liu et al. (2017);
Feature-based transfer	Action-based	Hengst (2002); da Silva et al. (2012); Azar et al. (2013)	Konidaris and Barto (2007); Topin et al. (2015)
	Feature function-based	Drummond (2002); Mahadevan and Maggioni (2007); Barreto et al. (2017);	Ferguson and Mahadevan (2006)
Model-based transfer		Wilson et al. (2007); Rusu et al. (2015); Yin and Pan (2017)	Taylor et al. (2005); Taylor and Stone (2007); Rusu et al. (2015)

8.2.4 Taxonomy of Transfer Reinforcement Learning

In this section, we discuss the taxonomy of transfer learning algorithms for reinforcement learning concerning three dimensions.

First, we categorize all methods according to the problem setting by emphasizing the difference between the source and target MDPs. The inter-task transfer learning requires the source and target MDPs to lie in the same state and action spaces. The transition and reward functions are allowed to be different. In comparison, inter-domain transfer learning is a more complicated problem than same-domain learning because the state or action spaces are different across domains.

Second, we consider what is transferred by different algorithms. The potential solutions to solve each problem include instance-based, feature-based and model-based transfer. As we discussed earlier, the representation for an MDP problem concerns the states, actions and the feature functions for the value function approximation. Accordingly, we discuss action-based transfer and feature function-based transfer separately.

Finally, transfer learning algorithms within a category differ in how to transfer. We summarize the taxonomy and the representative works in Table 8.1. The rest of this chapter is organized in the same manner as the taxonomy.

8.3 Inter-task Transfer Learning

In this section, we introduce transfer learning algorithms for MDPs within the same domain but different tasks. The source and target MDPs are denoted by $\{M_{s_i} | i = 1 \dots m\}$ and M_t, respectively. The source and target MDPs share the same state and action spaces, that is, $S_{s_i} = S_t = S$ and $A_{s_i} = A_t = A$. The transition function or reward function, however, is different in source and target MDPs, that is,

$P_{s_i} \neq P_t$ or $R_{s_i} \neq R_t$. For instance, a dialogue system (Genevay and Laroche, 2016) utilizes reinforcement learning to learn a policy to interact with users. To magnify the personalization, the dialogue system formulates the interaction with each user as an independent MDP. To reduce the number of interactions with users, Genevay and Laroche (2016) adapt the experiences of existing users to an incoming user. As all users are using the same language, the state space S and the action space A are invariant across users. Users, however, differ in habits and interests, leading to the personalized transition function P_t and reward function R_t.

According to "what to transfer," we discuss three families of solutions for inter-task transfer learning, including the instance-based transfer, feature-based transfer and model-based transfer. Then we discuss "when to transfer" for inter-task transfer learning.

8.3.1   Instance-Based Transfer

Transfer learning in reinforcement learning aims to reduce the necessity of the interactions with the environment. If an agent is capable of learning a reasonable policy from existing interactions of similar tasks, much fewer interactions with the target MDP are required. For instance, in a personalized dialogue system, an agent should contact an individual user many times to accumulate sufficient observations. If dialogues from other users are available, learning the general dialogue policy from existing observations of other users will accelerate the personalized policy learning.

The instance-based transfer is an intuitive idea to achieve knowledge transfer between MDPs within the same domain. The instance-based transfer directly or indirectly adopts accumulated experiences in source MDPs to improve the performance of a target MDP.

As far as we know, Lazaric et al. (2008) propose the first instance-based transfer method for reinforcement learning. In Lazaric et al. (2008), a source MDP is selected according to the probability of being compliant with the target MDP and then the experience is reused according to the distribution of being relevant to the target MDP. More specifically, the task compliance is defined as the probability that the target experiences are drawn from the specific source MDP. Suppose that $\hat{M}_{s_i}$ denotes the estimation of i-th source MDP according to finite interactions and that N_t interactions $< s_n, a_n, r_n, s'_n >$ are available in the target MDP. The task compliance is defined as

$$\Lambda_{s_i} = \frac{1}{N_t} \sum_{n=1}^{N_t} \mathbb{P}\left(\langle s_n, a_n, r_n, s'_n \rangle | \hat{M}_{s_i} \right). \tag{8.4}$$

Given the task compliance, all the source experiences are weighted and the weighted source experiences are used to help the learning of the target MDP.

Genevay and Laroche (2016) apply an instance-based transfer method to the spoken dialogue system. Different from Lazaric et al. (2008) where the compliance of a source MDP is manually defined, Genevay and Laroche (2016) formulate the source selection problem as a multi-armed stochastic bandit problem that treats each learned policy π_{s_i} from the i-th source MDP as an arm. Pulling the i-th arm is equivalent to applying π_{s_i} to the target user and observing the corresponding discounted reward in the dialogue system. The multi-armed bandit guarantees that the most useful source MDP can be identified with high probability. Furthermore, the usefulness of certain source experience is defined by whether it contains complementary information to the target MDP. As a result, Genevay and Laroche (2016) select source experiences that are far from the target training data via a density-based criterion. Finally, the proposed method learns from the transferred experiences by using any batch reinforcement learning algorithm as the initialization. Empirically, this method successfully achieves both the jumpstart improvement and asymptotic improvement.

Laroche and Barlier (2017) propose an instance-based transfer learning method named transfer reinforcement learning with shared dynamics (TRLSD) that aims at improving the learning speed when facing MDPs with the shared dynamics. TRLSD is inspired by robotics applications where an agent takes advantage of the shared transition function P to understand the complex environment. TRLSD learns the shared transition function by using experiences from all MDPs and estimates the task-specific reward function using the target experiences only. More concretely, TRLSD first translates the source experience $< s_m, a_m, r_m, s'_m >$ to the target MDP via the reward proxy $\hat{r}_m$ and then learns the target policy from all the translated source experiences added to target experiences using the fitted-Q iteration. In the process, it is found that the reward proxy learned from limited target experiences suffers from a high uncertainty. To explore the shared dynamics and reward function more efficiently, TRLSD adopts the *optimism in the face of uncertainty* heuristic and explicitly models the uncertainty of the reward function with the upper confidence reinforcement learning.

8.3.2   Feature-Based Transfer

The feature-based transfer-learning algorithms leverages the high-level knowledge from the source MDPs by adapting the feature representation of a target MDP. As we introduced earlier, the state spaces, the action spaces and the feature functions for the value function approximation are the representation of an MDP. The feature-based transfer learning methods can be classified into two categories, the action-based transfer and the feature function-based transfer. We discuss them separately in the following.

Action-Based Transfer

The action-based transfer learning methods assume that our aim is to adapt the target action space by leveraging high-level knowledge from the source MDPs.

Among all action-based transfer learning algorithms, the option-based transfer is a dominating method. The option-based transfer assumes that abstract actions named *options* (Sutton et al., 1999) can be generalized to the target MDP. An option $o \in O$ is defined by three components $\{s_o, \pi_o, \beta_o\}$, including the state where the option can be executed s_o, the option-specific policy π_o and the terminating condition β_o. When an agent arrives at s_o, it must decide whether to take the abstract action via π_o until the termination or not. Intuitively, the options summarize the internal structure of the source MDPs and are regarded as subgoals to achieve the final objective. The option-based transfer method discovers the options O_s in the source MDPs and augments the target action space with the options, that is, $A'_t = \{A_t, O_s\}$. In the "maze example" of Hengst (2002), as shown in Figure 8.4, a robot attempts to move from an initial position to a goal through three rooms, which are interconnected via doorways. Intuitively, the discovered options can be the subgoals such as to enter a nearby room via the doorway. When facing a target MDP that has a different goal position, entering a nearby room guided by the source options is still valuable.

The transferred options guide the agent to achieve the subgoals more efficiently, thereby improving the learning speed in the target MDP. The existing option-based transfer algorithms differ in how to discover options in the source MDPs. For MDPs with discrete state and action spaces, McGovern and Barto (2001) define the states that are frequently visited by the optimal source policy as the bottleneck. The bottleneck and the learned source policy combined are utilized to augment the target action space. For continuous MDPs, Kober et al. (2011) and da Silva et al. (2012) transfer the estimated parameterized options to similar MDPs. In particular, da Silva et al. (2012) discover low-dimensional manifolds where the invariant parameterized options lie.

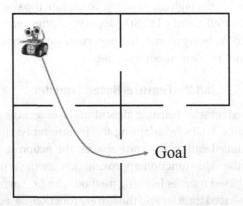

Figure 8.4 In this maze example (adapted from Hengst [2002]), the robot attempts to move from the initial position to the goal through three rooms

Unlike the option-based transfer, another line of the action-based transfer learning shrinks the action space and focuses more on potential optimal actions. Sherstov and Stone (2005) generate a set of synthetic MDPs by randomly perturbing a single source MDP. The actions that are not optimal in any generated MDPs are discarded. The agent solves the target MDP concerning only the remaining actions. Intuitively, by discarding non-optimal actions, the resulting smaller action space alleviates the need to explore all the actions, thereby improving the learning speed. Sherstov and Stone (2005) select actions by heuristics. Azar et al. (2013) propose a uncertain model upper confidence bound (umUCB) method that provides a theoretical mechanism to eliminate the actions. umUCB is tailored for the multi-armed bandit problem with multiple source tasks and guaranteed to avoid the negative transfer.

Feature Function Based Transfer

In reinforcement learning, searching for the optimal policy is equivalent to learning the optimal value function. Without loss of generality, we assume that the hypothesis space $\mathcal{H}$ of the value function can be represented approximately as the linear combination of d feature functions, that is,

$$\mathcal{H} = \left\{ h : h(s,a) = \sum_{j=1}^{d} \phi_j(s,a;\theta_\phi) w_j \right\}. \tag{8.5}$$

The feature function-based transfer extracts feature functions $\{\phi(s,a;\theta_\phi)\}_{i=1}^{d}$ in the source MDP and refines the target hypothesis space accordingly. For a discrete MDP, most reinforcement learning algorithms are guaranteed to converge to the optimal value function. Thus, the feature function-based transfer mainly provides informative feature functions to speed up the learning process. For a continuous MDP, the feature function-based transfer may enlarge the hypothesis space and achieve the asymptotic improvement. The feature function-based transfer algorithms differ in what and how feature functions are learned from the source MDP and encoded in the target MDP.

Proto-value functions (Ferguson and Mahadevan, 2006; Mahadevan and Maggioni, 2007) are a popular class of transferable feature functions. For an MDP M, the value function is usually smooth and it incorporates both information of the dynamics P_M and the reward function R_M. The key motivation of the proto-value functions method is twofold. First, proto-value functions serve as the feature function to parameterize the value function well. Second, the proto-value functions should summarize the dynamics of an MDP. To satisfy these two goals, Mahadevan and Maggioni (2007) first construct a graph or an adjacency matrix based on the state transition. More concretely, by using the n-th vertex to denote the state s_n, the vertexes s_n and $s_{n'}$ are connected via an edge if we can reach $s_{n'}$ from s_n in one step. An example is illustrated in Figure 8.5. Then, Mahadevan and Maggioni (2007) utilize the eigenvectors of the graph Laplacian as the proto-value functions. By assuming that the source and target MDPs share the same domain and dynamics, the adjacency matrix can also be invariant across domains. Thus, the proto-value functions can be directly used in the target MDP.

Successor feature functions (Barreto et al., 2017; Zhang et al., 2017a) are another successful high-level feature function tailored for the knowledge transfer. Assume

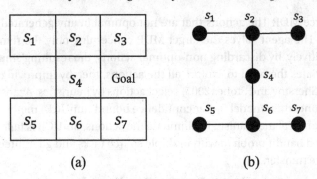

Figure 8.5 The dynamics of an MDP in (a) can be represented by the state transition graph in (b). The proto-value function method proposed in Mahadevan and Maggioni (2007) transfers the eigenvectors of the graph Laplacian

that the one-step expected reward is the linear combination of d feature functions $\phi_i(s, a; \theta_\phi)$, that is,

$$r(s, a) = \mathbb{E}_{s' \sim P}\left[r\left(s, a, s'\right)\right] = \sum_{i=1}^{d} \phi_i(s, a; \theta_\phi) w_i. \tag{8.6}$$

According to the Bellman equation, the action-value function under the policy π can be written as

$$Q^\pi(s, a) = \mathbb{E}^\pi\left[\sum_{t=\tau}^{\infty} \gamma^{t-\tau} \phi_{t+1} | s_t = s, a_t = a\right]^T \mathbf{w}, \tag{8.7}$$

where $\psi^\pi(s, a) \equiv \mathbb{E}^\pi\left[\sum_{t=\tau}^{\infty} \gamma^{t-\tau} \phi_{i+1} | s_t = s, a_t = a\right]$ is regarded as the successor feature functions. Clearly, when using the tabular representation of the state and action spaces, the successor feature functions represent the prediction on future occurrence of all other states under the policy π. For instance, in Figure 8.4, if the feature function $\phi(\cdot)$ represents the position of the robot, the successor feature functions can indicate the trajectory under the policy π. The successor feature functions can learn via the Bellman equation. Intuitively, in the MDP, the transition function is summarized by the successor feature functions and the reward function is modeled by $\mathbf{w}$. The successor feature functions decouple the dynamics and the reward function. When facing the source and target MDPs with the shared transition function but different reward functions, the agent could directly exploit the learned successor feature functions and estimate $\mathbf{w}$ in the target MDP.

Other definitions of the transferable feature functions also exist. For example, Drummond (2002) decomposes the state spaces of the source MDPs into subtasks and treats the independent value function of each subtask as the transferable feature functions. Snel and Whiteson (2014) adopt the feature functions selection to identify transferable feature functions. Walsh et al. (2006) and Lazaric (2008) share a similar idea to multi-task learning (Zhang and Yang, 2017b). When facing multiple source MDPs, Walsh et al. (2006) and Lazaric (2008) assume that the state aggregation or the subset of feature functions that perform well on all source MDPs is transferable. Bou-Ammar et al. (2014) solve a sequential transfer learning problem by assuming that feature functions for the source and target MDPs can be factorized into an invariant part and a task-specific part, and estimate both parts via sparse coding.

Deep reinforcement learning (Mnih et al., 2013), particularly the DQN algorithm, proposes the extraction of transferable feature functions in an end-to-end manner by taking advantage of powerful deep neural networks as the function approximator. For example, DQN successfully learns to play very complex Atari games based on the input images. To learn the complex deep neural networks, however, DQN calls for massive experience that emphasizes the necessity of the knowledge transfer. In the target MDP, DQN leverages the feature functions extracted by the deep neural network trained on the source MDPs. Therefore, the reasonable feature functions can speed up learning the policy in the target MDP.

8.3.3 Model-Based Transfer

The model-based transfer learning algorithms assume that the source and target MDPs share a part of the parameters that parameterize the MDPs. The model-based transfer mainly learns the shared parameters from the source MDPs. Then, it initializes the target MDP with the shared parameters. Model-based transfer can achieve both the jump start and learning speed improvements. According to different assumptions of shared parameters, various model-based transfer learning algorithms are proposed. In this section, we discuss two main categories of model-based transfer learning algorithms, including hierarchical Bayesian models and deep reinforcement learning.

Hierarchical Bayesian Models

Transfer learning algorithms based on hierarchical Bayesian models hypothesize that source and target MDPs are drawn from a global distribution that can be formulated as a hierarchical Bayesian model. More concretely, each MDP M is parameterized with the parameters θ_M, which is assumed to be independently and identically drawn from a fixed but unknown distribution Ω_ψ that is parameterized by ψ. The corresponding hierarchical Bayesian model is illustrated in Figure 8.6. Given N_{s_i} experiences for the i-th source MDP, that is, $K_{s_i} = \{< s_m, a_m, r_m, s'_m > \}_{m=1}^{N_{s_i}}$, the algorithm attempts to infer ψ according to

$$\mathbb{P}\left(\psi | \{K_{s_i}\}_{i=1}\right) \propto \prod_{i=1} \mathbb{P}\left(K_{S_i} | \psi\right) \mathbb{P}(\psi), \qquad (8.8)$$

and then initializes the target MDP accordingly. Intuitively, in the hierarchical Bayesian model, the global distribution Ω_ψ is estimated by using all the source MDPs and serves as an informative prior for the target MDP.

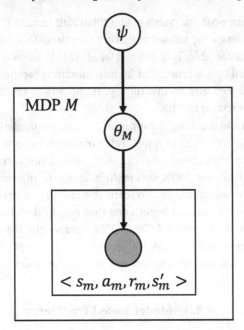

Figure 8.6 An illustration of a hierarchical Bayesian model (adapted from Lazaric [2012])

For instance, Wilson et al. (2007) parameterize the transition and reward functions and apply model-based Bayesian reinforcement learning to the target MDP. The model by Wilson et al. (2007) is not limited to the specific form of the prior of ψ. In comparison, Lazaric and Ghavamzadeh (2010) parameterize the value function based on a normal-inverse-Wishart hyper-prior.

Deep Reinforcement Learning

Deep reinforcement learning is regarded as a model-based transfer method. Policy distillation (Rusu et al., 2015) is proposed to train a single network for multiple MDPs. The policy distillation learns an independent teacher policy in each source MDP and accumulates that source experiences for the reply. The policy distillation method adopts the supervised loss function to train a student network that matches the action distribution predicted by the teacher policies. The framework of the policy distillation is illustrated in Figure 8.7. Moreover, DQN adopts convolutional neural networks that can automatically extract high-level feature functions from the pixels in the image data. Thus, for inter-task transfer learning problems, policy distillation shares both the convolutional filters and the fully connected layers. Yin and Pan (2017) argue that the task-specific convolutional feature functions are crucial for the performance. Thus, Yin and Pan (2017) only transfer the parameters of fully connected layers across MDPs.

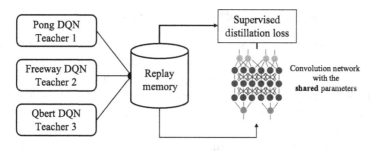

Figure 8.7 Illustration of the policy distillation framework

8.3.4   When to Transfer

Transferring irrelevant knowledge may jeopardize the performance of the target MDP. "When to transfer" mainly explores sound mechanisms of selective transfer to avoid negative transfer.

When transferring from a single source MDP, when to transfer mainly indicates whether to transfer or not. This decision heavily relies upon how to measure the similarity between the source and the target MDPs theoretically and empirically. We transfer knowledge when the source and target are close and pause knowledge transfer when the source and target are dramatically different. Ferns et al. (2004) first define the similarity between the states within one MDP. Given the similarity between all states, Phillips (2006) and Song et al. (2016) further extend (Ferns et al., 2004) to calculate the distance between two different MDPs via the Kantorovich and Hausdorff metrics.

When transferring from multiple source MDPs, when to transfer requires identifying relevant source MDPs. As discussed in Section 8.3.1, in the work by Lazaric et al. (2008), the source MDPs are selected according to the probability that they are compliant with the target MDP with the task compliance defined as the probability that the target experiences are drawn from the specific source MDP. Genevay and Laroche (2016) further formulate the source selection problem as a multi-armed stochastic bandit problem and guarantee that the relevant source MDPs are selected with a high probability.

In some studies, researchers theoretically analyze the performance improvement brought by the knowledge transfer and study the impact of when to transfer. Brunskill and Li (2013) propose a multi-task algorithm that theoretically reduces the per-task sample complexity of the exploration significantly. Brunskill and Li (2013) prove that the proposed algorithm can achieve a comparable per-task sample complexity in the worst case, which avoids negative transfer. Azar et al. (2013) focus on the knowledge transfer among the multi-armed bandit problems and provide theoretical regret analyses for the proposed umUCB method, and guarantee to avoid negative transfer.

8.4　Inter-domain Transfer Learning

Transferring across the MDPs within the same domain is limited in their range of applications. For instance, in the mountain car learning example in Figure 8.2, we anticipate the robot could learn to climb the two-dimensional mountain more efficiently if the three-dimensional mountain has already been conquered. The incompatible state and action spaces, however, pose challenges for knowledge transfer.

Inter-domain transfer learning is highly related to heterogeneous transfer learning, as introduced in Chapter 6, under the supervised learning setting. The key to solve this problem is how to align different spaces across domains. After the alignment, inter-domain transfer learning can be addressed by inter-task transfer learning algorithms introduced in the last section. The dominating ways to align the state or action space include the handcrafted mapping the learned mapping, and the invariant common representations. In this section, according to "what to transfer," we discuss the instance-based, feature-based and model-based transfer separately.

8.4.1　Instance-Based Transfer

The critical challenges for instance-based transfer methods include how to identify the similar experiences and how to reuse them efficiently. For the inter-task transfer learning problem, we focus on solving these two problems directly. In contrast, in this section, we survey the algorithms that address these two challenges within different state or action spaces.

Due to difference in state or action spaces, the experiences from the source MDPs cannot be directly incorporated into the learning process of the target MDP. Taylor et al. (2008a) propose a transferring instances for model-based reinforcement learning (TIMBREL) method that translates the source experiences into the target space. TIMBREL transforms source states into the target MDP via a given mapping $\chi_S : S_s \to S_t$. It also transforms source actions into the target MDP via a handcrafted mapping $\chi_A : A_s \to A_t$. In the mountain car example, the goal is to transfer from a three-dimensional problem to a two-dimensional case. The handcrafted mappings χ_S and χ_A are shown in Table 8.2. Given the mappings χ_S and χ_A, each source experience $< s_m, a_m, r_m, s'_m >$ is translated to $< \chi_S(s_m), \chi_A(a_m), r_m, \chi_S(s'_m) >$. Finally, TIMBREL adopts model-based reinforcement learning to learn from all the translated experiences and the target experiences. TIMBREL is tailored for a single source MDP and model-based reinforcement learning. Empirically, TIMBREL claims to improve both the learning speed and the asymptotic performance.

Liu et al. (2018) propose a new policy named transfer contextual bandit (TCB) to transfer the knowledge between contextual bandit domains with different contexts. To align different context spaces, TCB leverages the auxiliary information that indicates the similarity between m-th source experience and n-th target

Table 8.2 *The handcrafted inter-task mapping for the mountain car problem*
(Taylor et al., 2008a). The goal is to transfer from the three-dimensional problem to
the two-dimensional case

Inter-task mapping for the mountain car example	
Action mapping	χ_A(Neutral) =Neutral χ_A(North) =Right χ_A(East) =Right χ_A(South) =Left χ_A(South) =Left
State mapping	$\chi_S(x) = x$ $\chi_S(\dot{x}) = \dot{x}$ $\chi_S(y) = x$ $\chi_S(\dot{y}) = \dot{x}$

experience. TCB learns a mapping to preserve such geometry structure and, after learning the mapping, TCB adopts the translated source experiences to warm-start the target domain. To maximize the cumulative rewards, TCB not only explores the reward function, but also the learning process of the mappings. TCB achieves both the jump start and learning speed improvements in the application of recommender systems.

For other applications like the robotics, the auxiliary guidance may be unavailable. Bou-Ammar et al. (2012) present a tranfer fitted-Q-iteration (TrFQI) algorithm that automatically constructs the correspondence between source and target experiences and learns the inter-task mapping. More concretely, TrFQI and transfer least squares policy iteration (TrLSPI) calculate the similarity between each source and target experience pair via sparse coding. Based on the estimated correspondences, TrFQI and TrLSPI approximate the inter-task mapping with a Gaussian process.

When there is no auxiliary guidance, Bou-Ammar et al. (2015) propose the exploitation of the unsupervised loss to avoid this requirement. More concretely, all the source and target state variables are mapped to a common representation. The proposed method learns this mapping with an unsupervised loss by preserving the local manifold geometry. Then, similar to other instance-based transfer learning methods, Bou-Ammar et al. (2015) reuse the translated experiences as the initialization, which is far better than the random initialization.

8.4.2 Feature-Based Transfer

For the inter-domain transfer learning problems, the high-level feature representations, including state spaces, actions spaces and feature functions, may be heterogeneous in nature across MDPs. Such heterogeneity greatly undermines the use of existing feature-based transfer methods. In this section, we survey the action-based and feature function-based transfer methods that are generalized to the inter-domain problem.

Action-Based Transfer

In the option-based transfer, the agent discovers the options from the source MDPs and augments the target action space. The source options, however, are defined on the source state and action spaces. Therefore, the discovered options cannot be directly transferred to the target domain. Hence, the concept of options is generalized to abstract concepts to facilitate the reuse in the target domain.

Konidaris and Barto (2007) propose portable options that are transferable across MDPs with different state spaces but the same action space. Konidaris and Barto (2007) decompose the state space into the problem space and agent space. The problem space describes problem-specific properties and the agent space models the agent-specific characteristics that are invariant across learning problems. By taking the robot in Figure 8.4 as an example, the problem state records its location within the environment and the agent state includes the internal sensor and actuator of the robot. Clearly, when facing different environments, the agent state remains the same. Konidaris and Barto (2007) first discover the portable options within the fixed agent space and then augment the shared action space with the portable options.

Konidaris and Barto (2007), however, heavily rely on the manual decomposition of the state space. Topin et al. (2015) propose the portable option discovery (POD), which is tailored for the object-oriented MDP and automatically decides the mapping between source and target MDPs. First, POD creates an abstract domain with the abstract state space S'_s and decides the mapping $\chi_s : S_s \to S'$. The policy of an option can be mapped to the abstract states accordingly. Then, in the target MDP, POD searches for another mapping from the abstract domain to the target MDP, that is, $\chi_t : S' \to S_t$. In a word, POD translates the source options to the target MDP via an abstract domain. Furthermore, POD automatically decides the mappings χ_s and χ_t with the highest proportion of the state-action pairs that are preserved between the abstract policy and the source/target policy.

Feature Function-Based Transfer

The feature function-based transfer via the proto-value functions is discussed in the last section. The proto-value functions are generalized to the MDPs with different-sized state spaces. Intuitively, the constructed state graph expands while the patterns remain. Ferguson and Mahadevan (2006) discuss the usage of the Nyström method to reuse eigenvectors of the source graph Laplacian for the target MDP.

8.4.3   Model-Based Transfer

To reuse part of the parameters in the inter-domain transfer learning problem, the source and target parameter spaces are required to be aligned. Therefore, in this section, we discuss two kinds of algorithms according to whether the alignment mapping is given or learned.

Given a manually designed mapping, a general approach is to initialize the target MDP with the shared parameters and to continue fine-tuning the policy in the target MDP. Taylor and Stone (2005) and Taylor et al. (2005) prove the feasibility of the handcrafted mapping and the effectiveness of the value function transfer in different applications. Taylor et al. (2007) also transform and transfer the source policy to the target MDP via the given mapping.

Taylor and Stone (2007) propose the extraction of an abstract decision list that summarizes the source policy. The source decision list can guide the learning process in the target MDP. Based on the knowledge about qualitative characteristics of the source domain, Taylor and Stone (2007) also learn a translator for the decision list. Taylor et al. (2008b) propose the modeling approximate state transitions by exploiting regression (MASTER) algorithm, which is among the first such algorithms to automatically learn the inter-task mapping. MASTER relies on the estimation of the target-domain transition function from few experiences. For each possible mapping, MASTER transforms the source experiences accordingly and measures its compliance with the estimated target transition function and then it automatically decides the inter-task mapping with the highest compliance.

Deep reinforcement learning proves to be effective in solving the inter-domain transfer learning problems such as game playing (Devin et al., 2017). For instance, the policy distillation (Rusu et al., 2015) successfully plays ten Atari games with different action spaces. The policy distillation method relies on the shared convolutional filters to extract the abstract representation from raw images and the algorithm further learns domain-specific fully connected layers to adapt to different action spaces.

9
Multi-task Learning

9.1 Introduction

As discussed in Chapter 1, similar to transfer learning, multi-task learning (Caruana, 1997) also aims to generalize knowledge across different tasks. Different from transfer learning, which assumes some source domain(s) are available as inputs for solving a learning problem in a target domain, in multi-task learning, there are no source domains, but multiple target domains, each of which has insufficient labeled data to train a classifier independently. The goal of multi-task learning is to jointly learn the multiple target tasks by exploiting useful information from related learning tasks to help alleviate the data sparsity problem. In this sense, multi-task learning exhibits similar characteristics to transfer learning. However, multi-task learning is different from transfer learning in terms of the objective. That is, multi-task learning aims to improve the performance of all the tasks at hand, while transfer learning cares for the performance of the target task but not source tasks. Hence, the roles of different tasks in multi-task learning are equally important but, in transfer learning, the target task is more important than source tasks. From the perspective of the flow of knowledge transfer, in transfer learning there are flows targeting at the target task from source task(s) while multi-task learning has flows between any pair of tasks, which is illustrated in Figure 9.1. So multi-task learning and transfer learning are two different settings in terms of knowledge transfer. In terms of learning algorithms, many multi-task learning algorithms can be revised for transfer learning problems. Moreover, in the works by Xue et al. (2007) and Zhang and Yeung (2010a, 2014), a new multi-task learning setting called asymmetric multi-task learning is investigated and this setting considers a different scenario where a new task is arrived when multiple tasks have been learned jointly via some MTL method. This setting can be viewed as a hybrid of multi-task learning and transfer learning where multi-task learning happens for old tasks and transfer learning leverages knowledge from the old tasks to the new task.

Based on an assumption that all the tasks or some of them are related, learning multiple tasks together is empirically and theoretically found to have better performance than learning them individually. According to different natures of

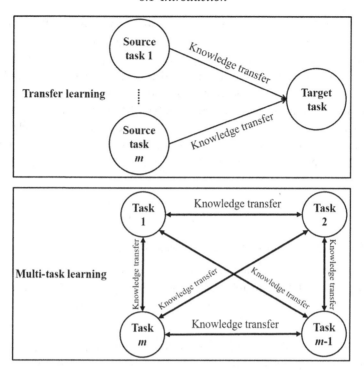

Figure 9.1 An illustration for the difference between transfer learning and multi-task learning from the perspective of the flow of knowledge transfer

learning tasks, multi-task learning can be categorized into multi-task supervised learning, multi-task unsupervised learning, multi-task semi-supervised learning, multi-task active learning, multi-task reinforcement learning, multi-task online learning and multi-task multi-view learning. Each task in the multi-task supervised learning setting is to make prediction on labels of unseen data based on a training data set that consists of training data instances as well as their labels. Each task in multi-task unsupervised learning is to discover useful patterns in a training data set that consists of data instances only. Similar to multi-task supervised learning, each task in multi-task semi-supervised learning is to make predictions on unseen data but based on a training set consisting of not only labeled data, but also unlabeled data. In multi-task active learning, each task exploits useful information in unlabeled data similar to multi-task semi-supervised learning but by choosing unlabeled data instances to query an oracle about their labels. Each task in multi-task reinforcement learning aims to maximize the cumulative reward by choosing actions. In multi-task online learning, each task is to process sequential data. Each task in multi-task, multi-view learning exploits multi-view data.

In this chapter, we overview different aspects of multi-task learning. First we present the definition of multi-task learning and then introduce different settings in multi-task learning, that is, multi-task supervised learning, multi-task unsupervised learning, multi-task semi-supervised learning, multi-task active learning, multi-task reinforcement learning, multi-task online learning and multi-task multi-view learning. For each setting, we introduce representative models. Moreover, we also present parallel and distributed multi-task models where there are a large number of tasks or data in different tasks located in different machines. For a more detailed survey on multi-task learning, please refer to the work by Zhang and Yang (2017b).

9.2   The Definition

At first, we give a definition for multi-task learning.

Definition 9.1   (multi-task learning) Given m learning tasks $\{\mathcal{T}_i\}_{i=1}^m$ where all the tasks or a subset of them are related but not identical, *multi-task learning* aims to help improve the learning of a model for $\mathcal{T}_i$ by using the knowledge contained in the m tasks.

According to the definition of multi-task learning, there are two basic elements. The first element is the task relatedness. The task relatedness is defined according to our understanding about how all the tasks are related and it can be used to design multi-task models. The second element is the nature of the learning task. In machine learning, learning tasks can have multiple choices, including supervised learning tasks such as classification and regression tasks, unsupervised learning tasks such as data clustering tasks, semi-supervised learning tasks, active learning tasks, reinforcement learning tasks, online learning tasks and multi-view learning tasks. Hence different learning tasks correspond to different settings in multi-task learning. In the following sections, we will introduce different settings in multi-task learning as well as representative models.

9.3   Multi-task Supervised Learning

In multi-task supervised learning, each task is a supervised learning task to learn the functional mapping from data instances to labels. Mathematically, given m supervised learning tasks $\{\mathcal{T}_i\}_{i=1}^m$, each task has a training data set $\mathcal{D}_i = \{(\mathbf{x}_j^i, y_j^i)\}_{j=1}^{n_i}$ consisting of n_i pairs of data instances and labels, where $\mathbf{x}_j^i \in \mathbb{R}^d$ and y_j^i is the label of $\mathbf{x}_j^i$. The goal of multi-task supervised learning is to learn m functions $\{f_i(\mathbf{x})\}_{i=1}^m$ based on the training data sets of the m tasks such that $f_i(\mathbf{x}_j^i)$ can approximate y_j^i well. After the learning process, $f_i(\cdot)$ will be used to make prediction on the labels of new data instances in the i-th task.

As discussed before, the design of multi-task supervised learning models depends on the understanding on task relatedness. Specifically, to reflect the task relatedness, there are three forms, that is, feature, model and instance, which correspond to three categories in multi-task supervised learning, that is, feature-based multi-task supervised learning, model-based multi-task supervised learning and instance-based multi-task supervised learning. The three classes exhibit different characteristics. For example, feature-based multi-task supervised learning aims to learn feature representations shared by all the tasks, while model-based multi-task supervised learning utilizes learning models in all the tasks as a bridge to learn the task relatedness. Different from them, instance-based multi-task supervised learning aggregates data instances in all the tasks to learn a model for each task via some ways such as instance weighting. In the following, representative models in the three categories are introduced.

9.3.1 Feature-Based Multi-task Supervised Learning

Feature-based multi-task supervised learning models assume that a feature representation, which is constructed based on the original feature representation, is shared by all the tasks. Based on different ways of the construction of the shared feature representation, feature-based multi-task supervised learning models can be categorized into three approaches, that is, feature transformation approach, feature selection approach and deep learning approach. Specifically, the feature transformation approach linearly or nonlinearly transforms the original feature representation to construct the shared feature representation, while the feature selection approach learns to select a subset of the original features to be the shared feature representation. As an extension of the feature transformation approach, the deep learning approach learns the shared feature representation via deep neural networks.

Feature Transformation Approach

In the feature transformation approach, the original feature representation is linearly or nonlinearly transformed to construct the shared feature representation. The multi-layer feedforward neural network (Caruana, 1997), with an example shown in Figure 9.2, is a representative model. In this example, the multi-layer feedforward neural network shown in Figure 9.2 has an input layer, a hidden layer and an output layer. By using the input layer to receive data instances from the m tasks, the multi-layer feedforward neural network treats the output of the hidden layer as the feature representation shared by all the tasks and the output of the output layer as the prediction on the corresponding data instance.

Formulated under the regularization framework, the multi-task feature learning (MTFL) method (Argyriou et al., 2006, 2008) and the multi-task sparse coding (MTSC) method (Maurer et al., 2013) linearly transform data instances as

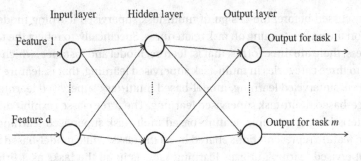

Figure 9.2 A multi-task feedforward neural network with one input layer, hidden layer and output layer

$\hat{\mathbf{x}}_j^i = \mathbf{U}^T\mathbf{x}_j^i$ to construct the share feature representation and then learn a linear function, which is defined as $f_i(\mathbf{x}_j^i) = (\mathbf{a}^i)^T\hat{\mathbf{x}}_j^i + b_i$, on the shared feature representation. The MTFL method formulates its objective function as

$$\min_{\mathbf{A},\mathbf{U},\mathbf{b}} \sum_{i=1}^m \frac{1}{n_i} \sum_{j=1}^{n_i} l(y_j^i, (\mathbf{a}^i)^T\mathbf{U}^T\mathbf{x}_j^i + b_i) + \lambda\|\mathbf{A}\|_{2,1}^2 \quad \text{s.t. } \mathbf{U}\mathbf{U}^T = \mathbf{I}, \qquad (9.1)$$

where $l(\cdot,\cdot)$ is a loss function, $\mathbf{b} = (b_1,\ldots,b_m)^T$ and $\mathbf{A} = (\mathbf{a}^1,\ldots,\mathbf{a}^m)$. It is easy to see that in (9.1) $\mathbf{U} \in \mathbb{R}^{d\times d}$ is orthogonal. Different from the MTFL method, the objective function of the MTSC method is formulated as

$$\min_{\mathbf{A},\mathbf{U},\mathbf{b}} \sum_{i=1}^m \frac{1}{n_i} \sum_{j=1}^{n_i} l(y_j^i, (\mathbf{a}^i)^T\mathbf{U}^T\mathbf{x}_j^i + b_i)$$

$$\text{s.t. } \|\mathbf{a}^i\|_1 \le \lambda \ \forall i \in [m], \ \|\mathbf{u}^j\|_2 \le 1 \ \forall j \in [D], \qquad (9.2)$$

where $\mathbf{U}$ has a larger number of columns than that of rows and $\mathbf{A}$ is assumed to be sparse based on the ℓ_1 constraint.

Feature Selection Approach

The feature selection approach learns to select a subset of original features as the shared feature representation for all the tasks. Overall, there are mainly two ways to perform the multi-task feature selection. The first way is to regularize the parameter matrix $\mathbf{W} = (\mathbf{w}^1,\ldots,\mathbf{w}^m)$ to make it row-sparse, while another one is to place probabilistic priors on $\mathbf{W}$ to make it row-sparse.

Among all the regularized techniques for multi-task feature selection, the most widely used technique is the $\ell_{p,q}$ regularization with the objective function formulated as

$$\min_{\mathbf{W},\mathbf{b}} \sum_{i=1}^m \frac{1}{n_i} \sum_{j=1}^{n_i} l(y_j^i, (\mathbf{w}^i)^T\mathbf{x}_j^i + b_i) + \lambda\|\mathbf{W}\|_{p,q}.$$

The $\ell_{p,q}$ regularization makes $\mathbf{W}$ row-sparse and hence only useful features for all the tasks will be preserved. The $\ell_{p,q}$ regularization has some instantiations, for example, the $\ell_{2,1}$ regularization (Obozinski et al., 2006, 2010) and the $\ell_{\infty,1}$ regularization (Liu et al., 2009b). To obtain a more compact subset of useful features for all the tasks, Gong et al. (2013) propose a capped-$\ell_{p,1}$ penalty, that is, $\sum_{i=1}^{d} \min(\|\mathbf{w}_i\|_p, \theta)$, which will reduce to the $\ell_{p,1}$ regularization when θ is large enough. Besides the $\ell_{p,q}$ regularization, Lozano and Swirszcz (2012) propose a multi-level Lasso to decompose w_{ji}, the (j,i)-th entry in $\mathbf{W}$, as $w_{ji} = \theta_j \hat{w}_{ji}$, where w_{ji} will be 0 when either θ_j or $\hat{w}_{ji}$ becomes 0. So, based on the ℓ_1 regularization on θ_j and $\hat{w}_{ji}$, the objective function of multi-level Lasso is formulated as

$$\min_{\theta, \hat{\mathbf{W}}, \mathbf{b}} \sum_{i=1}^{m} \frac{1}{n_i} \sum_{k=1}^{n_i} l(y_k^i, (\mathbf{w}^i)^T \mathbf{x}_k^i + b_i) + \lambda_1 \|\theta\|_1 + \lambda_2 \|\hat{\mathbf{W}}\|_1$$
$$\text{s.t.} \quad w_{ji} = \theta_j \hat{w}_{ji}, \theta_j \geq 0. \tag{9.3}$$

It is easy to see that a zero θ_j will filter out the j-th feature for all the tasks but a zero $\hat{w}_{ji}$ can do that for the i-th task only, making their impact different. Then the multi-level Lasso is extended in the works by Wang et al. (2014) and Han et al. (2014) to more general settings.

In the second way, Zhang et al. (2010c) give a probabilistic interpretation for $\ell_{p,1}$-regularized multi-task feature selection methods that the $\ell_{p,1}$ regularizer is corresponding to a generalized normal distribution prior:

$$w_{ji} \sim GN(0, \rho_j, p).$$

Then Zhang et al. (2010c) extend this prior to the matrix-variate generalized normal prior to learn pairwise relations among tasks. Different from that by Zhang et al. (2010c), the horseshoe prior is adopted by the works by Hernández-Lobato and Hernández-Lobato (2013) and Hernández-Lobato et al. (2015) to conduct multi-task feature selection. The difference between the works of Hernández-Lobato's (2013) and that of Hernández-Lobato et al. (2015) is that the former generalizes the horseshoe prior to learn feature covariance, while the latter directly uses the horseshoe prior.

Deep Learning Approach

Similar to the multi-layer feedforward neural network in the feature transformation approach, the deep learning approach relies on advanced neural networks such as convolutional neural networks and recurrent neural networks. However, neural networks used in the deep learning approach have a large number of hidden layers, which are different from those in the feature transformation approach with two or three layers. The output of one hidden layer in most deep learning models (Zhang et al., 2014; Li et al., 2015; Liu et al., 2015a; Mrkšic et al., 2015; Zhang et al., 2015a) is treated as the shared feature representation, which is similar to the multi-layer feedforward neural network in the feature transformation approach. One exception is the cross-stitch network (Misra et al., 2016). Specifically, by denoting by $x_{i,j}^A$ and $x_{i,j}^B$ hidden features in the j-th unit of the i-th hidden layer of two deep neural networks A and B for two tasks, the cross-stitch operation is defined as

$$\begin{pmatrix} \tilde{x}_{i,j}^A \\ \tilde{x}_{i,j}^B \end{pmatrix} = \begin{pmatrix} \alpha_{11} & \alpha_{12} \\ \alpha_{21} & \alpha_{22} \end{pmatrix} \begin{pmatrix} x_{i,j}^A \\ x_{i,j}^B \end{pmatrix},$$

where $\tilde{x}_{i,j}^A$ and $\tilde{x}_{i,j}^B$ denotes new hidden features by jointly learning the two tasks. Matrix $\boldsymbol{\alpha} = \begin{pmatrix} \alpha_{11} & \alpha_{12} \\ \alpha_{21} & \alpha_{22} \end{pmatrix}$ can be viewed as a quantitative measure for the task relatedness of the two tasks based on hidden features, making this method more flexible than only sharing hidden layers for multiple tasks.

9.3.2 Model-Based Multi-task Supervised Learning

Model-based multi-task supervised learning relates the learning of different tasks via model parameters. Based on different ways to relate model parameters of different tasks, model-based multi-task supervised learning models can be classified into four approaches, that is, low-rank approach, task clustering approach, task relation learning approach and multi-level approach. The low-rank approach assumes the parameter matrix $\mathbf{W}$ to be low rank since similar tasks have similar model parameters. The task clustering approach is to group tasks into several clusters each of which will have similar tasks with similar model parameters. The task relation learning approach aims to learn the pairwise task relations from data. The multi-level approach decomposes the parameter matrix into two or more component matrices to model complex relations among tasks. In the following sections, we will introduce each approach in details.

Low-Rank Approach

It is intuitive that similar tasks usually have similar model parameters and this intuition will lead to a low-rank $\mathbf{W}$. With an assumption that model parameters of the m tasks share a low-rank subspace, Ando and Zhang (2005) propose a parametrization of $\mathbf{w}^i$ as $\mathbf{w}^i = \mathbf{u}^i + \Theta^T \mathbf{v}^i$, where $\Theta \in \mathbb{R}^{h \times d}$ $(h < d)$ denotes the low-rank subspace shared by all the tasks and $\mathbf{u}^i$ is a task-specific parameter vector. Then, by placing an orthonormal constraint on Θ to remove the redundancy, the corresponding objective function is formulated as

$$\min_{\mathbf{U},\mathbf{V},\Theta,\mathbf{b}} \sum_{i=1}^{m} \frac{1}{n_i} \sum_{j=1}^{n_i} l\left(y_j^i, \left(\mathbf{u}^i + \Theta^T \mathbf{v}^i\right)^T \mathbf{x}_j^i + b_i\right) + \lambda \|\mathbf{U}\|_F^2$$

$$\text{s.t. } \Theta\Theta^T = \mathbf{I}. \tag{9.4}$$

Chen et al. (2009) generalize this model by adding a squared Frobenius regularization on $\mathbf{W}$, leading to an extended model with a convex objective function after some relaxation.

According to optimization theory, using the trace norm of a matrix, denoted by $\|\mathbf{W}\|_{S(1)}$, as a regularizer can lead to a low-rank matrix and hence the trace norm regularization (Pong et al., 2010) is widely used in multi-task learning, with the objective function typically formulated as

$$\min_{\mathbf{W},\mathbf{b}} \sum_{i=1}^{m} \frac{1}{n_i} \sum_{j=1}^{n_i} l\left(y_j^i, (\mathbf{w}^i)^T \mathbf{x}_j^i + b_i\right) + \lambda \|\mathbf{W}\|_{S(1)}. \tag{9.5}$$

Han and Zhang (2016) propose a capped trace regularizer, which is defined as $\sum_{i=1}^{\min(m,d)} \min(\mu_i(\mathbf{W}), \theta)$ with θ as a predefined hyperparameter. Minimizing the capped trace regularizer will only penalize small singular values of $\mathbf{W}$, leading to a matrix with a lower rank than the trace norm regularization.

Task Clustering Approach

Inspired by data clustering methods, the task clustering approach aims to group tasks into several clusters where all the tasks in a cluster are similar to each other in terms of model parameters.

Thrun and O'Sullivan (1996) propose the first task clustering algorithm, which has two stages. In the first stage, the proposed method clusters tasks in terms of model parameters learned separately under the single-task setting and after identifying the task clusters, the second stage is to aggregate the training data of all the tasks in a task cluster to learn a model for those tasks. Since this two-stage method to decouple the task clustering and the learning of model parameters may be suboptimal to the performance, follow-up works are willing to learn task clusters and model parameters simultaneously.

Bakker and Heskes (2003) propose a multi-task Bayesian neural network with a similar structure to the multi-layer neural network shown in Figure 9.2 to group tasks based on the Gaussian mixture model in terms of weights connecting the last hidden layer and the output layer. Xue et al. (2007) apply the Dirichlet process, a Bayesian model that is widely used in data clustering, to group tasks in terms of model parameters $\{\mathbf{w}^i\}_{i=1}^m$.

Different from the models (Bakker and Heskes, 2003) and (Xue et al., 2007), which rely on Bayesian models, several regularized methods (Jacob et al., 2008; Kang et al., 2011; Kumar and Daumé III, 2012; Barzilai and Crammer, 2015; Han and Zhang, 2015a) are proposed to group tasks. For example, built on the k-means clustering method, a regularizer is proposed by Jacob et al. (2008) to take between-cluster and within-cluster variances into consideration to help learn task clusters and the corresponding objective function is formulated as

$$\min_{\mathbf{W},\mathbf{b},\Sigma} \sum_{i=1}^{m} \frac{1}{n_i} \sum_{j=1}^{n_i} l(y_j^i, (\mathbf{w}^i)^T \mathbf{x}_j^i + b_i) + \lambda_1 \mathrm{tr}(\mathbf{W}\mathbf{U}\mathbf{W}^T) + \mathrm{tr}(\mathbf{W}\Pi\Sigma^{-1}\Pi\mathbf{W}^T)$$

$$\text{s.t. } \alpha\mathbf{I} \preceq \Sigma \preceq \beta\mathbf{I}, \ \mathrm{tr}(\Sigma) = \gamma, \tag{9.6}$$

where Π denotes an $m \times m$ centering matrix, $\mathbf{A} \preceq \mathbf{B}$ means that $\mathbf{B} - \mathbf{A}$ is positive semidefinite and α, β and γ are three hyperparameters. In (9.6), Σ encodes the information about task clusters and hence after solving (9.6), the task clusters can be identified based on the optimal Σ.

Kang et al. (2011) extend the MTFL method to the multiple-cluster case, in which the learning model of tasks in each cluster is the MTFL method, with the objective function formulated as

$$\min_{\mathbf{W},\mathbf{b},\{\mathbf{Q}_i\}} \sum_{i=1}^{m} \frac{1}{n_i} \sum_{j=1}^{n_i} l\left(y_j^i, (\mathbf{w}^i)^T \mathbf{x}_j^i + b_i\right) + \lambda \sum_{i=1}^{r} \|\mathbf{W}\mathbf{Q}_i\|_{S(1)}^2$$

$$\text{s.t. } \mathbf{Q}_i \in \{0,1\}^{m \times m} \ \forall i \in [r], \ \sum_{i=1}^{r} \mathbf{Q}_i = \mathbf{I},$$

where the 0/1 diagonal matrix $\mathbf{Q}_i$ is responsible of identifying the i-th cluster.

To automatically determine the number of clusters, Han and Zhang (2015a) propose a regularized objective function as

$$\min_{\mathbf{W},\mathbf{b}} \sum_{i=1}^{m} \frac{1}{n_i} \sum_{j=1}^{n_i} l\left(y_j^i, \left(\mathbf{w}^i\right)^T \mathbf{x}_j^i + b_i\right) + \lambda \sum_{j>i} \|\mathbf{w}^i - \mathbf{w}^j\|_2, \tag{9.7}$$

where the fused-Lasso-style regularizer in (9.7) enforces model parameters of each pair of tasks to be fused. After solving (9.7), columns in $\mathbf{W}$ are compared to identify the structure of task clusters and determine the number of task clusters.

Kumar and Daumé III (2012) and Barzilai and Crammer (2015) propose a decomposition of $\mathbf{W}$ as $\mathbf{W} = \mathbf{LS}$, where $\mathbf{L}$ contains basis parameter vectors of task clusters in its columns and $\mathbf{S}$ consists of combination coefficients. The objective functions in both methods can be unified as

$$\min_{\mathbf{L},\mathbf{S},\mathbf{b}} \sum_{i=1}^{m} \frac{1}{n_i} \sum_{j=1}^{n_i} l\left(y_j^i, (\mathbf{s}^i)^T \mathbf{L}^T \mathbf{x}_j^i + b_i\right) + \lambda_1 h(\mathbf{S}) + \lambda_2 \|\mathbf{L}\|_F^2, \tag{9.8}$$

where $\mathbf{L}$ is regularized by the squared Frobenius norm regularization but $\mathbf{S}$ is penalized by different $h(\cdot)$s in those two methods. Specifically, to identify overlapping task clusters where each task can belong to multiple clusters, Kumar and Daumé III (2012) define $h(\mathbf{S})$ as $h(\mathbf{S}) = \|\mathbf{S}\|_1$, while Barzilai and Crammer (2015) define $h(\mathbf{S})$ as $h(\mathbf{S}) = \begin{cases} 0 & \text{if } \mathbf{S} \in \{0,1\}^{r \times m}, \|\mathbf{s}^i\|_2 = 1 \\ +\infty & \text{otherwise} \end{cases}$ to assign one task to a task cluster, where r denotes the number of clusters and $\mathbf{s}^i$ denotes the i-th column in $\mathbf{S}$.

Task Relation Learning Approach

The task relation learning approach uses task relations to quantitatively measure the task relatedness with examples as task similarities and task covariances.

Earlier studies in this approach define task relations via model assumptions (Evgeniou and Pontil, 2004; Parameswaran and Weinberger, 2010) or assume that they are given by a priori information (Evgeniou et al., 2005; Kato et al., 2007, 2010a; Görnitz et al., 2011). However, model assumptions are not so easy to be verified for real world problems and the a priori information is unavailable for most problems, hence, those two ways are not so practical. The state-of-the-art way is to learn task relations from data and this is the focus of this section.

Bonilla et al. (2007) propose a multi-task Gaussian process to define a prior on $\mathbf{f} = (f_1^1, \ldots, f_{n_m}^m)^T$, where f_j^i denotes the functional value for $\mathbf{x}_j^i$, as

$$\mathbf{f} \sim N(\mathbf{0}, \Sigma).$$

The entry in Σ corresponding to the covariance between between f_j^i and f_q^p is defined as

$$\sigma(f_j^i, f_q^p) = \omega_{ip} k(\mathbf{x}_j^i, \mathbf{x}_q^p),$$

where $k(\cdot, \cdot)$ defines a kernel function and ω_{ip} denotes the covariance between tasks $\mathcal{T}_i$ and $\mathcal{T}_p$. So Ω, whose (i, p)-th entry is ω_{ip}, defines task relations in the form of task covariance. If the Gaussian likelihood is defined on labels based on $\mathbf{f}$, the marginal likelihood, which has a closed form, can be used to learn Ω. To improve the point estimation to reduce the risk of overfitting, Zhang and Yeung (2010b) propose a multi-task generalized t process by assigning an inverse-Wishart prior on Ω and adopting a generalized t likelihood.

Zhang and Yeung (2010a, 2014) propose a multi-task relationship learning (MTRL) model by assinging a matrix-variate normal distribution on $\mathbf{W}$ as

$$\mathbf{W} \sim MN(\mathbf{0}, \mathbf{I}, \Omega),$$

where $MN(\mathbf{M}, \mathbf{A}, \mathbf{B})$ denotes a matrix-variate normal distribution with $\mathbf{M}$, $\mathbf{A}$ and $\mathbf{B}$ as the mean, row covariance and column covariance. As a modified maximum a posterior solution, the objective function of the MTRL model is formulated as

$$\min_{\mathbf{W}, \mathbf{b}, \Omega} \sum_{i=1}^{m} \frac{1}{n_i} \sum_{j=1}^{n_i} l(y_j^i, (\mathbf{w}^i)^T \mathbf{x}_j^i + b_i) + \lambda_1 \|\mathbf{W}\|_F^2 + \lambda_2 \mathrm{tr}(\mathbf{W} \Omega^{-1} \mathbf{W}^T)$$

$$\text{s.t. } \Omega \succ \mathbf{0}, \ \mathrm{tr}(\Omega) \leq 1, \tag{9.9}$$

where Ω, the task covariance matrix, encodes the task relations among tasks. The MTRL method has been extended to multi-task boosting (Zhang and Yeung, 2012) and multi-label learning (Zhang and Yeung, 2013b), and generalized to learn sparse task relations in the work by Zhang and Yang (2017a). Zhang and Schneider (2010) propose a similar model to the MTRL method by placing a prior on $\mathbf{W}$ as $\mathbf{W} \sim MN(\mathbf{0}, \Omega_1, \Omega_2)$, and the proposed method assumes that the inverse matrices of Ω_1 and Ω_2 are sparse. As the prior used in the MTRL method implies that $\mathbf{W}^T \mathbf{W}$ follows a Wishart distribution $W(\mathbf{0}, \Omega)$, Zhang and Yeung (2013a) generalize the MTRL method to propose a new prior to learn high-order task relations as $(\mathbf{W}^T \mathbf{W})^t \sim W(\mathbf{0}, \Omega)$, where t is a positive integer. Lee et al. (2016) propose a regularizer similar to that of the MTRL method by defining a parametric form of Ω as $\Omega^{-1} = (\mathbf{I}_m - \mathbf{A})(\mathbf{I}_m - \mathbf{A})^T$, where $\mathbf{A}$ denotes asymmetric task relations proposed in (Lee et al., 2016).

Different from these methods that focus on global learning models, Zhang (2013) extends local learning methods such as the k-nearest-neighbor (kNN) classifier to the multi-task setting and formulates the objective function as

$$\min_{\Sigma} \sum_{i=1}^{m} \frac{1}{n_i} \sum_{j=1}^{n_i} l(y_j^i, f(\mathbf{x}_j^i)) + \frac{\lambda_1}{4} \|\Sigma - \Sigma^T\|_F^2 + \frac{\lambda_2}{2} \|\Sigma\|_F^2$$

$$\text{s.t. } \sigma_{ii} \geq 0 \; \forall i \in [m], -\sigma_{ii} \leq \sigma_{ij} \leq \sigma_{ii} \; \forall i \neq j, \tag{9.10}$$

where $\mathcal{N}_k(i, j)$ denotes the set of task and instance indices for kNNs of $\mathbf{x}_j^i$, $s(\cdot, \cdot)$ denotes the similarity between instances, σ_{ip} defines the similarity of task $\mathcal{T}_p$ to $\mathcal{T}_i$, and the learning function for the proposed multi-task kNN classifer is defined as

$$f(\mathbf{x}_j^i) = \sum_{(p,q) \in \mathcal{N}_k(i,j)} \sigma_{ip} s(\mathbf{x}_j^i, \mathbf{x}_q^p) y_q^p.$$

The regularizer in (9.10) is to enforce Σ, which is the task similarity matrix to encode task relations, to be a symmetric matrix.

Multi-level Approach

The multi-level approach assumes that the parameter matrix $\mathbf{W}$ can be decomposed as h component matrices $\{\mathbf{W}_i\}_{i=1}^{h}$, that is, $\mathbf{W} = \sum_{i=1}^{h} \mathbf{W}_i$, where h, the number of levels, is equal to or larger than 2. The objective functions of different models in this approach can be unified as

$$\min_{\mathbf{W} \in \mathscr{C}_W, \mathbf{b}} \sum_{i=1}^{m} \frac{1}{n_i} \sum_{j=1}^{n_i} l\left(y_j^i, (\mathbf{w}^i)^T \mathbf{x}_j^i + b_i\right) + \sum_{i=1}^{h} g_i(\mathbf{W}_i) \text{ s.t. } \mathbf{W} = \sum_{i=1}^{h} \mathbf{W}_i, \tag{9.11}$$

where $g_i(\mathbf{W}_i)$ defines the regularizer for the i-th component matrices, and $\mathscr{C}_W$ defines a set of constraints on $\{\mathbf{W}_i\}_{i=1}^{h}$. According to (9.11), the regularizers of different component matrices are decomposable and regularizers for different component matrices can be different.

Seven methods in this approach are introduced, that is, those by Jalali et al. (2010), Chen et al. (2010a, 2011), Gong et al. (2012b), Zweig and Weinshall (2013) and Han and Zhang (2015a, 2015b), and the corresponding choices of h, $\{g_i(\cdot)\}$ and $\mathscr{C}_W$ are shown in Table 9.1. According to Table 9.1, the first four methods have two component matrices while the last three ones can have two or more component matrices. The choice of $\{g_i(\cdot)\}$ varies among different methods. For example, based on the $\ell_{\infty,1}$ and $\ell_{2,1}$ norms, the $g_1(\cdot)$s in the works by Jalali et al. (2010) and Gong et al. (2012b) enforce $\mathbf{W}_1$ to be row-sparse. Different from them, the $g_1(\cdot)$'s proposed by Chen et al. (2010a, 2011) make $\mathbf{W}_1$ low rank by treating the trace norm as the the regularizer and constraint, respectively. For $\mathbf{W}_2$, the $g_2(\cdot)$'s proposed in the works by Jalali et al. (2010) and Chen et al. (2010a) enforce it to be sparse, while in Chen et al. (2011) and Gong et al. (2012b) they are enforced to be column-sparse to capture outlier tasks. Zweig and Weinshall (2013) assume that each component matrix is jointly sparse and row-sparse in different proportions related to the number of level. In the work by Han and Zhang (2015a), a multi-level task clustering method is to cluster all the tasks at each level via a fused-Lasso-style regularizer, which is operated on vectors instead of scalars, as in the fused

Lasso. By adopting the same regularizer as that in the works by Han and Zhang (2015a), Han and Zhang (2015b) aim to learn the hierarchical structure among tasks based on a sequential constraint $\mathscr{S}_W$ defined in Table 9.1.

Table 9.1 *Choices of $g_i(\cdot)$ for different methods in the multi-level approach, where $\{\lambda_1, \lambda_2, \lambda, \eta\}$ are regularization parameters, $\mathbf{w}_i^j$ denotes the j-th column in $\mathbf{W}_i$, $\emptyset$ denotes an empty set and $\mathscr{S}_W = \{\mathbf{W} \| \mathbf{w}_{i-1}^j - \mathbf{w}_{i-1}^k | \geq |\mathbf{w}_i^j - \mathbf{w}_i^k| \; \forall i \geq 2, \; \forall k > j\}$*

Reference	h	$\{g_i()\}$	$\mathscr{C}_W$
Jalali et al. (2010)	2	$g_1(\mathbf{W}_1) = \lambda_1 \|\mathbf{W}_1\|_{\infty,1}$ $g_2(\mathbf{W}_2) = \lambda_2 \|\mathbf{W}_2\|_1$	$\emptyset$
Chen et al. (2010a)	2	$g_1(\mathbf{W}_1) = \begin{cases} 0, & \text{if } \|\mathbf{W}_1\|_{S(1)} \leq \lambda_1 \\ +\infty, & \text{otherwise.} \end{cases}$ $g_2(\mathbf{W}_2) = \lambda_2 \|\mathbf{W}_2\|_1$	$\emptyset$
Chen et al. (2011)	2	$g_1(\mathbf{W}_1) = \lambda_1 \|\mathbf{W}_1\|_{S(1)}$ $g_2(\mathbf{W}_2) = \lambda_2 \|\mathbf{W}_2^T\|_{2,1}$	$\emptyset$
Gong et al. (2012b)	2	$g_1(\mathbf{W}_1) = \lambda_1 \|\mathbf{W}_1\|_{2,1}$ $g_2(\mathbf{W}_2) = \lambda_2 \|\mathbf{W}_2^T\|_{2,1}$	$\emptyset$
Zweig and Weinshall (2013)	≥ 2	$g_i(\mathbf{W}_i) = \frac{\lambda(h-i)}{h-1}\|\mathbf{W}_i\|_{2,1} + \frac{\lambda(i-1)}{h-1}\|\mathbf{W}_i\|_1$	$\emptyset$
Han and Zhang (2015a)	≥ 2	$g_i(\mathbf{W}_i) = \frac{\lambda}{\eta^{i-1}} \sum_{k>j} \|\mathbf{w}_i^j - \mathbf{w}_i^k\|_2$	$\emptyset$
Han and Zhang (2015b)	≥ 2	$g_i(\mathbf{W}_i) = \frac{\lambda}{\eta^{i-1}} \sum_{k>j} \|\mathbf{w}_i^j - \mathbf{w}_i^k\|_2$	$\mathscr{S}_W$

9.3.3 Instance-Based Multi-task Supervised Learning

To the best of our knowledge, there are few works in this category. A representative work is the multi-task distribution matching method proposed by Bickel et al. (2008). This work first estimates the ratio between the probability that each data instance comes from its own task and the probability that the same data instance is from a mixture of all the tasks. After learning such ratios, this work define instance weights based on these ratios and then learns a model for each task by aggregating weighted instances from all the tasks.

9.4 Multi-task Unsupervised Learning

The training set $\mathscr{D}_i$ of the i-th task in multi-task unsupervised learning, whose objective is to exploit the useful information contained in $\mathscr{D}_i$, consists of n_i data instances $\{\mathbf{x}_j^i\}$. This setting is different from multi-task supervised learning in which each data instance is assigned with a label. Tough unsupervised learning tasks contain diverse tasks, multi-task unsupervised learning mainly focuses on multi-task clustering, which is to do clustering on multiple data sets in all the tasks by leveraging useful information among them.

There are some models for multi-task unsupervised learning. For example, Zhang (2015a) proposes two multi-task clustering methods, which extend the MTFL model (Argyriou et al., 2006) and the MTRL method (Zhang and Yeung, 2010a) to clustering problems by treating labels as unknown cluster indicators to be learned from data.

9.5   Multi-task Semi-supervised Learning

Usually labeling data requires laborious efforts and, hence, in many applications, labeled data are very limited. However, in many situations, there are abundant unlabeled data. So semi-supervised learning aims to improve the generalization performance with the help of unlabeled data. The objective of multi-task semi-supervised learning is the same as semi-supervised learning by leveraging knowledge among multiple semi-supervised learning tasks.

Similar to the supervised learning setting where each task is for either classification or regression, multi-task semi-supervised learning has two settings, including multi-task semi-supervised classification and multi-task semi-supervised regression. There are some models for both settings. For example, Liu et al. (2007, 2009c) propose a multi-task semi-supervised classification model that uses the random walk method to make use of unlabeled data in each task and groups tasks into several clusters based on a relaxed Dirichlet process. For semi-supervised multi-task regression, Zhang and Yeung (2009) propose a method based on Gaussian processes to utilize unlabeled data to define the kernel function in the Gaussian process for each task, while different tasks share a prior on kernel parameters in different tasks.

9.6   Multi-task Active Learning

Similar to multi-task semi-supervised learning, each task in multi-task active learning has a training data set consisting of a small number of labeled data and a large number of unlabeled data. Different from multi-task semi-supervised learning, each task in multi-task active learning aims to choose informative unlabeled data to acquire their labels by querying an oracle. Therefore, in multi-task active learning, the research focus is to design the criterion to choose informative unlabeled data.

There are some models for multi-task active learning. For example, Reichart et al. (2008) propose two criteria to make selected unlabeled instances informative to all the tasks. Acharya et al. (2014) adopt the expected error reduction as the selection criterion. Fang and Tao (2015) design a selection strategy to make a trade-off between a confidence bound based on multi-armed bandits and the learning risk of a low-rank multi-task model based on the trace norm regularization.

9.7 Multi-task Reinforcement Learning

Reinforcement learning aims to learn how to take actions to maximize the cumulative reward in an environment. It has proved to be effective in many applications such as game playing and robotics. Given similar environments in different reinforcement learning tasks, it has been found that learning multiple reinforcement learning tasks together can have better performance than learning them individually, which leads to multi-task reinforcement learning.

There are some models for multi-task reinforcement learning. For example, Wilson et al. (2007) model each reinforcement learning task by a Markov decision process (MDP), while MDPs in all the tasks are clustered via a hierarchical Bayesian infinite mixture model. Li et al. (2009c) use a Dirichlet process to cluster tasks, each of which is learned via a regionalized policy. Lazaric and Ghavamzadeh (2010) use a Gaussian process temporal-difference value function model for each task and adopt a hierarchical Bayesian model to relate value functions in different tasks. By assuming that value functions in all the tasks share sparse parameters, Calandriello et al. (2014) learn all the value functions together by adapting the multi-task feature selection method with the $\ell_{2,1}$ regularization (Obozinski et al., 2006) and the MTFL method (Argyriou et al., 2006), respectively. Parisotto et al. (2016) propose an actor-mimic method to learn policy networks for multiple tasks by combining deep reinforcement learning and model compression techniques.

9.8 Multi-task Online Learning

When training data in multiple tasks arrive sequentially, multi-task online learning can handle them, while conventional multi-task models cannot.

There are some models for multi-task online learning. For example, by assuming that different tasks share a common goal, Dekel et al. (2006, 2007) propose the use of absolute norms as a global loss function, which combines the loss of each task together, to measure the relations among tasks. Lugosi et al. (2009) enforce constraints on actions for all the tasks to model task relations. Cavallanti et al. (2010) propose a perceptron-based multi-task online learning model by measuring task relations based on the geometric structure shared among tasks. Pillonetto et al. (2010) propose a multi-task Gaussian process with a Bayesian online algorithm to share kernel parameters among tasks. Saha et al. (2011) propose an online algorithm, which updates model parameters and task covariance together, for the MTRL method (Zhang and Yeung, 2010a).

9.9   Multi-task Multi-view Learning

In some applications, each data point can be represented by different feature representations, each of which is called view, and multi-view learning is able to handle such data with multiple views. As an extension of multi-view learning, multi-task, multi-view learning aims to leverage the knowledge among multiple multi-view learning tasks to improve the performance of each task.

There are some models for multi-task multi-view learning. For example, He and Lawrence (2011) first propose a multi-task multi-view classifier, which considers the consistency among views in each task and identifies the task relatedness based on common views shared by tasks. Zhang and Huan (2012) expect to achieve consensus on unlabeled data among views in each task , while the task relations can be either given as a priori information (Evgeniou et al., 2005) or learned as did in the MTRL method (Zhang and Yeung, 2010a).

9.10   Parallel and Distributed Multi-task Learning

When the number of tasks is large, the computational complexity of multi-task models may be high. With the use of powerful multi-CPU or multi-GPU facilities, it is possible and necessary to devise parallel multi-task algorithms to accelerate the learning process. For instance, Zhang (2015c) proposes the first parallel multi-task method to solve a widely used formulation, which is a subproblem of the MTRL model (Zhang and Yeung, 2010a) and many other models in the task relation learning approach in multi-task learning. The core idea of this parallel method is to utilize the fast iterative shrinkage thresholding algorithm to design a surrogate function, which is decomposable with respect to all the tasks and also parallelized. Zhang (2015c) studies the use of three loss functions, including the hinge, ϵ-insensitive and square losses, for both multi-task classification and regression models.

In some situation, training data of different tasks may locate in different machines, making the design of distributed multi-task algorithms necessary. Wang et al. (2016a) propose a distributed multi-task algorithm based on a debiased Lasso model to achieve efficient communications among machines, each of which possesses the training data of one task.

10

Transfer Learning Theory

10.1 Introduction

Besides investigating how to build models to transfer specific knowledge to solve target learning tasks, there have been theoretical studies on transfer learning. In transfer learning, we aim to improve the generalization performance, which measures the performance of a transfer learning model on unseen data generated from the underlying data distribution, of one or more tasks. However, since the underlying data distribution is unknown and hard to estimate accurately, the generalization performance is difficult to analyze and, in learning theory, generalization bounds are derived instead to upper-bound the generalization performance. The main focus of theoretical analyses in transfer learning is also to derive generalization bounds, which are upper-bounds of the generalization performance of transfer learning models on one or more tasks. Generalization bounds can bring much insight for transfer learning models, for example, sample complexity that can tell us how many samples are required to guarantee that the generalization performance is close to the training loss. So it is important to analyze the generalization bound in transfer learning.

In learning theory, there are mainly six mathematical tools to help derive generalization bounds, including Vapnik-Chervonenkis (VC) dimension (Vapnik, 1995), covering number (Zhang, 2002), algorithmic stability (Bousquet and Elisseeff, 2002), Rademacher/Gaussian complexity (Bartlett and Mendelson, 2002), probably approximately correct (PAC)-Bayesian theorem (McAllester, 1999) and Kolmogorov complexity. These tools are used to upper-bound the capacities of learning models. The VC dimension is defined as the cardinality of the largest set of points that a learning algorithm can shatter. The covering number is defined as the number of spherical balls with a given size that are needed to completely cover a given space. The algorithmic stability measures how a machine learning algorithm is perturbed by small changes to its training set. The Rademacher/Gaussian complexity measures the richness of a class of real-valued learning functions with respect to a probability distribution. The PAC-Bayesian theorem establishes inequalities to bound the Kullback–Leibler divergence between the prior and posterior distributions in Bayesian learning. The Kolmogorov complexity of a type of data such as texts is the shortest length of computer programs, which can produce the data as an output, in a predetermined programming language and it can be viewed as a measure of resources needed to specify the data. Among these tools, VC dimension is usually combined with a covering number to derive the generalization bound, while others can independently do the derivation.

Similarly, these tools are also used to analyze transfer learning models. In the following sections, we will show generalization bounds for three settings in transfer learning, including multi-task learning, supervised transfer learning, and unsupervised transfer learning.

10.2   Generalization Bounds for Multi-task Learning

The first formal generalization bound for multi-task learning is proposed in the work by Baxter (2000). In order to model the relations among different tasks, a concept called environment is presented. The environment can be viewed as a distribution to generate different tasks and, from the perspective of Bayesian learning, it acts as a hyperprior on tasks. With the assumption that such an environment exists for multiple tasks in multi-task learning, based on the tools including VC dimension and covering number, a generalization bound has been derived. Similar to the aforementioned analyses in transfer learning, the generalization bound consists of three terms. The first term is the empirical loss on the training data sets of multiple tasks, the second one is based on the capacity of the corresponding multi-task learner and the last term is the confidence term. Given such generalization bound, the sample complexity can be easily derived, that is, how many tasks and how many data points in a task can guarantee that the generalization performance is close to the training loss.

By following the work of Baxter (2000), the analysis in Ben-David et al.'s (2002) work considers jointly learning from multiple data sets/tasks, which is related to the data integration problem. Under this setting, different learners for all the tasks are assumed to be in an equivalence relation where any two learners can be transformed to each other via some function in a functional family. Built on such an assumption, the VC dimension of all the learners was studied and then a generalization bound was derived to help analyze the sample complexity. Then this work is extended in those by Ben-David and Schuller (2003) and Ben-David and Borbely (2008) by considering a similar setting where the distributions of two tasks are related via some function in a functional family. One benefit of this analysis is that it can give a bound the generalization performance of each task instead of the average generalization performance of all the tasks in previous studies.

In the work by Ando and Zhang (2005), the generalization bound of (9.4) is analyzed via the covering number. Maurer (2006a) analyzes the generalization bound of a linear multi-task learner that first learns a linear feature transformation for all the data points in all the tasks and then learns a linear classifier based on the transformed features. The learner considered here is similar to that in the work by Ando and Zhang (2005) but without the task-specific part $\mathbf{u}^i$ in (9.4). With the use of the Rademacher complexity, a generalization bound is derived as

$$\mathscr{E} \leq \hat{\mathscr{E}} + O\left(\frac{1}{\sqrt{mn_0}}\right), \tag{10.1}$$

where $\mathscr{E}$ denotes the average of the generalization errors of all the tasks, $\hat{\mathscr{E}}$ denotes the average of training errors of all the tasks, m denotes the number of tasks and n_0 denotes the average number of training samples in all the tasks. The second term on the right-hand side of bound (10.1) can show that the capacity of the linear multi-task learner is upper-bounded by the Frobenius norm of the task-averaged covariance matrix by assuming that the Frobenius norm of the feature transformation matrix is no smaller than 1. Different from previous bounds, the derived generalization bound here is data-dependent, implying that this bound can be estimated from training data due to the data-dependent nature of the Rademacher complexity.

In the work by Juba (2006), the Kolmogorov complexity in information theory is extended to multi-task learning to give uniform bounds to measure the difference between the empirical loss and generalization bound of different hypotheses provided by deterministic learning algorithms on independent samples drawn from a set of unknown computable distributions over tasks.

In the work by Maurer (2006b), two classes of multi-task algorithms are analyzed in terms of the generalization bound based on the Rademacher complexity. The first class to be analyzed include graph-regularized multi-task algorithms with those in the works by Evgeniou and Pontil (2004) and Evgeniou et al. (2005) as representative ones. In these algorithms, a graph $\mathbf{G}$ is used as a priori knowledge to describe similarities between any pair of tasks and, based on this graph, a regularizer is devised to encode such similarities to enforce similar tasks to have similar model parameters. Based on the generalization bound for this class of algorithms, their capacities are upper-bounded by $\sqrt{\text{tr}(\mathbf{G}^{-1})}$. The second class of multi-task algorithms to be analyzed include the Schatten norm regularization $\|\mathbf{W}\|_{S(p)}$ ($1 \leq p \leq \frac{4}{3}$) with the trace norm regularization (Pong et al., 2010) as a special case. According to the analysis by Maurer (2006b), the capacity of the corresponding multi-task learner is upper-bounded by the Schatten $\frac{q}{2}$ norm of the average data covariance over tasks, where q satisfies $\frac{1}{p} + \frac{1}{q} = 1$.

In the work by Kakade et al. (2012), some matrix regularizers, including the squared Schatten norm regularization and squared group sparse regularization, are proved to be strongly convex with respect to the trace norm and $\ell_{2,1}$ norm, respectively. Then, based on a widely used inequality in online learning (see Corollary 4 in the work by Kakade et al. (2012)) and such strongly convexity of matrix regularizers, a generalization bound is derived via the Rademacher complexity.

In the work by Crammer and Mansour (2012), a task clustering method is proposed to iteratively learn the model parameters for tasks in a task cluster and identify the cluster structure based on the training loss in a k-means style. Moreover, the lower- and upper-bound of its VC dimension is analyzed in order to derive the generalization bound and it shows that, when the logarithm of the number of clusters is lower than the number of samples per task and the number of clusters is much smaller than the total number of tasks, multi-task learning is significantly better than single-task learning in terms of the order of the complexity in the generalization bound.

In the work by Maurer et al. (2013), a generalization bound is presented for (9.3) where a dictionary is shared by all the tasks and coefficients in linear functions are task-specific. With the use of the Rademacher complexity, a generalization bound is derived to show that the capacity of multi-task sparse coding presented in (9.3) is upper-bounded with respect to the sum of both the average trace norm and spectral norm of data covariances over tasks. This model is extended to the transfer learning setting where the dictionary learned in source tasks will be used to the target task without learning it again and a similar generalization bound is also derived, showing again that both the average trace norm and spectral norm of data covariances in the target task affect the capacity of the target learner.

In the work by Pontil and Maurer (2013), the trace norm regularization in multi-task learning is analyzed. With recent advances on tail bounds for sums of random matrices and the Rademacher complexity, a dimension-independent bound is presented to analyze the generalization bound where the capacity is upper-bounded by the spectral norm of the average data covariance over tasks. Compared with Maurer (2006b) and Kakade et al.'s (2012) works, which can also analyze the trace norm regularization, the bound presented by Pontil and Maurer (2013) is tighter in terms of the orders on both the number of tasks and the number of data points per task.

In the work by Zhang (2015b), a multi-task extension of algorithmic stability is proposed and it is an extension of the conventional algorithmic stability in that the sensitivity of a multi-task learner is tested when a data point is removed from training data sets of all the tasks, respectively. In order to accommodate the newly defined multi-task algorithmic stability, a generalized McDiarmid's inequality is proved to allow more than one input argument of a function under investigation to be changed instead of only one in conventional McDiarmid's inequality. Then, with these new tools, a generalization bound is derived for general multi-task learning. Then, such general bound is applied to analyze the task relation learning approach (e.g., (9.9) with a fixed Ω), trace norm regularization and dirty approach (e.g., (Chen et al., 2010a) with a trace norm regularizer instead of a constraint).

In the work by Pentina and Ben-David (2015), the problem of learning the kernel function for support vector machines is studied under the multi-task and lifelong scenarios and some generalization bounds are presented to bound its generalization performance. The analyses show that, under mild conditions on the family of kernels used for learning, learning-related tasks simultaneously in multi-task learning are beneficial over single-task learning. Specifically, when the number of tasks increases, with an assumption that there exists a kernel function, which can achieve low approximation error on all the tasks, in the considered family of kernel functions, then the overhead for learning such a kernel vanishes and the corresponding complexity converges to that of the learner, which uses this good kernel function.

In the work by Maurer et al. (2016), multi-task representation learning, which learns a common representation for all the tasks, is analyzed and it accommodates the multi-task feature learning (i.e., (9.1)) and (deep) neural networks. With the use of the Gaussian complexity, which acts a similar role to the Rademacher complexity, a generalization bound is presented to reveal that the capacity of such learner depends on the complexity of the shared feature representation in terms of the ℓ_2 norm. Moreover, a similar bound is presented for the transfer learning setting. One benefit to use the Gaussian complexity is that it can analyze composite functions, which has the potential to analyze deep neural networks.

Besides analyzing generalization bounds, there are some other issues that have been analyzed. For example, in the works by Lounici et al. (2009), Obozinski et al. (2011) and Kolar et al. (2011), the oracle properties of the group sparsity in multi-task learning are studied to reveal under which conditions the group Lasso can identify features that can actually help the prediction of labels. In the works by Argyriou et al. (2009, 2010), sufficient and necessary conditions are investigated for the validness of the representer theorem in regularized multi-task methods. In the work by Solnon et al. (2012), the covariance matrix of the noise among multiple kernel ridge regressors adopted in multi-task learning is estimated based on the concept of minimal penalty and in a non-asymptotic setting, this estimator converges toward the true covariance matrix.

10.3 Generalization Bounds for Supervised Transfer Learning

In the work by Maurer (2005), a general transfer learning model is analyzed with a similar assumption to that by Baxter (2000) that both the source and target tasks are sampled from an environment. Under this setting, the source tasks can learn useful information about the environment and then provide it to the learning of the target task, hence, from this perspective transfer learning can be viewed as meta learning. For such meta algorithms, a general method is proposed for proving generalization bounds based on the algorithmic stability. This method can be applied to the bias learning model in the work by Baxter (2000) and to derive generalization bounds for meta algorithms that aim to learn uniformly stable algorithms. The proposed analysis method is also applied to analyze the regularized least squares regression.

In the work by Mahmud and Ray (2007), authors consider the definition of relatedness between tasks, which is an important problem, as understanding it can help design solutions about how much information to transfer and when and how to transfer it. This work uses the conditional Kolmogorov complexity between tasks to measure the amount of information one task contains about another. The analysis can neatly measure task relatedness and determine the transfer of the "right" amount of information in a Bayesian setting. In a very formal and precise sense, the analyses suggest that no other reasonable transfer method can do much better than the proposed Kolmogorov complexity theoretic transfer method. A practical approximation to the proposed method is devised to transfer information between tasks.

In Maurer (2009) work, by assuming that all the tasks are sampled from an environment as Baxter (2000) did, the Rademacher complexity is used to analyze transfer learning and the analysis shows that the spectral norm of the average data covariance upper-bounds the model capacity, which is similar to the conclusion made for multi-task learning by Maurer et al. (2013). Moreover, the analysis presented in this work explains the situations under which transfer learning is preferable to single-task learning. That is, the source tasks should be related to the target task, the input distribution needs to be high-dimensional and the number of source tasks should be larger than the data dimension and the number of data per task.

In the work by Yang et al. (2013), authors explore a transfer learning setting, in which tasks are sampled independently with an unknown distribution from a known family. The analysis studies how many labeled examples are required to achieve an arbitrary specified expected accuracy by focusing on the asymptotics in the number of tasks. The analysis can help understand the fundamental benefits of transfer learning by comparing single-task learning. The proposed analysis method is so general that it can be applied to other learning protocals, such as the combination of transfer learning and self-verifying active learning. Under this setting, authors find that the number of labeled examples required is significantly smaller than that required for single-task learning.

In the work by Kuzborskij and Orabona (2013), a hypothesis transfer learning scenario is studied, where the target learner can only access source learners but not source data directly. Specifically, a theoretical analysis based on the algorithmic stability is conducted to analyze a class of hypothesis transfer learning algorithms, that is, regularized least square regression with a biased regularization to the source learner. Based on the analysis, the relatedness of source and target tasks is found to accelerate the convergence of the leave-one-out error to the generalization error, which can inspire the use of the leave-one-out error to find the optimal target learner, even when the target domain is associated with a small training set. When the source domain is unrelated to the target domain, the analysis gives a theoretically principled way to prevent negative transfer such that the transfer learning method can reduce to the single-task model, an ideal solution in such a situation.

In the work by Pentina and Lampert (2014), built on the concept of the environment in the work by Baxter (2000), lifelong learning is analyzed from the PAC-Bayesian perspective by presenting a PAC-Bayesian generalization bound to offer a unified view on existing transfer learning paradigms such as the transfer of model parameters in a biased regularization or low-dimensional representations. Based on the generalization bound, two principled lifelong learning algorithms are derived. Then this work is generalized in the work by Pentina and Lampert (2015) to consider two scenarios in lifelong learning where observed tasks are not sampled independent and identically distributed (i.i.d.) from the task environment, while, in previous works, all the tasks are assumed to be i.i.d. The first scenario is that different tasks are sampled from the same environment but possibly with dependencies, and the second one allows the task environment to change over time in a consistent way. In the first case, a PAC-Bayesian bound is proved as a direct generalization of the analogous analysis for the i.i.d. case in the work by Pentina and Lampert (2014). For the second case, an inductive bias is learned in form of a transfer procedure.

In previous analyses for unsupervised transfer learning, the conditional probability of the label on the data is assumed to be identical in both source and target domains and it aims to match the marginal data distributions in both domains. To break this assumption, recent works propose a model shift setting, which allows conditional distributions to change across domains by providing a few target labels and assumes that the changes are smooth. In order to analyze such work under the model shift assumption, Wang and Schneider (2015) provide some analyses in their work based on the algorithmic stability. The analysis shows that, when the conditional distribution changes, a generalization error bound can be derived with respect to the number of labeled target samples and the smoothness of the change across domains. This analysis also derives conditions where transfer learning works better than no-transfer learning. Furthermore, transfer learning algorithms are proposed to handle both the single-source domain and multiple-source domain settings.

In the work by Perrot and Habrard (2015), the problem of transferring some a priori knowledge for metric learning is studied. Based on the notion of algorithmic stability, an on-average-replace-two-stability model is proposed for regularized metric learning where the metric in the target domain is enforced to approach the source metric. The newly proposed on-average-replace-two-stability proves generalization bounds with fast generalization rates for such biased regularized metric learning model. Furthermore, a consistency result is proposed to show the benefit of a biased weighted regularization formulation and a solution is proposed to learn the weights.

In the work by Balcan et al. (2015), the problem of learning from multiple tasks over time in the lifelong setting is studied and all the tasks are assumed to share certain commonalities in internal representations that are initially unknown. The goal is to learn such internal representation based on tasks at hand such that the learned representation can facilitate the efficient learning of subsequent tasks in such aspects, for example, reducing the need of labeled data. Efficient algorithms are developed to learn two different kinds of internal features shared by tasks, with the first type as low-dimensional subspaces and the second one as nonlinear Boolean combinations of features. For those two settings, the sample complexities are analyzed. Moreover, as a by-product, the proposed algorithm to learn nonlinear Boolean combinations of features has a dual interpretation, which can be used to construct near-optimal sparse Boolean autoencoders under an "anchor-set" assumption.

In deep learning, popular transfer learning approaches include the freeze method that directly uses the source network to make predictions for the target task and the fine-tune method that uses the parameters in a source network as initial values in the target network and then use labeled data in the target task to update the model parameters. These two simple approaches work well in many applications but they lacks a theoretical analysis to explain its success. In the work by McNamara and Balcan (2017), these two approaches are analyzed. For the freeze method, conditions are identified on how the tasks relate to obtain an upper bound on the generalization performance of the target task via the VC dimension. For the fine-tuned method, a PAC-Bayesian bound is presented to analyze the generalization performance of the target task under some suitable conditions. Moreover, the proposed bounds are used to analyze feedforward neural networks and a new approach is motivated by the analyses to transfer the source weights to the target task.

10.4   Generalization Bounds for Unsupervised Transfer Learning

In the works by Ben-David et al. (2006, 2010) and Blitzer et al. (2007a), two questions are studied for unsupervised transfer learning. First, under what conditions can a classifier trained for a source task be expected to have the good performance on the target task? Second, how should a small amount of labeled data in the target task be combined with the large amount of labeled data in the source task to achieve the lowest generalization error for the target task? To answer the first question, a generalization bound is presented to bound the target generalization error of a classifier by its source error and the divergence between the two domains. For the divergence, a classifier-induced divergence measure is introduced and it can be estimated from available unlabeled data from both domains. By assuming that there exists some hypothesis that has good performance on both domains, it has been proved that this divergence measure and the training error on the source task can be used together to characterize the generalization error of a source-trained classifier on the target task. For the second question, a learning model that aims to minimize a convex combination of the empirical losses for both source and target tasks is studied and its generalization bound is derived. Different from previous theoretical studies that aim to minimize just the error in the source task, just the error in the target task or equally weighting data from both domains, in this work the optimal combination coefficients of source and target errors can be learned as a function of the divergence measure, the sample sizes in both domains and the complexity of the hypothesis class. Hence, the resulting bound is a generalization of previous bounds and it is at least as tight as some previous bounds that minimize only the target error and consider the same weighting for source and target errors.

Different from most existing algorithms that first determine the data distributions in two domains and then make appropriate corrections based on the estimated distributions, in the work by Huang et al. (2006) a nonparametric method is proposed to estimate the ratio of two data distributions without distribution estimation. Built on kernel methods, the proposed method matches the two distributions in two domains via the mean value, which is referred to as the kernel mean matching method.

In the work by Mansour et al. (2008), a theoretical analysis is presented for the problem of unsupervised transfer learning with multiple sources tasks. For each source task, the distribution over the data as well as a hypothesis with error at most ϵ are given. In order to learn a good learner with small error for the target task, combining these hypotheses is a good strategy. First, standard convex combinations of the source learners have been proved to possibly perform very poorly. However, the analysis shows that there are theoretical guarantees for combinations weighted by the source distributions. The main result shows that, for any fixed target learner, there exists a distribution weighted combination that has an error of, at most, ϵ with respect to any mixture of source distributions. This setting is then generalized from a single target learner to multiple consistent target learners and the analysis shows that there exists a distribution weighted combination with an error of, at most, 3ϵ.

As a generalization of a previous work (Ben-David et al., 2006), in the work by Mansour et al. (2009), a novel distance between distributions, discrepancy distance, is introduced and it is suitable for unsupervised transfer learning problems with any loss function. Bounds based on the Rademacher complexity are proposed to estimate the discrepancy distance from finite data samples for different loss functions. Based on this distance, new generalization bounds for unsupervised transfer learning are derived for a wide family of loss functions. Based on these bounds and the empirical estimation of the discrepancy distance, a series of novel bounds are presented for large classes of regularized algorithms, including support vector machines and kernel ridge regression. These bounds motivate the proposal of several unsupervised transfer learning algorithms to minimize the empirical estimation of the discrepancy distance for various loss functions.

In the work by Cortes et al. (2010), an analysis of importance weighting is presented to learn from finite samples and a series of theoretical and algorithmic results are given. First, this work shows some simple cases in which importance weighting can perform badly and this suggests the importance to analyze this technique. Then both upper and lower bounds for the generalization performance for bounded importance weights are presented. More importantly, learning guarantees for the more common case where importance weights are unbounded but their second moment is bounded are given. The assumption that the second moment is bounded is related to the Rényi divergence between the data distributions in both domains. These bounds are then used to design an alternative reweighting algorithm. Moreover, the properties of a widely used normalized importance weighting are analyzed.

In Zhang et al.'s (2012) work, a new framework is proposed to study the generalization bound for unsupervised transfer learning. Two kinds of representative unsupervised transfer learning settings are considered: one is unsupervised transfer learning with multiple source tasks and the other is unsupervised transfer learning by combining source and target data. Specifically, the integral probability metric is used to measure the difference between two domains. Then, a specific Hoeffding-type deviation inequality and symmetrization inequality are developed for either setting to obtain the corresponding generalization bound based on the uniform entropy number. Based on the newly derived generalization bound, the asymptotic convergence and the rate of convergence are analyzed. Moreover, factors to affect the asymptotic behavior of the learning process in unsupervised transfer learning are discussed.

In the work by Germain et al. (2013), the first PAC-Bayesian analysis for unsupervised transfer learning is proposed. In order to derive the generalization bound, a novel distribution pseudodistance is defined based on a disagreement averaging. Using this measure, a PAC-Bayesian bound for stochastic Gibbs classifier is derived under the unsupervised transfer learning setting. This bound has the advantage, that is, it can be directly optimized for any hypothesis space. Hence, it is applied to linear classifiers, leading to the design of a learning algorithm for linear classifers.

In the work by Cortes et al. (2015), based on the discrepancy minimization algorithm that outperforms a number of popular unsupervised transfer learning algorithms, a new algorithm is proposed. Different from most previous approaches that rely on a fixed reweighting of the losses over training samples in different tasks, the newly proposed algorithm uses a reweighting method that depends on the hypothesis considered and it aims to minimize a new measure of generalized discrepancy. In the detailed description of the proposed algorithm, the analysis shows that it can be formulated as a convex optimization problem that brings benefits for the optimization. Moreover, a detailed theoretical analysis of its learning guarantees is presented and it can help select its parameters.

11

Transitive Transfer Learning

11.1 Introduction

In this chapter, we study a new type of transfer learning problem where there is a very large gap between the source and target domains, making most traditional transfer learning solutions invalid. For example, as shown in Figure 11.1, the source domain is to classify objects among images collected from the Web, but the target domain is to predict the poverty level of an area from its satellite images. This is a problem faced by researchers at Stanford University studying how to predict the poverty levels of African regions based on satellite images in order to provide assistance to UN aid (Jean et al., 2016). These tasks are conceptually distant and hence the knowledge learned in the source domain cannot directly be used in the target domain. This problem is difficult for transfer learning algorithms because there may not be direct linkage between source and target domains. However, we human beings are naturally capable of making indirect inference and learning via transitivity (Bryant and Trabasso, 1971). This ability helps humans connect many concepts and transfer the knowledge between two seemingly unrelated concepts. A typical methodology adopted by human learning is to introduce a few intermediate concepts as a bridge to connect these concepts. For example, a student who has solid mathematical knowledge may find it hard to understand theoretical computer science. However, if the student has taken some elementary computer science courses, then the elementary computer science concepts can act as a bridge between the mathematical knowledge and theoretical computer science courses. The elementary computer science concepts hereby serve as mappings between mathematical theories and deep computer science concepts, and can be considered as an intermediate domain.

The ability for humans to conduct transitive inference and learning inspires a novel learning paradigm known as transitive transfer learning (TTL). As illustrated in Figure 11.2, in TTL, the source and target domains have few common factors, but they can be connected by one or more intermediate domains through some shared factors. For example, in the poverty prediction problem described in Figure 11.1, the knowledge such as the high-level representations of images learned

Source domain: Object recognition   Target domain: Poverty-level estimation

Figure 11.1 An illustration of a TTL problem. The source and target domains have distant concepts, where the source domain is to do object recognition but the target domain is to predict the poverty level from satellite images, which are from Google Maps

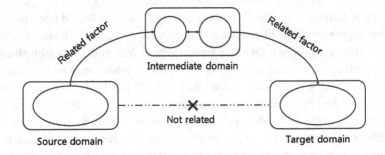

Figure 11.2 An illustration of the main idea of TTL

from the object recognition task cannot be transferred to the target task directly, as satellite images in the target domain are captured from an aerial view. Jean et al. (2016) introduce an intermediate domain that is the nighttime light intensity information of cities, and use this information as a bridge to connect the knowledge on object detection and poverty-level prediction. They transfer the knowledge from object recognition tasks to help learn a model that predicts nighttime light intensities from daytime images and then predict the poverty levels based on the light intensities. The knowledge of object recognition tasks can help identify hills, rivers, roads and buildings, which are highly relevant to the light intensities of a city. The light intensities are key factors in estimating the poverty level. In text sentiment classification problems, knowledge in a corpus of book reviews can hardly be transferred to music reviews because the words used in the two domains are quite different and they follow very different word distributions. Using TTL, Tan et al. (2015) introduce a set of movie reviews as a bridge. Reviews on movies share some words with book reviews, and, at same time, share some words with reviews on the background music of the movies. The movie reviews can be crawled from online movie websites. Thus, the movie reviews help build connections between the book and music domains. This forms a transitive knowledge-transfer structure to obtain a more versatile sentiment classification system.

In general, the TTL paradigm is important to extend the ability of transfer learning as it is able to transfer knowledge between domains with a huge distribution gap. This helps in reusing as much previous knowledge as possible. Overall, traditional machine learning uses knowledge learned with data from the same domain and transfer learning borrows knowledge from similar domains, while TTL pushes the transfer learning boundary even further to allow connection with distant domains.

There are two major research issues in designing the TTL paradigm. The first one is how to select appropriate intermediate domain data that serve as the connecting bridges between distant domains. The second issue is how to transfer knowledge effectively among transitively connected domains. In this chapter, we will introduce three different learning algorithms under the TTL paradigm. In particular, in Section 11.2, we manually select an intermediate domain and transfer the knowledge by using random walk with restarts. In Section 11.3, we select the intermediate domain data by distribution measurement, such as the Kulback–Leibler divergence and $\mathscr{A}$-distance in the work by Blitzer et al. (2007a), and transfer the knowledge via matrix factorization. In Section 11.4, we use deep learning to make intermediate domain data selection and knowledge transfer, by simultaneously conducting domain data selection and knowledge transfer via deep neural networks.

11.2 TTL over Mixed Graphs

We first consider a version of the TTL problem when the source and target domains have heterogeneous feature spaces such as text and images; for example, our source domain consists of texts describing springtime scenery and the target domain are images that describe the same scenery. To solve this problem, we can bridge the two domains by co-occurrence data stored in an intermediate domain. For example, on the Flickr website, there are a large number of images with text annotations or tags. These co-occurrence data can be used as the intermediate domain data for transferring knowledge from text data to image data. This setting is related to heterogeneous transfer learning introduced in Chapter 6.

However, the situation is more complicated than heterogeneous transfer learning. For example, in our experiments, the co-occurrence data are crawled from the Internet and contain much noise. For instance, lots of image annotations in Flickr are imprecise and meaningless or plainly wrong, and only around 50 percent of them are actually related to the image content (Liu et al., 2009a). This is

Source documents   Image with tags   Target images

Figure 11.3 An example of text-to-image TTL with annotated images as the inter-mediate domain data. Images are from Wikipedia and Flickr.

illustrated in Figure 11.3, where the words "eos," "400d" and "business" are irrel-evant to the images about architecture . These irrelevant data might degrade the accuracy of the cross-domain connection if we use them to build the knowledge transfer bridge directly. Besides irrelevant noises, thousands of tags are used when people annotate pictures from one peculiar category, and vocabularies in the tags are very different from those in formal documents. For example, articles from Wikipedia have different writing styles under different contexts. Hence, only a few image tags are useful for knowledge transfer, but they may be well hidden. To find a unbiased and clean channel for knowledge transfer, Tan et al. (2014) propose a mixed-transfer algorithm, which is able to transfer knowledge across domains ef-fectively even with noisy co-occurrence data. Their algorithm determines which source instances and which features are actually helping the knowledge transfer. The mixed-transfer algorithm models the relationship between the source and target domains as a joint transition probability graph of mixed instances and fea-tures, which is illustrated in Figure 11.4. In the graph, we have two types of node, the square nodes indicate the instances (e.g., documents and images) and the cir-cles represent the features (e.g., words in the documents and texture in the im-ages). The transition probabilities between two cross-domain features are con-structed from the co-occurrence data and measured by a cross-domain harmonic function, which is robust to irrelevant data.

In this graph-based algorithm, the label propagation process is simulated as a random walk with restarts. The advantage is that we can transfer knowledge with the help of all the instances and features globally and simultaneously. From the structure of the graph, we can see that the feature nodes play the role of hubs for information transmission within a domain and across domains. The label prop-agation process continues until it converges. During this process, some features have high probabilities of being visited. These are the features that carry the most label knowledge and can be automatically detected by the random-walk process. When the label propagation converges to a fixed point, the weights on instance nodes indicate the label preference and can be used to build a model for making predictions.

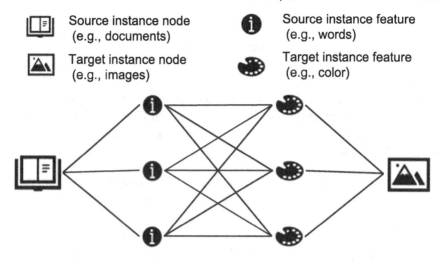

Figure 11.4 An illustration of the joint transition probability graph of mixed instances and features. In the graph, there are two types of nodes with the square nodes indicating the instances (e.g., documents and images) and the circles representing the features (e.g., words in the documents and texture in the images). The transition probabilities between two cross-domain features are constructed from the co-occurrence data

11.2.1   Problem Definition

Let $\mathscr{D}_s$ and $\mathscr{D}_t$ be the source and target domains respectively. $\mathscr{D}_S = \{\mathbf{X}_s, \mathbf{y}_s\}$ is composed of n_s labeled instances. $\mathscr{D}_t = \{\mathbf{X}_t, \mathbf{y}_t\} \cup \{\mathbf{X}_t^u\}$ contains n_t^l labeled instances and n_t^u unlabeled instance.

In order to build connections between the source and target domains, there are co-occurrence data. Let $\mathscr{O} = \{\tilde{\mathbf{x}}_k^s, \tilde{\mathbf{x}}_k^t\}_{k=1}^{n_o}$ denote the co-occurrence data, each instance of which contains two sub-instances $\tilde{\mathbf{x}}_k^s$ and $\tilde{\mathbf{x}}_k^t$. $\tilde{\mathbf{x}}_k^s$ is represented by a feature vector in the source domain feature space. $\tilde{\mathbf{x}}_k^t$ is represented by a feature vector in the target domain feature space.

The objective of the mixed-transfer learning algorithm is to learn a classifier $f(\cdot)$ that has the lowest possible prediction error on unlabeled instances $U = \mathbf{X}_t^u$ in the target domain by using all the data from the source, target and intermediate data. Formally, we have

$$\underset{f}{\arg\min} \mathbb{L}(f, \mathscr{X}, \mathbf{y}) + \mathbb{R}(f, U | \mathscr{O}), \qquad (11.1)$$

where $\mathscr{X}$ contains all the labeled data, and $\mathbf{y}$ are the labels, $\mathbb{L}(\cdot)$ is the loss function and $\mathbb{R}(\cdot)$ indicates the relationship between the classifier and the unlabeled data given the co-occurrence data $\mathscr{O}$.

11.2.2   The Mixed-Transfer Algorithm

Cross-Domain Feature Similarity

We first describe the strategy in measuring the cross-domain feature similarity. In this chapter, without loss of generality, we assume that the feature values of all the instances are non-negative. For some features that have negative values, we can normalize them to appear non-negative. Given a feature $\mathcal{X}_k^s$ in the source domain, the relevance value between this feature and the target domain feature space is defined as

$$\gamma_k^{(s,t)} = \frac{1}{|\tilde{\mathcal{X}}_k^t| \times (1 - |\tilde{\mathcal{X}}_k^t|)} \sum_{\tilde{\mathbf{x}}_i^t \in \tilde{\mathcal{X}}^t} \sum_{\tilde{\mathbf{x}}_j^t \in \tilde{\mathcal{X}}^t, \tilde{\mathbf{x}}_j^t \neq \tilde{\mathbf{x}}_i^t} \Phi(\tilde{\mathbf{x}}_i^t, \tilde{\mathbf{x}}_j^t), \tag{11.2}$$

where $\tilde{\mathcal{X}}_k^t$ denotes the set of target instances, each of which has a positive value for the k-th feature, $\Phi(\tilde{\mathbf{x}}_t^t, \tilde{\mathbf{x}}_{t'}^t) = \exp(-\frac{\|\tilde{\mathbf{x}}_t^t - \tilde{\mathbf{x}}_{t'}^t\|^2}{2\sigma^2})$, and $|\tilde{\mathcal{X}}_k^t|$ is the cardinality of $\tilde{\mathcal{X}}_k^t$. A larger $r_k^{(s,t)}$ indicates that the k-th feature has higher relevance to the target domain. For instance, a set of annotated images that share a tag should be similar to each other. Otherwise, the tag is irrelevant to these images.

On the set $\{\mathcal{X}_k^1, \mathcal{X}_k^2\}$, we calculate the similarity between the k-th feature in the source domain and the l-th feature in the target domain with correlation coefficient (Mitra et al., 2002):

$$s_{k,l}^{(s,t)} = 1 - \frac{|\text{cov}(f_k^s, f_l^t)|}{\sqrt{\text{var}(f_k^1) \times \text{var}(f_l^t)}} \tag{11.3}$$

where f_k^s and f_l^t are the feature vectors from $\tilde{\mathcal{X}}_k^s$ and $\tilde{\mathcal{X}}_k^t$ respectively, $\text{var}(\cdot)$ is the variance of a variable, $\text{cov}(\cdot, \cdot)$ is the covariance between two variables.

Combining these two criteria, we obtain the final similarity $a_{k,l}^{(s,t)}$:

$$a_{k,l}^{(s,t)} = \gamma_k^{(s,t)} \times s_{k,l}^{(s,t)} \tag{11.4}$$

Finally, we can construct the feature similarity matrix $A^{(s,t)}$ between two domains, where the (k, l)-th element of $A^{(s,t)}$ is equal to $a_{k,l}^{(s,t)}$, and then we have $a_{k,l}^{(s,t)} = a_{l,k}^{(t,s)}$, that is, $A^{(s,t)}$ is the transpose of $A^{(t,s)}$.

Graph Construction

For the i-th domain, where $i \in \{s, t\}$, we have an n_i-by-m_i matrix $\mathbf{A}^{(i,i)}$, with its (k, l)-th entry given by the value of the l-th feature of the k-th instance. It is clear that $\mathbf{A}^{(i,i)}$ is a matrix with all the entries being non-negative. We also have cross-domain feature similarity matrix $\mathbf{A}^{(s,t)}$.

In order to perform label propagation on this mixed graph, we have to construct a joint transition probability graph. In other words, we have to normalize the weights of the edges so that they are probability values.

By using $\mathbf{A}^{(i,i)}$, we can further construct an n_i-by-m_i Markov probability transition matrix $\mathbf{P}^{(i,i)}$ by normalizing the entries of $\mathbf{A}^{(i,i)}$ with respect to each column, that is, the sum of each column in $\mathbf{P}^{(i,i)}$ equals 1.

Similarly, we can make use of the transpose of $\mathbf{A}^{(i,i)}$ to construct an m_i-by-n_i Markov probability transition matrix $\mathbf{Q}^{(i,i)}$ by normalizing the entries of the transpose of $\mathbf{A}^{(i,i)}$ with respect to each column, that is, the sum of each column in $\mathbf{Q}^{(i,i)}$ is equal to one.

For such $\mathbf{P}^{(i,i)}$ and $\mathbf{Q}^{(i,i)}$, we can model the probabilities of visiting the instances from current features in a random walk process.

By using $\mathbf{A}^{(s,t)}$, we can construct an m_s-by-m_t matrix $\mathbf{F}^{(s,t)}$ by normalizing the entries of $\mathbf{A}^{(st,t)}$ with respect to each column, that is, the sum of each column in $\mathbf{F}^{(st,t)}$ is equal to 1. We note that there may be some columns of $\mathbf{F}^{(s,t)}$ to be zero as we may not find the co-occurrences for some features. In this case, all the entries of this column is set to be $\frac{1}{m_s}$, which indicates an equal chance of visiting an instance in a random walk. For such $\mathbf{F}^{(s,t)}$, the probabilities of visiting features in the source domain from current feature in the target domain can be modeled. Since $\mathbf{A}^{(s,t)}$ is a symmetric matrix, we have $\mathbf{F}^{(s,t)} = \mathbf{F}^{(t,s)}$.

Although the characteristics of the entries in $\mathbf{A}^{(i,i)}$ are different from those in $\mathbf{A}^{(s,t)}$, we make use of a coupled Markov chain model to combine their corresponding probability matrices $\mathbf{P}^{(i,i)}$, $\mathbf{Q}^{(i,i)}$, $\mathbf{F}^{(s,t)}$ and $\mathbf{F}^{(t,s)}$ together to build a joint transition probability graph of mixed instances and features for a random walk.

Mixed-Transfer Algorithm

In the mixed-transfer algorithm over the mixed graphs, we perform a random walk that starts from nodes corresponding to labeled instances. The 'walker' moves by traversing an edge to their neighboring nodes with the joint transition probability graph, or has a probability α to stay at the same node. The corresponding model is formulated as

$$\mathbf{R}^{(i)}(t+1) = (1-\alpha)\mathbf{P}^{(i,i)}\mathbf{V}^{(i)}(t) + \alpha\mathbf{D}^{(i)}, \quad i = s, t, \tag{11.5}$$

and

$$\mathbf{V}^{(i)}(t+1) = \lambda_{i,i}\mathbf{Q}^{(i,i)}\mathbf{R}^{(i)}(t+1) + \sum_{j=1, j\neq i}^{2} \lambda_{i,j}\mathbf{F}^{(i,j)}\mathbf{V}^{(j)}(t), \, i = 1, 2, \tag{11.6}$$

where $l_d^{(i)}$ is the number of labeled instances belonging to the d-th class and $\mathbf{D}^{(i)}$ is an n_i-by-c matrix with the (k, d)-th element $d_{k,d}^{(i)}$ equal to $1/l_d^{(i)}$ if and only if the k-th instance is labeled and belongs to the d-th class and is otherwise equal to 0.

Theorem 11.1 *Assume that α and $\lambda_{i,j}$ ($1 \le i, j \le 2$) are non-negative. Then there are unique non-negative matrices $\{\bar{\mathbf{R}}^{(i)}\}_{i=1}^{2}$, and $\{\bar{\mathbf{V}}^{(1)}\}_{i=1}^{2}$ satisfying* (11.5) *and* (11.6).

The steady probability distribution matrices on $\mathbf{R}^{(i)}(t)$ and $\mathbf{V}^{(i)}(t)$ ($1 \le i \le 2$) can be solved by the iterative method described in Algorithm 11.1. The convergence of the algorithm is proved in the work by Tan et al. (2014).

Algorithm 11.1 Mixed-transfer

1: **Input:** $P^{(i,i)}$, $Q^{(i,i)}$, $F^{(i,j)}$, $d^{(i)}$, threshold σ, α, $\lambda_{i,i}$, $\lambda_{i,j}$, $i, j = 1, 2$, $i \neq j$,
2: **Output:** $r^{(i)}(t)$
3: set $t = 1$, $r^{(i)}(0) = d^{(i)}$
4: compute $r^{(i)}(t)$ and $v^{(i)}(t)$ according to (11.5) and (11.6), respectively.
5: let $\text{Diff}_1 = \sum_{i=1}^{2} \| \mathbf{R}^{(i)}(t) - \mathbf{R}^{(i)}(t-1) \|_F^2$ and $\text{Diff}_2 = \sum_{i=1}^{2} \| \mathbf{V}^{(i)}(t) - \mathbf{V}^{(i)}(t-1) \|_F^2$
6: if $\text{Diff}_1 < \sigma$ and $\text{Diff}_2 < \sigma$, then stop; otherwise, set $t = t + 1$ and go to step 4

11.3 TTL with Hidden Feature Representations

In the previous section, we introduced a TTL solution by using one intermediate domain and transferring knowledge by cross-domain feature similarities. However, in many real world applications, there may be many intermediate domains and we are not sure which one is helpful for TTL. Moreover, the source, target and intermediate domains may be from different data providers, where each pair of domains has a distributional shift. In this section, we introduce a new learning algorithm for the TTL problem to address these issues. The algorithm is composed of two steps. The first step is to find an appropriate domain to bridge the given source and target domains. The second step is to do effective knowledge transfer among all domains. In the first step, a probability model is introduced to select appropriate domains that are able to draw the source and target domains closer. The selection is based on domain characteristics such as domain difficulty and pairwise closeness. In the second step, we consider both domain relationship and distributional shift, and learn a common feature subspace among these domains to propagate the label information through them.

11.3.1 Problem Definition

In this problem setting, we have labeled source domain data $\mathbb{S} = \{(\mathbf{x}_i^s, y_i)\}_{i=1}^{n_s}$, unlabeled target domain data $\mathbb{T} = \{\mathbf{x}_i^t\}_{i=1}^{n_t}$ and k unlabeled intermediate domains $\mathbb{D}_j = \{\mathbf{x}_i^{d_j}\}_{i=1}^{n_j}$, $j = 1, \ldots, k$, where $\mathbf{x}^* \in R^{m^*}$ is represented as a m^*-dimensional feature vector. The data from different domains can have different dimensions. $\mathbb{S}$ and $\mathbb{T}$ have a large distribution gap, thus directly transferring knowledge between them may cause a substantial performance loss in the target domain. The algorithm introduced aims at finding intermediate domains to bridge $\mathbb{S}$ and $\mathbb{T}$ and minimize the training loss in $\mathbb{T}$.

Formally, given a measure $g(\cdot, \cdot)$ for the domain distribution gap, the first step is to find an intermediate domain that satisfies $g(\mathbb{S}, \mathbb{T}|\mathbb{D}_i) < g(\mathbb{S}, \mathbb{T})$. The second step performs transfer learning from the source domain $\mathbb{S}$ to the target domain $\mathbb{T}$ via the intermediate domain $\mathbb{D}_i$. This is implemented via learning two feature clustering functions $p_{sd}(\mathbb{S}, \mathbb{D}_i)$ and $p_{dt}(\mathbb{D}_i, \mathbb{T})$, the outputs of which are the largest common subspaces between $\mathbb{S}$ and $\mathbb{D}_i$ and between $\mathbb{D}_i$ and $\mathbb{T}$, respectively. The label information in the source domain is propagated to the intermediate and target data on the selected common subspaces.

11.3.2 Coupled Matrix Tri-factorization Algorithm

Intermediate Domain Selection

The selection of intermediate domains is task-specific and hence different problems may require different strategies. In this section, we introduce a specific intermediate domain selection algorithm for the problem of sentiment classification. As studied in previous research, the task difficulty (Ponomareva and Thelwall, 2012) and domain distance (Ben-David et al., 2006) are two major issues that affect transfer learning performance for any given pairs of domains. Intuitively, if a task in a source domain is not difficult to solve than tasks in the intermediate and target domains, the model learned from the source data may perform well and can be very helpful in achieving good performance in the intermediate and target domains as well. If the intermediate domain is able to draw the source and target domains closer than directly transferring between them, then the knowledge transfer process between the source and target domains will have lower information loss, and result in good performance in the target domain. Hence, we introduce the domain difficulty and domain distance, respectively as follows.

- Domain difficulty: The domain difficulty measure is problem-specific as different problems may have different types of features. In this problem, the domain complexity (Ponomareva and Thelwall, 2012) is used to measure the difficulty. The domain complexity is calculated as the percentage of long tail features that have low frequencies and defined as

$$\text{cplx}(\boldsymbol{D}) = \frac{|\{x|c(x) < t \times n\}|}{m}, \tag{11.7}$$

where for non-negative features, $c(x)$ is the number of instances whose feature x is larger than zero, and $|\{x|c(x) < t \times n\}|$ denotes the number of features that appear in less than $t \times n$ instances.

- $\mathscr{A}$ distance: The $\mathscr{A}$ distance estimates the distribution difference of two sets of data samples that are drawn from two probability distributions. In Ben-David et al. (2006), it is proved that the prediction error of the target domain is bounded by the error of the source domain and the $\mathscr{A}$ distance as well as constant factors. Practically, given data $\boldsymbol{D}_i$ and $\boldsymbol{D}_j$ from two domains, the $\mathscr{A}$-distance can be computed as

$$dis_{\mathscr{A}}(\boldsymbol{D}_i, \boldsymbol{D}_j) = 2(1 - 2\min_{h \in \mathscr{H}} \text{error}(h|\boldsymbol{D}_i, \boldsymbol{D}_j)), \tag{11.8}$$

where $\mathscr{H}$ is a hypothesis space, h is a proxy classifier that discriminates data points from two domains and error($\cdot$) denotes the classification error. To learn h, which uses the logistic regression as the proxy classifier, the source data is

Table 11.1 *Domain characteristic features*

feature	description
cplx_src (c_1)	source domain complexity
cplx_inter (c_2)	intermediate domain complexity
cplx_tar (c_3)	target domain complexity
$dis_{\mathscr{A}}^{si}$ (c_4)	a_distance between source and intermediate
$dis_{\mathscr{A}}^{st}$ (c_5)	a_distance between source and target
$dis_{\mathscr{A}}^{it}$ (c_6)	a_distance between intermediate and target

treated as positive and the target data is assigned to be negative. After learning h, we can estimate the error$(h|\boldsymbol{D}_i, \boldsymbol{D}_j))$ in the $\mathscr{A}$ distance.

Given a triple $\boldsymbol{t} = \{\mathbb{S}, \mathbb{D}, \mathbb{T}\}$, we can extract six features, as described in Table 11.1. The first three features summarize individual in-domain characteristics and the other three features capture the pairwise cross-domain distances. These features together affect the success probability of a transfer learning algorithm. However, it is impossible to design a universal domain selection criteria, as different problems may have different preferences (weights) on these features. To model the success probability of the introduced intermediate domain, the following logistic function is used:

$$f(\boldsymbol{t}) = \delta(\beta_0 + \sum_{i=1}^{6} \beta_i c_i), \tag{11.9}$$

where $\delta(x) = \frac{1}{1+\exp\{-x\}}$. We estimate the parameters $\boldsymbol{\beta} = \{\beta_0, \cdots, \beta_6\}$ to maximize the log likelihood defined as:

$$\mathscr{L}(\boldsymbol{\beta}) = \sum_{i=1}^{t} l^{(i)} \log f(\boldsymbol{t}_i) + (1 - l^{(i)}) \log(1 - f(\boldsymbol{t}_i)), \tag{11.10}$$

where $l^{(i)}$ is a binary label, indicating whether the intermediate domain in the i-th triple is able to bridge the source and target domains. Such labels are obtained via the following strategy. A semi-supervised label propagation algorithm is performed on $\mathbb{S}$ and $\mathbb{T}$ and a prediction accuracy acc_{st} can be obtained on the target domain. The same algorithm is also performed on $\mathbb{S}$, $\mathbb{D}$ and $\mathbb{T}$ and another accuracy acc_{sit} is obtained on the target domain. If $acc_{sit} > acc_{st}$, we set $l^{(i)} = 1$, otherwise, $l^{(i)} = 0$.

Hence, we transform the intermediate domain selection problem to a probability estimation problem. A candidate intermediate domain with a high $f(\boldsymbol{t})$ is more likely to be selected.

In the second step, a transfer learning algorithm, which considers both of the transitive relationship and distribution shift among all the domains, is used. This algorithm is based on non-negative matrix tri-factorization (NMTF) that can perform feature clustering and label propagation simultaneously. In the following, we first present some background knowledge.

Non-negative Matrix Tri-factorization

In NMTF, the feature-instance matrix is decomposed into three sub-matrices. In general, given a feature-instance matrix $\mathbf{X} \in \mathbb{R}^{m \times n}$ where m is the data dimension and n is the number of instances, we can obtain factorized sub-matrices by solving an optimization problem as follows

$$\underset{\mathbf{F}, \mathbf{A}, \mathbf{G}}{\arg\min} \quad \mathscr{L} = ||\mathbf{X} - \mathbf{FAG}^T||_F.$$

$\mathbf{F} \in \mathbb{R}^{m \times p}$ indicates the information of feature clusters, with p as the number of feature clusters. The element $F_{i,j}$ indicates the possibility that the i-th feature belongs to the j-th feature cluster.

$\mathbf{G} \in \mathbb{R}^{n \times c}$ is the instance cluster assignment matrix, with c as the number of instance clusters. If the largest element of the i-th row in $\mathbf{G}$ is located in the j-th column, it means that the i-th instance belongs to the j-th instance cluster.

$\mathbf{A} \in \mathbb{R}^{p \times c}$ is the association matrix. The element $A_{i,j}$ denotes the possibility that the i-th feature cluster is associated with the j-th instance cluster.

NMTF for Transfer Learning

NMTF can used as a basic model for transfer learning. Given the source and target domains $\mathbb{S}$ and $\mathbb{T}$ with $\mathbf{X}_s$ and $\mathbf{X}_t$ as their respective feature-instance matrices, one can decompose these two matrices simultaneously and allow decomposed matrices to share some cross-domain information (sub-matrices). Formally, given two related domains $\mathbb{S}$ and $\mathbb{T}$, their feature-instance matrices can be decomposed simultaneously as

$$\mathscr{L}_{ST} = ||\mathbf{X}_s - \mathbf{F}_s \mathbf{A}_s \mathbf{G}_s^T||_F + ||\mathbf{X}_t - \mathbf{F}_t \mathbf{A}_t \mathbf{G}_t^T||_F$$

$$= \left\| \mathbf{X}_s - [\mathbf{F}^1, \mathbf{F}_s^2] \begin{bmatrix} \mathbf{A}^1 \\ \mathbf{A}_s^2 \end{bmatrix} \mathbf{G}_s^T \right\|_F + \left\| \mathbf{X}_t - [\mathbf{F}^1, \mathbf{F}_t^2] \begin{bmatrix} \mathbf{A}^1 \\ \mathbf{A}_t^2 \end{bmatrix} \mathbf{G}_t^T \right\|_F, \tag{11.11}$$

where $\mathbf{F}^1 \in \mathbb{R}_+^{m \times p_1}$ and $\mathbf{A}_1 \in \mathbb{R}_+^{p_1 \times c}$ contain the common factors shared by the source and target domains, $\mathbf{F}_s^2, \mathbf{F}_t^2 \in \mathbb{R}_+^{m \times p_2}, \mathbf{A}_s^2, \mathbf{A}_t^2 \in \mathbb{R}_+^{p_2 \times n}$ contain domain-specific information, p_1, p_2 are two parameters that indicate the number of hidden feature clusters, $\mathbf{G}_s \in \mathbb{R}^{n \times c}$ is the 0/1 label indicator matrix in the source domain and $\mathbf{G}_t$ is the unknown label indicator matrix of the target domain and will be learned during the training process.

According to (11.11), we can see that the label information of the source domain is propagated to the target domain through the shared factors $\mathbf{F}_1$ and $\mathbf{A}_1$.

The Coupled Matrix Tri-factorization Algorithm

The source, intermediate and target domains have a transitive relationship, which means that the intermediate domain bridges the source and target domains, but has different common factors from them respectively. Hence, to capture these properties, a coupled NMTF (CMTF) algorithm is proposed in

Figure 11.5 An illustration of the CMTF algorithm in the TTL framework. The algorithm learns two coupled feature representations by feature clustering, and then propagates the label information from the source domain to the target domain through the intermediate domain based on the coupled feature representation

Tan et al.'s (2015) work. The CMTF algorithm is illustrated in Figure 11.5 and its objective function is formulated as

$$
\begin{aligned}
\mathcal{L} = & \|\mathbf{X}_s - \mathbf{F}_s \mathbf{A}_s \mathbf{G}_s^T\|_F + \|\mathbf{X}_I - \mathbf{F}_I \mathbf{A}_I \mathbf{G}_I^T\|_F + \|\mathbf{X}_I - \mathbf{F}_I' \mathbf{A}_I' \mathbf{G}_I^T\|_F + \|\mathbf{X}_t - \mathbf{F}_t \mathbf{A}_t \mathbf{G}_t^T\|_F \\
= & \left\| \mathbf{X}_s - [\hat{\mathbf{F}}^1, \hat{\mathbf{F}}_s^2] \begin{bmatrix} \hat{\mathbf{A}}^1 \\ \hat{\mathbf{A}}_s^2 \end{bmatrix} \mathbf{G}_s^T \right\|_F + \left\| \mathbf{X}_I - [\hat{\mathbf{F}}^1, \hat{\mathbf{F}}_I^2] \begin{bmatrix} \hat{\mathbf{A}}^1 \\ \hat{\mathbf{A}}_I^2 \end{bmatrix} \mathbf{G}_I^T \right\|_F \\
& + \left\| \mathbf{X}_I - [\tilde{\mathbf{F}}^1, \tilde{\mathbf{F}}_I^2] \begin{bmatrix} \tilde{\mathbf{A}}^1 \\ \tilde{\mathbf{A}}_I^2 \end{bmatrix} \mathbf{G}_I^T \right\|_F + \left\| \mathbf{X}_t - [\tilde{\mathbf{F}}^1, \tilde{\mathbf{F}}_t^2] \begin{bmatrix} \tilde{\mathbf{A}}^1 \\ \tilde{\mathbf{A}}_t^2 \end{bmatrix} \mathbf{G}_t^T \right\|_F .
\end{aligned} \quad (11.12)
$$

According to (11.12), we can see that the first two terms correspond to the first feature clustering and label propagation between the source and intermediate domains in Figure 11.5 and the last two terms refer to the second feature clustering and label propagation between the intermediate and target domains. In (11.12), it is worth noting that $\mathbf{X}_I$ is decomposed twice with different decomposition matrices, since $\mathbf{X}_I$ shares different knowledge with $\mathbf{X}_s$ and $\mathbf{X}_t$. At the same time, we couple these two decomposition processes via the label matrix $\mathbf{G}_I$. It is reasonable as instances in the intermediate domain should have the same labels in different decomposition processes.

Overall, the CMTF algorithm defines a transitive property among domains. The label information in the source domain is transferred through $\hat{\mathbf{F}}_1$ and $\hat{\mathbf{A}}^1$ to the intermediate domain and affects the learning of $\mathbf{G}_I$. The knowledge on class labels encoded in $\mathbf{G}_I$ is further transferred from the intermediate domain to the target domain through $\tilde{\mathbf{F}}_1$ and $\tilde{\mathbf{A}}^1$.

11.4   TTL with Deep Neural Networks

In previous problems, we transitively transfer knowledge with one intermediate domain, which can be selected by domain knowledge or by some predefined selection criteria. However, in some applications, the source and target domains cannot be connected by one intermediate domain. Multiple intermediate domains are needed to construct the bridge to connect the source and target domains. In this section, we present a method proposed in the work by Tan et al. (2017) to transfer knowledge between distant domains by gradually selecting multiple subsets of instances from a mixture of intermediate domains as a bridge. Tan et al. (2017) use the reconstruction error as a distance measure between two domains. That is, if the reconstruction error on some data points in the source and intermediate domains is small based on a model trained on the target domain, then we consider that these data points from the source and intermediate domains are helpful for the target domain. Based on this measure, a selective learning algorithm (SLA) is proposed in Tan et al.'s (2017) work for the TTL problem. It simultaneously selects useful instances from the source and intermediate domains, learns high-level representations for selected data and trains a classifier for the target domain based on the high-level representations. The learning process of SLA is an iterative procedure that selectively adds new data points from intermediate domains and removes unhelpful data in the source domain to revise the source-specific model toward a target-specific model step by step until some stopping criterion is satisfied.

11.4.1 Problem Definition

We denote by $\mathscr{D}_S = \{(\mathbf{x}_S^1, y_S^1), \cdots, (\mathbf{x}_S^{n_S}, y_S^{n_S})\}$ the source domain labeled data of size n_S, which are assumed to be sufficient enough to train an accurate classifier for the source domain, and by $\mathscr{D}_T = \{(\mathbf{x}_T^1, y_T^1), \cdots, (\mathbf{x}_T^{n_T}, y_T^{n_T})\}$ the target domain labeled data of size n_T, which are assumed to be too insufficient to learn an accurate classifier for the target domain. Moreover, we denote by $\mathscr{D}_I = \{\mathbf{x}_I^1, \cdots, \mathbf{x}_I^{n_I}\}$ the mixture of unlabeled data of multiple intermediate domains, where n_I is assumed to be large enough. Here a domain corresponds to a concept or class for a specific classification problem, such as face or airplane recognition from images. Without loss of generality, we suppose the classification problems in the source domain and the target domain are both binary. All data points are supposed to lie in the same feature space. Let $p_S(\mathbf{x}), p_S(y|\mathbf{x})$ and $p_S(\mathbf{x}, y)$ be the marginal, conditional and joint distributions of the source domain data, respectively, $p_T(\mathbf{x}), p_T(y|\mathbf{x})$ and $p_T(\mathbf{x}, y)$ be the parallel definitions for the target domain, and $p_I(\mathbf{x})$ be the marginal distribution for the intermediate domains. In a TTL problem, we have

$$p_T(\mathbf{x}) \neq p_S(\mathbf{x}), \ p_T(\mathbf{x}) \neq p_I(\mathbf{x}), \text{ and } p_T(y|\mathbf{x}) \neq p_S(y|\mathbf{x}).$$

The goal of TTL is to exploit the unlabeled data in the intermediate domains to build a bridge between the source and target domains, which are originally distant to each other, and train an accurate classifier for the target domain by transferring supervised knowledge from the source domain with the help of the bridge. Note that not all the data in the intermediate domains are supposed to be similar to the source domain data, and some of them may be quite different. Therefore, simply using all the intermediate data to build the bridge may fail to work.

11.4.2   The Selective Learning Algorithm

In this section, we present the SLA proposed in the work by Tan et al. (2017).

Auto-encoders and Its Variant

As a basis component in SLA is the autoencoder (Bengio, 2009) and its variant; we review them here. An autoencoder is an unsupervised feedforward neural network with an input layer, one or more hidden layers, and an output layer. It usually includes two processes: encoding and decoding. Given an input $\mathbf{x} \in \mathbb{R}^q$, an autoencoder first encodes it through an encoding function $f_e(\cdot)$ to map it to a hidden representation, and then decodes it through a decoding function $f_d(\cdot)$ to reconstruct $\mathbf{x}$. The process of the autoencoder can be summarized as

$$\text{encoding}: \mathbf{h} = f_e(\mathbf{x}), \text{ and decoding}: \hat{\mathbf{x}} = f_d(\mathbf{h}),$$

where $\hat{\mathbf{x}}$ is the reconstructed input to approximate $\mathbf{x}$. The learning of the pair of encoding and decoding functions, $f_e(\cdot)$ and $f_d(\cdot)$, is done by minimizing the reconstruction error over all training data, that is, $\min_{f_e, f_d} \sum_{i=1}^{n} \|\hat{\mathbf{x}}_i - \mathbf{x}_i\|_2^2$.

After the pair of encoding and decoding functions are learned, the output of encoding function of an input $\mathbf{x}$, that is, $\mathbf{h} = f_e(\mathbf{x})$, is considered as a higher-level and robust representation for $\mathbf{x}$. Note that an autoencoder takes a vector as the input. When an input instance represented by a matrix or tensor, such as images, is presented to an autoencoder, the spatial information of the instance may be discarded. In this case, a convolutional autoencoder is more desired, and it is a variant of the autoencoder by adding one or more convolutional layers to characterize inputs, and one or more correspondingly deconvolutional layers to generate outputs.

Instance Selection via Reconstruction Error

A motivation behind SLA is that, in an ideal case, if the data from the source domain are useful for the target domain, then one should be able to find a pair of encoding and decoding functions such that the reconstruction errors on the source domain data and the target domain data are both small. In practice, as the source domain and the target domain are distant, there may be only a subset of the source domain data that is useful for the target domain. The situation is similar in the intermediate domains. Therefore, to select useful instances from the intermediate domains, and remove irrelevant instances from the source domain for the target domain, SLA learns a pair of encoding and decoding functions by minimizing reconstruction errors on the selected instances in the source and intermediate domains and all the instances in the target domain simultaneously.

The objective function to be minimized is formulated as follows:

$$\mathscr{J}_1(f_e, f_d, \mathbf{v}_S, \mathbf{v}_T) = \frac{1}{n_S} \sum_{i=1}^{n_S} v_S^i \|\hat{\mathbf{x}}_S^i - \mathbf{x}_S^i\|_2^2 + \frac{1}{n_I} \sum_{i=1}^{n_I} v_I^i \|\hat{\mathbf{x}}_I^i - \mathbf{x}_I^i\|_2^2$$

$$+ \frac{1}{n_T} \sum_{i=1}^{n_T} \|\hat{\mathbf{x}}_T^i - \mathbf{x}_T^i\|_2^2 + R(\mathbf{v}_S, \mathbf{v}_T), \tag{11.13}$$

where $\hat{\mathbf{x}}_S^i, \hat{\mathbf{x}}_I^i$ and $\hat{\mathbf{x}}_T^i$ are reconstructions of $\mathbf{x}_S^i, \mathbf{x}_I^i$ and $\mathbf{x}_T^i$ based on the autoencoder, $\mathbf{v}_S = (v_S^1, \cdots, v_S^{n_S})^\top$, $\mathbf{v}_I = (v_I^1, \cdots, v_I^{n_I})^\top$ and $v_S^i, v_I^j \in \{0, 1\}$ are selection indicators for the i-th instance in the source domain and the j-th instance in the intermediate domains, respectively. When the value is equal to 1, the corresponding instance is selected and otherwise unselected. $R(\mathbf{v}_S, \mathbf{v}_T)$ is a regularization function on $\mathbf{v}_S$ and $\mathbf{v}_T$ to avoid a trivial solution by setting all values of $\mathbf{v}_S$ and $\mathbf{v}_T$ to be zero. In SLA, $R(\mathbf{v}_S, \mathbf{v}_T)$ is defined as $R(\mathbf{v}_S, \mathbf{v}_T) = -\frac{\lambda_S}{n_S} \sum_{i=1}^{n_S} v_S^i - \frac{\lambda_I}{n_I} \sum_{i=1}^{n_I} v_I^i$. Minimizing this term is equivalent to encouraging the selection of as many instances as possible from the source and intermediate domains. Two regularization parameters, λ_S and λ_I, control the importance of this regularization term.

Incorporation of Side Information

By solving the minimization problem, (11.13), one can select useful instances from the source and intermediate domains for the target domain through $\mathbf{v}_S$, $\mathbf{v}_T$ and learn high-level hidden representations for data in different domains through the encoding function $f_e(\mathbf{x})$ simultaneously. However, the learning process is in an unsupervised manner. As a result, the learned hidden representations may not be relevant to the classification problem in the target domain. This motivates to incorporate side information into the learning of the hidden representations for different domains. For the source and target domains, labeled data can be used as the side information, while, for the intermediate domains, there is no label information. SLA considers the predictions on the intermediate domains as the side information and use the confidence on the predictions to guide the learning of the hidden representations. To be specific, we propose to incorporate the side information into learning by minimizing the following function

$$\mathscr{J}_2(f_c, f_e, f_d) = \frac{1}{n_S} \sum_{i=1}^{n_S} v_S^i \ell(y_S^i, f_c(\mathbf{h}_S^i)) + \frac{1}{n_T} \sum_{i=1}^{n_T} \ell(y_T^i, f_c(\mathbf{h}_T^i)) + \frac{1}{n_I} \sum_{i=1}^{n_I} v_I^i g(f_c(\mathbf{h}_I^i)),$$

$$\tag{11.14}$$

where $f_c(\cdot)$ is a classification function to output classification probabilities, and $g(\cdot)$ is the entropy function defined as $g(z) = -z \ln z - (1-z) \ln(1-z)$ for $0 \leq z \leq 1$, which is used to select instances with high prediction confidences in the intermediate domains.

Overall Objective Function

By combining the two objectives in (11.13) and (11.14), we obtain the final objective function for TTL as follows:

$$\min_{\Theta, \mathbf{v}} \mathscr{J} = \mathscr{J}_1 + \mathscr{J}_2, \text{ s.t. } v_S^i, v_I^i \in \{0, 1\}, \tag{11.15}$$

where $\mathbf{v} = \{\mathbf{v}_S, \mathbf{v}_T\}$ and Θ denotes all parameters of the functions $f_c(\cdot)$, $f_e(\cdot)$, and $f_d(\cdot)$.

To solve (11.15), SLA uses the block coordinate decedent method, where, in each iteration, variables in each block are optimized while keeping other variables fixed. In (11.15), there are two blocks of variables: Θ and $\mathbf{v}$. When the variables in $\mathbf{v}$ are fixed, we can update Θ using the back propagation algorithm where the gradients can be computed easily. Alternatively, when the variables in Θ are fixed, we can obtain an analytical solution for $\mathbf{v}$ as follows,

$$v_S^i = \begin{cases} 1 & \text{if } \ell(y_s^i, f_c(f_e(\boldsymbol{x}_S^i))) + \|\hat{\mathbf{x}}_S^i - \mathbf{x}_S^i\|_2^2 < \lambda_S \\ \\ 0 & \text{otherwise} \end{cases} \tag{11.16}$$

$$v_I^i = \begin{cases} 1 & \text{if } \|\hat{\mathbf{x}}_I^i - \mathbf{x}_I^i\|_2^2 + g(f_c(f_e(\mathbf{x}_I^i))) < \lambda_I \\ \\ 0 & \text{otherwise} \end{cases} \tag{11.17}$$

Based on (11.16), we can see that for data in the source domain, only those with low reconstruction errors and low training losses will be selected during the optimization procedure. Similarly, based on (11.17), it can be found that, for data in the intermediate domains, only those with low reconstruction errors and high prediction confidences will be selected.

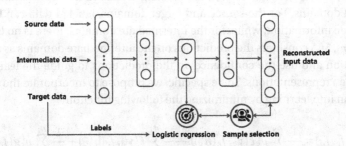

Figure 11.6 The network architecture used in SLA (adapted from Tan et al. [2017])

An intuitive explanation of this learning strategy is twofold: (1) When updating $\mathbf{v}$ with a fixed Θ, "useless" data in the source domain will be removed and intermediate data that can bridge the source and target domains will be selected for training; and (2) when updating Θ with fixed $\mathbf{v}$, the model is trained only on the selected "useful" data samples. The overall algorithm for solving (11.15) is summarized in Algorithm 11.2.

The network architecture corresponding to (11.15) is illustrated in Figure 11.6. From Figure 11.6, we note that, except for the instance selection component **v**, the rest of the architecture in Figure 11.6 can be viewed as a generalization of an autoencoder or a convolutional autoencoder by incorporating the side information.

Algorithm 11.2 The SLA

1: **Input:** Data in $\mathscr{S}$, $\mathscr{T}$ and $\mathscr{I}$, and parameters λ_S, λ_I and T;
2: Initialize Θ, $\mathbf{v}_S = \mathbf{1}$, $\boldsymbol{v}_I = \mathbf{0}$; // *All source data are used*
3: **while** $t < T$ **do**
4:    Update Θ via the back propagation algorithm; // *Update the network*
5:    Update **v** by (11.16) and (11.17); // *Select "useful" instances*
6:    $t = t + 1$
7: **end while**
8: **Output:** Θ and **v**

12

AutoTL: Learning to Transfer Automatically

12.1 Introduction

Three key research issues in transfer learning, discussed in Chapter 1, are when to transfer, how to transfer and what to transfer. Once a source domain is considered to be helpful for a target domain (when to transfer), a transfer learning algorithm (how to transfer) can help learn the transferable knowledge across domains (what to transfer). Usually different transfer learning algorithms are likely to learn different knowledge, leading to uneven transfer learning effectiveness, which can be measured by the improvement of the performance over non-transfer algorithms in the target domain. To obtain good performance in the target domain, many transfer learning algorithms can be treated as candidate algorithms to try, including instance-based transfer learning algorithms (Dai et al., 2007b), model-based transfer learning algorithms (Tommasi et al., 2014) and feature-based transfer learning algorithms (Pan et al., 2011). It is computationally expensive and practically impossible to try all the transfer learning algorithms in a brute-force way. As a trade-off, researchers usually heuristically choose a transfer learning algorithm, which may lead to a suboptimal performance.

It is not the only way to optimize what to transfer by exploring the whole space of transfer learning algorithms. Actually transfer learning experiences are helpful. It has been widely accepted in educational psychology (Luria, 1976; Belmont et al., 1982) that learning from experience is a good methodology. To improve transfer learning skills of deciding what to transfer, humans can conduct meta-cognitive reflection on diverse experiences. Unfortunately, by ignoring previous transfer learning experiences, all existing transfer learning algorithms learn from scratch.

With machine learning models getting increasingly complex, the need for automated machine learning, or AutoML (Yao et al., 2018), has emerged as a strong trend in machine learning. As machine learning involves many tedious steps that require much experience from human experts, ranging from sample selection, feature engineering, algorithm selection, architectural design, model tuning and evaluation, and so on, machine learning practice desires an end-to-end solution where many of these steps can be automated. Recognizing the need to design sophisticated architectures and engage in complex parameter tuning by AI experts, AutoML aims to liberate humans from the manual-labor-driven tasks to optimize a machine learning model, by introducing automation through machine learning itself. Several research prototypes and solutions have been applied in real world applications, for example see the works by Kotthoff et al. (2017), Wong et al. (2018), Liu et al. (2018c), Bello et al. (2017) and Feurer et al. (2015). AutoML has several advantages compared to traditional manual-based model construction, including fast deployment in practice, optimized selection of model and a lower cost. There have been several applications of AutoML, including image and speech recognition, recommendation systems and predictive analytics.

Similar to AutoML, transfer learning can also be packaged in an end-to-end process. We can call the automated transfer learning framework collectively as AutoTL, which stands for automated transfer learning. In this chapter we present a novel AutoTL framework called Learning to Transfer (L2T), which selects transfer learning algorithms automatically through experience. This framework was first proposed by Wei et al. (2018). L2T is a special case of AutoTL, with an aim of identifying the suitable algorithm and model parameters based on previous transfer learning experience.

By exploiting previous transfer learning experiences, the L2T framework is to improve the transferring performance from a source to a target domain to determine what and how to transfer between them. To achieve this goal, L2T consists of two phases. In the first phase, given transfer learning experiences, each of which consists of three elements, including a pair of source and target domains, the knowledge transferred between them and the performance improvement, a reflection function, which functionally maps a pair of domains and the transferred knowledge to the performance improvement, is learned from all the experiences. During the second phase, for a new pair of domains, the learned reflection function as an approximation of the performance improvement is maximized to determine what to transfer between the two domains.

12.2 The L2T Framework

An L2T agent keeps a record of N_e transfer learning experiences by conducting transfer learning several times. Each transfer learning experience is defined as $E_e = (\langle \mathscr{S}_e, \mathscr{T}_e \rangle, a_e, l_e)$ where $\mathscr{S}_e = \{\mathbf{X}_e^s, \mathbf{y}_e^s\}$ and $\mathscr{T}_e = \{\mathbf{X}_e^t, \mathbf{y}_e^t\}$ denote a source domain and a target domain, respectively. $\mathbf{X}_e^* \in \mathbb{R}^{n_e^* \times m}$ denotes the data matrix and each domain has n_e^* examples in an m-dimensional feature space $\mathscr{X}_e^*$, where the superscript $*$ denotes s or t as a source or target domain. $\mathbf{y}_e^* \in \mathscr{Y}_e^*$ denotes an $n_{le}^* \times 1$ vector consisting of labels for $\mathbf{X}_e^*$. Usually the number of labeled examples in the source domain is much larger than that of the target domain, that is, $n_{le}^t \ll n_{le}^s$. We consider the setting of homogeneous feature space and

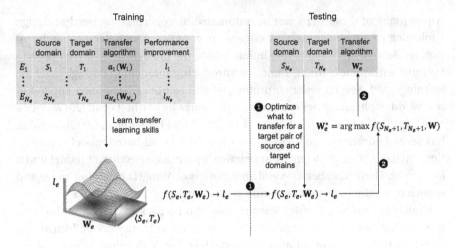

Figure 12.1 An illustration of the L2T framework. The training stage learns a reflection function f, which encrypts transfer learning skills, based on N_e transfer learning experiences $\{E_1, \cdots, E_{N_e}\}$. In the testing stage, for the $(N_e + 1)$-th source-target pair, the learned reflection function f is maximized to learn the transferred knowledge between them, that is, $\mathbf{W}^*_{N_e+1}$.

heterogeneous label spaces for each pair of domains, that is, $\mathcal{X}^s_e = \mathcal{X}^t_e$ and $\mathcal{Y}^s_e \neq \mathcal{Y}^t_e$. $a_e \in \mathcal{A} = \{a_1, \cdots, a_{N_a}\}$ denotes a transfer learning algorithm that has been conducted between $\mathcal{S}_e$ and $\mathcal{T}_e$. Here the transferred knowledge by the algorithm a_e is parameterized as $\mathbf{W}_e$. Finally, $l_e = p^{st}_e / p^t_e$ denotes the performance improvement ratio that is the label of the corresponding transfer learning experience, where p^{st}_e is the performance (e.g., classification accuracy) of a test data set in $\mathcal{T}_e$ after transferring $\mathbf{W}_e$ from $\mathcal{S}_e$ and p^t_e is that of the same test data set without transfer.

In the training stage as illustrated in Figure 12.1, the L2T aims to learn a *reflection* function f based on N_e transfer learning experiences $\{E_1, \cdots, E_{N_e}\}$ by approximating l_e by $f(\mathcal{S}_e, \mathcal{T}_e, \mathbf{W}_e)$. When a new pair of domains $\langle \mathcal{S}_{N_e+1}, \mathcal{T}_{N_e+1} \rangle$ comes, the L2T model can maximize f to learn the knowledge to be transferred, that is, $\mathbf{W}^*_{N_e+1}$, as shown in the testing stage in Figure 12.1.

12.3 Parameterizing What to Transfer

Transfer learning algorithms used in different experiences are usually different. A prerequisite for learning the reflection function is to uniformly parameterize "what to transfer" for each algorithm in the candidate set $\mathcal{A}$. Here $\mathcal{A}$ is assumed to contain algorithms transferring single-level latent features, because existing model-based and instance-based algorithms cannot be applied to the transfer learning setting we study (i.e., $\mathcal{X}^e_s = \mathcal{X}^e_t$ and $\mathcal{Y}^e_s \neq \mathcal{Y}^e_t$). As a result, what to transfer is parameterized with a latent feature matrix $\mathbf{W}$, as elaborated in the following.

Latent feature-based algorithms are to learn domain-invariant features across domains. In those algorithms, what to transfer denotes the shared features across domains. The way to define domain-invariant features includes two classes of algorithms, that is, common latent space-based and manifold ensemble-based algorithms.

12.3.1 Common Latent Space-Based Algorithms

By assuming that domain-invariant features lie in a single shared latent space, this class of algorithms includes but is not limited to TCA (Pan et al., 2011), LSDT (Zhang et al., 2016) and DIP (Baktashmotlagh et al., 2013). With φ denoting a function mapping the original feature representation into the latent space, when φ is a linear function, it can be represented as an embedding matrix $\mathbf{W} \in \mathbb{R}^{m \times u}$, where u is the dimensionality of the latent space. Therefore, what to transfer can be parameterized with $\mathbf{W}$. Otherwise, although the feature mapping of a nonlinear φ may not be explicitly defined in most cases, what to transfer can still be parameterized with $\mathbf{W}$ based on the similarity metric matrix (Cao et al., 2013) in the latent space, that is, $\mathbf{G} = (\mathbf{X}_e^t)^{\dagger} \mathbf{Z}_e^t (\mathbf{Z}_e^t)^T [(\mathbf{X}_e^t)^T]^{\dagger} \in \mathbb{R}^{m \times m}$ according to $\mathbf{X}_e^t \mathbf{G}(\mathbf{X}_e^t)^T = \mathbf{Z}_e^t (\mathbf{Z}_e^t)^T$, where $(\mathbf{X}_e^t)^{\dagger}$ is the pseudo-inverse of $\mathbf{X}_e^t$. Then, the LDL decomposition applied to $\mathbf{G} = \mathbf{L}\mathbf{D}\mathbf{L}^T$ can lead to the latent feature matrix $\mathbf{W} = \mathbf{L}\mathbf{D}^{1/2}$.

12.3.2 Manifold Ensemble-Based Algorithms

Initiated by Gopalan et al. (2011), manifold ensemble algorithms assume that multiple subspaces, which are treated as points on the Grassmann manifold, with the same dimension shared by a source domain and a target domain. Then the latent representation of target examples becomes $\mathbf{Z}_e^{t(n_u)} = [\varphi_1(\mathbf{X}_e^t), \cdots, \varphi_{n_u}(\mathbf{X}_e^t)]$ when n_u subspaces are sampled from the Grassmann manifold. When n_u approaches the infinity, which implies that all the subspaces are sampled, Gong et al. (2012a) has proved that $\mathbf{Z}_e^{t(\infty)} (\mathbf{Z}_e^{t(\infty)})^T = \mathbf{X}_e^t \mathbf{G}(\mathbf{X}_e^t)^T$, where $\mathbf{G}$ denotes the similarity metric matrix. Then the latent feature representation can be defined by $\mathbf{W} = \mathbf{L}\mathbf{D}^{1/2}$.

12.4 Learning from Experiences

Given all experiences $\{E_1, \cdots, E_{N_e}\}$, the training stage is to learn the reflection function f as an approximation of the improvement ratio. The improvement ratio l_e is closely related to two factors. The first factor is the divergence between a source domain and a target domain in the latent space, while the second one denotes the discriminative ability of the target domain in the latent space. Therefore, the reflection function f is built by taking both factors into consideration. In the following section, we discuss how to define these two factors.

12.4.1   Divergence between Source and Target Domains

Similar to the work by Pan et al. (2011), the maximum mean discrepancy (MMD) is used to measure the divergence between domains. MMD empirically calculates the distance between the mean of source examples and that of target examples as

$$
\hat{d}_e^2(\mathbf{X}_e^s \mathbf{W}_e, \mathbf{X}_e^t \mathbf{W}_e)
$$

$$
= \left\| \frac{1}{n_e^s} \sum_{i=1}^{n_e^s} \phi(\mathbf{x}_{ei}^s \mathbf{W}_e) - \frac{1}{n_e^t} \sum_{j=1}^{n_e^t} \phi(\mathbf{x}_{ej}^t \mathbf{W}_e) \right\|_{\mathcal{H}}^2
$$

$$
= \frac{1}{(n_e^s)^2} \sum_{i,i'=1}^{n_e^s} \mathcal{K}(\mathbf{x}_{ei}^s \mathbf{W}_e, \mathbf{x}_{ei'}^s \mathbf{W}_e) + \frac{1}{(n_e^t)^2} \sum_{j,j'=1}^{n_e^t} \mathcal{K}(\mathbf{x}_{ej}^t \mathbf{W}_e, \mathbf{x}_{ej'}^t \mathbf{W}_e)
$$

$$
- \frac{2}{n_e^s n_e^t} \sum_{i,j=1}^{n_e^s, n_e^t} \mathcal{K}(\mathbf{x}_{ei}^s \mathbf{W}_e, \mathbf{x}_{ej}^t \mathbf{W}_e), \tag{12.1}
$$

where $\mathbf{x}_{ej}^t$ denotes the j-th example in $\mathbf{X}_e^t$, ϕ maps from the u-dimensional latent space to the RKHS $\mathcal{H}$ and $\mathcal{K}(\cdot,\cdot) = \langle \phi(\cdot), \phi(\cdot) \rangle$ denotes the kernel function. Different kernels $\mathcal{K}$ leads to different MMDs, leading to different forms of f and hence learning f is to identifying the optimal $\mathcal{K}$. By following multi-kernel MMD (Gretton et al., 2012), $\mathcal{K}$ is parameterized as a linear combination of N_k kernels with non-negative combination coefficients, that is, $\mathcal{K} = \sum_{k=1}^{N_k} \beta_k \mathcal{K}_k \ (\beta_k \geq 0, \forall k)$, and the coefficients $\boldsymbol{\beta} = [\beta_1, \cdots, \beta_{N_k}]^T$ will be learned instead. Then the MMD can be simplified as

$$
\hat{d}_e^2(\mathbf{X}_e^s \mathbf{W}_e, \mathbf{X}_e^t \mathbf{W}_e) = \sum_{k=1}^{N_k} \beta_k \hat{d}_{e(k)}^2(\mathbf{X}_e^s \mathbf{W}_e, \mathbf{X}_e^t \mathbf{W}_e) = \boldsymbol{\beta}^T \hat{\mathbf{d}}_e,
$$

where $\hat{\mathbf{d}}_e = \left[\hat{d}_{e(1)}^2, \cdots, \hat{d}_{e(N_k)}^2 \right]^T$ with $\hat{d}_{e(k)}^2$ calculated based on the k-th kernel $\mathcal{K}_k$.

However, it is insufficient to the MMD alone to measure the divergence between domains. A pair of domains with a small MMD have little distributional overlapping if the variance of the distance between them is high. The distance variance among all pairs of instances across domains is also required to fully characterize the difference. According to Gretton et al. (2012), (12.1) is the empirical estimation of $d_e^2(\mathbf{X}_e^s \mathbf{W}_e, \mathbf{X}_e^t \mathbf{W}_e) = \mathbb{E}_{\mathbf{x}_e^s \mathbf{x}_e^{s'} \mathbf{x}_e^t \mathbf{x}_e^{t'}} h(\mathbf{x}_e^s, \mathbf{x}_e^{s'}, \mathbf{x}_e^t, \mathbf{x}_e^{t'})$ with $h(\mathbf{x}_e^s, \mathbf{x}_e^{s'}, \mathbf{x}_e^t, \mathbf{x}_e^{t'})$ defined as

$$
h(\mathbf{x}_e^s, \mathbf{x}_e^{s'}, \mathbf{x}_e^t, \mathbf{x}_e^{t'})
$$

$$
= \mathcal{K}(\mathbf{x}_e^s \mathbf{W}_e, \mathbf{x}_e^{s'} \mathbf{W}_e) + \mathcal{K}(\mathbf{x}_e^t \mathbf{W}_e, \mathbf{x}_e^{t'} \mathbf{W}_e) - \mathcal{K}(\mathbf{x}_e^s \mathbf{W}_e, \mathbf{x}_e^{t'} \mathbf{W}_e) - \mathcal{K}(\mathbf{x}_e^{s'} \mathbf{W}_e, \mathbf{x}_e^t \mathbf{W}_e).
$$

Consequently, the distance variance, σ_e^2, can be computed as

$$
\sigma_e^2(\mathbf{X}_e^s \mathbf{W}_e, \mathbf{X}_e^t \mathbf{W}_e) = \mathbb{E}_{\mathbf{x}_e^s \mathbf{x}_e^{s'} \mathbf{x}_e^t \mathbf{x}_e^{t'}} [(h(\mathbf{x}_e^s, \mathbf{x}_e^{s'}, \mathbf{x}_e^t, \mathbf{x}_e^{t'}) - \mathbb{E}_{\mathbf{x}_e^s \mathbf{x}_e^{s'} \mathbf{x}_e^t \mathbf{x}_e^{t'}} h(\mathbf{x}_e^s, \mathbf{x}_e^{s'}, \mathbf{x}_e^t, \mathbf{x}_e^{t'}))^2].
$$

As the MMD is characterized with N_k positive semi-definite kernels, we can obtain $\sigma_e^2 = \boldsymbol{\beta}^T \mathbf{Q}_e \boldsymbol{\beta}$, where $\mathbf{Q}_e = \text{cov}(h) = \begin{bmatrix} \sigma_{e(1,1)} & \cdots & \sigma_{e(1,N_k)} \\ \cdots & \cdots & \cdots \\ \sigma_{e(N_k,1)} & \cdots & \sigma_{e(N_k,N_k)} \end{bmatrix}$ with each

entry $\sigma_{e(k_1,k_2)}$ calculated as $\sigma_{e(k_1,k_2)} = \text{cov}(h_{k_1}, h_{k_2}) = \mathbb{E}\left[(h_{k_1} - \mathbb{E}h_{k_1})(h_{k_2} - \mathbb{E}h_{k_2}) \right]$, where $\mathbb{E}h_{k_1}$ stands for $\mathbb{E}_{\mathbf{x}_e^s \mathbf{x}_e^{s\prime} \mathbf{x}_e^t \mathbf{x}_e^{t\prime}} h_{k1}(\mathbf{x}_e^s, \mathbf{x}_e^{s\prime}, \mathbf{x}_e^t, \mathbf{x}_e^{t\prime})$ with h_{k_1} calculated via the k_1-th kernel.

12.4.2 Discriminative Ability of Target Domain

Since there are a limited number of labeled examples in the target domain, unlabeled examples are used to help evaluate the discriminative ability based on the unlabeled discriminant criterion proposed by Yang et al. (2007a) as

$$\tau_e = \text{tr}(\mathbf{W}_e^T \mathbf{S}_e^N \mathbf{W}_e) / \text{tr}(\mathbf{W}_e^T \mathbf{S}_e^L \mathbf{W}_e),$$

where $\mathbf{S}_e^L = \sum_{j,j'=1}^{n_e^t} \frac{H_{jj'}}{(n_e^t)^2} (\mathbf{x}_{ej}^t - \mathbf{x}_{ej'}^t)(\mathbf{x}_{ej}^t - \mathbf{x}_{ej'}^t)^T$ is the local scatter covariance matrix, $\mathbf{S}_e^N = \sum_{j,j'=1}^{n_e^t} \frac{\mathcal{K}(\mathbf{x}_{ej}^t, \mathbf{x}_{ej'}^t) - H_{jj'}}{(n_e^t)^2} (\mathbf{x}_{ej}^t - \mathbf{x}_{ej'}^t)(\mathbf{x}_{ej}^t - \mathbf{x}_{ej'}^t)^T$ is the non-local scatter covariance matrix, and $H_{jj'}$ is defined as

$$H_{jj'} = \begin{cases} \mathcal{K}(\mathbf{x}_{ej}^t, \mathbf{x}_{ej'}^t), & \text{if } \mathbf{x}_{ej}^t \in \mathcal{N}_r(\mathbf{x}_{ej'}^t) \text{ and } \mathbf{x}_{ej'}^t \in \mathcal{N}_r(\mathbf{x}_{ej}^t) \\ 0, & \text{otherwise} \end{cases}.$$

It is noted that the calculation of τ_e depends on kernels. With $\tau_{e(k)}$ obtained from the k-th kernel $\mathcal{K}_k$, τ_e can be reformulated as $\tau_e = \sum_{k=1}^{N_k} \beta_k \tau_{e(k)} = \boldsymbol{\beta}^T \boldsymbol{\tau}_e$, where $\boldsymbol{\tau}_e = [\tau_{e(1)}, \cdots, \tau_{e(N_k)}]^T$.

12.4.3 Optimization Problem

By combining the two aforementioned factors to build the reflection function f, the optimization problem to learn f can be formulated as

$$\boldsymbol{\beta}^*, \lambda^*, \mu^*, b^* = \arg \min_{\boldsymbol{\beta}, \lambda, \mu, b} \sum_{e=1}^{N_e} \mathcal{L}_h\left(\boldsymbol{\beta}^T \hat{\mathbf{d}}_e + \lambda \boldsymbol{\beta}^T \hat{\mathbf{Q}}_e \boldsymbol{\beta} + \frac{\mu}{\boldsymbol{\beta}^T \boldsymbol{\tau}_e} + b, \frac{1}{l_e} \right) + \gamma_1 R(\boldsymbol{\beta}, \lambda, \mu, b),$$

$$\text{s.t. } \beta_k > 0, \ \forall k \in \{1, \cdots, N_k\}, \ \lambda \geq 0, \ \mu \geq 0, \tag{12.2}$$

where f is defined as $f = 1 / \left(\boldsymbol{\beta}^T \hat{\mathbf{d}}_e + \lambda \boldsymbol{\beta}^T \hat{\mathbf{Q}}_e \boldsymbol{\beta} + \frac{\mu}{\boldsymbol{\beta}^T \boldsymbol{\tau}_e} + b \right)$, λ and μ are two variables to balance the importance of the three terms in f, b is a bias, $\mathcal{L}_h(\cdot)$ is the Huber regression loss (Huber, 1964), the regularizer R defines the ℓ_2 norm regularization and γ_1 is a regularization parameter. (12.2) combines the difference between domains, including the MMD distance $\boldsymbol{\beta}^T \hat{\mathbf{d}}_e$ and the distance variance $\boldsymbol{\beta}^T \hat{\mathbf{Q}}_e \boldsymbol{\beta}$, and the discriminant criterion $\boldsymbol{\beta}^T \boldsymbol{\tau}_e$ in the target domain to approximate the performance improvement ratio l_e.

12.5   Inferring What to Transfer

Once the reflection function $f(\mathcal{S}, \mathcal{T}, \mathbf{W}; \boldsymbol{\beta}^*, \lambda^*, \mu^*, b^*)$ is learned in the training stage, the L2T agent will utilize the learned reflection function to optimize what to transfer, that is, the latent feature matrix $\mathbf{W}$, for a new pair of a source domain $\mathcal{S}_{N_e+1}$ and a target domain $\mathcal{T}_{N_e+1}$. As the optimal latent feature matrix $\mathbf{W}^*_{N_e+1}$ is to maximize the value of f, the corresponding objective function is formulated as

$$
\begin{aligned}
\mathbf{W}^*_{N_e+1} &= \arg\min_{\mathbf{W}} \, 1/f(\mathcal{S}_{N_e+1}, \mathcal{T}_{N_e+1}, \mathbf{W}; \boldsymbol{\beta}^*, \lambda^*, \mu^*, b^*) + \gamma_2 \|\mathbf{W}\|_F^2 \\
&= \arg\min_{\mathbf{W}} \, (\boldsymbol{\beta}^*)^T \hat{\mathbf{d}}_{\mathbf{W}} + \lambda^* (\boldsymbol{\beta}^*)^T \hat{\mathbf{Q}}_{\mathbf{W}} \boldsymbol{\beta}^* + \mu^* \frac{1}{(\boldsymbol{\beta}^*)^T \boldsymbol{\tau}_{\mathbf{W}}} + \gamma_2 \|\mathbf{W}\|_F^2,
\end{aligned}
\quad (12.3)
$$

where γ_2 is a regularization parameter. The first and second terms in (12.3) are computed as

$$
(\boldsymbol{\beta}^*)^T \hat{\mathbf{d}}_{\mathbf{W}} = \sum_{k=1}^{N_k} \beta_k^* \Big[\frac{1}{a^2} \sum_{i,i'=1}^{a} \mathcal{K}_k(\mathbf{v}_i \mathbf{W}, \mathbf{v}_{i'} \mathbf{W}) + \frac{1}{b^2} \sum_{j,j'=1}^{b} \mathcal{K}_k(\mathbf{w}_j \mathbf{W}, \mathbf{w}_{j'} \mathbf{W})
$$

$$
- \frac{2}{ab} \sum_{i,j=1}^{a,b} \mathcal{K}_k(\mathbf{v}_i \mathbf{W}, \mathbf{w}_j \mathbf{W}) \Big]
$$

$$
(\boldsymbol{\beta}^*)^T \hat{\mathbf{Q}}_{\mathbf{W}} \boldsymbol{\beta}^* = \frac{1}{n^2-1} \sum_{i,i'=1}^{n} \sum_{k=1}^{N_k} \Big\{ \beta_k^* \big[\mathcal{K}_k(\mathbf{v}_i \mathbf{W}, \mathbf{v}_{i'} \mathbf{W}) + \mathcal{K}_k(\mathbf{w}_i \mathbf{W}, \mathbf{w}_{i'} \mathbf{W}) - 2\mathcal{K}_k(\mathbf{v}_i \mathbf{W}, \mathbf{w}_{i'} \mathbf{W})
$$

$$
- \frac{1}{n^2} \sum_{i,i'=1}^{n} \Big(\mathcal{K}_k(\mathbf{v}_i \mathbf{W}, \mathbf{v}_{i'} \mathbf{W}) + \mathcal{K}_k(\mathbf{w}_i \mathbf{W}, \mathbf{w}_{i'} \mathbf{W}) - 2\mathcal{K}_k(\mathbf{v}_i \mathbf{W}, \mathbf{w}_{i'} \mathbf{W}) \big) \Big] \Big\}^2,
$$

where shorthands, including $\mathbf{v}_i = \mathbf{x}^s_{(N_e+1)i}$, $\mathbf{v}_{i'} = \mathbf{x}^s_{(N_e+1)i''}$, $\mathbf{w}_j = \mathbf{x}^t_{(N_e+1)j}$, $\mathbf{w}_{j'} = \mathbf{x}^t_{(N_e+1)j'}$ and $a = n^s_{N_e+1}$, and $b = n^t_{N_e+1}$, are used. The third term in (12.3) can be calculated as $(\boldsymbol{\beta}^*)^T \boldsymbol{\tau}_{\mathbf{W}} = \sum_{k=1}^{N_k} \beta_k^* \frac{\mathrm{tr}(\mathbf{W}^T \mathbf{S}^N_k \mathbf{W})}{\mathrm{tr}(\mathbf{W}^T \mathbf{S}^L_k \mathbf{W})}$. The non-convex (12.3) can be optimized via the conjugate gradient method.

12.6   Connections to Other Learning Paradigms

12.6.1   Transfer Learning

Three key research issues, that is, when, what and how to transfer, are identified in Chapter 1 for transfer learning. Models (Yang et al., 2007b; Tommasi et al., 2014), instances (Dai et al., 2007b) or features (Pan et al., 2011) can be transferred between domains. Some works (Yang et al., 2007b; Tommasi et al., 2014) use *the source models* to regularize the target model that is based on SVM. In (Dai et al., 2007b), the target learner is boosted by utilizing useful source *instances*. Various techniques that are able to learn transferable *features* between domains have been studied extensively. These techniques are based on pivot features selected manually (Blitzer et al., 2006), dimensionality reduction (Pan et al., 2011; Baktashmotlagh et al., 2013, 2014), collective matrix factorization (Long et al., 2014), dictionary learning/sparse coding (Raina et al., 2007; Zhang et al., 2016), manifold learning (Gopalan et al., 2011; Gong et al., 2012a) and deep learning (Yosinski et al., 2014; Long et al., 2015; Tzeng et al., 2015). Different from L2T, all existing studies focus on transferring from scratch.

12.6.2 Multi-task Learning

Multi-task learning (Caruana, 1997; Zhang and Yang, 2017b) learns multiple related tasks together by sharing knowledge among tasks to improve the generalization performance of all the tasks, which is different from transfer learning and L2T, as shown in Figure 12.2.

	Training	Testing
Transfer learning	Task 1	Task 2
Multi task learning	Task 1 ⋯ Task N	Task 1 ⋯ Task N
Lifelong learning	Task 1 ⋯ Task N	Task N+1
Learning to transfer	Task 1 → Task 2 ⋯ Task 2N-1 → Task 2N	Task 2N+1 → Task 2N+2

Figure 12.2 Illustration of the differences between L2T and other related learning paradigms

12.6.3 Lifelong Machine Learning

Lifelong machine learning, to be introduced in Chapter 14, transfers knowledge contained in existing learning tasks to a new task, which is assumed to lie in the same environment as existing tasks. Ruvolo and Eaton (2013) study lifelong machine learning from the perspective of online meta-learning. The commonality between L2T and lifelong machine learning is that they both aim to exploit historical experiences to improve the performance of a learning system, while the difference between them is that each historical experience in lifelong machine learning is a traditional learning task but that in L2T is a transfer learning task, which is illustrated in Figure 12.2.

12.6.4 Automated Machine Learning

As mentioned earlier in this chapter, the L2T framework aims to automatically tune a suitable transfer learning model for a transfer learning task. Hence, it is strongly related to AutoML, which aims to construct machine learning programs without human assistance and within limited computational budgets.

Several successful attempts have been made in AutoML. For instance, Kotthoff et al. (2017) present a system designed to automate the search in the machine learning system Waikato environment for knowledge analysis' learning algorithm space and their respective hyperparameter settings to maximize performance. Wong et al. (2018) apply transfer learning to help improve the AutoML process, making it more cost-effective to apply the technique. Feurer et al. (2015) present an AutoML system based on scikit-learn that automatically considers the past performance of a system on similar data sets in the past. The technique is based on an ensemble of learning systems that are to be optimized. Bello et al. (2017) present an approach to automate the process of discovering optimization methods for deep learning architectures and their method uses a reinforcement learning algorithm to maximize the performance of a model based on a few functional primitives to update a model. Liu et al. (2018c) present a method for learning the structure of convolutional neural networks with a sequential-model-based optimization strategy. This method is shown to be more efficient than the contemporary reinforcement-learning-based solutions.

The L2T framework introduced in this chapter is a special case of the AutoTL framework, which applies AutoML to transfer learning tasks. In particular, L2T belongs to the model selection module in AutoML. Different AutoML techniques can be applied here to transfer learning. However, AutoML and AutoTL also have differences. Specifically, the former focuses on automating the supervised learning algorithms, whereas the latter (i.e., the L2T framework) focuses on transfer learning only. Hence, the L2T framework can be viewed as an AutoML case for transfer learning.

13
Few-Shot Learning

13.1 Introduction

The concept of "few-shot learning" is inspired by the observation that human beings are capable of learning a novel concept with only a few examples, or even without any examples! Babies are especially capable of capturing typical characteristics of a concept by few observations. For instance, when presented with an image and told that the object in the image is an apple, humans can rapidly capture the key features about its shape, color and texture, and naturally associate such features with the concept "fruit apple." Next time, when we encounter a particular kind of apple, say a wax apple, we immediately recognize it no matter whether the scale or the viewing angle is different from the previous observations. Sometimes, even if we are not informed of the characteristics of the image, it is still possible for us to guess that the object may belong to a species akin to apple, because they share some physical properties such as red skin, smooth texture and shape. We do not need to be taught the concept through massive examples with a variety of deformations such as positive and negative examples.

However, such an easy task is difficult for a majority of contemporary machine learning algorithms, especially for deep learning models that perform competitively in many perception tasks. In contrast with the ability for humans to learn from a small set of examples, the learning part of machine learning algorithms is often based on the existence of a large number of examples. Typically, the more complicated a model is, the more labeled data the model needs to be fed during training. As a result, when a machine learning model encounters an entirely new concept, the chance that a previous experience can help in making a right judgment is random at best. In most cases, machine learning algorithms require a large amount of new examples to be updated for new tasks.

To endow machine learning algorithms with the ability to capture useful information from only a small number of examples, researchers have tried to simulate the delicate process in which humans learn from small samples, instead of brutally training an end-to-end model with "big data." The core of this group of models is built on a characteristic of human cognitive ability with which humans learn a new concept based on all previous experiences "pretraining." There are many phases of cognition ranging from physical observation to mental comprehension and memory. Take the recognition of fruits as an example. Although different kinds of fruits, such as wax apple and fruit apple, have distinctive appearances, flavors and textures, they share something in common. Both their skins are smooth and their shapes are similar. Those similar features support that the knowledge can be "transferred" from one type of apple to the other. If an algorithm possesses such a generalization ability based on universal features, a model can also easily be adaptable to a novel concept with a few correcting examples.

Following this insight, researchers have proposed few-shot learning to mimic the learning ability of humans. There are many variants of few-shot learning, including zero-shot learning, one-shot learning, Bayesian program learning (BPL), poor resource learning and domain generalization. They all can be understood as some variants of transfer learning. Thus, in the context of transfer learning, we will review them one by one.

Compared with the previously introduced transfer learning settings, in few-shot learning, the target domain are generally assumed to have very limited data, including both labeled and unlabeled data. In some extreme cases, no data instances in the target domain are assumed to be available in advance; for example, this might be the case in domain generalization problems. In the following, we introduce some representative state-of-the-art models under the settings of zero-shot learning (Section 13.2), one-shot learning (Section 13.3), BPL (Section 13.4), poor resource learning (Section 13.5) and, finally, domain generalization learning (Section 13.6).

13.2   Zero-Shot Learning

13.2.1   Overview

In the zero-shot learning setting, a learning system handles testing samples from novel classes that do not appear in the training data set. Compared with conventional machine learning settings, the critical difference is that new concepts or labels appear in the test samples, and this difference requires a "bridge" from knowledge of existing classes to that of the novel classes. The main bridge employed in most zero-shot learning methods is the so-called semantic features. These features make the transfer learning possible.

In particular, semantic features of a certain class are the attributes characterizing this class. Thus, instead of learning a mapping from $\mathscr{X}$ to $\mathscr{Y}$, where $\mathscr{X}$ is an m-dimensional feature space and $\mathscr{Y}$ is a label space, we try to learn a function: $\mathscr{X} \to \mathscr{F}$ where $\mathscr{F}$ is a semantic feature space. Apart from that, we need a knowledge base $\mathscr{K}$, which lists all the class labels and their associated semantic features, which act as a bridge. The knowledge base $\mathcal{K}$ has the information about both the existing classes and novel classes. Thus, after we obtain semantic features of an example, we match the features in the knowledge base to obtain the most similar classe as the one to which the data sample belongs. In the following, we introduce some useful terminologies used in the work by Palatucci et al. (2009).

A *semantic feature space*, denoted by $\mathcal{F}$, is a d-dimensional space. Each dimension in the space represents an implicit or explicit attribute that can be either continuous or categorical. In the explicit case, the dimension denotes an explicit semantic attribute such as whether the object has a pair of wings or how many legs the object has. In the implicit case, it is hard to give the feature an explicit description, but we know that the feature helps us to distinguish between different classes. The most well-known example of such kind of features is the word embedding, where words with similar semantic meanings are close to each other in the embedding space.

A *semantic knowledge base* is denoted by $\mathcal{K} = \{(\mathbf{f}_1, y_1), \cdots, (\mathbf{f}_k, y_k)\}$, where $y_i \in \mathcal{Y}$ represents a label and $\mathbf{f}_i \in \mathcal{F}$ represents the corresponding representation in the semantic feature space. It is assumed that there is a one-to-one mapping between $\mathcal{F}$ and $\mathcal{Y}$. Therefore, as long as we get a semantic feature representation $\mathbf{f}$, we can find the class it belongs to, and vice versa.

The knowledge base $\mathcal{K}$ can be constructed either by the manual annotation or via machine learning. With manual annotation, each assigned label is given by human annotators, which is often explainable. In images, an annotator labels the objects appearing in an image with tags indicating the presence or absence of a certain attributes. Machine learning-based annotation is based on a corpus of text, which consists of the terms of all the class labels. A model is trained to imitate the ability of human of learning new concepts via reading. For example, we may not know the meaning of "liger," but after going through a description such as "The liger is a hybrid cross between a male lion and a female tiger," we can extrapolate that the appearance of a liger is akin to both a tiger and a lion, to some extent. The word embedding is critical in capturing the semantic similarity of words. If two words occur in a similar context, then their semantic similarity may be high. Technically, the core of this category of methods is to encode words into a distributional representation by maximizing the probability of the term occurrence in a context given pivot terms or maximizing the probability of the occurrence of the pivot term given terms in the context.

Shen et al. (2006b) present one of the first works in zero-shot learning via a "bridging classifier". This work won the Championship of 2005 ACM KDD CUP data-mining competition (Shen et al., 2005), and has been subsequently applied to several commercial search engine and advertisement systems. We will give a detailed description of this solution below.

13.2.2   Algorithms for Zero-Shot Learning

Many zero-shot learning algorithms have been proposed and they can be classified into two categories. The first class is from the perspective of the classification or regression. The other is from the perspective of the energy function ranking.

Classification and Regression

As mentioned earlier, in zero-shot learning a mapping process is needed, which is divided into two phases, $\mathcal{X} \to \mathcal{F}$ and $\mathcal{F} \to \mathcal{Y}$. $\mathcal{F}$ is the semantic feature space to bridge different classes. Each dimension in the semantic feature space can either be continuous or be categorical.

To enable zero-shot learning, in the first step, we first need to translate the labels in training examples to semantic features $\mathbf{f}$ based on the knowledge base. In the second step, we can fit a collection of functions to training examples, where the function can be either a classifier for categorical feature or a regression model for continuous feature. We have $\{(\mathbf{x}_1^s, \mathbf{f}_1^s), \cdots, (\mathbf{x}_{n_s}^s, \mathbf{f}_{n_s}^s)\}$, because $\mathbf{f}$ is multi-dimensional and each dimension among them requests for a prediction model.

During the testing phase, we apply the classifier to the target task. Our first step is to map $\mathbf{x}_i^t$ to $\mathbf{f}_i^t$ for each $i \in \{1, 2, \cdots, n_t\}$ by the collection of prediction models that we have just learned. The second step is to go through the knowledge base to identify the class with the highest similarity between the predicted semantic features and the prototype semantic features of the class, and output the highest ranked one.

Shen et al. (2006b) present one of the first works in zero-shot learning via a "bridging classifier." This work won the Championship of 2005 ACM KDD CUP data-mining competition, and has been subsequently applied to several commercial search engine and advertisement systems (Shen et al., 2005). In this algorithm, the goal is to classify a given query into new category labels, when there is few or no training data given for the labels.

To solve this problem, two phases were used to build a zero-shot classifier model. Phase I corresponds to the training phase of a typical machine learning algorithm, in which data from the Web are collected for training a collection of intermediate classifiers that map text documents to the intermediate categories that can potentially cover a huge label space (300,000 in all). Phase II maps the labels in the base classifiers to the new labels in the target domain to fully connect the base documents to the target labels, which is less than 100. The intermediate class label space corresponds to the semantic labels mentioned earlier, and the Web provides the data that connects an incoming query to the semantic features and then to the target labels.

A full description of the algorithm with experiments on query classification can be found in the work by Shen et al. (2006a). Let $p(C_i^T | q)$ be the probability of conditional probability of the query q belonging to class C_i^T. $p(C_i^T | C_j^I)$ and $p(q_j | C_j^I)$ are similarly defined. Here $p(C_j^I)$ is the prior probability of the intermediate class label C_j^I, which can be estimated from the Web pages in C^I. Their relationship is computed by applying the Bayes rule:

$$p(C_i^T|q) = \Sigma_{C_j^I} p(C_i^T, C_j^I|q)$$

$$= \sigma_{C_j^I} p(C_i^T|C_j^I, q) p(C_j^I|q)$$

$$\propto \sigma_{C_j^I} p(C_i^T|C_j^I) p(q|C_j^I) p(C_j^I).$$

The terms in the last equation can be estimated by term frequency of words or phrases in a category. For example,

$$p(C_i^T|C_j^I) = \Pi_{k=1}^n (p(w_k|C_j^I))^{n_k}. \tag{13.1}$$

Finally, the class to be output is determined by the maximum likelihood formula:

$$c^* = \arg\max_{C_i^T} p(C_i^T|q). \tag{13.2}$$

A schematic figure showing how the mappings from queries to the target classes through the intermediate classes is shown in Figure 13.1. In this figure, a query q_k is mapped to the target class label C^T with a certain probability that is calculated through the intermediate classifiers from Q to C^I, and then from C^I to the target C^T.

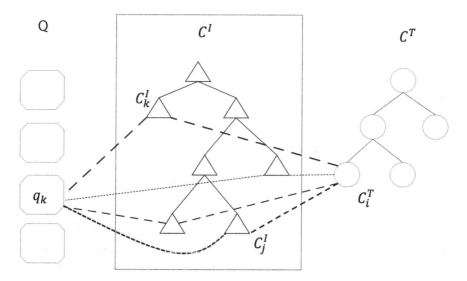

Figure 13.1 The schematic graph shows the bridging classifier for query classification through intermediate domains (adapted from Shen et al. [2006b])

The semantic feature can be represented in an explicit form such as annotated attributes or an implicit form such as semantic label encodings. Socher et al. (2013a) propose a regression model to project a raw feature representation into a label encoding space. Under such setting, $\mathbf{f}_i$ can be represented as $f(y_i)$ for

$i \in \{1, \cdots, n\}$, where $f(y_i)$ is a distributional representation of label y_i learned from a large corpus. The regression model is a two-layer neural network and its objective function is defined as

$$l(\mathbf{x}, y) = \| f(y) - \boldsymbol{\theta}^{(2)} \tanh(\boldsymbol{\theta}^{(1)} \mathbf{x}) \|^2,$$

where $\boldsymbol{\theta}^{(1)} \in \mathbb{R}^{h \times d}$, $\boldsymbol{\theta}^{(2)} \in \mathbb{R}^{m \times h}$ and $\tanh(\cdot)$ denotes the hyperbolic tangent function. They also consider that, if existing and novel classes are mixed together in the test set, this model may mistakenly classify an image from a novel class to an existing one. This is a typical issue dealt in transfer learning literature. Since the target and source domains have separate distributions, the model trained by the source data cannot be applied to the prediction task of the target data directly. If the model is given access to some examples from the target domain, it can employ some domain adaptation techniques to alleviate the distribution difference.

To address the data-shortage issue, Socher et al. (2013a) add a step before the classification step to detect novel samples that are the samples belonging to unseen classes. Then they employ two kinds of strategies to perform the classification task for the two groups, respectively, with one strategy handling novelties or outliers and the other one dealing with normal samples.

Another interesting model in this category is the convex combination of semantic embeddings (ConSE) (Norouzi et al., 2013). The distinction between ConSE and Socher et al.'s (2013a) model is on the choice of the objective function. In fact, it hides the regression process in a standard classification process, so the mean squared error is substituted by the classification error. The classifier is trained in the source domain to estimate the probability of a data point belonging to each of the classes. In the test phase, the trained classifier is applied to the target data to output the probability that this data point is drawn from each source class. Next, the representation of the sample in the semantic feature space is computed by a convex combination of label encodings corresponding to each source class with the estimated probabilities as the weights and mathematically it can be defined as

$$f(\mathbf{x}) = \frac{1}{Z} \sum_{t=1}^{T} \mathbb{P}(\hat{y}(\mathbf{x}, t) | x) f(\hat{y}(\mathbf{x}, t)),$$

where top T most likely classes are involved, $\hat{y}(\mathbf{x}, t)$ denotes the label with the t-th highest probability, and Z is the normalization factor. The intuition behind the method is to derive the representation with the similarity between the current sample and different classes. Suppose the appearance of a liger is half akin to a lion and half akin to a tiger, we have f(liger) is approximately $\frac{1}{2} f$(lion) $+ \frac{1}{2} f$(tiger). With the predicted embedding in the semantic space, we can easily find its nearest neighbors in the semantic knowledge base.

Energy Function Ranking
Another category of methods estimates the matching score between a raw feature and the encoding of a class label directly. Naturally, the class with the highest

score will be the one that the sample belongs to. The formulation in this setting is to map from $\mathscr{X} \times \mathscr{F}$ to $\mathscr{S}$ where $\mathscr{S}$ is the score space. After predicting the matching scores for all the classes, we can rank the scores in descending order and select the most likely one or several to produce the predicted label. The form of the mapping function can either be simply bilinear (i.e., $\mathbf{x}^T \mathbf{Wf}$), where $\mathbf{W}$ is a $d_x \times d_f$ parameter matrix to be learned, or nonlinear such as deep neural networks. Another difference lies in the choice of the loss function.

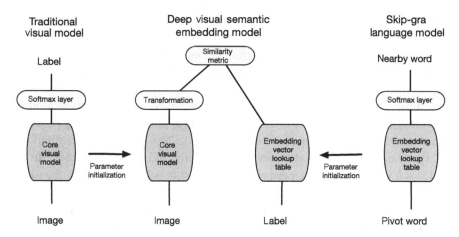

Figure 13.2 The architecture of deep visual-semantic embedding model (adapted from Frome et al. [2013]). The left part is an image recognition model, the right part is a skip-gram language model and the central part is the joint model based on the two components

Take deep visual-semantic embedding model (DeViSE) (Frome et al., 2013) as a concrete example. The architecture is depicted in Figure 13.2. The goal here is to predict labels for novel instances. The label encoding component in this model is transferred from a pretrained language model, and the visual feature learning component is transferred from a conventional classification model. They replace the softmax layer of visual model with a projection layer to map the visual representation to the label encoding. The objective of the model is to make the similarity of the visual representation with the label encoding of the correct class higher than other classes. As a result, the loss function is defined as

$$l\left(\mathbf{x}, y_{label}\right) = \sum_{j \neq label} \max\left[0, m - f(y_{label})^T \mathbf{W} g(\mathbf{x}) + f(y_j)^T \mathbf{W} g(\mathbf{x})\right],$$

where $g(\mathbf{x}) \in \mathbb{R}^{d_h}$ is the compressed representation of an image, m is the margin, $f(\cdot) \in \mathbb{R}^{d_f}$ represents the label encoding and $\mathbf{W}$ is a $d_h \times d_f$ matrix utilized to compute a matching score between the image representation and the label encoding.

In the training phase, parameters in the visual model, language model (i.e., label embedding) and $\mathbf{W}$ can be tuned to minimize the training loss on training samples. In the test phase, given a test image, there is no need to compute the matching score between the test image and each label. We can only identify the nearest neighbor of $\mathbf{W}g(\mathbf{x})$ in the label encoding space.

13.3   One-Shot Learning

13.3.1   Overview

In the one-shot learning setting, we are only given one sample from each class. One labeled data is clearly insufficient for most machine learning algorithms to function well, especially for deep learning. Models can overfit to the single example that a small variation on testing data can negatively influence the prediction result. There are two strategies to prevent overfitting. One is to incorporate a prior knowledge to leverage previous experience. Using generative model is a natural way to assimilate external knowledge to prevent the training process from concentrating on the only sample (Li et al., 2006). The prior distribution of a generative model encodes previous experience. BPL (Lake et al., 2011, 2013, 2015) is a representative framework in this area that will be detailed in the next section.

The other line of methods transforms a one-shot classification task into a verification task (Koch, 2015). To be specific, when given a testing sample, the model matches the example to prototypes stored in a support set of labeled samples. The predicted label of the testing sample is the class that the prototype with the highest matching score belongs to.

In this section, we will focus on a deep learning model for the one-shot learning task.

13.3.2   One-Shot Learning Algorithms

One advantage of the verification-based method is that it is simple. Despite its simplicity, the verification-based method can be easily substituted by more sophisticated methods such as the deep learning algorithms. Here we present the Siamese neural network to demonstrate the basic idea of this type of methods.

Siamese Neural Networks

The Siamese neural network was first proposed by Bromley et al. (1993) to solve a signature verification task. It can be viewed as a pair of identical neural networks connected by an objective function on top of the outputs from two neural networks. The twin neural networks have the same architecture and share the same set of parameters. Going through either of the neural networks can be seen as embedding the exemplar to a new representation to simplify diverse variations in the raw feature representation and to erase noises. The symmetric structure ensures that the embedding process is the same and, as a result, the prototype sample and the testing sample are projected into the same latent feature space. The motivation is to enable the model to have some discriminative ability. For instance, given two objects, although humans may not be able to name them respectively, humans can easily distinguish whether they are from the same category by comparing their key features, As long as the model possesses the discrimination ability, it can make its judgment by comparison. A typical architecture of the Siamese neural network is shown in Figure 13.3.

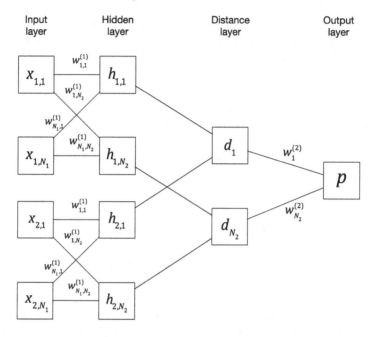

Figure 13.3 The architecture of the Siamese neural network (adapted from Koch [2015])

The inputs to the Siamese neural network are denoted by $\mathbf{x}^{(1)}$ and $\mathbf{x}^{(2)}$ respectively and the output is denoted by $\mathbb{P}(\mathbf{x}^{(1)}, \mathbf{x}^{(2)})$. Within the twin neural networks, L layers, which can be any of linear layer, convolutional layer, pooling layer or other nonlinear layer, are connected in sequence. We use $\mathbf{h}^{(i,l)}$, where $i \in \{1,2\}$ and $l \in \{1, \cdots, L\}$, to denote the output of the l-th layer in the i-th neural network. The outputs of the two neural networks, $\mathbf{h}^{(i,L)}$ for $i \in \{1,2\}$, are separately transformed into two vectors $\mathbf{z}^{(i)}$. Finally, we use a metric to measure the distance between them as the output $\mathbb{P}(\mathbf{x}^{(1)}, \mathbf{x}^{(2)})$. In Koch's (2015) work, the distance metric is defined as

$$d(\mathbf{z}^{(1)}, \mathbf{z}^{(2)}) = \sigma\left(\sum_j \alpha_j |\mathbf{z}_j^{(1)} - \mathbf{z}_j^{(2)}|\right),$$

where $\mathbf{z}_j^{(i)}$ is the j-th entry in vector $\mathbf{z}^{(i)}$. The metric can naturally be used to approximate the probability of the pair of inputs to twin network owning the same label.

In the training phase, for each pair of inputs $(\mathbf{x}^{(1)}, \mathbf{x}^{(2)})$ from the support set, the output y is set to 1 if $\mathbf{x}^{(1)}$ and $\mathbf{x}^{(2)}$ belong to the same class, or to 0 otherwise. The loss function is defined as

$$l(\mathbf{x}^{(1)}, \mathbf{x}^{(2)}) = y \log(\mathbb{P}(\mathbf{x}^{(1)}, \mathbf{x}^{(2)})) + (1 - y) \log(1 - \mathbb{P}(\mathbf{x}^{(1)}, \mathbf{x}^{(2)})).$$

We can adopt various optimization techniques, such as stochastic gradient descent (SGD) and Adam, to learn the parameters.

In the testing phase, we simply match the test sample to each sample in the support set to identify the one with largest confidence. Finally, we regard the associated label as the prediction.

Other Variations

The Siamese neural network can be viewed as a hard classification method, as it assigns the label of the most similar exemplar in the support set to the testing sample without considering less similar ones. As a hard decision may be misled by outliers, its deficiency is inevitable. Since if we only get one exemplar from each class, which is independent of the rest, we do not have more evidence to support the judgment. In other words, there is no way to borrow knowledge via comparison with other exemplars to make the current comparison result more compelling.

This issue can be addressed if we take two or more shots from the same class or from other related classes, then we can exploit more information from more relevant shots. In this situation, a soft classification is preferred. Vinyals et al. (2016) propose an algorithm to use the exemplars in the whole library to make a soft decision. Technically, the algorithm estimates the probability of the new observation belonging to each category.

Given a support set of n_s labeled examples $\mathscr{S} = \{(\mathbf{x}_i^s, y_i^s)\}_{i=1}^{n_s}$, the goal is to map from this support set to a classifier $cs(\mathbf{x})$, which can predict the probability distribution over all the candidate class labels y. A general form of the probability distribution is defined as

$$\mathbb{P}(y|\mathbf{x}, \mathscr{S}) = \sum_{i=1}^{n_s} a(\mathbf{x}, \mathbf{x}_i^s) \, (y_i^s) \quad \text{subject to} \sum_{i=1}^{n_s} a(\mathbf{x}, \mathbf{x}_i^s) = 1,$$

where $\mathbf{x}$ is a data point, y represents a label and $a(\mathbf{x}, \mathbf{x}_i^s) = \frac{\exp(c(f(\mathbf{x}), g(\mathbf{x}_i^s)))}{\sum_{j=1}^{k} \exp(c(f(\mathbf{x}), g(\mathbf{x}_i^s)))}$ denotes the probability of $\mathbf{x}$ belonging to the same class as $\mathbf{x}_i^s$ based on two transformation functions $f(\cdot)$ and $g(\cdot)$.

In this way, the one-shot learning problem is transformed to a classification problem. In the testing phase, we need to scan the whole support set to classify a testing data point.

13.4 Bayesian Program Learning

13.4.1 Overview

The BPL algorithm is proposed in the works by Lake et al. (2011, 2013, 2015). It is an instance of *unsupervised transfer learning*, in which the label information is not observed in the training data. The core of this framework is to model the concept in a generative way.

Despite the complexity of the method, BPLs are composed of common primitives at a more abstract level. The process of generating concepts from primitives follows the intuition of human learning. For example, a character is constructed by strokes and connections between strokes. Strokes are basic components and some strokes constitute a more complex part of character that is also shared across characters. Finally, a character comes out based on the structural composition of different parts. Lake et al. (2015) indicate that there are three key ideas in BPL, which are compositionality, causality and learning to learn. The compositionality property refers to the characteristic that a concept is composed by primitives, as illustrated in the character-stroke example. The causality property means that a probabilistic model captures the causal generative process from primitives to concepts. This allows the method to practice the philosophy of *learning to learn*, which means that it applies experience from a different but related task to current task. Thus, the BPL framework is also a variant of transfer learning. In the following, we will formalize the BPL framework by introducing its details.

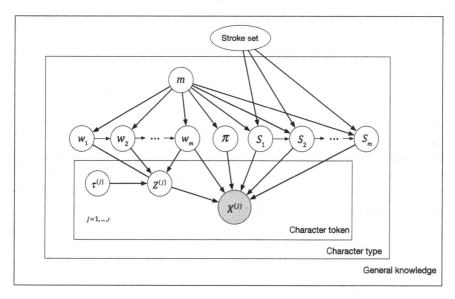

Figure 13.4 An illustration for the generative process of a character token, where a character type acts like a template that can be used to generate a group of tokens (adapted from Lake et al. [2011])

13.4.2 BPL for Identifying Character Strokes

We follow the definitions in the works by Lake et al. (2011, 2013, 2015). Suppose that we have a library of n black and white images with a character drawn in each. In one-shot learning setting, there is only one example in the data set for each character, for example, $(A, B, C, \cdots)$. The i-th image is represented by a $w \times h$ binary matrix $\mathbf{X}^{(i)}$, where w denotes the width and h denotes the height. $\mathbf{X}^{(i)}_{(x,y)} = 1 (0 \leq x \leq w, 0 \leq y \leq h)$ indicates that the pixel in location (x, y) is black and otherwise $\mathbf{X}^{(i)}_{(x,y)} = 0$. From the image of the character, we need to infer the generative process that gives rise to the character outlook. Specifically, the basic elements include the number of strokes m, the specification of each stroke $S_j (1 \leq j \leq m)$, the starting position of each stroke $\{W_j\}_{j=1}^m$ and the mixing weights $\boldsymbol{\pi}$. Figure 13.4 describes the generative process. We will detail the process as follows.

Generative Models for Character Types

A character type is composed of the basic elements mentioned earlier. First, we sample m from a uniform distribution ranging from 1 to 10. Then, we sample m strokes one by one. The first stroke S_1 is sampled from uniform distribution $\mathbb{P}(S_1) = \frac{1}{K}$, where K is the size of the stroke set. The starting position of a stroke is also sampled uniformly across the image, which has wh pixel points. The probability of each position to be chosen is $\frac{1}{wh}$. The style and position of subsequent strokes are sampled from two transition probability distributions $\mathbb{P}(S_{i+1}|S_i)$ and $\mathbb{P}(W_{i+1}|W_i)$, which means that the drawing of the current stroke depends on the previous stroke. In the last step, we sample mixing weights $\boldsymbol{\pi}$ from a Dirichlet distribution.

Generative Models for Character Tokens

A character token is the observed image of a character. You can regard it as the writing criterion, while the actual token or image heavily relies on personal habit that varies from writer to writer. Here, we allow systematic and random displacements. The systematic displacement means that layout of a character skews from its standard position in the image and the random displacement means that starting point of each stroke may not be exactly in the standard position of the character. $\mathbf{Z} = \{Z_1, Z_2, \cdots, Z_m\}$ denotes the distorted starting point and $\boldsymbol{\tau}$ represents the systematic displacement. So, the prior distributions of $\mathbf{Z}$ and $\boldsymbol{\tau}$ are defined as

$$\mathbb{P}(\boldsymbol{\tau}) \propto \exp\left(-\frac{1}{2\sigma_t^2}||\boldsymbol{\tau}||_2^2\right),$$

$$\mathbb{P}(\mathbf{Z}|\mathbf{W}, \boldsymbol{\tau}) \propto \prod_{i=1}^m \exp\left(-\frac{1}{2\sigma_z^2}||(Z_i - W_i - \boldsymbol{\tau}||_2^2\right).$$

After acquiring the actual starting position of each stroke, we are now able to generate a character token, or a ink track on an image, according to an adjusted ink model proposed by Revow et al. (1996). As we know, when writing down a character, the ink would flow to surrounding positions when a pen is pressed on a point. It would be necessary to model the diffusion process, otherwise the ink would be mistakenly considered as other strokes. The probability that color of a position (x, y) is white is

$$\mathbb{P}(\mathbf{X}_{(x,y)}^{(i)} = 0 | \mathbf{S}^{(i)}, \mathbf{Z}^{(i)}, \boldsymbol{\pi}^{(i)}) = \left(1 - Q\left(\mathbf{X}_{(x,y)}^{(i)} | \mathbf{S}^{(i)}, \mathbf{Z}^{(i)}, \boldsymbol{\pi}^{(i)}\right)\right)^{G},$$

and the probability of it being black is

$$\mathbb{P}(\mathbf{X}_{(x,y)}^{(i)} = 1 | \mathbf{S}^{(i)}, \mathbf{Z}^{(i)}, \boldsymbol{\pi}^{(i)}) = 1 - \mathbb{P}(\mathbf{X}_{(x,y)}^{(i)} = 0 | \mathbf{S}^{(i)}, \mathbf{Z}^{(i)}, \boldsymbol{\pi}^{(i)}).$$

The form of Q will be defined later and it can be intuitively viewed as a mixture of random noises and the influence from all the m strokes.

Heuristically, if the track of a stroke is distant from position (x, y), it is unlikely that $\mathbf{X}_{(x,y)}$ is black due to such stroke. A Gaussian distribution can be used to express this heuristic, in which, as the distance becomes larger, the probability drops rapidly. As a single stroke traverses across many pixels of an image, which results in a high complexity, the ink model discretizes continuous strokes to multiple beads. Take a vertical line as an example, we can use multiple points or beads along it to approximate the stroke, instead of a complete line. In this way, we can control the number of beads to be sampled along the line. We can define Q as

$$Q(\mathbf{X}_{(x,y)}^{(i)} | \mathbf{S}^{(i)}, \mathbf{Z}^{(i)}, \boldsymbol{\pi}^{(i)}) = \frac{\beta}{R^2} + (1 - \beta) \sum_{j=1}^{m} \pi_j^{(i)} V(\mathbf{X}_{(x,y)}^{(i)} | S_j^{(i)}, Z_j^{(i)}),$$

$$V(\mathbf{X}_{(x,y)}^{(i)} | S_j^{(i)}, Z_j^{(i)}) = \frac{1}{B} \sum_{b=1}^{B} N(\mathbf{X}_{(x,y)}^{(i)} | C_b + Z_j^{(i)}, \sigma_b^2 \mathbf{I}),$$

where B is the number of beads to induce the stroke shape and $C_b \in \mathbb{R}^2$ is a bead coordinate for stroke S_i.

Inference for BPL

As the BPL approach is classified under the one-shot learning paradigm, the setting is the same as the general case of one-shot learning. In our model, we have one observation $\mathbf{X}^l$ of each character type from the target domain and several observations of character types from a source domain. Based on the labeled data, the model makes an inference for unlabeled character tokens $\mathbf{X}^u$. Then a Markov chain Monte Carlo process along with the Metropolis-Hastings algorithm can be used to make an inference in BPL for a newly arriving sample, in order to draw a final conclusion on which character is seen by the system.

13.5　Poor Resource Learning

13.5.1　Overview

In machine learning, "few-shot learning" and "zero-shot learning" are normally used to describe learning methods suffering the insufficiency of training data in computer vision applications. However, similar scenarios occur frequently in natural language processing (NLP) tasks as well. In the NLP community, researchers resort to other terminologies such as "poor resource learning," "zero resource learning" and "low resource learning," where the "resource" refers to the training data.

There are more than 7,000 languages in the world, most of which do not have any annotated data or corpus for building a NLP system. Treebank, a well-known parsed text corpus that is annotated with syntactic or semantic sentence structure, covers forty languages, which are still a small portion of the entire language set. Even within the scope of English language, there are many kinds of tasks in plenty of domains. Part of speech tagging and dependency parsing require distinctive formats of data, and sentiment analysis for political news or sports news also requires domain-specific texts. Thus, the poor-resource problem exists across not only different languages, but also tasks of the same language.

The poor-resource problem in NLP is not as easy to be addressed as the few-shot problem in computer vision. Even for humans, it is a long and tough trip to grasp a new language. We need to remember a large number of vocabulary and grammars. Fortunately, different languages more or less share some common characteristics in different levels. First, each lexicon in a language, often has a correspondence in another language. Second, at a higher level, every lexicons in each language can be categorized into universal types such as verbs, nouns and adjectives. Third, at the sentence level, the dependency relationship is shared across some languages. Therefore, it may be less painstaking if we have some specific background knowledge, where transfer learning can help learn a new task or language. Although poor-resource learning has been broadly applied to diverse NLP tasks, we only use machine translation as a typical example in this section.

13.5.2　Machine Translation

Research in machine translation community frequently encounters a major challenge that most languages in the world only have limited resources for training a machine learning model. Although there are ample English–Chinese and French–English parallel sentences to be used as samples, there are only scarce Chinese–Portuguese parallel sentences. Here, "parallel sentences" denotes a pair of sentences in two different languages that can be translated to each other. Direct mapping from a source language to a target language means that each pair of languages forms a unique learning task, which is independent of other pairs. As a consequence, it is not trivial to transfer knowledge from an already powerful machine-translation model to other poor-resource language translation tasks. Therefore, we should come up with a mechanism allowing for some form of mutual enhancement.

We first introduce a basic tool for translation tasks. The encoder-decoder framework (see Figure 13.5) has an inherent advantage to make it possible for various tasks to share the same components. Specifically, we can assign the same encoder to the same language whenever it acts as a source domain in a translation task, Such a design is plausible as no matter which language is taken as a target, the first step is to understand the semantic of the source sentence. Then, based on the semantic meaning that is independent of the language, we can transform the semantic to the target language.

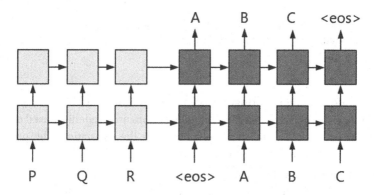

Figure 13.5 An illustration of the encoder-decoder architecture (adapted from Zoph and Knight [2016]). Light units denote the encoder and dark units are for the decoder

Low-Resource Learning

When some data resources are available for a target learning task in the form of parallel language pairs, it is possible to train a target-domain model. Zoph et al. (2016) train a parent model from a high-resource domain (i.e., source domain) in which a large number of French–English language pairs are available, as shown in Figure 13.6. A portion of parameters in the parent model is used to initialize the parameters in a child model that aims at the translation task in the low-resource Uzbek–English language pair. The parent model and the child model are constrained to share the identical architecture that is a two-layer encoder-decoder model with long short-term memory units. The model uses an attention component to look back at the source domain.

Zero Resource Learning

In an extreme case when there is no parallel corpus available in the target domain, we have a zero resource translation problem. In this case, some researchers find an intermediate or pivot language to bridge the gap. For instance, although it

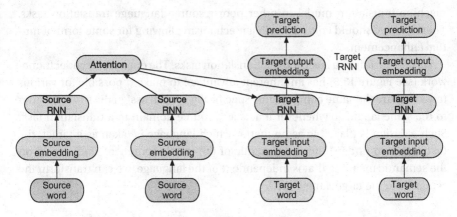

Figure 13.6 The architecture for machine translation by showing six blocks of parameters (adapted from Zoph et al. [2016])

is hard to find a Chinese–Portuguese parallel corpus, a few Chinese-English parallel copora and English-Portuguese parallel copora are available. Based on these corpora, we can employ English as a pivot to guide the translation. This process is similar to transitive transfer learning (TTL).

Specifically, given a Chinese sentence, we translate it to English first and then to Portuguese based on the English translation. However, connecting two translators trained on two corpora separately without any tailoring would still have some deficiencies. The most critical issue is that the quality of intermediate translations cannot be guaranteed Technically, the distribution of generated sentences may not match the distribution of raw sentences in a training corpus, even if they are drawn from the same domain.

Firat et al. (2016) introduce a pseudo-parallel corpus method to fine-tune the model parameters in order to alleviate the distribution difference to some extent. In their work, the researchers decompose the translating procedure from Spanish to French into a pipeline from Spanish to English and then from English to French. The pseudo-parallel corpus is generated as follows. First, they randomly select N sentence pairs from English to French. Second, they make use of a trained English–Spanish translator to restore corresponding sentences from the pivot language (English) to the source language (Spanish). Third, they exploit ground truth sentences in the target language (French) and the corresponding pseudo-expressions in the source language (Spanish) to train a translator with an encoder and a decoder initialized from Spanish–English and English–French translators respectively. Since a source sentence is created by the model instead of human experts, which may not be entirely accurate, it may mislead the subsequent learning process. In order to avoid impairing the robustness of the encoder and decoder trained from the ground truth data, they fix the parameters in the two components and only fine-tune the attention units. With such constraints, the attention units are expected to capture more general knowledge despite the fact that the source features may have some noises.

There are some concerns about the chosen language pairs as intermediate domains to conduct the TTL. For example, French people often acquires English more rapidly than Chinese people because English and French share some common characteristics in many aspects. When facing the translation task, despite the fact that there is no solid theory supporting the choice, we can expect that different pairs result in different effects in the transitive learning process.

13.6 Domain Generalization

13.6.1 Overview

Domain generalization handles a learning problem where data from the target task is inaccessible to the model during the training phase. Unlike domain adaptation, domain generalization makes no assumption on the availability of samples from the target domain. Our requirement is that the model can handle testing samples in target domain even no training samples are provided.

While it sounds difficult, with transfer learning, domain generalization can work based upon three strategies. The first strategy is based on domain similarity, which independently learns a model for each domain (Xu et al., 2014b). When a new domain comes, it identifies the most similar existing domain and applies the corresponding model to the new domain. The second strategy is a special case of parameter-based transfer learning in that all available domains engage in learning cooperatively by learning a set of domain-agnostic parameters that are shared among the multiple domains (Khosla et al., 2012; Li et al., 2017a). For each individual domain, there is still a set of domain-specific parameters. This strategy follows multitask learning paradigm. The third strategy is a variant of feature-based transfer learning, which assumes that, although the distribution over the original space varies from one domain to another, there exists an invariant distribution shared by all the domains (Ghifary et al., 2015). According to such an intuition, all domains are first projected into a common subspace. In the following sections, we will introduce two representative algorithms to illustrate these strategies.

13.6.2 Biased SVM

Khosla et al. (2012) employ a common visual world model for all domains to learn some general knowledge as well as a collection of specific models for each individual domain to capture the specialty of each domain. The visual world model may not be the most accurate on an individual task, but it performs well on all the tasks on average. Each task is solved by the visual world model and the corresponding domain-specific model jointly.

There are m source domains $\{\mathbb{S}_i\}_{i=1}^{m}$, and the i-th domain has a training data set $\mathscr{D}_{s_i}$. Each data set $\mathscr{D}_{s_i} = \{(\mathbf{x}_j^{s_i}, y_j^{s_i})\}_{j=1}^{n_{s_i}}$, consists of n_{s_i} training examples, where $\mathbf{x}_j^{s_i} \in \mathbb{R}^d$ is the j-th data point in $\mathscr{D}_{s_i}$ and $y_j^{s_i} \in \{-1,1\}$ is its label. In the proposed algorithm, they learn one set of parameters, $\Delta^{s_i} \in \mathbb{R}^d$, which corresponds to the bias for data set $\mathscr{D}_{s_i}$. It also learns a set of specific parameters, $\mathbf{w}_{vw}$, corresponding to the visual world. The parameters of the biased model is a combination of them, that is, $\mathbf{w}^{s_i} = \mathbf{w}_{vw} + \Delta^{s_i}$. The objective function is formulated as

$$\min_{\mathbf{w}_{vw}, \Delta^{s_i}, \xi, \rho} \quad \frac{1}{2}\|\mathbf{w}_{vw}\|^2 + \frac{\lambda}{2}\sum_{i=1}^{m}\|\Delta^{s_i}\|^2 + C_1\sum_{i=1}^{m}\sum_{j=1}^{n_{s_i}}\xi_j^{s_i} + C_2\sum_{i=1}^{m}\sum_{j=1}^{n_{s_i}}\rho_j^{s_i},$$

$$\text{subject to} \quad \mathbf{w}^{s_i} = \mathbf{w}_{vw} + \Delta^{s_i}, \tag{13.3}$$

$$y_j^{s_i}\mathbf{w}_{vw}\mathbf{x}_j^{s_i} \geq 1 - \xi_j^{s_i} \quad (i \in \{1,\cdots,m\}, j \in \{1,\cdots,n_{s_i}\}), \tag{13.4}$$

$$y_j^{s_i}\mathbf{w}^{s_i}\mathbf{x}_j^{s_i} \geq 1 - \rho_j^{s_i} \quad (i, \in \{1\cdots,m\}, j \in \{1,\cdots,n_{s_i}\}), \tag{13.5}$$

$$\xi_j^{s_i} \geq 0, \rho_j^{s_i} \geq 0 \quad (i \in \{1,\cdots,m\}, j \in \{1,\cdots,n_{s_i}\}),$$

where C_1, C_2 and λ are hyperparameters, and $\xi_j^{s_i}$ and $\rho_j^{s_i}$ are slack variables. (13.3) defines a linear relationship between $\mathbf{w}_{vw}$, $\mathbf{w}^{s_i}$ and Δ^{s_i}. (13.4) corresponds to the loss incurred across all data sets when using the visual world weights $\mathbf{w}_{vw}$, since the visual world model is expected to generalize across all data sets. (13.5) corresponds to the loss incurred by the private model.

13.6.3 Multi task Autoencoder

A multitask autoencoder (Ghifary et al., 2015) follows the essence of feature-based transfer learning. Basically, it assumes that variations across domains are generated from a common subspace. Although the mapping from the feature space to the label space varies from domain to domain, the mapping from the common subspace can be shared. To explore the subspace automatically, the multitask autoencoder employs an architecture derived from an autoencoder. The difference between the multitask autoencoder and the conventional autoencoder lies in the decoding part where the multitask autoencoder has different decoders for different domains. Recovering the subspace from a domain forms a task, so that there are multiple tasks to learn. The encoder is shared to ensure the consistency of the learned subspace. An example of the architecture is shown in Figure 13.7.

Ghifary et al. (2015) present a specific case. Here we introduce a generalized version to reflect its core idea. There are m source domains $\{\mathbb{S}\}_{i=1}^{m}$. Each of them

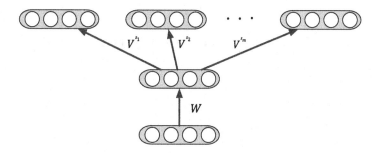

Figure 13.7 The architecture of the multitask autoencoder (adapted from Ghifary et al. [2015]), where all the domains share the same encoder and have separate decoders

has a training set $\mathscr{D}_{s_i} = \left\{ \mathbf{x}_j^{s_i} \right\}_{j=1}^{n_{s_i}}$. The encoder and decoders are defined as

$$\mathbf{h}_j^{s_i} = \sigma_{enc}(\mathbf{W}^\top \mathbf{x}_j^{s_i}),$$

$$f_{\Theta^{s_i}}(\mathbf{x}_i^{s_i}) = \sigma_{dec}(\mathbf{V}^{s_i \top} \mathbf{h}_j^{s_i}),$$

where $\Theta^{s_i} = \left\{ \mathbf{W}, \mathbf{V}^{s_i} \right\}$ contains the shared and individual parameters. The loss function is defined as

$$J(\Theta^{s_i}) = \sum_{j=1}^{n_{s_i}} l(f_{\Theta^{s_i}}(\mathbf{x}_j^{s_i}), \mathbf{x}_j^{s_i}).$$

The entire objective function is formulated as

$$\hat{\Theta}^{s_i} = \underset{\Theta^{s_i}}{\operatorname{argmin}} \sum_{i=1}^m J(\Theta^{s_i}) + \eta R(\Theta^{s_i}),$$

where $R(\Theta^{s_i})$ is a regularization term. Ghifary et al. (2015) use the squared l_2 norm regularization, that is, $R(\Theta^{s_i}) = \|\mathbf{W}\|_F^2 + \sum_{i=1}^m \|\mathbf{V}^{s_i}\|_F^2$. The SGD is applied to solve the objective function.

14

Lifelong Machine Learning

14.1 Introduction

In the past decades, there have been significant advances in machine learning. However, there is a missing part in most proposed learning algorithms if we compare them with how humans learn to solve problems. We can observe that humans solve problems by continuously learning and improving their capabilities for various tasks in their lifetime. In contrast, most contemporary machine learning theory and algorithms still only focus on a one-time solution to learning problems. We can see many examples in text classification, image classification, image segmentation and so on.

But humans typically learn to solve various problems in a sequential way, one after another, and in a continuous way as well. For example, a musician might learn how to play many different instruments and study how to compose and perform different music year after year. Because of their ability to continuously learn, musicians can learn how to play guitar quickly if he or she already knows how to play the piano, and read and compose music. We call the paradigm in which learning happens continuously such that later learning can benefit from previous learning "lifelong machine learning."

An important reason for why lifelong machine learning is important for machine learning is that a large amount of labeled data from diverse learning tasks become available in time. That is largely driven by the prevalence of data collection devices such as cameras and mobile phones, and the Internet of Things technology. Deep learning requires a lot of labeled data to learn complex models, and these data can increasingly enable the learning to be increasingly effective. In addition, over time, the prevalence of highly popular machine learning platforms such as Tensorflow (Abadi et al., 2016a) along with more powerful and cheaper computing hardware makes developing machine learning much easier and more efficient. These are the context to make lifelong machine learning feasible. In this chapter, we will explain in detail the lifelong machine learning paradigm.

Lifelong machine learning has a long history in machine learning, mainly in the transfer learning community (Thrun, 1995; Ruvolo and Eaton, 2013; Silver et al., 2013; Chen and Liu, 2016). We will review some of these main approaches.

14.2 Lifelong Machine Learning: A Definition

In this section, we start by giving the formal definitions of lifelong machine learning first, following the formalism in the work by Silver et al. (2013).

Lifelong machine learning does not assume the same training and test data distribution as assumed in traditional machine learning. Instead, lifelong machine learning studies the complicated scenario where a large number of tasks come over time and therefore a new knowledge retention strategy as well as more sophisticated knowledge transfer approaches need be designed. We first give a formal definition of lifelong machine learning.

Definition 14.1 (lifelong machine learning)   Lifelong machine learning is a machine learning system that completes multiple learning tasks $\mathcal{T} = \{T_1, T_2, T_3, \cdots\}$ from different domains $\mathcal{D} = \{D_1, D_2, D_3, \cdots\}$ over time, and solves the later tasks more effectively with the help of previously solved tasks.

A typical lifelong machine learning system (see Figure 14.1) uses a knowledge base $\mathcal{KB}$ that stores previously learned knowledge learned over time. At time t, the system receives a task T_t coming from a corresponding domain D_t. A typical lifelong machine learning system first builds a new model for T_t based on the training data from D_t and the knowledge in $\mathcal{KB}$. Then, lifelong machine learning extracts the transferable knowledge from (D_t, T_t) and updates the knowledge base $\mathcal{KB}$. The updated knowledge base $\mathcal{KB}$ is used to refine the models trained for the previous $t-1$ tasks.

There are two essential elements for a successful lifelong machine learning system. First, there needs be a retention system for learned knowledge on previous tasks to store the previous examples and models in the universal knowledge base. Second, there needs be a selective transfer mechanism on how to select the previous domains and tasks to transfer to the current task, which is the domain knowledge part at the center.

Knowledge retention enables lifelong machine learning from the perspective of the knowledge representation for the universal knowledge. Learned knowledge can be stored in various forms. The simplest method of retaining task knowledge is in a functional form such as the training examples (Silver and Mercer, 1996). An advantage of functional knowledge is the accuracy and purity of the knowledge to allow for effective retention.

A disadvantage of functional knowledge is that there may be need for a large amount of storage space that is searched frequently, which is time consuming. Alternatively, we can retain the models learned previously in some form understandable by the current task; for example, the previous knowledge can be a

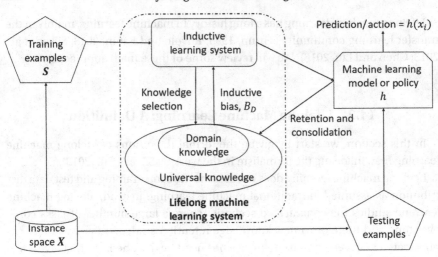

Figure 14.1 The overall architecture of a lifelong machine learning system (adapted from Silver et al. [2013])

compressed form that has the same representation as the current task. The advantage of the latter approach is that the compact size of the retained model requires relative small space for storing the previous training examples. In addition, having a model allows for a more efficient way for the generalization of models. In the past, many knowledge representation forms have been used for knowledge retention, including neural networks and probability distributions.

Transfer learning enables lifelong machine learning from the perspective knowledge reuse. The knowledge transfer component in lifelong machine learning pushes the limit of transfer learning in two directions. Instead of leveraging the limited knowledge obtained from selected previous source tasks, lifelong machine learning targets the large-scale knowledge transfer from all related source tasks learned over time. An important issue includes how to identify related tasks to transfer knowledge from and scale the knowledge transfer to hundreds of source tasks.

14.3   Lifelong Machine Learning through Invariant Knowledge

A good example of lifelong machine learning is in Thrun (1995), which describes one of the earliest lifelong machine learning systems. In this work on lifelong machine learning, a collection of related learning problems is encountered over the lifetime of the learner. When learning the next task, the lifelong learner may employ the invariant knowledge gathered in previous learning sessions to enhance the learning of the next task. This process iterates as the overall lifelong machine learning system evolves.

Thrun (1995) defines a support set of previously learned tasks along with their training examples. For any pair of training example, they are considered candidates of a training data set for the invariant function if their outcomes agree on that task. These are the positive examples. When examples' outcome disagree, they constitute the negative examples.

Given a set of previously encountered tasks, their training examples can be used to define an invariant function to be learned via a neural network algorithm. When learning the new function for the next task, the invariance network can be used to improve the effectiveness of training by providing additional information on gradient descent.

In the case of object recognition, for example, there may be many images of objects such as shoes, hats, and so on to be learned. Having learned to recognize images of shoes, for example, certain image features can be identified as invariant, which can in turn be used to recognize hats.

14.4 Lifelong Machine Learning in Sentiment Classification

Perhaps the simplest and most commonly used strategy to represent and store knowledge is to treat the supervised information, such as labeled data, as the knowledge directly. In this framework, the supervised information obtained from previous tasks are stored in a database. When a new task comes, the supervised information will be used as auxiliary information to help build a model for the new task.

As an example, Chen et al. (2015) propose a lifelong sentiment classification method for the classification of user comments based on the naive Bayes method. Sentiment classification is the task for classifying user product reviews or opinions into positive or negative orientations. Many products have some product-specific terms to express different opinions, such as "blurred" that can be used to express a negative opinion about a camera and "inspiring" that gives a very high praise to a book. Sentiment classification is a very important task in natural language process where transfer learning techniques are widely used for cross-domain classification; the task is to classify the user opinions in a new domain using the knowledge gained from a related domain. Chen et al. (2015) store two types of supervised information in the knowledge base: document-level knowledge and domain-level knowledge. The document-level supervised information is the frequency of a word w appearing among the positive examples (denoted as $n_{+,w}^{KB}$) and negative examples $n_{-,w}^{KB}$, respectively, in all previous tasks. The document-level word frequency serves as a priori knowledge about the sentiment of a word.

However, as we discussed earlier, sentiment classification is very product-specific in which the same word might express totally different sentiments for different products. For example, "fast" is usually used to appraise the performance of a computer while also being used to express a negative opinion about a bad battery, such as "battery drains fast."

In order to overcome this bias, domain-level knowledge can be added to ensure that only unambiguous words are stored in the knowledge base. The domain-level knowledge can be viewed as how likely a word expresses the same sentiment in different domains. More specifically, $m_{+,w}^{KB}$ and $m_{-,w}^{KB}$ denote the numbers of domains in which word w appears more in positive and negative examples, respectively. In the knowledge transfer step, $n_{+,w}^{KB}$ and $n_{-,w}^{KB}$ are used to compute the positive and negative word counts combined with the empirical word counts. The computed word counts are then used to estimate the conditional probability $P(+|w)$ and $P(-|w)$. The domain-level knowledge $m_{+,w}^{KB}$ and $m_{-,w}^{KB}$ is used to select the words that at least appear in more than a certain number of different domains.

Besides the classification problem, shared supervised knowledge has also been used to build topic models in transfer learning (Chen and Liu, 2014a, 2014b; Wang et al., 2016b). Topic models, such as probabilistic latent semantic analysis (PLSA) (Hofmann, 1999) and latent Dirichlet allocation (LDA), are statistical models used to discover topics from a collection of text documents. A topic is defined as a list of words with the probabilities representing how likely the words belong to that topic. PLSA assumes the following generative process for word and document co-occurrences:

- select a document d_i with probability $\mathbb{P}(D = d_i)$,
- draw a topic z_k with probability $\mathbb{P}(Z = z_k | D = d_i)$,
- select a word w_j with probability $\mathbb{P}(W = w_j | Z = z_k)$.

The probabilities of $\mathbb{P}(D = d_i)$, $\mathbb{P}(Z = z_k | D = d_i)$ and $\mathbb{P}(W = w_j | Z = z_k)$ over $\{d_i, z_k, w_j\}_{i,j,k}$ are estimated by maximizing the likelihood of all observed word and document co-occurrences.

In the lifelong topic modeling (LTM) (Chen and Liu, 2016), a must-link, which implies that the corresponding two words should belong to the same topic, is extracted from previous topic models and used to help train better topic models for future tasks. More specifically, the LTM algorithm has two steps: prior topic generation and topic modeling in test domain. Those two steps correspond to knowledge retention and knowledge transfer, respectively, as discussed before.

In the LTM algorithm, prior topic generation or knowledge retention is done via a standard topic model such as LDA. This model is used to learn a set of topics $\mathbf{z}^t = (z_1^t, z_2^t, \cdots, z_{k^t}^t)$ for each domain $\mathbf{d}^t = (d_1^t, d_2^t, \cdots, d_{n^t}^t)$. The learned topics from different domains are put together to form a unified topic set $\mathcal{Z} = \bigcup_{t=1}^{T} \mathbf{z}^t$. This unified topic set $\mathcal{Z}$ can be viewed as the knowledge base used in many lifelong machine learning algorithms.

In the topic modeling approach to knowledge transfer, a transfer learning algorithm is used to transfer knowledge from the knowledge base $\mathcal{Z}$ to a current domain $\mathbf{d}^{T+1}$. First, a standard topic modeling algorithm is used to learn initial topics

$\mathbf{z}^{T+1} = (z_1^{T+1}, z_2^{T+1}, \cdots, z_{k^{T+1}}^{T+1})$ for the current domain $\mathbf{d}^{T+1} = (d_1^{T+1}, d_2^{T+1}, \cdots, d_{n^{T+1}}^{T+1})$. Then, for each topic $z_k^{T+1} \in \mathbf{z}^{T+1}$, its similar topics from the knowledge base $\mathcal{Z}$ will be identified based on the Kulback–Leibler divergence between z_k^{T+1} and any topic in $\mathcal{Z}$. The similar topics are put together to form a topic set $\mathcal{M}_k^{T+1}$. A frequent item set-mining algorithm (Han and Kamber, 2000) is then used to find the words that co-occur in many different topics from $\mathcal{M}_k^{T+1}$. The intuition is that, if two words appear together many times in different topics, we should be confident to say that they are related. By limiting the topics to the similar topics $\mathcal{M}_k^{T+1}$, we can increase the chance of successful transfer by eliminating unrelated topics. All the word pairs learned from the previous process for all the topics are used to generate a "must-link" set, which is used as the prior knowledge to guide the topic mining for current domain $\mathbf{d}^{T+1}$. In LTM, a specific type of topic model, the generalized Pólya Urn model, is adopted to incorporate this knowledge in its Gibbs sampling process to encourage such a pair of words to be in the same topic. Figure 14.2 shows the architecture of LTM.

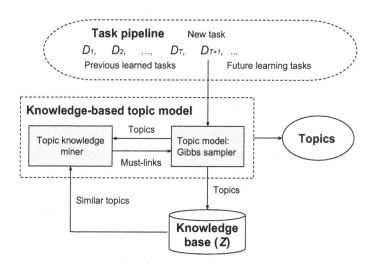

Figure 14.2 The architecture of the LTM model (adapted from Chen and Liu [2016])

Besides the "must-link" constraint, the "cannot-link" constraint is also used as knowledge for topic modeling in lifelong machine learning. Chen and Liu (2014a) propose a new LTM called AMC that stands for topic modeling with automatically generated must-links and cannot-links. In addition to adopting cannot-links as the knowledge, AMC learns must-links by using information from past tasks instead of the current task only. Because the LTM model needs a certain amount of data from a current task to learn the initial topics and also the must-links, learning must-links without the data from a current task can increase the coverage of the algorithm to the problems where very limited data are available in the current task. However, without those data, the learned must-links might be unrelated to the current task and therefore might hurt the performance of the knowledge transfer. Although the must-links are learned from past tasks only in AMC, these cannot-links are learned together with the topic modeling.

The overall architecture of AMC is presented in Figure 14.3. The design of AMC is similar to that of LTM. But, as AMC does not use any data from the target task to learn must-links, the MustLinkMiner component in Figure 14.3 is different from that in LTM. In AMC, MustLinkMiner uses a multiple minimum supports frequent item set mining (MS-FIM) algorithm (Liu et al., 1999) to extract must-links between two words. The reason that the traditional single minimum-support frequent item set-mining algorithm does not work for this problem is that generic topics, such as price, quality, customer service and so on, are shared among many topics. That means the frequency of generic topics are much higher than specific ones that pose a challenge to learn must-links for both generic and specific topics. The MS-FIM algorithm is applied to mine a frequent item set that contains a set of terms that have appeared many times in the knowledge base.

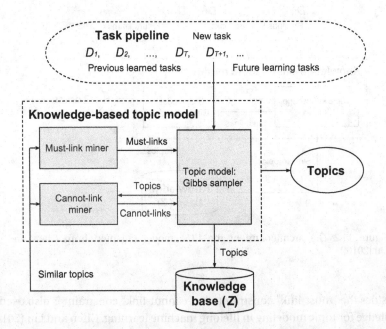

Figure 14.3 The architecture of the AMC model (adapted from Chen and Liu [2016])

Different from LTM, AMC mines both must-links and cannot-links. As the potential cannot-links for a term w can be any words in the vocabulary list except the ones that co-occur with w in a document before, the candidate set is too large to consider directly without any a priori knowledge. In AMC, the topics from the current task are served as the candidate pool for mining the cannot-links. Formally, given a knowledge base $\mathcal{Z}$ that contains all the topics from previous tasks and $z_i^{T+1} \in \mathbf{z}^{T+1}$ from the current task, AMC only considers two top terms w_i and w_j from $z_i^{T+1} \in \mathbf{z}^{T+1}$ as the candidates, and then uses the topics in the knowledge base $z_i^{T+1} \in \mathbf{z}^{T+1}$ to decide whether a cannot-link should be added to the two terms or not. To determine the cannot-link relation, AMC examines all topics from $\mathcal{Z}$ and labels the term pairs that seldom appear together in the topics of $\mathcal{Z}$ as cannot-linked terms. Once AMC gets both the must-links and cannot-links, the same knowledge-based topic modeling algorithm used in the LTM can be used to learn a better topic model by incorporating the knowledge as a priori knowledge to guide the topic modeling.

14.5 Shared Model Components as Multi-task Learning

The shared model component approach is inspired by the hierarchical models in Bayesian statistics. These works assume that the models of all tasks are generated by a high-level hidden model. This assumption can be represented as

$$\forall i \quad \boldsymbol{\theta}^i \sim \mathbf{M}, \tag{14.1}$$

where $\boldsymbol{\theta}^i$ is the model for the i-th task and $\mathbf{M}$ is the high-level hidden model. A similar idea is used in many multi-task learning methods (Zhang and Yang, 2017b) to share knowledge among tasks.

In the ELLA framework (Ruvolo and Eaton, 2013), a model dictionary $\mathbf{M} \in \mathbb{R}^{d \times k}$ shared by different tasks is used to represent latent model components. The model parameter $\boldsymbol{\theta}^t$ for a task t is represented as a linear combination of latent model components in $\mathbf{M}$. If $\mathbf{s}^t \in \mathbb{R}^k$ denotes the linear combination weight, $\boldsymbol{\theta}^t$ can be represented as

$$\boldsymbol{\theta}^t = \mathbf{M}\mathbf{s}^t. \tag{14.2}$$

Because $\mathbf{M}$ is shared among all tasks, which are learned continuously, after seeing more training data from different tasks, $\mathbf{M}$ should be able to improve over time.

More specifically, define $\{\mathbf{x}_i^t, y_i^t\}_{i=1}^{n^t}$ as the training set for task t. The objective function of ELLA is formulated as follows

$$\frac{1}{T}\sum_{t=1}^{T}\min_{\mathbf{s}^t}\left\{\frac{1}{n^t}\sum_{i-1}^{n^t}L(f(\mathbf{x}_i^t;\mathbf{M}\mathbf{s}^t),y_i^t)+\mu\|\mathbf{s}^t\|_1\right\},$$

where T is the total number of tasks seen so far and L is the loss function.

However, because this objective function depends on all of the previous training data and every model $\mathbf{s}^t$ also depends on the shared model components $\mathbf{M}$, the optimization for this objective function is very expensive to compute as more tasks arrive. Ruvolo and Eaton (2013) use approximation techniques to ensure the computational efficiency in the lifelong-learning setting.

Wang and Pineau (2016) extend ELLA to cover nonlinear cases where the model components are not limited to linear hypotheses. More specifically, instead of learning a dictionary of basis vectors as in the work by Kumar and Daumé III (2012), Wang and Pineau (2016) propose the learning of a more generalized dictionary $\mathbf{F} = [f^1, f^2, \cdots, f^T]$ that contains a set of basis functions in a functional space where $\{f^t\}_{t=1}^T$ can be any hypothesis instead of the linear hypothesis assumed in the ELLA. The objective function of the proposed method is formulated as

$$\min_{\mathbf{F},\{\gamma^t\}} \sum_{t=1}^{T} \sum_{i=1}^{n^t} L(\langle \mathbf{F}(\mathbf{x}_i^t), \gamma^t \rangle, y_i^t) + \mu \sum_{t=1}^{T} \|\gamma^t\|_1. \tag{14.3}$$

By relaxing the linear assumption for the model, Wang and Pineau (2016) can handle more complicated learning tasks that expand the scope of the "shared model components" approach.

This line of research on lifelong machine learning follows the perspective of multi-task learning. By modeling the different tasks hierarchically, the knowledge retention step can be easily expressed as the shared high-level hidden model. However, similar to many hidden models, in this approach, it is hard to understand the learned knowledge stored in the knowledge base $\mathcal{KB}$. In addition, it might be an oversimplification to assume that a large number of tasks share a set of base model components for complex lifelong machine learning problems. For example, learning how to classify documents should be quite different from learning how to classify images.

14.6 Never-Ending Language Learning

Lifelong machine learning must scale to deal with a large number of tasks. The outputs of these tasks are predictions of various forms, which may also arrive in large volume. These model outputs can be used as the auxiliary in lifelong machine learning. They can be used as auxiliary features or constraints to help improve the performance of the current task.

The never-ending language learning system (NELL) has been running around the clock at Carnegie Mellon University since 2010 (Carlson et al., 2010; Mitchell et al., 2015) to learn concepts from web pages on the World Wide Web. NELL gives a prime example of lifelong machine learning by making use of the auxiliary information continuously to increase the knowledge base. NELL is designed to learn important concepts from the web pages of the World Wide Web by trawling millions of the pages and learning important concepts and their relations in a continuous manner (thus never-ending). Once it learns a new concept, it relates the concept with the concepts already learned in its knowledge base, and thus its knowledge base keeps growing. For example, when seeing the term "Peking University," it realizes that the word refers to a university in China because of the upper case for university used in the phrase, and Peking is a name used to refer to the city of Beijing in the past.

In the work by Mitchell et al. (2015), the never-ending learning problem $\mathscr{L}$ is defined as a set of learning tasks and a set of coupling constraints among solutions to these learning tasks. More specifically, a NELL learning task is defined as a tuple $\mathscr{L}_i = \{\mathscr{T}_i, P_i, \mathscr{E}_i\}$, where $\mathscr{T}_i$ is the performance task, P_i is a pre-defined metric for task $\mathscr{T}_i$ and $\mathscr{E}_i$ is the training experience. $\mathscr{T}_i = (\mathbf{X}_i, \mathbf{Y}_i)$ defines the problem domain and model space $f_i : \mathbf{X}_i \to \mathbf{Y}_i$. The performance metric P_i is used to measure the performance of each model f_i. $\mathscr{E}_i$ is the training data used to train the model. The goal of the learning task $\mathscr{T}_i$ is to learn an optimal model f_i^* for the i-th learning task given the training data $\mathscr{E}_i$ and the predefined metrics P_i as

$$f_i^* = \arg\max_{f \in \mathscr{F}_i} P_i(f), \tag{14.4}$$

where $\mathscr{F}_i$ is the set of all possible models.

In NELL, many different learning tasks are trained together twenty-four hours a day since early 2010. All the learning tasks are linked together through the relational constraints derived from the model outputs. These different learning tasks are learned in five main learning functional categories listed as follows:

- Phrase classification: NELL is given an initial ontology defining 280 categories such as "sport" and "athlete." NELL learns different predictive functions to classify noun phrases to one or more categories in the ontology. That means each noun phrase (e.g., apple) can be assigned one or multiple classes (e.g., food and company). In order to leverage the power of co-training, NELL builds five different predictive functions for each category based on five different views of the data, and lets them reinforce each other in a co-training (Blum and Mitchell, 1998) manner to improve the learning.

- Relation classification: NELL is also given 327 distinct relations defined between two noun phrases. The goal of relation classification is to learn functions that can predict whether two noun phrases can be correlated with given relations. For example, <"Shanghai", "China"> satisfies the relation "CityLocatedInCountry(x,y)."

- Entity resolution: NELL can predict whether two noun phrases are synonyms. Thus, these phrases should be identified to represent the same meaning.

- Inference rules among belief (i.e., rule) triples: Functions that predict new beliefs. NELL represents a function that maps the current knowledge base of NELL to new beliefs by a collection of restricted Horn clause rules learned by the path ranking algorithm (PRA) system, which can derive new beliefs based on old ones (Ni et al. 2011).

All of these functions can be represented as a main learning task $f : \mathbf{X} \to \mathbf{Y}$. The performance metric of each task, that is, P_i, is simply the accuracy of the corresponding model.

In addition to a wide range of learning tasks, another unique component of NELL is how it connects different concepts. These relations are formulated as constraints, listed as follows in the form of "coupling":

- Multiview co-training coupling: NELL builds models through different views of noun phrases. This provides a natural co-training setting where the predictions of different models are enforced to be the same as long as the input noun phrases or noun phrases pairs are the same.
- Subset/superset coupling: NELL enforces that the model prediction for a category should be consistent with that of a parent category.
- Multi-label mutual exclusion coupling: Similar to subset/superset coupling, NELL enforces the mutual exclusion between model predictions from two mutually exclusive categories.
- Coupling relations to their argument types: A relation is defined on top of two noun phrase categories. For example, "CityLocated-InCountry(x,y)" can only be defined for "City" and "Country." This adds another set of constraints for the inputs of relation learning tasks.
- Horn clause coupling: A Horn clause is a set of logic literals in which at least one literal is positive. All the Horn clauses that are used to infer new knowledge-based beliefs from the existing ones are used as coupling constraints for NELL.

From these descriptions, those constraints are derived directly or indirectly from the outputs of distinct learning tasks. The overall architecture of NELL is shown in Figure 14.4.

A distinguishing feature of the NELL system is its knowledge base, which is the core of NELL. In NELL, the knowledge base includes all the beliefs predicted by different models with high confidence. Over time, millions of coupling constraints have been constructed to link all the tasks. The knowledge retention and knowledge transfer processes are engineered to work in sync. NELL uses an expectation-maximization-style learning paradigm (Dempster et al., 1977) to iteratively perform the knowledge retention (E-step) and knowledge transfer (M-step). In the E-step, the parameters of all models are fixed and the models are used to output the current best prediction for various tasks.

For example, after determining whether "Shanghai" is a "City" and "China" is a country, it infers that <"Shanghai", "China"> satisfies the relation "CityLocated-InCountry(x,y)." The predictions are called beliefs in NELL. Each prediction comes with a confidence score that represents how confident the model is about the prediction. If the confidence score of a belief is higher than a certain predetermined threshold, NELL adds it to the knowledge base as the new knowledge.

In addition to adding highly confident model predictions as knowledge components, NELL also includes an active learning component to acquire supervised knowledge from humans. In the M-step, all the beliefs in the knowledge base are

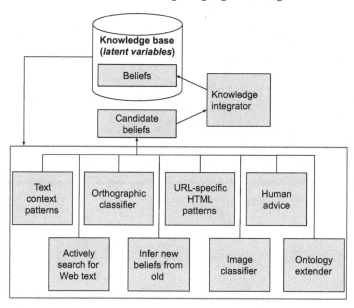

Figure 14.4 The architecture of NELL

used to construct the coupling constraints. For example, if <"Shanghai", "China"> satisfies the relation "CityLocated-InCountry(x,y)," "Shanghai" must be a "City" and "China" must be a country. The coupling constraints serve as an inductive bias that is the key for machine learning models. The M-step updates the parameters of all models based on training data and the coupling constraints.

PART II

APPLICATIONS OF TRANSFER LEARNING

Recently, many machine learning algorithms have been modified to achieve the differential privacy, including logistic regression (Chaudhuri et al., 2011), tree models (Emekçi et al., 2007; Fong and Weber-Jahnke, 2012; Jagannathan et al., 2012), deep neural networks (Shokri and Shmatikov, 2015; Abadi et al., 2016b), and so on.

When applying transfer learning, however, the issue becomes more critical as transfer learning models typically map across different domains and data sets and bridges different organizations. Therefore, transfer learning faces user privacy challenge as well, especially when it is applied across different organizations. Designing differentially privacy-preserving mechanisms to extract and transfer knowledge becomes a challenge. In this chapter, we first introduce the definition of differential privacy as well as related differentially private algorithms, and then introduce some state-of-the-art methods for privacy-preserving transfer learning.

15.2   Differential Privacy

15.2.1   Definition

Differential privacy (Dwork et al., 2006b; Dwork and Roth, 2014) has been established as a rigorous standard to guarantee the privacy for algorithms that access private data. Intuitively, given a privacy budget ϵ, an algorithm preserves ϵ-differential privacy if changing one entry in the data set does not change the log-likelihood of any output of the algorithm by more than ϵ (see Figure 15.1). Formally, it is defined as follows.

Definition 15.1 (differential privacy)   A randomized mechanism $\mathcal{M}$ is ϵ-differentially private if for any output t of $\mathcal{M}$ and for any two input data sets $\mathcal{D}_1, \mathcal{D}_2$ differing by one element, $\mathbb{P}(\mathcal{M}(\mathcal{D}_1) = t) \leq e^{\epsilon} \, \mathbb{P}(\mathcal{M}(\mathcal{D}_2) = t)$.

To meet the ϵ-differential privacy guarantee, careful perturbations or noises usually need to be added to the learning algorithm. A smaller ϵ provides the stricter privacy guarantee but at the expense of heavier noise, leading to larger performance deterioration (Chaudhuri et al., 2011; Bassily et al., 2014). To solve this issue, a relaxed version of ϵ-differentially private, called (ϵ, δ)-differentially privacy where δ measures the loss in the privacy, was proposed in the work by Dwork and Roth (2014) and defined as follows.

Definition 15.2 ((ϵ, δ)-differentially private)   A randomized mechanism $\mathcal{M}$ is (ϵ, δ)-differentially private if for any output t of $\mathcal{M}$ and for any two input data sets $\mathcal{D}_1, \mathcal{D}_2$ differing by one element, $\mathbb{P}(\mathcal{M}(\mathcal{D}_1) = t) \leq e^{\epsilon} \, \mathbb{P}(\mathcal{M}(\mathcal{D}_2) = t) + \delta$.

In the following, we introduce some differentially private learning algorithms.

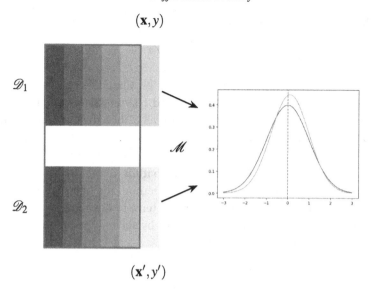

$(\mathbf{x}, y)$

Figure 15.1 When using a differentially private algorithm, the distributions of outputs of two data sets that only differs in one single entry are close to each other

15.2.2 Privacy-Preserving Regularized Empirical Risk Minimization

For a training data set $\mathscr{D}$, the regularized empirical risk minimization (ERM) chooses a predictor f over a hypothesis space $\mathscr{H}$ to minimize the regularized empirical loss as

$$\min_{f \in \mathscr{H}} J(f, \mathscr{D}) = \frac{1}{n} \sum_{j=1}^{n} l(f(\mathbf{x}_j), y_j) + \lambda r(f), \tag{15.1}$$

where the regularization term $r(f)$ prevents the overfitting and λ is a regularization parameter. Regularized ERM methods are widely used in practice, for example, the logistic regression and support vector machines. For simplicity, in the following we only focus on linear functions, that is, $f(\mathbf{x}) = \mathbf{w}^T \mathbf{x}$.

In the following sections, we introduce several techniques for creating privacy-preserving ERM algorithms, including output perturbation, objective perturbation and gradient perturbation.

Output Perturbation

The output perturbation method (Chaudhuri et al., 2011) is derived from the sensitivity method proposed by Dwork et al. (2006b), which is a general method for generating a privacy-preserving approximation to any function. For the minimizer $\mathbf{w}^* = \operatorname{argmin}_{\mathbf{w}} J(\mathbf{w}, \mathscr{D})$, it outputs a predictor

$$\mathbf{w}_{priv} = \mathbf{w}^* + \mathbf{b},$$

where **b** is random noise with density

$$\mathbb{P}(\mathbf{b}) = \frac{1}{\alpha} e^{-\beta \|\mathbf{b}\|_2}, \tag{15.2}$$

where α is a normalizing constant and $\beta = \frac{n\epsilon\lambda}{2}$. Chaudhuri et al. (2011) prove that, if the regularizer $r(\cdot)$ is differentiable and 1-strongly convex, and the loss l is convex and differentiable with $|l'(z)| \leq 1$ for all z, then the output perturbation method provides ϵ-differential privacy.

Objective Perturbation

Differently from the output perturbation method, the objective perturbation method (Chaudhuri et al., 2011) adds a noise term to the objective function. Instead of minimizing J, it learns the predictor by solving the following objective function as

$$\mathbf{w}_{priv} = \underset{\mathbf{w}}{\text{argmin}} \, J(\mathbf{w}, \mathscr{D}) + \frac{1}{n} \mathbf{b}^T \mathbf{w} + \frac{1}{2} \Delta \|\mathbf{w}\|_2^2,$$

where **b** is sampled according to (15.2) with $\beta = \epsilon'/2$ and ϵ', Δ are computed as:

(1) $\epsilon' = \epsilon - \log(1 + \frac{2c}{n\lambda} + \frac{c^2}{n^2\lambda^2})$.

(2) If $\epsilon' > 0$, then $\Delta = 0$, else $\Delta = \frac{c}{n(e^{\epsilon/4}-1)} - \lambda$ and $\epsilon' = \epsilon/2$.

Here, c is a constant. Similarly, if $r(\cdot)$ is 1-strongly convex and doubly differentiable, and $l(\cdot)$ is convex and doubly differentiable with $|l'(z)| \leq 1$ and $|l''(z)| \leq c$ for all z, the objective perturbation method is ϵ-differentially private. Specifically, if the regularized logistic regression is used as the ERM model, that is $r(\mathbf{w}) = \frac{1}{2}\|\mathbf{w}\|_2^2$ and $l(z) = \log(1 + e^{-z})$, then $c = \frac{1}{4}$.

15.2.3 Gradient Perturbation

As discussed earlier, the output perturbation and objective perturbation methods require the objective function to be convex with a strongly convex regularizer. This precondition is not satisfied in some algorithms such as deep models. To solve this problem, Abadi et al. (2016b) propose a gradient perturbation method to guarantee differential privacy in deep learning algorithms.

Specifically, in the t-th iteration, a group of samples L_t are randomly selected and their gradients $g_t(\mathbf{x}_i)$ are clipped to an upper bound C as

$$\bar{g}_t(\mathbf{x}_i) = g_t(\mathbf{x}_i) / \max(1, \|g_t(\mathbf{x}_i)\|_2 / C),$$

where $\mathbf{x}_i \in L_t$. Then random Gaussian noises are added to this group as

$$\tilde{g}_t = \frac{1}{L} (\sum_i \bar{g}_t(\mathbf{x}_i) + \mathcal{N}(0, \sigma^2 C^2 \mathbf{I})),$$

where L is the size of L_t and σ is a constant. The gradient $\tilde{g}_t$ is used to update the model. Abadi et al. (2016b) prove that, with carefully selected instance sampling rate, σ, and the iteration number, the gradient perturbation method guarantees the (ϵ, δ)-differential privacy.

15.3 Privacy-Preserving Transfer Learning

15.3.1 Problem Setting

In many transfer learning applications, the source domains and the target domain can be located at different organizations such that information cannot be transported directly to each other due to the privacy concern. In this chapter, we will discuss several settings where the user privacy issues are critical.

Target improvement In most transfer learning applications, one or several source data sets are used to help improve the performance of the model trained in the target domain. Thus, there is a need to design a privacy-preserving mechanism for extracting and transferring the knowledge from source domains to preserve the leak of sensitive information.

Multiparty learning In this scenario, several organizations wish to build a model together, while keeping their sensitive data private.

Multitask learning In multitask learning, each task borrows the information from each other to improve its learning model. So, the privacy mechanism needs to guarantee that each side does not leak its privacy.

15.3.2 Target Improvement

Differentially Private Hypothesis Transfer Learning

Wang et al. (2018d) propose to train local differentially private logistic models and transfer them to the target domain, as illustrated in Figure 15.2. To do this, a public data set (not necessarily labeled) that is accessible to both source domains and the target domain is needed, and it serves as an information intermediary. Specifically, this model takes the following steps:

(1) Each source domain uses its labeled samples to train a differentially private logistic regression model $\mathbf{w}_{priv}^{s_i}$ under parameters ϵ. All the hypotheses $\{\mathbf{w}_{priv}^{s_i}\}_{i=1}^{m}$ are then sent to the target domain.

(2) Each source domain fetches the public data set, and computes the differentially private "importance weight" vector $\mathbf{v}^{s_i}$ with its unlabeled samples and the public data set. Then $\{\mathbf{v}^{s_i}\}_{i=1}^{m}$ are sent to the target.

(3) The target domain fetches the public data set and computes the non-private "importance weight" vector $\mathbf{v}$.

(4) The target domain computes the "hypothesis weight" vector $\mathbf{v}_H \in \mathbb{R}^m$ such that the Kulback–Leibler divergence between $\mathbf{v}$ and the linear combination of $\mathbf{v}^{s_i}$ weighted by $\mathbf{v}_H$ is minimized.

(5) The target model constructs an informative Gaussian prior using $\mathbf{v}_H$ and $\{\mathbf{w}_{priv}^{s_i}\}_{i=1}^{m}$ from the source domains.
(6) The target domain trains a Bayesian logistic regression model with limited labeled target data and the informative Gaussian prior by following Marx et al. (2008), and returns the parameters $\mathbf{w}_{priv}$.

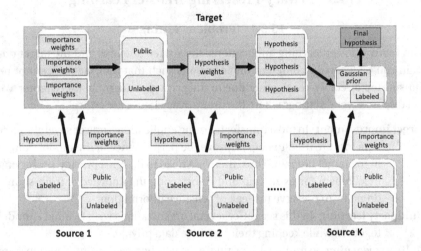

Figure 15.2 The diagram of the multiple-source transfer learning system (adapted from Wang et al. [2018d])

Differentially Private Transfer Learning with Feature Split and Stacking

To preserve the privacy, adding noises may bring negative influence on the learning procedure. As a result, transferring such models can be helpless or even harmful to the learning in the target domain.

Guo et al. (2018b) propose an approach to alleviate this problem. For simplicity, there is only one source domain. In the work by Guo et al. (2018b), the source data set is first split into K subsets in terms of features, and a differentially private logistic regression model is trained for each subset by using a variant of the objective perturbation method (Chaudhuri et al., 2011). Then those models are transferred to the target domain and combined by stacking in a differentially private manner. Moreover, the feature importance can be incorporated into the training process so that subsets with larger importance can be trained and transferred with less perturbation, while the privacy for the whole data set is still guaranteed. The whole framework is shown in Figure 15.3. The proposed algorithm works as follows:

(1) Partition the source data set to K disjoint sets based on features.
(2) Scale samples in each subset with its importance and train K differentially private logistic regression models on these subsets with a total privacy budget ϵ_s to obtain $\{\mathbf{w}_k^s\}_{k=1}^{K}$ based on a variant of the objective perturbation method.

(3) Split the target data set by samples into two parts with equal size, that is, $\mathscr{D}_l$ and $\mathscr{D}_h$, and partition both of them into K disjoint sets in the same way as the source data set.

(4) In the K subsets of $\mathscr{D}_l$, obtain $\{\mathbf{w}_k^l\}_{k=1}^K$ by differentially private hypotheses transfer. Here Guo et al. (2018b) use a different method from Wang et al. (2018d). The same method in step 2 is applied with the regularization term as $r_k(\mathbf{w}) = \frac{1}{2}\|\mathbf{w} - \mathbf{w}_k^s\|_2^2$. The whole privacy budget is set to be ϵ.

(5) Construct a meta-data set $\mathscr{D}_f = \{\sigma(\mathbf{x}_{(1)}^T \mathbf{w}_1^l), \ldots, \sigma(\mathbf{x}_{(K)}^T \mathbf{w}_K^l)\}$ by using all $\{\mathbf{x}, y\} \in \mathscr{D}_h$, where $\mathbf{x}_{(k)}$ denotes the part of $\mathbf{x}$ in the k-th subset.

(6) Train an ϵ-differentially private logistic regression with privacy budget ϵ on $\mathscr{D}_f$ and obtain the model parameter $\mathbf{w}^h$.

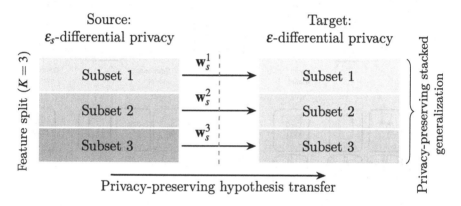

Figure 15.3 The framework of differentially private transfer learning with feature split and stacking with $K = 3$.

In the work by Guo et al. (2018b), the privacy of both the source domain (by ϵ_s) and the target domain (by ϵ) is guaranteed. In addition, a variant of the objective perturbation method is used so that the feature importance can be leveraged to define the noise, while keeping the overall privacy fixed. As shown in Guo et al.'s (2018b) work, the proposed method obtains better generalization performance, especially when the feature importance is known.

15.3.3 Multiparty Learning

In multiparty learning, there is no distinction among different data sets. The goal is to learn a common model over all the data sets. Its private variant needs to preserve the privacy of each data set. Suppose for the i-th data set, a local classifier $h_i(\cdot)$ is trained on it. In the work by Hamm et al. (2016), local classifiers are collected by a trusted central server, and a common differentially private model is built based on an auxiliary unlabeled data set $\mathscr{D}_u$ with n samples and the local classifiers. The workflow is shown in Figure 15.4. There are two approaches to train the common model, that is, majority-voted ERM and weighted ERM. In the following sections, we introduce those two approaches based on following assumptions:

- the loss-hypothesis has a form $l(h(\mathbf{x};\mathbf{w}),v) = l(v\mathbf{w}^T\mathbf{x})$;
- the loss $l(\cdot)$ is convex and continuously differentiable;
- $|l'(z)| < 1, \forall z \in \mathbb{R}$;
- for all $\mathbf{x}$, $\|\mathbf{x}\|_2 \le 1$.

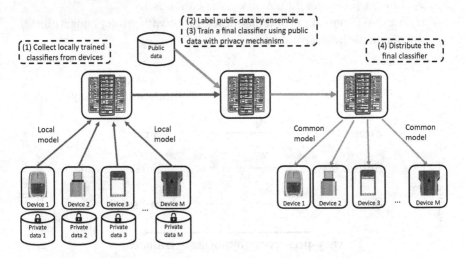

Figure 15.4 The workflow of multiparty learning (adapted from Hamm et al. [2016]). Each party holds a small amount of private data and uses the data to train a local classifier. The ensemble of local classifiers then generates labels for the auxiliary data, which in turn are used for training a global classifier. The final classifier is released after the sanitization for the privacy.

Majority-Voted ERM

The majority-voted ERM method works as follows.

(1) Generate majority voted labels $v(\mathbf{x})$ for $\mathbf{x} \in \mathscr{D}_u$ by

$$v(\mathbf{x}) = \begin{cases} 1, & \text{if } \sum_{i=1}^m I[h_i(\mathbf{x}) = 1] \ge \frac{m}{2} \\ 0, & \text{otherwise} \end{cases};$$

(2) find minimizer $\mathbf{w}^*$ by

$$\mathbf{w}^* = \underset{\mathbf{w}}{\operatorname{argmin}} \frac{1}{n} \sum_{\mathbf{x} \in \mathscr{D}_u} l(h(\mathbf{x};\mathbf{w}), v(\mathbf{x})) + \frac{\lambda}{2} \|\mathbf{w}\|_2^2;$$

(3) sample a random vector $\mathbf{b}$ from $\mathbb{P}(\mathbf{b}) \propto e^{-0.5\epsilon\|\mathbf{b}\|_2}$;

(4) output $\mathbf{w}_{priv} = \mathbf{w}^* + \mathbf{b}$.

Theoretical analyses show that the perturbed output $\mathbf{w}_{priv}$ is ϵ-differentially private.

Weighted ERM

The main problem with the majority-voted ERM approach is its sensitivity to the decision of a single party. The weighted ERM method is thus proposed to solve this problem. Specifically, $\alpha(\mathbf{x})$ is defined to be the fraction of positive votes from m classifiers for a sample $\mathbf{x}$ as

$$\alpha(\mathbf{x}) = \frac{1}{m} \sum_{i=1}^{m} I[h_i(\mathbf{x}) = 1].$$

Then, the weighted ERM algorithm works as follows:

(1) Compute $\alpha(\mathbf{x}_i)$ for all i;
(2) find the minimizer $\mathbf{w}^*$ by

$$\mathbf{w}^* = \underset{\mathbf{w}}{\arg\min} \frac{1}{n} \sum_{\mathbf{x} \in \mathcal{D}_u} l^{\alpha}(h(\mathbf{x}; \mathbf{w}), \alpha(\mathbf{x})) + \frac{\lambda}{2} \|\mathbf{w}\|_2^2,$$

where

$$l^{\alpha}(\cdot) = \alpha(\mathbf{x}) l(\mathbf{w}^T \mathbf{x}) + (1 - \alpha(\mathbf{x})) l(-\mathbf{w}^T \mathbf{x});$$

(3) sample a random vector $\mathbf{b}$ from $\mathbb{P}(\mathbf{b}) \propto e^{-0.5\epsilon \|\mathbf{b}\|_2}$;
(4) output $\mathbf{w}_{priv} = \mathbf{w}^* + \mathbf{b}$.

Theoretical analyses show that $\mathbf{w}_{priv}$ is ϵ-differentially private.

15.3.4 Multitask Learning

For multitask learning, which is introduced in Chapter 9, the privacy should be taken into consideration when all the tasks help each other in the learning process and hence the privacy problem also exists. In the work by Xie et al. (2017), a differentially privacy-preserving multi-task learning method is proposed. The model parameter $\mathbf{w}^i$ is assumed to be decomposed into two components, that is, $\mathbf{w}^i = \mathbf{p}^i + \mathbf{q}^i$, where $\mathbf{p}^i \in \mathbb{R}^d$ is the component to learn the task relatedness and $\mathbf{q}^i \in \mathbb{R}^d$ is the task-specific component, leading to $\mathbf{W} = \mathbf{P} + \mathbf{Q}$. Thus, the proposed objective function is formulated as

$$\min_{\mathbf{P}, \mathbf{Q}} \sum_{i=1}^{m} \left(\frac{1}{n_i} \sum_{j=1}^{n_i} l_j^i(\mathbf{p}^i + \mathbf{q}^i) \right) + \lambda_1 r_P(\mathbf{P}) + \lambda_2 r_Q(\mathbf{Q}),$$

where $l_j^i(\mathbf{w}^i)$ denotes the loss on the j-th data point in the i-th task with the model parameter $\mathbf{w}^i$, $r_P(\mathbf{P})$ performs the knowledge transfer and $r_Q(\mathbf{Q})$ penalizes the model complexity. Here $r_Q(\mathbf{Q})$ is assumed to be decomposable in terms of tasks, that is, $r_Q(\mathbf{Q}) = \sum_{i=1}^{m} r_Q^i(\mathbf{q}_i)$. Thus, each column $\mathbf{q}^i$ in $\mathbf{Q}$ can be distributed to a computing node and it can be updated locally. For $\mathbf{P}$, the gradient information about $\mathbf{p}^i$ is computed locally and then collected by a central server to update $\mathbf{P}$. Since only $\mathbf{p}^i$ is passed to the central server, noises can be added to it to guarantee the differential privacy.

16

Transfer Learning in Computer Vision

16.1 Introduction

Understanding the visual world around us has been a research focus in AI for decades and significant contributions have been made. AI has already achieved human-level performance in various visual tasks and contexts, such as face recognition, handwritten character recognition, lip reading and so on. In AI's early days, most visual models had been developed on the basis of handcrafted features for general visual tasks such as image classification and video classification. Recently, deep neural network models become a new trend due to their powerful ability to learn hierarchical feature representations.

However, the advances of visual models heavily rely on large-scale labeled data. As labeled data are difficult to obtain, transfer learning is desired. To transfer the knowledge from a source domain to a target domain, feature-based methods are widely adopted. Some models augment target domain features with source domain features. Some models learn a mapping from the source domain to the target domain. Some other models learn a shared dictionary across the two domains. In deep neural networks, some learned features are highly "transferable" and hence the features learned from one data set can naturally be generalized and transferred to another domain and context.

This chapter is organized as follows. Section 16.2 focuses on image applications, where image classification, as the most widely studied visual application, is first discussed. Then, transfer learning models for other visual applications such as video classification and object detection are addressed. Transfer learning models for medical image applications are specifically discussed in Section 16.3, where classification, detection and segmentation tasks are investigated. We pick medical imaging as an application domain for transfer learning particularly because the high-quality labeled data are difficult to obtain to enable this very important application.

16.2 Overview

Image data are ubiquitous. For example, users share photos on social networks, traffic cameras monitor road environments, advertisements are displayed with images on online-shopping sites and so on. Understanding images plays a key role in various applications, including self-driving cars, video surveillance, recommender systems and so on. Thanks to large-scale labeled databases and the advancement of vision models, remarkable progress has been made in understanding the visual world. Yet labeled data are scarce in real world applications. For example, when a traffic camera is set up in a new city, the distribution of the traffic flow is likely to differ from that in other cities. As manually labeling video frames is time-consuming and it costs moderate human effort, it is necessary to transfer the knowledge from labeled data in other cities or public data sets, where transfer learning models can be applied.

In this section, we review transfer learning models for vision tasks. We first focus on the image classification task and then discuss other vision tasks such as video classification, captioning, object detection and so on. For survey papers that address visual domain adaptation, readers may refer to the works by Csurka (2017) and Patel et al. (2015).

Most transfer learning models are general-purpose, and they can be directly used in visual applications without particular adjustments. For transfer learning models pertaining to image classification, there are a plethora of approaches, as shown in Figure 16.1. They are first categorized into *shallow* models and *deep* models. Deep models are usually artificial neural networks and learn hierarchical representations, while shallow models do not. For shallow models, there are mainly four transfer approaches, namely feature augmentation-based, feature transformation-based, parameter adaptation and dictionary-based approaches. For deep models, they can be divided into feature-based and model-based approaches, and these two approaches are usually used together. In the following, we introduce those two categories of transfer learning models.

16.2.1 Shallow Transfer Learning Models

In this section, we introduce shallow transfer learning models for image classification, which can be categorized into the following four approaches: feature augmentation-based, feature transformation-based, parameter adaptation and dictionary-based approaches.

Feature Augmentation-Based Approach

Daumé III (2007) proposes a transfer learning method by augmenting the target feature space. The augmented feature space is composed of three parts, namely general features that are shared across domains, private features of the source domain and private features of the target domain. The feature augmentation is

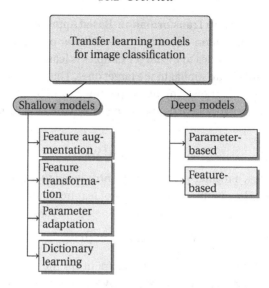

Figure 16.1 Categorization of transfer learning models for image classification

attained by concatenating the three parts as

$$\phi_s(\mathbf{x}) = [\mathbf{x}, \mathbf{x}, \mathbf{0}]^T \qquad\qquad \phi_t(x) = [\mathbf{x}, \mathbf{0}, \mathbf{x}]^T, \qquad (16.1)$$

where $\mathbf{0}$ denotes a zero vector of dimension d and ϕ_s and ϕ_t denote the feature augmentation mapping in the source and target domains, respectively. Knowledge transfer across domains is achieved by considering domain-shared and domain-specific features simultaneously. This method can be extended to the multiple domain setting.

The feature augmentation-based method has been extended by considering intermediate subspaces that connect the source and target domains (Gopalan et al., 2011, 2014; Gong et al., 2012a). The geodesic flow sampling method (Gopalan et al., 2011) views the generative subspaces of the source and target domains as points on a Grassmann manifold, and then samples point along the geodesic to obtain intermediate subspace representations. Original feature representations from the two domains are projected into these subspaces and they are concatenated into high-dimensional feature representations. A discriminative classifier is constructed on the resulting feature representation. Instead of sampling finite subspaces, the geodesic flow kernel method (Gong et al., 2012a) defines a kernel function that integrates an infinite number of subspaces that lie on the geodesic flow from the source domain to the target one. A more general framework is proposed by Gopalan et al. (2014), which considers feature representations in a reproducing kernel Hibert space using kernel methods and a low-dimensional manifold representation using Laplacian eigenmaps.

Feature Transformation-Based Approach

For feature transformation-based methods, a linear or nonlinear transformation from the source samples to the target samples is learned such that the transformed source samples are similar to the target ones. This idea is first proposed by Saenko et al. (2010). The transformation is parameterized by $\mathbf{W}$ and the similarity between the transformed source domain sample and the target domain sample is defined as

$$\text{sim}(\mathbf{x}_s, \mathbf{x}_t) = (\mathbf{x}_s)^T \mathbf{W} \mathbf{x}_t.$$

To avoid overfitting, a regularization term is introduced to the transformation $\mathbf{W}$, denoted by $r(\mathbf{W})$. The optimization problem of feature transformation transfer is formulated as

$$\min_{\mathbf{W}} r(\mathbf{W}) \quad \text{s.t.} \ c_i(\mathbf{X}_s^T \mathbf{W} \mathbf{X}_t) \geq 0 \ 1 \leq i \leq c, \tag{16.2}$$

where c_i denotes the i-th supervision constraint. In the work by Saenko et al. (2010), the regularizer is defined as $r(\mathbf{W}) = \text{tr}(\mathbf{W}) - \log \det(\mathbf{W})$ and two types of constraints, namely class-based constraints and correspondence-based constraints, are considered. For the class-based constraints, a random labeled sample is selected from the source domain and the target domain, respectively. This distance between the two samples should be smaller than a threshold if they have the same label; otherwise, the distance should exceed a threshold. Alternatively, correspondence-based constraints can be constructed if the relationship other than the label information of two samples is known. The similarity and dissimilarity constraints help learning a domain-invariant transformation. The constrained optimization problem defined in (16.2) is first converted to an unconstrained problem and then it is solved by an information-theoretic metric learning method.

Later, Kulis et al. (2011) propose a more general formulation where the model proposed by Saenko et al. (2010) becomes a special case. It learns an asymmetric nonlinear transformation, which makes the model capable of handling changes in the feature type and dimension.

The feature transformation method works well even when the source and target domains have different representations, which belongs to heterogeneous transfer learning. Dai et al. (2008) present one of the first such works known as **translated learning**, where the training data and test data can be from totally different feature spaces. For example, the source can be text while the target can be text or audio. Translated learning is an example of heterogeneous transfer learning. A main method for this approach is to obtain a "dictionary" that can be a translator to link the different feature spaces.

An intuitive idea for translated learning is to translate some or all of the training data from the source domain as well as the target domain into a common target feature space, such that learning can be done in this single space. This approach can be used for applications such as cross-lingual text classification and cross-domain image understanding. It can also be used to link the knowledge between text and images, in applications where one can use text to explain the semantics of images. Compared with the machine translation methods typically used in natural language understanding, the key difference lies in how different feature spaces are connected; instead of focusing on the sequential nature of texts to be translated, in translated learning the target data may be of any order.

Dai et al. (2008) present a solution to the translated learning problem, which is to make the best use of available data to construct a dictionary or translator. While the target data alone may not be sufficient in building a good classifier for the target domain, by leveraging the available labeled data in the source domain, we can indeed build effective translators, which in turn can enhance the training data in the target domain. An example is to translate between the text and image feature spaces using the social tagging data available on the World Wide Web.

The translated learning model assumes that the learning tasks are represented by a common label space c, which is the same in both the source and the target domains. The learning process can be represented using a Markov chain $c \to f \to x$, where f represents the features of the data instances x. The source domain data x_s are represented by the features f_s in the source feature space, while the test data in the target domain x_t are represented by the features f_t in the target feature space. Translated learning models the learning in the source space through a Markov chain $c \to f_s \to x_s$, which can be connected to another Markov chain $c \to f_t \to x_t$ in the target space. An important feature of translated learning is to show how to connect these two paths, so that a new chain $c \to f_s \to f_t \to x$, can be formed to translate the knowledge from the source space to the target space. In this process, the mapping $f_s \to f_t$ acts as a feature-level translator. The algorithm, known as TLRisk, exploits the risk minimization framework in the work by Lafferty and Zhai (2001) to model translated learning.

We first express the overall objective of translated learning. We can use the risk function $R(c, x_t)$ to measure the the risk for classifying x_t to the category c. To predict the label for an instance x_t, we need only to find the class-label c that minimizes the risk function $R(c, x_t)$, so that the hypothesis h_t can be estimated with

$$h_t(x_t) = \arg\min_{c \in C} R(c, x_t) \tag{16.3}$$

The risk function $R(c, x_t)$ can be formulated as the expected loss when c and x_t are relevant. Since C only depends on c and X_t only depends on x_t, we can use $p(C|c)$ to replace $p(C|c, x_t)$, and use $p(X_t|x_t)$ to replace $p(X_t|c, x_t)$.

Dai et al. (2008) represent the risk function as follows:

$$R(c, x_t) - \int_{\Theta_C} \int_{\Theta_{X_t}} L(\theta_C, \theta_{X_t}, r = 1) p(\theta_C|c) p(\theta X_t|x_t) d\theta_{X_t} d\theta_C \tag{16.4}$$

where Θ_C and Θ_{X_t} are the model spaces corresponding to the label space C and the target data space X_t, respectively. $L(\theta_C, \theta_{X_t}, r = 1)$ represent the loss function as a result of a wrong prediction of instance-class label association. θ are variables representing the particular models. In this objective function, the loss function $L(\theta_C, \theta_{X_t}, r = 1)$ can be estimated by the Kullback–Leibler divergence (Kullback and Leibler, 1951) of the two distribution spaces behind models θ_C and θ_{X_t}. This divergence estimation in turn requires a translator from the feature space f_s to feature space f_t, which can be estimated using the occurrence data acquired from the Web. Of course, one has to be careful in constructing the dictionary, as there may be much bias and noise inherent in the web data (Dai et al., 2008).

Parameter Adaptation Approach

Several algorithms were proposed to adapt a model trained with the source domain data for model learning in the target domain. Yang et al. (2007c) propose an adaptive support vector machine (A-SVM), which learns a "delta function" between the source domain model and the target domain model. The adaptation is formulated as

$$f_t(\mathbf{x}) = f_s(\mathbf{x}) + \delta f(\mathbf{x}),$$

where f_s, f_t and δf denote the source domain model, the target domain model and the delta function, respectively. Further, the delta function is defined as $\delta f(\mathbf{x}) = \mathbf{w}^T \phi(\mathbf{x})$, where $\mathbf{w}$ denotes the parameter of the delta function and the mapping ϕ projects the data sample into a high-dimensional space. To estimate the parameter $\mathbf{w}$, the objective of A-SVM is extended from standard SVMs as

$$\min_{\mathbf{w}} \frac{1}{2} \|\mathbf{w}\|^2 + C \sum_i^{n_t} \epsilon_i$$

$$\text{s.t.} \epsilon_i \geq 0, \ y_i f_s(\mathbf{x}_i) + y_i \mathbf{w}^T \phi(\mathbf{x}_i) \geq 1 - \epsilon_i \ \forall (\mathbf{x}_i, y_i) \in \mathscr{D}_t, \tag{16.5}$$

where ϵ_i measures the classification error and C controls the trade-off between the two terms. (16.5) learns a target domain model that correctly classifies labeled samples in the target domain and is close to the source domain model at the same time.

Domain transfer SVM, proposed by Duan et al. (2009), improves over the A-SVM by reducing the domain discrepancy measured by maximum mean discrepancy (MMD) and learns a target decision function simultaneously. Adaptive multiple kernel learning (Duan et al., 2012c) learns a kernel function based on multiple base kernels. There are also methods that learn the feature transformation and classifier parameters jointly (Shi and Sha, 2012; Donahue et al., 2013; Hoffman et al., 2013).

Dictionary-Based Approach

Dictionary learning represents high-dimensional data as a linear combination of basic elements. The basic elements are referred to as "atoms" and the atoms compose a dictionary. Dictionary learning has been successfully applied in various vision tasks, such as face recognition, image reconstruction, image de-blurring and so on. However, dictionary learning is challenging in the cross-domain setting because the dictionary learned in the source domain might be unsuitable for the target domain due to the domain shift. Several models are proposed to address this issue (Qiu et al., 2012; Ni et al., 2013; Shekhar et al., 2013).

Shekhar et al. (2013) propose a shared domain-adapted dictionary learning framework that learns a shared dictionary for both the source and target domains in a low-dimensional space. Two costs are considered, namely a reconstruction cost and a regularization cost denoted by C_1 and C_2, respectively. The data are first projected into a low-dimensional space where the parameters for the mappings are denoted by $\mathbf{W}_s$ and $\mathbf{W}_t$, respectively. The shared dictionary denoted by $\mathbf{K}$ is learned by minimizing the reconstruction cost in the low-dimensional space. The reconstruction cost C_1 is defined as

$$C_1(\mathbf{K}, \mathbf{W}_s, \mathbf{W}_t) = \|\mathbf{W}_s \mathbf{X}_s - \mathbf{K} \mathbf{V}_s\|_F^2 + \|\mathbf{W}_t \mathbf{X}_t - \mathbf{K} \mathbf{V}_t\|_F^2, \tag{16.6}$$

where $\mathbf{V}_s$ and $\mathbf{V}_t$ denote the sparse representation of $\mathbf{X}_s$ and $\mathbf{X}_t$ over the dictionary $\mathbf{K}$, respectively.

Meanwhile, the regularization cost C_2 is introduced to ensure that the projection does not lose too much information and it is defined as

$$C_2(\mathbf{W}_s, \mathbf{W}_t) = \|\mathbf{X}_s - \mathbf{W}_s^T \mathbf{W}_s \mathbf{X}_s\|_F^2 + \|\mathbf{X}_t - \mathbf{W}_t^T \mathbf{W}_t \mathbf{X}_t\|_F^2. \tag{16.7}$$

Combining (16.6) and (16.7) and applying algebraic calculations, the overall optimization problem is formulated as

$$\min_{\mathbf{K}, \tilde{\mathbf{W}}, \tilde{\mathbf{V}}} \|\tilde{\mathbf{W}} \tilde{\mathbf{X}} - \mathbf{K} \tilde{\mathbf{V}}\|_F^2 - \lambda \text{tr}((\tilde{\mathbf{W}} \tilde{\mathbf{X}})(\tilde{\mathbf{W}} \tilde{\mathbf{X}})^T)$$
$$\text{s.t. } \mathbf{W}_s \mathbf{W}_s^T = \mathbf{I}, \ \mathbf{W}_t \mathbf{W}_t^T = \mathbf{I}, \ \|\tilde{\mathbf{v}}_j\|_0 \leq T_0, \forall j,$$

where λ is a positive constant, T_0 denotes the sparsity level, $\|\cdot\|_0$, the ℓ_0 norm, is defined as the number of non-zero elements in a vector, and $\tilde{\mathbf{W}}$, $\tilde{\mathbf{X}}$ and $\tilde{\mathbf{V}}$ are defined as

$$\tilde{\mathbf{W}} = [\mathbf{W}_s, \mathbf{W}_t], \ \tilde{\mathbf{X}} = \begin{bmatrix} \mathbf{X}_s & \mathbf{0} \\ \mathbf{0} & \mathbf{X}_t \end{bmatrix}, \tilde{\mathbf{V}} = [\mathbf{V}_s, \mathbf{V}_t].$$

This framework can be extended to a kernelized version and it can handle multiple source domains as well.

16.2.2 Deep Transfer Learning Models

In the context of deep learning, there are mainly two approaches for transfer learning, namely model-based and feature-based transfer learning, and these two approaches are usually used simultaneously in a deep transfer learning model. As deep transfer learning models are already discussed in previous chapters, we provide an overview of deep transfer learning models for image classification and do not delve into details.

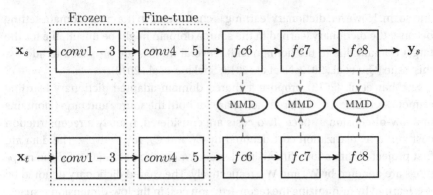

Figure 16.2 An illustration of the domain adaptation network (adapted from Long et al. [2015]), which applies both model-based and feature-based transfer learning approaches. It adopts the AlexNet architecture with eight layers.

Model-based transfer learning via the parameter sharing and fine-tuning is the most widely adopted method. This is because parameters in a deep neural network are *transferable* in that they are suitable for multiple domains (Donahue et al., 2014; Oquab et al., 2014; Yosinski et al., 2014). The generalization ability of parameters is referred as "transferability." Two popular model-based transfer learning methods are *parameter-sharing* and *fine-tuning*. Parameter-sharing assumes that parameters are highly transferable, and it directly copies parameters in the source network to the target network. The fine-tuning method assumes that parameters in the source network are useful but they need to be trained with the target data to better adapt to the target domain.

Feature-based transfer learning models learn a common feature space that is shared by both the source and target domains (Long et al., 2015; Ganin et al., 2016). For deep neural networks, feature-based transfer learning is usually used in conjunction with model-based transfer learning. A typical example is shown in Figure 16.2. The first three layers are copied from a source network and this corresponds to parameter sharing in model-based transfer learning and also feature sharing in the feature-based transfer learning. The next two layers are initialized with parameters from the source network and they are fine-tuned during the training process. The last three layers are domain-specific and learned based on the target data.

He et al. (2018b) show that, by learning from scratch, some vision tasks achieve comparable performance with the fine-tuning approach based on the ImageNet data set. We think this phenomena occurs based on a prerequisite that the target domain has enough training data. So, when the target domain has few training data, the fine-tuning approach can perform better than the pure supervised learning approach.

16.2.3   Transfer Learning for Other Vision Tasks

So far, we have focused on transfer learning models for image classification. Transfer learning models have also been developed for other vision tasks such as video classification, image/video captioning, object detection and so on. The generalization ability of features learned with a convolutional neural network (CNN) on a video classification data set is empirically investigated by Karpathy et al. (2014). While it achieves an accuracy of 41.3 percent when the network is trained on the target domain alone, a signification improvement can be obtained by taking a parameter-based transfer learning approach. The accuracy reaches 65.4 percent when retaining the low-level layers from the source network and retraining the top layers of the network. A similar result is reported by Abu-El-Haija et al. (2016). The mean average precision of ActivityNet is improved from 53.8 to 77.6 percent by pretraining on a large-scale YouTube-8M data set. In image/video captioning tasks, initializing the convolutional network with the parameters pretrained on the ImageNet data set is a widely adopted technique (Venugopalan et al., 2015a, 2015b; Vinyals et al., 2015; Xu et al., 2015). Parameter-based transfer learning has also been used in object detection where the model decides whether a region of interest in an image contains a certain object (Sermanet et al., 2013; Girshick et al., 2014; Hoffman et al., 2014). In addition to parameter-based transfer learning, a region with CNN features detector can be adapted by aligning feature subspaces of localized bounding boxes between the source domain and the target domain (Raj et al., 2015).

16.3   Transfer Learning for Medical Image Analysis

In the past decades, medical imaging technologies, for example, computed tomography (CT), magnetic resonance (MR), positron emission tomography, mammography, ultrasound, X-ray and so on, have played important roles in the early detection, the diagnosis and the treatment of diseases. In the clinic, interpreting medical images relies on human experts such as radiologists and physicians. Therefore, medical image analysis (MIA), a subfield of computer vision, emerged in the 1990s to automatically complete tasks such as classification, detection and segmentation for clinical care and biomedical research.

Although MIA is a subfield of computer vision, compared to images in general, medical images have some specific characteristics.

- *Small data and expensive labeling*: Medical image data are collected through special equipment under very private contexts, hence, medical image data often only have small sample, measured in the order of hundreds of samples only. This is much smaller than general image data sets such as ImageNet and CIFAR. The labeling of medical images often relies on experienced and well-trained human experts such as doctors and radiologists, making the labeling for medical images much more expensive.

- *Complex data*: Computer vision tasks usually focus on two-dimensional (2D) images or videos. However, medical images have a much more complex data formation. X-ray images often consist of several views for a body area of a patient. Some examination equipment such as CT offers three-dimensional (3D) images or videos instead of 2D ones. MR images (MRI) even have several modalities in 3D images. Ultrasound devices often generate sequential image data.

- *Imbalanced labels*: In practice, medical image data are imbalanced. Positive results such as true confirmations of cancer cases have a much lower chance of appearing than negative results, since most patients are healthy. This makes the data have an imbalanced distribution, which in turn makes it difficult to learn. Additionally, the abnormality of the data usually occurs in a small patch of the images and these local patches will determine the label of the whole image. For example, a small tumor in a CT scan of a lung will lead to a positive label no matter what other patches are classified. This is a typical case of multi-instance learning (Dietterich et al., 1997).

In the following , we discuss how transfer learning helps MIA tasks under different settings.

16.3.1   Medical Image Classification

Since the size of medical image data sets is typically small, the popularity of transfer learning for this applications is not surprising. Using a pretrained network as a feature extractor and fine-tuning a pretrained network are both widely used in medical image classification based on transfer learning. In the work by Antony et al. (2016), the fine-tuning clearly outperforms the feature extraction, achieving 57.6 percent accuracy in multi-class grade assessment of knee osteoarthritis compared with 53.4 percent. However, Kim et al. (2016) show that using a CNN as a feature extractor outperforms the fine-tuning in the cytopathology image classification.

Similar to the general computer vision, the medical imaging community initially focuses on unsupervised pretraining. Those early attempted works (Brosch and Tam, 2013; Plis et al., 2013; Suk and Shen, 2013; Suk et al., 2014) focus on neuroimaging from brain MRI, as shown in the Figure 16.3. They apply deep belief networks to unsupervisedly learn the MRI data distribution $P(x|h)$ and the hidden representation $P(h|x)$. Specifically, generative models like restricted Boltzmann machines or stacked autoencoder learn to reconstruct the inputs x by minimizing $\prod_{x \in X} P(x)$ or $\sum_{x \in X} |x - f_w(x)|^2$ and inferring the hidden representation h. Then, the hidden representation h can be directly reused or further fine-tuned with the label information to do the classification for the diagnosis of Alzheimer's disease.

In later studies, researchers make attempts to transfer the representations in supervised learning from large image data sets such as ImageNet to improve the learning on small medical image data sets. Despite the fact that there are many

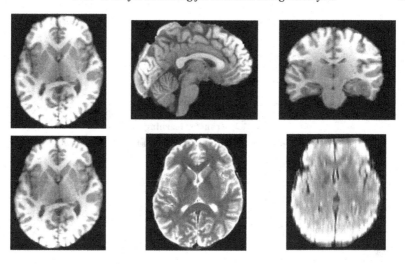

Figure 16.3 MRI images from the public BRATS data set (Menze et al., 2015; Bakas et al., 2017) in 3D and multimodality. The upper row shows three different views of the 3D MRI image in T1, and the lower row shows the images of the T1, T2 and flair modalities.

differences between general images and medical images, the transferred representations help the learned model to achieve comparable or even better performance than human experts in many diagnosis tasks including retinal diseases (Kermany et al., 2018), pneumonia (Rajpurkar et al., 2017) and skin cancer (Esteva et al., 2017).

Taking the diagnosis of retinal diseases as an example (Kermany et al., 2018), fine-tuning from the ImageNet data set has the following four steps: (1) the inception network is chosen as the backbone model and randomly initialized at the beginning. (2) The inception network is first trained on the ImageNet data set with a final classifier layer outputting one of 1,000 classes. (3) After pretraining on the ImageNet data set, the last classifier layer with 1,000 output nodes is replaced by another randomly initialized classifier layer to predict four retinal status, while other previous layers remain unchanged. (4) The whole network continues to fine-tune the last several fully connected layers with all previous CNN layers frozen. The whole process is illustrated in Figure 16.4. It turns out that this strategy can achieve a high accuracy like 93.4 percent with limited labeled data.

16.3.2 Abnormality Detection in Medical Images

In some works on the abnormality detection problem, transferring from large-scale general image data sets (e.g., the ImageNet data set) has been found to be consistently beneficial. Shin et al. (2016) exploit and extensively evaluate transfer learning with different deep CNN architectures, including CifarNet, AlexNet and GoogLeNet. What's more, this work also investigates and compares different

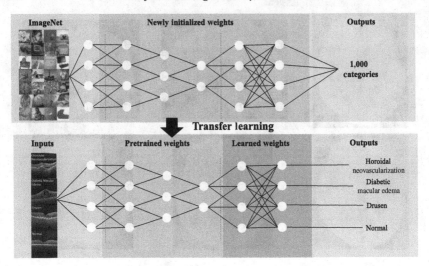

Figure 16.4 An example of the fine-tuning method from the ImageNet data set about how to achieve comparable or better performance than human experts on the retinal disease diagnosis (adapted from Kermany et al. [2018])

training protocols of transfer learning: (1) fine-tuning: the model is initialized from a pretrained network and then it is trained with labeled data from the target domain. (2) Off-the-shelf: the network pretrained from the source domain is frozen except the last classifier layer, which is randomly initialized and trained on the target data. In the two studied problems, that is, the thoracoabdominal lymph node detection and interstitial lung disease classification, transfer learning making use of the ImageNet data can achieve the state-of-the-art performance.

Samala et al. (2016) study transfer learning between two similar medical image domains for mass detection of the breast cancer. The proposed method develops a computer-aided detection system for masses in digital breast tomosynthesis volumes using a CNN to transfer knowledge from mammograms. Empirical studies show that using transfer learning improves the area under curve score.

16.3.3 Medical Image Segmentation

Segmentation is a common task in both general CV and MIA. It is defined as the process of partitioning a digital image into multiple segments (sets of pixels, also known as super-pixels). A segmentation model is to classify pixels in an image to perform the segmentation that carries some semantic meaning. Dou et al. (2018) use adversarial learning to conduct unsupervised domain adaptation from source MRI domain to the target CT domain. This work employs a residual network to conduct pixelwise predictions for the segmentation and the whole network is first trained on the MRI images in the source domain. It assumes that the distributional differences between the MRI domain and CT domain are in the primarily low-level features (e.g., gray-scale values) rather than high-level features (e.g., geometric structures). Therefore, the domain adaptation module (DAM) is introduced to replace the low-level layer for the target domain and the domain critic module (DCM) will concatenate the multiple high-level features as its input to learn to tell the source domain from the target domain. The DCM and DAM are trained together by optimizing the adversarial loss as

$$\min_{M} L_M(X^t, D) = -\mathbb{E}_{(M(x^t), F_H(x^t)) \sim \mathbb{P}_g}(D(M(x^t), F_H(x^t))$$

$$\min_{D} L_D(X^s, X^t, M) = \mathbb{E}_{(M(x^t), F_H(x^t)) \sim \mathbb{P}_g}(D(M(x^t), F_H(x^t)))$$

$$- \mathbb{E}_{(M(x^s), F_H(x^s)) \sim \mathbb{P}_s}(D(M(x^s), F_H(x^s))),$$

where M denotes the DAM and D denotes the DCM. As shown in Figure 16.5, the DCM and DAM work together to learn how to align high-level features between the source and target domains, and then the high-level layers of the segmentation model can be reused by the target domain.

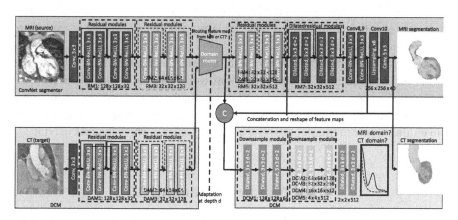

Figure 16.5 The framework of the unsupervised domain adaptation from MRI segmentation to CT segmentation (adapted from Dou et al. [2018])

17

Transfer Learning in Natural Language Processing

17.1 Introduction

Transfer learning is often referred to as domain adaptation in natural language processing (NLP) tasks. Transfer learning plays a significant role in various NLP tasks, especially when there are limited data for training a model. In this case, transfer learning can help these tasks by leveraging the knowledge gained from other related learning tasks.

This chapter will give an overview of transfer learning in NLP. We give an overview in two sections. In the first section, we give a general introduction about how transfer learning can be used in NLP tasks. In the second section, we focus on how transfer learning helps sentiment analysis. In the next chapter, we will devote an entire chapter to transfer learning in dialog systems, which is a task in NLP.

17.2 Transfer Learning in NLP

A basic model for transfer learning in NLP is neural networks. As neural networks are usually trained with gradient descent methods, it is straightforward to use gradient information in both source and target domains for optimization to accomplish the knowledge transfer. Depending on how samples in source and target domains are used, there are two main approaches to neural network-based transfer learning, including parameter initialization (INIT) and multitask learning (MTL). In some cases, we can use a hybrid of the two methods, which pre-trains on the source domain in the spirit of the INIT approach and then trains on the source and target domains simultaneously based on the MTL approach.

17.2.1 Problem Settings

Under the transfer learning setting, we suppose there are m source tasks $\{\mathbb{S}_i\}_{i=1}^{m}$ and one target task $\mathbb{T}$ where $m \geq 1$. The i-th source task $\mathbb{S}_i$ has a training data set $\mathscr{D}_{s_i}$, which contains n_{s_i} pairs of data points and labels $\{(\mathbf{x}_j^{s_i}, y_j^{s_i})\}_{j=1}^{n_{s_i}}$ where the j-th data point $\mathbf{x}_j^{s_i} \in \mathbb{R}^{d_{s_i}}$ lies in a d_{s_i}-dimensional space and $y_j^{s_i}$ belongs to $\{-1,1\}$ for a classification task and otherwise is a scalar. $\mathcal{D}_t$, the training data set of the target task $\mathbb{T}$, has n_t data points $\{\mathbf{x}_i^t\}_{i=1}^{n_t}$ where $\mathbf{x}_i^t \in \mathbb{R}^{d_t}$. The data matrix for the i-th source task is denoted by $\mathbf{X}_{s_i} = (\mathbf{x}_1^{s_i}, \ldots, \mathbf{x}_{n_{s_i}}^{s_i})$ and the label vector by $\mathbf{y}_{s_i} = (y_1^{s_i}, \ldots, y_{n_{s_i}}^{s_i})^T$. The data matrix and label vector for the target task are denoted by $\mathbf{X}_t$ and $\mathbf{y}_t$. The distribution of the data points in the i-th source task $\mathbb{S}_i$ is denoted by $\mathbb{P}_{s_i}^X$, the condition distribution of the label given the data point by $\mathbb{P}_{s_i}^{Y|X}$, and the joint distribution by $\mathbb{P}_{s_i}^{X \times Y}$. The corresponding distributions in the target task are denoted by $\mathbb{P}_t^X$, $\mathbb{P}_t^{X|Y}$ and $\mathbb{P}_t^{X \times Y}$, respectively.

17.2.2 Parameter Initialization in NLP Applications

The INIT approach first trains neural networks on m source tasks $\{\mathbb{S}_i\}_{i=1}^m$ and then uses the learned parameters to initialize a neural network for a target task $\mathbb{T}$. After that, if labeled data are available in $\mathbb{T}$, they are used to update the parameters of the target neural network. There are two methods to apply parameter initialization.

(1) Freezing: It applies the neural network trained on a source domain to the target domain without any modification.
(2) Fine-tuning: In this method, a neural network is trained on a source domain. Then this neural network is applied to the target domain with parameters of some layers fixed while parameters of other layers will be learned on the target domain data. An illustration of the fine-tuning method is shown in Figure 17.1.

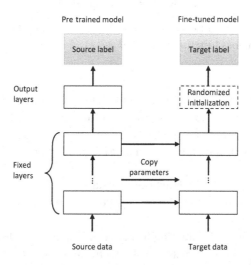

Figure 17.1 An illustration of the fine-tuning method by training the top layer on the target domain with other layers fixed

With the popularity of distributed representations, pretrained word embedding models such as word2vec (Mikolov et al., 2013a) and glove (Pennington et al., 2014) are widely used and word representations pretrained from a large source data set are used to initialize the word embedding layer in a target model for many NLP tasks. When the size of the target data set is much smaller than that of the source data set used for word embeddings, it is observed that freezing representations outperforms fine-tuning them (Seo et al., 2016) and otherwise the fine-tuning method is better than the freezing method (Kim, 2014).

Min et al. (2017) train a BiDAF model (Seo et al., 2016) on a source data set, Stanford question answering (SQuAD) (Rajpurkar et al., 2016), which is a span-supervised question and answering (QA) data set and then adapt it to two other QA data sets, WikiQA and SemEval 2016. Moreover, specific layers trained on a sentence scoring task are applied to a different task – the entailment task.

Devlin et al. (2018) pretrain a proposed bidirectional encoder representations from transformers (BERT) model on two tasks, that is, masked language modeling and next sentence prediction, and then fine-tune the pretrained BERT model on eleven NLP tasks/data sets, including multi-genre natural language inference, Quora question pairs, question natural language inference, Stanford sentiment treebank, the corpus of linguistic acceptability, semantic textual similarity benchmark, Microsoft research paraphrase corpus, recognizing textual entailment, Winograd natural language inference, SQuAD data set, the CoNLL 2003 named entity recognition (NER) data set and the situations with adversarial generations data set, to achieve the state-of-the-art performance.

17.2.3   MTL in NLP Applications

The MTL approach simultaneously learns from both the source and target domains. The overall loss function is defined as

$$J = \lambda J_t + (1 - \lambda) J_s, \tag{17.1}$$

where J_t and J_s are the individual loss function of each domain, and $\lambda \in (0, 1)$ is a regularization parameter to balance the loss functions of two domains.

In the rest of this section, we will introduce the use of the MTL approach on NLP tasks by highlighting different strategies and rationales.

Machine Translation

Different models to use MTL for machine translation can be classified into two categories.

The first category is by training a unified translation model under the MTL framework, thus simultaneously translating from one source language into several different target languages. The general model could be regarded as a variation of an encoder-decoder framework. Dong et al. (2015) build a recurrent neural network (RNN)-based encoder-decoder model with multiple target tasks, each of which is for a target language. Different tasks share the same encoder, as shown in Figure 17.2. Different from Dong et al. (2015), Zoph and Knight (2016) define a specific encoder for each target language and jointly train them. Malaviya et al. (2017) build a massive many-to-one neural machine translation system from 1,017 languages to English. Moreover, Johnson et al. (2016b) jointly train encoders and decoders.

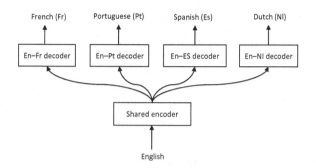

Figure 17.2 MTL for multiple language translation

The second category of machine translation works is to utilize other related tasks as auxiliary tasks to help the machine translation task. Luong et al. (2016) use the parsing and image captioning as auxiliary tasks. Wu et al. (2017) jointly model the target word sequence and its dependency tree structure to help the machine translation task. As shown in Figure 17.3, Niehues and Cho (2017) build a model that can learn three NLP tasks, including part-of-speech (POS) tagging, NER as well as machine translation by using an attention-based encoder-decoder model. Here POS tagging and NER can also be modeled as translation problems. For example, instead of translating the source words into the target language, they translate words into labels such as POS tags or NER labels.

Multilingual Tasks

Similar to machine translation, it is often beneficial to use the MTL approach to jointly train models for various NLP tasks such as POS tagging (Fang and Cohn, 2017), dependency parsing (Duong et al., 2015; Guo et al., 2016b), discourse segmentation (Braud et al., 2017), sequence tagging (Yang et al., 2016), NER (Gillick et al., 2016) and document classification (Pappas and Popescu-Belis, 2017).

Relation Extraction

For relation extraction, the information related to different relations or roles can often be shared. Specifically, the knowledge learned from other types of relations or even other tasks, could be transferred to the target relation and help to improve the performance of the relation extractor.

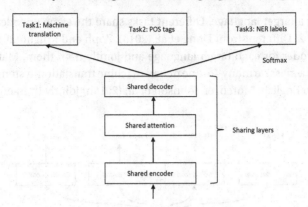

Figure 17.3 Learning three NLP tasks in a neural network based on the MTL approach

Jiang (2009) analyzes on relation extraction in a weakly supervised learning setting, which only has a few seed instances of the target relation and a large number of labeled instances of other types of relations. Jiang (2009) proposes a general MTL framework where classifiers for a number of related tasks share a common component and are trained together.

Liu et al. (2015b) propose a multitask deep neural network (DNN) to combine the multiple-domain classification for query classification and information retrieval for ranking in a Web search. Experimental results demonstrate that the proposed MTL model outperforms baseline methods without MTL.

Yang and Mitchell (2017) propose a bidirectional long short-term memory (LSTM) network that predicts semantic role labels and a relational network that predicts semantic roles for individual text expressions. The integrated model is a relational neural model that is learned by using the knowledge distilled from the sequential LSTM network.

Katiyar and Cardie (2017) use a method that jointly extracts entity mentions and relations. They show that the attention-based LSTM network can extract semantic relations between entities without using dependency trees. Experiments on the ACE05 data set show that the proposed model can significantly outperform the joint structured perceptron model (Li and Ji, 2014).

Question Answering

For the NLP task of QA and the task of reading comprehension, many effective approaches are based on RNNs that learn a mapping from a text document and a given question to an answer. Conventional approaches regard a document as a long sentence and encode it word by word. However, model quality and training efficiency would decrease once given a relatively long document. Inspired by studies on how people do reading comprehension by first skimming the document, identifying relevant parts and carefully reading these parts, it is beneficial to jointly learn different parts for the QA and reading comprehension tasks.

Choi et al. (2017) present a framework that has two parts, including a simple and fast model for sentence selection and a more complex model for answer generation based on the question and those selected sentences for the QA task. These two parts are learned jointly.

Wang et al. (2018c) jointly train a ranker, which learns to rank retrieved passages, and an answer-extraction reader for the open-domain QA, where the model is given a question and can access to a large corpus (e.g., Wikipedia) instead of a preselected passage.

Semantic Parsing

A long-standing problem in NLP research is the task of semantic parsing, which aims to parse natural language texts to meanings. A challenge is the limitation on data resources because the parsers are often manually designed and the text are labeled by humans. Thus, for the task of semantic parsing, an MTL approach is often adopted when given multiple labeled text data to help leverage as much shared information as possible.

Guo et al. (2016a) describe a universal framework that can exploit multi-typed source treebanks to improve the parsing of a target treebank. Specifically, the proposed framework considers two kinds of source treebanks, including multilingual universal treebanks and monolingual heterogeneous treebanks.

Peng et al. (2017) learn three semantic dependency graph formalisms, including the DELPH-IN bi-lexical dependencies representation, Enju predicate-argument structures representation and Prague semantic dependencies representation, in parallel.

Fan et al. (2017) jointly learn different Alexa-based semantic parsing formalisms with different levels of parameter sharing. They explore three multitask architectures for sequence-to-sequence modeling, including one-to-many, one-to-one and one-to-shared-many.

Zhao and Huang (2017) propose the first end-to-end discourse parser that jointly trains a syntactic and a discourse parser as well as the first syntacto-discourse treebank by integrating the Penn Treebank with the RST Treebank.

Representation Learning

For learning the vectorized representations of text, for example, words and sentences, the challenge is to define the objective function. Most existing representation learning models have been based on a single task with a loss function, such as predicting the next word (Mikolov et al., 2013b) or sentence (Kiros et al., 2015) or training on a certain task such as entailment (Conneau et al., 2017) or machine translation (McCann et al., 2017). Thus, the performance on these tasks are often limited by the small amount of training data. Rather than learning representations from only one task, intuitively learning from multiple tasks for representation learning could leverage more supervised data from many tasks. Moreover, the use of MTL also benefits from a regularization effect such as reducing the risk of the overfitting, thus making the learned representations universal across tasks.

Jernite et al. (2017) adopt three auxiliary tasks for sentence representation learning. The first task is to learn to arrange the order of sentences in a passage. The second task is to select the next sentence out of five candidates given the first three sentences of a paragraph. The third task is trained to recover the conjunction category in sentences.

Hashimoto et al. (2017) introduce a joint many-task (JMT) model to utilize linguistic hierarchies by successively growing the depth of the model to solve increasingly complex tasks, as shown in Figure 17.4. The JMT model can be trained in an end-to-end manner for the POS tagging, chunking, dependency parsing, semantic relatedness and textual entailment. In the JMT model, higher layers have shortcut connections to lower layers.

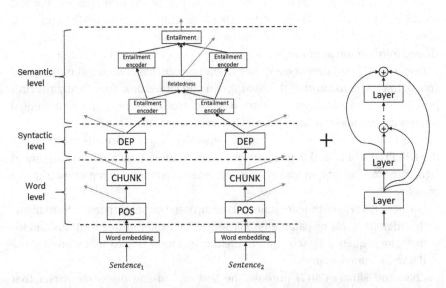

Figure 17.4 The JMT model (adapted from Hashimoto et al. [2017])

Chunking

Chunking (Chomsky, 1956), an effective NLP technique in which linguistic structures are grouped by hierarchical components, has been shown to benefit from being jointly trained with low-level tasks such as POS tagging.

Collobert and Weston (2008) first propose a general DNN architecture, which enables the model to learn multiple NLP tasks such as semantic role labeling (SRL), NER, POS, chunking and language modeling simultaneously.

Søgaard and Goldberg (2016) show that low-level tasks such as POS tagging and NER can be learned to generate feature representations at bottom layers in neural networks when used as auxiliary tasks for chunking. Moreover, the authors show how this hierarchical architecture can be used for domain adaptation.

Ruder et al. (2017) define chunking, NER and a simplified version of SRL as main tasks, and pair them with POS tagging as an auxiliary task. The collection of tasks are then used in an MTL setting.

Automatic Speech Recognition

MTL approaches for automatic speech recognition (ASR) typically use additional supervised information that is available in speech recognition as auxiliary tasks to train an ASR model in an end-to-end manner. For example, phonetic recognition and frame-level state classification can be used as auxiliary tasks to learn helpful intermediate representations.

Toshniwal et al. (2017) find that placing an auxiliary loss at an intermediate layer improves performance due to the combined advantages of the end-to-end training and traditional pipeline approaches. Similarly, Arık et al. (2017) present Deep Voice, a production-quality text-to-speech system based on DNNs. This system comprises five major building blocks, including a segmentation model to locate phoneme boundaries, a grapheme-to-phoneme conversion model, a phoneme duration prediction model, a fundamental frequency prediction model and an audio synthesis model.

Other NLP Tasks

Besides the aforementioned tasks, there are some other NLP tasks that have benefited from the MTL setting.

Balikas et al. (2017) study the problem of fine-grained sentiment classification where tweets are classified according to five-point ratings, and show how to jointly learn a ternary problem with three categories and a fine-grained sentiment classification problem.

Augenstein and Søgaard (2017) use several auxiliary tasks, including semantic super-sense tagging and identification of multi-word expressions for keyphrase boundary classification, that is to detect keyphrases in scientific articles and label them in terms of predefined types.

Luo et al. (2017) propose an attention-based neural network to jointly model the charge prediction task and the relevant article extraction task in a unified framework.

17.3 Transfer Learning in Sentiment Analysis

One of the successful NLP applications of transfer learning is sentiment analysis of user reviews. Often, users leave many textual comments on products in e-commerce sites, or opinions about social events as social media messages. Sentiment analysis aims to take these comments as input and produce their polarity such as positive or negative as output. In this section, we will introduce how transfer learning techniques are applied to sentiment analysis.

As mentioned earlier, users tend to use natural language texts to express opinions and attitudes about products or services on social media or review sites. Thus, it is helpful to build models that take these user comments and correctly interpret their emotional tendency. Sentiment analysis, which aims to automatically determine the overall sentiment polarity of the text, achieves this objective by producing positive or negative polarity as output. As the needs for understanding user feedback in modern society grow, sentiment analysis has attracted increasing attention over the past decades (Pang et al., 2002; Hu and Liu, 2004; Pang and Lee, 2008; Liu, 2012). The characterization of sentiment polarity can be deployed in practical systems that gauge market reaction and summarize opinion in various scenarios such as Web pages, discussion boards and blogs. Successful sentiment analysis can greatly facilitate service-oriented societies.

Supervised learning has been widely used in sentiment analysis using techniques such as DNNs. These supervised models often require massive labeled data as the training data to build sentiment classification models for a specific domain (Wang and Manning, 2012; Socher et al., 2013b; Tang et al., 2015). A major bottleneck in building a sentiment model is the cost spent on annotating new corpora for new application domains, as data labeling in these new domains may be time-consuming and expensive. This is a typical cold-start problem.

To address the afore mentioned cold-start problem, cross-domain sentiment classification is desirable. Cross-domain sentiment analysis aims to leverage the knowledge from a related source domain that has abundant labeled data to improve the performance of a target domain that has no or few labeled data. Because cross-domain sentiment analysis can speed up the launching of a new service, in many fast growing industry sectors, it has become a chosen tool to use.

For cross-domain sentiment classification, a main challenge lies in that features in the source and target domains may be mismatched or have discrepancy in their meanings. This is caused by variations of sentiment expression in different domains. For example, "light" means positively in one domain while negative in another. An examples is illustrated in Figure 17.5.

Therefore, in cross-domain sentiment analysis, we envision a scenario in which, once we have obtained a good sentiment classifier in a source domain, we wish to transfer the knowledge to a target domain with minimal human labeling of data. For example, we may have a good sentiment model for the *movie* domain already, and we wish to transfer the knowledge to a new domain, the *electronics* domain. We need to overcome several challenges in cross-domain sentiment classification. First, the target domain usually contains sentiment words or phrases that do not appear or rarely appear in the source domain. For example, in the *movie* do-

Source domain (**movie**)   Target domain (**electronics**)

 Great movie. The characters are *engaging* and *thoughtful*.   This **great** touchpad feels *glossy* and is *responsive*.

 An **awful** movie and it is very *plotless* and *insipid*.   It is very *lightweight*, an **excellent** transition from PC.

 I think this film is so **terrible** and *lightweight*.   It is *blurry* and *fuzzy* in very dark settings. So **terrible** HP PC.

Figure 17.5 Illustrated examples for cross-domain (movie→electronics) sentiment classification. Words that are in italics and bold are non-pivots and those that are underlined and in bold are pivots. Up-thumbing denotes the positive sentiment while down-thumbing denotes the negative sentiment

main, the words *engaging* and *thoughtful* are used to express positive sentiment, whereas *insipid* and *plotless* often indicate negative sentiment. However, in the *electronics* domain, *glossy* and *responsive* are often used to express positive sentiment, whereas the words *fuzzy* and *blurry* are used to express negative sentiment.

Second, the semantic meaning of a word often differs from one domain to another. For example, *lightweight* is usually used to express a positive sentiment toward portable electronic devices in the *electronics* domain because a lightweight device is easier to carry. However, the same word has a negative sentiment in the *movie* domain since movies that do not invoke deep thoughts in viewers are considered to be lightweight. Therefore, due to this domain discrepancy, a sentiment classifier trained in a source domain may not work well when directly applied to a target domain.

In the following sections, we introduce some of the representative techniques for cross-domain sentiment analysis based on transfer learning.

17.3.1 Problem Definition and Notations

In this section, we introduce some useful notations and definitions used for cross-domain sentiment classification.

- **Pivot**: Blitzer et al. (2006) introduce the concept of the pivot. Pivots are the features with two attributes. First, they are frequently occurring in both domains. Second, they behave in the same way for discriminative learning in both domains, that is, the semantic and the polarity of them are preserved across domains.

- **Non-pivot**: Blitzer et al. (2006) propose the concept of a non-pivot phrase as opposite to the pivot. Non-pivots are usually the features with two characteristics. First, in terms of occurrence, non-pivots are much more frequent in one domain than in another one and their existence highly depends on the domains. Second, the semantic meanings of non-pivots vary across domains.

Cross-domain sentiment classification can be divided into two categories depending on whether labeled data are available for the target domain. In this chapter, we focus on the more challenging case, where there are unlabeled data but no labeled data for the target domain to guide the model learning from the labeled source domain. In the following, we give the formal definition of the cross-domain sentiment classification.

Definition 17.1 (cross-domain sentiment classification)   We are given two domains $\mathbb{S}$ and $\mathbb{T}$, which denote a source domain and a target domain, respectively. Suppose that we have a set of labeled data points $\mathbf{X}_s = \left\{\mathbf{x}_i^s, y_i^s\right\}_{i=1}^{n_s}$ in the source domain $\mathbb{S}$. Besides, a set of unlabeled data points $\mathbf{X}_t = \{\mathbf{x}_j^t\}_{j=1}^{n_t}$ is available in the target domain $\mathbb{T}$. The goal of cross-domain sentiment classification is to train an accurate classifier for the target domain based on labeled source data and unlabeled target data.

Here we divide the solutions to the cross-domain sentiment classification problem into shallow models an deep models.

17.3.2   Shallow Models

In order to align non-pivots from both domains, shallow models can be used. Shallow models refer to those machine learning models that do not rely on deep architectures such as DNNs. These models are based on knowledge on pivots that link the source and target domains. Then more correspondence between domains can be found by correlating pivots and non-pivots. Non-pivots, which are correlated with the same pivots in different domains, are assumed to have correspondence with pivots and hence they should be aligned with each other.

Here we introduce two typical shallow methods, the structural-correspondence-based method and spectral-clustering-based method.

Structural Correspondence-Based Methods

Blitzer et al. (2007a) propose a structural correspondence learning (SCL) method for cross-domain sentiment classification. The intuition of this method is to notice that non-pivots can predict the occurrence of pivot in the unlabeled data of both domains. If a non-pivot can predict the existence of a pivot well, the learned weights for this pair can be used to map all non-pivots from both domains corresponding to a pivot into a common feature space.

Suppose that we are performing a cross-domain sentiment classification task. Suppose that we wish to transfer the knowledge from a *movie* domain to an *electronics* domain. While many features of a movie review are the same as an electronics review, that is, the pivots like "great" and "awful," many words are totally different, such as "glossy" and "responsive." Likewise, many words are useful for the movie domain, but they are not useful for sentiment classification for the electronics domain. For example, words like "engaging" and "thoughtful" are not useful. The key intuition of SCL is that even when ("engaging," "thoughtful") and ("glossy," "responsive") are domain specific, if they have high correlation with pivot words such as "great" and have low correlations with words like "awful," then they can still be aligned with these pivot words, and thus with each other.

	engaging	thoughtful	responsive	glossy	⋯	great	awful	⋯
review1:	1	1	0	0	⋯	1	0	⋯
review2:	0	0	1	1	⋯	1	0	⋯

n non-pivot **features** (bag-of-words)　　　　**m** pseudo **labels**

Figure 17.6 An illustrated example for the multiple pivot prediction tasks

Given the labeled data from a source domain and unlabeled data from both domains, SCL first selects m pivots, which occur frequently in both domains and have high mutual-information values with sentiment labels. These pivots act as a bridge between the source and target domains. Then, all other n features are regarded as the non-pivots. As shown in Figure 17.6, SCL models the correlation between the pivots and the non-pivots by utilizing m linear pivot predictors to predict the occurrence of each pivot from both domains and induces a projected feature space that works well for both domains.

We can denote the weight vector of the i-th pivot predictor as $\mathbf{w}_i \in \mathbb{R}^n$. This allows positive entries in $\mathbf{w}_i$ to mean that the corresponding non-pivots are positively correlated with the i-th pivot. All the weight vectors can be arranged into a matrix $\mathbf{W} = [\mathbf{w}_i]_{i=1}^m \in \mathbb{R}^{n \times m}$ and $\Theta \in \mathbb{R}^{n \times k}$ consists of the top k left singular vectors of $\mathbf{W}$. Here Θ are the principal predictors for the weight space. Given a feature vector $\mathbf{x} \in \mathbb{R}^d$ where $d = m + n$, let $DS(\mathbf{x})$ denote its non-pivot part. SCL applies the projection $\Phi(\mathbf{x}) = DS(\mathbf{x})\Theta$ to obtain new k-dimensional features and learns a sentiment predictor for the augmented instance $\langle \mathbf{x}, DS(\mathbf{x})\Theta \rangle$, where $\langle \cdot, \cdot \rangle$ is a concatenation operation.

Spectral Feature-Based Methods

Pan et al. (2010a) propose a spectral feature alignment (SFA) algorithm. This approach aims at learning model from the cooccurrence matrix formed by pivot and non-pivot mapping. If a pivot feature and a non-pivot feature frequently cooccur in some context, then the non-pivot feature is highly correlated with the pivot, and this knowledge can be used to project a mapping from the cooccurrence matrix.

Based on this intuition, we can group non-pivots in the source and target domains into meaningful clusters by using the pivots as a bridge. The SFA algorithm transforms the cooccurrence relations between pivots and non-pivots into a bipartite graph between domains and adapts a spectral clustering algorithm (Ng et al., 2002) on the bipartite graph to solve the domain mismatch problem.

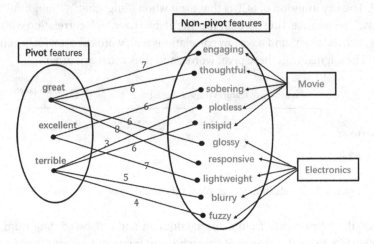

Figure 17.7 An example of the bipartite graph between pivots and non-pivots

SFA constructs a bipartite graph between domains. It first chooses l words that have high term frequencies in both domains and low mutual-information values as pivots and the remaining $m - l$ words are treated as non-pivots, where m is the total number of words. Let $\mathbf{W}_P \in \mathbb{R}^l$ and $\mathbf{W}_{NP} \in \mathbb{R}^{(m-l)}$ denote the vocabulary of the pivots and non-pivots, respectively. SFA leverages the cooccurrence relationship between pivots and non-pivots to construct a bipartite graph $G = (V_P \cup V_{NP}, E)$. In G, each vertex in V_P corresponds to a pivot in $\mathbf{W}_P$ and each vertex in V_{NP} corresponds to a non-pivot in $\mathbf{W}_{NP}$. An edge in E connects two vertices in V_P and V_{NP}, respectively. For each edge $e_{ij} \in E$, there is a non-negative weight r_{ij} to measure the relation between the pivot $w_i \in \mathbf{W}_P$ and the non-pivot $w_j \in \mathbf{W}_{NP}$ according to their cooccurrence. In this way, they form a cooccurrence matrix $\mathbf{M} \in \mathbb{R}^{(m-l) \times l}$. An example for the bipartite graph is shown in Figure 17.7. Finally, we use the constructed bipartite graph to model the intrinsic relationship between pivots and non-pivots.

17.3.3   Deep Learning Based Methods

DNNs have been successfully applied in various NLP tasks such as text classification (Kim, 2014), machine translation (Bahdanau et al., 2014) and QA (Wang et al., 2017c). With the superior transferability of intermediate layers, DNNs are also exploited in transfer learning to automatically learn domain-invariant feature representations for cross-domain sentiment classification. In this section, we introduce four categories based on DNNs, including autoencoder-based models (Glorot et al., 2011; Chen et al., 2012a; Zhou et al., 2016; Ziser and Reichart, 2017), embedding-based models (Bollegala et al., 2015), adversarial learning models (Goodfellow et al., 2014) and pivot-based neural models (Ziser and Reichart, 2017, 2018).

Autoencoder-Based Models

Autoencoder-based models aims to align domain-specific features based on a reconstruction criterion and learn intermediate representations shared across domains. In the following, we introduce several representative autoencoder-based models.

Stacked Denoising Autoencoder

An autoencoder is a feedforward neural network that is trained in an unsupervised manner to reproduce a given input from its latent representation (Bengio et al., 2007). As shown in Figure 17.8, an autoencoder has three layers, including the input layer, the hidden layer and the output layer and hence consists of two parts, namely the encoder and the decoder. Mathematically, given an input $\mathbf{x} \in \mathbb{R}^d$, the encoder f attempts to map $\mathbf{x}$ into a latent representation $\mathbf{z} \in \mathbb{R}^k$, where k is equal to the number of neurons in the hidden layer and typically is smaller than the dimension of the input. f is usually defined as a nonlinear function as

$$\mathbf{z} = f(\mathbf{x}) = \sigma_e(\mathbf{W}_e\mathbf{x} + \mathbf{b}_e), \tag{17.2}$$

where σ_e is a nonlinear activation function in the encoder such as the Sigmoid or hyperbolic tangent function, $\mathbf{W}_e \in \mathbb{R}^{k \times d}$ is a linear transformation matrix, and $\mathbf{b}_e \in \mathbb{R}^k$ is the bias. The decoder g aims to reproduce the input by mapping the latent representation $\mathbf{z}$ to a reconstruction as

$$\hat{\mathbf{x}} = g(\mathbf{z}) = \sigma_d(\mathbf{W}_d\mathbf{z} + \mathbf{b}_d), \tag{17.3}$$

where σ_d is a activation function of the decoder and $\mathbf{W}_d \in \mathbb{R}^{d \times k}, \mathbf{b}_d \in \mathbb{R}^d$ are learnable parameters. The objective of the autoencoder is to minimize the average reconstruction error:

$$\mathscr{L}(\mathbf{x}, \hat{\mathbf{x}}) = \min_{\mathbf{W}_e, \mathbf{b}_e, \mathbf{W}_d, \mathbf{b}_d} \sum_{i=1}^{n} \|\mathbf{x}_i - \hat{\mathbf{x}}_i\|_2^2, \tag{17.4}$$

where $\mathbf{x}_i$ is the i-th training sample out of the total n training samples.

The denoising autoencoder (DAE) (Vincent et al., 2008) is an alternative to the ordinary autoencoder. In DAE, each input $\mathbf{x}$ is stochastically corrupted to $\bar{\mathbf{x}}$, and its objective is to reconstruct input data from their corruptions, that is, minimizing a denoising reconstruction error $\mathscr{L}(\mathbf{x}, g(\mathbf{f}(\bar{\mathbf{x}}))$, as shown in Figure 17.9. Multiple DAEs can be stacked into a deep learning architecture, which is called stacked DAE (SDA).

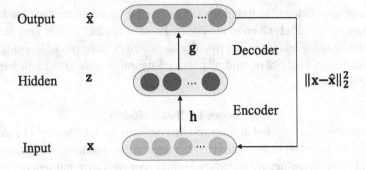

Figure 17.8 The architecture of an autoencoder

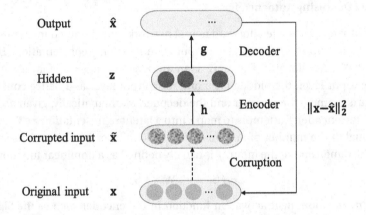

Figure 17.9 The architecture of a DAE

Glorot et al. (2011) successfully adapt the SDA to learn general feature representations for cross-domain sentiment classification. Based on unlabeled data from both domains and the label information in the source domain, the proposed method tackles the cross-domain sentiment classification problem with a two-step procedure. Glorot et al. (2011) train an SDA to reconstruct the input based on the union of the source and target data. Then a linear classifier such as support vector machine is trained on the resulting feature representation $f(\mathbf{x})$ of the source labeled data. The SDA is able to disentangle hidden factors, which explains the variations in the input data and automatically group the features according to their relatedness to these factors.

Bi-transferring Autoencoder

Zhou et al. (2016) propose a bi-transferring autoencoder (BTAE) for cross

-domain sentiment classification. Bi-transferring means that the autoencoder can transfer the source domain data to the target domain and, at the same time, transfer the target domain data to the source domain. Compared with the traditional autoencoder, BTAE consists of one encoder f_c and two decoders g_s and g_t for the source and target domains, respectively. The framework of the BTAE is illustrated in Figure 17.10.

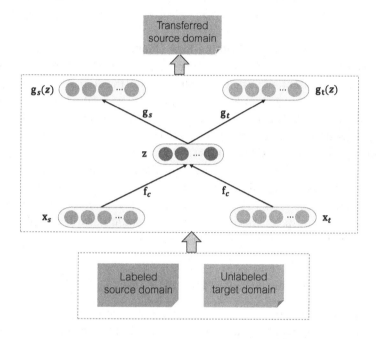

Figure 17.10 The framework of the BTAE (adapted from Zhou et al. [2016])

Specifically, the encoder f_c aims to map an input example $\mathbf{x}$ from both domains into a latent feature representation $\mathbf{z}$:

$$\mathbf{z} = f_c(\mathbf{x}) = \sigma_e(\mathbf{W}_e\mathbf{x} + \mathbf{b}_e). \tag{17.5}$$

The decoders g_s and g_t attempt to map the latent representation to the source or target domain as

$$g_s(z) = \sigma_d(\mathbf{W}_s\mathbf{z} + \mathbf{b}_s), \quad g_t(z) = \sigma_d(\mathbf{W}_t\mathbf{z} + \mathbf{b}_t).$$

The two domains can be generally reconstructed from each other. The objective function for the BTAE system is formulated as

$$\min_{f_c, g_s, g_t, \mathbf{B}_s, \mathbf{B}_t} \left\| \mathbf{X}_s - g_s\left(f_c(\mathbf{X}_s)\right) \right\|_2^2 + \left\| g_t\left(f_c(\mathbf{X}_s)\right) - \mathbf{X}_t\mathbf{B}_t \right\|_2^2 + \left\| \mathbf{X}_t - g_t\left(f_c(\mathbf{X}_t)\right) \right\|_2^2$$

$$+ \left\| g_s\left(f_c(\mathbf{X}_t)\right) - \mathbf{X}_s\mathbf{B}_s \right\|_2^2 + \gamma\left(\|\mathbf{B}_s\|_F^2 + \|\mathbf{B}_t\|_F^2 \right) \tag{17.6}$$

where γ is a regularization parameter. The first term in the objective function of

(17.6) is to minimize the reconstruction error in the source domain. The second term of the equation minimizes the reconstruction error of the target domain data based on the source domain data with the help of a linear transformation matrix $\mathbf{B}_t$. The third and fourth terms are defined similarly. After solving (17.6), the transferred source domain data $g_t\left(f_c\left(\mathbf{X}_s\right)\right)$ have a similar distribution to that of the target domain and hence can be used to train a sentiment classifier for the target domain.

Embedding-Based Models

Embedding-based models (Bollegala et al., 2015) focus on learning domain-specific word representations that accurately capture the domain-specific aspects of semantic meanings of words. Actually, this type of methods can solve both problems of feature mismatch and semantic variation. Bollegala et al. (2015) propose a cross-domain word representation learning (CDWRL) method for cross-domain sentiment analysis. The goal of CDWRL is to predict the surrounding non-pivots of every pivot such that the semantic meaning and orientation of non-pivots are captured. Therefore, there exist two requirements for learning the cross-domain word embeddings. First, for both domains, pivots must accurately predict the cooccurring non-pivots. Second, word representations learned for pivots must be similar in the two domains. Thus, the objective function for CDWRL is formulated as

$$\min L(C_s, W_s) + L(C_t, W_t) + \lambda R(C_s, C_t),$$

where s and t denote the source and target domain, respectively, and C and W denote the pivot and non-pivot, respectively. $L(C_s, W_s)$ is defined as a rank-based predictive hinge loss:

$$L(C_s, W_s) = \sum_{d \in D_s} \sum_{(c_s, w_s) \in d} \sum_{w_s^* \sim p(w_s)} \max(0, 1 - c_s^T w_s + c_s^T w_s^*),$$

where indices c_s and w_s denote a pivot and a non-pivot cooccurring in a document, w_s^* denotes a non-pivot that does not cooccur with c_s, and $p(w)$, the marginal distribution of non-pivots, can be estimated from the corpus counts. Similarly, $L(C_t, W_t)$ is defined as

$$L(C_t, W_t) = \sum_{d \in D_t} \sum_{(c_t, w_t) \in d} \sum_{w_t^* \sim p(w_t)} \max(0, 1 - c_t^T w_t + c_t^T w_t^*).$$

The regularizer $R(C_s, C_t)$ is defined as

$$R(C_s, C_t) = \frac{1}{2} \sum_{i=1}^{K} \left\| c_s^{(i)} - c_t^{(i)} \right\|.$$

Through learning the embeddings for the pivots and non-pivots, their semantic relation and sentiment orientation can be captured for domain adaptation.

Adversarial Learning Models

A generative adversarial network (GAN) (Goodfellow et al., 2014) is a popular deep generative model for a diverse range of tasks from style transfer in images to data augmentation. The goal of GAN is to learn a generative distribution $\mathbb{P}_G^X$ that imitates the real data distribution $\mathbb{P}_{real}^X$. Specifically, GAN learns a generative network G and a discriminative network D, where G generates samples from the generator distribution $\mathbb{P}_G^X$ and D learns to determine whether a sample is from $\mathbb{P}_G^X$ or $\mathbb{P}_{real}^X$. The objective of GANs is to optimize the following min-max risk as

$$\phi = \min_G \max_D \left(\mathbb{E}_{x \sim \mathbb{P}_{real}^X} \left[\log D(x) \right] + \mathbb{E}_{z \sim \mathbb{P}_G^Z} \left[\log(1 - D(G(z))) \right] \right). \qquad (17.7)$$

The success of GANs inspires innovations in which adversarial learning be used to measure the discrepancy between distributions. Formally, Ganin and Lempitsky (2015) and Ganin et al. (2016) apply the adversarial loss to measure the *H*-divergence between two distributions and propose a domain-adversarial training of neural network (DANN) for domain adaptation.

Compared with the GAN, the DANN consists of three parts, the feature extractor G_f, the class predictor G_y and the domain classifier G_d. The input **x** is first mapped by G_f to a D-dimensional feature representation $\mathbf{f} = G_f(\mathbf{x}; \boldsymbol{\theta}_f) \in \mathbb{R}^D$, where $\boldsymbol{\theta}_f$ denotes parameters in G_f. Then, the feature representation **f** is mapped by G_y to the label y, where the parameters of G_y are denoted by $\boldsymbol{\theta}_y$. At the same time, the feature representation **f** is also mapped by G_d to the domain label d with the parameters denoted by $\boldsymbol{\theta}_d$.

In the learning stage, the DANN aims to minimize the label prediction loss on the source labeled data. Thus, the parameters of the feature extractor and the class predictor, that is, $\boldsymbol{\theta}_f$ and $\boldsymbol{\theta}_y$, are both optimized to minimize the empirical loss on the source domain. This guarantees the features **f** to be discriminative on the source domain. At the same time, the DANN attempts to make the feature **f** invariant across the domain, which is equivalent to making the distributions of the source and target domains similar. In order to obtain domain-invariant feature representations, the parameters $\boldsymbol{\theta}_f$ are optimized to maximize the classification loss of the domain classifier such that the distributions of the two domains are similar as much as possible, while simultaneously optimizing the parameters $\boldsymbol{\theta}_d$ of the domain classifier to minimize the loss of the domain classifier and make the domain classifier discriminate the feature representations from the source and target domains.

On the surface, adversarial generative learning systems such as DANN can be directly applied to transfer sentiment classification models between domains. However, these aforementioned deep neural methods cannot directly identify the pivots and they lack of the interpretability for what to transfer. In fact, interpretability is a major problem in deep learning based models, where the model is often referred to as the "black-box" models. In practice, it would be nice to explain to the

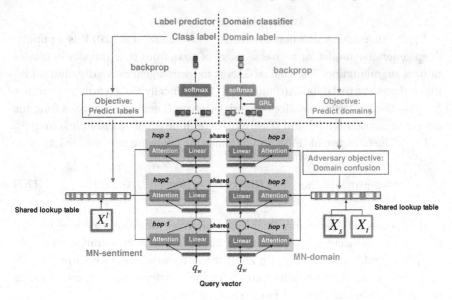

Figure 17.11 The framework of the adversarial memory network

users why a model picks a certain word as pivot and non-pivot words, to provide more confidence that the system is making a correct decision.

Another limitation of previous cross-domain sentiment classification works is that, for the most part, pivots and non-pivots are hand-picked by humans. It would be nice to automatically learn the pivots from two domains. Li et al. (2017b) propose a method known as the adversarial memory network (AMN), which is shown in Figure 17.11, to automatically capture pivots in a cross-domain setting. They also introduced a novel word attention mechanism into the domain adversarial learning framework to allow for interpretability. They make use of the attention mechanism of a memory network, which can automatically visualize which words are more likely to be pivots and contribute more to the domain-invariant representations based on attention scores, to interpret what to transfer.

Several illustrative examples of the learned result are shown in Figure 17.12 to visualize the attentions of the AMN model. We can see that the words with high attention weights such as *great, good, best, beautiful, fantastic, gorgeous, terrible, disappointed, disappointment* and *poor* are pivots. These are indeed the words chosen by humans.

Despite superior experimental performance, AMN is limited to only focusing on word-level attention because it ignores the hierarchical structure of documents. In practice, we wish to accurately capture pivots in long documents, which often follow a hierarchical structure. Besides, it cannot automatically capture and exploit the relationship between non-pivots and pivots, which may result in the degraded performance when the source and target domains only have few overlapping pivots.

To simultaneously harness the collective power of pivots and non-pivots, and to interpret what to transfer, Li et al. (2017b) introduce a hierarchical attention transfer network (HATN) for cross-domain sentiment classification. HATN jointly train two hierarchical attention networks named P-net and NP-net.

The first part is P-net, which aims to capture the pivots. To achieve this goal, the labeled data X_s in the source domain is fed into the P-net for sentiment classification and, in the meantime, all the data X_s and X_t in both domains are fed into the P-net for domain classification based on adversarial learning to make the domain classifier indiscriminative between the representations from the source and target domains. In this way, it guarantees that representations from the P-net are both domain-shared and useful for sentiment classification. It can thus identity the pivot features with the attention mechanism.

The second part is NP-net, which aims to align the non-pivots. To reach this goal, the transformed labeled data $g(X_s)$ in the source domain $\mathbb{S}$ generated by hiding all the pivots identified by the P-net are fed into the NP-net for sentiment classification. At the same time, all transformed data $g(X_s)$ and $g(X_t)$ in both domains $\mathbb{S}$ and $\mathbb{T}$ generated in the same way are fed to NP-net for +(positive)/-(negative) pivot predictions.

The P-Net and the NP-net work together to predict whether an original sample x contains positive or negative pivots based on the transformed sample $g(x)$. The transformed sample $g(x)$ has two labels, a label z^+ indicating whether x contains at least one positive pivot and a label z^- indicating whether x contains at least one negative pivot. The intuition behind it is that positive non-pivots tend to cooccur with positive pivots and negative non-pivots tend to cooccur with negative pivots. In this way, the NP-net can discover domain-specific features with the pivots as a bridge and capture the non-pivots that are expected to correlate closely to the pivots with the attention mechanism.

The NP-net needs positive and negative pivots as a bridge across domains. Since the P-net possesses the ability of automatically capturing the pivots with attentions, the training procedure of HATN consists of two stages.

- Individual attention learning: The P-net is trained for cross-domain sentiment classification. We use the best parameters for P-net with early stopping on the validation set and then select positive pivots based on the highest attention scores in positive reviews. The negative pivots are obtained in a similar way.
- Joint attention learning: The P-net and the NP-net are jointly trained for cross-domain sentiment classification. The labeled data X_s and its transformed data $g(X_s)$ in the source domain $\mathbb{S}$ are simultaneously fed into the P-net and the NP-net respectively and their representations are concatenated for sentiment classification. Note that, the transformed labeled data $g(X_s)$ fed to the NP-net are used for sentiment classification and +(positive)/-(negative) pivot predic-

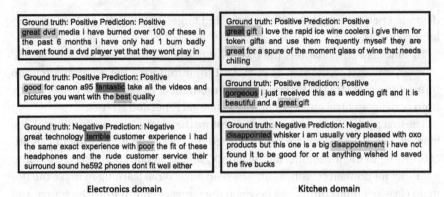

Electronics domain   **Kitchen domain**

Figure 17.12 The visualization of attentions of the electronics→kitchen adaptation task. Deeper color implies larger attention weights and higher probability to be pivots

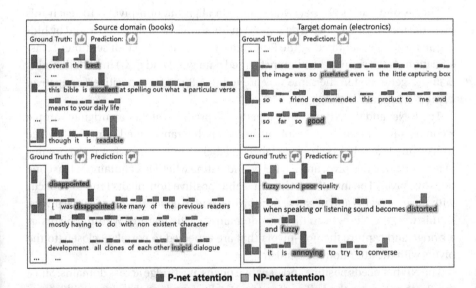

■ **P-net attention**   □ **NP-net attention**

Figure 17.13 Visualization of attentions of the HATN model in the book→electronics adaptation task (adapted from Li et al. [2017b]). Label 1 denotes the positive sentiment and label 0 denotes the negative sentiment

tions simultaneously, but transformed unlabeled data $g(\mathbf{X}_t)$ fed to the NP-net can only be used for the +(positive)/-(negative) pivot predictions.

Several illustrative examples are shown in Figure 17.13 to visualize attentions of the HATN model. Figure 17.13 illustrates that the P-net tends to pay higher word attentions to pivots between domains such as positive pivots *best, excellent* and *good* and negative pivots *disappointed, poor* and *annoying*. The sentences that contain these pivots also get higher sentence attentions in the P-net. Different from the P-net, the NP-net aims to pay higher word attentions to the non-pivots in the two domains, such as source non-pivots *readable* and *insipid* in the books domain and target non-pivots *pixelated, fuzzy* and *distorted* in the electronics domain. The sentences that contain these non-pivots also get higher sentence attentions in the NP-net.

Pivot-Based Neural Models

Pivot-based neural models aim to learn a correlation mapping between the non-pivots and pivots via neural networks. Ziser and Reichart (2017) propose an autoencoder SCL (AE-SCL) method that applies the idea of SCL to autoencoder-based neural networks. AE-SCL learns to encode the non-pivots of a data point into a low-dimensional representation so that the existence of pivot features in the example can be decoded from that representation. The architecture of the AE-SCL is shown in Figure 17.14.

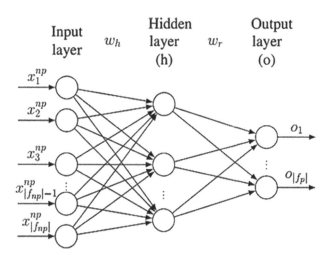

Figure 17.14 The architecture of the AE-SCL model (adapted from Ziser and Reichart [2017])

Specifically, the feature set is denoted by f, the subset of pivots by $f_p \subseteq \{1,\ldots,|f|\}$, and the subset of non-pivots by $f_{np} \subseteq \{1,\ldots,|f|\}$ such that $f_p \cup f_{np} = f$ and $f_p \cap f_{np} = \emptyset$. Besides, the representations of a pivot and a non-pivot of an input $\mathbf{x}$ are denoted by $\mathbf{x}^p$ and $\mathbf{x}^{np}$, respectively.

The goal of the AE-SCL aims to induce a robust and compact feature representation by learning a nonlinear prediction function from $\mathbf{x}^p$ to $\mathbf{x}^{np}$. The prediction function is based on the framework of the autoencoder. Based on $\mathbf{x}^{np}$, the AE-SCL first encodes $\mathbf{x}^{np}$ into an intermediate representation $h_{\mathbf{w}^h}(\mathbf{x}^{np}) = \sigma\left(\mathbf{w}^h \mathbf{x}^{np}\right)$ and then predicts the occurrence of the pivot x^p with a decoder function

$o = r_{\mathbf{w}^r}(h_{\mathbf{w}^h}(\mathbf{x}^{np})) = \sigma\left(w^r h_{\mathbf{w}^h}(\mathbf{x}^{np})\right)$, which reflects the probability that the pivot appears in the input. Hence, the cross-entropy loss function is naturally used.

Two observations are in order. First, pivots with similar semantic meanings often have similar word embeddings. Second, pivots that occur in an input are much fewer than pivots that do not occur in it. Thus, Ziser and Reichart (2017) propose an AE-SCL with similarity regularization, where pretrained word embeddings of the pivots are injected into the AE-SCL model to improve the generalization across examples with semantically similar pivots. Moreover, Ziser and Reichart (2018) propose a pivot-based language modeling that incorporates pivots into a language modeling method.

18

Transfer Learning in Dialogue Systems

18.1 Introduction

Dialogue systems can be roughly categorized into open-domain dialogue systems (Sutskever et al., 2014; Shang et al., 2015; Serban et al., 2016, 2017) and task-oriented dialogue systems (Young et al., 2013). Open-domain dialogue systems do not limit their dialogue domains and can be used for chit-chat. Task-oriented dialogue systems aim to guide a user to finish a certain task in a restricted domain. It can be deployed in a call center, an online chatting platform or a customer service center. It can reduce the need of human staff and thus the cost.

Open-domain dialogue systems do not have a restricted domain, so the topics of questions can be very diversified and the domain knowledge can hardly be incorporated. Sequence-to-sequence models or the encoder-decoder models (Sutskever et al., 2014; Shang et al., 2015; Serban et al., 2016, 2017) are widely used in the open-domain dialogue systems. There has been few works on applying transfer learning to open-domain dialogue systems, and we will focus more on transfer learning in task-oriented systems in this chapter.

A task-oriented dialogue system takes text inputs from a user and generates text responses to the user based on the context and the question. The design of current task-oriented dialogue systems requires much human knowledge and manual data labeling. Frame-based task-oriented dialogue systems are widely used. In the frame-based systems, a slot is a basic piece of information with a set of possible values. For example, with respect to the choices of food, we can have Chinese food, Japanese food, Indian food and so on.

Based on their functionalities, a dialogue system can be divided into different components. Each component is responsible for a specific subtask, and the communications between components are through a set of slots and their values. There are four basic components in a task-oriented dialogue system, including the spoken language understanding module, the dialogue state tracker module, the dialogue policy learning (DPL) module and the natural language generation module. The spoken language understanding module (He and Young, 2006; Mairesse et al., 2009; Henderson et al., 2012; Yao et al., 2013, 2014) is respon-

Figure 18.1 The architecture of a task-oriented dialogue system

sible for detecting speech-acts, slots and the corresponding slot values. It takes a user utterance as the input and identifies the speech-acts and slot values appeared in the user utterance. The dialogue state tracker (Wang and Lemon, 2013; Henderson et al., 2014; Zilka and Jurcicek, 2015; Lee and Kim, 2016; Sun et al., 2016) is responsible of inferring and maintaining dialogue states. It takes a parsed user utterance (including speech-acts, slots and slot values) as the input and keeps the track of current dialogue state based on the user utterance and the previous dialogue state. The DPL module (Williams, 2008a, 2008b; Lefèvre et al., 2009; Young et al., 2010) takes current dialogue state as the input and decides the next action to take. The natural language generation module (Wen et al., 2015a) converts the system action back to text response. Among these four modules, the DPL module is the core component.

According to their training approaches, task-oriented dialogue systems can be categorized into modular dialogue systems and end-to-end dialogue systems. The components in modular dialogue systems can be built separately with different objective functions, while end-to-end dialogue systems are trained jointly with a single objective function. Modular dialogue systems have a low inter-modular dependency, thus we can plug-in different components freely. Hence, components can be trained or handcrafted independently and the data needed to train each component can be obtained easily. However, without a consistent objective function, the whole system with different components might not work well. End-to-end dialogue systems have a single objective function. When trained jointly, the whole system can learn together and achieve the better performance, and it does not require intermediate annotation thus to reduce human efforts. However, since all components are learned jointly, we cannot switch components without retraining. Moreover, the training of an end-to-end dialogue system is more difficult.

The rest parts of this chapter are organized as follows. We first introduce the problem formulation, then we introduce each of the four modules one by one from Section 18.3 to Section 18.6, and finally we introduce the end-to-end dialogue systems in Section 18.7.

18.2 Problem Formulation

In a task-oriented dialogue system, given a sequence of historical dialogues and current question, the goal is to predict the response. We use X to denote the questions and use Y to denote the responses. The n-th question is denoted by $X_n = \{x_1, x_2, \cdots, x_{N_n^x}\}$ with N_n^x as the number of associated words. Similarly the n-th response is denoted by $Y_n = \{y_1, y_2, \cdots, y_{N_n^y}\}$ where N_n^y denotes the number of words in Y_n. N denotes the number of dialogue rounds in a dialogue. Given the dialogue history $H_n = \{\{X_j, Y_j\}_{j=1}^{n-1}, X_n\}$, our task is to predict Y_n.

As discussed before, there are four components in a task-oriented dialogue system.

(1) The spoken language understanding module. It takes a text utterance X_n as input and identifies the abstract user action $\tilde{X}_n$ of the utterance at every time step n.

(2) The dialogue state tracker module. Given a previous dialogue state $\tilde{H}_{n-1}$, an abstract system action $\tilde{Y}_{n-1}$ and an abstract user utterance $\tilde{X}_n$, the dialogue state tracker aims to keep track of current dialogue state $\tilde{H}_n$.

(3) The DPL module. It takes the dialogue state $\tilde{H}_n$ as the input and predict the abstract system action $\tilde{Y}_n$.

(4) The natural language generation module. It takes an abstract system action $\tilde{Y}_n$ as the input and generates the final system response sentence Y_n.

In the following four sections, we will introduce how transfer learning can help the learning of the four modules.

18.3 Transfer Learning in Spoken Language Understanding

The spoken language understanding module is responsible for mapping a text utterance to a structured output such as speech-acts, slots and slot values. In this section, we summarize the transfer learning methods used for spoken language understanding. There are mainly three methods to transfer knowledge, including model adaptation, instance-based transfer and parameter transfer.

18.3.1 Problem Definition

The spoken language understanding module takes a raw text utterance X_n as the input to identify the abstract user action $\tilde{X}_n$ in the utterance. The abstract user action $\tilde{X}_n = \{a_n, \mathbf{s}_n = \{s_j = v_j\}\}$ consists of a user speech-act a_n (also known as intention) and a sequence of slot value pairs $\mathbf{s}_n = \{s_1 = v_1, s_2 = v_2, \cdots\}$.

There are two major problems in spoken language understanding. The first problem is known as the speech-act classification and the other is known as slot-filling.

(1) Speech-act classification: The input is a user utterance X_n and the output is the speech-act a_n of the user utterance. The speech-act classification can be viewed as a multi-label classification problem.

(2) Slot-filling: The problem is to find all possible slot value pairs $\mathbf{s}_n = \{s_1 = v_1, s_2 = v_2, \cdots\}$ in the user utterance X_n. The slot-filling task can be viewed as a sequential classification problem based on the word sequence of a sentence. For an input sentence "who played Zeus in the 2010 action movie Titans," the expected output is a semantic tag for each word in the input sentence like "who:{} played:{} zeus:{character=zeus} in:{} the:{} 2010:{year=2010} action:{genre=action} movie:{type=movie} Titans:{name=Titans}."

18.3.2 Model Adaptation

Tür (2005) proposes to use model adaptation and boosting for the speech-act classification. The source and target domains share the same set of speech-acts labels but have different distributions. In this work, the objective is to regularize the target domain model by minimizing the Kulback–Leibler (KL) divergence between the source and target models. The loss function in the target domain is defined as

$$L(\mathbf{w}) = \sum_n \sum_{a'} (\ln(1 + \exp(-A_n[a']f(X_n, a'; \mathbf{w})))) + \eta \mathrm{KL}(P(A_n[a']=1|X_n)||\sigma(f(X_n, a'; \mathbf{w}))),$$

where n is the index of an instance, a' is an element in the label set, $P(A_n[a'] = 1|\mathbf{X}_n)$ denotes the probability that $\mathbf{X}_n$ belongs to label a' in the source domain and $\sigma(f(\mathbf{X}_n), a')$ defines the probability that X_n belongs to label a' in the target domain. In this objective function, the first term measures the training loss on the target domain and the second term denotes the KL divergence between the source and target models.

18.3.3 Instance-Based Transfer

Tür (2006) proposes transferring instances on the speech-act classification problem. There are a number of similar intention classes in the source and target domains, but no mapping is available. Instances with similar labels in the source domain are chosen to help build a model for intention classification in the target domain. Denote the target domain data set as $\{X, a\}$ and the source domain data set as $\{X^s, a^s\}$. We can denote the classifier in the source domain by $p(a^s|X^s) = f_{a^s}^s(X^s)$. The classifier in the target domain is denoted by $p(a|X) = f_a^t(X)$.

To ensure the quality instances being transferred, Tür (2006) applies the target domain classifier to each instance X^s in the source domain. If the predicted probability that the source instance X^s belongs to a target class a is above a threshold, that is, $f_a^t(X^s) > \rho$, then X^s is transferred to the target domain as an instance of target domain class a. After some instances are transferred, the target-domain classifier can be retrained with the transferred source domain instances and the target domain instances.

18.3.4   Parameter Transfer

Yazdani and Henderson (2015) propose sharing model parameters between classifiers with similar labels, so that similar classifiers can have similar decision functions. The classification model for each speech-act a is a linear classifier, and the parameter for the classifier corresponding to label $a_j(s_k = v_m)$ is a weight vector $\mathbf{w}_{a_j(s_k=v_m)}$. For each label $a_j(s_k = v_m)$, the classifier is a logistic regression formulated as $y = \sigma(\mathbf{w}_{a_j(s_k=v_m)}^T \phi(x_i))$. Yazdani and Henderson (2015) assume that the weight vector $\mathbf{w}_{a_j(s_k=v_m)}$ can be modeled by a two-layer perceptron given the embeddings of the label words. Specifically, the weight parameters for label $a_j(s_k = v_m)$ is defined based on the word embedding of a_j, s_k and v_m as

$$\mathbf{w}_{a_j(s_k=v_m)} = \sigma([\phi(a_j), \phi(s_k), \phi(v_m)] \mathbf{W}_{ih}) \mathbf{W}_{ho},$$

where $\phi(x_i)$ denotes the word embedding for word x_i, σ is an activation function, $\mathbf{W}_{ih}$ is a $3d \times h$ matrix and $\mathbf{W}_{ho}$ is a $d \times d$ matrix. The parameter $\mathbf{W}_{ih}$ and $\mathbf{W}_{ho}$ are shared for all labels, making it a transfer learning method.

Jeong and Lee (2009) propose dividing the model parameters into domain-dependent and domain-independent parameters, where the domain-independent parameters are shared across domains to transfer knowledge. A conditional random field is used as the base model for the slot-filling problem. The probability of the slot set is given by

$$\mathbf{s} = \underset{\mathbf{s}'}{\arg\max} \, P(\mathbf{s}'|X),$$

where $X = \{x_1, x_2, \cdots\}$ is the input word sequence and $\mathbf{s} = \{s_1, s_2, \cdots\}$ is the associated class label sequence. The probability of the slot set can be factorized by

$$P(\mathbf{s}|X) = \prod_t P(s_t|x_t, s_{t-1}),$$

$$P(s_t|x_t, s_{t-1}) = \frac{1}{Z(x_t, s_{t-1})} \exp(\phi_d(s_{t-1}, s_t, x_t) + \phi_{ind}(s_{t-1}, s_t, x_t),$$

where $Z(x_t, s_{t-1})$ is the normalization term, $\phi_d(s_{t-1}, s_t, x_t)$ is the domain-dependent component and $\phi_{ind}(s_{t-1}, s_t, x_t)$ is the domain-independent component. The model considers features such as n-gram lexical features in the sliding window and state transition probability. The domain-independent component is shared across domains for knowledge transfer.

In summary, model adaptation can be used to adapt an existing model from a source domain to improve the performance in a target domain. Given the target domain data, the pretrained model is fine-tuned on a few instances in the target domain. However, the source and target domains have to use the same kind of models. Instance transfer can work without modifying the structure of the classifier and it is easy to train. However, the source and the target models need to be trained for multiple times, which is time consuming. Parameter transfer can transfer common model parameters from a source domain to a target domain. However, the model parameters have to be partitioned into shared parameters and domain-dependent parameters and, as a result, some classifiers could not be used.

18.4   Transfer Learning in Dialogue State Tracker

The dialogue state tracker module tracks the dialogue state according to the system action, the user utterance and the previous dialogue state. In this section, we review the multi-domain transfer learning works for the dialogue state tracking problem. These algorithms can be categorized into the feature-based approach (Ren et al., 2014) and the model-based approach (Williams, 2013; Mrkšic et al., 2015).

Feature-based multi-domain dialogue state trackers aim to learn general domain-independent features so that the trained models can be reused in multi-domain setting. Model-based multi-domain dialogue state trackers adapt a general domain-independent tracking model with the domain-dependent data to build a dialogue state tracker for multiple domains.

18.4.1   Feature-Based Multi-domain Dialogue State Tracker

A feature-based multi-domain dialogue state tracker aims to build general domain-independent features that can be reused in multiple domains.

Ren et al. (2014) propose to share the dialogue state tracker model across different domains by using a domain-dependent feature set. For each utterance, a joint feature representation is extracted. In the joint feature representation of the utterance, different features are extracted for each domain. The extracted features for each domain are specially designed, so that, for different domains, we can use the same dialogue state tracker.

18.4.2   Model-Based Multi-domain Dialogue State Tracker

A model-based multi-domain dialogue state tracker adapts a general domain-independent tracking model trained in the domain-dependent data sets to build a dialogue state tracker for multiple domains.

Williams (2013) proposes to decompose the model into two parts, including the domain-shared component and domain-specific component. To do this, the original feature representation is expanded to construct a new feature representation. For example, assuming we have three domains, the new feature representation of an instance in the first domain is $(\mathbf{f}_1^T, \mathbf{0}, \mathbf{0}, \mathbf{f}_1^T)^T$ where $\mathbf{f}_1$ is the original feature representation, that for an instance in the second domain take the form of $(\mathbf{0}, \mathbf{f}_2^T, \mathbf{0}, \mathbf{f}_2^T)^T$ and for the third domain is $(\mathbf{0}, \mathbf{0}, \mathbf{f}_3^T, \mathbf{f}_3^T)^T$. Then the parameter of the corresponding linear learner is formulated as $(\mathbf{w}_1^T, \mathbf{w}_2^T, \mathbf{w}_3^T, \mathbf{w}_0^T)^T$, where $\mathbf{w}_1, \mathbf{w}_2$ and $\mathbf{w}_3$ are the domain-shared model parameters, while $\mathbf{w}_0^T$ is shared by all the domains.

Mrkšic et al. (2015) propose to first train a generalize dialogue state tracker recurrent neural network (RNN) for all domains and then they initialize the domain-dependent tracker RNN with this general RNN. The key idea is to use delexicalized features before processing. For example, the sentence "want available internet" is preprocessed and turns into "want tag-slot-value tag-slot-name." The delexicalized features allow knowledge transfer between not only domains, but also fine granularity slots. However, due to different data distributions in different slots, a model adaptation step is still required to make the general model work well for each slot.

18.5 Transfer Learning in DPL

A popular model for the DPL module is the Markov decision process (MDP) (Biermann and Long, 1996; Levin et al., 1997; Walker et al., 1998; Singh et al., 1999). The DPL module is modeled as a system that tries to achieve a goal through a series of interactions with the user. The information about the current dialogue situation is modeled by the dialogue state and the DPL module can choose the optimal system action. The next dialogue state depends only on the current state and the action taken by the system, which follows the Markov assumption. In some situations, the current state of a system cannot be fully determined. A partially observable MDP (POMDP) (Young et al., 2013) is then used to model the dialogue policy. At each step, instead of tracking the ground-truth dialogue state, POMDP keeps track of a probability distribution on all possible dialogue states, which is called a belief state. The belief state is assumed to follow the Markov assumption, which means the next belief state depends only on current belief state and the action taken. The POMDP policy decides the best system action based on the current belief state instead of the true state.

Based on whether multiple domains are considered, dialogue systems can be categorized into single-domain dialogue systems and multi-domain dialogue systems. The single domain means the training and testing data are in the same domain and the goal of single-domain DPL is to learn the optimal dialogue policy in this domain. Multi-domain dialogue systems aim to use the knowledge in a source domain to help the policy learning in a target domain. In this section, we introduce the multi-domain transfer learning works for the DPL problem. Most methods under this setting are based on the Q-learning framework and we categorize these works into three categories, including transferred linear model, transferred Gaussian process and transferred Bayesian committee machine.

Before presenting these three approaches, we first introduce some notations. In a modular dialogue system, without loss of generality, we formulate the DPL as an MDP since a POMDP policy could be represented by an MDP on the belief state. The MDP is defined as $\{H, Y, P, \mathscr{R}, \gamma\}$, where H denotes the dialogue state, Y denotes the reply of the agent, P is the state transition probability function, $\mathscr{R}$ is the reward function and $\gamma \in [0, 1]$ is the discounted factor. At time step n, $\tilde{H}_n$ denotes the dialogue state, $\tilde{Y}_n$ denotes the agent reply and r_n denotes the reward. We assume the spoken language understanding module and the dialogue state tracker have provided the current state $\tilde{H}_n$ at time step n, so we can observe $\tilde{H}_n$, $\tilde{Y}_n$ and r_n. The goal is to find an optimal policy that can maximize the cumulative return, defined as $G_n = \sum_{k=0}^{\infty} \gamma^k r_{n+k}$.

18.5.1   Transferred Linear Model for Q-learning

Genevay and Laroche (2016) adapt an existing user model to a new user by transferring a liner model. Specifically, the action value function can be approximated by $Q(\tilde{H}, \tilde{Y}) = \sigma(\phi(\tilde{H}, \tilde{Y})^T \mathbf{w})$, where $\phi(\tilde{H}, \tilde{Y})$ denotes the feature vector extracted for the state-action pair $(\tilde{H}, \tilde{Y})$, $\mathbf{w}$ is the weight vector of this linear function and σ is an activation function. The proposed method selects only transitions that are dissimilar to the the target domain data. That is, for each trajectory in the source domain $< \tilde{H}^s, \tilde{Y}^s, \tilde{H}'^s, r^s >$, if there exists a trajectory in the target domain $< \tilde{H}, \tilde{Y}, \tilde{H}', r >$ whose $\tilde{Y} = \tilde{Y}^s$ and $\|\tilde{H} - \tilde{H}^s\| \leq \eta$, then this source trajectory will not be transferred to the target domain. The policy is initially trained on the selected source data points $\mathscr{D}^s = \{< \tilde{H}^s, \tilde{Y}^s, \tilde{H}'^s, r^s >\}$. Then the policy parameters are transferred to the target domain and updated on the target domain data.

Genevay and Laroche (2016) aim to adapt an existing user model to a new user. The similarity between the source and target domains $\|\tilde{H} - \tilde{H}^s\|$ is calculated based on a set of predefined features, including the utility loss between the last time slot and the next one, the number of time slots, the length of the dialogue and the speech recognition score.

Transferred linear models for Q-learning are simple and efficient, but they can only work when the source and target data are in the same feature space.

18.5.2   Transferred Gaussian Process for Q-learning

In Gašić et al. (2013, 2014, 2015a, 2015b, 2015c), the authors use a Gaussian process to learn the Q-function, which is defined as

$$Q^\pi(\tilde{H}, \tilde{Y}) \sim \mathcal{N}(m(\tilde{H}, \tilde{Y}), k((\tilde{H}, \tilde{Y}), (\tilde{H}, \tilde{Y}))),$$

where $m(\tilde{H}, \tilde{Y})$ is the mean function and $k((\tilde{H}, \tilde{Y}), (\tilde{H}', \tilde{Y}'))$ is the kernel function. The kernel function $k((\tilde{H}, \tilde{Y}), (\tilde{H}', \tilde{Y}'))$ can be factorized into separate kernels over the state and action spaces via

$$k((\tilde{H}, \tilde{Y}), (\tilde{H}', \tilde{Y}')) = k_{\tilde{H}}(\tilde{H}, \tilde{H}') k_{\tilde{Y}}(\tilde{Y}, \tilde{Y}').$$

Given training state-action sequences $\mathbf{B} = [(\tilde{H}_0, \tilde{Y}_0), \cdots, (\tilde{H}_n, \tilde{Y}_n)]^T$ and the corresponding immediate rewards $\mathbf{r} = [r_0, \cdots, r_n]^T$, the Q-function $Q^{\pi}(\tilde{H}, \tilde{Y})$ for any state-action pair $(\tilde{H}, \tilde{Y})$ is given by

$$Q(\tilde{H}, \tilde{Y}) | \mathbf{B}, \mathbf{r} \sim \mathcal{N}(\bar{Q}(\tilde{H}, \tilde{Y}), \text{cov}((\tilde{H}, \tilde{Y})(\tilde{H}, \tilde{Y}))),$$

where the posterior mean is given by

$$\bar{Q}(\tilde{H}, \tilde{Y}) = \mathbf{k}(\tilde{H}, \tilde{Y})^T \mathbf{H}^T (\mathbf{HKH}^T + \sigma^2 \mathbf{HH}^T)^{-1} (\mathbf{r} - \mathbf{m}),$$

and the covariance is given by

$$\text{cov}((\tilde{H}, \tilde{Y}), (\tilde{H}, \tilde{Y})) = k((\tilde{H}, \tilde{Y}), (\tilde{H}, \tilde{Y})) - \mathbf{k}(\tilde{H}, \tilde{Y})^T \mathbf{H}^T (\mathbf{HKH}^T + \sigma^2 \mathbf{HH}^T)^{-1} \mathbf{Hk}(\tilde{H}, \tilde{Y}),$$

where $\mathbf{m} = [m(\tilde{H}_0, \tilde{Y}_0), \cdots, m(\tilde{H}_n, \tilde{Y}_n)]^T$, $\mathbf{K}$ is the kernel matrix, $\mathbf{H}$ is the band matrix with diagonal $[1, -\gamma]$, $\mathbf{k}(\tilde{H}, \tilde{Y}) = [k((\tilde{H}_0, \tilde{Y}_0), (\tilde{H}, \tilde{Y})), \cdots, k((\tilde{H}_n, \tilde{Y}_n), (\tilde{H}, \tilde{Y}))]^T$ and σ^2 is the variance for the noise.

To transfer a Gaussian process policy, there are basically two approaches.

(1) Transferring the mean function $\bar{Q}(\tilde{H}, \tilde{Y})$. In the works by Gašić et al. (2015a, 2015b, 2015c), source data are used to build a good Q-function $\bar{Q}(\tilde{H}, \tilde{Y})$ for the target domain. In the works by Gašić et al. (2013, 2014) and Casanueva et al. (2015), the mean function in the source domain is used as a prior on that of the target domain.

(2) Transferring the covariance function $k((\tilde{H}, \tilde{Y}), (\tilde{H}, \tilde{Y}))$. In the works by Gašić et al. (2013, 2014, 2015a, 2015b, 2015c) and Casanueva et al. (2015), the kernel function on state-action pairs is defined from different domains.

The kernel function $k((\tilde{H}, \tilde{Y}), (\tilde{H}', \tilde{Y}'))$ is the core of transfer learning methods. Based on different definitions of kernel functions, we have different kinds of methods.

In Gašić et al. (2014), only the slots in the source domain $\mathcal{S}$ are used. In this work, the belief state is defined according to Bayesian update of dialogue states (Thomson and Young, 2010) and the cross-domain kernel function is

$$k_{\tilde{H}}(\tilde{H}^s, \tilde{H}) = \sum_{s \in \mathcal{S}} <\tilde{H}_s^s, \tilde{H}_s>$$

where s denotes a source slot. The kernel function between a source speech-act a^s and a target speech-act a is defined as

$$k_A(a^s, a) = \begin{cases} \delta_{a^s}(a) & a \in \mathcal{A}^s \\ 0 & a \notin \mathcal{A}^s \end{cases},$$

where $\mathscr{A}^s$ and $\mathscr{A}^t$ are the collections of speech-acts in the source and the target domains, respectively, and $\delta_{a^s}(a)$ is the kernel function defined in the source domain.

Gašić et al. (2013) define the cross-domain kernel function based on common slots in the source and the target domains. For slots only appeared in the target domain, the most similar slots are used to calculate the kernel function. Specifically, the kernel function is defined as

$$k_{\tilde{H}}(\tilde{H}^s, \tilde{H}) = \sum_{s^s \in \mathscr{S}} < \tilde{H}^s_{s^s}, \tilde{H}_{s^s} > + \sum_{s^t \notin \mathscr{S}} < \tilde{H}^s_{l(s^t)}, \tilde{H}_{s^t} >$$

where s^s denotes a slot in the source domain $\mathscr{S}$, s^t denotes a slot in the target domain $\mathscr{T}$ and function $l : \mathscr{T} \to \mathscr{S}$ finds a source slot $l(s^t)$ that is the most similar to the target slot s^t. The kernel function for actions is defined as

$$k_a(a^s, a) = \begin{cases} \delta_{a^s}(a) & a \in \mathscr{A}^s \\ \delta_{a^s}(L(a)) & a \notin \mathscr{A}^s, \end{cases}$$

where function $L : \mathscr{A}^t \to \mathscr{A}^s$ maps an action that does not exist in the source domain to a replaced action in the source domain and $\delta_{a^s}(a)$ is the kernel function defined in the source domain.

By assuming that the source and target domains are from different users with the same set of slots, Casanueva et al. (2015) propose to use additional features to determine the kernel function as

$$k((\tilde{H}^s, \tilde{Y}^s), (\tilde{H}, \tilde{Y})) = k_{\tilde{H}}(\tilde{H}^s, \tilde{H})k_{\tilde{Y}}(\tilde{Y}^s, \tilde{Y})k_{\tilde{H}}(\mathbf{l}^s, \mathbf{l}),$$

where $\mathbf{l}^s$ is an acoustic feature vector for the state-action pair in the source domain and similarly $\mathbf{l}$ is for the target domain. Hence, the kernel depends on some external features to help calculate the cross-domain similarity.

Gašić et al. (2015a) propose building a distributed policy for each node in a knowledge graph. A dialogue policy is decomposed into a set of topic-specific policies that are distributed across the class nodes in the graph. The root node in the knowledge graph is general for all its children nodes and so this policy can work for all sub-domains. The proposed method matches only the common slots with

$$k_{\tilde{H}}(\tilde{H}^s, \tilde{H}) = \sum_{s \in \mathscr{S} \cup \mathscr{T}} < \tilde{H}^s_s, \tilde{H}_s > \text{ and } k_A(a^s, a) = \begin{cases} \delta_{a^s}(a) & a \in \mathscr{A}^s \\ 0 & a \notin \mathscr{A}^s, \end{cases}$$

where $\delta_{a^s}(a)$ is the kernel function defined in the source domain. If there is no common slots, the none-matching slots are treated as abstract slots and then renamed to be some names such as "slot-1" and "slot-2." The abstract slots in the source and target domains are matched one-by-one in order.

Transferred Gaussian processes for Q-learning do not assume a completely identical feature space in the two domains, but they still assume that there are common slots between the two domains. Moreover, transferred Gaussian processes are computationally expensive, thus they could not support large training data sets.

18.5.3 Transferred Bayesian Committee Machine for Q-learning

Previous methods assume the existence of common slots but this assumption is not always true. When there is no common slot, we can use the Bayesian committee machine to transfer a dialogue policy. The Bayesian committee machine combines policies trained in different domains and it is particularly suitable for Gaussian process (Gašić et al., 2015b, 2015c).

A Bayesian committee machine is a Gaussian process, where the combined mean function $\bar{Q}(\tilde{H}, \tilde{Y})$ is calculated as

$$\bar{Q}(\tilde{H}, \tilde{Y}) = \Sigma^Q(\tilde{H}, \tilde{Y}) \sum_{i=1}^{M} \Sigma_i^Q(\tilde{H}, \tilde{Y})^{-1} \bar{Q}_i(\tilde{H}, \tilde{Y}),$$

and the covariance function Σ^Q is calculated as

$$\Sigma^Q(\tilde{H}, \tilde{Y})^{-1} = -(M-1) \times k((\tilde{H}, \tilde{Y}), (\tilde{H}, \tilde{Y}))^{-1} + \sum_{i=1}^{M} \Sigma_i^Q(\tilde{H}, \tilde{Y})^{-1},$$

where M is the number of policies in the Bayesian committee machine, $Q_i(\tilde{H}, \tilde{Y})$ is the Q-function of the i-th policies, $\bar{Q}_i$ is the mean of $Q_i(\tilde{H}, \tilde{Y})$ and Σ_i^Q is the covariance of $Q_i(\tilde{H}, \tilde{Y})$. Note that $Q_i(\tilde{H}, \tilde{Y})$ is trained on a set of state-action and reward pairs. To evaluate a state-action pair $(\tilde{H}, \tilde{Y})$, the Bayesian committee machine requires this state-action pair to be predicted by all $Q_i(\tilde{H}, \tilde{Y})$. In this case, a kernel function has to be defined between state-action pairs in different domains and similar to the Gaussian process, it is core to transfer learning methods.

In the works by Gašić et al. (2015b, 2015c), no slot is assumed to be shared in the source and target domains. The source and target slots are matched one-by-one based on the normalized entropy. For each domain $c \in \{\mathscr{S}, \mathscr{T}\}$, the slots are sorted based on their normalized entropy so that $\eta(s_i^c) \geq \eta(s_j^c)$ for $i \leq j$ in domain c. The kernel function between the source domain $\mathscr{S}$ and the target domain $\mathscr{T}$ is calculated as

(1) Iteratively, for s_i^c in domain $c \in \{\mathscr{S}, \mathscr{T}\}$ when index i satisfies $i \leq \min(|\mathscr{S}|, |\mathscr{T}|)$ ($|c|$ denotes the number of slots in domain c), we match the corresponding elements of belief state and actions.

(2) Otherwise, we disregard the elements of the belief state related to the unpaired slot j and if one of the actions is related to slot j, we set the action kernel to be 0.

The Bayesian committee machine does not assume the existence of common slots in the source and target domains. Instead, an entropy-based cross-domain kernel function is defined to estimate the data similarity between different domains. However, each committee is a Gaussian process model, which is still computationally expensive, and thus it could not support large data sets.

18.6 Transfer Learning in Natural Language Generation

In this section, we review some transfer learning works for the natural language generation module. The natural language generation module aims to convert a system action into a sentence with an appropriate adequacy, fluency and readability. Walker et al. (2007) and Mairesse and Walker (2008, 2011) propose adapting general sentence planning models to different personal linguistic styles. Although these models can handle many linguistic problems, they are heavily dependent on the human knowledge and handcrafted rules. Different from them, RNN-based language models (Shi et al., 2015; Wen et al., 2015b, 2016) are flexible and general to generate natural language and they do not require much human efforts. Here we focus on transfer learning for RNN-based language models.

There are mainly three types of transfer learning techniques in the RNN-based language models.

(1) Model fine-tuning: A model is first trained on a source domain and then it is retrained with the target domain data.
(2) Curriculum learning: In each training epoch, the training instances are sorted such that general instances are fed into the training of the model first and then the specific target domain data are fed.
(3) Instance synthesis: Synthetic target domain sentences are built from delexicalized source domain sentences by substituting slot values.

18.6.1 Model Fine-tuning for Natural Language Generation

Wen et al. (2013, 2015b) propose to fine-tune an out-of-domain model with the in-domain data to achieve transfer learning. The base model is the semantically conditioned long short-term memory networks (SC-LSTM) model (Wen et al., 2015a). First, the authors train an out-of-domain model with all source domain data. Second, the authors fine-tune the model parameters on various proportion of target domain data. Two baseline models are used, including an encoder-decoder model and the SC-LSTM model. The authors find that the fine-tuned SC-LSTM model and SC-LSTM model perform better than the encoder-decoder model when the data in the target domain is sufficient. However, when data in the target domain is insufficient, the simple encoder-decoder model performs better.

18.6.2 Curriculum Learning for Natural Language Generation

Shi et al. (2015) propose to use curriculum learning (Elman, 1993) to adapt an RNN language model. The authors propose two curriculum learning strategies. The first strategy is via data-sorting such that the model is first trained on plenty of source domain data and then trained on a few target domain data. The second curriculum learning strategy is based on the model fine-tuning to train the whole model on the source domain first and then fine-tune this model with the target domain data. The data-sorting strategy and the model fine-tuning strategy differ in the ordering under which the source and the target domain data are used. In the data-sorting strategy, at each training epoch the model utilizes the source domain data first and then the target domain data. In the model fine-tuning strategy, the model is fully optimized on the source domain data and then adapted to the target domain.

18.6.3 Instance Synthesis for Natural Language Generation

Wen et al. (2016) propose combining the model fine-tuning and the instance synthesis based on the SC-LSTM model (Wen et al., 2015a) for domain adaptation in natural language generation. First, the SC-LSTM model is trained on the delexicalized source domain and fine-tuned in the delexicalized target domain. In this case, for sentences with new slot values that appear only in the target domain, the model learns from scratch and no knowledge can be transferred. Second, some synthetic instances are generated by adapting the source domain instances with new slot values. In details, the slot values in the source data are substituted with similar new slot values in the target domain. Then the synthetic data can be used to train the model for the target domain to achieve knowledge transfer for new slot values in the target domain. In this approach, a similarity metric between source and target slot values is required and usually this similarity function is defined based on the slot type.

In summary, both model fine-tuning and curriculum learning can be used to transfer low-level language modeling knowledge but they differ in terms of how the source domain data is used to help the target domain. Moreover, these two approaches cannot handle new slot values that appear only in the target domain. The instance synthesis approach can transfer language modeling knowledge to new slot values in the target domain by assuming that the expressions of different slot values are similar.

18.7 Transfer Learning in End-to-End Dialogue Systems

In this section, we introduce a special class of dialogue systems called end-to-end task-oriented dialogue systems. Traditional modular dialogue systems require a large amount of handcrafted rules or a large amount of labeled data for each component. Unlike modular dialogue systems whose modules are handcrafted or trained separately, the components in an end-to-end dialogue system are trained together by optimizing a single objective function. End-to-end dialogue systems do not require intermediate annotations and hence they can reduce the amount of human labor required for building a dialogue system.

Unlike modular dialogue systems that first identify current dialogue state and then decide the next action, there is no unique definition of a ground-truth dialogue state in an end-to-end dialogue system. Instead, in each time step, the dialogue system directly takes current question as the input and generates an output sentence based on an internal state. The internal state is updated at each time step and in some aspect, it represents the abstract dialogue state at each time step. So the whole end-to-end dialogue system can be viewed as a policy function with the input as the dialogue history as well as current question and the output as the answer of the system. Unlike modular dialogue systems, the action space of an end-to-end dialogue system is the space of all possible sentences.

Based on the the type of knowledge being transferred, we categorize relevant works into the following two categories.

(1) The complete parameter fine-tuning methods: They first pretrain an end-to-end dialogue model on the source domain with sufficient training data and then fine-tune all parameters in the target domain with a few training data.

(2) The partial parameter sharing methods: They share only a part of model parameters across domains, in contrast to the model fine-tuning methods where all parameters are transferred.

18.7.1   Complete Parameter Fine-tuning

The parameter fine-tuning methods consists of two steps. First, an end-to-end dialogue model is pretrained on a source domain with a lot of training data. Second, the pretrained model are fine-tuned in a target domain with a few data.

Serban et al. (2016) pretrained the word embeddings and the hierarchical recurrent encoder-decode (HRED) dialogue model (Sordoni et al., 2015) on a large-scale question answer corpus, and then adapted this model to the target domain. Specifically, the word embeddings were pre-trained in a Google News Corpus (Mikolov et al., 2013b), the source domain uses the SubTle data set to pretrain the HRED dialogue model and the target domain uses the MovieTriples data set. Experimental results show that pretraining the word embeddings can greatly improve the performance of the dialogue model.

Zhang et al. (2017b) transferred an encoder-decoder dialogue model to a chatting task among five volunteers. The encoder-decoder model was pretrained on a large scale corpus with pairs of the post and response. The proposed method contained two phrases, that is, the initialization and adaptation, to generate responses that have a personalized style. The source data set consisted of one million Chinese one-to-one post-response pairs collected from several Chinese online forums. The target data set had 2,000 chatting messages without personal information collected from five volunteers. In order to evaluate the personal style of the responses, they proposed the use of the lexical distributions and word overlapping proportion as evaluation metrics. Experimental results show that the five transferred models can indeed capture the personal responding styles of the five volunteers.

Yang et al. (2017) transfer a pretrained long short-term memory network-based encoder-decoder dialogue model to a target domain with dual learning. They initialized a post agent and a response agent separately, then treated the post agent as the primal task and the response agent as the dual task, and perform dual learning. The primal and dual tasks can form a closed loop and generate informative feedbacks to train the dialogue system even with only a small number of training data in the target domain. In the adaptation process, the post agent first generated an intermediate response and then the response agent generated a post based on the intermediate response. This dual process can monitor the quality of generated responses, and improve the post agent and the response agent simultaneously.

Joshi et al. (2017) aimed to share parameters in a memory network among multiple users with different profiles. For each profile, the per-response accuracy is used as an evaluation metric. In the experiment, the proposed multi-profile transfer learning model outperforms the baselines trained with data from only one user.

18.7.2 Partial Parameter Sharing

In contrast to the complete parameter fine-tuning method, the partial parameter sharing methods share only a part of model parameters. Due to domain differences, some model parameters are domain-dependent and should not be transferred. Transferring all model parameters may lead to the negative transfer, which will harm the performance in the target domain. In order to alleviate the negative transfer, in a typical partial parameter sharing method, the model parameters are divided into multiple parts, where some parameters are shared or transferred across domains, while others keep private to its own domain.

Li et al. (2016) proposed a personalized neural response model to tackle the speaker consistency problem for a group of users. The proposed model was an encoder-decoder model, where general parameters in the encoder-decoder model was learned and shared between all users. In addition, personal parameters were learned for each user to capture the characteristic of individual users such as the background information and the speaking style.

In the following two sections, we introduce two recent works about building personalized dialogue systems based on transfer learning.

Transfer Reinforcement Learning through Personalized Q-function

Mo et al. (2018) aimed to transfer the general dialogue policy from a group of source users to a target user to build a personalized dialogue policy for the target user. Due to the difference in user preferences, directly fine-tuning the whole dialogue model might lead to the negative transfer. They proposed a PErsonalized Task-oriented diALogue (PETAL) system, which is a transfer learning framework based on the POMDP for learning a personalized dialogue system. The PETAL sys-

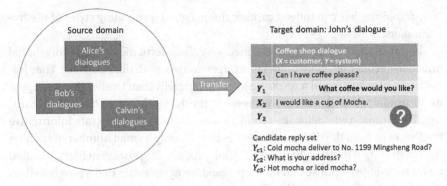

Figure 18.2 An illustration of the setting in the PETAL system

tem first learns common dialogue knowledge from the source domain and then adapts this knowledge to the target user.

An example about the coffee ordering dialogue is shown in Figure 18.2. X denotes users' utterances and Y denotes the replies of the agent. In this example, given the dialogue context $H_2^u = \{X_1, Y_1, X_2\}$ and the candidate reply set $\{Y_{c1}, Y_{c2}, Y_{c3}\}$, the dialogue policy should decide which reply is more appropriate. Formally, the inputs for this problem include abundant dialogue data $\{\{X_n^{u_s}, Y_n^{u_s}\}_{n=0}^T\}$ of source customers $\{u_s\}$, and a few dialogue data $\{\{X_n^{u_t}, Y_n^{u_t}\}_{n=0}^T\}$ of the target customer u_t. The expected output is a policy π^{u_t} for target user.

A personalized coffee ordering dialogue can be formulated as a reinforcement learning problem, and the flowchart is illustrated in Figure 18.3. In each turn of the dialogue, based on the question Y asked by the system and the answer X of the user, the dialogue belief state transits from one state to another. By asking a personalized question Y^p, the system can make the whole dialogue significantly shorter. For example, if the system knows that a user always orders a cup of cold mocha and delivers to his home, the system can ask a personalized question "Cold mocha deliver to No. 1199 Mingsheng Road?," and the user might say yes with a high probability, making the dialogue shorter.

Due to the difference in user preferences, directly fine-tuning the whole dialogue model might lead to the negative transfer. In a reinforcement learning dialogue policy, Mo et al. (2018) propose a personalized Q-function, which consists of a general part Q_g and a personal part Q_p as

$$Q^{\pi^u}(H_n^u, Y_n^u) = Q_g(H_n^u, Y_n^u; \mathbf{w}) + Q_p(H_n^u, Y_n^u; \mathbf{p}_u, w_p)$$

$$\approx \mathbb{E}_{\pi^u}\left[\sum_{k=0}^{\infty} \gamma^k r_{t+k+1}^{u,g} | H_n^u, Y_n^u\right] + \mathbb{E}_{\pi_u}\left[\sum_{k=0}^{\infty} \gamma^k r_{t+k+1}^{u,p} | H_n^u, Y_n^u\right], \quad (18.1)$$

where $r_t^{u,g}$ and $r_t^{u,p}$ denote the general and personal rewards for user u at time t, respectively, the general Q-function $Q_g(H_n^u, Y_n^u; \mathbf{w})$ captures the expected reward related to the general dialogue policy for all users, $\mathbf{w}$ is the set of parameters for

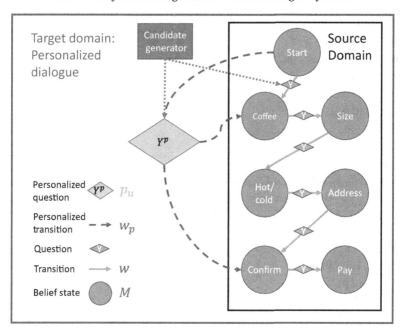

Figure 18.3 The flowchart of the PETAL system on the coffee-ordering task

the general Q-function and contains a large number of parameters such that it requires a lot of training data, and the personal Q-function $Q_p(H_n^u, Y_n^u; \mathbf{p}_u, w_p)$ captures the expected reward related to the preference of each user.

The general part accounts for the general dialogue policy, and it is pretrained in the source domain and transferred to the target domain, while the personal part is for personal preferences of each user and is learned with the target domain data only. $\mathbf{M}$, $\mathbf{w}$ and w_p are shared across different users, and they could be trained on source domains and then transferred to the target domain. These parameters contain the common dialogue knowledge, which is independent of users' preferences. Moreover, $\mathbf{p}_u$, which is user-specific, captures the preferences of different users.

The detailed PETAL algorithm is shown in Algorithm 18.1. The PETAL algorithm trains a model for each user in the source domain. $\mathbf{M}$, $\mathbf{w}$ and w_p are shared by all users and there is a separate $\mathbf{p}_u$ for each user in the source domain. The PETAL algorithm transfers $\mathbf{M}$, $\mathbf{w}$ and w_p to the target domain by using them to initialize the corresponding variables in the target domain, and then it trains them as well as $\mathbf{p}_u$ for each target user with limited training data. Since the source and target users might have different preferences, $\mathbf{p}_u$ learned in the source domain is not very useful in the target domain. The personal preference of each target user will be learned separately in each $\mathbf{p}_u$. Without modeling $\mathbf{p}_u$ for each user, different

---

Algorithm 18.1 The PETAL algorithm

Input: $\mathcal{D}^s, \mathcal{D}^t$
Output: $\Theta = \{\mathbf{M}, \mathbf{w}, w_p \{\mathbf{p}_u\}\}$
 1: **for** $\{X_n^u, Y_n^u\}$ in $\mathcal{D}^s$ **do**
 2:    **if** $\mathbf{p}_u$ exist **then**
          load $\mathbf{p}_u$
 3:    **else**
          $\mathbf{p}_u \leftarrow 0$
 4:    **end if**
 5:    **for** $(H_n^u, Y_n^u, r_n^u, H_{n+1}^u, Y_{n+1}^u)$ in $\{X_n^u, Y_n^u\}$ **do**
 6:       $\Theta_{t+1} \leftarrow \Theta_t + \alpha \Delta_\Theta \mathcal{L}(\Theta_t)$
 7:    **end for**
 8: **end for**
 9: **for** $\{\{X_n^u, Y_n^u\}_n^T\}$ in $\mathcal{D}^t$ **do**
10:    **if** $\mathbf{p}_u$ exist **then**
          load $\mathbf{p}_u$
11:    **else**
          $\mathbf{p}_u \leftarrow 0$
12:    **end if**
13:    **for** $(H_n^u, Y_n^u, r_n^u, H_{n+1}^u, Y_{n+1}^u)$ in $\{X_n^u, Y_n^u\}$ **do**
14:       $\Theta_{t+1} \leftarrow \Theta_t + \alpha \Delta_\Theta \mathcal{L}(\Theta_t)$
15:    **end for**
16: **end for**

---

preferences of the source and target users might interfere with each other and thus cause the negative transfer.

Transfer Reinforcement Learning through Personal Word Gating

Mo et al. (2017) transfer the general dialogue policy between end-to-end personalized dialogue policies. Since different users have different preferences, directly transferring dialogue policies might lead to negative transfer. For example, the transferred policy might generate a wrong address for the target user according to the data of the source users. Mo et al. (2017) propose a personalized decoder that can transfer shared phrase-level knowledge between different users while keeping the personalized information of each user intact. A novel personal control gate is introduced in the proposed personalized decoder, enabling the decoder to switch between generating shared phrases and personal phrases.

An example problem is illustrated in Figure 18.4. User u's question in the n-th turn is denoted by $X_n^u = \{x_{n,t}^u\}_{t=1}^{N_n^{u,x}}$, and $N_n^{u,x}$ is the number of words in X_n^u. Agent's response in the n-th turn is denoted by $Y_n^u = \{y_{n,t}^u\}_{t=1}^{N_n^{u,y}}$, where $N_n^{u,y}$ is the number of words in Y_n^u. In the example, given the dialogue context $H_2^u = \{X_1, Y_1, X_2\}$, the dialogue system is to generate an appropriate reply Y_2 word by word. The

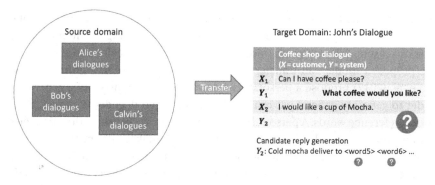

Figure 18.4 An illustration of the setting in the personalized decoder

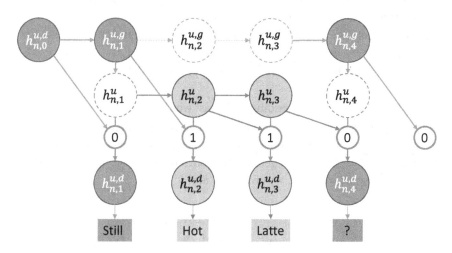

Figure 18.5 Personalized response generation with the personalized decoder. The personal control gate at different time steps are denoted in gray circles

transfer learning problem is to learn an end-to-end personalized task-oriented dialogue system for each user by leveraging the conversation history of multiple other users. The input of this problem include the historical dialogue sessions $\mathcal{T}^u = \{X_n^u, Y_n^u, r_n^u\}_{n=1}$ of each user, where r_n^u is the reward obtained at n-th dialogue turn. Another input is the personal word label $\mathcal{O}_n^u = \{o_{n,t}^u\}_{t=1}^N$ for each word in Y_n^u, where $o_{n,t}^u = 1$ means that $x_{n,t}^u$ is a personal word and $o_{n,t}^u = 0$ means the word $x_{n,t}^u$ is a general word. Personal words are defined as the words related to all possible user choices in the domain slots. For the example in Figure 18.5, "hot latte" is a personal phrase and "still" and "?" are shared phrases. The output of this problem is a dialogue policy π^u for each user u, which generates a response Y_n^u for each dialogue history $H_n^u = \{\{X_i^u, Y_i^u\}_{i=1}^{n-1}, X_n^u\}$.

Since different users have different preferences, directly transferring dialogue sentences might lead to negative transfer. For example, the transferred policy might make a wrong suggestion to the target user according to the preferences of source users. Different from traditional methods that transfer entire sentences, the proposed model can transfer fine-grain phrases between a group of users. Mo et al. (2017) propose a personalized decoder, which consists of a general decoder to generate general patterns and a personalized decoder to generate personal preference words. A personal word gating mechanism is introduced to select the appropriate decoder for each generated word, making the personalized decoder switch between generating general pattern words and personalized phrases. For the example in Figure 18.5, the personal control gate selects the personal decoder to generate the personal phrase "hot latte", and uses the common decoder to generate common phrases "Still" and "?." The personalized decoder can generate different personal phrases for different users in a sentence, while the knowledge for the shared phrases is shared among all users.

Basic decoder: The hidden state for the t-th word in the n-th turn is defined as

$$\mathbf{h}_{n,t}^{u,d} = \tanh(\mathbf{W}^d \mathbf{h}_{n,t-1}^{u,d} + \mathbf{U}^d \hat{y}_{n,t-1}^u + \mathbf{V}^d \mathbf{h}_n^{u,c}),$$

where $\hat{y}_{n,t-1}^u$ is the word embedding of the last word $\hat{y}_{n,t-1}^u$ in the same sentence, and $\tanh(\cdot)$ denotes the hyperbolic tangent function. The decoder RNN takes $\mathbf{h}_{n,0}^{u,d}$ and $\mathbf{h}_n^{u,c}$ as inputs and then generates the response word by word, where $\mathbf{h}_n^{u,c}$ is the embedding vector used to generate the current response. The probability of generating the next word $\hat{y}_{n,t}^u = y$ given $\mathbf{h}_{n,t}^{u,d}$ and $\hat{y}_{n,t-1}^u$ is

$$\omega(\mathbf{h}_{n,t}^{u,d}, \hat{y}_{n,t-1}^u) = \mathbf{H}_0 \mathbf{h}_{n,t}^{u,d} + \mathbf{E}_0 \hat{y}_{n,t-1}^u + \mathbf{b}_o \tag{18.2}$$

$$g(\mathbf{h}_{n,t}^{u,d}, \hat{y}_{n,t-1}^u, y) = \mathbf{o}_y^T \omega(\mathbf{h}_{n,t}^{u,d}, \hat{y}_{n,t-1}^u) \tag{18.3}$$

$$p(\hat{y}_{n,t}^u = y) = \frac{\exp(g(\mathbf{h}_{n,t}^{u,d}, \hat{y}_{n,t-1}^u, y))}{\sum_{\forall y'} \exp(g(\mathbf{h}_{n,t}^{u,d}, \hat{y}_{n,t-1}^u, y'))} \tag{18.4}$$

where $\mathbf{o}_y$ is the output embedding for word y, and $\mathbf{H}_0$, $\mathbf{E}_0$ and $\mathbf{b}_o$ are parameters.

Personalized dialogue decoder for phrase-level transfer learning: The proposed personalized decoder is illustrated in Figure 18.5. While the sentence-level transfer is to transfer entire sentences, the proposed personalized decoder is on the phrase level and is to transfer a shared fraction of the sentences to the target domain, where a phrase is a short sequence of words containing a coherent meaning. To achieve maximum knowledge transfer and to avoid negative transfer caused by differences in user preferences, the proposed personalized decoder has a shared component and a personalized component. To learn to switch between the shared and personal components in the phrase level, Mo et al. (2017) introduce a personal control gate $o_{n,t}^u$, which is learned from the training data, for each word.

Given the the embedding vector for the n-th response $\mathbf{h}_n^{u,c}$ and initial hidden state $\mathbf{h}_{n,0}^{u,d}$ for the predicted word $\hat{y}_{n,0}^{u}$, the initial states are computed as

$$\mathbf{h}_{n,0}^{u,g} = \mathbf{h}_{n,0}^{u,d}, \mathbf{h}_{n,0}^{u} = \mathbf{h}_{n,0}^{u,d}, \hat{o}_{n,0}^{u} = 0$$
$$\hat{y}_{n,0}^{u} = 0, \hat{y}_{n,0}^{u,g} = 0$$

where $\mathbf{h}_{n,t}^{u,g}$ is the hidden state for the shared component, and $\hat{y}_{n,t}^{u,g}$ records the last word generated by the shared component, $\mathbf{h}_{n,t}^{u}$ is the hidden state for the personal component and $\mathbf{h}_{n,t}^{u,d}$ is the hidden state for generating the word $\hat{y}_{n,t}^{u}$.

The shared component adopts the gated recurrent unit model to capture the long-term dependency and is shared by all users. Specifically, at each time step t, the shared component is defined as

$$z_{n,t}^{u} = \sigma(\mathbf{W}_z^g \mathbf{h}_{n,t-1}^{u,g} + \mathbf{U}_z^g \hat{y}_{n,t-1}^{u,g} + \mathbf{V}_z^g \mathbf{h}_n^{u,c} + \mathbf{b}_z) \tag{18.5}$$

$$r_{n,t}^{u} = \sigma(\mathbf{W}_r^g \mathbf{h}_{n,t-1}^{u,g} + \mathbf{U}_r^g \hat{y}_{n,t-1}^{u,g} + \mathbf{V}_r^g \mathbf{h}_n^{u,c} + \mathbf{b}_r) \tag{18.6}$$

$$\tilde{\mathbf{h}}_{n,t}^{u,g} = \sigma(\mathbf{W}_h^g (r_{n,t}^{u} \odot \mathbf{h}_{n,t-1}^{u,g}) + \mathbf{U}_h^g \hat{y}_{n,t-1}^{u,g} + \mathbf{V}_h^g \mathbf{h}_n^{u,c} + \mathbf{b}_h) \tag{18.7}$$

$$\hat{\mathbf{h}}_{n,t}^{u,g} = z_{n,t}^{u} \odot \mathbf{h}_{n,t-1}^{u,g} + (1 - z_{n,t}^{u}) \odot \tilde{\mathbf{h}}_{n,t}^{u,g}, \tag{18.8}$$

where $\odot$ denotes the element-wise product between vectors or matrices, $\sigma(\cdot)$ is the sigmoid function, $z_{n,t}^{u}$ is the update gate, $r_{n,t}^{u}$ is the forget gate and $\hat{\mathbf{h}}_{n,t}^{u,g}$ is the tentative updated hidden state. If the t-th word is a shared word (i.e., $\hat{o}_{n,t}^{u} = 0$), then the model updates the shared hidden state and last general word as usual and otherwise $\mathbf{h}_{n,t}^{u,g}$ and $\hat{y}_t^{u,g}$ remain unchanged. Thus, $\mathbf{h}_{n,t}^{u,g}$ and $\hat{y}_t^{u,g}$ can be updated as

$$\mathbf{h}_{n,t}^{u,g} = (1 - \hat{o}_{n,t}^{u}) \odot \hat{\mathbf{h}}_{n,t}^{u,g} + \hat{o}_{n,t}^{u} \odot \mathbf{h}_{n,t-1}^{u,g} \tag{18.9}$$

$$\hat{y}_t^{u,g} = (1 - \hat{o}_{n,t}^{u}) \odot \hat{y}_{t-1}^{u} + \hat{o}_{n,t}^{u} \odot \hat{y}_{t-1}^{u,g}. \tag{18.10}$$

The personal component is an RNN model, which generates personalized sequence based on sentence context $\mathbf{h}_{n,t}^{u,g}$ from the shared component. There is a separate RNN model for each user. At each time step t, the personal component receives $\hat{y}_{t-1}^{u}, \hat{o}_{n,t}^{u}, \mathbf{h}_{n,t-1}^{u}$ and $\mathbf{h}_{n,t-1}^{u,g}$ as inputs and outputs $\hat{\mathbf{h}}_{n,t}^{u}$, which is defined as

$$\hat{\mathbf{h}}_{n,t}^{u} = \sigma(\mathbf{W}^u \mathbf{h}_{n,t-1}^{u} + \mathbf{U}^u \hat{y}_{n,t-1}^{u} + \mathbf{V}^u \mathbf{h}_{n,t-1}^{u,g}). \tag{18.11}$$

The personal hidden state will be update as

$$\mathbf{h}_{n,t}^{u} = (1 - \hat{o}_{n,t}^{u}) \odot \mathbf{h}_{n,t}^{u,g} + \hat{o}_{n,t}^{u} \odot \hat{\mathbf{h}}_{n,t}^{u}. \tag{18.12}$$

$\mathbf{h}_{n,t}^{u}$ equals $\hat{\mathbf{h}}_{n,t}^{u}$ if the control gate is corresponding to $\hat{o}_{n,t}^{u} = 1$. If $\hat{o}_{n,t}^{u}$ equals 0, $\mathbf{h}_{n,t}^{u}$ will take the value of $\mathbf{h}_{n,t}^{u,g}$.

The personal control gate $o_{n,t}^{u}$ is binary, that is, $o_{n,t}^{u} \in \{0,1\}$. The predicted control gate $\hat{o}_{n,t}^{u}$ at time t is a function of $\hat{o}_{n,t-1}^{u}$, $\mathbf{h}_{n,t-1}^{u,g}$, $\mathbf{h}_{n,t-1}^{u}$ and $\hat{y}_{n,t-1}^{u}$ as[1]

$$p(\hat{o}_{n,t}^{u} = 1) = \begin{cases} \sigma(\mathbf{W}_o^g \mathbf{h}_{n,t-1}^{u,g} + \mathbf{U}_o^g \hat{y}_{n,t-1}^{u} + \mathbf{b}_o) & \text{if } \hat{o}_{n,t-1}^{u} = 0 \\ \sigma(\mathbf{W}_o^u \mathbf{h}_{n,t-1}^{u} + \mathbf{U}_o^u \hat{y}_{n,t-1}^{u} + \mathbf{b}_o^u) & \text{if } \hat{o}_{n,t-1}^{u} = 1 \end{cases}. \tag{18.13}$$

---

[1] In training process, the ground-truth $o_{n,t}^{u}$ is used as a label to train the prediction function for $\hat{o}_{n,t}^{u}$.

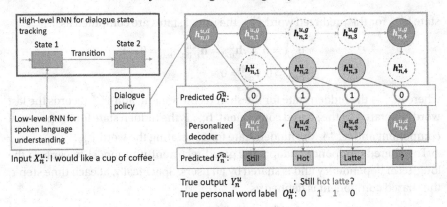

Figure 18.6 The architecture for personalized HRED, obtained by combining HRED with a personalized decoder

$\hat{o}_{n,t}^u$ decides whether to use the personal component to generate the next word. $\mathbf{h}_{n,t}^{u,d}$ is defined as

$$\mathbf{h}_{n,t}^{u,d} = (1 - \hat{o}_{n,t}^u) \odot \mathbf{h}_{n,t}^{u,g} + \hat{o}_{n,t}^u \odot \mathbf{h}_{n,t}^u, \qquad (18.14)$$

where $\mathbf{h}_{n,t}^{u,d}$ is the hidden vector that directly generates the next word $\hat{y}_{n,t}^u$ and the probability of generating the next word $y_{n,t}^u$ is defined by the generation process in (18.2)–(18.4).

The decoding procedure is as follows:

(1) Initialize $\mathbf{h}_{n,0}^{u,g}, \mathbf{h}_{n,0}^u, \hat{o}_{n,0}^u, \hat{\mathbf{y}}_{n,0}^u$ and $\hat{\mathbf{y}}_{n,0}^{u,g}$ based on $\mathbf{h}_{n,0}^{u,d}$ and $\mathbf{h}_n^{u,c}$. $\hat{o}_{n,0}^u$ is initialized to be 0 and $\hat{\mathbf{y}}_{n,0}^u$ is initialized to be a zero vector $\mathbf{0}$.
(2) Compute personal control gate $\hat{o}_{n,t}^u$ based on $\mathbf{h}_n^{u,c}, \hat{o}_{n,t-1}^u, \mathbf{h}_{n,t-1}^{u,g}, \mathbf{h}_{n,t-1}^u$ and $\hat{\mathbf{y}}_{t-1}^u$ with (18.13).
(3) Compute $\mathbf{h}_{n,t}^{u,g}, \mathbf{h}_{n,t}^u$ and the outputted hidden state $\mathbf{h}_{n,t}^{u,d}$ based on the personal control gate $\hat{o}_{n,t}^u$.
(4) Generate $\hat{y}_{n,t}^u$ based on the outputted hidden state $\mathbf{h}_{n,t}^{u,d}$ with (18.14).
(5) Repeat step 2 to step 4 until the ending symbol.

The shared and personal components can be trained together with supervised learning and reinforcement learning.

The personalized decoder is capable of transferring dialogue knowledge, and it can easily be combined with many models including the Seq2seq model (Sutskever et al., 2014) and the HRED model (Serban et al., 2015). The architecture for personalized HRED, obtained by combining HRED with personalized decoder, is shown in Figure 18.6.

19

Transfer Learning in Recommender Systems

19.1 Introduction

Recommender systems are a critical component in many intelligent systems. There are many examples of recommender systems in our everyday lives, ranging from news recommendation to product recommendation, and to online advertisement. In Amazon, Netflix and Facebook, for example, recommendation techniques are used for the suggestions of books, movies and friends. Among all recommendation techniques, collaborative filtering and its extensions are among the first techniques used in many applications.

However, collaborative recommendation suffers from the data sparsity problem, that is, users' preference data on products or items are usually too few to be used to learn their true preferences. This is especially a limitation for personalized recommendation. In addition, to support new recommendation applications, the data sparsity implies that we face a cold-start problem, which makes it difficult to boost a new recommendation service.

Recommendation technology can often be mapped to a matrix completion operation, whose aim is to fill in the missing values in the matrix. These matrices are often referred to as preference matrices. A preference matrix is often built in terms of users and items. These matrices are often very sparse, but, fortunately, there may often be some related source data that we may explore to alleviate the data sparsity problem in the target domain. This can be done through transfer learning.

In many applications, transfer learning has achieved great success in text mining, mobile computing, bioinformatics and so on. Like in many other machine learning areas, transfer learning has indeed been proposed in recommendation system area to improve the target learning task by extracting and transferring the knowledge from the source data. Many auxiliary data exist to make the recommendation performance in a target domain better. The main problem solved by transfer learning in recommendation systems is the cold-start problem, which is typically solved using variants of collaborative learning algorithms. In this chapter, we survey approaches to transfer learning in collaborative recommendation.

Li et al. (2009a) propose one of the first algorithms for integrating recommendation systems with transfer learning with an algorithm known as codebook transfer (CBT). Subsequently, many research works appear that allow transfer learning to be applied to recommender systems, which include all instance-based, feature-based and model-based transfer learning frameworks.

The organization of this chapter is as follows. We first discuss some representative transfer learning methods for recommendation in Section 19.2. We then present two transfer learning applications in news recommendation and VIP recommendation in Section 19.3 and Section 19.4, respectively.

19.2   What to Transfer in Recommendation

In this section, we take the perspective of "what to transfer" in transfer learning and discuss three types of transfer learning methods in recommendation. These methods include instance-based transfer learning, feature-based transfer learning and model-based transfer learning in recommendation. Before we discuss some representative works in each category, we propose a unified framework for knowledge transfer in recommendation as

$$\min_{\Theta, \mathcal{K}_I, \mathcal{K}_F, \mathcal{K}_M} l(\Theta, \mathcal{K}_I, \mathcal{K}_F, \mathcal{K}_M | \mathbb{T}, \mathbb{S}) + r(\Theta | \mathcal{K}_I, \mathcal{K}_F, \mathcal{K}_M, \mathbb{S}) + r(\mathcal{K}_F), \quad (19.1)$$
$$\text{s.t.} \quad \Theta \in c(\mathcal{K}_I, \mathbb{T}, \mathbb{S}),$$

where $\mathbb{T}$ is the target data, $\mathbb{S}$ is the source data, Θ is the parameter to be learned and $\mathcal{K}_I$, $\mathcal{K}_F$ and $\mathcal{K}_M$ denote the knowledge in instance-based transfer learning, feature-based transfer learning and model-based transfer learning, respectively. We can see that the framework in (19.1) contains a loss function, two regularization terms and a constraint.

In the previous equation, the function $l(\cdot)$ is the loss function, and $r(\cdot)$ is a regularization function. We wish the loss to be as small as possible provided that the model size is also under control to ensure the generalization ability of learning.

19.2.1   Instance-Based Transfer Learning in Recommendation

Instance-based transfer learning methods in recommendation aim to transfer knowledge such as users' feedback or ratings as instances from the source data $\mathbb{S}$ to the target data $\mathbb{T}$. Mathematically, the optimization problem based on (19.1) is formulated as

$$\min_{\Theta, \mathcal{K}_I} l(\Theta, \mathcal{K}_I | \mathbb{T}, \mathbb{S}) + r(\Theta | \mathcal{K}_I, \mathbb{S}), \text{ s.t., } \Theta \in c(\mathcal{K}_I, \mathbb{T}, \mathbb{S}). \quad (19.2)$$

In this equation, there are a loss function $l(\cdot)$, a regularization term $r(\cdot)$ and a constraint $c(\cdot)$. Different transfer learning methods may instantiate different parts of problem statement. Examples are $l(\cdot)$ and $r(\cdot)$ in the works by Pan et al. (2015b, 2016b) and Hu et al. (2019) and $l(\cdot)$ and $c(\cdot)$ in the works by Pan et al. (2012, 2017).

Pan et al. (2015b) study two types of one-class feedback that have different uncertainties such as transactions and examinations for preference learning and item ranking. Specifically, they propose learning the confidence of each examination instance and then transfering the confidence-weighted examination instances to the target preference learning task with transaction records by an adaptive Bayesian personalized ranking (ABPR) algorithm.

Pan et al. (2016b) study labeled feedback such as numerical ratings and unlabeled feedback such as examinations, and design a self transfer learning (sTL) algorithm, which iteratively identifies some likely-to-prefer examination instances and transfers them to improve the target rating prediction task.

Hu et al. (2019) develop a deep learning model called transfer meets hybrid (TMH) to selectively transfer the interacted source item instances by the corresponding target user via an attentive weighting scheme, as well as to exploit the unstructured text information of the target (user, item) pair by a memory network in a hybrid manner.

Pan et al. (2012) take users' uncertain actions, that is, feedback in the form of rating intervals, as source rating instances, and integrate them into the target five-star rating matrix factorization task for preference learning via a transfer by integrative factorization (TIF) method.

Pan et al. (2017) propose a transfer to rank (ToR) method to first exploit the union of the target explicit feedback and source implicit feedback to obtain a candidate list of item instances of users' potential interest, and then transfer them to the target matrix factorization task with explicit feedback only to re-rank the candidate list.

Observe that instance-based transfer learning methods have been applied to different recommendation problems in terms of the input such as ratings, transactions, examinations and installation, and the output including rating prediction and item ranking. The transferred knowledge of *instances* can be in different forms, including examination instances (Pan et al., 2015b, 2016b), installation instances (Hu et al., 2019), rating instances (Pan et al., 2012) and candidate item instances (Pan et al., 2017). Furthermore, the transfer learning algorithms can also be formulated in different styles such as adaptive styles (Pan et al., 2015b), iterative styles (Pan et al., 2016b), integrative styles (Pan et al., 2012; Hu et al., 2019) and two-stage styles (Pan et al., 2017).

19.2.2 Feature-Based Transfer Learning in Recommendation

Feature-based transfer learning methods in recommendation usually choose to share and transfer the knowledge in some latent feature factors learned from the source data, or from both the source data and the target data. Mathematically, the instantiated optimization problem based on (19.1) is formulated as

$$\min_{\Theta, \mathcal{K}_\mathrm{F}} l(\Theta, \mathcal{K}_\mathrm{F} | \mathbb{T}, \mathbb{S}) + r(\Theta | \mathcal{K}_\mathrm{F}, \mathbb{S}) + r(\mathcal{K}_\mathrm{F}), \tag{19.3}$$

which includes a loss function $l(\cdot)$ and two regularization terms $r(\cdot)$.

Singh and Gordon (2008) study users' rating behaviors and items' attributes in a single framework, and bridge two different domains via sharing the knowledge of items' latent features. More specifically, they design a collective matrix factorization (CMF) model that jointly factorizes a rating matrix in terms of users and items and a data matrix about items, and share the collectively learned item-specific latent feature matrix to achieve bidirectional knowledge transfer. Besides, Shi et al. (2013b) propose a joint matrix factorization (JMF) method for a rating matrix and an item similarity matrix defined on the contextual information.

Pan et al. (2010b) aim to leverage both user-side and item-side source examination information to improve the target rating prediction problem. In particular, they design a coordinate system transfer (CST) algorithm, where the coordinate systems are actually the user-specific and item-specific latent features learned from the user-side and item-side source examination data, respectively. Such latent features are then transferred to the target rating prediction task via two biased regularization terms. We can see that the CST method is a two-stage approach, including the coordinate system construction and transfer learning.

Pan and Yang (2013) turn to exploit the front-side binary feedback such as users' likes and dislikes to assist the target rating prediction task. In order to acquire the rich knowledge for sharing, they design a transfer by collective factorization (TCF) approach, which models the data-independent knowledge via two shared latent matrices and the data-dependent effect via two non-shared matrices simultaneously for the target numerical ratings and the source like/dislike binary ratings. In TCF, the two shared latent feature matrices, that is, the user-specific latent feature matrix and the item-specific latent feature matrix, are designed to bridge two heterogeneous data in a collective manner.

Pan et al. (2016a) study two one-class feedback such as purchases and browses via a transfer via joint similarity learning (TJSL) method from the perspective of joint similarity learning by sharing the item-specific latent feature matrix. In particular, the TJSL method proposes to learn a similarity between a candidate item and a purchased item and also a similarity between a candidate item and a browsed item. Such joint similarity learning via sharing item-specific latent features is empirically shown to achieve better performance in terms of item ranking.

Hu et al. (2018) develop a deep transfer learning model for shared user cross-domain recommendation. They propose a collaborative cross network (CoNet), which can transfer source domain knowledge in a way of deep representations. The knowledge transfer happens in both directions, from the source to target domain and from the target to source domain. The idea is to feed the representations from the source network into the hidden layers in the target network. This makes the preference learning in the target domain easier even in the sparse data case since the target network only needs to learn an incremental "residual" representations with the reference of source representations.

He et al. (2018a) design a deep learning model called General Cross-domain framework via BAyesian Neural network (GCBAN) to bridge two recommendation domains by sharing the latent representation of both the users and their profile attributes.

Gao et al. (2019) develop a neural attentive transfer recommendation (NATR) model to transfer items' latent features, that is, embeddings, from an auxiliary rating matrix, which are further weighted via an item-level attention and a domain-level attention for more effective knowledge transfer.

There are also some works combining deep learning, feature engineering and hybrid methods in order to exploit different information and knowledge in a recommendation system more sufficiently (Cheng et al., 2016; Covington et al., 2016; Zhang et al., 2017d). Moreover, some recent works turn to explore a deep model for a nonlinear mapping from a source feature matrix to a target feature matrix for better knowledge transfer in comparison with that of traditional linear mapping (Man et al., 2017; Zhu et al., 2018).

From the aforementioned representative works, we can see that latent feature transfer can be applied to different learning tasks in recommendation, for example, rating prediction with item-side source text information in the work by Singh and Gordon (2008), both user-side and item-side examination information in the work by Pan et al. (2010b), frontal-side binary ratings in the work by Pan and Yang (2013), item ranking with both purchases and examinations in that by Pan et al. (2016a), item-side numerical ratings in the wo Gao et al. (2019) and rating prediction with user-side source text information and numerical ratings in the work by He et al. (2018a). The shared common knowledge of latent features can be transferred from the source domain to the target domain in a collective manner as in the work by Singh and Gordon (2008), Pan and Yang (2013), Pan et al. (2016a) and He et al. (2018a) or an adaptive manner in the work by Pan et al. (2010b), Hu et al. (2018) and Gao et al. (2019).

19.2.3 Model-Based Transfer Learning in Recommendation

For model-based transfer learning methods in recommendation, we focus on extracting some common model or compressed knowledge from the source domain and transfer the knowledge to a target domain. Mathematically, we have the reduced optimization problem from the general framework in (19.1), as

$$\min_{\Theta, \mathcal{K}_{\mathrm{M}}} l(\Theta, \mathcal{K}_{\mathrm{M}} | \mathbb{T}, \mathbb{S}) + r(\Theta | \mathcal{K}_{\mathrm{M}}, \mathbb{S}), \qquad (19.4)$$

which includes a loss function $l(\cdot)$ and a regularization term $r(\cdot)$.

Li et al. (2009a) propose one of the first algorithms for integrating recommendation systems with transfer learning with an algorithm known as CBT. The CBT model first constructs a codebook from the source rating data, which reflects the correlation knowledge of user groups and item clusters, and then transfers the codebook to the target rating prediction task in a non-negative matrix factorization framework. Empirical studies show that the codebook can help alleviate the sparsity problem in the target domain. The transferred knowledge in the code-book can also be shared in a collective manner as done in the rating-matrix generative model (RMGM) (Li et al., 2009b). Besides, Gao et al. (2013) propose a cluster-level latent factor model (CLFM) with two types of codebooks, one for the shared common rating pattern and another for the domain-specific rating pattern.

Pan et al. (2015a) propose a compressed knowledge transfer via factorization machine (CKT-FM) to integrate explicit and implicit feedbacks. First, CKT-FM mines the compressed knowledge of users and items via a clustering method, where the extracted knowledge of membership information for both users and items are assumed to be stable across two types of feedback. Second, CKT-FM transfers the mined compressed knowledge to the target rating prediction task via a generic feature engineering based factorization approach, that is, factorization machine.

Kanagawa et al. (2019) apply a recent deep learning method called domain separation networks (DSNs) (Bousmalis et al., 2016) to a content-based cross-domain recommendation problem with two preference data, where a common encoder and a common decoder are shared between the source and target preference prediction tasks, while two private encoders are also kept for the source data and the target data.

We can see that the main idea of most model-based transfer learning in recommendation is to share or transfer high-level rating behaviors such as clusters or memberships of users and items, which are assumed to be relatively stable and consistent across explicit and implicit feedbacks. The transferred knowledge is particularly useful when the target domain is extremely sparse in terms of ratings.

Finally, we summarize the aforementioned transfer learning methods in recommendation in Table 19.1. We can see that most transfer learning models are designed to transfer knowledge from the frontal-side source information such as examinations, uncertain ratings and binary ratings.

19.3   News Recommendation

In this section, we introduce a recommendation problem, that is, news recommendation, as a target problem for transfer learning.

News recommendation has been an important service in mobile devices for most users to know what has happened in the world. In this section, we focus on recommending latest news articles to new users. We assume that users have newly registered in a certain news recommendation service and have not read any news article before. This task is associated with the new user cold-start challenge and the new item (i.e., news article) cold-start challenge, and is thus termed as *dual cold-start recommendation* (DCSR).

For the DCSR problem, existing news recommendation methods (Das et al.,

Table 19.1 *A brief summary of transfer learning methods in recommendation*

Categorization	Method and problem setting
Instance-based	ABPR: from frontal-side examinations to transactions for item ranking sTL: from frontal-side examinations to numerical ratings for rating prediction TMH: from user-side installation behaviors to reading feedback for item ranking TIF: from frontal-side uncertain rating to numerical rating for rating prediction ToR: from frontal-side examinations to numerical ratings for item ranking
Feature-based	CMF, JMF: from item-side information to ratings for rating prediction CST: from two-sided examinations to numerical ratings for rating prediction TCF: from frontal-side binary ratings to numerical ratings for rating predition TJSL: from frontal-side examinations to transactions for item ranking CoNet: from user-side information to ratings for item ranking GCBAN: from user-side information to ratings for rating prediction NATR: from item-side numerical ratings to ratings for item recommendation
Model-based	CBT, RMGM, CLFM: from numerical ratings to numerical ratings for rating prediction CKT-FM: from frontal-side examinations to numerical ratings for rating prediction DSNs: from interactions to interactions for item recommendation

2007; Liu et al., 2010a) are not applicable, because they rely on users' historical reading behaviors and news articles' content information that are not available in the DCSR problem.

The DCSR problem can be solved from the perspective of transfer learning. Although there are no users' behaviors about the cold-start users and cold-start items in the news domain, there may be some other related domains with users' behaviors. Specifically, we leverage some knowledge from a related domain, that is, the app domain, where the users' app-installation behaviors are available. Most cold-start users in the news domain have already installed some apps, and this information may be helpful in determining his/her preferences in news articles. In particular, we assume that users with similar app-installation behaviors are likely to have similar interests in news articles. With this assumption, the neighborhood in the APP domain can be used as the knowledge to be transferred to the target domain of news articles.

19.3.1 Problem Definition

In the news recommendation problem, we have two domains, an APP domain acting as the source domain and a news domain as the target domain.

In the APP domain, we have a set of triples, that is, (u, g, G_{ug}), indicating that user u has installed G_{ug} times of mobile apps belonging to the genre g. The data of the APP domain can then be represented as a user-genre matrix $\mathbf{G}$, as shown in Figure 19.1.

In the news domain, we have a user-item matrix $\mathbf{R}$ to denote whether a user has read an item or not. Each item i is associated with a level-1 category $c_1(i) \in \mathscr{C}_1$ and a level-2 category $c_2(i) \in \mathscr{C}_2$. We thus have a set of quadruples, that is, $(u, i, c_1(i), c_2(i))$, denoting that user u has read an item i belonging to $c_1(i)$ and

$c_2(i)$. After pre-processing, we have a user-category matrix **C**, in which each entry denotes the number of items belonging to a certain category that a user has read.

The goal is to recommend a ranking list of new items (i.e., latest news articles) to each new user who has not read any items before. Note that, under the DCSR setting, we only make use of category information for items but not the content information.

19.3.2 Challenges

The main difficulty of the DCSR problem is the lack of previous preference data for new users and new items. We face the new user cold-start challenge, where the target users to whom we will provide recommendations have not read any items before. We also face the new item cold-start challenge, where the target items that we will recommend to the target users are totally new for all users. Under such challenges, most existing recommendation algorithms are not applicable.

To address the two challenges in the DCSR problem, we make a preference assumption across the APP domain and news domain that neighborhood structure in the two domains are similar. A neighborhood-based transfer learning (NTL) method is introduced to transfer the knowledge of the neighborhood from the APP domain to the news domain, which can address the new user cold-start challenge. For the new item cold-start challenge, a category-level preference is designed to replace the traditional item-level preference because the latter is not available for the new items in the DCSR problem. With these two techniques addressing the two challenges, some well-studied neighborhood-based recommendation methods are applicable to the DCSR problem.

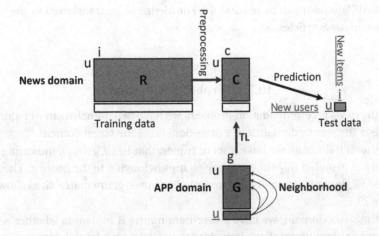

Figure 19.1 An illustration of the NTL method for the DCSR problem

19.3.3 A Solution: NTL

In most recommendation methods, the user-user (or item-item) similarity is a central concept, because the neighborhood can be constructed for like-minded users' preference aggregation and then for the target user's preference prediction. Mathematically, the preference prediction rule for user u on item i can be formulated as

$$\hat{r}_{u,i} = \frac{1}{|\mathcal{N}_u|} \sum_{u' \in \mathcal{N}_u} \hat{r}_{u',i}, \tag{19.5}$$

where $\mathcal{N}_u$ denotes a set of nearest neighbors of user u in terms of a similarity measure such as the cosine similarity, and $\hat{r}_{u',i}$ is the estimated preference of user u' on item i. The average score $\hat{r}_{u,i}$ is taken as the preference of user u on item i and it will be used for item ranking and top-k recommendation.

For the DCSR problem, we cannot build correlations between a cold-start user in the test data and a warm-start user in the training data using the data from the news domain only. The main idea of the NTL method is to leverage the correlations among users in the APP domain with the preference assumption that users with similar app-installation behaviors are likely to be similar in the news domain. For instance, two users with the installed apps in the same genre such as business may both prefer news articles on the finance topic.

With the preference assumption, we first compute the cosine similarity between a cold-start user u and a warm-start user u' in the APP domain as

$$s_{u,u'} = \frac{G_{u.} G_{u'.}^T}{\sqrt{G_{u.} G_{u.}^T} \sqrt{G_{u'.} G_{u'.}^T}}, \tag{19.6}$$

where $G_{u.}$ is a row vector w.r.t. user u in the user-genre matrix $\mathbf{G}$. Once we have calculated the cosine similarity, for each cold-start user u, we first remove users with small similarity values (e.g., $s_{u,u'} < 0.1$), and then take the most similar users to construct the neighborhood $\mathcal{N}_u$.

For the item-level preference $\hat{r}_{u',i}$ in (19.5), we are unable to have such a score directly because item i is new to all users, including the warm-start users and the target cold-start user u'. We can propose approximating the item-level preference by a category-level preference as

$$\hat{r}_{u',i} \approx \hat{r}_{u',c(i)}, \tag{19.7}$$

where $c(i)$ can be the level-1 or level-2 category. We can have two types of category-level preferences as

$$\hat{r}_{u',c(i)} = \hat{r}_{u',c_1(i)} = N_{u',c_1(i)}, \tag{19.8}$$

$$\hat{r}_{u',c(i)} = \hat{r}_{u',c_2(i)} = N_{u',c_2(i)}, \tag{19.9}$$

where $N_{u',c_1(i)}$ and $N_{u',c_2(i)}$ denote the number of items (by user u') belonging to the level-1 category $c_1(i)$ and the level-2 category $c_2(i)$, respectively.

Finally, with (19.7)–(19.9), we can rewrite (19.5) as

$$\hat{r}_{u,i} \approx \frac{1}{|\mathcal{N}_u|} \sum_{u' \in \mathcal{N}_u} N_{u',c_1(i)}, \tag{19.10}$$

$$\hat{r}_{u,i} \approx \frac{1}{|\mathcal{N}_u|} \sum_{u' \in \mathcal{N}_u} N_{u',c_2(i)}, \tag{19.11}$$

which will be used for the preference prediction. Specifically, the neighborhood $\mathcal{N}_u$ helps address the new user cold-start challenge and the category-level preference $N_{u',c_1(i)}$ or $N_{u',c_2(i)}$ addresses the new item cold-start challenge.

19.4   VIP Recommendation in Social Networks

In this section, we introduce another recommendation problem, that is, VIP or key-opinion-leader (KOL) recommendation in social media and social networks.

Social network services such as microblogging (e.g., Twitter) and instant messenger (e.g., Skype, etc.) are playing an increasingly important role in our everyday life. Similar to the fundamental motivation of information overload (Toffler, 1970) in recommender systems (Resnick and Varian, 1997), users may feel difficult to find other interesting users to follow from hundreds of millions of users within the same social network platform. One example of this challenge is that, in microblogging services, a large number of new users join the network every day. Effective solutions for recommendation must overcome the challenge of "user overload" in such a social network, similar to the challenge of "information overload" in online shopping sites like Amazon.

In a social network, some famous users known as VIPs contribute to the dissemination of information and growth in social networks significantly. VIP recommendation aims to recommend VIP users to other users. This is a strategically important task for social network sustainability, since good VIP recommendation brings in more relations and activities in the online social community. However, even for VIP recommendation, the problem of user overload or more precisely VIP overload still exists, since there are a large number of VIPs.

There are two main challenges for the task of VIP recommendation. First, the "following" relation data in a microblogging social network are very sparse, making it difficult to apply traditional similarity-based techniques. Second, this data is extremely large, thus pairwise similarity calculation would be computationally infeasible. To solve these two problems, in this section, we present a SOcial Relation based Transfer (SORT) method, which extracts useful knowledge from the source data consisting of other services and applies the common knowledge to help improve the VIP recommendation.

The SORT method has two major advantages over traditional memory-based methods such as the Resnick's rule (Resnick et al., 1994). First, it is very efficient for an extremely large user set as it avoids the similarity calculation, the bottleneck step in traditional approaches. Second, it recommends accurately by leveraging additional knowledge from a mature social network of instant messenger via transfer learning techniques.

19.4.1 Problem Definition

In a target domain consisting of a microblogging social network, we have n users and m VIPs, where the m VIPs are selected by considering the various factors including social impact and business influence. The goal is to recommend the top-k VIPs among the given m VIPs for each of n users. Due to the sparsity of the user-VIP matrix of the *following* relations, we concern the efficiency and effectiveness of the solution, and wish to exploit the source data under the transfer learning setting.

Mathematically, we have a matrix $\mathbf{R} = [r_{ui}]_{n \times m} \in \{1, ?\}^{n \times m}$, where "1" denotes the observed *following* relation between user u and VIP i and "?" denotes a missing or unobserved value. Note that the *following* relations are usually considered as weak ties. We use a mask matrix $\mathbf{Y} = [y_{ui}]_{n \times m} \in \{0, 1\}^{n \times m}$ to denote whether the entry (u, i) is observed ($y_{ui} = 1$) or not ($y_{ui} = 0$). Similarly, in the source domain of instant messenger, we have a matrix $\mathbf{X} = [x_{uw}]_{n \times n} \in \{1, ?\}^{n \times n}$, where "?" denotes the missing value and "1" denotes the observed *friendship* relation between users u and w. Since instant messenger services have been developed for a long time, the *friendship* relations represent strong ties. Thus, we can simplify the *friendship* relation matrix as $\mathbf{X} = [x_{uw}]_{n \times n} \in \{1, 0\}^{n \times n}$, where "0" denotes the non-friend relation between user u and user w. Note that there is a one-one mapping between the users of $\mathbf{R}$ and $\mathbf{X}$. The goal is to help each user u find a personalized list of top-k VIPs by transferring knowledge from $\mathbf{X}$.

Note that the source social network of the instant messenger, $\mathbf{X}$, can be replaced by the *following* relations between users $\mathbf{S}_1 \in \{1, ?\}^{n \times n}$ or VIPs $\mathbf{S}_2 \in \{1, ?\}^{m \times m}$ within the same target social network of microblog, where $\mathbf{S}_1$ and $\mathbf{S}_2$ represent the user–user *following* and VIP–VIP *following* relations, respectively. Considering the "distance" or "analogy" of $\mathbf{X}$ and $\mathbf{R}$, and that of $\mathbf{S}_1$ (or $\mathbf{S}_2$) and $\mathbf{R}$, these two settings can be considered as *far transfer* and *near transfer*, respectively (Hinrichs and Forbus, 2011).

In a brief summary, the proposed problem setting can be considered as transferring knowledge over two real heterogeneous social networks of instant messenger and microblog as

$$\left\{ \begin{array}{ll} \mathbf{X} \Rightarrow \mathbf{R}, & \textit{far transfer} \\ \mathbf{S}_1, \mathbf{S}_2 \Rightarrow \mathbf{R}, & \textit{near transfer} \end{array} \right. \tag{19.12}$$

where *far transfer* represents knowledge transfer across two heterogeneous social networks of instant messenger and microblog, and *near transfer* for that within the target social network of microblog. The goal is to predict the missing values in **R**, and thus we can rank and recommend VIPs for each user. An illustration is shown in Figure 19.2.

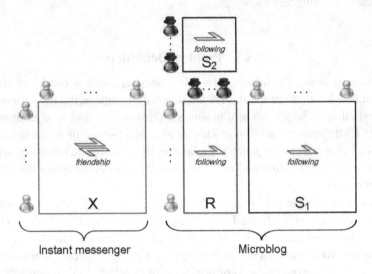

Figure 19.2 An illustration of the VIP recommendation

19.4.2 Challenges

VIP recommendation is basically a one-class collaborative filtering problem (Pan et al., 2008a), since the rating of user u on VIP i is either "1" or unknown (missing value). Hence, most memory-based collaborative filtering methods for rating prediction cannot be used directly, which we will explain later. We observe two very fundamental challenges in VIP recommendation.

(1) The first challenge is the scalability, since it's extremely time consuming to estimate the similarity between every two users when there are millions of users.

(2) The second challenge is the sparsity, since the observed *following* relations in **R** are very few, and thus the estimated similarities between users may be not accurate.

We can see that these two challenges are rooted in the "similarity" in memory-based collaborative filtering methods, for example, the Resnick's rule (Resnick et al., 1994). As far as we know, distributed algorithms can address the first challenge and most transfer learning works focus on addressing the second challenge. However, few works study to address those two challenges in a single framework. In the following section, we will introduce a solution to achieve this.

19.4.3 A Solution: Social Relation-Based Transfer

A Simplified Prediction Rule

The Pearson correlation coefficient (PCC) is a widely adopted similarity measure for two users u and w based on the ratings on their commonly rated items (Resnick et al., 1994) and it can be defined as

$$PCC(u, w) = \frac{\sum_i y_{ui} y_{wi} (r_{ui} - m_{u\cdot})(r_{wi} - m_{w\cdot})}{\sqrt{\sum_i y_{ui} y_{wi}(r_{ui} - m_{u\cdot})^2}\sqrt{\sum_i y_{ui} y_{wi}(r_{wi} - m_{w\cdot})^2}},$$

where $m_{u\cdot} = \sum_i y_{ui} y_{wi} r_{ui} / \sum_i y_{ui} y_{wi}$ is the average rating of user u and $m_{w\cdot} = \sum_i y_{ui} y_{wi} r_{wi} / \sum_i y_{ui} y_{wi}$ is the average rating of user w. Then the normalized similarity between users u and w can be calculated as

$$s_{uw} = \frac{PCC(u, w)}{\sum_{u' \in N_u} PCC(u, u')},$$

where N_u is the set of nearest neighboring users of user u according to the PCC. Finally, according to Resnick et al. (1994), we can predict the rating of user u on item i as

$$\hat{r}_{ui} = \bar{r}_{u\cdot} + \sum_{w \in N_u} y_{wi} s_{uw}(r_{wi} - m_{w\cdot}), \tag{19.13}$$

where $\bar{r}_{u\cdot} = \sum_i y_{ui} r_{ui} / \sum_i y_{ui}$ is the average rating of user u on all items rated by user u. (19.13) can equivalently be reformulated as

$$\hat{r}_{ui} = \bar{r}_{u\cdot} - \sum_{w \in N_u} y_{wi} s_{uw} m_{w\cdot} + \sum_{w \in N_u} y_{wi} s_{uw} r_{wi}, \tag{19.14}$$

where the first term represents the globally average rating of user u and the second term represents the aggregation of local average ratings of its nearest neighbors. For the one-class collaborative filtering for VIP recommendation, we have $\bar{r}_{u\cdot} = 1$ and $m_{w\cdot} = 1$, thus such average ratings do not contain any discriminative information and can be safely discarded. Finally, we obtain a simplified prediction rule as

$$\hat{r}_{ui} = \sum_{w \in N_u} y_{wi} s_{uw} r_{wi}, \tag{19.15}$$

which means that the rating of user u on item i can be estimated from the preferences of nearest neighbors of user u on item i via a weighted aggregation.

The SORT Method

As mentioned before, there are two challenges for the simplified prediction rule in (19.15), including the scalability and the sparsity. Here we introduce the SORT method to replace the similarity calculation in the target domain with existing relations from a source domain. Specifically, we use a well-developed source social network of instant messenger, which can avoid the procedures of the similarity calculation and neighborhood search. We replace N_u and s_{uw} in (19.15) with

$\tilde{N}_u$ and x_{uw} to obtain a revised prediction rule as

$$\hat{r}_{ui} = \sum_{w \in \tilde{N}_u} y_{wi} x_{uw} r_{wi}, \qquad (19.16)$$

where $\tilde{N}_u$ denotes the set of user u's friends in the social network of instant messenger and x_{uw} denotes the relationship of user u and his/her friend w. To consider each friend equally, we set $x_{uw} = 1$ in (19.16) and then we have

$$\hat{r}_{ui} = \sum_{w \in \tilde{N}_u} y_{wi} r_{wi}. \qquad (19.17)$$

For the one-class collaborative filtering problem in microblog, we can further replace the term $y_{wi} r_{wi}$ in (19.17) with $f_{wi} = \begin{cases} 1, & \text{user } w \text{ has followed VIP } i \\ 0, & \text{otherwise} \end{cases}$ to get

$$\hat{r}_{ui} = \sum_{w \in \tilde{N}_u} f_{wi}, \qquad (19.18)$$

which implies that, if user u has $|\tilde{N}_u|$ friends in the social network of instant messenger and $\sum_{w \in \tilde{N}_u} f_{wi}$ of them have followed VIP i in the social network of microblog, then the preference of user u on VIP i is equal to $\sum_{w \in \tilde{N}_u} f_{wi}$. We can see that two heterogeneous social networks of microblog (the *following* relation f_{wi}) and instant messenger (the *friendship* relations $\tilde{N}_u$) are integrated together in such an intuitive way as shown in (19.18). The knowledge of social relations, $\tilde{N}_u$, of instant messenger is naturally embedded in the prediction method.

According to (19.18), we can see that the predicted score $\hat{r}_{ui}$ must be an integer since f_{wi} is either 1 or 0, and user u may have the same score on several different VIPs, where we cannot distinguish the ranking positions. To address this problem, we further introduce a popularity score for each VIP i, $0 \le p_i \le 1, i = 1, \ldots, m$, to obtain the prediction rule as

$$\hat{r}_{ui} = p_i + \sum_{w \in \tilde{N}_u} f_{wi}. \qquad (19.19)$$

The SORT method transfers *friendship* relations, $\tilde{N}_u$, from a source social network of instant messenger to a target VIP recommendation in microblog. We can see that the procedures of similarity calculation and neighbor search in Resnick's rule (Resnick et al., 1994) is avoided.

20

Transfer Learning in Bioinformatics

20.1 Introduction

With the fast-growing biological technology comes the rapid growth in the amount of biological data. These data are made available with increasingly lower cost in bio-sensor technologies, and, as a result, in the next few years we expect to witness a dramatic increase in the application of personal genomic and personalized medicine.

Bioinformatics is an interdisciplinary field in nature, covering diverse areas such as biology, biochemistry, machine learning, data management, information retrieval, computer science and so on. Researchers have exploited data from a wide spectrum of devices such as microarray, genomic sequencing, medical imaging and so on (Larrañaga et al., 2006). Based on these data, bioinformatics target the task of learning statistical models to infer biological properties from them. Various techniques such as supervised learning and unsupervised learning have been developed with promising results and biological insights for different problems such as sequence classification, gene expression data analysis, biological network reconstruction and so on.

One common assumption in learning from biological data is that a sufficient amount of annotated training data are available so that an accurate learning model can be trained. However, in many real world bioinformatics problems, labeled training data are limited or can only be obtained by paying a huge cost. This data sparsity problem has become a major bottleneck for applying machine learning methods in bioinformatics. Moreover, when the data sparsity problem occurs, the overfitting can easily happen. As a result, the learned model will experience a reduction in the performance.

In response to the data sparsity problem, various novel machine learning methods have been developed. Among them, transfer learning and multitask learning are good solutions. In the following sections, we introduce how to use transfer learning and multitask learning to solve bioinformatics problems.

20.2 Machine Learning Problems in Bioinformatics

In this chapter, we focus on several problems in bioinformatics, including biological sequence analysis, gene expression analysis, genetic analysis, systems biology and biomedical text and image mining.

Biological sequence analysis mainly aims to assign functional annotations to sequences of DNA segments, and it is important for our understanding of a genome. One example is the identification of splice sites in terms of the exon and intron boundaries, which is a complex task due to alternative splicing, which allows many different protein products. Other examples include the prediction of regulatory regions that allow the binding of proteins and determine their functions, the prediction of transcription start and initiation sites, and the prediction of coding regions. Another important sequence analysis problem is the major histocompatibility complex (MHC) binding prediction from the perspective of the sequence, where sequences from pathogens provide a huge amount of potential vaccine candidates (Dönnes and Elofsson, 2002). MHC molecules are key in the human immune system, and the prediction of their binding peptides helps the design of peptide-based vaccines. Despite much success in the prediction of MHC bindings, lacking sufficient training data for the majority of these molecules has hindered the application of machine learning to this problem. In addition, the protein subcellular localization prediction based on sequences, an important problem in biological sequence analysis, targets to provide location annotations to the protein sequences.

Gene expression analysis and genetic analysis through microarrays or gene chips is an important task for the understanding of proteins and mRNAs. A microarray measures the relative mRNA level of genes. One application is to compare the gene expression levels of some biological samples over time to understand differences between normal and cancer cells (Aas, 2001). One characteristics of this task is that the number of features that correspond to genes are usually larger than the number of samples and it makes it difficult to apply traditional feature selection approaches directly on these data to reduce the dimensionality (Xing et al., 2001). Another techinque applied to the gene expression data is co-clustering, which aims to cluster both the samples and genes at the same time (Yang et al., 2011). In genetic analysis, recent advances have allowed genome-wide association studies (GWASs) to assay hundreds of thousands of single nucleotide polymorphisms (SNPs) and relate them to clinical conditions or measurable traits, where a combination of statistical and machine learning methods has been exploited (Yang et al., 2008; Wan et al., 2009).

Systems biology refers to the tasks of modeling gene-protein regulatory networks and making inferences based on protein–protein interaction networks and so on. Data fusion and data integration become an important issue as many different types of data are considered, therefore computational challenges in systems biology lie in how to integrate and explore large-scale, multi-dimension and various types of data. Besides the automatic prediction based on statistical models, mixed initiative approaches such as visualization have also been developed to tackle the large-scale data and complex modeling problems in systems biology.

Biomedical text mining refers to using information retrieval techniques to extract information on genes, proteins and their functional relationships from scientific literature (Krallinger and Valencia, 2005). Today we face a vast amount of biological findings that are published as articles, journals, blogs, books and conference proceedings. For example, PubMed and MEDLINE provide much up-to-date information for biological researchers. If we follow a traditional way of acquiring the information, a researcher has to read through this huge volume of information to discover potential findings in his/her field. With text mining technologies, new findings that are published in text can be automatically detected and then presented to researchers.

Biomedical image mining is an important problem in many applications. The manual classification of images is time-consuming, repetitive and unreliable. Given a set of training images classified into a number of classes, the goal of an automatic image classification method is to train a model to accurately predict the category of new images. A typical example is breast cancer identification from medical imaging data through computer-aided detection in screening mammography. An important issue for such models is how to reduce the false positive rates of the classification.

Transfer learning is important to solving the data sparsity problem for each of the aforementioned problems in bioinformatics. In the following sections, we will survey recent transfer learning studies in these areas.

We introduce some notations that are used in this chapter. The data of the source domain $\mathcal{D}_s$ is composed of data instances $\mathbf{x}_i$ and their corresponding labels y_i, thus, the source domain data $(\mathbf{X}_s, \mathbf{Y}_s)$ is denoted by $\{(\mathbf{x}_i^s, y_i^s)\}_{i=1}^{n_s}$. Similarly, the data of the target domain $\mathcal{D}_t$ is composed of data instances $\mathbf{x}_i^t$ and their corresponding labels y_i^t, thus the target domain data $(\mathbf{X}_t, \mathbf{Y}_t)$ is denoted by $\{(\mathbf{x}_i^t, y_i^t)\}_{i=1}^{n_t}$. The functions $f_s(\cdot)$ and $f_t(\cdot)$ denote the predictive functions in the source domain D_s and the target domain D_t, respectively. In multitask learning, the data $(\mathbf{X}_i, \mathbf{Y}_i)$ of task i for $i = 1, \ldots m$ can be represented by $\{(\mathbf{x}_j^i, y_j^i)\}_{j=1}^{n_i}$, where m is the total number of tasks.

20.3   Biological Sequence Analysis

In sequence classification, the goal is to annotate gene sequences or protein sequences from a given set of training data. As mentioned earlier, learning to annotate sequences often suffers from the data sparsity problem and hence easily causes the overfitting. To solve this problem, multitask learning methods are often used to annotate two or more sets of sequence data together. In this approach, the sequence data can be from different domains. By learning these tasks together, the data sparsity problem can be alleviated.

In multitask learning, the regularization approach is often exploited. Under a regularization framework, the objective function of this approach consists of two terms, including an empirical loss on the training data of all tasks and a regularization term that encodes the relationships among tasks.

As a pioneer work, Evgeniou and Pontil (2004) propose a multitask extension of a support vector machine (SVM), which minimizes the following objective function as

$$\xi(\{\mathbf{w}_t\}) = \sum_{t=1}^{m} \sum_{i=1}^{n_t} l(y_i^t, \mathbf{w}_t^{\mathsf{T}} \mathbf{x}_i^t) + \lambda_1 \sum_{t=1}^{m} \|\mathbf{w}_t\|_2^2 + \lambda_2 \sum_{t=1}^{m} \|\mathbf{w}_t - \frac{1}{m} \sum_{t'=1}^{m} \mathbf{w}_{t'}\|_2^2. \quad (20.1)$$

The first and second terms in (20.1) denote the empirical error and the squared ℓ_2 norm regularization of parameter vectors, respectively, which are the same as those of single-task SVMs. A difference between single-task SVMs and multitask SVMs lies in the third term of (20.1), which is designed to penalize a large deviation between each parameter vector and the mean parameter vector of all tasks. This penalized term enforces the parameter vectors in all tasks to be similar to each other.

One of the earliest works in multitask sequence classification is the one by Widmer et al. (2010a), which proposes two regularization-based multitask learning methods to predict the splice sites across different organisms. In order to leverage information from related organisms, Widmer et al. (2010a) suggest two principal approaches to incorporate relations across organisms. The proposed methods modify the regularization term in the work by Evgeniou and Pontil (2004). However, different from Evgeniou and Pontil (2004), the relation among the organisms in the work by Widmer et al. (2010a) is defined by a tree or a graph implied by their taxonomy or phylogeny. The first approach trains the models in a top-down manner, where a model is learned for each node in the hierarchy over the data set of the corresponding task and the parent node provide the a priori information, and its objective function is formulated as

$$\xi(\{\mathbf{w}_t\}) = \sum_{t=1}^{m} \sum_{i=1}^{n_t} l(y_i^t, \mathbf{w}_t^{\mathsf{T}} \mathbf{x}_i^t) + \lambda_1 \sum_{t=1}^{m} \|\mathbf{w}_t - \mathbf{w}_{parent(t)}\|_2^2. \quad (20.2)$$

In biology, an organism and its ancestors should be similar, due to the inheritance in the evolution. This information leads to the second approach in Widmer et al. (2010a) with the objective function formulated as

$$\xi(\{\mathbf{w}_t\}) = \sum_{t=1}^{m} \sum_{i=1}^{n_t} l(y_i^t, \mathbf{w}_t^{\mathsf{T}} \mathbf{x}_i^t) + \lambda_1 \sum_{t=1}^{m} \sum_{t'=1}^{m} \gamma_{tt'} \|\mathbf{w}_t - \mathbf{w}_{t'}\|_2^2, \quad (20.3)$$

where the regularization term enforces $\mathbf{w}_t$ to be similar to $\mathbf{w}_{t'}$ depending on $\gamma_{tt'}$ which reflects the evolutionary similarity between two organisms.

In addition, Widmer et al. (2010a) consider not only the data of the task t, but also the data of its corresponding ancestor r_t according to a hierarchy structure R.

The objective function is formulated as

$$\xi(\{\mathbf{w}_t\}) = \sum_{t=1}^{m}\sum_{i=1}^{n_t} l(y_i^t, \mathbf{w}_t^T \mathbf{x}_i^t) + \lambda_1 \sum_{t=1}^{m} \|\mathbf{u}_t\|_2^2 + \lambda_2 \sum_{t=1}^{m}\sum_{r_t=1}^{R} \|\mathbf{v}_{r_t}\|_2^2, \qquad (20.4)$$

where $\mathbf{u}_t$ is the parameter vector of a leaf node and $\mathbf{v}_{r_t}$ denotes the parameter vector of its corresponding ancestor that are internal nodes in the hierarchy structure.

Similarly, Schweikert et al. (2008) consider a number of *domain transfer learning* methods for the splice site recognition across several organisms by using a model of a well-analyzed source domain with its associated data to obtain or refine a model for a less analyzed target domain. In the work by Schweikert et al. (2008), is the source domain, while *Caenorhabditis remanei*, *Pristionchus pacificus*, *Drosophila melanogaster* and *Arabidopsis thaliana* are treated as target domains. The domain transfer learning methods used include

- Combination: As a baseline, the simplest way is to combine the source domain data and the target domain data directly with equal weights.
- Convex combination:

$$F(x) = \alpha f_t(x) + (1 - \alpha) f_s(x), \qquad (20.5)$$

where α is the trade-off parameter to balance the contributions of the source data and the target data.

- Dual-task learning:

$$\xi(\{\mathbf{w_s}, \mathbf{w_t}\}) = C \sum_{i=1}^{n_s+n_t} l(y_i^{s+t}, \mathbf{w}^t \mathbf{x}_i^{s+t}) + \lambda \|\mathbf{w}_s - \mathbf{w}_t\|, \qquad (20.6)$$

where both $\mathbf{w_s}$ and $\mathbf{w_t}$ are optimized.

- Kernel mean matching:

$$\hat{\Phi}(\mathbf{x}_k) = \Phi(\mathbf{x}_k) - \alpha \left(\frac{1}{n_s}\sum_{i=1}^{n_s} \Phi(\mathbf{x}_i) - \frac{1}{n_t}\sum_{i=n_s+1}^{n_s+n_t} \Phi(\mathbf{x}_i) \right) \forall_i = 1, \ldots, n_s \qquad (20.7)$$

where Φ is a kernel mapping to project the data into a RKHS.

It is verified by the experiments in the work by Schweikert et al. (2008) that the differences of classification functions for recognizing splice site in these organisms will increase with increasing evolutionary distance.

Jacob and Vert (2007) design an algorithm to learn peptide-MHC-I binding models for many alleles simultaneously by sharing binding information across alleles. The sharing of information is controlled by a user-defined measure of similarity between alleles, where the similarity can be defined in terms of supertypes or more directly by comparing key residues that are known to play a role in the peptide-MHC binding. The pair of an allele a and a peptide candidate p is represented in a feature vector. Then, based on the kernel trick, Jacob and Vert (2007) define the kernel function between pairs of alleles and peptides as

$$K((p,a),(p',a')) = K_{pep}(p,p')K_{all}(a,a'), \qquad (20.8)$$

where, for the peptide kernel K_{pep}, any kernel between the peptide representation can be used and, for the allele kernel K_{all}, the authors exploit some methods to model the relationships across alleles including the multitask kernel and super-type kernel.

Jacob et al. (2008) propose a regularized multitask method for MHC class I binding prediction to group similar tasks in a cluster. To achieve this goal, the regularization term is formulated as

$$\Omega(\mathbf{W}) = \varepsilon_M \Omega_{mean}(\mathbf{W}) + \varepsilon_B \Omega_{between}(\mathbf{W}) + \varepsilon_W \Omega_{within}(\mathbf{W}),$$

where $\Omega_{mean}(\mathbf{W})$ measures on the average of weight vectors, $\Omega_{between}(\mathbf{W})$ is a measure of between-cluster variance and $\Omega_{within}(\mathbf{W})$ is a measure of within-cluster variance.

Following Jacob and Vert (2007) and Jacob et al. (2008), Widmer et al. (2010b) propose to improve the predictive power of a multitask kernel method for the MHC class I binding prediction by developing an advanced kernel based on Jacob and Vert (2007). In addition, Widmer et al. (2010c) investigate multitask learning scenarios where a latent structural relation across tasks exists and apply the proposed method for the splice site recognition as well as the MHC class I binding prediction. More specifically, they model the relatedness between tasks based on meta-tasks such that the information is transferred between two tasks t and t' according to the number of meta-tasks co-occurred in tasks t and t'.

As mentioned in Section 20.2, the protein subcellular localization prediction based on protein sequences can be categorized into biological sequence analysis. Xu et al. (2011) compare a multitask learning method under SVMs (implementation (1) with a common feature representation-based approach (implementation (2), which is based on Argyriou et al.'s (2006, 2008) works, for the protein subcellular location prediction problem. To answer the question "can multi-task learning generate more accurate classifiers than single-task learning?," Xu et al. (2011) conduct several experiments on different organisms by comparing the test accuracy among the proposed multitask learning methods and baselines. Through experimental results, we can see that multitask learning techniques can generally help improve the prediction performance for protein subcellular localization in comparison with supervised single-task learning techniques and that the relatedness of tasks may affect the performance of multitask learning techniques.

Liu et al. (2010b) propose a cross-platform model based on a multitask linear regression model for the siRNA efficacy prediction. Given a vectorized representation of siRNAs, a linear ridge regression model is applied to predict the novel siRNA efficacy from a set of siRNAs with known efficacy. It is shown that, in the siRNA efficacy prediction, there exists certain efficacy distribution diversity across siRNAs binding to different mRNAs and that common properties across different siRNAs have some influence on the potent siRNA design.

20.4 Gene Expression Analysis and Genetic Analysis

One way to represent the gene expression data is in the form of a matrix, where each row corresponds to a data sample and each column is for a gene expression pattern. There are two classes, including "control" and "case," for a data sample. The objective of the gene expression classification is to accurately classify new samples into the two classes. This problem is particularly challenging because this is a small sample problem, where the number of samples is much smaller than the features, and the data are noisy.

Chen and Huang (2010) propose a multi-task support vector sample learning (MTSVSL) method to classify the cancer gene expression data. The MTSVSL method constructs two learning tasks, with the first task classifying the data and the second one answering "is this sample a support vector sample?." For the learning of the two tasks, the MTSVSL method first extracts important samples out of support vectors and then learn the two tasks in a neural network simultaneously.

In genetic analysis, a main issue is the GWAS. To perform a joint GWAS from multiple populations, Puniyani et al. (2010) develop a novel multi-task regressor to use the $\ell_{1,2}$ regularizer to identify useful SNPs for multiple populations with the objective function formulated as

$$\xi(\mathbf{B}) = \frac{1}{2} \sum_t \|\mathbf{y}^t - \mathbf{X}^t \boldsymbol{\beta}^t\|_2^2 + \lambda \|\mathbf{B}\|_{1,2},$$

where $\mathbf{B}$ is a $m \times P$ matrix, m is the number of SNPs and the j-th row $\boldsymbol{\beta}_j$ corresponds to the j-th SNP. Here the $\ell_{1,2}$ regularizer is used to select features for all the tasks.

20.5 Systems Biology

Over recent years, the application of transfer learning to systems biology has become increasingly popular. Transfer learning techniques such as the task regularization approach, distribution matching approach, matrix factorization approach and Bayesian approach have been employed for systems biology.

Gene interaction network analysis has been very useful in gaining insights into various cellular properties. Tamada et al. (2005) utilize the evolutionary information between two organisms to reconstruct individual gene networks. Given two organisms, A and B, with respective gene expression data, D_A and D_B, the networks of the two organisms, G_A and G_B, are built simultaneously by a hill-climbing algorithm that maximizes the posterior probability $P(G_A, G_B | D_A, D_B,$

H_{AB}), where H_{AB} models the evolutionary information between A and B. In order to calculate $P(H_{AB}|G_A, G_B)$ based on gene expression data D_A and D_B, two free parameters are chosen empirically. As follow-up work, Nassar et al. (2008) propose a new score function to capture the evolutionary information between A and B by a parameter β instead of choosing two free parameters. The parameter β represents the similarity between the underlying Bayesian networks.

Kato et al. (2010b) consider multiple assays where the learning happens via sharing the local knowledge and the objective function is formulated as

$$\xi(\{\mathbf{w}_t\}) = \sum_{t=1}^{m} \sum_{i=1}^{n_t} l(y_i^t, \mathbf{w}_t^T \mathbf{x}_i^t) + \lambda_1 \sum_{t=1}^{m} \|\mathbf{w}_t\|_2^2 + \lambda_2 \sum_{t=1}^{m} \sum_{v \in V_t} (\|\mathbf{w}_v\|^2 + \lambda_3 \|\mathbf{w}_v - \mathbf{w}_t\|),$$

(20.9)

where V_t represents the set of neighbors of a node t. Intuitively, this formulation improves a task with the help of its neighbors.

The protein–protein interaction prediction is an important problem in systems biology. Qi et al. (2010) propose a semi-supervised multitask model to predict protein–protein interactions from not only labeled, but also partially labeled reference sets. The basic idea is to perform multitask learning on a supervised classification task and a semi-supervised auxiliary task via a regularization term. This is equivalent to learning two tasks jointly with the loss function as

$$\xi(\{\mathbf{w}\}) = \sum_{i=1}^{n_{labeled}} l(y_i, \mathbf{w}^T \mathbf{x}_i) + Loss(AuxiliaryTask).$$

(20.10)

Xu et al. (2010) also exploit to solve this problem by borrowing the idea of the collective matrix factorization (CMF) method (Singh and Gordon, 2008). The proposed method uses the similarities of proteins between two interaction networks and shows that, when the source matrix is sufficiently dense and similar to the target network, transfer learning is effective for predicting protein–protein interactions in a sparse network. Consider a similarity matrix $\mathbf{S} \in \mathbb{R}^{m \times n}$ as the correspondence between networks G and P. The rows and columns of $\mathbf{S}$ correspond to proteins in networks G and P, respectively, and each element S_{ij} of $\mathbf{S}$ represents the similarity between node i in network G and node j in network P. The objective function of the proposed method is formulated as

$$\min_{\mathbf{Z}, \mathbf{V}, \mathbf{U}} D(\mathbf{X}^t, \mathbf{Z}\mathbf{V}^T) + \lambda^s D(\mathbf{X}^a, \mathbf{U}\mathbf{V}^T) + \lambda^U \|\mathbf{U}\|_F^2 + \lambda^V \|\mathbf{V}\|_F^2 + \lambda^Z \|\mathbf{Z}\|_F^2,$$

(20.11)

where $\mathbf{X}^t = \begin{bmatrix} \mathbf{L}_{m \times m} & 0 \\ 0 & \mathbf{L}_{n \times n} \end{bmatrix}$, $\mathbf{X}^a = \begin{bmatrix} 0 & \mathbf{S} \\ \mathbf{S}^T & 0 \end{bmatrix}$, $D(\cdot, \cdot)$ denotes the divergence between the two input arguments. Based on (20.11), we can see that $\mathbf{Z}\mathbf{V}^T$ is to approximate $\mathbf{X}^t$ while $\mathbf{U}\mathbf{V}^T$ approximates $\mathbf{X}^a$ with a shared factor $\mathbf{V}$ that is to transfer useful knowledge between two networks.

A sparse multitask regression approach is presented in Zhang et al. (2010b), where a co-clustering algorithm is applied to gene expression data with phenotypic signatures. This algorithm can uncover the dependency between genes and phenotypes. The objective function is formulated as

$$\min_{\mathbf{T},\mathbf{P}_d} \sum_{d=0}^{D} ||\mathbf{X}_0\mathbf{T}\mathbf{P}_d - \mathbf{Y}_d||_F^2 + \lambda ||\mathbf{T}||_1 \ \text{s.t.} \ ||\mathbf{P}_d||_F = 1, \forall d \in \{1,\dots,D\},$$

where $\mathbf{T}_d = \mathbf{T}\mathbf{P}_d$ means that the phenotype responses under different experimental conditions are lying on the same low-dimensional space $\mathbf{T}$. Hence, the first term in this objective function enforces the fitting between the gene expression and the phenotypic signature under each condition, while the second term enforces the sparsity on $\mathbf{T}$.

Bickel et al. (2008) study the problem of predicting the HIV therapy outcomes of different drug combinations based on observed genetic properties of patients, where each task corresponds to a particular drug combination. The authors propose to jointly train models for different drug combinations by pooling data together for all tasks and use the weights to adapt the data for each particular task. The goal is to learn a hypothesis $f_t : x \to y$ for each task t by minimizing the loss function with respect to $p(x, y | t)$, where x describes the genotype of the virus that a patient carries as well as the patient's treatment history and y denotes the class label indicating whether the therapy is successful or not. Simply pooling the available data for all tasks will generate a set of training samples $D = \{(\mathbf{x}_j^i, y_j^i, i)\}$. The proposed method is to create a task-specific weight function $r_t(x, y)$ for each sample.

20.6 Biomedical Text and Image Mining

In the biomedical domain, an important problem is semantic role labeling (SRL), which labels the roles for genes, proteins and biological entities in the textual form. These texts are often manually labeled but such labeling is time consuming. To solve this problem, Dahlmeier and Ng (2010) formulate the SRL problem as a transfer learning problem to leverage existing SRL resources for a new domain. They employ three domain transfer learning methods, including instance weighting, augment method and instance pruning.

In addition to biomedical text mining, biomedical image mining is also an important problem in bioinformatics. For example, Bi et al. (2008) formulate the detection of different types of clinically related abnormal structures in medical images from the perspective of multitask learning. The proposed method captures the task dependence by sharing common feature representation, which is shown to be effective in eliminating irrelevant features and identifying discriminative features. Given m tasks, for task t, the training data set is composed of the data matrix $\mathbf{X}^t$ and the label vector $\mathbf{y}^t$. In the work by Bi et al. (2008), the model parameter for the linear learning function for tasks t, $\boldsymbol{\alpha}_t$, can be defined as $\boldsymbol{\alpha}_t = \mathbf{C}\boldsymbol{\beta}_t$, where $\boldsymbol{\beta}_t$ is task-specific while $\mathbf{C}$ is a diagonal matrix with c as the non-negative diagonal vector. The objective function can be rewritten as

$$\min_{\boldsymbol{\beta},\mathbf{c}} \sum_{t=1}^{m} \left(l(\mathbf{C}\boldsymbol{\beta}_t, \mathbf{X}^t, \mathbf{y}^t) + P_1(\boldsymbol{\beta}_t) \right) \quad \text{s.t. } P_2(\mathbf{c}) \le \gamma,$$

where P_1 and P_2 are regularization functions. Based on this objective function, we can see that $\mathbf{c}$ is a vector indicating whether each feature will be used in the model and hence this is to learn a common feature representation for all tasks.

20.7   Deep Learning for Bioinformatics

20.7.1   Deep Neural Pursuit

The emergence of deep learning has impacted numerous applications. There have been some studies to apply deep transfer learning techniques to bioinformatics.

Liu et al. (2017) present a deep learning-based algorithm for gene selection in genetic data. The problem to be solved is typical in bioinformatics: phenotype prediction using genetic variants suffers from the growing challenges of high dimensionality and low sample size. Until 2008, biologists had identified 15 million genetic variants (SNPs) for *Homo sapiens*. The number of recognized genetic variants quadrupled in 2011 and increased to 150 million in 2016. In contrast, only thousands of samples are available (1000 Genomes Project Consortium, 2015). This kind of *high dimension, low sample size (HDLSS)* data is also vital for scientific discoveries in other areas such as chemistry, financial engineering and so on (Fan and Li, 2006).

When training on this kind of "fat data," the severe overfitting and high-variance gradients are the major challenges for the majority of machine learning algorithms (Friedman et al., 2001).

First, selecting the optimal subset of features reduces the size of feature space, thereby alleviating the risk of overfitting. Second, new scientific knowledge can be discovered through selecting features.

For instance, selecting features from genotype-cancer data sets helps accumulate the knowledge of cancer-related genetic variants. However, selecting the optimal subset of features is known to be nondeterministic polynomial-time hard (Amaldi and Kann, 1998). Instead, a large body of compromised methods for feature selection have been proposed. Among these methods, representative methods include sparse linear models such as least absolute shrinkage and selection operator (Tibshirani, 1996). Unfortunately, sparse linear models ignore the nonlinear input–output relations and interactions among features, both of which have been proved to be important in explaining the missing heritability in phenotype prediction. Although some attempts have been made to achieve nonlinear feature selection via kernel methods (Li et al., 2005; Yamada et al., 2014) or gradient boosted tree (Xu et al., 2014c), almost all of them address the curse of dimensionality under the blessing of large sample size.

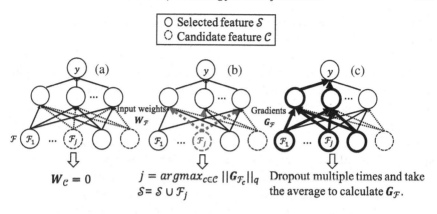

Figure 20.1 An illustration of the DNP algorithm: (a) The selected features and the corresponding subnetwork; (b) the selection of a single feature; (c) gradients with lower variance via multiple dropouts

Liu et al. (2017) introduce a deep neural network model tailored for the HDLSS data, which is named *deep neural pursuit* (DNP). DNP selects a subset of features from a very long sequence of genes (approximately 200,000 long) with very small sample sizes. To alleviate the problem of overfitting, DNP takes the average over multiple dropouts to calculate gradients with low variance. By using a deep neural network, DNP enjoys the advantages of the high nonlinearity, robustness to high dimensionality and the capability of learning from a small number of samples. This allows it to maintain the stability in feature selection in an end-to-end style of model training.

For a feedforward neural network, we can select a specific input feature if at least one of the connections associated with that feature has non-zero weight. To achieve this goal, we place the $l_{p,1}$ norm to constrain the input weights, that is, $\|\mathbf{W}_{\mathscr{F}}\|_{p,1}$. We use $\mathbf{W}_{\mathscr{F}_j}$ to denote the weights associated with the j-th input node in $\mathbf{W}_{\mathscr{F}}$. We can define the $l_{p,1}$ norm of the input weights as $\|\mathbf{W}_{\mathscr{F}}\|_{p,1} = \sum_j \|\mathbf{W}_{\mathscr{F}_j}\|_p$, where $\|\cdot\|_p$ is the l_p norm on a vector. One effect of the $l_{p,1}$ norm is to enforce the group sparsity (Evgeniou and Pontil, 2007) and here we assume that weights in $\mathbf{W}_{\mathscr{F}_j}$ form a group. A general form of the objective function for training the feedforward network in formulated as:

$$\min_{\mathbf{W}} \sum_i^n \ell(y_i, f(\mathbf{x}_i|\mathbf{W})) \quad \text{s.t.} \quad \|\mathbf{W}_{\mathscr{F}}\|_{p,1} \leq \lambda. \tag{20.12}$$

Without loss of generality, we only consider the binary classification problem and use the logistic loss in (20.12).

The whole process of the feature selection in the DNP consists of training a deep neural network. We graphically illustrate DNP's greedy feature selection in Figure 20.1 and detail the learning process in Algorithm 20.1.

In DNP, we maintain two sets, that is, a selected set $\mathscr{S}$ and a candidate set $\mathscr{C}$, with $\mathscr{S} \cup \mathscr{C} = \mathscr{F}$.

Initially, $\mathscr{S}$ starts from a bias to avoid the case that all rectified linear hidden units are inactive. Except for the weights corresponding to the bias, all weights in the neural network are initialized to be zero. Upon the selected set $\mathscr{S}$, input weights $\mathbf{W}_{\mathscr{F}}$ comprise of selected input weights $\mathbf{W}_{\mathscr{S}}$, which are input weights associated with features in $\mathscr{S}$, and candidate weights $\mathbf{W}_{\mathscr{C}}$. We update the whole neural network until convergence while fixing all candidate weights $\mathbf{W}_{\mathscr{C}}$ to zero (i.e., steps 4 and 5 of Algorithm 20.1). In Figure 20.1(a), we plot $\mathscr{S}$ and $\mathscr{C}$ with solid circles and dotted circles, respectively. All dotted connections are fixed zero. Then, $\mathbf{G}_{\mathscr{F}}$ is employed to select one feature, say the j-th one from $\mathscr{C}$ (step 7).

After initialization, $\mathbf{W}_{\mathscr{F}}$ is updated by initializing newly selected input weights $\mathbf{W}_{\mathscr{F}_j}$ with the Xavier initializer (Glorot and Bengio, 2010) and reusing earlier weights $\mathbf{W}_{\mathscr{S}}$ (step 9). $\mathscr{S}$ and $\mathscr{C}$ are updated by adding and removing j, respectively (step 10).

One question is how to select features using $\mathbf{G}_{\mathscr{F}}$. Without loss of generality, we assume that all features are normalized.

The gradient's magnitude implies how much the objective function may decrease by updating the corresponding weight (Perkins et al., 2003).

Similarly, the norm of a group of gradients infers how much the loss may decrease by updating this group of weights together. According to Tewari et al. (2011), there exists an equivalence between minimizing the $l_{p,1}$ norm in (20.12) and greedily selecting features with the maximum l_q norm of gradients, where q satisfies $1/p + 1/q = 1$.

We assume that the larger the $\|\mathbf{G}_{\mathscr{F}_j}\|_q$ is, the more j-th feature contributes to minimizing (20.12). Consequently, we select the features with the maximum $\|\mathbf{G}_{\mathscr{F}_j}\|_q$. Throughout our experiments, we choose $p = q = 2$ provided that our empirical comparisons among different settings of p show a limited difference. On the other hand, DNP can satisfy the norm constraint, that is, $\|\mathbf{W}_{\mathscr{F}}\|_{p,1} \leq \lambda$, by early stopping at the k-th iteration. We illustrate the selection of a single feature in Figure 20.1(b).

Due to the small sample size, the backpropagated gradients in DNP have especially high variance. This makes selecting the features according to gradients misleading. As shown in Figure 20.1(c), DNP utilizes multiple dropouts technique to avoid high-variance gradients. As a regularizer, the dropout (Srivastava et al., 2014) randomly drops neurons and features during forward training and back propagation. Therefore, gradients $\mathbf{G}$ are calculated on the subnetwork composed of the rest neurons.

Multiple dropouts in DNP can improve the quality of the features selected. First, according to step 6 of Algorithm 20.1, DNP randomly drops neurons multiple times, computes $\mathbf{G}_{\mathscr{F}_c}$ based on the remaining neurons and connections, and averages multiple $\mathbf{G}_{\mathscr{F}_c}$. Such multiple dropouts technique obtains averaged gradients with low variance.

More importantly, multiple dropouts empower DNP with the stable feature se-

Algorithm 20.1 Deep neural pursuit

1: **Input:** $\mathbf{X} \in \mathbb{R}^{n \times d}$, $\mathbf{y} \in \mathbb{R}^n$, the maximum number of selected features k.
2: **Initialize:** $\mathscr{S} = \{bias\}$, $\mathscr{C} = \mathscr{F}$ and $\mathbf{W}_{\mathscr{C}} = 0$.
3: **while** $|\mathscr{S}| \leq k + 1$ **do**
4:     Fix candidate weights $\mathbf{W}_{\mathscr{C}} = 0$;
5:     Update weights of hidden layer and input $\mathbf{W}_{\mathscr{S}}$;
6:     Dropout multiple times and average out $\mathbf{G}_{\mathscr{F}_c}$;
7:     $j = \mathrm{argmax}_{c \in \mathscr{C}} \|\mathbf{G}_{\mathscr{F}_c}\|_q$;
8:     Update learning rates using Adagrad;
9:     Initialize $\mathbf{W}_{\mathscr{F}_j}$ with Xavier Initializer;
10:     $\mathscr{S} = \mathscr{S} \cup \mathscr{F}_j$ and $\mathscr{C} = \mathscr{C} \setminus \mathscr{F}_j$;
11: **end while**

lection. Stability, as a vital criterion for feature selection, indicates that identical features should be consistently selected even using slightly changed training data sets (Kalousis et al., 2007). Multiple dropouts combine selected features over many random subnetworks to make the DNP method more stable and powerful.

20.7.2 Deep Transfer Learning in Bioinformatics

Sevakula et al. (2018) present a novel transfer learning framework for molecular cancer classification. The data from all the types of tumors are used to learn a powerful feature representation based on stacked sparse auto-encoders and then built on the learned feature representation, a classifier is learned to classify different types of tumor data.

Deep transfer learning is adapted to the task of biomedical named-entity recognition and for example, Giorgi and Bader (2018) demonstrate that transferring a deep neural network trained on a large noisy corpora to a smaller but more reliable corpora improves the performance.

Deep learning has also been applied to biomedical image mining. Specifically, Zhang et al. (2017c) employ the deep convolutional neural network as a multilayer feature extractor to generate generic representations for in situ hybridization (ISH) images. They first directly use the model trained on natural images as feature extractors and then fine-tune the pretrained model with labeled ISH images. The experimental results show that the proposed approach can get the better classification performance and reduce the labeling cost.

Wang et al. (2017b) apply deep transfer learning methods for membrane protein contact prediction and folding. They predict MP contacts by concatenating two deep residual neural networks (He et al., 2016). MPs are important for drug design, but experimental study of MP structures is challenging and thus training data is few. However, machine learning methods are challenging to apply due to a lack of sufficient MPs with solved structures. To overcome this difficulty, Wang et al. (2017b) train a deep learning model using thousands of non-MPs with solved structures. The non-MPs serve as the source data, while the MPs as the target data. The transfer learning model works well for MP contact prediction by increasing the determination accuracy by a large margin. The authors went on to study why transfer learning worked well in MP prediction. They found that the underlying contact occurrence patterns in both MPs and non-MPs are similar, implying that the structure of the problem space is similar.

A data set is composed of enzyme–ligand interaction data, G-protein-coupled receptors (GPCRs)–ligand interaction data and ion channel–ligand interaction data. Another released ligand interaction data set contains four subsets for enzymes, ion channels, GPCRs, and nuclear receptors (Kashima et al., 2009), respectively.

21

Transfer Learning in Activity Recognition

21.1 Introduction

Human behavior recognition from sensor observations is an important topic in both AI and mobile computing. It is also a difficult task as the sensor and behavior data are usually noisy and limited. In this chapter, we review two major problems in human behavior recognition, including location estimation and activity recognition. Solving these two problems helps answer typical questions in human behavior recognition, such as where a user is, what the user is doing and whether the user will be interested in doing something at somewhere. In the prior attempts to solve these problems, we find that in practice the biggest challenge comes from the data sparsity. Such data sparsity can be because we have limited labeled data for new contexts in localization, or limited sensor data for users and activities in activity recognition. In order to address these challenges, transfer learning, which can effectively incorporate domain-dependent auxiliary data in the training process and thus greatly relieve the data sparsity problem, becomes a viable approach. In the remainder part of this chapter, we introduce research works on using transfer learning for wireless localization and sensor-based activity recognition.

21.2 Transfer Learning for Wireless Localization

Figure 21.1 shows an example of the indoor location estimation using the WiFi signal strength. A user moving in an indoor environment carries a mobile device such as a smartphone or laptop. The mobile device can detect multiple WiFi signals from various access points (APs). Then, the detected WiFi signal strength values are used to form a feature vector. As shown in Figure 21.1, in an environment with $d_1 \in \mathbb{Z}^+$ APs, a mobile device receives wireless signals from these APs. The received signal strength (RSS) values at one location are used as a feature vector $\mathbf{x} \in \mathbb{R}^{d_1}$, for example, $\mathbf{x} = [-30\text{dBm}, -50\text{dBm}, -70\text{dBm}]$, where dBm is a standard signal strength measurement. The device's location corresponds to a label $y \in \mathcal{Y}$, where $\mathcal{Y}$ is the set of possible locations in the environment. Generally, the mobile device receives different signal strength vectors at different locations. As a result, given a signal-to-location mapping function, we can predict the user's location with her current signal strength vector. Such a signal-to-location mapping function is also referred as a localization model, which is capable of transforming a signal vector to a location. In the offline training stage, given sufficient labeled data $\{(\mathbf{x}_i, y_i)\}$, we learn a mapping function $f : \mathbb{R}^{d_1} \to \mathcal{Y}$. In the online testing stage, we use f to predict the location for a new signal vector $\mathbf{x}$ (Pan et al., 2007a).

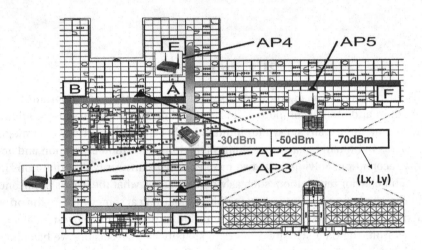

Figure 21.1 WiFi indoor localization

21.2.1 Context-Dependent Data Sparsity Challenges

A major drawback of traditional localization methods is that they assume the collected signal data are context-independent. In other words, the signal data distribution stays the same even when the context changes. However, this assumption usually does not hold in practice. For example, sensor signals may vary from device to device due to their different signal sensing capacities, or from time to time due to multipath fading effects with signal refraction or diffraction, or from space to space due to different APs. Figure 21.2 gives such an evidence. The RSS can vary significantly on different devices or time periods, even though they were detected from the same AP at the same location. Through some real world studies, we find that, if we collect sufficient labeled data in the new context including time, devices and spaces, we can provide localization results with the error around 1.5 meters. However, if we do not collect labeled data in the new context, but use the data in the old context, the localization error greatly increases to 6 meters for the time-varying case and 18 meters for the device-varying case. This observation mo-

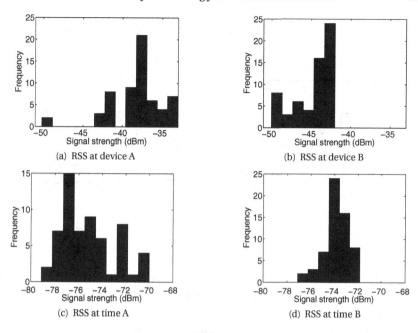

Figure 21.2 Signal variations over devices and time periods

tivates us to well consider such signal variation problem, where few/sparse data are available in the new context.

As we cannot afford collecting a large amount of labeled data all the time when the context changes, we are facing the data sparsity challenge in learning some localization model for a new mobile device, or a new time period, or a new space. Traditional learning algorithms may just ignore the signal data difference between different contexts, and use the existing data in another context to train a model. In general, such a simple strategy by overlooking the difference may greatly deteriorate the localization performance. This motivates us to take the difference of these data into account and carefully design transfer learning algorithms. In the following section, we review transfer learning algorithms in the application of wireless localization according to different transfer strategies, including feature-based, instance-based and model-based transfer learning.

21.2.2 Feature-Based Transfer Learning for Localization

Let us take cross-device wireless localization as an example to introduce feature-based transfer learning. Consider a two-dimensional (2D) indoor localization problem. In the environment, there are m APs, from which we collect the RSS data. Each RSS data point is denoted by $\mathbf{x} = (x_1, \ldots, x_d)^T \in \mathbb{R}^d$, and its location label denoting the coordinates is $\mathbf{y} = (y_1, y_2) \in \mathbb{R}^2$. For the source device, we have

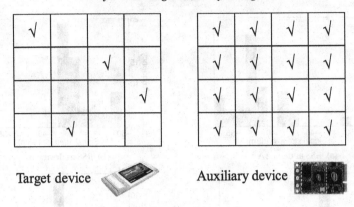

Figure 21.3 An illustration for the cross-device wireless localization

collected a large amount of labeled data $D_s = \{(\mathbf{x}_s^{(i)}, \mathbf{y}_s^{(i)}) | i = 1, ..., n_s\}$. On the target device, we may collect a small amount of labeled data $D_t = \{(\mathbf{x}_t^{(i)}, \mathbf{y}_t^{(i)}) | i = 1, ..., n_t\}$. Finally, we also have a test data set from the target device $D_t^{tst} = \{(\mathbf{x}_t^{tst(i)}, \mathbf{y}_t^{tst(i)}) | i = 1, ..., n_t^{tst}\}$. This setting is illustrated in Figure 21.3, where a matrix in the figure denotes a 2D location space and a tick indicates labeled data collected in that location.

Target device with data (i.e., $D_s \neq \emptyset$): MeanShift (Haeberlen et al., 2004) treats the signal variation as a Gaussian mean-value shift, and use a linear model as

$$x_{t,j} = c_1 \cdot x_{s,j} + c_2, \tag{21.1}$$

to fit the RSS value $x_{t,j}$ of the j-th AP on a target device based on the RSS value $x_{s,j}$ on a source device. Here, c_1 and c_2 are model parameters to be estimated by the least square fit. Once c_1 and c_2 are learned, we can transform all the data from the source device $\{\mathbf{x}_s^{(i)} | i = 1, ..., n_s\}$ into the target device. Finally, we can have much more data for the target device and thus be able to train an accurate classifier for the localization.

Similar to MeanShift, ModelTree (Yin et al., 2005) also applies a regression analysis to learn the temporal predictive relationship between the RSS values received by sparsely located reference points and that received by the mobile device. Then it uses the newly observed RSS values at the device and the reference points for the localization with some decision tree algorithm.

Target device without data (i.e., $D_{aux} = \emptyset$): Kjaergaard and Munk (2008) propose a hyperbolic location fingerprinting (HLF) method to address the device signal variation problem. The intuition is that, each single RSS from a certain AP is vulnerable to the device heterogeneity, but the relative value between two RSS from two certain APs may be more stable. Therefore, the HLF method tries to turn the absolute RSS values into ratios among different APs and uses them as the new feature representation to train a localization model.

The high-order pairwise (HOP) model proposed in Zheng et al. (2016) is motivated by the HLF model to learn a device-robust feature representation $g : \mathbb{R}^{d_1} \to \mathbb{R}^{d_2}$ such that for two RSS vectors $\mathbf{x}_s$ and $\mathbf{x}_t$ collected at the same location $\tilde{y} \in \mathcal{Y}$ by the source device S and target device T, we assume

$$g(\mathbb{E}[\mathbf{x}^s] | y^s = \tilde{y}) = g(\mathbb{E}[\mathbf{x}^t] | y^t = \tilde{y}), \tag{21.2}$$

where the expectation is taken over each dimension of $\mathbf{x}$ to account for the randomness in the RSS from each AP. Finally, given $g(\cdot)$, we can build a function $f : \mathbb{R}^{d_2} \to \mathcal{Y}$ to locate the heterogeneous devices. Because pairwise RSS values can be shown to be insufficient to discriminate different locations, the HOP model designs some higher-order features as follows.

Definition 21.1 (HOP feature): A HOP feature h is defined as

$$h = \delta \left(\sum_{(k_1, k_2)} c_{k_1, k_2} (x_{k_1} - x_{k_2}) + b > 0 \right). \tag{21.3}$$

We then learn a set of hs such that they are representative for the data by solving the following problem

$$\max_{\mathbf{h} \in \{0,1\}^{d_2}} \sum_{k=1}^{n_L} \log P(\mathbf{x}^{(k)}; \mathbf{h}), \tag{21.4}$$

where $\mathbf{h} = [h_1, ..., h_{d_2}]$ is a vector of d_2 HOP features and $P(\mathbf{x}; \mathbf{h})$ is the data likelihood to be defined later based on $\mathbf{h}$. Directly learning $\mathbf{h}$ leads to optimizing an excessive number of parameters. We can reduce the number of parameters by rewriting (21.3) to an equivalent form as

$$\sum_{(k_1, k_2)} c_{k_1, k_2} (x_{k_1} - x_{k_2}) + b = \sum_{i=1}^{d_1} \alpha_i x_i + b, \tag{21.5}$$

where $\alpha_i = \sum_{(k_1, k_2)} \left[c_{k_1, k_2} \delta(k_1 = i) - c_{k_1, k_2} \delta(k_2 = i) \right]$. Zheng et al. (2016) prove

$$\sum_{i=1}^{d_1} \alpha_i = 0, \tag{21.6}$$

which means that a HOP feature defined in (21.3) corresponds to a special feature transformation function with a constraint as

$$h = \delta \left(\sum_{i=1}^{d_1} \alpha_i x_i + b > 0 \right), \text{ s.t. } \sum_{i=1}^{d_1} \alpha_i = 0. \tag{21.7}$$

As a result, to learn HOP features, we only need to focus on learning linear weights for each individual RSS value x_i subject to a zero-sum constraint. A careful derivation shows that (21.4) can be learned through a constrained restricted Boltzmann machine (RBM) as

$$P(\mathbf{x}; \mathbf{h}) = \frac{1}{Z} \sum_{\mathbf{h}} e^{-E(\mathbf{x}, \mathbf{h})}, \tag{21.8}$$

where $E(\mathbf{x}, \mathbf{h}) = \sum_{i=1}^{d_1} \frac{(x_i - a_i)^2}{2\pi_i^2} - \sum_{j=1}^{d_2} b_j h_j - \sum_{i,j} \frac{x_i}{\pi_i} h_j w_{ij}$ is an energy function and $Z = \sum_{\mathbf{x}, \mathbf{h}} e^{-E(\mathbf{x}, \mathbf{h})}$ is a partition function. The first term of $E(\mathbf{x}, \mathbf{h})$ models a Gaussian distribution over each x_i, where a_i and π_i are the mean and standard deviation. The second term models the bias b_j for each h_j. The third term models the linear mapping between $\mathbf{x}$ and h_j. In RBM, each h_j can be seen as $h_j = \delta(\sum_{i=1}^{d_1} \frac{x_i}{\pi_i} w_{i,j} + b_j > 0)$, and it is sampled by a conditional probability (Krizhevsky and Hinton, 2009) as

$$P(h_j = 1|\mathbf{x}) = \sigma\left(\sum_{i=1}^{d_1} \frac{x_i}{\pi_i} w_{i,j} + b_j\right), \tag{21.9}$$

where $\sigma(r) = \frac{1}{1+e^{-r}}$ is the sigmoid function. To take the zero-sum constraint into account, we compare (21.9) with (21.7), and set $\alpha_i = \frac{1}{\pi_i} w_{ij}$. Finally, the objective function is formulated as

$$\min -\frac{1}{n_L} \sum_{k=1}^{n_L} \log P(\mathbf{x}^{(k)}) \text{ s.t. } \sum_{i=1}^{d_1} \frac{1}{\pi_i} w_{ij} = 0, \forall j. \tag{21.10}$$

These HOP features can be learned together with the localization classifier.

In addition to this feature-based transfer learning methods, there are some feature-based transfer learning methods for cross-space localization (Wang et al., 2010) and cross-device and cross-time localization (Zhang et al., 2013).

21.2.3   Instance-Based Transfer Learning for Localization

Let us take cross-time wireless localization as an example to introduce instance-based transfer learning for the localization. Given a 2D indoor localization problem with m APs, we assume that there are ℓ reference points placed at various locations to obtain real-time RSS values over different time periods. In a source time period, we have collected some labeled data $D_s = \{(\mathbf{x}_s^{(i)}, \mathbf{y}_s^{(i)})|i=1,...,n_s\}$ and in the target time period, we optionally collect a small amount of labeled data $D_t = \{(\mathbf{x}_t^{(i)}, \mathbf{y}_t^{(i)})|i=1,...,n_t\}$. Finally, we also have a test data set from the target device $D_t^{tst} = \{(\mathbf{x}_t^{tst(i)}, \mathbf{y}_t^{tst(i)})|i=1,...,n_t^{tst}\}$. The setting is illustrated in Figure 21.4 where the matrix denotes a 2D location space and a tick indicates labeled data collected in that location. Optionally, we may have some trajectories in the blue arrow line, which are collected in both the source and target time periods.

The LANDMARC model (Ni et al., 2003) and the LEASE model (Krishnan et al., 2004) both utilize some additional hardware equipments, including stationary emitters and sniffers, to obtain up-to-date RSS values and further apply some K nearest neighbor (KNN) style algorithms to estimate the location. However, such methods may suffer from the limited number of sniffers and the limited modeling power of KNN.

Pan et al. (2007b) propose a LeManCoR model, which is a semi-supervised manifold method. The LeManCoR model treats different time periods as multiple views and uses a multiview learning framework to constrain the predictions on reference points to be consistent. Specifically, the objective function of the LeManCoR

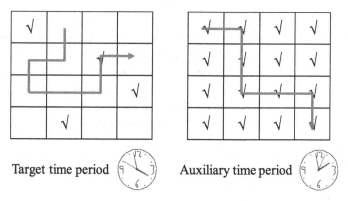

Figure 21.4 An illustration for cross-time wireless localization

model is formulated as

$$(f^{(s)*}, f^{(t)*}) = \arg \min_{f^{(s)}, f^{(t)}} \frac{\mu}{n_s} \sum_{i=1}^{n_s} V(\mathbf{x}_s^{(i)}, y_s^{(i)}, f^{(s)}) + \gamma_A \|f^{(s)}\|^2_{H_{K_1}} + \gamma_I^{(1)} \|f^{(s)}\|^2_I$$
$$+ \frac{1}{n_s} \sum_{i=1}^{n_s} V(\mathbf{x}_t^{(i)}, y_t^{(i)}, f^{(t)}) + \gamma_A \|f^{(t)}\|^2_{H_{K_2}} + \gamma_I^{(2)} \|f^{(t)}\|^2_I$$
$$+ \frac{\gamma_I}{\ell} \sum_{i=1}^{\ell} [f^{(s)}(\mathbf{x}_s^{(i)}) - f^{(t)}(\mathbf{x}_t^{(i)})]^2. \tag{21.11}$$

The first term in (21.11) is to minimize the localization loss at the source time period, and the second and third terms are for the manifold regularization. The next three terms are defined similarly for the target time period. The last term in (21.11) is to enforce the location prediction on the reference points, which can receive real time RSS values, to be consistent by two localization classifiers $f^{(s)}$ and $f^{(t)}$. In this way, the training instances in different time periods can be leveraged together.

Xu et al. (2017) propose a metric transfer learning framework (MTLF). Many previous studies use the Euclidean distance to measure the dissimilarity between instances from two different domains. However, the Euclidean distance may be suboptimal in some real world applications. In MTLF, instance weights are learned and exploited to bridge the distributions of different domains, while the Mahalanobis distance is learned simultaneously to maximize the interclass distances and minimize the intraclass distances for the target domain. In addition to these instance-based transfer learning methods for the cross-time localization, there is an instance-based transfer learning method for the cross-space localization (Pan et al., 2008c).

This work on instance-based transfer learning focuses on handling localization with wireless data. There exist some work that uses instance-based transfer learning for the localization based on the image data. For example, in the work by

Lu et al. (2016), the localization system considers two kinds of inputs, including red green blue (RGB) images that are obtained under a normal light condition and thermal images that are obtained under an emergency power outage condition. As thermal images are not obtained as easily as color images, an active transfer learning method is proposed to treat RGB images as the source domain and thermal images as the target domain. On the one hand, it uses an adaptive multi-kernel learning framework to train the model with both labeled RGB images and thermal images. On the other hand, it also tries to carefully choose thermal images to be labeled by the human expert so as to maximize the performance gain.

21.2.4 Model-Based Transfer Learning for Localization

In this section, model-based transfer learning for the wireless localization is introduced. We mainly introduce two works that consider nonsequential and sequential model-based transfer learning.

Non-sequential model: Let us take cross-device wireless localization as an example to introduce model-based transfer learning. The LatentMTL method (Zheng et al., 2008a) models different devices as different tasks and exploits the task relatedness by cross-task parameter sharing for improving the localization performance. We model the localization with a regression function $f(\mathbf{z}) = \mathbf{w}^T \mathbf{z} + b$ to estimate locations from some transformed signal vector $\mathbf{z} = \varphi(\mathbf{x}) \in \mathbb{R}^k$, where $\mathbf{w}$ is a weight vector, b is a bias term and φ is a feature mapping function. In this multi-device problem, we treat T devices as T tasks, where T is simply set to 2 as we consider one target device and one source device, and each task $t \in \{1, ..., T\}$ has a regression function parameterized as $\mathbf{w}_t$ with a shared b for the computational simplicity. By following (Evgeniou and Pontil, 2004), $\mathbf{w}_t$ is defined as

$$\mathbf{w}_t = \mathbf{w}_0 + \mathbf{v}_t, \forall t = 1, ..., T,$$

where $\mathbf{w}_0$ is shared by all the tasks and $\mathbf{v}_t$ is specific to task t. We are interested in finding appropriate feature mappings φ_t which can map the raw signal data to a k-dimensional latent feature space where the learned hypotheses across tasks are similar, that is, $\mathbf{v}_t$ is "small."

The objective function of the LatentMTL model is formulated as

$$\min_{\mathbf{w}_0, \mathbf{v}_t, \xi_{it}, \xi_{it}^*, b, \varphi_t} \underbrace{\sum_{t=1}^{T} \pi_t \sum_{i=1}^{n_t} (\xi_{it} + \xi_{it}^*)}_{\text{loss}} + \underbrace{\frac{\lambda_1}{T} \sum_{t=1}^{T} \|\mathbf{v}_t\|^2}_{\text{knowledge share}} + \underbrace{\lambda_2 \|\mathbf{w}_0\|^2 + \frac{\lambda_3}{T} \sum_{t=1}^{T} \Omega(\varphi_t)}_{\text{regularization}}$$

$$\text{s.t. } y_{it} - (\mathbf{w}_0 + \mathbf{v}_t) \cdot \varphi_t(\mathbf{x}_{it}) - b \leq \varepsilon + \xi_{it}$$

$$(\mathbf{w}_0 + \mathbf{v}_t) \cdot \varphi_t(\mathbf{x}_{it}) + b - y_{it} \leq \varepsilon + \xi_{it}^*$$

$$\xi_{it}, \xi_{it}^* \geq 0 \tag{21.12}$$

We explain each term in (21.12) as follows.

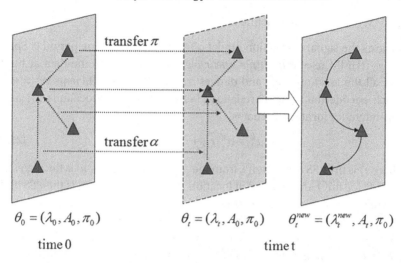

$$\theta_0 = (\lambda_0, A_0, \pi_0) \qquad \theta_t = (\lambda_t, A_0, \pi_0) \qquad \theta_t^{new} = (\lambda_t^{new}, A_t, \pi_0)$$

time 0   time t

Figure 21.5 The TrHMM model to adapt a localization model from time 0 to time t

- In the *loss* term, ξ_{it} and ξ_{it}^* are slack variables measuring the errors. π_t are the weight parameters for each task t.
- In the *knowledge share* term, minimizing $\|\mathbf{v}_t\|^2$ regularizes the dissimilarities among the task hypotheses in the latent feature space $\varphi_t(\mathbf{x})$.
- In the *regularization* term, minimizing $\|\mathbf{w}_0\|^2$ corresponds to maximizing the margin of the learned models to provide the generalization ability. Generally, the regularization parameter λ_1 is set to be larger than λ_2 to force the task hypotheses to be similar. $\Omega(\varphi_t)$ penalizes the complexity of the mapping function φ_t. To make our problem tractable, we consider $\varphi_t \in \mathbb{R}^{k \times d}$ as a linear transformation by letting $\varphi_t(\mathbf{x}) = \varphi_t \mathbf{x}$. We use the squared Frobenius norm for $\Omega(\varphi_t)$, that is, $\Omega(\varphi_t) = \|\varphi_t\|_F^2$.
- The constraints follow the routine of the standard ϵ-SVR (Scholkopf and Smola, 2001) with b as the bias term and ϵ as the tolerance parameter.

Sequential model: The TrHMM model (Zheng et al., 2008b) exploits the trajectories (i.e., the blue lines in Figure 21.4) by using the hidden Markov model (HMM) and then for transfer learning, it allows HMM parameters to be shared and updated carefully across different time periods.

For an HMM $\theta = (\lambda, A, \pi)$, the radio map $\lambda = \{P(\mathbf{x}_i | y_i)\}$ models the signal distribution, for example, Gaussian distribution $P(\mathbf{x}|y) = \frac{1}{(2\pi)^{k/2}|\Sigma|^{1/2}} e^{-\frac{1}{2}(\mathbf{x}-\boldsymbol{\mu})^T \Sigma (\mathbf{x}-\boldsymbol{\mu})}$ at each location, where $\boldsymbol{\mu}$ is the mean and Σ is the covariance matrix. By assuming the independence among the APs according to Ladd et al. (2002), we can simplify Σ as a diagonal matrix. The transition matrix $A = \{P(y_{i+1}|y_i)\}$ encodes the probability for a user to move from one location to another. The location prior π is set to be a uniform distribution over all the locations as a user can start from any location.

TrHMM has three stages defined as follows.

- It learns the signal correlation model α from the source time period 0. Specifically, TrHMM uses a *multiple linear regression* model on the data at time 0 over all the location grids and derives the regression coefficients $\boldsymbol{\alpha}^k = \{\alpha_{ij}^k\}$, which encode the signal correlations between reference locations $\{l_c\}$ and a non-reference location k. That is,

$$s_j^k = \alpha_{0j}^k + \alpha_{1j}^k r_{1j} + \ldots + \alpha_{nj}^k r_{nj} + \epsilon_j, \tag{21.13}$$

where s_j^k is the RSS at location k from the j-th AP, α_{ij}^k ($1 \le i \le n$) is the regression weights for the j-th AP signal at location k and r_{ij} ($1 \le i \le n$) is the RSS at the i-th reference point from the j-th AP.

- It applies the signal correlation model α to the target time period t and re-estimates the radio map using up-to-date signal data $D_{tar}^{\in L}$. Specifically, it uses the αs to update the non-reference point locations' signal strengths with the newly collected signal strengths on the reference point locations $\{l_c\}$. As there is a possible shift for the regression parameters over time, a trade-off constraint is added to derive the new λ_t as

$$\boldsymbol{\mu}_t = \beta \boldsymbol{\mu}_0 + (1 - \beta) \boldsymbol{\mu}_t^{reg}$$
$$\boldsymbol{\Sigma}_t = \beta \left[\Sigma_0 + (\boldsymbol{\mu}_t - \boldsymbol{\mu}_0)(\boldsymbol{\mu}_t - \boldsymbol{\mu}_0)^T \right] + (1 - \beta) \left[\Sigma_t^{reg} + (\boldsymbol{\mu}_t - \boldsymbol{\mu}_t^{reg})(\boldsymbol{\mu}_t - \boldsymbol{\mu}_t^{reg})^T \right],$$

where we balance the regressed radio map $\lambda_t^{reg} = (\boldsymbol{\mu}_t^{reg}, \Sigma_t^{reg})$ and the base radio map $\lambda_0 = (\boldsymbol{\mu}_0, \Sigma_0)$ by introducing a parameter $\beta \in [0, 1]$.

- It updates the model, whose the location prior π and transition matrix A are shared from the source time 0, by using the trace data T_t. Specifically, we first trained an HMM $\theta_0 = (\lambda_0, A_0, \pi_0)$ at time 0 as the base model. Then, in another time period t, we improve λ_0 by applying the regression analysis and obtain a new HMM $\theta_t = (\lambda_t, A_0, \pi_0)$.

21.3   Transfer Learning for Activity Recognition

21.3.1   Background

In the activity recognition, the goal is to recognize human activities in their daily lives such as walking, running or cycling by using wearable sensors like accelerometers, GPS locations, object-based sensors like radio-frequency identification tags and so on.

Traditional approaches: For activity recognition, one of the most common formulation is to simply consider it as a supervised learning problem. Typically, a data set is collected from several types of sensors and different kinds of features are extracted based on domain and expert knowledge. Some ways of extracting features (Bulling et al., 2014) include statistical features like the mean, variance or kurtosis of the raw sensor readings, or some frequency-domain features like mel-frequency cepstral coefficients, Fourier transform, wavelet transform and so on. After the feature extraction stage, different machine learning approaches ranging from decision trees (Bao and Intille, 2004), SVM (Bulling and Roggen, 2011), hidden Markov models (Bulling et al., 2008) and conditional random fields (van Kasteren et al., 2008) have been successfully applied to a variety of activity recognition data sets.

Deep learning approaches: Although a lot of traditional machine learning approaches have been successfully applied to the activity recognition problem, in recent years more researchers have started looking into deep learning-based approaches. Wang et al. (2017a) mention two major drawbacks of traditional machine learning approaches. The first is that it would take a long time to handcraft the features required to build a successful activity recognition system in a general environment. Next, handcrafted features can only be used to recognize simple and low-level activities like running and walking, but hard to infer high-level or context-aware activities. Hammerla et al. (2016) explore deep feedforward neural networks, convolutional neural networks (CNNs), and recurrent neural networks on three different activity recognition data sets. Hammerla et al. (2016) discover that recurrent neural networks outperform CNNs significantly on activities that are short in duration but have a natural ordering. For prolonged and repetitive activities, they recommend using CNNs.

Data sparsity challenges: One particular challenge for formulating activity recognition as a supervised learning problem is the difficulty in collecting enough labeled data. The annotator has to go through the raw sensor readings and manually segments the activities. In some cases where the input contains motion sensor readings like accelerometers or gyroscopes, it is extremely difficult to accurately interpret the data (Bulling et al., 2014). As a result, almost all of the publicly available activity recognition data sets are small in terms of number of subjects, duration of the collected data sets and the number of activities monitored.

For example, for the three data sets evaluated by Hammerla et al. (2016), the Opportunity data set (Chavarriaga et al., 2013) consists of sensor readings from only four subjects and eighteen common kitchen activities like opening and closing the dishwasher as well as opening and closing fridge, the PAMAP2 data set (Reiss and Stricker, 2012) consists of readings from nine subjects and twelve lifestyle activities, and the Daphnet Gait data set (Bächlin et al., 2009) consists of readings from ten subjects and two activity classes. None of these has a rich activity hierarchy that one can observe in "real world" activities of daily living.

In the context of activity recognition, the classic requirement of supervised learning manifest itself as: (1) the same feature space requirement meaning that training and testing data should use the same set of sensors; (2) the same underlying distribution requirement meaning that the preferences or the habit of the subjects should be similar in both training and testing data; and (3) the same label space requirement meaning that the activity sets recognized in the training and testing data are the same.

With such severe labeled data sparsity problem, it becomes natural to consider transfer learning in real world activity scenarios. In the context of transfer learning, we would hope that: (1) the source and target domains can have different feature spaces, for example, using sensor readings collected from smartphones (the source domain) to help recognize activities from smart watch sensor readings (the target domain); (2) the source and target domains can have different probability distributions, for example, using the sensor readings collected on one person to help recognize activities for another person; and (3) the source and target domains can have different label spaces, for example, using sensor readings collected for walking and running to help recognize activities for swimming.

Different transfer learning approaches have been proposed in recent years to tackle different aspects of the aforementioned transfer learning settings. For transferring between different feature spaces, Khan et al. (2018) propose a transductive transfer learning model based on CNNs. The proposed CNN model minimized layerwise Kulback–Leibler divergence between the source and target domains. For transferring between different persons, Deng et al. (2014) propose a cross-person activity recognition approach that uses a reduced kernel extreme learning machine to realize the initial activity recognition model. Deng et al. (2014) also propose an online learning algorithm to use highly confident recognition results to adapt the online model. For transferring between different label spaces, Wang et al. (2018b) propose a stratified transfer learning framework to first obtain pseudo labels on the target domain and then transform labels from both the source and target domains into a subspace.

In the remainder part of this section, we will discuss some transfer learning approaches in details. In particular we will discuss how to relax the same feature space requirement and the same label space requirement, that is, activity recognition from different sets of sensors and activity recognition between different sets of activities.

21.3.2   Problem Setting

We first define the problem setting for activity recognition based on transfer learning. We study two domains that have different sets of sensors and different activity labels. Specifically, we have a source domain S, where the labeled sensor readings are in the form of $\{(\mathbf{x}_s, \mathbf{y}_s)\}$, and a target domain T, which is assumed to have only unlabeled sensor readings in the form of $\{\mathbf{x}_t\}$.

We make an assumption that the label spaces in the source and target domains are related through a probability function $p(y_s, y_t)$, where y_s and y_t are source and target-domain activity labels, respectively. This probability function between the label spaces can be learned by labeling some of the target domain instances or through some distance/similarity functions that can be approximated via Web information.

Our goal is to estimate $p(\mathbf{y}_t|\mathbf{x}_t)$. To achieve that, we have

$$p(\mathbf{y}_t|\mathbf{x}_t) = \sum_{\mathbf{c}} p(\mathbf{c}|\mathbf{x}_t)p(\mathbf{y}_t|\mathbf{c}),$$

where $\mathbf{c}$ is an activity label. Since the activity-label spaces may be large, for simplicity, we approximate the value of $p(\mathbf{y}_t|\mathbf{x}_t)$ by the *mode*, which is the most frequent label of $p(\mathbf{c}|\mathbf{x}_t)$ and denoted by $\hat{\mathbf{c}}$. In other words,

$$p(\mathbf{y}_t|\mathbf{x}_t) \approx p(\hat{\mathbf{c}}|\mathbf{x}_t)p(\mathbf{y}_t|\hat{\mathbf{c}}), \quad \hat{\mathbf{c}} = \arg\max_{\mathbf{c}} p(\mathbf{c}|\mathbf{x}_t).$$

We assume that the two label spaces are different but related. Therefore, the joint distribution $p(\mathbf{y}_s, \mathbf{y}_t)$ should have high mutual information in general and that $p(\mathbf{y}_t|\hat{\mathbf{c}})$ should also be high.

From this equation, the introduced transfer learning framework takes two steps. In the first step, we will estimate $p(\hat{\mathbf{c}}|\mathbf{x}_t)$ where $\hat{\mathbf{c}}$ is labeled according to the source domain label space. Briefly speaking, we aim to use the source domain label space to explain the target domain sequences $\mathbf{x}_t$ first. Since the two domains have different feature spaces, in the first step we need to transfer across different feature spaces. Next, we estimate $p(\mathbf{y}_t|\hat{\mathbf{c}})$ where $\mathbf{y_t}$ is defined on the target domain label space and $\hat{\mathbf{c}}$ is defined on the source domain label space, hence, in the second step, we need to transfer across different label spaces.

21.3.3 Transfer across Feature Spaces

Based on these discussions, in this section we first need to transfer knowledge between different feature spaces and estimate $p(\hat{\mathbf{c}}|\mathbf{x}_t)$.

For each sensor reading $\mathbf{x}_s$ in the source domain S, it is represented by features f_s. Similarly, for each sensor reading $\mathbf{x}_t$ in the target domain T, it is represented by features f_t. For example, f_s can be an on-body three-dimensional accelerometer attached to the wrist and f_t can be the WiFi signals from a cellphone. Here we need to build a bridge between f_s and f_t.

Inspired by translated learning (Dai et al., 2008), when transferring across different feature spaces, an important step is to find a *translator* $\phi(f_t, f_s) \propto p(f_t|f_s)$ between the source and target domains. Since f_t and f_s are conditionally independent given $\mathbf{x}_s$, we have

$$p(f_t, f_s) = \int_{\mathcal{X}_s} p(f_t|\mathbf{x}_s)p(f_s|\mathbf{x}_s)p(\mathbf{x}_s)d\mathbf{x}_s = \int_{\mathcal{X}_s} p(f_t, \mathbf{x}_s)p(f_s|\mathbf{x}_s)d\mathbf{x}_s.$$

In order to measure the joint distribution $p(f_t, f_s)$, we need to measure $p(f_t, \mathbf{x}_s)$, or, more precisely, the joint distribution between each feature in T with the source domain sensor readings $\mathbf{x}_s$. Depending on computing based on the difference on distributions or difference on signal data, we can use two basic tools to approximate $p(f_t, \mathbf{x}_s)$, including Jeffrey's J-divergence (Jeffreys, 1946), which is a symmetric version of the KL divergence, and dynamic time warping (DTW) (Keogh and Pazzani, 2000).

We can extract two kinds of information from sensor readings. The first is that, given a sequence of sensor reading, we can estimate the generative distribution from which such a sensor reading is generated. Since we only care about the relative distance between two distributions of sensor readings instead of describing these distributions accurately, we simply plot the frequency of each sensor value, which will be discretized if it is continuous, and then smooth the discretized probability distribution. Since we have quite different feature spaces, we first normalize all our sensor readings into the range of [0,1].

In particular, suppose that we have a training set in the source domain $\{x_i, y_i\}$, where x_i is a sensor reading and y_i is the corresponding label. For each activity y_i, we can select all sequences of sensor readings x that have y_i as its label. Next, we could count the occurrences of sensor values x_{ij}, and then estimate the probability distribution for each of the sensor in the sensor reading sequence x_i. An intuitive explanation of aforementioned method is that we try to link each generative distribution of different sensors to a target activity.

Following a similar approach, we can also estimate the probability distribution for each sensor reading sequence in the target domain. Now that for each sensor reading sequence, we have an estimated distribution Q and we wish to find a close distribution P in the source domain. Since KL divergence is asymmetric, that is, $D_{KL}(P \parallel Q) \neq D_{KL}(Q \parallel P)$. Therefore, instead of calculating $D_{KL}(P \parallel Q)$, we use $D_{KL}(P \parallel Q) + D_{KL}(Q \parallel P)$, which is a symmetric measurement, to measure the distance between two distributions generating sensor readings.

Two issues need to be addressed for the selection of candidate labels based on the relative entropy measurements. The first issue is that, although $D_{KL}(P \parallel Q) + D_{KL}(Q \parallel P)$ equals zero if and only if the two distributions P and Q are identical, the fact that sensors have a very large value does not necessarily mean the two distributions are highly uncorrelated. Consider two accelerometers where the directions of accelerations are different. In this case, whenever the first accelerometer senses a high value, the second accelerometer will sense a low value. Therefore, we need to consider distribution pairs at both high divergence and low divergence values. The second issue we consider is the different sampling rates of different sensors when plotting their signal values versus time. Different kinds of sensors have very different sampling rates and the accuracy of distributions estimated can vary a lot. When calculating the correlation between different sensors, another important step is to use a distance metric that can take different sampling rates into account. Now given two series of sensor readings of only one dimension, Q and C of length n and m, we wish to align two sequences based on DTW (Keogh and Pazzani, 2000).

The idea of DTW is simple. We could construct an n-by-m matrix where the (i, j)-th element contains the distance $d(q_i, c_j)$ between the two points q_i and c_j, which is measured as the absolute value of difference of q_i and c_j, that is, $d(q_i, c_j) = |q_i - c_j|$. Since the (i, j)-th element corresponds to the alignment between q_i and c_j, the objective is to find a warping path W that is a contiguous set

Algorithm 21.1 Projecting the labels in the source domain to the unlabeled sensor readings in the target domain

Input: Source domain activities $\S_s$, source domain data $\mathcal{D}_s = \{(\mathbf{x}_s, \mathbf{y}_s)\} = \{(x_i, y_i)|y_i \in L_s\}$, target domain data $\mathcal{D}_t = \{\mathbf{x}_t\}$

Output: Pseudo-labeled target domain data $\mathcal{D}'_t = \{(\mathbf{x}_s, \mathbf{y}'_s)\}$

begin

  1: Normalize each sensor reading sequence in S and T.
  2: For each pair of sensor reading and activity in $(\mathbf{x}_s, \mathbf{y}_s) \in S$, estimate its probability distribution $p(f_s|y_s)$.
  3: For each unlabeled sequence in the target domain $\mathbf{x}_t$, estimate the distribution of its feature values: $P(f_t)$.
  4: Calculate the relative entropy between distributions in T and all the distributions in S. Take the top-K similar and the bottom-K similar distributions out and record their labels as candidates.
  5: Calculate the DTW score between this sensor reading sequence $\mathbf{x}_t$ and all the labeled sensor reading sequences $(\mathbf{x}_s, \mathbf{y}_s)$ in the source domain. Take the top-K highest and the bottom-K lowest similar sensor readings out and record their labels as candidates.
  6: Label an unlabeled sequence $\mathbf{x}_t$ with the label that appeared maximum times in the candidate label set.

end

of elements that define the mapping between Q and C. Thus, the element at position K of the warping path W is defined as $w_k = (i, j)_k$. This warping path can be found via dynamic programming with a quadratic time complexity.

Algorithm 21.1 shows the step for projecting the labels in the source domain to the unlabeled sensor readings in the target domain. Notice that in Algorithm 21.1, we introduce a parameter K, which is used to control the number of candidate label sequences in the source domain.

21.3.4 Transfer across Label Spaces

In the previous section, we had already estimated the value for $\arg\max_c p(\hat{c}|\mathbf{x}_t)$. In this section, we aim to estimate $p(\mathbf{y}_t|\hat{c})$. Since $p(\mathbf{y}_t|c) = p(\mathbf{y}_t, c)/p(c)$, if we assume that there is no distinction between the prior distribution $p(c)$, then we can get $p(\mathbf{y}_t|c) \propto p(\mathbf{y}_t, c)$.

Based on the Markov assumption, we have

$$p(\mathbf{y}_t, \mathbf{c}) = p(y_t^0) \prod_i p(y_t^i|y_t^{i-1}) \prod_i p(c^i|y_t^i) \propto \prod_i p(y_t^i|y_t^{i-1}) \prod_i p(c^i|y_t^i)$$

$$\log p(\mathbf{y}_t, \mathbf{c}) \propto \sum_i \log p(y_t^i|y_t^{i-1}) + \sum_i \log p(c^i|y_t^i).$$

From this formulation, we can see that such a problem can be reduced to esti-

---

Algorithm 21.2 Projecting target domain sequences with source domain labels to target domain sequences with target domain labels

---

Input: Pseudo-labeled target domain data $\mathscr{D}'_t = \{(\mathbf{x}_t, \hat{\mathbf{c}})\}$
Output: Labeled target domain data: $\mathscr{D}^*_t = \{(\mathbf{x}_t, \mathbf{y}_t)\}$
begin

1: For each pseudo-labeled target domain instance d'_t, calculate its minimum loss value $R(i,j)$ based on the recurrence relation $R(i,j) = \min_{k \in L_t}\{R(i-1,k) + NGD(\hat{\mathbf{c}}^i, j) + NGD(k,j)\}$, where NGD denotes the Google similarity distance metric.

2: Relabel d'_t using the labels in the target domain label space, thereby creating a new sequence d^*_t.

end

---

mating $p(l_s|l_t)$, where $l_s \in L_s, l_t \in L_t$, and $p(l^1_t|l^2_t)$, where $l^1_t, l^2_t \in L_t$. Since the number of labeled training data in the target domain is not sufficient, we need extra knowledge sources to estimate such probabilities. For example, Shen et al. (2006b) use web pages from the Open Directory Project as a bridge to estimate the probabilities. Zheng et al. (2009) calculate the cosine similarity of two word vectors, which are composed by the words in the Web search results when two activity names are used as queries. In practice, such algorithms based on Web pages could be extremely slow. Instead of measuring the conditional probabilities directly, we choose to optimize a similar measurement that intrinsically can be optimized similarly to $p(\mathbf{y}_t, \mathbf{c})$, as stated later.

We define $R(i,j)$ as the expected loss of assigning $j \in L_t$ to y^i_t and $Q(l_1, l_2)$ as the "information distance" between l_1 and l_2, which are activity labels from the source and target domains, respectively. Then $R(i,j)$ is defined recursively as

$$R(i,j) = \min_{k \in L_t}\{R(i-1,k) + Q(\hat{\mathbf{c}}^i, j) + Q(k,j)\}.$$

We briefly explain the nature of this recursive relation. In order to minimize the loss up to time slice i, we need to consider the minimum loss up to time slice $i-1$. To do that, we need to enumerate all possible $R(i-1,k)$, where $k \in L_t$ is the label we assigned to time slice $i-1$. Next, we need to minimize the distance between the original "pseudo-label" $\hat{\mathbf{c}}^i$ and this new label $j \in L_t$. Furthermore, $Q(k,j)$ is also considered in the recursive function to minimize the distance between successive slices $\mathbf{y}^i_t$ and $\mathbf{y}^{i-1}_t$. It can be seen that this recurrence relation could be solved via dynamic programming. Here we use the Google similarity distance (Cilibrasi and Vitányi, 2007) as Q to approximate the information distance between two entities.

The Google similarity distance is defined as

$$NGD(x,y) = \frac{\max\{\log f(x), \log f(y)\} - \log f(x,y)}{\log N - \min\{\log f(x), \log f(y)\}},$$

where $f(x)$ denotes the number of pages containing x as reported by Google, $f(x, y)$ denotes the number of pages containing both x and y, and N is a normalized factor. Therefore, what we need to know is just a count of the search results. By using the Google similarity distance, we have

$$R(i, j) = \min_{k \in L_t}\{R(i - 1, k) + NGD(\hat{c}^i, j) + NGD(k, j)\}.$$

Algorithm 21.2 further explains the procedure we use to bridge the gap between different labels.

After these two steps, we now have the label $y_t^i \in L_t$ for each unlabeled sensor reading in the target domain and then we can apply *any* machine learning algorithm used for activity recognition such as hidden Markov models (Patterson et al., 2005) or conditional random fields (Vail et al., 2007) to train an activity recognition classifier in the target domain.

22
Transfer Learning in Urban Computing

22.1 Introduction

Nowadays, cell phones, vehicles and infrastructures (e.g., traffic cameras and air-quality monitoring stations) continuously generate a huge amount of data related to our cities in heterogeneous formats such as GPS points, online posts, road conditions and weather conditions. This opens a new door for us to know about the dynamics of our city from different perspectives and facilitates various urban computing applications for traffic monitoring, society security, urban planning, health care and so on. The current solutions can help streamline citywide planning and decision-making in the following way:

Fine-grained data inference: In many urban monitoring tasks, the obtained data cannot cover the whole city area. A representative example is air-quality monitoring where the stations for air-quality sensing are only sparsely located in a city. Then, how to infer a more fine-grained data distribution based on the sparsely collected data becomes an important research issue.

Future phenomenon prediction: Another important and hot research area is the urban-event prediction problem, such as air quality and traffic prediction. Note that, in traditional statistics, such a problem can often be modeled as a time-series modeling problem and be solved via statistical models such as the autoregressive integrated moving average. However, in complex urban computing applications, in order to obtain a more accurate prediction, usually a more complicated machine learning model is constructed to take heterogeneous data sources into consideration. For example, in the air-quality prediction, many conditions such as road maps, weather conditions and traffic conditions can all be used to make the prediction.

Event detection: Detecting abnormal events is very important in urban computing applications. For example, under destructive weather conditions such as typhoons and hurricanes, it is a critical issue to detect road obstacles, such as fallen trees and ponding water, in a real-time manner. City authorities can restore road transportation in a timely manner to reduce losses.

Facility deployment: Finding appropriate sites for deploying a new facility such as the placement of shopping malls, electronic car-charging stations or environment monitoring stations is another major research topic. It is worth noting that, for most facilities, once they are built, it will be difficult to move the facilities to other sites. Hence, mechanisms for facility deployment tasks usually cannot adopt a trial-and-error methodology, which makes this task more challenging.

Despite extensive research efforts in urban computing research, most existing studies build their applications with an assumption that the amount of service-relevant data is adequate and easily available, for example, traffic flow records for the traffic prediction application. However, this is not always the case in reality. Many cities may just start the urban digitization process and do not have much historical service-relevant data. Hence, one key question in urban computing, while rarely studied yet, emerges: that is, *how to cold-start a new urban computing service given the problem of the data scarcity?* For example, suppose that we want to build a facility deployment assistant system to recommend sites of various facilities such as large shopping malls or five-star hotels, but no such facilities exist in the city yet. Then, how can we make such a site recommendation with little data in this city?

In the remainder of this chapter, we will study how transfer learning can help build such an urban computing application when the data scarcity problem exists. First, we will introduce how "what to transfer" materializes in urban computing applications. Generally, this is an application-dependent issue, but, given the common characteristics of urban computing applications, we can classify this issue into three categories, *cross-modality transfer, cross-region or city transfer,* and *cross-application transfer.* We then demonstrate several key issues in transfer learning of smart-city applications, including *identifying the appropriate source domain, linking source and target domains,* and *assessing the transferability of smart-city knowledge.* Finally, two practical applications are elaborated to illustrate the state-of-the-art transfer learning techniques in urban computing.

22.2 "What to Transfer" in Urban Computing

To leverage transfer learning for building urban computing applications with the data scarcity problem, the first critical issue to address is finding the appropriate source domain knowledge to transfer, that is, *"what to transfer."* In urban computing applications, this knowledge can primarily come from the following sources:

Cross-modality transfer: One of the key characteristics of urban computing applications is that they are often dependent on heterogeneous data modalities. For example, in the air-quality prediction task, a variety of data modalities such as city-road maps, vehicle GPS trajectories, points-of-interest (POI) distributions, weather information and so on, can help increase the prediction accuracy. However, in some cities or regions, it is possible that some data modalities are absent and thus the prediction accuracy is not satisfactory. In such cases, if we can first infer the information of the missing modality by transferring knowledge from other modalities, then we may improve the performance of the target application.

Cross-region and cross-city transfer: The auxiliary knowledge source for building a new application in a city or region is the experience from other cities/regions where the same (or similar) application has already been built in the past. In such scenarios, we can also call the source city/region as the *data-rich* city/region and the target city/region as the *data-scarce* city/region. While the basic idea of the cross-city/region transfer is intuitive, we highlight that it practically faces plenty of difficulties. For example, different cities have distinct development levels, which makes a direct transfer usually useless and perhaps leads to "negative transfer."

Cross-application transfer: For a new smart-city application to be developed, another important knowledge source for transfer learning is from an existing and related application that has already collected a lot of data. For example, suppose we want to open a new ridesharing industry in a city, but we do not have any data about the behaviors of ridesharing cars. Then, to implement an urban computing application related to ridesharing such as the demand-supply prediction, it is possible to leverage existing data from taxi-related applications.

It is worth noting that these knowledge sources can be combined together in a transfer learning application in urban computing. For example, suppose that we want to build a reliable and useful connection between different data modalities within a city for a target application. We can first learn the connection in a source city where all the data modalities are adequate and then transfer it to a target city where some data modalities and the target application data are lacking.

22.3   Key Issues of Transfer Learning in Urban Computing

In this section, we summarize several key issues that should be considered in applying transfer learning to urban computing.

(1) *Identifying the appropriate source domain*: Although the previous section elaborates some ways to obtain source domain knowledge for urban computing applications, finding an appropriate source domain is still the most difficult part in practice. First, for many applications, it may be hard to find a perfect source domain that includes all the desired information for building the target application. Even worse, we may not be able to find any data modality, region/city or application from which to transfer. In such a scenario, we may need to rely on simulation software to generate data as the source domain or attempt to crawl data from websites and apps. In many cases, social media platforms such as Facebook and Twitter will be a useful data source because the activities of users on those platforms (e.g., check-ins) can often be mapped to real-life physical spaces and reflect urban dynamics.

(2) *Linking source and target domains*: Once determining the source domain, the second step is to learn the knowledge that can be transferred from the source domain to the target domain. In other words, the "invariant" part of the knowl-

edge needs to be extracted between the two domains. While this part is usually application specific and no single method can be always effective, here we give some guidelines and suggestions.

- *Building with privacy-preserving solutions in a systematic way:* In urban computing applications, many data can only be collected and shared in a privacy-preserving way. This may incur the inconsistency between the source and target domain data. For example, taxi trajectory records published by many cities only include coarse pick-up and drop-off regions rather than detailed GPS coordinates. Then, when we want to build a taxi-related urban computing application by the cross-city transfer, probably we can only obtain the privacy-preserving taxi data from the source city, while more fine-grained data can be retrieved from the target city. Hence, some systematic ways to deal with such privacy-preserving data may be desired to facilitate the transfer learning.
- *Learning common representations via neural networks for transferability:* With the recent development of deep neural networks, it has become a very powerful tool to automatically learn the feature representation for a large scope of tasks. Similarly, in transfer learning applications in urban computing, it also becomes a popular method recently. For example, we can use neural networks to learn a new feature representation for a city region while its original feature can include POI distribution, temperature, traffic conditions and so on. Then, other useful prior knowledge (e.g., two regions in two cities, such as central business districts, are similar to each other) can be added into the neural network to help learn a new feature representation with better transferability.

(3) *Assessing transferability:* Another fundamental issue is to quantitatively measure the transferability between the source and target domains. For example, given several source city candidates, assessing the transferability will help select appropriate cities as the source cities. It is probable that we can consider the size, population, culture, economics and so on to quantify the intercity similarity and also the intercity transferability. However, up to date, there is still little work focusing on mathematically quantifying such intercity transferability. We believe that this will be an important future research direction, which will significantly boost the applications of transfer learning in urban computing.

In the next two sections, we introduce two practical problems in urban computing, that is, the chain store recommendation problem and the air-quality prediction problem to elaborate how transfer learning can effectively address the data scarcity issue in urban computing.

22.4 Chain Store Recommendation

Chain business dominates the market in the world. One critical issue to address in the chain business is to select optimal locations for chain stores when a chain enterprise wants to start the business in a new city. Traditionally, operators address this problem via questionnaire surveys to understand the needs of citizens and detailed investigations to learn characteristics of candidate locations, based on which locations for new stores will be selected. Obviously, these traditional methods are too time-consuming to adopt, especially when cities are developing rapidly nowadays. On the other hand, to adopt traditional machine learning technologies to solve this problem, we face the cold-start issue, that is, there is not enough data about the chain stores in the target city.

In this situation, we turn to transfer learning for a solution. For example, Guo et al. (2018a) propose a CityTransfer model to conduct the intercity knowledge transfer between cities and the intracity knowledge transfer between enterprises. In the following, we will introduce their problem settings and the CityTransfer model in detail.

22.4.1 Problem Settings

Consider two large cities in China, that is, Beijing and Shanghai. Each city is divided into uniform-sized grids as $G = \{g_1, \ldots, g_m\}$. A vector of features, denoted by f_i, is extracted for each grid. Three popular economic chain hotel enterprises in China are considered, that is, 7 Days Inn, Home Inn and Hanting Inn, which are denoted by $H = \{h_1, h_2, h_3\}$.

Suppose that in Beijing there has already been chain stores for these three enterprises while Shanghai has chain stores only for the "7 Days Inn" and "Home Inn." If "Hanting Inn" wants to start its business in Shanghai, it faces a cold-start problem, which can be solved via a transfer learning method. The CityTransfer method conducts inter- and intra-city knowledge transfer to adapt the knowledge between different cities and enterprises. In our case, Beijing is treated as the source city s, which has grids $G^s = \{g_1^s, \ldots, g_{m_1}^s\}$, while Shanghai is treated as a target city t, which has grids $G^t = \{g_1^t, \ldots, g_{m_2}^t\}$. Besides, h_1 and h_2 are the source enterprises, while h_3 is the target one.

The CityTransfer model leverages multiple heterogeneous data sources to conduct the store-location recommendation. The adopted data sources are from two categories, that is, the urban characteristics data and chain hotel enterprise data. The former includes the POIs in each grid crawled from the Gaode map, one of the most popular digital map service provider in China, and the house prices in each grid crawled from the Soufang, a popular website for real estate in China. The latter includes the enterprise profile information crawled from the company Ctrip (www.ctrip.com), a popular travel reservation website in China, and consumer reviews crawled from the Sina Weibo (www.sina.com), one of the most famous microblogging service in China. We show the details of the data in Table 22.1. As the business performance of an enterprise in a grid is reflected by theo number of related reviews to this enterprise in this grid, the CityTransfer model approximates r_{ij}, which denotes the rating of a store of the enterprise h_i in grid g_j, by the number of reviews in g_j related to h_i.

Table 22.1 *Urban characteristics and chain hotel enterprise data (Guo et al., 2018a)*

Source	Beijing	Shanghai
7 Days Inn hotels	160	46
Home Inn hotels	179	156
Hanting Inn hotels	123	147
7 Days Inn reviews	31,215	8,610
Home Inn reviews	35,310	45,146
Hanting Inn reviews	18,195	22,875
POIs	348,863	444,703
Check-ins	21,222070	16,928,489
House prices	55,030	50,224

22.4.2 The CityTransfer Model

The CityTransfer model (Guo et al., 2018a) extends the traditional singular value decomposition (SVD)-based collaborative filtering model to conduct inter- and intra-city knowledge transfer. First, as the original feature representation extracted from multimodal data for each grid is redundant and noisy, the intracity semantic extraction component is designed to construct a more robust and informative feature representation from the original one for each grid, that is, $f_i \rightarrow v_i$. Second, as the feature and rating distributions in different cities may be different, the inter-city knowledge association component is designed to guarantee that the new feature representation is in a shared semantic space. Third, based on the SVD-based collaborative filtering model, the rating score of each grid for each enterprise can be predicted via a transfer rating prediction model.

Intra-city semantic extraction: An autoencoder is adopted to construct a new feature vector v_i from the original feature f_i. The construction process is defined as

$$v_i^s = \sigma \left(W_s f_i^s + y_1^s \right) \tag{22.1}$$
$$v_i^t = \sigma \left(W_t f_i^t + y_1^t \right), \tag{22.2}$$

where W_s, W_t, y_1^s and y_1^t are parameters and σ denotes an activation function. Meanwhile, the original grid feature vectors can be reconstructed as

$$\hat{f}_i^s = \sigma \left(W_s^T v_i^s + y_2^s \right) \tag{22.3}$$
$$\hat{f}_i^t = \sigma \left(W_t^T v_i^t + y_2^t \right), \tag{22.4}$$

where y_2^s and y_2^t are parameters. The parameters in the autoencoder are estimated by minimizing the reconstruction error as

$$O_1 = \sum_{i=1}^{m_1} \left\| \hat{f}_i^s - f_i^s \right\|_2^2 + \sum_{i=1}^{m_2} \left\| \hat{f}_i^t - f_i^t \right\|_2^2. \tag{22.5}$$

Inter-city knowledge association: To guarantee the new feature representations from different cities can be comparable, they should be projected to a shared semantic space. One way to achieve that is to follow the following method. We first calculate the Pearson correlation coefficient between any two cities based on the original feature representations, that is, $\rho_{ij} = \rho\left(f_i^s, f_j^t\right)$. According to these coefficients, for each grid in the source city, we choose its top k similar grids in the target city, and similarly for each grid in the target city, we choose its top k similar grids in the source city, generating a set of similar grid pairs between the two cities as $\Delta = \left\{\left(g_i^s, g_j^t\right)\right\}$. To make these pairs of grids similar in the shared semantic space, we can use the following function as a regularization term to obtain the new representations:

$$O_2 = \sum_{\left(g_i^s, g_j^t\right) \in \Delta} \rho\left(f_i^s, f_j^t\right)\left(v_i^s - v_j^t\right)^2. \qquad (22.6)$$

Transfer rating prediction model: An SVD-based collaborative filtering model is extended to predict the rating for each enterprise in a grid. We use u_i to represent the feature representation of enterprise h_i. The rating for an enterprise $h_i \in H$ in grid j of the source city is estimated as

$$\hat{r}_{ij}^s = b_i + e_j^s + u_i^T v_j^s. \qquad (22.7)$$

Similarly, the rating for enterprise h_i in grid j of the target city is estimated as

$$\hat{r}_{ij}^t = b_i + e_j^t + u_i^T v_j^t. \qquad (22.8)$$

To minimize the prediction error, the optimization objective is defined as

$$O_3 = \sum_{r_{ij}^t \in R^t} \left(\hat{r}_{ij}^t - r_{ij}^t\right)^2 + \lambda_1 \sum_{r_{ij}^s \in R^s} \left(\hat{r}_{ij}^s - r_{ij}^s\right)^2. \qquad (22.9)$$

By combining these three components as well as a regularization term denoted by R, the final objective function is formulated as

$$O = \frac{\lambda_1}{2} O_1 + \frac{\lambda_2}{2} O_2 + \frac{\lambda_3}{2} O_3 + \frac{\lambda_4}{2} R. \qquad (22.10)$$

As we can see, the CityTransfer model is a feature-based transfer learning method, where the feature representations of grids and enterprises are transferred from the source city and enterprises to the target ones.

22.5   Air-Quality Prediction

Air pollution is a severe issue in urban life in many parts of the world as contributed by an increasing number of factories, vehicles, human activities and so on. Being able to accurately predicting the air quality in each region in a city is important for citizens to plan their outdoor activities in advance. Clearly, the air quality in a region is impacted by many factors, for example, POIs, traffic, production factories and so on. Thus, the level of pollution largely varies with the location. In a pollution forecasting system, we wish to leverage these multimodal data to estimate the fine-grained air quality in a city in advance.

More specifically, our task is to classify the air quality into *good, moderate, unhealthy* and so on. We can formulate the air-quality prediction as a classification problem. Given the multimodal data in each region during a specific period, we wish to classify the corresponding air quality to a class. We note that the traditional classification models cannot address this problem ideally for two reasons. First, the air-quality data are very scarce because many cities have only a few air-quality monitoring stations, resulting in a label scarcity issue. Second, there is a data insufficiency issue because some multimodel data about important impacting factors may be missing in some regions or some periods, or even totally missing; for example, the meteorology data in Shanghai may be missing for some hours. Likewise, the taxi trajectory data may not be available for some regions and for some periods in certain areas of Shanghai.

Therefore, we consider the problem of whether it is feasible to transfer the knowledge from a city to another city to help predict the air quality. In this section, we explain one of the solutions known as the FLORAL model (Wei et al., 2016b) to transfer multimodal data between cities.

22.5.1 Problem Settings

Suppose that Beijing, as a source domain, has collected sufficient labeled and unlabeled data to build a predictive model on traffic while the target domain, Shanghai, has only few labeled and some unlabeled data. Each data instance stands for a region during a period and is denoted as a multimodal tuple, including the data about various impacting factors to air quality. We assume that there are M modalities and denote the labeled and unlabeled instances in the target domain as $T_l = \{t_{li}^1, t_{li}^2, ..., t_{li}^M\}$ and $T_u = \{t_{ui}^1, t_{ui}^2, ..., t_{ui}^M\}$. Labeled and unlabeled instances in the source domain are denoted in a similar way by $S_l = \{s_{li}^1, s_{li}^2, ..., s_{li}^M\}$ and $S_u = \{s_{ui}^1, s_{ui}^2, ..., s_{ui}^M\}$. As $|S_l| \gg |T_l|$ and some modalities are missing in some instances in T_l, we wish to leverage S_u and S_l to help learn a classifier for the target domain more effectively and efficiently.

In our problem, there are four data modalities, that is, the road networks and POIs data from Bing Maps, the meteorology data crawled from a public website and the taxi trajectory data. Note that the taxi trajectory data are only available in Beijing and some modalities for some instances are missing in Shanghai. The details of the data for the other three modalities are summarized in Table 22.2.

Table 22.2 *Statistics of the modality used in (Wei et al., 2016b)*

Modalities	Beijing	Shanghai
# Road segments	249,080	313,736
Highways	994 km	2,016 km
Roads	24,643 km	40,944 km
# POIs	379,022	433,016
Time span(2014)	Feb. 1–May 31	Aug. 1–Sept. 10

22.5.2 The FLORAL Model

In this section, we introduce the FLORAL model for urban computing. The FLO-RAL model includes two major components, that is, one component for learning semantically related dictionaries for the multiple modalities in the source domain and another for transferring the dictionaries and instances from the source domain to the target domain. Based on the sparse coding of each instance from both the source and target domains, a classification model is to be learned to predict the air quality in the target city. Here we introduce each component in turn.

Learning semantically related dictionaries: Dictionaries in the FLORAL model are obtained by clustering, which has three steps, that is, graph construction, graph clustering and dictionary inference. First, a similarity graph $G = (V, E)$ is constructed. The vertex set includes all modalities of each instance in the source domain and the edges describe pairwise relations between vertices, that is, intra-edges within each modality and inter-edges across different modalities. For each pair of vertices s_i^m and s_j^m in the m-th modality, we measure their similarity with the Euclidean distance on their feature representations. They are connected with an intra-edge if each of them is among the top k similar vertices of each other. The weight of each inter-edge is calculated by a Gaussian kernel between them. For a pair of vertices s_i^m and s_j^n in different modalities, we connect them with an inter-edge whose weight is 1 if the two instance s_i and s_j are known to be correlated, for example, two neighbored regions. Second, a submodular graph clustering is designed to cluster the obtain similarity graph into K groups by guaranteeing some properties that the numbers of labeled instances are balanced across different clusters and that modalities in each cluster are diverse enough. Third, the dictionary for each modality can be inferred based on the obtained clusters. That is, for each cluster k, we calculate the center of the vertices in modality m as the dictionary element d_k^m and, therefore, the final dictionary for modality m combines the K dictionary elements inferred from the K clusters, that is, $D^m = [d_1^m, d_2^m, ..., d_K^m]$, $m = 1, 2, ..., M$. These M dictionaries have the same size and are semantically related.

Transfer dictionaries and instances to the target domain: The dictionaries obtained from the source domain can be reused in the target domain and then sparse codings of both the source and target instances are calculated. By leveraging the sparse codings of the labeled instances from both the source and target domains, a multimodal transfer AdaBoost algorithm based on TrAdaBoost (Dai et al., 2007b) is designed to learn a classifier for the target domain. As an extension of TrAdaBoost, this system can additionally learn the weights of different modalities.

23

Concluding Remarks

In this book, we have explained the mathematical principles and computational foundations of transfer learning. We have introduced the basic concepts underlying transfer learning and explored various types of knowledge transfer and model adaptation algorithms. In terms of domain differences, we have looked at both homogeneous and heterogeneous transfer learning settings and discussed three research issues: when to transfer, what to transfer and how to transfer.

For the"what to transfer" issue, we considered four basic forms, including instance, feature, model and relations that can be the target of knowledge transfer. In terms of "how to transfer," we considered algorithms of four types, including instance-based, feature-based, model-based and relation-based transfer learning algorithms. In the mathematical foundations of transfer learning, we introduced the notion of distribution divergence and domain distance measure. We also explored strong ties to other types of machine learning paradigms including supervised learning, semi-supervised, active learning and multitask learning.

We have also taken a closer look at some advanced transfer learning algorithms, including deep learning-based transfer learning, transitive transfer learning, lifelong machine learning and AutoTL algorithms for learning to how to conduct transfer learning. We have introduced adversarial transfer learning, as well as transfer learning in reinforcement learning.

We have also considered important application areas such as computer vision, natural language processing, dialogue systems, recommender systems, bioinformatics, activity recognition and urban computing. There are more areas in which transfer learning continues to play a major role, which we cannot cover in the space of this book, and we believe that more and more application areas will emerge.

Transfer learning addresses a major problem facing the AI field, that is, the data is often in short supply. Sometimes this lack of data is due to the difficulty in data collection in a field, for example, in the medical domain, to confirm a complete case requires years of treatment and operation. Sometimes though it is because that the society demands more management and control over ownership of the data. More laws and regulations are placed on the sharing of data with third parties. Thus, data are increasingly difficult to obtain in many domains. Furthermore, as more areas in our society move to digitalization and datalization, predictive modeling is on increasing demand. In the "long tail" of application fields where the distribution is over decreasing available data, only the heads are benefiting from machine learning and AI. If we cannot provide the "have-nots" with the benefits of the "haves," our society will become more polarized.

Transfer learning can be a technical solution for this "small-data challenge." If we can take the models from a data-rich areas and transfer them to data-poor areas, we can potentially enable these data-poor areas with faster progress toward an information- and knowledge-based society. Indeed, through many of the application examples given in this book, we have seen that transfer learning can effectively alleviate the small data problem.

One of the areas to explore in the future is to continue to explore lifelong machine learning and automated transfer learning. One of humans' intelligence sources lies in our ability to quickly and effortlessly adapt to new tasks and new environment. In fact, humans cannot only transfer knowledge to a new domain, but also learn how to automatically transfer given new tasks and environments. This indeed is a wonderful puzzle in nature that cannot be solved by computational means alone. Neural science and experimental neurology can potentially shed light on the nature of such abilities, and we hope AI in general and transfer learning in particular can benefit from such insights.

As we are witnessing one of the fundamental AI revolutions in human history, transfer learning distinguishes itself as a deep research area that inspires new ideas and thoughts into the nature of intelligence. In answering Turing's question "Can Machines Think?," we hope to start shed light into the question by giving answers to "How Can Machines Think in New Environments and for New Tasks?"

References

1000 Genomes Project Consortium. 2015. A global reference for human genetic variation. *Nature*, **526**(7571), 68–74.

Aas, Kjersti. 2001. *Microarray Data Mining: A Survey*. Tech. report Norwegian Computing Center.

Abadi, Martín, Barham, Paul, Chen, Jianmin, et al. 2016a. TensorFlow: A system for large-scale machine learning. Pages 265–283 of: Keeton, Kimberly, and Roscoe, Timothy (eds.), *Proceedings of the 12th USENIX Symposium on Operating Systems Design and Implementation*.

Abadi, Martín, Chu, Andy, Goodfellow, Ian J., et al. 2016b. Deep learning with differential privacy. Pages 308–318 of: *Proceedings of ACM Conference on Computer and Communications Security*.

Abu-El-Haija, Sami, Kothari, Nisarg, Lee, et al. 2016. Youtube-8M: A large-scale video classification benchmark. *arXiv preprint*, arXiv:1609.08675.

Acharya, Ayan, Mooney, Raymond J., and Ghosh, Joydeep. 2014. Active multitask learning using both latent and supervised shared topics. Pages 190–198 of: *Proceedings of the 2014 SIAM International Conference on Data Mining*.

Amaldi, Edoardo, and Kann, Viggo. 1998. On the approximability of minimizing nonzero variables or unsatisfied relations in linear systems. *Theoretical Computer Science*, **209**(1), 237–260.

Ando, Rie Kubota, and Zhang, Tong. 2005. A framework for learning predictive structures from multiple tasks and unlabeled data. *Journal of Machine Learning Research*, **6**, 1817–1853.

Antony, Joseph, McGuinness, Kevin, O'Connor, Noel E., and Moran, Kieran. 2016. Quantifying radiographic knee osteoarthritis severity using deep convolutional neural networks. Pages 1195–1200 of: *23rd International Conference on Pattern Recognition*.

Argyriou, Andreas, Evgeniou, Theodoros, and Pontil, Massimiliano. 2006. Multi-task feature learning. Pages 41–48 of: *Advances in Neural Information Processing Systems*.

Argyriou, Andreas, Evgeniou, Theodoros, and Pontil, Massimiliano. 2008. Convex multi-task feature learning. *Machine Learning*, **73**(3), 243–272.

Argyriou, Andreas, Micchelli, Charles A., and Pontil, Massimiliano. 2009. When is there a representer theorem? Vector versus matrix regularizers. *Journal of Machine Learning Research*, **10**, 2507–2529.

Argyriou, Andreas, Micchelli, Charles A., and Pontil, Massimiliano. 2010. On spectral learning. *Journal of Machine Learning Research*, **11**, 935–953.

Arık, Sercan Ö., Chrzanowski, Mike, Coates, Adam, et al. 2017. Deep voice: Real-time neural text-to-speech. Pages 195–204 of: *Proceedings of International Conference on Machine Learning*.

Arjovsky, Martín, and Bottou, Léon. 2017. Towards principled methods for training generative adversarial networks. *CoRR*, abs/1701.04862.

Arjovsky, Martín, Chintala, Soumith, and Bottou, Léon. 2017. Wasserstein generative adversarial networks. Pages 214–223 of: *Proceedings of the 34th International Conference on Machine Learning*.

Ashley, Kevin D. 1991. Reasoning with cases and hypotheticals in HYPO. *International Journal of Man-Machine Studies*, **34**(6), 753–796.

Augenstein, Isabelle, and Søgaard, Anders. 2017. Multi-task learning of keyphrase boundary classification. Pages 341–346 of: *Proceedings of the 55th Annual Meeting of the Association for Computational Linguistics*.

Aytar, Yusuf, and Zisserman, Andrew. 2011. Tabula rasa: Model transfer for object category detection. Pages 2252–2259 of: *Proceedings of IEEE International Conference on Computer Vision*.

Azar, Mohammad Gheshlaghi, Lazaric, Alessandro, and Brunskill, Emma. 2013. Sequential transfer in multi-armed bandit with finite set of models. Pages 2220–2228 of: *Advances in Neural Information Processing Systems*.

Bächlin, Marc, Roggen, Daniel, Tröster, Gerhard, et al. 2009. Potentials of enhanced context awareness in wearable assistants for Parkinson's disease patients with the freezing of gait syndrome. Pages 123–130 of: *Proceedings of the 13th IEEE International Symposium on Wearable Computers*.

Bahdanau, Dzmitry, Cho, Kyunghyun, and Bengio, Yoshua. 2014. Neural machine translation by jointly learning to align and translate. *CoRR*, abs/1409.0473.

Bakas, Spyridon, Akbari, Hamed, Sotiras, Aristeidis, et al. 2017. Advancing the cancer genome atlas glioma MRI collections with expert segmentation labels and radiomic features. *Scientific Data*, **4**, 170117.

Bakker, Bart, and Heskes, Tom. 2003. Task clustering and gating for Bayesian multitask learning. *Journal of Machine Learning Research*, **4**, 83–99.

Baktashmotlagh, Mahsa, Harandi, Mehrtash T., Lovell, Brian C., and Salzmann, Mathieu. 2013. Unsupervised domain adaptation by domain invariant projection. Pages 769–776 of: *Proceedings of IEEE International Conference on Computer Vision*.

Baktashmotlagh, Mahsa, Harandi, Mehrtash T., Lovell, Brian C., and Salzmann, Mathieu. 2014. Domain adaptation on the statistical manifold. Pages 2481–2488 of: *Proceedings of IEEE Conference on Computer Vision and Pattern Recognition*.

Balcan, Maria-Florina, Blum, Avrim, and Vempala, Santosh. 2015. Efficient representations for lifelong learning and autoencoding. Pages 191–210 of: *Proceedings of the 28th Conference on Learning Theory*.

Balikas, Georgios, Moura, Simon, and Amini, Massih-Reza. 2017. Multitask learning for fine-grained Twitter sentiment analysis. Pages 1005–1008 of: *Proceedings of the 40th International ACM SIGIR Conference on Research and Development in Information Retrieval*.

Bao, Ling, and Intille, Stephen S. 2004. Activity recognition from user-annotated acceleration data. Pages 1–17 of: *Proceedings of the Second International Conference on Pervasive Computing*.

Barreto, André, Dabney, Will, Munos, Rémi, et al. 2017. Successor features for transfer in reinforcement learning. Pages 4058–4068 of: *Advances in Neural Information Processing Systems*.

Bartlett, Peter L., and Mendelson, Shahar. 2002. Rademacher and Gaussian complexities: Risk bounds and structural results. *Journal of Machine Learning Research*, **3**, 463–482.

Barzilai, Aviad, and Crammer, Koby. 2015. Convex multi-task learning by clustering. Pages 65–73 of: *Proceedings of the 18th International Conference on Artificial Intelligence and Statistics*.

Bassily, Raef, Smith, Adam D., and Thakurta, Abhradeep. 2014. Private empirical risk minimization: Efficient algorithms and tight error bounds. Pages 464–473 of: *Proceedings of IEEE Annual Symposium on Foundations of Computer Science*.

Baxter, Jonathan. 2000. A model of inductive bias learning. *Journal of Artifical Intelligence Research*, **12**, 149–198.

Bay, Herbert, Ess, Andreas, Tuytelaars, Tinne, and Van Gool, Luc. 2008. Speeded-up robust features (SURF). *Computer Vision and Image Understanding*, **110**(3), 346–359.

Bello, Irwan, Zoph, Barret, Vasudevan, Vijay, and Le, Quoc V. 2017. Neural optimizer search with reinforcement learning. Pages 459–468 of: *Proceedings of the 34th International Conference on Machine Learning*.

Belmont, John M., Butterfield, Earl C., and Ferretti, Ralph P. 1982. To secure transfer of training instruct self-management skills. Pages 147–154 of: Detterman, Douglas K., and Sternberg, Robert J. (eds.), *How and How Much Can Intelligence Be Increased*. Ablex Publishing Corporation.

Ben-David, Shai, and Borbely, Reba Schuller. 2008. A notion of task relatedness yielding provable multiple-task learning guarantees. *Machine Learning*, **73**(3), 273–287.

Ben-David, Shai, and Schuller, Reba. 2003. Exploiting task relatedness for multiple task learning. Pages 567–580 of: *Proceedings of the 16th Annual Conference on Computational Learning Theory*.

Ben-David, Shai, Gehrke, Johannes, and Schuller, Reba. 2002. A theoretical framework for learning from a pool of disparate data sources. Pages 443–449 of: *Proceedings of the 8th ACM SIGKDD International Conference on Knowledge Discovery and Data Mining*.

Ben-David, Shai, Blitzer, John, Crammer, Koby, and Pereira, Fernando. 2006. Analysis of representations for domain adaptation. Pages 137–144 of: *Advances in Neural Information Processing Systems*.

Ben-David, Shai, Blitzer, John, Crammer, et al. 2010. A theory of learning from different domains. *Machine Learning*, **79**(1–2), 151–175.

Bengio, Yoshua. 2009. Learning deep architectures for AI. *Foundations and Trends in Machine Learning*, **2**(1), 1–127.

Bengio, Yoshua. 2012. Deep learning of representations for unsupervised and transfer learning. Pages 17–36 of: *Proceedings of ICML Workshop on Unsupervised and Transfer Learning*.

Bengio, Yoshua, Lamblin, Pascal, Popovici, Dan, and Larochelle, Hugo. 2007. Greedy layerwise training of deep networks. Pages 153–160 of: *Advances in Neural Information Processing Systems*.

Bengio, Yoshua, Courville, Aaron, and Vincent, Pascal. 2013. Representation learning: A review and new perspectives. *IEEE Transactions on Pattern Analysis and Machine Intelligence*, **35**(8), 1798–1828.

Bi, Jinbo, Xiong, Tao, Yu, Shipeng, Dundar, Murat, and Rao, R. Bharat. 2008. An Improved multi-task learning approach with applications in medical diagnosis. Pages 117–132 of: *Proceedings of European Conference on Machine Learning and Practice of Knowledge Discovery in Databases*.

Bickel, Steffen, Brückner, Michael, and Scheffer, Tobias. 2007. Discriminative learning for differing training and test distributions. Pages 81–88 of: *Proceedings of the 24th International Conference on Machine Learning*.

Bickel, Steffen, Bogojeska, Jasmina, Lengauer, Thomas, and Scheffer, Tobias. 2008. Multi-task learning for HIV therapy screening. Pages 56–63 of: *Proceedings of the Twenty-Fifth International Conference on Machine Learning*.

Biermann, Alan W., and Long, Philip M. 1996. The composition of messages in speech-graphics interactive systems. Pages 97–100 of: *Proceedings of the 1996 International Symposium on Spoken Dialogue*.

Blitzer, John, McDonald, Ryan, and Pereira, Fernando. 2006. Domain adaptation with structural correspondence learning. Pages 120–128 of: *Proceedings of the 2006 Conference on Empirical Methods in Natural Language Processing*.

Blitzer, John, Crammer, Koby, Kulesza, Alex, Pereira, Fernando, and Wortman, Jennifer. 2007a. Learning bounds for domain adaptation. Pages 129–136 of: *Advances in Neural Information Processing Systems*.

Blitzer, John, Dredze, Mark, and Pereira, Fernando. 2007b. Biographies, bollywood, boom-boxes and blenders: Domain adaptation for sentiment classification. Pages 440–447 of: *Proceedings of the 45th Annual Meeting of the Association for Computational Linguistics*.

Blum, Avrim, and Mitchell, Tom M. 1998. Combining labeled and unlabeled data with co-training. Pages 92–100 of: Bartlett, Peter L., and Mansour, Yishay (eds.), *Proceedings of the Eleventh Annual Conference on Computational Learning Theory*.

Bollegala, Danushka, Maehara, Takanori, and Kawarabayashi, Ken-ichi. 2015. Unsupervised cross-domain word representation learning. Pages 730–740 of: *Proceedings of the 53rd Annual Meeting of the Association for Computational Linguistics*.

Bonilla, Edwin V., Chai, Kian Ming Adam, and Williams, Christopher K. I. 2007. Multi-task Gaussian process prediction. Pages 153–160 of: *Advances in Neural Information Processing Systems 20*.

Bou-Ammar, Haitham, Tuyls, Karl, Taylor, Matthew E., Driessens, Kurt, and Weiss, Gerhard. 2012. Reinforcement learning transfer via sparse coding. Pages 383–390 of: *Proceedings of International Conference on Autonomous Agents and Multiagent Systems*.

Bou-Ammar, Haitham, Eaton, Eric, Ruvolo, Paul, and Taylor, Matthew E. 2014. Online multi-task learning for policy gradient methods. Pages 1206–1214 of: *Proceedings of the 31th International Conference on Machine Learning*.

Bou-Ammar, Haitham, Eaton, Eric, Ruvolo, Paul, and Taylor, Matthew E. 2015. Unsupervised cross-domain transfer in policy gradient reinforcement learning via manifold alignment. Pages 2504–2510 of: *Proceedings of the Twenty-Ninth AAAI Conference on Artificial Intelligence*.

Bousmalis, Konstantinos, Trigeorgis, George, Silberman, Nathan, Krishnan, Dilip, and Erhan, Dumitru. 2016. Domain separation networks. Pages 343–351 of: *Advances in Neural Information Processing Systems*.

Bousquet, Olivier, and Elisseeff, André. 2002. Stability and generalization. *Journal of Machine Learning Research*, **2**, 499–526.

Braud, Chloé, Lacroix, Ophélie, and Søgaard, Anders. 2017. Cross-lingual and cross-domain discourse segmentation of entire documents. Pages 237–243 of: *Proceedings of the 55th Annual Meeting of the Association for Computational Linguistics*.

Bromley, Jane, Guyon, Isabelle, LeCun, Yann, Säckinger, Eduard, and Shah, Roopak. 1993. Signature verification using a Siamese time delay neural network. Pages 737–744 of: *Advances in Neural Information Processing Systems*.

Brosch, Tom, and Tam, Roger C. 2013. Manifold learning of brain MRIs by deep learning. Pages 633–640 of: *Proceedings of the 16th International Conference on Medical Image Computing and Computer-Assisted Intervention*.

Brunskill, Emma, and Li, Lihong. 2013. Sample complexity of multi-task reinforcement learning. In: *Proceedings of the Twenty-Ninth Conference on Uncertainty in Artificial Intelligence.*

Bruzzone, Lorenzo, and Marconcini, Mattia. 2010. Domain adaptation problems: A DASVM classification technique and a circular validation strategy. *IEEE Transactions on Pattern Analysis and Machine Intelligence*, 32(5), 770–787.

Bryant, Peter E., and Trabasso, Thomas. 1971. Transitive inferences and memory in young children. *Nature*, 232, 456–458.

Bulling, Andreas, and Roggen, Daniel. 2011. Recognition of visual memory recall processes using eye movement analysis. Pages 455–464 of: *Proceedings of the 13th International Conference on Ubiquitous Computing.*

Bulling, Andreas, Ward, Jamie A., Gellersen, Hans, and Tröster, Gerhard. 2008. Robust recognition of reading activity in transit using wearable electrooculography. Pages 19–37 of: *Proceedings of the 6th International Conference on Pervasive Computing.*

Bulling, Andreas, Blanke, Ulf, and Schiele, Bernt. 2014. A tutorial on human activity recognition using body-worn inertial sensors. *ACM Computing Surveys*, 46(3), 33:1–33:33.

Calandriello, Daniele, Lazaric, Alessandro, and Restelli, Marcello. 2014. Sparse multi-task reinforcement learning. Pages 819–827 of: *Advances in Neural Information Processing Systems.*

Cao, Qiong, Ying, Yiming, and Li, Peng. 2013. Similarity metric learning for face recognition. Pages 2408–2415 of: *Proceedings of IEEE International Conference on Computer Vision.*

Cao, Zhangjie, Long, Mingsheng, Wang, Jianmin, and Jordan, Michael I. 2017. Partial transfer learning with selective adversarial networks. *CoRR*, abs/1707.07901.

Carbonell, Jaime G. 1981. A computational model of analogical problem solving. Pages 147–152 of: *Proceedings of the 7th International Joint Conference on Artificial Intelligence.*

Carbonell, Jaime G., Etzioni, Oren, Gil, Yolanda, et al. 1991. PRODIGY: An integrated architecture for planning and learning. *SIGART Bulletin*, 2(4), 51–55.

Carlson, Andrew, Betteridge, Justin, Kisiel, Bryan, et al. 2010. Toward an architecture for never-ending language learning. In: *Proceedings of the 24th AAAI Conference on Artificial Intelligence.*

Caruana, Rich. 1997. Multitask learning. *Machine Learning*, 28(1), 41–75.

Casanueva, Inigo, Hain, Thomas, Christensen, Heidi, Marxer, Ricard, and Green, Phil. 2015. Knowledge transfer between speakers for personalised dialogue management. Pages 12–21 of: *Proceedings of the 16th Annual Meeting of the Special Interest Group on Discourse and Dialogue.*

Castrejon, Lluis, Aytar, Yusuf, Vondrick, Carl, Pirsiavash, Hamed, and Torralba, Antonio. 2016. Learning aligned cross-modal representations from weakly aligned data. Pages 2940–2949 of: *Proceedings of IEEE Conference on Computer Vision and Pattern Recognition.*

Cavallanti, Giovanni, Cesa-Bianchi, Nicolò, and Gentile, Claudio. 2010. Linear algorithms for online multitask classification. *Journal of Machine Learning Research*, 11, 2901–2934.

Chaudhuri, Kamalika, Monteleoni, Claire, and Sarwate, Anand D. 2011. Differentially private empirical risk minimization. *Journal of Machine Learning Research*, 12, 1069–1109.

Chavarriaga, Ricardo, Sagha, Hesam, Calatroni, Alberto, et al. 2013. The opportunity challenge: A benchmark database for on-body sensor-based activity recognition. *Pattern Recognition Letters*, 34(15), 2033–2042.

Chen, Austin H., and Huang, Zone-Wei. 2010. A new multi-task learning technique to predict classification of leukemia and prostate cancer. Pages 11–20 of: *Proceedings of the Second International Conference on Medical Biometrics.*

Chen, Jianhui, Tang, Lei, Liu, Jun, and Ye, Jieping. 2009. A convex formulation for learning shared structures from multiple tasks. Pages 137–144 of: *Proceedings of the 26th International Conference on Machine Learning.*

Chen, Jianhui, Liu, Ji, and Ye, Jieping. 2010a. Learning incoherent sparse and low-rank patterns from multiple tasks. Pages 1179–1188 of: *Proceedings of the 16th ACM SIGKDD International Conference on Knowledge Discovery and Data Mining.*

Chen, Jianhui, Zhou, Jiayu, and Ye, Jieping. 2011. Integrating low-rank and group-sparse structures for robust multi-task learning. Pages 42–50 of: *Proceedings of the 17th ACM SIGKDD International Conference on Knowledge Discovery and Data Mining.*

Chen, Minmin, Xu, Zhixiang, Sha, Fei, and Weinberger, Kilian Q. 2012a. Marginalized denoising autoencoders for domain adaptation. Pages 767–774 of: *Proceedings of the 29th International Conference on Machine Learning.*

Chen, Minmin, Xu, Z., Weinberger, Kilian Q., and Sha, Fei. 2012b. Marginalized stacked denoising autoencoders. In: *Proceedings of the Learning Workshop.*

Chen, Wei-Yu, Hsu, Tzu-Ming Harry, Tsai, Yao-Hung Hubert, Wang, Yu-Chiang Frank, and Chen, Ming-Syan. 2016a. Transfer neural trees for heterogeneous domain adaptation. Pages 399–414 of: *Proceedings of European Conference on Computer Vision.*

Chen, Xi, Duan, Yan, Houthooft, Rein, Schulman, John, Sutskever, Ilya, and Abbeel, Pieter. 2016b. InfoGAN: Interpretable representation learning by information maximizing generative adversarial nets. Pages 2172–2180 of: *Advances in Neural Information Processing Systems.*

Chen, Yuqiang, Jin, Ou, Xue, Gui-Rong, Chen, Jia, and Yang, Qiang. 2010b. Visual contextual advertising: Bringing textual advertisements to images. In: *Proceedings of 24th AAAI Conference on Artificial Intelligence.*

Chen, Zhiyuan, and Liu, Bing. 2016. *Lifelong Machine Learning.* Morgan & Claypool.

Chen, Zhiyuan, Ma, Nianzu, and Liu, Bing. 2015. Lifelong learning for sentiment classification. Pages 750–756 of: *Proceedings of the 53rd Annual Meeting of the Association for Computational Linguistics.*

Cheng, Heng-Tze, Koc, Levent, Harmsen, Jeremiah, et al. 2016. Wide & deep learning for recommender systems. Pages 7–10 of: *Proceedings of the 1st Workshop on Deep Learning for Recommender Systems.*

Choi, Eunsol, Hewlett, Daniel, Uszkoreit, Jakob, et al. 2017. Coarse-to-fine question answering for long documents. Pages 209–220 of: *Proceedings of the 55th Annual Meeting of the Association for Computational Linguistics.*

Chomsky, Noam. 1956. Three models for the description of language. *IRE Transactions on Information Theory,* **2**(3), 113–124.

Cilibrasi, Rudi, and Vitányi, Paul M. B. 2007. The Google similarity distance. *IEEE Transactions on Knowledge and Data Engineering,* **19**(3), 370–383.

Collobert, Ronan, and Weston, Jason. 2008. A unified architecture for natural language processing: Deep neural networks with multitask learning. Pages 160–167 of: *Proceedings of the 25th International Conference on Machine Learning.*

Conneau, Alexis, Kiela, Douwe, Schwenk, Holger, Barrault, Loïc, and Bordes, Antoine. 2017. Supervised learning of universal sentence representations from natural language inference data. Pages 670–680 of: *Proceedings of the 2017 Conference on Empirical Methods in Natural Language Processing.*

Cortes, Corinna, Mansour, Yishay, and Mohri, Mehryar. 2010. Learning bounds for importance weighting. Pages 442–450 of: *Advances in Neural Information Processing Systems.*

Cortes, Corinna, Mohri, Mehryar, and Medina, Andres Muñoz. 2015. Adaptation algorithm and theory based on generalized discrepancy. Pages 169–178 of: *Proceedings of the 21th ACM SIGKDD International Conference on Knowledge Discovery and Data Mining*.

Covington, Paul, Adams, Jay, and Sargin, Emre. 2016. Deep neural networks for YouTube recommendations. Pages 191–198 of: *Proceedings of the 10th ACM Conference on Recommender Systems*.

Crammer, Koby, and Mansour, Yishay. 2012. Learning multiple tasks using shared hypotheses. Pages 1484–1492 of: *Advances in Neural Information Processing Systems*.

Cree, V., and Macaulay. 2000. *Transfer of Learning in Professional and Vocational Education*. Routledge.

Csurka, Gabriela. 2017. Domain adaptation for visual applications: A comprehensive survey. *CoRR*, **abs/1702.05374**.

da Silva, Bruno Castro, Konidaris, George, and Barto, Andrew G. 2012. Learning parameterized skills. *Proceedings of the 29th International Conference on Machine Learning*.

Dahlmeier, Daniel, and Ng, Hwee Tou. 2010. Domain adaptation for semantic role labeling in the biomedical domain. *Bioinformatics*, **26**(8), 1098–1104.

Dai, Wenyuan, Xue, Gui-Rong, Yang, Qiang, and Yu, Yong. 2007a. Transferring naive Bayes classifiers for text classification. Pages 540–545 of: *Proceedings of the Twenty-Second AAAI Conference on Artificial Intelligence*.

Dai, Wenyuan, Yang, Qiang, Xue, Gui-Rong, and Yu, Yong. 2007b. Boosting for transfer learning. Pages 193–200 of: *Proceedings of the 24th International Conference on Machine Learning*.

Dai, Wenyuan, Chen, Yuqiang, Xue, Gui-Rong, Yang, Qiang, and Yu, Yong. 2008. Translated learning: Transfer learning across different feature spaces. Pages 353–360 of: *Advances in Neural Information Processing Systems*.

Das, Abhinandan S., Datar, Mayur, Garg, Ashutosh, and Rajaram, Shyam. 2007. Google news personalization: Scalable online collaborative filtering. Pages 271–280 of: *Proceedings of the 16th International Conference on World Wide Web*.

Daumé III, Hal. 2007. Frustratingly easy domain adaptation. Pages 256–263 of: *Proceedings of the 45th Annual Meeting of the Association for Computational Linguistics*.

Davis, Jesse, and Domingos, Pedro. 2009. Deep transfer via second-order Markov logic. Pages 217–224 of: *Proceedings of the 26th International Conference on Machine Learning*.

Dekel, Ofer, Long, Philip M., and Singer, Yoram. 2006. Online multitask learning. Pages 453–467 of: *Proceedings of the 19th Annual Conference on Learning Theory*.

Dekel, Ofer, Long, Philip M., and Singer, Yoram. 2007. Online learning of multiple tasks with a shared loss. *Journal of Machine Learning Research*, **8**, 2233–2264.

Dempster, A. P., Laird, N. M., and Rubin, D. B. 1977. Maximum likelihood from incomplete data via the EM algorithm. *Journal of the Royal Statistical Society*, **39**(1), 1–38.

Deng, Wan-Yu, Zheng, Qing-Hua, and Wang, Zhong-Min. 2014. Cross-person activity recognition using reduced kernel extreme learning machine. *Neural Networks*, **53**, 1–7.

Denton, Emily L., Chintala, Soumith, Fergus, Rob, et al. 2015. Deep generative image models using a Laplacian pyramid of adversarial networks. Pages 1486–1494 of: *Advances in Neural Information Processing Systems*.

Devin, Coline, Gupta, Abhishek, Darrell, Trevor, Abbeel, Pieter, and Levine, Sergey. 2017. Learning modular neural network policies for multi-task and multi-robot transfer. Pages 2169–2176 of: *Proceedings of IEEE International Conference on Robotics and Automation*.

Devlin, Jacob, Chang, Ming-Wei, Lee, Kenton, and Toutanova, Kristina. 2018. BERT: Pre-training of deep bidirectional transformers for language understanding. *CoRR*, **abs/1810.04805**.

Dietterich, Thomas G., Lathrop, Richard H., and Lozano-Pérez, Tomás. 1997. Solving the multiple instance problem with axis-parallel rectangles. *Artificial Intelligence*, **89**(1–2), 31–71.

Donahue, Jeff, Hoffman, Judy, Rodner, Erik, Saenko, Kate, and Darrell, Trevor. 2013. Semi-supervised domain adaptation with instance constraints. Pages 668–675 of: *Proceedings of IEEE Conference on Computer Vision and Pattern Recognition*.

Donahue, Jeff, Jia, Yangqing, Vinyals, Oriol, et al. 2014. Decaf: A deep convolutional activation feature for generic visual recognition. Pages 647–655 of: *Proceedings of the 31th International Conference on Machine Learning*.

Donahue, Jeff, Krähenbühl, Philipp, and Darrell, Trevor. 2016. Adversarial feature learning. *CoRR*, **abs/1605.09782**.

Dong, Daxiang, Wu, Hua, He, Wei, Yu, Dianhai, and Wang, Haifeng. 2015. Multi-task learning for multiple language translation. Pages 1723–1732 of: *Proceedings of the 53rd Annual Meeting of the Association for Computational Linguistics and the 7th International Joint Conference on Natural Language Processing*.

Dönnes, Pierre, and Elofsson, Arne. 2002. Prediction of MHC Class I binding peptides, using SVMHC. *BMC Bioinformatics*, **3**, 25.

Dou, Qi, Ouyang, Cheng, Chen, Cheng, Chen, Hao, and Heng, Pheng-Ann. 2018. Unsupervised cross-modality domain adaptation of ConvNets for biomedical image segmentations with adversarial loss. Pages 691–697 of: *Proceedings of the Twenty-Seventh International Joint Conference on Artificial Intelligence*.

Drummond, Chris. 2002. Accelerating reinforcement learning by composing solutions of automatically identified subtasks. *Journal of Artificial Intelligence Research*, **16**, 59–104.

Duan, Lixin, Tsang, Ivor W., Xu, Dong, and Maybank, Stephen J. 2009. Domain transfer SVM for video concept detection. Pages 1375–1381 of: *Proceedings of IEEE Conference on Computer Vision and Pattern Recognition*.

Duan, Lixin, Tsang, Ivor W., and Xu, Dong. 2012a. Domain transfer multiple kernel learning. *IEEE Transactions on Pattern Analysis and Machine Intelligence*, **34**(3), 465–479.

Duan, Lixin, Xu, Dong, and Tsang, Ivor W. 2012b. Learning with augmented features for heterogeneous domain adaptation. Pages 711–718 of: *Proceedings of International Conference on Machine Learning*.

Duan, Lixin, Xu, Dong, Tsang, Ivor Wai-Hung, and Luo, Jiebo. 2012c. Visual event recognition in videos by learning from web data. *IEEE Transactions on Pattern Analysis and Machine Intelligence*, **34**(9), 1667–1680.

Dumoulin, Vincent, Belghazi, Ishmael, Poole, Ben, et al. 2016. Adversarially learned inference. *CoRR*, **abs/1606.00704**.

Duong, Long, Cohn, Trevor, Bird, Steven, and Cook, Paul. 2015. Low resource dependency parsing: Cross-lingual parameter sharing in a neural network parser. Pages 845–850 of: *Proceedings of the 53rd Annual Meeting of the Association for Computational Linguistics and the 7th International Joint Conference on Natural Language Processing*.

Dwork, Cynthia. 2008. Differential privacy: A survey of results. Pages 1–19 of: *Proceedings of the 5th Annual Conference on Theory and Applications of Models of Computation*.

Dwork, Cynthia, and Roth, Aaron. 2014. The algorithmic foundations of differential privacy. *Foundations and Trends in Theoretical Computer Science*, **9**(3–4), 211–407.

Dwork, Cynthia, Kenthapadi, Krishnaram, McSherry, Frank, Mironov, Ilya, and Naor, Moni. 2006a. Our data, ourselves: Privacy via distributed noise generation. Pages 486–503 of: *Proceedings of the 25th Annual International Conference on the Theory and Applications of Cryptographic Techniques.*

Dwork, Cynthia, McSherry, Frank, Nissim, Kobbi, and Smith, Adam D. 2006b. Calibrating noise to sensitivity in private data analysis. Pages 265–284 of: *Proceedings of the 3rd Theory of Cryptography Conference.*

Ellis, Henry Carlton. 1965. *The Transfer of Learning.* MacMillan.

Elman, Jeffrey L. 1993. Learning and development in neural networks: The importance of starting small. *Cognition,* **48**(1), 71–99.

Emekçi, Fatih, Sahin, Ozgur D., Agrawal, Divyakant, and El Abbadi, Amr. 2007. Privacy preserving decision tree learning over multiple parties. *Data and Knowledge Engineering,* **63**(2), 348–361.

Esteva, Andre, Kuprel, Brett, Novoa, Roberto A., et al. 2017. Dermatologist-level classification of skin cancer with deep neural networks. *Nature,* **542**(7639), 115–118.

Evgeniou, A., and Pontil, Massimiliano. 2007. Multi-task feature learning. *Advances in Neural Information Processing Systems,* **19**, 41.

Evgeniou, Theodoros, and Pontil, Massimiliano. 2004. Regularized multi-task learning. Pages 109–117 of: *Proceedings of the 10th ACM SIGKDD International Conference on Knowledge Discovery and Data Mining.*

Evgeniou, Theodoros, Micchelli, Charles A., and Pontil, Massimiliano. 2005. Learning multiple tasks with Kernel methods. *Journal of Machine Learning Research,* **6**, 615–637.

Fan, Jianqing, and Li, Runze. 2006. Statistical challenges with high dimensionality: Feature selection in knowledge discovery. *arXiv,* arXiv:math/0602133.

Fan, Xing, Monti, Emilio, Mathias, Lambert, and Dreyer, Markus. 2017. Transfer learning for neural semantic parsing. Pages 48–56 of: *Proceedings of the 2nd Workshop on Representation Learning for NLP.*

Fang, Meng, and Cohn, Trevor. 2017. Model transfer for tagging low-resource languages using a bilingual dictionary. Pages 587–593 of: *Proceedings of the 55th Annual Meeting of the Association for Computational Linguistics.*

Fang, Meng, and Tao, Dacheng. 2015. Active multi-task learning via bandits. Pages 505–513 of: *Proceedings of the 2015 SIAM International Conference on Data Mining.*

Fang, Meng, Yin, Jie, and Zhu, Xingquan. 2013. Transfer learning across networks for collective classification. Pages 161–170 of: *Proceedings of IEEE International Conference on Data Mining.*

Fang, Meng, Yin, Jie, Zhu, Xingquan, and Zhang, Chengqi. 2015. TrGraph: Cross-network transfer learning via common signature subgraphs. *IEEE Transactions on Knowledge and Data Engineering,* **27**(9), 2536–2549.

Ferguson, Kimberly, and Mahadevan, Sridhar. 2006. Proto-transfer learning in Markov decision processes using spectral methods. *Proceedings of ICML Workshop on Transfer Learning.*

Ferns, Norm, Panangaden, Prakash, and Precup, Doina. 2004. Metrics for finite Markov decision processes. Pages 162–169 of: *Proceedings of the 20th Conference in Uncertainty in Artificial Intelligence.*

Feurer, Matthias, Klein, Aaron, Eggensperger, Katharina, et al. 2015. Efficient and robust automated machine learning. Pages 2962–2970 of: *Advances in Neural Information Processing Systems 28.*

Firat, Orhan, Sankaran, Baskaran, Al-Onaizan, Yaser, et al. 2016. Zero-resource translation with multi-lingual neural machine translation. Pages 268–277 of: *Proceedings of the 2016 Conference on Empirical Methods in Natural Language Processing.*

Fong, Pui Kuen, and Weber-Jahnke, Jens H. 2012. Privacy preserving decision tree learning using unrealized data sets. *IEEE Transactions on Knowledge and Data Engineering*, **24**(2), 353–364.

Forbus, Kenneth D., Gentner, Dedre, Markman, Arthur B., and Ferguson, Ronald W. 1998. Analogy just looks like high level perception: Why a domain-general approach to analogical mapping is right. *Journal of Experimental and Theoretical Artificial Intelligence*, **10**(2), 231–257.

Friedman, Jerome, Hastie, Trevor, and Tibshirani, Robert. 2001. *The Elements of Statistical Learning*. Springer.

Frome, Andrea, Corrado, Gregory S., Shlens, Jonathon, et al. 2013. DeViSE: A deep visual-semantic embedding model. Pages 2121–2129 of: *Advances in Neural Information Processing Systems*.

Ganguly, Soumyajit, and Pudi, Vikram. 2017. Paper2vec: Combining graph and text information for scientific paper representation. Pages 383–395 of: *Proceedings of European Conference on Information Retrieval*.

Ganin, Yaroslav, and Lempitsky, Victor. 2015. Unsupervised domain adaptation by backpropagation. Pages 1180–1189 of: *Proceedings of the 32nd International Conference on Machine Learning*.

Ganin, Yaroslav, Ustinova, Evgeniya, Ajakan, Hana, et al. 2016. Domain-adversarial training of neural networks. *Journal of Machine Learning Research*, **17**, 2096–2030.

Gao, Chen, Chen, Xiangning, Feng, Fuli, et al. 2019. Cross-domain recommendation without sharing user-relevant data. Pages 491–502 of: *Proceedings of the 2019 World Wide Web Conference on World Wide Web*.

Gao, Sheng, Luo, Hao, Chen, Da, et al. 2013. Cross-domain recommendation via cluster-level latent factor model. Pages 161–176 of: *Proceedings of the European Conference on Machine Learning and Practice of Knowledge Discovery in Databases*.

Gašić, M., Kim, Dongho, Tsiakoulis, Pirros, and Young, Steve. 2015a. Distributed dialogue policies for multi-domain statistical dialogue management. Pages 5371–5375 of: *Proceedings of IEEE International Conference on Acoustics, Speech and Signal Processing*.

Gašić, M., Mrkšic, N., Barahona, L. Rojas, et al. 2015b. Multi-agent learning in multi-domain spoken dialogue systems. In: *Proceedings of NIPS workshop on Spoken Language Understanding and Interaction*.

Gašić, Milica, Breslin, Catherine, Henderson, Matthew, et al. 2013. POMDP-based dialogue manager adaptation to extended domains. In: *Proceedings of the 14th Annual Meeting of the Special Interest Group on Discourse and Dialogue*.

Gašić, Milica, Kim, Dongho, Tsiakoulis, Pirros, et al. 2014. Incremental on-line adaptation of POMDP-based dialogue managers to extended domains. Pages 140–144 of: *Proceedings of the 15th Annual Conference of the International Speech Communication Association*.

Gašić, Milica, Mrkšic, Nikola, Su, Pei-hao, et al. 2015c. Policy committee for adaptation in multi-domain spoken dialogue systems. Pages 806–812 of: *Proceedings of 2015 IEEE Workshop on Automatic Speech Recognition and Understanding*.

Gatys, Leon A., Ecker, Alexander S., and Bethge, Matthias. 2016. Image style transfer using convolutional neural networks. Pages 2414–2423 of: *Proceedings of IEEE Conference on Computer Vision and Pattern Recognition*.

Genevay, Aude, and Laroche, Romain. 2016. Transfer learning for user adaptation in spoken dialogue systems. Pages 975–983 of: *Proceedings of the 2016 International Conference on Autonomous Agents and Multiagent Systems*.

Germain, Pascal, Habrard, Amaury, Laviolette, François, and Morvant, Emilie. 2013. A PAC-Bayesian approach for domain adaptation with specialization to linear classifiers. Pages 738–746 of: *Proceedings of the 30th International Conference on Machine Learning*.

Getoor, Lise, and Taskar, Ben. 2007. *Introduction to Statistical Relational Learning*. MIT Press.

Ghifary, Muhammad, Bastiaan Kleijn, W., Zhang, Mengjie, and Balduzzi, David. 2015. Domain generalization for object recognition with multi-task autoencoders. Pages 2551–2559 of: *Proceedings of the IEEE International Conference on Computer Vision*.

Ghifary, Muhammad, Kleijn, W. Bastiaan, Zhang, Mengjie, Balduzzi, David, and Li, Wen. 2016. Deep reconstruction-classification networks for unsupervised domain adaptation. Pages 597–613 of: *Proceedings of European Conference on Computer Vision*.

Gillick, Dan, Brunk, Cliff, Vinyals, Oriol, and Subramanya, Amarnag. 2016. Multilingual language processing from bytes. Pages 1296–1306 of: *Proceedings of the 2016 Conference of the North American Chapter of the Association for Computational Linguistics: Human Language Technologies*.

Giorgi, John M., and Bader, Gary. 2018. Transfer learning for biomedical named entity recognition with neural networks. *Bioinformatics*, **34**(23), 4087–4094.

Girshick, Ross, Donahue, Jeff, Darrell, Trevor, and Malik, Jitendra. 2014. Rich feature hierarchies for accurate object detection and semantic segmentation. Pages 580–587 of: *Proceedings of the IEEE Conference on Computer Vision and Pattern Recognition*.

Glorot, Xavier, and Bengio, Yoshua. 2010. Understanding the difficulty of training deep feedforward neural networks. Pages 249–256 of: *Proceedings of International Conference on Artificial Intelligence and Statistics*.

Glorot, Xavier, Bordes, Antoine, and Bengio, Yoshua. 2011. Domain adaptation for large-scale sentiment classification: A deep learning approach. Pages 513–520 of: *Proceedings of the 28th International Conference on Machine Learning*.

Gong, Boqing, Shi, Yuan, Sha, Fei, and Grauman, Kristen. 2012a. Geodesic flow kernel for unsupervised domain adaptation. Pages 2066–2073 of: *Proceedings of IEEE Conference on Computer Vision and Pattern Recognition*.

Gong, Pinghua, Ye, Jieping, and Zhang, Changshui. 2012b. Robust multi-task feature learning. Pages 895–903 of: *Proceedings of the 18th ACM SIGKDD International Conference on Knowledge Discovery and Data Mining*.

Gong, Pinghua, Ye, Jieping, and Zhang, Changshui. 2013. Multi-stage multi-task feature learning. *Journal of Machine Learning Research*, **14**, 2979–3010.

Goodfellow, Ian, Pouget-Abadie, Jean, Mirza, Mehdi, et al. 2014. Generative adversarial nets. Pages 2672–2680 of: *Advances in Neural Information Processing Systems*.

Gopalan, Raghuraman, Li, Ruonan, and Chellappa, Rama. 2011. Domain adaptation for object recognition: An unsupervised approach. Pages 999–1006 of: *Proceedings of IEEE International Conference on Computer Vision*.

Gopalan, Raghuraman, Li, Ruonan, and Chellappa, Rama. 2014. Unsupervised adaptation across domain shifts by generating intermediate data representations. *IEEE Transactions on Pattern Analysis and Machine Intelligence*, **36**(11), 2288–2302.

Görnitz, Nico, Widmer, Christian, Zeller, Georg, et al. 2011. Hierarchical multitask structured output learning for large-scale sequence segmentation. Pages 2690–2698 of: *Advances in Neural Information Processing Systems*.

Gouws, Stephan, Bengio, Yoshua, and Corrado, Greg. 2015. BilBOWA: Fast bilingual distributed representations without word alignments. Pages 748–756 of: *Proceedings of the 32nd International Conference on Machine Learning*.

Gretton, Arthur, Bousquet, Olivier, Smola, Alex, and Schölkopf, Bernhard. 2005. Measuring statistical dependence with Hilbert-Schmidt norms. Pages 63–77 of: *Proceedings of International Conference on Algorithmic Learning Theory.*

Gretton, Arthur, Borgwardt, Karsten M., Rasch, Malte, Schölkopf, Bernhard, and Smola, Alex J. 2007. A kernel method for the two-sample-problem. Pages 513–520 of: *Advances in Neural Information Processing Systems.*

Gretton, Arthur, Sejdinovic, Dino, Strathmann, Heiko, et al. 2012. Optimal kernel choice for large-scale two-sample tests. Pages 1214–1222 of: *Advances in Neural Information Processing Systems.*

Guo, Bin, Li, Jing, Zheng, Vincent W., Wang, Zhu, and Yu, Zhiwen. 2018a. CityTransfer: Transferring inter- and intra-city knowledge for chain store site recommendation based on multi-source urban data. Pages 135:1–135:23 of: *Proceeding of the 2018 ACM International Joint Conference on Pervasive and Ubiquitous Computing.*

Guo, Jiang, Che, Wanxiang, Wang, Haifeng, and Liu, Ting. 2016a. Exploiting multi-typed treebanks for parsing with deep multi-task learning. *CoRR*, **abs/1606.01161.**

Guo, Jiang, Che, Wanxiang, Wang, Haifeng, and Liu, Ting. 2016b. A universal framework for inductive transfer parsing across multi-typed treebanks. Pages 12–22 of: *Proceedings of the 26th International Conference on Computational Linguistics.*

Guo, Xiawei, Yao, Quanming, Tu, Wei-Wei, et al. 2018b. Privacy-preserving transfer learning for knowledge sharing. *CoRR*, **abs/1811.09491.**

Guo, Zhenyu, and Wang, Z. Jane. 2013. Cross-domain object recognition via input-output Kernel analysis. *IEEE Transactions on Image Processing*, **22**(8), 3108–3119.

Gupta, Sunil Kumar, Phung, Dinh, Adams, Brett, Tran, Truyen, and Venkatesh, Svetha. 2010. Nonnegative shared subspace learning and its application to social media retrieval. Pages 1169–1178 of: *Proceedings of the 16th ACM SIGKDD International Conference on Knowledge Discovery and Data Mining.*

Haeberlen, Andreas, Flannery, Eliot, Ladd, Andrew M., et al. 2004. Practical robust localization over large-scale 802.11 wireless networks. Pages 70–84 of: *Proceedings of the 10th Annual International Conference on Mobile Computing and Networking.*

Ham, Ji Hun, Lee, Daniel D., and Saul, Lawrence K. 2003. Learning high dimensional correspondences from low dimensional manifolds. *Proceedings of ICML Workshop on the Continuum from Labeled to Unlabeled Data in Machine Learning and Data Mining.*

Hamm, Jihun, Cao, Yingjun, and Belkin, Mikhail. 2016. Learning privately from multiparty data. Pages 555–563 of: *Proceedings of the 33rd International Conference on Machine Learning.*

Hammerla, Nils Y., Halloran, Shane, and Plötz, Thomas. 2016. Deep, convolutional, and recurrent models for human activity recognition using wearables. Pages 1533–1540 of: *Proceedings of the Twenty-Fifth International Joint Conference on Artificial Intelligence.*

Han, Jiawei, and Kamber, Micheline. 2000. *Data Mining: Concepts and Techniques.* Morgan Kaufmann.

Han, Lei, and Zhang, Yu. 2015a. Learning multi-level task groups in multi-task learning. Pages 2638–2644 of: *Proceedings of the 29th AAAI Conference on Artificial Intelligence.*

Han, Lei, and Zhang, Yu. 2015b. Learning tree structure in multi-task learning. *Proceedings of the 21st ACM SIGKDD Conference on Knowledge Discovery and Data Mining.*

Han, Lei, and Zhang, Yu. 2016. Multi-stage multi-task learning with reduced rank. Pages 1638–1644 of: *Proceedings of the 30th AAAI Conference on Artificial Intelligence.*

Han, Lei, Zhang, Yu, Song, Guojie, and Xie, Kunqing. 2014. Encoding tree sparsity in multi-task learning: A probabilistic framework. Pages 1854–1860 of: *Proceedings of the 28th AAAI Conference on Artificial Intelligence.*

Harris, Zellig S. 1954. Distributional structure. *Word*, **10**(2–3), 146–162.

Hashimoto, Kazuma, Tsuruoka, Yoshimasa, Socher, Richard, et al. 2017. A joint many-task model: Growing a neural network for multiple NLP tasks. Pages 1923–1933 of: *Proceedings of the 2017 Conference on Empirical Methods in Natural Language Processing*.

Hausknecht, Matthew J., and Stone, Peter. 2015. Deep recurrent Q-learning for partially observable MDPs. *CoRR*, **abs/1507.06527**.

He, Jia, Liu, Rui, Zhuang, Fuzhen, et al. 2018a. A general cross-domain recommendation framework via Bayesian neural network. Pages 1001–1006 of: *Proceedings of the 2018 IEEE International Conference on Data Mining*.

He, Jingrui, and Lawrence, Rick. 2011. A graph-based framework for multi-task multi-view learning. Pages 25–32 of: *Proceedings of the 28th International Conference on Machine Learning*.

He, Kaiming, Zhang, Xiangyu, Ren, Shaoqing, and Jian, Sun. 2016. Identity mappings in deep residual networks. Pages 630–645 of: *European Conference on Computer Vision*.

He, Kaiming, Girshick, Ross B., and Dollár, Piotr. 2018b. Rethinking ImageNet pre-training. *CoRR*, **abs/1811.08883**.

He, Yulan, and Young, Steve. 2006. Spoken language understanding using the hidden vector state model. *Speech Communication*, **48**(3), 262–275.

Henderson, Matthew, Gašić, Milica, Thomson, Blaise, et al. 2012. Discriminative spoken language understanding using word confusion networks. Pages 176–181 of: *Proceedings of IEEE Spoken Language Technology Workshop*.

Henderson, Matthew, Thomson, Blaise, and Young, Steve. 2014. Word-based dialog state tracking with recurrent neural networks. Pages 292–299 of: *Proceedings of the 15th Annual Meeting of the Special Interest Group on Discourse and Dialogue*.

Hengst, Bernhard. 2002. Discovering hierarchy in reinforcement learning with HEXQ. Pages 243–250 of: *Proceedings of the Nineteenth International Conference on Machine Learning*.

Hernández-Lobato, Daniel, and Hernández-Lobato, José Miguel. 2013. Learning feature selection dependencies in multi-task learning. Pages 746–754 of: *Advances in Neural Information Processing Systems*.

Hernández-Lobato, Daniel, Hernández-Lobato, José Miguel, and Ghahramani, Zoubin. 2015. A probabilistic model for dirty multi-task feature selection. Pages 1073–1082 of: *Proceedings of the 32nd International Conference on Machine Learning*.

Hinrichs, Thomas R., and Forbus, Kenneth D. 2011. Transfer learning through analogy in games. *AI Magazine*, **32**(1), 70–83.

Hoffman, Judy, Rodner, Erik, Donahue, Jeff, Saenko, Kate, and Darrell, Trevor. 2013. Efficient learning of domain-invariant image representations. *CoRR*, **abs/1301.3224**.

Hoffman, Judy, Guadarrama, Sergio, Tzeng, Eric S., et al. 2014. LSDA: Large scale detection through adaptation. Pages 3536–3544 of: *Advances in Neural Information Processing Systems*.

Hofmann, Thomas. 1999. Probabilistic latent semantic analysis. Pages 289–296 of: *Proceedings of the Fifteenth Conference on Uncertainty in Artificial Intelligence*.

Holyoak, Keith J., and Thagard, Paul. 1989. Analogical mapping by constraint satisfaction. *Cognitive Science*, **13**(3), 295–355.

Hu, Guangneng, Zhang, Yu, and Yang, Qiang. 2018. CoNet: Collaborative cross networks for cross-domain recommendation. Pages 667–676 of: *Proceedings of the 27th ACM International Conference on Information and Knowledge Management*.

Hu, Guangneng, Zhang, Yu, and Yang, Qiang. 2019. Transfer meets hybrid: A synthetic approach for cross-domain collaborative filtering with text. Pages 2822–2829 of: *Proceedings of the Web Conference*.

Hu, Minqing, and Liu, Bing. 2004. Mining and summarizing customer reviews. Pages 168–177 of: *Proceedings of the tenth ACM SIGKDD International Conference on Knowledge Discovery and Data Mining.*

Huang, Jiayuan, Smola, Alexander J., Gretton, Arthur, Borgwardt, Karsten M., and Schölkopf, Bernhard. 2006. Correcting sample selection bias by unlabeled data. Pages 601–608 of: *Advances in Neural Information Processing Systems.*

Huang, Jui-Ting, Li, Jinyu, Yu, Dong, Deng, Li, and Gong, Yifan. 2013. Cross-language knowledge transfer using multilingual deep neural network with shared hidden layers. Pages 7304–7308 of: *Proceedings of the IEEE International Conference on Acoustics, Speech and Signal Processing.*

Huber, Peter J. 1964. Robust estimation of a location parameter. *The Annals of Mathematical Statistics*, **35**(1), 73–101.

Isola, Phillip, Zhu, Jun-Yan, Zhou, Tinghui, and Efros, Alexei A. 2017. Image-to-image translation with conditional adversarial networks. Pages 1125–1134 of: *Proceedings of the IEEE Conference on Computer Vision and Pattern Recognition.*

Jacob, Laurent, and Vert, Jean-Philippe. 2007. Efficient peptide-MHC-I binding prediction for alleles with few known binders. *Bioinformatics*, **24**(3), 358–366.

Jacob, Laurent, Bach, Francis R., and Vert, Jean-Philippe. 2008. Clustered multi-task learning: A convex formulation. Pages 745–752 of: *Advances in Neural Information Processing Systems.*

Jagannathan, Geetha, Pillaipakkamnatt, Krishnan, and Wright, Rebecca N. 2012. A practical differentially private random decision tree classifier. *Transactions on Data Privacy*, **5**(1), 273–295.

Jalali, Ali, Ravikumar, Pradeep, Sanghavi, Sujay, and Ruan, Chao. 2010. A dirty model for multi-task learning. Pages 964–972 of: *Advances in Neural Information Processing Systems 23.*

Jean, Neal, Burke, Marshall, Xie, Michael, et al. 2016. Combining satellite imagery and machine learning to predict poverty. *Science*, **353**(6301), 790–794.

Jeffreys, Harold. 1946. An invariant form for the prior probability in estimation problems. *Proceedings of the Royal Society of London. Series A, Mathematical and Physical Sciences*, **86**(1007).

Jeong, Minwoo, and Lee, Gary Geunbae. 2009. Multi-domain spoken language understanding with transfer learning. *Speech Communication*, **51**(5), 412–424.

Jernite, Yacine, Bowman, Samuel R., and Sontag, David. 2017. Discourse-based objectives for fast unsupervised sentence representation learning. *CoRR*, **abs/1705.00557**.

Ji, Zhanglong, Jiang, Xiaoqian, Wang, Shuang, Xiong, Li, and Ohno-Machado, Lucila. 2014. Differentially private distributed logistic regression using private and public data. *BMC Medical Genomics*, **7**(1), S14.

Jia, Yangqing, Salzmann, Mathieu, and Darrell, Trevor. 2010. Factorized latent spaces with structured sparsity. Pages 982–990 of: *Advances in Neural Information Processing Systems.*

Jiang, Jing. 2009. Multi-task transfer learning for weakly-supervised relation extraction. Pages 1012–1020 of: *Proceedings of the 47th Annual Meeting of the Association for Computational Linguistics and the 4th International Joint Conference on Natural Language Processing of the AFNLP.*

Jiang, Jing, and Zhai, Chengxiang. 2007. Instance weighting for domain adaptation in NLP. Pages 264–271 for: *Proceedings of the 45th Annual Meeting of the Association of Computational Linguistics.*

Jiang, Wei, Zavesky, Eric, Chang, Shih-Fu, and Loui, Alex. 2008. Cross-domain learning methods for high-level visual concept classification. Pages 161–164 of: *Proceedings of the 15th IEEE International Conference on Image Processing*.

Jie, Luo, Tommasi, Tatiana, and Caputo, Barbara. 2011. Multiclass transfer learning from unconstrained priors. Pages 1863–1870 of: *Proceedings of IEEE International Conference on Computer Vision*.

Joachims, Thorsten. 1999. Transductive inference for text classification using support vector machines. Pages 200–209 of: *Proceedings of the Sixteenth International Conference on Machine Learning*.

Johnson, Justin, Alahi, Alexandre, and Fei-Fei, Li. 2016a. Perceptual losses for real-time style transfer and super-resolution. Pages 694–711 of: *Proceedings of European Conference on Computer Vision*.

Johnson, Melvin, Schuster, Mike, Le, Quoc V., et al. 2016b. Google's multilingual neural machine translation system: Enabling zero-shot translation. *CoRR*, **abs/1611.04558**.

Joshi, Chaitanya K., Mi, Fei, and Faltings, Boi. 2017. Personalization in goal-oriented dialog. *CoRR*, **abs/1706.07503**.

Juba, Brendan. 2006. Estimating relatedness via data compression. Pages 441–448 of: *Proceedings of the 23rd International Conference on Machine Learning*.

Kakade, Sham M., Shalev-Shwartz, Shai, and Tewari, Ambuj. 2012. Regularization techniques for learning with matrices. *Journal of Machine Learning Research*, **13**, 1865–1890.

Kalousis, Alexandros, Prados, Julien, and Hilario, Melanie. 2007. Stability of feature selection algorithms: A study on high-dimensional spaces. *Knowledge and Information Systems*, **12**(1), 95–116.

Kanagawa, Heishiro, Kobayashi, Hayato, Shimizu, Nobuyuki, Tagami, Yukihiro, and Suzuki, Taiji. 2019. Cross-domain recommendation via deep domain adaptation. Pages 20–29 of: *Proceedings of the 41st European Conference on Information Retrieval*.

Kanamori, Takafumi, Hido, Shohei, and Sugiyama, Masashi. 2009. A least-squares approach to direct importance estimation. *Journal of Machine Learning Research*, **10**, 1391–1445.

Kang, Zhuoliang, Grauman, Kristen, and Sha, Fei. 2011. Learning with whom to share in multi-task feature learning. Pages 521–528 of: *Proceedings of the 28th International Conference on Machine Learning*.

Karpathy, Andrej, Toderici, George, Shetty, Sanketh, et al. 2014. Large-scale video classification with convolutional neural networks. Pages 1725–1732 of: *Proceedings of the IEEE Conference on Computer Vision and Pattern Recognition*.

Kashima, Hisashi, Yamanishi, Yoshihiro, Kato, Tsuyoshi, Sugiyama, Masashi, and Tsuda, Koji. 2009. Simultaneous inference of biological networks of multiple species from genome-wide data and evolutionary information: A semi-supervised approach. *Bioinformatics*, **25**(22), 2962–2968.

Katiyar, Arzoo, and Cardie, Claire. 2017. Going out on a limb: Joint extraction of entity mentions and relations without dependency trees. Pages 917–928 of: *Proceedings of the 55th Annual Meeting of the Association for Computational Linguistics*.

Kato, Tsuyoshi, Kashima, Hisashi, Sugiyama, Masashi, and Asai, Kiyoshi. 2007. Multi-task learning via conic programming. Pages 737–744 of: *Advances in Neural Information Processing Systems*.

Kato, Tsuyoshi, Kashima, Hisashi, Sugiyama, Masashi, and Asai, Kiyoshi. 2010a. Conic Programming for multitask learning. *IEEE Transactions on Knowledge and Data Engineering*, **22**(7), 957–968.

Kato, Tsuyoshi, Okada, Kinya, Kashima, Hisashi, and Sugiyama, Masashi. 2010b. A transfer learning approach and selective integration of multiple types of assays for biological network inference. *International Journal of Knowledge Discovery in Bioinformatics*, **1**(1), 66–80.

Keogh, Eamonn J., and Pazzani, Michael J. 2000. Scaling up dynamic time warping for datamining applications. Pages 285–289 of: *Proceedings of the Sixth ACM SIGKDD International Conference on Knowledge Discovery and Data Mining*.

Kermany, Daniel S., Goldbaum, Michael, Cai, Wenjia, et al. 2018. Identifying medical diagnoses and treatable diseases by image-based deep learning. *Cell*, **172**(5), 1122–1131.

Khan, Md Abdullah Al Hafiz, Roy, Nirmalya, and Misra, Archan. 2018. Scaling human activity recognition via deep learning-based domain adaptation. Pages 1–9 for: *Proceedings of IEEE International Conference on Pervasive Computing and Communications*.

Khosla, Aditya, Zhou, Tinghui, Malisiewicz, Tomasz, Efros, Alexei A., and Torralba, Antonio. 2012. Undoing the damage of dataset bias. Pages 158–171 of: *Proceedings of European Conference on Computer Vision*.

Kim, Edward, Corte-Real, Miguel, and Baloch, Zubair. 2016. A deep semantic mobile application for thyroid cytopathology. *Proceedings of Medical Imaging 2016: PACS and Imaging Informatics: Next Generation and Innovations*.

Kim, Taeksoo, Cha, Moonsu, Kim, Hyunsoo, Lee, Jung Kwon, and Kim, Jiwon. 2017. Learning to discover cross-domain relations with generative adversarial networks. Pages 1857–1865 of: *Proceedings of International Conference on Machine Learning*.

Kim, Yoon. 2014. Convolutional neural networks for sentence classification. Pages 1746–1751 of: *Proceedings of the 2014 Conference on Empirical Methods in Natural Language Processing*.

Kiros, Ryan, Zhu, Yukun, Salakhutdinov, Ruslan R., et al. 2015. Skip-thought vectors. Pages 3294–3302 of: *Advances in Neural Information Processing Systems*.

Kjaergaard, Mikkel Baun, and Munk, Carsten Valdemar. 2008. Hyperbolic location fingerprinting: A calibration-free solution for handling differences in signal strength. Pages 110–116 of: *Proceedings of the Sixth IEEE International Conference on Pervasive Computing and Communications*.

Kober, Jens, Öztop, Erhan, and Peters, Jan. 2011. Reinforcement learning to adjust robot movements to new situations. Pages 2650–2655 of: *Proceedings of the 22nd International Joint Conference on Artificial Intelligence*.

Koch, Gregory. 2015. *Siamese Neural Networks for One-Shot Image Recognition*. M.Phil. thesis, University of Toronto.

Kolar, Mladen, Lafferty, John D., and Wasserman, Larry A. 2011. Union support recovery in multi-task learning. *Journal of Machine Learning Research*, **12**, 2415–2435.

Koller, Daphne, and Friedman, Nir. 2009. *Probabilistic Graphical Models: Principles and Techniques*. MIT Press.

Kolodner, Janet. 1993. *Case-Based Reasoning*. Morgan Kaufmann.

Konidaris, George, and Barto, Andrew G. 2007. Building portable options: skill transfer in reinforcement learning. Pages 895–900 of: *Proceedings of the 20th International Joint Conference on Artificial Intelligence*.

Kotthoff, Lars, Thornton, Chris, Hoos, Holger H., Hutter, Frank, and Leyton-Brown, Kevin. 2017. Auto-WEKA 2.0: Automatic model selection and hyperparameter optimization in WEKA. *Journal of Machine Learning Research*, **18**, 25:1–25:5.

Krallinger, Martin, and Valencia, Alfonso. 2005. Text-mining and information-retrieval services for molecular biology. *Genome Biology*, **6**, 224.

Krishnan, P., Krishnakumar, A. S., Ju, Wen-Hua, Mallows, Colin, and Ganu, Sachin. 2004. A system for LEASE: Location estimation assisted by stationery emitters for indoor RF wireless networks. In: *Proceedings of IEEE International Conference on Computer Communications*.

Krizhevsky, Alex, and Hinton, Geoffrey. 2009. *Learning Multiple Layers of Features from Tiny Images*. Computer Science Department, University of Toronto, Technical Report.

Kulis, Brian, Saenko, Kate, and Darrell, Trevor. 2011. What you saw is not what you get: Domain adaptation using asymmetric kernel transforms. Pages 1785–1792 of: *Proceedings of the IEEE Conference on Computer Vision and Pattern Recognition*.

Kullback, S., and Leibler, R. A. 1951. On information and sufficiency. *Annals of Mathematical Statistics*, **22**(1), 79–86.

Kumar, Abhishek, and Daumé III, Hal. 2012. Learning task grouping and overlap in multitask learning. *Proceedings of the 29th International Conference on Machine Learning*.

Kumaraswamy, Raksha, Odom, Phillip, Kersting, Kristian, Leake, David, and Natarajan, Sriraam. 2015. Transfer learning via relational type matching. Pages 811–816 of: *Proceedings of IEEE International Conference on Data Mining*.

Kuzborskij, Ilja, and Orabona, Francesco. 2013. Stability and hypothesis transfer learning. Pages 942–950 of: *Proceedings of the 30th International Conference on Machine Learning*.

Ladd, Andrew M., Bekris, Kostas E., Rudys, Algis, et al. 2002. Robotics-based location sensing using wireless Ethernet. Pages 227–238 of: *Proceedings of the 8th Annual International Conference on Mobile Computing and Networking*.

Lafferty, John D., and Zhai, ChengXiang. 2001. Document language models, query models, and risk minimization for information retrieval. Pages 111–119 of: Croft, W. Bruce, Harper, David J., Kraft, Donald H., and Zobel, Justin (eds.), *SIGIR 2001: Proceedings of the 24th Annual International ACM SIGIR Conference on Research and Development in Information Retrieval*.

Lai, Tze Leung, and Robbins, Herbert. 1985. Asymptotically efficient adaptive allocation rules. *Advances in Applied Mathematics*, **6**(1), 4–22.

Lake, B. M., Salakhutdinov, R., and Tenenbaum, J. B. 2015. Human-level concept learning through probabilistic program induction. *Science*, **350**(6266), 1332–1338.

Lake, Brenden, Salakhutdinov, Ruslan, Gross, Jason, and Tenenbaum, Joshua. 2011. One shot learning of simple visual concepts. Pages 2568–2573 for: *Proceedings of the Annual Meeting of the Cognitive Science Society*.

Lake, Brenden M., Salakhutdinov, Ruslan, and Tenenbaum, Joshua B. 2013. One-shot learning by inverting a compositional causal process. Pages 2526–2534 of: *Advances in Neural Information Processing Systems*.

Laroche, Romain, and Barlier, Merwan. 2017. Transfer reinforcement learning with shared dynamics. Pages 2147–2153 of: *Proceedings of the Thirty-First AAAI Conference on Artificial Intelligence*.

Larrañaga, Pedro, Calvo, Borja, Santana, Roberto, et al. 2006. Machine learning in bioinformatics. *Briefings in Bioinformatics*, **7**(1), 86–112.

Lawrence, Neil D., and Platt, John C. 2004. Learning to learn with the informative vector machine. *Proceedings of the Twenty-First International Conference on Machine Learning*.

Lazaric, Alessandro. 2008. *Knowledge Transfer in Reinforcement Learning*. Ph.D. thesis, Politecnico di Milano.

Lazaric, Alessandro. 2012. Transfer in reinforcement learning: A framework and a survey. Pages 143–173 of: Wiering, Marco, and van Otterlo, Martijn (eds), *Reinforcement Learning: State-of-the-Art*.

Lazaric, Alessandro, and Ghavamzadeh, Mohammad. 2010. Bayesian multi-task reinforcement learning. Pages 599–606 of: *Proceedings of the 27th International Conference on Machine Learning*.

Lazaric, Alessandro, Restelli, Marcello, and Bonarini, Andrea. 2008. Transfer of samples in batch reinforcement learning. Pages 544–551 of: *Proceedings of the Twenty-Fifth International Conference on Machine Learning*.

Ledig, Christian, Theis, Lucas, Huszar, Ferenc, et al. 2017. Photo-realistic single image super-resolution using a generative adversarial network. Pages 4681–4690 of: *Proceedings of the IEEE Conference on Computer Vision and Pattern Recognition*.

Lee, Byung-Jun, and Kim, Kee-Eung. 2016. Dialog history construction with long-short term memory for robust generative dialog state tracking. *Dialogue & Discourse*, **7**(3), 47–64.

Lee, Giwoong, Yang, Eunho, and Hwang, Sung Ju. 2016. Asymmetric multi-task learning based on task relatedness and loss. Pages 230–238 of: *Proceedings of the 33rd International Conference on Machine Learning*.

Lee, Honglak, Battle, Alexis, Raina, Rajat, and Ng, Andrew Y. 2007. Efficient sparse coding algorithms. Pages 801–808 of: *Advances in Neural Information Processing Systems*.

Lee, Jaewoo, and Kifer, Daniel. 2018. Concentrated differentially private gradient descent with adaptive per-iteration privacy budget. Pages 1656–1665 of: *Proceedings of the 24th ACM SIGKDD International Conference on Knowledge Discovery and Data Mining*.

Lefèvre, Fabrice, Gašić, Milica, Jurčíček, F., et al. 2009. k-Nearest neighbor Monte-Carlo control algorithm for POMDP-based dialogue systems. Pages 272–275 of: *Proceedings of the 10th Annual Meeting of the Special Interest Group on Discourse and Dialogue*.

Levin, Esther, Pieraccini, Roberto, and Eckert, Wieland. 1997. Learning dialogue strategies within the Markov decision process framework. Pages 72–79 of: *Proceedings of IEEE Workshop on Automatic Speech Recognition and Understanding*.

Li, Bin, Yang, Qiang, and Xue, Xiangyang. 2009a. Can movies and books collaborate? Cross-domain collaborative filtering for sparsity reduction. Pages 2052–2057 of: *Proceedings of the 21st International Joint Conference on Artificial Intelligence*.

Li, Bin, Yang, Qiang, and Xue, Xiangyang. 2009b. Transfer learning for collaborative filtering via a rating-matrix generative model. Pages 617–624 of: *Proceedings of the 26th Annual International Conference on Machine Learning*.

Li, Da, Yang, Yongxin, Song, Yi-Zhe, and Hospedales, Timothy M. 2017a. Deeper, broader and artier domain generalization. Pages 5543–5551 of: *Proceedings of IEEE International Conference on Computer Vision*.

Li, Fan, Yang, Yiming, and Xing, Eric P. 2005. From lasso regression to feature vector machine. Pages 779–786 of: *Advances in Neural Information Processing Systems*.

Li, Fangtao, Pan, Sinno Jialin, Jin, Ou, Yang, Qiang, and Zhu, Xiaoyan. 2012. Cross-domain co-extraction of sentiment and topic lexicons. Pages 410–419 for: *Proceedings of the 50th Annual Meeting of the Association for Computational Linguistics*.

Li, Fei-Fei, Fergus, Robert, and Perona, Pietro. 2006. One-shot learning of object categories. *IEEE Transactions on Pattern Analysis and Machine Intelligence*, **28**(4), 594–611.

Li, Hui, Liao, Xuejun, and Carin, Lawrence. 2009c. Multi-task reinforcement learning in partially observable stochastic environments. *Journal of Machine Learning Research*, **10**, 1131–1186.

Li, Jiwei, Galley, Michel, Brockett, Chris, Spithourakis, et al. 2016. A persona-based neural conversation model. Pages 994–1003 for:*Proceedings of the 54th Annual Meeting of the Association for Computational Linguistics*.

Li, Lihong, Chu, Wei, Langford, John, and Schapire, Robert E. 2010. A contextual-bandit approach to personalized news article recommendation. Pages 661–670 of: *Proceedings of the 19th International Conference on World Wide Web*.

Li, Qi, and Ji, Heng. 2014. Incremental joint extraction of entity mentions and relations. Pages 402–412 of: *Proceedings of the 52nd Annual Meeting of the Association for Computational Linguistics*.

Li, Sijin, Liu, Zhi-Qiang, and Chan, Antoni B. 2015. Heterogeneous multi-task learning for human pose estimation with deep convolutional neural network. *International Journal of Computer Vision*, **113**(1), 19–36.

Li, Wen, Duan, Lixin, Xu, Dong, and Tsang, Ivor W. 2014. Learning with augmented features for supervised and semi-supervised heterogeneous domain adaptation. *IEEE Transactions on Pattern Analysis and Machine Intelligence*, **36**(6), 1134–1148.

Li, Zheng, Zhang, Yu, Wei, Ying, Wu, Yuxiang, and Yang, Qiang. 2017b. End-to-end adversarial memory network for cross-domain sentiment classification. Pages 2237–2243 of: *Proceedings of the International Joint Conference on Artificial Intelligence*.

Liao, Renjie, Schwing, Alexander G., Zemel, Richard S., and Urtasun, Raquel. 2016. Learning deep parsimonious representations. Pages 5076–5084 of: *Advances in Neural Information Processing Systems*.

Liao, Xuejun, Xue, Ya, and Carin, Lawrence. 2005. Logistic regression with an auxiliary data source. Pages 505–512 of: *Proceedings of the 22nd International Conference on Machine Learning*.

Ling, Xiao, Xue, Gui-Rong, Dai, Wenyuan, et al. 2008. Can Chinese web pages be classified with English data source? Pages 969–978 of: *Proceedings of the 17th International Conference on World Wide Web*.

Liu, Bing. 2012. Sentiment analysis and opinion mining. *Synthesis Lectures on Human Language Technologies*, **5**(1), 1–167.

Liu, Bing, Hsu, Wynne, and Ma, Yiming. 1999. Mining association rules with multiple minimum supports. Pages 337–341 of: *Proceedings of the Fifth ACM SIGKDD International Conference on Knowledge Discovery and Data Mining*.

Liu, Bo, Wei, Ying, Zhang, Yu, and Yang, Qiang. 2017. Deep neural networks for high dimension, low sample size data. Pages 2287–2293 of: Sierra, Carles (ed.), *Proceedings of the Twenty-Sixth International Joint Conference on Artificial Intelligence*.

Liu, Bo, Wei, Ying, Zhang, Yu, Yan, Zhixian, and Yang, Qiang. 2018. Transferable contextual bandit for cross-domain recommendation. Pages 3619–3626 of: *Proceedings of the Thirty-Second AAAI Conference on Artificial Intelligence*.

Liu, Chenxi, Zoph, Barret, Neumann, Maxim, et al. 2018c. Progressive neural architecture search. Pages 19–35 of: *Proceedings of 15th European Conference on Computer Vision*.

Liu, Dong, Hua, Xian-Sheng, Yang, Linjun, Wang, Meng, and Zhang, Hong-Jiang. 2009a. Tag ranking. Pages 351–360 of: *Proceedings of the 18th International Conference on World Wide Web*.

Liu, Han, Palatucci, Mark, and Zhang, Jian. 2009b. Blockwise coordinate descent procedures for the multi-task lasso, with applications to neural semantic basis discovery. Pages 649–656 of: *Proceedings of the 26th International Conference on Machine Learning*.

Liu, Jiahui, Dolan, Peter, and Pedersen, Elin Rønby. 2010a. Personalized news recommendation based on click behavior. Pages 31–40 of: *Proceedings of the 15th International Conference on Intelligent User Interfaces*.

Liu, Qi, Xu, Qian, Zheng, Vincent W., et al. 2010b. Multi-task learning for cross-platform siRNA efficacy prediction: an in-silico study. *BMC Bioinformatics*, **11**, 181.

Liu, Qiuhua, Liao, Xuejun, and Carin, Lawrence. 2007. Semi-supervised multitask learning. Pages 937–944 of: *Advances in Neural Information Processing Systems.*

Liu, Qiuhua, Liao, Xuejun, Li, Hui, Stack, Jason R., and Carin, Lawrence. 2009c. Semisupervised multitask learning. *IEEE Transactions on Pattern Analysis and Machine Intelligence*, **31**(6), 1074–1086.

Liu, Wu, Mei, Tao, Zhang, Yongdong, Che, Cherry, and Luo, Jiebo. 2015a. Multi-task deep visual-semantic embedding for video thumbnail selection. Pages 3707–3715 of: *Proceedings of IEEE Conference on Computer Vision and Pattern Recognition.*

Liu, Xiaodong, Gao, Jianfeng, et al. 2015b. Representation learning using multi-task deep neural networks for semantic classification and information retrieval. Pages 912–921 of: *Proceedings of the 2015 Conference of the North American Chapter of the Association for Computational Linguistics: Human Language Technologies.*

Long, Mingsheng, Wang, Jianmin, Ding, Guiguang, Shen, Dou, and Yang, Qiang. 2014. Transfer learning with graph co-regularization. *IEEE Transactions on Knowledge and Data Engineering*, **26**(7), 1805–1818.

Long, Mingsheng, Cao, Yue, Wang, Jianmin, and Jordan, Michael I. 2015. Learning transferable features with deep adaptation networks. Pages 97–105 of: *Proceedings of the 32nd International Conference on Machine Learning.*

Long, Mingsheng, Zhu, Han, Wang, Jianmin, and Jordan, Michael I. 2017. Deep transfer learning with joint adaptation networks. Pages 2208–2217 of: *Proceedings of International Conference on Machine Learning.*

Lounici, Karim, Pontil, Massimiliano, Tsybakov, Alexandre B., and van de Geer, Sara A. 2009. Taking advantage of sparsity in multi-task learning. *Proceedings of the 22nd Conference on Learning Theory.*

Lozano, Aurelie C., and Swirszcz, Grzegorz. 2012. Multi-level lasso for sparse multi-task regression. *Proceedings of the 29th International Conference on Machine Learning.*

Lu, Guoyu, Yan, Yan, Ren, Li, et al. 2016. Where am I in the dark: Exploring active transfer learning on the use of indoor localization based on thermal imaging. *Neurocomputing*, **173**, 83–92.

Lugosi, Gábor, Papaspiliopoulos, Omiros, and Stoltz, Gilles. 2009. Online multi-task learning with hard constraints. *Proceedings of the 22nd Conference on Learning Theory.*

Luo, Bingfeng, Feng, Yansong, Xu, Jianbo, Zhang, Xiang, and Zhao, Dongyan. 2017. Learning to predict charges for criminal cases with legal basis. Pages 2727–2736 of: *Proceedings of the 2017 Conference on Empirical Methods in Natural Language Processing.*

Luong, Minh-Thang, Le, Quoc V., Sutskever, Ilya, Vinyals, Oriol, and Kaiser, Lukasz. 2016. Multi-task sequence to sequence learning. *Proceedings of the 4th International Conference on Learning Representations.*

Luria, Aleksandr R. 1976. *Cognitive Development: Its Cultural and Social Foundations.* Harvard University Press.

Ma, Zhigang, Yang, Yi, Nie, Feiping, et al. 2014. Harnessing lab knowledge for real-world action recognition. *International Journal of Computer Vision*, **109**(1–2), 60–73.

Mahadevan, Sridhar, and Maggioni, Mauro. 2007. Proto-value functions: A Laplacian framework for learning representation and control in Markov decision processes. *Journal of Machine Learning Research*, **8**, 2169–2231.

Mahajan, Dhruv, Girshick, Ross B., Ramanathan, Vignesh, et al. 2018. Exploring the limits of weakly supervised pretraining. *CoRR*, abs/1805.00932.

Mahmud, M. M., and Ray, Sylvian R. 2007. Transfer learning using Kolmogorov complexity: Basic theory and empirical evaluations. Pages 985–992 of: *Advances in Neural Information Processing Systems.*

Mairesse, François, and Walker, Marilyn A. 2008. Trainable generation of big-five personality styles through data-driven parameter estimation. Pages 165–173 of: *Proceedings of the 46th Annual Meeting of the Association for Computational Linguistics*.

Mairesse, François, and Walker, Marilyn A. 2011. Controlling user perceptions of linguistic style: Trainable generation of personality traits. *Computational Linguistics*, **37**(3), 455–488.

Mairesse, François, Gašić, Milica, Jurcícek, Filip, et al. 2009. Spoken language understanding from unaligned data using discriminative classification models. Pages 4749–4752 of: *Proceedings of IEEE International Conference on Acoustics, Speech and Signal Processing*.

Malaviya, Chaitanya, Neubig, Graham, and Littell, Patrick. 2017. Learning language representations for typology prediction. Pages 2529–2535 of: *Proceedings of the 2017 Conference on Empirical Methods in Natural Language Processing*.

Man, Tong, Shen, Huawei, Jin, Xiaolong, and Cheng, Xueqi. 2017. Cross-domain recommendation: An embedding and mapping approach. Pages 2464–2470 of: *Proceedings of the 26th International Joint Conference on Artificial Intelligence*.

Mansour, Yishay, Mohri, Mehryar, and Rostamizadeh, Afshin. 2008. Domain adaptation with multiple sources. Pages 1041–1048 of: *Advances in Neural Information Processing Systems*.

Mansour, Yishay, Mohri, Mehryar, and Rostamizadeh, Afshin. 2009. Domain adaptation: Learning bounds and algorithms. *Proceedings of the 22nd Conference on Learning Theory*.

Mao, Xiangbo, Lin, Binbin, Cai, Deng, He, Xiaofei, and Pei, Jian. 2013. Parallel field alignment for cross media retrieval. Pages 897–906 of: *Proceedings of the 21st ACM International Conference on Multimedia*.

Marx, Zvika, Rosenstein, Michael T., Dietterich, Thomas G., and Kaelbling, Leslie Pack. 2008. Two algorithms for transfer learning. *Inductive Transfer: 10 Years Later*.

Maurer, Andreas. 2005. Algorithmic stability and meta-learning. *Journal of Machine Learning Research*, **6**, 967–994.

Maurer, Andreas. 2006a. Bounds for linear multi-task learning. *Journal of Machine Learning Research*, **7**, 117–139.

Maurer, Andreas. 2006b. The Rademacher complexity of linear transformation classes. Pages 65–78 of: *Proceedings of the 19th Annual Conference on Learning Theory*.

Maurer, Andreas. 2009. Transfer bounds for linear feature learning. *Machine Learning*, **75**(3), 327–350.

Maurer, Andreas, Pontil, Massimiliano, and Romera-Paredes, Bernardino. 2013. Sparse coding for multitask and transfer learning. Pages 343–351 of: *Proceedings of the 30th International Conference on Machine Learning*.

Maurer, Andreas, Pontil, Massimiliano, and Romera-Paredes, Bernardino. 2016. The benefit of multitask representation learning. *Journal of Machine Learning Research*, **17**, 1–32.

McAllester, David A. 1999. Some PAC-Bayesian theorems. *Machine Learning*, **37**(3), 355–363.

McCann, Bryan, Bradbury, James, Xiong, Caiming, and Socher, Richard. 2017. Learned in translation: Contextualized word vectors. Pages 6297–6308 of: *Advances in Neural Information Processing Systems*.

McGovern, Amy, and Barto, Andrew G. 2001. Automatic discovery of subgoals in reinforcement learning using diverse density. Pages 361–368 of: *Proceedings of the Eighteenth International Conference on Machine Learning*.

McNamara, Daniel, and Balcan, Maria-Florina. 2017. Risk bounds for transferring representations with and without fine-tuning. Pages 2373–2381 of: *Proceedings of the 34th International Conference on Machine Learning*.

Menze, Bjoern H., Jakab, András, Bauer, Stefan, et al. 2015. The multimodal brain tumor image segmentation benchmark (BRATS). *IEEE Transactions on Medical Imaging*, **34**(10), 1993–2024.

Mihalkova, Lilyana, and Mooney, Raymond J. 2008. Transfer learning by mapping with minimal target data. In: *Proceedings of the AAAI-08 Workshop on Transfer Learning for Complex Tasks*.

Mihalkova, Lilyana, Huynh, Tuyen N., and Mooney, Raymond J. 2007. Mapping and revising Markov logic networks for transfer learning. Pages 608–614 of: *Proceedings of the Twenty-Second AAAI Conference on Artificial Intelligence*.

Mikolov, Tomas, Chen, Kai, Corrado, Greg, and Dean, Jeffrey. 2013a. Efficient estimation of word representations in vector space. *CoRR*, abs/1301.3781.

Mikolov, Tomas, Sutskever, Ilya, Chen, Kai, Corrado, Greg S., and Dean, Jeff. 2013b. Distributed representations of words and phrases and their compositionality. Pages 3111–3119 of: *Advances in Neural Information Processing Systems*.

Min, Sewon, Seo, Minjoon, and Hajishirzi, Hannaneh. 2017. Question answering through transfer learning from large fine-grained supervision data. Pages 510–517 of: *Proceedings of the 55th Annual Meeting of the Association for Computational Linguistics*.

Misra, Ishan, Shrivastava, Abhinav, Gupta, Abhinav, and Hebert, Martial. 2016. Cross-stitch networks for multi-task learning. Pages 3994–4003 of: *Proceedings of IEEE Conference on Computer Vision and Pattern Recognition*.

Mitchell, T., Cohen, W., Hruschka, E., et al. 2015. Never-ending learning. Pages 2302–2310 of: *Proceedings of the Twenty-Ninth AAAI Conference on Artificial Intelligence*.

Mitra, Pabitra, Murthy, C. A., and Pal, Sankar K. 2002. Unsupervised feature selection using feature similarity. *IEEE Transactions on Pattern Analysis and Machine Intelligence*, **24**(3), 301–312.

Mitzlaff, Folke, Atzmüller, Martin, Hotho, Andreas, and Stumme, Gerd. 2014. The social distributional hypothesis: A pragmatic proxy for homophily in online social networks. *Social Network Analysis and Mining*, **4**(1), 216.

Mnih, Volodymyr, Kavukcuoglu, Koray, Silver, David, et al. 2013. Playing Atari with deep reinforcement learning. *CoRR*, abs/1312.5602.

Mnih, Volodymyr, Kavukcuoglu, Koray, Silver, David, et al. 2015. Human-level control through deep reinforcement learning. *Nature*, **518**(7540), 529–533.

Mo, Kaixiang, Zhang, Yu, Yang, Qiang, and Fung, Pascale. 2017. Fine grained knowledge transfer for personalized task-oriented dialogue systems. *CoRR*, abs/1711.04079.

Mo, Kaixiang, Zhang, Yu, Li, Shuangyin, Li, Jiajun, and Yang, Qiang. 2018. Personalizing a dialogue system with transfer reinforcement learning. Pages 5317–5324 of: *Proceedings of the Thirty-Second AAAI Conference on Artificial Intelligence*.

Moore, Andrew W. 1991. Variable resolution dynamic programming: Efficiently learning action maps in multivariate real-valued state-spaces. Pages 333–337 of: *Proceedings of the Eighth International Conference on Machine Learning*.

Mou, Lili, Meng, Zhao, Yan, Rui, et al. 2016. How transferable are neural networks in NLP applications? Pages 479–489 of: *Proceedings of the 2016 Conference on Empirical Methods in Natural Language Processing*.

Mrkšic, Nikola, Séaghdha, Diarmuid Ó., Thomson, Blaise, et al. 2015. Multi-domain dialog state tracking using recurrent neural networks. Pages 794–799 of: *Proceedings of the 53rd Annual Meeting of the Association for Computational Linguistics*.

Nassar, Marcel, Abdallah, Rami, Zeineddine, Hady Ali, Yaacoub, Elias, and Dawy, Zaher. 2008. A new multitask learning method for multiorganism gene network estimation. Pages 2287–2291 of: *Proceedings of IEEE International Symposium on Information Theory*.

Ng, Andrew Y., Jordan, Michael I., and Weiss, Yair. 2002. On spectral clustering: Analysis and an algorithm. Pages 849–856 of: *Advances in Neural Information Processing Systems*.

Nguyen, Hien Van, Ho, Huy Tho, Patel, Vishal M., and Chellappa, Rama. 2015. DASH-N: Joint hierarchical domain adaptation and feature learning. *IEEE Transactions on Image Processing*, **24**(12), 5479–5491.

Nguyen, Khanh, III, Hal Daumé, and Boyd-Graber, Jordan L. 2017. Reinforcement learning for bandit neural machine translation with simulated human feedback. Pages 1464–1474 of: *Proceedings of the 2017 Conference on Empirical Methods in Natural Language Processing*.

Ni, Jie, Qiu, Qiang, and Chellappa, Rama. 2013. Subspace interpolation via dictionary learning for unsupervised domain adaptation. Pages 692–699 of: *Proceedings of IEEE Conference on Computer Vision and Pattern Recognition*.

Ni, Lionel M., Liu, Yunhao, Lau, Yiu Cho, and Patil, Abhishek P. 2003. LANDMARC: Indoor location sensing using active RFID. Pages 407–415 of: *Proceedings of IEEE International Conference on Pervasive Computing and Communications*.

Nickel, Maximilian, Murphy, Kevin, Tresp, Volker, and Gabrilovich, Evgeniy. 2016. A review of relational machine learning for knowledge graphs. *Proceedings of the IEEE*, **104**(1), 11–33.

Niehues, Jan, and Cho, Eunah. 2017. Exploiting linguistic resources for neural machine translation using multi-task learning. Pages 80–89 of: *Proceedings of the Second Conference on Machine Translation*.

Norouzi, Mohammad, Mikolov, Tomas, Bengio, Samy, et al. 2013. Zero-shot learning by convex combination of semantic embeddings. *CoRR*, abs/1312.5650.

Nowozin, Sebastian, Cseke, Botond, and Tomioka, Ryota. 2016. f-GAN: Training generative neural samplers using variational divergence minimization. Pages 271–279 of: *Advances in Neural Information Processing Systems*.

Obozinski, Guillaume, Taskar, Ben, and Jordan, Michael. 2006. *Multi-task Feature Selection*. Tech. Report, Department of Statistics, University of California, Berkeley.

Obozinski, Guillaume, Taskar, Ben, and Jordan, Michael. 2010. Joint covariate selection and joint subspace selection for multiple classification problems. *Statistics and Computing*, **20**(2), 231–252.

Obozinski, Guillaume, Wainwright, Martin J., and Jordan, Michael I. 2011. Support union recovery in high-dimensional multivariate regression. *The Annals of Statistics*, **39**(1), 1–47.

Olshausen, Bruno A., and Field, David J. 1997. Sparse coding with an overcomplete basis set: A strategy employed by V1? *Vision Research*, **37**(23), 3311–3325.

Oquab, Maxime, Bottou, Leon, Laptev, Ivan, and Sivic, Josef. 2014. Learning and transferring mid-level image representations using convolutional neural networks. Pages 1717–1724 of: *Proceedings of IEEE Conference on Computer Vision and Pattern Recognition*.

Palatucci, Mark, Pomerleau, Dean, Hinton, Geoffrey E., and Mitchell, Tom M. 2009. Zero-shot learning with semantic output codes. Pages 1410–1418 of: *Advances in Neural Information Processing Systems*.

Pan, Jialin. 2010. *Feature-based Transfer Learning with Real-world Applications*. Ph.D. thesis, Hong Kong University of Science and Technology.

Pan, Rong, Zhao, Junhui, Zheng, Vincent Wenchen, et al. 2007a. Domain-constrained semi-supervised mining of tracking models in sensor networks. Pages 1023–1027 of: *Proceedings of the 13th ACM SIGKDD International Conference on Knowledge Discovery and Data Mining.*

Pan, Rong, Zhou, Yunhong, Cao, Bin, et al. 2008a. One-class collaborative filtering. Pages 502–511 of: *Proceedings of the Eighth IEEE International Conference on Data Mining.*

Pan, Sinno J., Kwok, James T., Yang, Qiang, and Pan, Jeffrey J. 2007b. Adaptive localization in a dynamic WiFi environment through multi-view learning. Pages 1108–1113 of: *Proceedings of the 22nd National Conference on Artificial Intelligence.*

Pan, Sinno Jialin. 2014. Transfer Learning. Pages 537–570 of: *Data Classification: Algorithms and Applications.* Chapman & Hall/CRC.

Pan, Sinno Jialin, and Yang, Qiang. 2010. A survey on transfer learning. *IEEE Transactions on Knowledge and Data Engineering,* **22**(10), 1345–1359.

Pan, Sinno Jialin, Kwok, James T., and Yang, Qiang. 2008b. Transfer learning via dimensionality reduction. Pages 677–682 of: *Proceedings of the 23rd AAAI Conference on Artificial Intelligence.*

Pan, Sinno Jialin, Shen, Dou, Yang, Qiang, and Kwok, James T. 2008c. Transferring localization models across space. Pages 1383–1388 of: *Proceedings of the 23rd AAAI Conference on Artificial Intelligence.*

Pan, Sinno Jialin, Ni, Xiaochuan, Sun, Jian-Tao, Yang, Qiang, and Chen, Zheng. 2010a. Cross-domain sentiment classification via spectral feature alignment. Pages 751–760 of: *Proceedings of the 19th International Conference on World Wide Web.*

Pan, Sinno Jialin, Tsang, Ivor W., Kwok, James T., and Yang, Qiang. 2011. Domain adaptation via transfer component analysis. *IEEE Transactions on Neural Networks,* **22**(2), 199–210.

Pan, Weike, and Yang, Qiang. 2013. Transfer learning in heterogeneous collaborative filtering domains. *Artificial Intelligence,* **197**, 39–55.

Pan, Weike, Xiang, Evan W., Liu, Nathan N., and Yang, Qiang. 2010b. Transfer learning in collaborative filtering for sparsity reduction. Pages 230–235 of: *Proceedings of the Twenty-Fourth AAAI Conference on Artificial Intelligence.*

Pan, Weike, Xiang, Evan Wei, and Yang, Qiang. 2012. Transfer learning in collaborative filtering with uncertain ratings. Pages 662–668 of: *Proceedings of the Twenty-Sixth AAAI Conference on Artificial Intelligence.*

Pan, Weike, Liu, Zhuode, Ming, et al. 2015a. Compressed knowledge transfer via factorization machine for heterogeneous collaborative recommendation. *Knowledge-Based Systems,* **85**, 234–244.

Pan, Weike, Zhong, Hao, Xu, Congfu, and Ming, Zhong. 2015b. Adaptive Bayesian personalized ranking for heterogeneous implicit feedbacks. *Knowledge-Based Systems,* **73**, 173–180.

Pan, Weike, Liu, Mengsi, and Ming, Zhong. 2016a. Transfer learning for heterogeneous one-class collaborative filtering. *IEEE Intelligent Systems,* **31**(4), 43–49.

Pan, Weike, Yang, Qiang, Duan, Yuchao, and Ming, Zhong. 2016b. Transfer learning for semisupervised collaborative recommendation. *ACM Transactions on Interactive Intelligent Systems,* **6**(2), 10:1–10:21.

Pan, Weike, Yang, Qiang, Duan, Yuchao, Tan, Ben, and Ming, Zhong. 2017. Transfer learning for behavior ranking. *ACM Transactions on Intelligent Systems and Technology,* **8**(5), 65:1–65:23.

Pang, Bo, and Lee, Lillian. 2008. Opinion mining and sentiment analysis. *Foundations and Trends in Information Retrieval,* **2**(1–2), 1–135.

Pang, Bo, Lee, Lillian, and Vaithyanathan, Shivakumar. 2002. Thumbs up? Sentiment classification using machine learning Techniques. Pages 79–86 of: *Proceedings of the 2002 Conference on Empirical Methods in Natural Language Processing*.

Pappas, Nikolaos, and Popescu-Belis, Andrei. 2017. Multilingual Hierarchical attention networks for document classification. Pages 1015–1025 of: *Proceedings of the 8th International Joint Conference on Natural Language Processing*.

Parameswaran, Shibin, and Weinberger, Kilian Q. 2010. Large margin multi-task metric learning. Pages 1867–1875 of: *Advances in Neural Information Processing Systems*.

Parisotto, Emilio, Ba, Jimmy, and Salakhutdinov, Ruslan. 2016. Actor-mimic: Deep multitask and transfer reinforcement learning. *Proceedings of the 4th International Conference on Learning Representations*.

Patel, Vishal M., Gopalan, Raghuraman, Li, Ruonan, and Chellappa, Rama. 2015. Visual domain adaptation: A survey of recent advances. *IEEE Signal Processing Magazine*, **32**(3), 53–69.

Patterson, Donald J., Fox, Dieter, Kautz, Henry A., and Philipose, Matthai. 2005. Fine-grained activity recognition by aggregating abstract object usage. Pages 44–51 of: *Proceedings of the Ninth IEEE International Symposium on Wearable Computers*.

Pei, Zhongyi, Cao, Zhangjie, Long, Mingsheng, and Wang, Jianmin. 2018. Multi-adversarial domain adaptation. Pages 3934–3941 of: *Proceedings of the Thirty-Second AAAI Conference on Artificial Intelligence*.

Peng, Hao, Thomson, Sam, and Smith, Noah A. 2017. Deep multitask learning for semantic dependency parsing. Pages 2037–2048 of: *Proceedings of the 55th Annual Meeting of the Association for Computational Linguistics*.

Pennington, Jeffrey, Socher, Richard, and Manning, Christopher. 2014. Glove: Global vectors for word representation. Pages 1532–1543 of: *Proceedings of the 2014 Conference on Empirical Methods in Natural Language Processing*.

Pentina, Anastasia, and Ben-David, Shai. 2015. multi-task and lifelong learning of kernels. Pages 194–208 of: *Proceedings of the 26th International Conference on Algorithmic Learning Theory*.

Pentina, Anastasia, and Lampert, Christoph H. 2014. A PAC-Bayesian bound for lifelong learning. Pages 991–999 of: *Proceedings of the 31th International Conference on Machine Learning*.

Pentina, Anastasia, and Lampert, Christoph H. 2015. Lifelong learning with non-i.i.d. tasks. Pages 1540–1548 of: *Advances in Neural Information Processing Systems*.

Perkins, Simon, Lacker, Kevin, and Theiler, James. 2003. Grafting: Fast, incremental feature selection by gradient descent in function space. *Journal of Machine Learning Research*, **3**, 1333–1356.

Perrot, Michaël, and Habrard, Amaury. 2015. A theoretical analysis of metric hypothesis transfer learning. Pages 1708–1717 of: *Proceedings of the 32nd International Conference on Machine Learning*.

Phillips, Caitlin. 2006. *Knowledge Transfer in Markov Decision Processes*. Tech. reptort, McGill University.

Pillonetto, Gianluigi, Dinuzzo, Francesco, and Nicolao, Giuseppe De. 2010. Bayesian online multitask learning of Gaussian processes. *IEEE Transactions on Pattern Analysis and Machine Intelligence*, **32**(2), 193–205.

Plis, Sergey M., Hjelm, Devon R., Salakhutdinov, Ruslan, and Calhoun, Vince D. 2013. Deep learning for neuroimaging: A validation study. *CoRR*, abs/1312.5847.

Pong, Ting Kei, Tseng, Paul, Ji, Shuiwang, and Ye, Jieping. 2010. Trace norm regularization: Reformulations, algorithms, and multi-task learning. *SIAM Journal on Optimization*, **20**(6), 3465–3489.

Ponomareva, Natalia, and Thelwall, Mike. 2012. Biographies or blenders: Which resource is best for cross-domain sentiment analysis? Pages 488–499 of: *Proceedings of International Conference on Intelligent Text Processing and Computational Linguistics.*

Pontil, Massimiliano, and Maurer, Andreas. 2013. Excess risk bounds for multitask learning with trace norm regularization. Pages 55–76 of: *Proceedings of the 26th Annual Conference on Learning Theory.*

Pugh, K. J., and Bergin, D. A. 2006. Motivational influences on transfer. *Educational Psychologist,* **41**, 147–160.

Puniyani, Kriti, Kim, Seyoung, and Xing, Eric P. 2010. Multi-population GWA mapping via multi-task regularized regression. *Bioinformatics,* **26**, i208–i216.

Qi, Guo-Jun, Aggarwal, Charu, and Huang, Thomas. 2011a. Towards semantic knowledge propagation from text corpus to web images. Pages 297–306 of: *Proceedings of the 20th International Conference on World Wide Web.*

Qi, Guo-Jun, Aggarwal, Charu, Rui, Yong, et al. 2011b. Towards cross-category knowledge propagation for learning visual concepts. Pages 897–904 of: *Proceedings of the IEEE Conference on Computer Vision and Pattern Recognition.*

Qi, Yanjun, Tastan, Oznur, Carbonell, Jaime G., and Klein-Seetharaman, Judith. 2010. Semi-supervised multi-task learning for predicting interactions between HIV-1 and human proteins. *Bioinformatics,* **26**, i645–i652.

Qiu, Qiang, Patel, Vishal M., Turaga, Pavan, and Chellappa, Rama. 2012. Domain adaptive dictionary learning. Pages 631–645 of: *Proceedings of European Conference on Computer Vision.*

Quionero-Candela, Joaquin, Sugiyama, Masashi, Schwaighofer, Anton, and Lawrence, Neil D. 2009. *Dataset Shift in Machine Learning.* MIT Press.

Radford, Alec, Metz, Luke, and Chintala, Soumith. 2015. Unsupervised representation learning with deep convolutional generative adversarial networks. *CoRR,* abs/1511.06434.

Raina, Rajat, Battle, Alexis, Lee, Honglak, Packer, Benjamin, and Ng, Andrew Y. 2007. Self-taught learning: Transfer learning from unlabeled data. Pages 759–766 of: *Proceedings of the 24th International Conference on Machine Learning.*

Raj, Anant, Namboodiri, Vinay P., and Tuytelaars, Tinne. 2015. Subspace alignment based domain adaptation for RCNN detector. Pages 166.1–166.11 of: *Proceedings of the British Machine Vision Conference.*

Rajpurkar, Pranav, Zhang, Jian, Lopyrev, Konstantin, and Liang, Percy. 2016. SQuAD: 100,000+ questions for machine comprehension of text. Pages 2383–2392 of: *Proceedings of the 2016 Conference on Empirical Methods in Natural Language Processing.*

Rajpurkar, Pranav, Irvin, Jeremy, Zhu, Kaylie, et al. 2017. CheXNet: Radiologist-level pneumonia detection on chest X-rays with deep learning. *CoRR,* abs/1711.05225.

Ranzato, Marc'Aurelio, Chopra, Sumit, Auli, Michael, and Zaremba, Wojciech. 2015. Sequence level training with recurrent neural networks. *CoRR,* abs/1511.06732.

Recanzone, Gregg H. 2009. Interactions of auditory and visual stimuli in space and time. *Hearing Research,* **258**(1), 89–99.

Reichart, Roi, Tomanek, Katrin, Hahn, Udo, and Rappoport, Ari. 2008. Multi-task active learning for linguistic annotations. Pages 861–869 of: *Proceedings of the 46th Annual Meeting of the Association for Computational Linguistics.*

Reiss, Attila, and Stricker, Didier. 2012. Introducing a new benchmarked dataset for activity monitoring. Pages 108–109 of: *Proceedings of the 16th International Symposium on Wearable Computers.*

Ren, Hang, Xu, Weiqun, and Yan, Yonghong. 2014. Markovian discriminative modeling for cross-domain dialog state tracking. Pages 342–347 of: *Proceedings of IEEE Spoken Language Technology Workshop*.

Resnick, Paul, and Varian, Hal R. 1997. Recommender systems. *Communications of the ACM*, **40**(3), 56–58.

Resnick, Paul, Iacovou, Neophytos, Suchak, Mitesh, Bergstrom, Peter, and Riedl, John. 1994. GroupLens: An open architecture for collaborative filtering of netnews. Pages 175–186 of: *Proceedings of the 1994 ACM Conference on Computer Supported Cooperative Work*.

Revow, Michael, Williams, Christopher K. I., and Hinton, Geoffrey E. 1996. Using generative models for handwritten digit recognition. *IEEE Transactions on Pattern Analysis and Machine Intelligence*, **18**(6), 592–606.

Richards, Bradley L., and Mooney, Raymond J. 1992. Learning relations by pathfinding. Pages 50–55 of: *Proceedings of the 10th National Conference on Artificial Intelligence*.

Richardson, Matthew, and Domingos, Pedro. 2006. Markov logic networks. *Machine Learning*, **62**(1–2), 107–136.

Rohrbach, Marcus, Stark, Michael, Szarvas, György, Gurevych, Iryna, and Schiele, Bernt. 2010. What helps where – and why? Semantic relatedness for knowledge transfer. Pages 910–917 of: *Proceedings of the IEEE Conference on Computer Vision and Pattern Recognition*.

Ruder, Sebastian, Bingel, Joachim, Augenstein, Isabelle, and Søgaard, Anders. 2017. Sluice networks: Learning what to share between loosely related tasks. *CoRR*, abs/1705.08142.

Rusu, Andrei A., Colmenarejo, Sergio Gomez, Gülçehre, Çaglar, et al. 2015. Policy distillation. *CoRR*, abs/1511.06295.

Ruvolo, Paul, and Eaton, Eric. 2013. ELLA: An efficient lifelong learning algorithm. Pages 507–515 of: *Proceedings of the 30th International Conference on Machine Learning*.

Saenko, Kate, Kulis, Brian, Fritz, Mario, and Darrell, Trevor. 2010. Adapting visual category models to new domains. Pages 213–226 of: *Proceedings of European Conference on Computer Vision*.

Saha, Avishek, Rai, Piyush, III, Hal Daumé, and Venkatasubramanian, Suresh. 2011. Online learning of multiple tasks and their relationships. Pages 643–651 of: *Proceedings of the Fourteenth International Conference on Artificial Intelligence and Statistics*.

Salimans, Tim, Goodfellow, Ian, Zaremba, Wojciech, et al. 2016. Improved techniques for training GANs. Pages 2234–2242 of: *Advances in Neural Information Processing Systems*.

Samala, Ravi K., Chan, Heang-Ping, Hadjiiski, Lubomir, et al. 2016. Mass detection in digital breast tomosynthesis: Deep convolutional neural network with transfer learning from mammography. *Medical physics*, **43**(12), 6654–6666.

Schank, Roger C. 1983. *Dynamic Memory – A Theory of Reminding and Learning in Computers and People*. Cambridge University Press.

Scholkopf, Bernhard, and Smola, Alexander J. 2001. *Learning with Kernels: Support Vector Machines, Regularization, Optimization, and Beyond*. MIT Press.

Schunk, D. 1965. *Learning Theories: An Educational Perspective*. Pearson.

Schwaighofer, Anton, Tresp, Volker, and Yu, Kai. 2005. Learning Gaussian process kernels via hierarchical Bayes. Pages 1209–1216 of: *Advances in Neural Information Processing Systems*.

Schweikert, Gabriele Beate, Widmer, Christian, Schölkopf, Bernhard, and Rätsch, Gunnar. 2008. An empirical analysis of domain adaptation algorithms for genomic sequence analysis. Pages 1433–1440 of: *Advances in Neural Information Processing Systems*.

Seo, Minjoon, Kembhavi, Aniruddha, Farhadi, Ali, and Hajishirzi, Hannaneh. 2016. Bidirectional attention flow for machine comprehension. *CoRR*, abs/1611.01603.

Serban, Iulian V., Sordoni, Alessandro, Bengio, Yoshua, Courville, Aaron, and Pineau, Joelle. 2015. Building end-to-end dialogue systems using generative hierarchical neural network models. *arXiv preprint*, arXiv:1507.04808.

Serban, Iulian V., Sordoni, Alessandro, Bengio, Yoshua, Courville, Aaron, and Pineau, Joelle. 2016. Building end-to-end dialogue systems using generative hierarchical neural network models. Pages 3776–3784 of: *Proceedings of the 30th AAAI Conference on Artificial Intelligence*.

Serban, Iulian Vlad, Sordoni, Alessandro, Lowe, Ryan, et al. 2017. A hierarchical latent variable encoder-decoder model for generating dialogues. Pages 3295–3301 of: *Proceedings of the Thirty-First AAAI Conference on Artificial Intelligence*.

Sermanet, Pierre, Eigen, David, Zhang, Xiang, et al. 2013. Overfeat: Integrated recognition, localization and detection using convolutional networks. *CoRR*, abs/1312.6229.

Sevakula, R. K., Singh, V., Verma, N. K., Kumar, C., and Cui, Y. 2018. Transfer learning for molecular cancer classification using deep neural networks. *IEEE/ACM Transactions on Computational Biology and Bioinformatics*.

Shang, Lifeng, Lu, Zhengdong, and Li, Hang. 2015. Neural responding machine for short-text conversation. Pages 1577–1586 of: *Proceedings of the 53rd Annual Meeting of the Association for Computational Linguistics*.

Shekhar, Shashi, Patel, Vishal M., Nguyen, Hien, and Chellappa, Rama. 2013. Generalized domain-adaptive dictionaries. Pages 361–368 of: *Proceedings of the IEEE Conference on Computer Vision and Pattern Recognition*.

Shen, Dou, Pan, Rong, Sun, Jian-Tao, et al. 2005. Q^2C@UST: Our winning solution to query classification in KDDCUP 2005. *SIGKDD Explorations*, **7**(2), 100–110.

Shen, Dou, Pan, Rong, Sun, Jian-Tao, et al. 2006a. Query enrichment for web-query classification. *ACM Transactions on Information Systems*, **24**(3), 320–352.

Shen, Dou, Sun, Jian-Tao, Yang, Qiang, and Chen, Zheng. 2006b. Building bridges for web query classification. Pages 131–138 of: *Proceedings of the 29th Annual International ACM SIGIR Conference on Research and Development in Information Retrieval*.

Sherstov, Alexander A., and Stone, Peter. 2005. Improving action selection in MDP's via knowledge transfer. Pages 1024–1029 of: *Proceedings of the Twentieth National Conference on Artificial Intelligence*.

Shi, Xiaoxiao, Liu, Qi, Fan, Wei, Yang, Qiang, and Yu, Philip S. 2010a. Predictive modeling with heterogeneous sources. Pages 814–825 of: *Proceedings of the SIAM International Conference on Data Mining*.

Shi, Xiaoxiao, Liu, Qi, Fan, Wei, Yu, Philip S., and Zhu, Ruixin. 2010b. Transfer learning on heterogenous feature spaces via spectral transformation. Pages 1049–1054 of: *Proceedings of the IEEE International Conference on Data Mining*.

Shi, Xiaoxiao, Paiement, Jean-François, Grangier, David, and Yu, Philip S. 2012. Learning from heterogeneous sources via gradient boosting consensus. Pages 224–235 of: *Proceedings of the SIAM International Conference on Data Mining*.

Shi, Xiaoxiao, Liu, Qi, Fan, Wei, and Philip, S. Yu. 2013a. Transfer across completely different feature spaces via spectral embedding. *IEEE Transactions on Knowledge and Data Engineering*, **25**(4), 906–918.

Shi, Yangyang, Larson, Martha, and Jonker, Catholijn M. 2015. Recurrent neural network language model adaptation with curriculum learning. *Computer Speech and Language*, **33**(1), 136–154.

Shi, Yuan, and Sha, Fei. 2012. Information-theoretical learning of discriminative clusters for unsupervised domain adaptation. Pages 1275–1282 of: *Proceedings of the 29th International Conference on Machine Learning.*

Shi, Yue, Larson, Martha, and Hanjalic, Alan. 2013b. Mining contextual movie similarity with matrix factorization for context-aware recommendation. *ACM Transactions on Intelligent Systems and Technology,* **4**(1), 16:1–16:19.

Shin, Hoo-Chang, Roth, Holger R., Gao, Mingchen, et al. 2016. Deep convolutional neural networks for computer-aided detection: CNN architectures, dataset characteristics and transfer learning. *IEEE Transactions on Medical Imaging,* **35**(5), 1285–1298.

Shokri, Reza, and Shmatikov, Vitaly. 2015. Privacy-preserving deep learning. Pages 1310–1321 of: *Proceedings of ACM Conference on Computer and Communications Security.*

Shrivastava, Ashish, Pfister, Tomas, Tuzel, Oncel, et al. 2017. Learning from simulated and unsupervised images through adversarial training. Pages 2242–2251 of: *Proceedings of the IEEE Conference on Computer Vision and Pattern Recognition.*

Shu, Xiangbo, Qi, Guo-Jun, Tang, Jinhui, and Wang, Jingdong. 2015. Weakly-shared deep transfer networks for heterogeneous-domain knowledge propagation. Pages 35–44 of: *Proceedings of the 23rd ACM International Conference on Multimedia.*

Si, Si, Tao, Dacheng, and Geng, Bo. 2010. Bregman divergence-based regularization for transfer subspace learning. *IEEE Transactions on Knowledge and Data Engineering,* **22**(7), 929–942.

Silver, Daniel L., and Mercer, Robert E. 1996. The parallel transfer of task knowledge using dynamic learning rates based on a measure of relatedness. *Connection Science Special Issue: Transfer in Inductive Systems,* **8**(2), 277–294.

Silver, Daniel L., Yang, Qiang, and Li, Lianghao. 2013. Lifelong machine learning systems: Beyond learning algorithms. *Proceedings of the 2013 AAAI Spring Symposium on Lifelong Machine Learning,* AAAI Technical Report, vol. SS-13-05.

Silver, David, Huang, Aja, Maddison, Chris J., et al. 2016. Mastering the game of Go with deep neural networks and tree search. *Nature,* **529**(7587), 484–489.

Singh, Ajit P., and Gordon, Geoffrey J. 2008. Relational learning via collective matrix factorization. Pages 650–658 of: *Proceeding of the 14th ACM SIGKDD International Conference on Knowledge Discovery and Data Mining.*

Singh, Satinder P., Kearns, Michael J., Litman, Diane J., and Walker, Marilyn A. 1999. Reinforcement learning for spoken dialogue systems. Pages 956–962 of: *Advances in Neural Information Processing Systems.*

Smola, Alexander J., and Schölkopf, Bernhard. 2004. A tutorial on support vector regression. *Statistics and Computing,* **14**(3), 199–222.

Smola, Alex, Gretton, Arthur, Song, Le, and Schölkopf, Bernhard. 2007a. A Hilbert space embedding for distributions. Pages 13–31 of: *Proceedings of International Conference on Algorithmic Learning Theory.*

Smola, Alexander J., Gretton, Arthur, Song, Le, and Schölkopf, Bernhard. 2007b. A Hilbert space embedding for distributions. Pages 40–41 of: *Proceedings of the 10th International Conference on Discovery Science.*

Snel, Matthijs, and Whiteson, Shimon. 2014. Learning potential functions and their representations for multi-task reinforcement learning. *Autonomous Agents and Multi-Agent Systems,* **28**(4), 637–681.

Socher, Richard, Ganjoo, Milind, Manning, Christopher D., and Ng, Andrew Y. 2013a. Zero-shot learning through cross-modal transfer. Pages 935–943 of: *Advances in Neural Information Processing Systems.*

Socher, Richard, Perelygin, Alex, Wu, Jean Y., et al. 2013b. Recursive deep models for semantic compositionality over a sentiment treebank. Pages 1631–1642 of: *Proceedings of the 2013 Conference on Empirical Methods in Natural Language Processing*.

Søgaard, Anders, and Goldberg, Yoav. 2016. Deep multi-task learning with low level tasks supervised at lower layers. Pages 231–235 of: *Proceedings of the 54th Annual Meeting of the Association for Computational Linguistics*.

Solnon, Matthieu, Arlot, Sylvain, and Bach, Francis R. 2012. Multi-task regression using minimal penalties. *Journal of Machine Learning Research*, **13**, 2773–2812.

Song, Jinhua, Gao, Yang, Wang, Hao, and An, Bo. 2016. Measuring the distance between finite markov decision processes. Pages 468–476 of: *Proceedings of the 2016 International Conference on Autonomous Agents & Multiagent Systems*.

Sordoni, Alessandro, Bengio, Yoshua, Vahabi, Hossein, et al. 2015. A hierarchical recurrent encoder-decoder for generative context-aware query suggestion. Pages 553–562 of: *Proceedings of the 24th ACM International on Conference on Information and Knowledge Management*.

Srivastava, Nitish, Hinton, Geoffrey E., Krizhevsky, Alex, Sutskever, Ilya, and Salakhutdinov, Ruslan. 2014. Dropout: A simple way to prevent neural networks from overfitting. *Journal of Machine Learning Research*, **15**(1), 1929–1958.

Sugiyama, Masashi, Nakajima, Shinichi, Kashima, Hisashi, von Bünau, Paul, and Kawanabe, Motoaki. 2008. Direct importance estimation with model selection and its application to covariate shift adaptation. Pages 1433–1440 of: *Advances in Neural Information Processing Systems*.

Suk, Heung-Il, and Shen, Dinggang. 2013. Deep learning-based feature representation for AD/MCI classification. Pages 583–590 of: *Proceedings of the 16th International Conference on Medical Image Computing and Computer-Assisted Intervention*.

Suk, Heung-Il, Lee, Seong-Whan, and Shen, Dinggang. 2014. Hierarchical feature representation and multimodal fusion with deep learning for AD/MCI diagnosis. *NeuroImage*, **101**, 569–582.

Sun, Kai, Xie, Qizhe, and Yu, Kai. 2016. Recurrent polynomial network for dialogue state tracking. *Dialogue and Discourse*, **7**(3), 65–88.

Sutskever, Ilya, Vinyals, Oriol, and Le, Quoc V. 2014. Sequence to sequence learning with neural networks. Pages 3104–3112 of: *Advances in Neural Information Processing Systems*.

Sutton, Richard S., and Barto, Andrew G. 1998. *Reinforcement Learning – An Introduction*. MIT Press.

Sutton, Richard S., Precup, Doina, and Singh, Satinder. 1999. Between MDPs and semi-MDPs: A framework for temporal abstraction in reinforcement learning. *Artificial Intelligence*, **112**(1–2), 181–211.

Sweeney, Latanya. 2002. k-Anonymity: A model for protecting privacy. *International Journal of Uncertainty, Fuzziness and Knowledge-Based Systems*, **10**(5), 557–570.

Tai, Lei, Paolo, Giuseppe, and Liu, Ming. 2017. Virtual-to-real deep reinforcement learning: Continuous control of mobile robots for mapless navigation. Pages 31–36 of: *Proceedings of 2017 IEEE/RSJ International Conference on Intelligent Robots and Systems*.

Tamada, Yoshinori, Bannai, Hideo, Kanehisa, Minoru, and Miyano, Satoru. 2005. Utilizing evolutionary information and gene expression data for estimating gene networks with Bayesian network models. *Journal of Bioinformatics and Computational Biology*, **3**(6), 1295–1313.

Tan, Ben, Zhong, Erheng, Ng, Michael K., and Yang, Qiang. 2014. Mixed-transfer: Transfer learning over mixed graphs. Pages 208–216 of: *Proceedings of the SIAM International Conference on Data Mining*.

Tan, Ben, Song, Yangqiu, Zhong, Erheng, and Yang, Qiang. 2015. Transitive transfer learning. Pages 1155–1164 of: *Proceedings of the 21th ACM SIGKDD International Conference on Knowledge Discovery and Data Mining.*

Tan, Ben, Zhang, Yu, Pan, Sinno Jialin, and Yang, Qiang. 2017. Distant domain transfer learning. Pages 2604–2610 of: *Proceedings of the Thirty-First AAAI Conference on Artificial Intelligence.*

Tang, Duyu, Qin, Bing, Feng, Xiaocheng, and Liu, Ting. 2015. Target-dependent sentiment classification with long short term memory. *CoRR*, abs/1512.01100.

Taylor, Matthew E., and Stone, Peter. 2005. Behavior transfer for value-function-based reinforcement learning. Pages 53–59 of: *Proceedings of the 4th International Joint Conference on Autonomous Agents and Multiagent Systems.*

Taylor, Matthew E., and Stone, Peter. 2007. Cross-domain transfer for reinforcement learning. Pages 879–886 of: *Proceedings of the Twenty-Fourth International Conference on Machine Learning.*

Taylor, Matthew E., and Stone, Peter. 2009. Transfer learning for reinforcement learning domains: A survey. *Journal of Machine Learning Research*, **10**, 1633–1685.

Taylor, Matthew E., Stone, Peter, and Liu, Yaxin. 2005. Value functions for RL-based behavior transfer: A comparative study. Pages 880–885 of: *Proceedings of the Twentieth National Conference on Artificial Intelligence and the Seventeenth Innovative Applications of Artificial Intelligence Conference.*

Taylor, Matthew E., Whiteson, Shimon, and Stone, Peter. 2007. Transfer via inter-task mappings in policy search reinforcement learning. *Proceedings of the 6th International Joint Conference on Autonomous Agents and Multiagent Systems.*

Taylor, Matthew E., Jong, Nicholas K., and Stone, Peter. 2008a. Transferring instances for model-based reinforcement learning. Pages 488–505 of: *Proceedings of European Conference on Machine Learning and Practice of Knowledge Discovery in Databases.*

Taylor, Matthew E., Kuhlmann, Gregory, and Stone, Peter. 2008b. Autonomous transfer for reinforcement learning. Pages 283–290 of: *Proceedings of the 7th International Joint Conference on Autonomous Agents and Multiagent Systems.*

Tewari, Ambuj, Ravikumar, Pradeep K., and Dhillon, Inderjit S. 2011. Greedy algorithms for structurally constrained high dimensional problems. Pages 882–890 of: *Advances in Neural Information Processing Systems.*

Thomson, Blaise, and Young, Steve. 2010. Bayesian update of dialogue state: A POMDP framework for spoken dialogue systems. *Computer Speech and Language*, **24**(4), 562–588.

Thorndike, Edward. L., and S. Woodworth, R. 1901. The influence of improvement in one mental function upon the efficiency of other functions. II. The estimation of magnitudes. *Psychological Review*, **8**(01), 384–395.

Thrun, Sebastian. 1995. *Explanation-Based Neural Network Learning a Lifelong Learning Approach.* Ph.D. thesis, University of Bonn.

Thrun, Sebastian, and O'Sullivan, Joseph. 1996. Discovering structure in multiple learning tasks: The TC algorithm. Pages 489–497 of: *Proceedings of the 13th International Conference on Machine Learning.*

Tibshirani, Robert. 1996. Regression shrinkage and selection via the lasso. *Journal of the Royal Statistical Society. Series B (Methodological)*, **58**(1), 267–288.

Toffler, Alvin. 1970. *Future Shock.* Random House.

Tommasi, Tatiana, Orabona, Francesco, and Caputo, Barbara. 2010. Safety in numbers: Learning categories from few examples with multi model knowledge transfer. Pages 3081–3088 of: *Proceedings of IEEE Conference on Computer Vision and Pattern Recognition.*

Tommasi, Tatiana, Orabona, Francesco, and Caputo, Barbara. 2014. Learning categories from few examples with multi model knowledge transfer. *IEEE Transactions on Pattern Analysis and Machine Intelligence*, **36**(5), 928–941.

Tompson, Jonathan, Stein, Murphy, Lecun, Yann, and Perlin, Ken. 2014. Real-time continuous pose recovery of human hands using convolutional networks. *ACM Transactions on Graphics*, **33**(5), 169:1–169:10.

Topin, Nicholay, Haltmeyer, Nicholas, Squire, Shawn, et al. 2015. Portable option discovery for automated learning transfer in object-oriented Markov decision processes. Pages 3532–3536 of: Pages 3856–3864 of: *Proceedings of the Twenty-Fourth International Joint Conference on Artificial Intelligence*.

Toshniwal, Shubham, Tang, Hao, Lu, Liang, and Livescu, Karen. 2017. Multitask learning with low-level auxiliary tasks for encoder-decoded based speech recognition. *Proceedings of the 18th Annual Conference of the International Speech Communication Association*.

Tsuboi, Yuta, Kashima, Hisashi, Hido, Shohei, Bickel, Steffen, and Sugiyama, Masashi. 2009. Direct density ratio estimation for large-scale covariate shift adaptation. *Journal of Information Processing*, **17**, 138–155.

Tür, Gökhan. 2005. Model adaptation for spoken language understanding. Pages 41–44 of: *Proceedings of IEEE International Conference on Acoustics, Speech, and Signal Processing*.

Tür, Gökhan. 2006. Multitask learning for spoken language understanding. Pages 585–588 of: *Proceedings of IEEE International Conference on Acoustics Speech and Signal Processing*.

Tzeng, Eric, Hoffman, Judy, Zhang, Ning, Saenko, Kate, and Darrell, Trevor. 2014. Deep domain confusion: Maximizing for domain invariance. *CoRR*, abs/1412.3474.

Tzeng, Eric, Hoffman, Judy, Darrell, Trevor, and Saenko, Kate. 2015. Simultaneous deep transfer across domains and tasks. Pages 4068–4076 of: *Proceedings of IEEE International Conference on Computer Vision*.

Tzeng, Eric, Hoffman, Judy, Saenko, Kate, and Darrell, Trevor. 2017. Adversarial discriminative domain adaptation. Pages 2962–2971 of: *Proceedings of IEEE Conference on Computer Vision and Pattern Recognition*.

Vail, Douglas L., Veloso, Manuela M., and Lafferty, John D. 2007. Conditional random fields for activity recognition. In: *Proceedings of the Sixth International Joint Conference on Autonomous Agents and Multiagent Systems*.

van Haaren, Jan, Kolobov, Andrey, and Davis, Jesse. 2015. TODTLER: Two-order-deep transfer learning. Pages 3007–3015 of: *Proceedings of the Twenty-Ninth AAAI Conference on Artificial Intelligence*.

van Kasteren, Tim, Noulas, Athanasios K., Englebienne, Gwenn, and Kröse, Ben J. A. 2008. Accurate activity recognition in a home setting. Pages 1–9 of: *Proceedings of the 10th International Conference on Ubiquitous Computing*.

Vapnik, Vladimir. 1995. *The Nature of Statistical Learning Theory*. Springer.

Vapnik, Vladimir N. 1998. *Statistical Learning Theory*. Wiley-Interscience.

Venugopalan, Subhashini, Rohrbach, Marcus, Donahue, Jeffrey, et al. 2015a. Sequence to sequence – Video to text. Pages 4534–4542 of: *Proceedings of the IEEE International Conference on Computer Vision*.

Venugopalan, Subhashini, Xu, Huijuan, Donahue, Jeff, et al. 2015b. Translating videos to natural language using deep recurrent neural networks. Pages 1494–1504 of: *Proceedings of the 2015 Conference of the North American Chapter of the Association for Computational Linguistics: Human Language Technologies*.

Vincent, Pascal, Larochelle, Hugo, Bengio, Yoshua, and Manzagol, Pierre-Antoine. 2008. Extracting and composing robust features with denoising autoencoders. Pages 1096–1103 of: *Proceedings of the 25th International Conference on Machine Learning*.

Vinyals, Oriol, Toshev, Alexander, Bengio, Samy, and Erhan, Dumitru. 2015. Show and tell: A neural image caption generator. Pages 3156–3164 of: *Proceedings of IEEE Conference on Computer Vision and Pattern Recognition*.

Vinyals, Oriol, Blundell, Charles, Lillicrap, Tim, Kavukcuoglu, Koray, and Wierstra, Daan. 2016. Matching networks for one shot learning. Pages 3630–3638 of: *Advances in Neural Information Processing Systems*.

Vondrick, Carl, Pirsiavash, Hamed, and Torralba, Antonio. 2016. Generating videos with scene dynamics. Pages 613–621 of: *Advances In Neural Information Processing Systems*.

Walker, Marilyn A., Fromer, Jeanne C., and Narayanan, Shrikanth. 1998. Learning optimal dialogue strategies: A case study of a spoken dialogue agent for email. Pages 1345–1351 of: *Proceedings of the 36th Annual Meeting of the Association for Computational Linguistics and 17th International Conference on Computational Linguistics*.

Walker, Marilyn A., Stent, Amanda, Mairesse, François, and Prasad, Rashmi. 2007. Individual and domain adaptation in sentence planning for dialogue. *Journal of Artificial Intelligence Research*, **30**, 413–456.

Walsh, Thomas J., Li, Lihong, and Littman, Michael L. 2006. Transferring state abstractions between MDPS. *Proceedings of ICML Workshop on Structural Knowledge Transfer for Machine Learning*.

Wan, Xiang, Yang, Can, Yang, Qiang, et al. 2009. MegaSNPHunter: A learning approach to detect disease predisposition SNPs and high level interactions in genome wide association study. *BMC Bioinformatics*, **10**, 13.

Wang, Boyu, and Pineau, Joelle. 2016. Generalized dictionary for multitask learning with boosting. Pages 2097–2103 of: *Proceedings of the Twenty-Fifth International Joint Conference on Artificial Intelligence*.

Wang, Chang, and Mahadevan, Sridhar. 2009. Manifold alignment without correspondence. Pages 1273–1278 of: *Proceedings of the 21st International Joint Conference on Artificial Intelligence*.

Wang, Chang, and Mahadevan, Sridhar. 2011. Heterogeneous domain adaptation using manifold alignment. Pages 1541–1546 of: *Proceedings of the 22nd International Joint Conference on Artificial Intelligence*.

Wang, Daixin, Cui, Peng, and Zhu, Wenwu. 2018a. Deep asymmetric transfer network for unbalanced domain adaptation. Pages 443–450 of: *Proceedings of the 32th AAAI Conference on Artificial Intelligence*.

Wang, Hua, Huang, Heng, Nie, Feiping, and Ding, Chris. 2011. Cross-language web page classification via dual knowledge transfer using nonnegative matrix tri-factorization. Pages 933–942 of: *Proceedings of the 34th International ACM SIGIR Conference on Research and Development in Information Retrieval*.

Wang, Hua-Yan, and Yang, Qiang. 2011. Transfer learning by structural analogy. Pages 513–518 of: *Proceedings of the Twenty-Fifth AAAI Conference on Artificial Intelligence*.

Wang, Hua-Yan, Zheng, Vincent Wenchen, Zhao, Junhui, and Yang, Qiang. 2010. Indoor localization in multi-floor environments with reduced effort. Pages 244–252 of: *Proceedings of the 8th Annual IEEE International Conference on Pervasive Computing and Communications*.

Wang, Jialei, Kolar, Mladen, and Srebro, Nathan. 2016a. Distributed multi-task learning. Pages 751–760 of: *Proceedings of the 19th International Conference on Artificial Intelligence and Statistics*.

Wang, Jindong, Chen, Yiqiang, Hao, Shuji, Peng, Xiaohui, and Hu, Lisha. 2017a. Deep learning for sensor-based activity recognition: A survey. *CoRR*, abs/1707.03502.

Wang, Jindong, Chen, Yiqiang, Hu, Lisha, Peng, Xiaohui, and Yu, Philip S. 2018b. Stratified transfer learning for cross-domain activity recognition. *CoRR*, abs/1801.00820.

Wang, Sheng, Li, Zhen, Yu, Yizhou, and Xu, Jinbo. 2017b. Folding membrane proteins by deep transfer learning. *CoRR*, abs/1708.08407.

Wang, Shenlong, Zhang, Lei, Liang, Yan, and Pan, Quan. 2012. Semi-coupled dictionary learning with applications to image super-resolution and photo-sketch synthesis. Pages 2216–2223 of: *Proceedings of the IEEE Conference on Computer Vision and Pattern Recognition*.

Wang, Shuai, Chen, Zhiyuan, and Liu, Bing. 2016b. Mining aspect-specific opinion using a holistic lifelong topic model. Pages 167–176 of: *Proceedings of the 25th International Conference on World Wide Web*.

Wang, Shuohang, Yu, Mo, Guo, Xiaoxiao, et al. 2018c. R^3: Reinforced ranker-reader for open-domain question answering. Pages 5981–5988 of: *Proceedings of the Thirty-Second AAAI Conference on Artificial Intelligence*.

Wang, Sida, and Manning, Christopher D. 2012. Baselines and bigrams: Simple, good sentiment and topic classification. Pages 90–94 of: *Proceedings of the 50th Annual Meeting of the Association for Computational Linguistics*.

Wang, Wenhui, Yang, Nan, Wei, Furu, Chang, Baobao, and Zhou, Ming. 2017c. Gated self-matching networks for reading comprehension and question answering. Pages 189–198 of: *Proceedings of the 55th Annual Meeting of the Association for Computational Linguistics*.

Wang, Xin, Bi, Jinbo, Yu, Shipeng, and Sun, Jiangwen. 2014. On multiplicative multitask feature learning. Pages 2411–2419 of: *Advances in Neural Information Processing Systems*.

Wang, Xuezhi, and Schneider, Jeff G. 2015. Generalization bounds for transfer learning under model shift. Pages 922–931 of: *Proceedings of the Thirty-First Conference on Uncertainty in Artificial Intelligence*.

Wang, Yang, Gu, Quanquan, and Brown, Donald E. 2018d. Differentially private hypothesis transfer learning. Pages 811–826 of: *Proceedings of European Conference on Machine Learning and Knowledge Discovery in Databases*.

Wang, Zhuoran, and Lemon, Oliver. 2013. A simple and generic belief tracking mechanism for the dialog state tracking challenge: On the believability of observed information. Pages 423–432 of: *Proceedings of the 14th Annual Meeting of the Special Interest Group on Discourse and Dialogue*.

Wei, Ying, Zhu, Yin, Leung, Cane Wing-ki, Song, Yangqiu, and Yang, Qiang. 2016a. Instilling social to physical: Co-regularized heterogeneous transfer learning. Pages 1338–1344 of: *Proceedings of the 30th AAAI Conference on Artificial Intelligence*.

Wei, Ying, Zheng, Yu, and Yang, Qiang. 2016b. Transfer knowledge between cities. Pages 1905–1914 of: *Proceedings of the 22nd ACM SIGKDD International Conference on Knowledge Discovery and Data Mining*.

Wei, Ying, Zhang, Yu, Huang, Junzhou, and Yang, Qiang. 2018. Transfer learning via learning to transfer. Pages 5072–5081 of: *Proceedings of the 35th International Conference on Machine Learning*.

Weinberger, Kilian Q., Sha, Fei, and Saul, Lawrence K. 2004. Learning a kernel matrix for nonlinear dimensionality reduction. *Proceedings of the Twenty-First International Conference on Machine Learning*.

Wen, Tsung-Hsien, Heidel, Aaron, Lee, Hung-yi, Tsao, Yu, and Lee, Lin-Shan. 2013. Recurrent neural network based language model personalization by social network crowdsourcing. Pages 2703–2707 of: *Proceedings of the 14th Annual Conference of the International Speech Communication Association*.

Wen, Tsung-Hsien, Gašić, Milica, Mrkšic, Nikola, et al. 2015a. Semantically conditioned LSTM-based natural language generation for spoken dialogue systems. Pages 1711–1721 of: *Proceedings of the 2015 Conference on Empirical Methods in Natural Language Processing*.

Wen, Tsung-Hsien, Gašić, Milica, Mrkšic, Nikola, et al. 2015b. Toward multi-domain language generation using recurrent neural networks. *NIPS Workshop on ML for SLU and Interaction*.

Wen, Tsung-Hsien, Gašić, Milica, Mrkšic, Nikola, et al. 2016. Multi-domain neural network language generation for spoken dialogue systems. Pages 120–129 of: *Proceedings of the 2016 Conference of the North American Chapter of the Association for Computational Linguistics: Human Language Technologies*.

Widmer, Christian, Leiva, Jose, Altun, Yasemin, and Rätsch, Gunnar. 2010a. Leveraging sequence classification by taxonomy-based multitask learning. Pages 522–534 of: *Proceedings of 14th the Annual International Conference on Research in Computational Molecular Biology*.

Widmer, Christian, Toussaint, Nora C., Altun, Yasemin, Kohlbacher, Oliver, and Rätsch, Gunnar. 2010b. Novel machine learning methods for MHC Class I binding prediction. Pages 98–109 of: *Proceedings of the 5th IAPR International Conference on Pattern Recognition in Bioinformatics*.

Widmer, Christian, Toussaint, Nora C., Altun, Yasemin, and Rätsch, Gunnar. 2010c. Inferring latent task structure for multitask learning by multiple kernel learning. *BMC Bioinformatics*, 1(Suppl. 8), 55.

Williams, Jason. 2013. Multi-domain learning and generalization in dialog state tracking. Pages 433–441 of: *Proceedings of the 14th Annual Meeting of the Special Interest Group on Discourse and Dialogue*.

Williams, Jason D. 2008a. The best of both worlds: Unifying conventional dialog systems and POMDPs. Pages 1173–1176 of: *Proceedings of the 9th Annual Conference of the International Speech Communication Association*.

Williams, Jason D. 2008b. Integrating expert knowledge into POMDP optimization for spoken dialog systems. *Proceedings of the AAAI Workshop on Advancements in POMDP Solvers*.

Wilson, Aaron, Fern, Alan, Ray, Soumya, and Tadepalli, Prasad. 2007. Multi-task reinforcement learning: A hierarchical Bayesian approach. Pages 1015–1022 of: *Proceedings of the Twenty-Fourth International Conference on Machine Learning*.

Winston, Patrick H. 1980. Learning and reasoning by analogy. *Communications of the ACM*, 23(12), 689–703.

Wong, Catherine, Houlsby, Neil, Lu, Yifeng, and Gesmundo, Andrea. 2018. Transfer learning with neural AutoML. Pages 8366–8375 of: *Advances in Neural Information Processing Systems 31*.

Wood, Erroll, Baltrušaitis, Tadas, Morency, Louis-Philippe, Robinson, Peter, and Bulling, Andreas. 2016. Learning an appearance-based gaze estimator from one million synthesised images. Pages 131–138 of: *Proceedings of the Ninth Biennial ACM Symposium on Eye Tracking Research and Applications*.

Wu, Pengcheng, and Dietterich, Thomas G. 2004. Improving SVM accuracy by training on auxiliary data sources. Pages 111–117 of: *Proceedings of the 21st International Conference on Machine Learning*.

Wu, Shuangzhi, Zhang, Dongdong, Yang, Nan, Li, Mu, and Zhou, Ming. 2017. Sequence-to-dependency neural machine translation. Pages 698–707 of: *Proceedings of the 55th Annual Meeting of the Association for Computational Linguistics*.

Wu, Xinxiao, Wang, Han, Liu, Cuiwei, and Jia, Yunde. 2013. Cross-view action recognition over heterogeneous feature spaces. Pages 609–616 of: *Proceedings of the IEEE International Conference on Computer Vision*.

Xie, Liyang, Baytas, Inci M., Lin, Kaixiang, and Zhou, Jiayu. 2017. Privacy-preserving distributed multi-task learning with asynchronous updates. Pages 1195–1204 of: *Proceedings of the 23rd ACM SIGKDD International Conference on Knowledge Discovery and Data Mining*.

Xie, Michael, Jean, Neal, Burke, Marshall, Lobell, David, and Ermon, Stefano. 2016. Transfer learning from deep features for remote sensing and poverty mapping. Pages 3929–3935 of: *Proceedings of the Thirtieth AAAI Conference on Artificial Intelligence*.

Xing, Eric P., Jordan, Michael I., and Karp, Richard M. 2001. Feature selection for high-dimensional genomic microarray data. Pages 601–608 of: *Proceedings of the 8th International Conference on Machine Learning*.

Xu, Jiaolong, Ramos, Sebastian, Vázquez, David, and López, Antonio M. 2014a. Domain adaptation of deformable part-based models. *IEEE Transactions on Pattern Analysis and Machine Intelligence*, **36**(12), 2367–2380.

Xu, Kelvin, Ba, Jimmy, Kiros, Ryan, et al. 2015. Show, attend and tell: Neural image caption generation with visual attention. Pages 2048–2057 of: *Proceedings of the 32nd International Conference on Machine Learning*.

Xu, Qian, and Yang, Qiang. 2011. A survey of transfer and multitask learning in bioinformatics. *Journal of Computing Science and Engineering*, **5**(3), 257–268.

Xu, Qian, Xiang, Evan Wei, and Yang, Qiang. 2010. Protein–protein interaction prediction via collective matrix factorization. Pages 62–67 of: *Proceedings of IEEE International Conference on Bioinformatics and Biomedicine*.

Xu, Qian, Pan, Sinno Jialin, Xue, Hannah Hong, and Yang, Qiang. 2011. Multitask learning for protein subcellular location prediction. *IEEE/ACM Transactions on Computational Biology and Bioinformatics*, **8**(3), 748–759.

Xu, Yonghui, Pan, Sinno Jialin, Xiong, Hui, Wu, et al. 2017. A unified framework for metric transfer learning. *IEEE Transactions on Knowledge and Data Engineering*, **29**(6), 1158–1171.

Xu, Zheng, Li, Wen, Niu, Li, and Xu, Dong. 2014b. Exploiting low-rank structure from latent domains for domain generalization. Pages 628–643 of: *Proceedings of the 13th European Conference on Computer Vision*.

Xu, Zhixiang, Huang, Gao, Weinberger, Kilian Q., and Zheng, Alice X. 2014c. Gradient boosted feature selection. Pages 522–531 of: *Proceedings of the 20th ACM SIGKDD International Conference on Knowledge Discovery and Data Mining*. ACM.

Xue, Ya, Liao, Xuejun, Carin, Lawrence, and Krishnapuram, Balaji. 2007. Multi-task learning for classification with Dirichlet process priors. *Journal of Machine Learning Research*, **8**, 35–63.

Yamada, Makoto, Jitkrittum, Wittawat, Sigal, Leonid, Xing, Eric P., and Sugiyama, Masashi. 2014. High-dimensional feature selection by feature-wise kernelized lasso. *Neural Computation*, **26**(1), 185–207.

Yang, Bishan, and Mitchell, Tom. 2017. A joint sequential and relational model for frame-semantic parsing. Pages 1247–1256 of: *Proceedings of the 2017 Conference on Empirical Methods in Natural Language Processing*.

Yang, Can, He, Zengyou, Wan, Xiang, et al. 2008. SNPHarvester: A filtering-based approach for detecting epistatic interactions in genome-wide association studies. *Bioinformatics*, **25**(4), 504–511.

Yang, Jian, Zhang, David, Yang, Jing-Yu, and Niu, Ben. 2007a. Globally maximizing, locally minimizing: Unsupervised discriminant projection with applications to face and palm biometrics. *IEEE Transactions on Pattern Analysis and Machine Intelligence*, **29**(4), 650–664.

Yang, Jianchao, Wright, John, Huang, Thomas S., and Ma, Yi. 2010. Image super-resolution via sparse representation. *IEEE Transactions on Image Processing*, **19**(11), 2861–2873.

Yang, Jun, Yan, Rong, and Hauptmann, Alexander G. 2007b. Adapting SVM classifiers to data with shifted distributions. Pages 69–76 of: *Workshops Proceedings of the 7th IEEE International Conference on Data Mining*.

Yang, Jun, Yan, Rong, and Hauptmann, Alexander G. 2007c. Cross-domain video concept detection using adaptive SVMs. Pages 188–197 of: *Proceedings of the 15th ACM International Conference on Multimedia*.

Yang, Liu, Hanneke, Steve, and Carbonell, Jaime G. 2013. A theory of transfer learning with applications to active learning. *Machine Learning*, **90**(2), 161–189.

Yang, Min, Zhao, Zhou, Zhao, Wei, et al. 2017. Personalized response generation via domain adaptation. Pages 1021–1024 of: *Proceedings of the 40th International ACM SIGIR Conference on Research and Development in Information Retrieval*.

Yang, Qiang, Chen, Yuqiang, Xue, Gui-Rong, Dai, Wenyuan, and Yu, Yong. 2009. Heterogeneous transfer learning for image clustering via the social web. Pages 1–9 of: *Proceedings of the Joint Conference of the 47th Annual Meeting of the ACL and the 4th International Joint Conference on Natural Language Processing of the AFNLP*.

Yang, Wen Hui, Dai, Dao Qing, and Yan, Hong. 2011. Finding correlated biclusters from gene expression data. *IEEE Transaction on Knowledge and Data Engineering*, **23**(4), 568–584.

Yang, Zhilin, Salakhutdinov, Ruslan, and Cohen, William. 2016. Multi-task cross-lingual sequence tagging from scratch. *CoRR*, abs/1603.06270.

Yao, Kaisheng, Zweig, Geoffrey, Hwang, Mei-Yuh, Shi, Yangyang, and Yu, Dong. 2013. Recurrent neural networks for language understanding. Pages 2524–2528 of: *Proceedings of the 14th Annual Conference of the International Speech Communication Association*.

Yao, Kaisheng, Peng, Baolin, Zhang, Yu, et al. 2014. Spoken language understanding using long short-term memory neural networks. Pages 189–194 of: *Proceedings of IEEE Spoken Language Technology Workshop*.

Yao, Quanming, Wang, Mengshuo, Escalante, Hugo Jair, et al. 2018. Taking human out of learning applications: A survey on automated machine learning. *CoRR*, abs/1810.13306.

Yazdani, Majid, and Henderson, James. 2015. A model of zero-shot learning of spoken language understanding. Pages 244–249 of: *Proceedings of the 2015 Conference on Empirical Methods in Natural Language Processing*.

Ye, Jihang, Cheng, Hong, Zhu, Zhe, and Chen, Minghua. 2013. Predicting positive and negative links in signed social networks by transfer learning. Pages 1477–1488 of: *Proceedings of the 22nd International Conference on World Wide Web*.

Yi, Zili, Zhang, Hao, Tan, Ping, and Gong, Minglun. 2017. DualGAN: Unsupervised dual learning for image-to-image translation. Pages 2849–2857 of: *Proceedings of the IEEE Conference on Computer Vision and Pattern Recognition*.

Yin, Haiyan, and Pan, Sinno Jialin. 2017. Knowledge transfer for deep reinforcement learning with hierarchical experience replay. Pages 1640–1646 of: *Proceedings of the Thirty-First AAAI Conference on Artificial Intelligence*.

Yin, Jie, Yang, Qiang, and Ni, Lionel M. 2005. Adaptive temporal radio maps for indoor location estimation. Pages 85–94 of: *Proceedings of the 3rd IEEE International Conference on Pervasive Computing and Communications*.

Yosinski, Jason, Clune, Jeff, Bengio, Yoshua, and Lipson, Hod. 2014. How transferable are features in deep neural networks? Pages 3320–3328 of: *Advances in Neural Information Processing Systems*.

Young, Steve, Gašić, Milica, Keizer, Simon, Mairesse, et al. 2010. The hidden information state model: A practical framework for POMDP-based spoken dialogue management. *Computer Speech and Language*, **24**(2), 150–174.

Young, Steve, Gašić, Milica, Thomson, Blaise, and Williams, Jason D. 2013. POMDP-based statistical spoken dialog systems: A review. *Proceedings of the IEEE*, **101**(5), 1160–1179.

Yu, Lantao, Zhang, Weinan, Wang, Jun, and Yu, Yong. 2017. SeqGAN: Sequence generative adversarial nets with policy gradient. Pages 2852–2858 of: *Proceedings of the Thirty-First AAAI Conference on Artificial Intelligence*.

Yu, Zhou, Wu, Fei, Yang, Yi, et al. 2014. Discriminative coupled dictionary hashing for fast cross-media retrieval. Pages 395–404 of: *Proceedings of the 37th International ACM SIGIR Conference on Research and Development in Information Retrieval*.

Zadrozny, Bianca. 2004. Learning and evaluating classifiers under sample selection bias. *Proceedings of the Twenty-First International Conference on Machine Learning*.

Zhang, Chao, Zhang, Lei, and Ye, Jieping. 2012. Generalization bounds for domain adaptation. *Advances in Neural Information Processing Systems*.

Zhang, Duo, Mei, Qiaozhu, and Zhai, Chengxiang. 2010a. Cross-lingual latent topic extraction. Pages 1128–1137 of: *Proceedings of the 48th Annual Meeting of the Association for Computational Linguistics*.

Zhang, Jing, Ding, Zewei, Li, Wanqing, and Ogunbona, Philip. 2018. Importance weighted adversarial nets for partial domain adaptation. Pages 8156–8164 of: *Proceedings of the IEEE Conference on Computer Vision and Pattern Recognition*.

Zhang, Jingwei, Springenberg, Jost Tobias, Boedecker, Joschka, and Burgard, Wolfram. 2017a. Deep reinforcement learning with successor features for navigation across similar environments. Pages 2371–2378 of: *Proceedings of 2017 IEEE/RSJ International Conference on Intelligent Robots and Systems*.

Zhang, Jintao, and Huan, Jun. 2012. Inductive multi-task learning with multiple view data. Pages 543–551 of: *Proceedings of the 18th ACM SIGKDD International Conference on Knowledge Discovery and Data Mining*.

Zhang, Kai, Gray, Joe W., and Parvin, Bahram. 2010b. Sparse multitask regression for identifying common mechanism of response to therapeutic targets. *Bioinformatics*, **26**, i97–i105.

Zhang, Kai, Zheng, Vincent W., Wang, Qiaojun, et al. 2013. Covariate shift in Hilbert space: A solution via surrogate kernels. Pages 388–395 of: *Proceedings of the 30th International Conference on Machine Learning*.

Zhang, Lei, Zuo, Wangmeng, and Zhang, David. 2016. LSDT: Latent sparse domain transfer learning for visual adaptation. *IEEE Transactions on Image Processing*, **25**(3), 1177–1191.

Zhang, Tong. 2002. Covering number bounds for certain regularized linear function classes. *Journal of Machine Learning Research*, **2**, 527–550.

Zhang, Weinan, Liu, Ting, Wang, Yifa, and Zhu, Qingfu. 2017b. Neural personalized response generation as domain adaptation. *CoRR*, abs/1701.02073.

Zhang, Wenlu, Li, Rongjian, Zeng, Tao, Sun, et al. 2015a. Deep model based transfer and multi-task learning for biological image analysis. Pages 1475–1484 of: *Proceedings of the 21th ACM SIGKDD International Conference on Knowledge Discovery and Data Mining.*

Zhang, Wenlu, Li, Rongjian, Zeng, Tao, et al. 2017c. Deep model based transfer and multi-task learning for biological image analysis. *IEEE Transactions on Big Data.*

Zhang, Xiao-Lei. 2015a. Convex discriminative multitask clustering. *IEEE Transactions on Pattern Analysis and Machine Intelligence,* **37**(1), 28–40.

Zhang, Xucong, Sugano, Yusuke, Fritz, Mario, and Bulling, Andreas. 2015b. Appearance-based gaze estimation in the wild. Pages 4511–4520 of: *Proceedings of the IEEE Conference on Computer Vision and Pattern Recognition.*

Zhang, Yi, and Schneider, Jeff G. 2010. Learning multiple tasks with a sparse matrix-normal penalty. Pages 2550–2558 of: *Advances in Neural Information Processing Systems.*

Zhang, Yongfeng, Ai, Qingyao, Chen, Xu, and Croft, W. Bruce. 2017d. Joint representation learning for top-N recommendation with heterogenous information sources. Pages 1449–1458 of: *Proceedings of the 2017 ACM on Conference on Information and Knowledge Management.*

Zhang, Yu. 2013. Heterogeneous-neighborhood-based multi-task local learning algorithms. Pages 1896–1904 of: *Advances in Neural Information Processing Systems.*

Zhang, Yu. 2015b. Multi-task learning and algorithmic stability. Pages 3181–3187 of: *Proceedings of the 29th AAAI Conference on Artificial Intelligence.*

Zhang, Yu. 2015c. Parallel multi-task learning. Pages 629–638 of: *Proceedings of the IEEE International Conference on Data Mining.*

Zhang, Yu, and Yang, Qiang. 2017a. Learning sparse task relations in multi-task learning. Pages 2914–2920 of: *Proceedings of the 31st AAAI Conference on Artificial Intelligence.*

Zhang, Yu, and Yang, Qiang. 2017b. A survey on multi-task learning. *CoRR,* abs/1707.08114v2.

Zhang, Yu, and Yeung, Dit-Yan. 2009. Semi-supervised multi-task regression. Pages 617–631 of: *Proceedings of European Conference on Machine Learning and Knowledge Discovery in Databases.*

Zhang, Yu, and Yeung, Dit-Yan. 2010a. A convex formulation for learning task relationships in multi-task learning. Pages 733–742 of: *Proceedings of the 26th Conference on Uncertainty in Artificial Intelligence.*

Zhang, Yu, and Yeung, Dit-Yan. 2010b. Multi-task learning using generalized t process. Pages 964–971 of: *Proceedings of the 13th International Conference on Artificial Intelligence and Statistics.*

Zhang, Yu, and Yeung, Dit-Yan. 2012. Multi-task boosting by exploiting task relationships. Pages 697–710 of: *Proceedings of European Conference on Machine Learning and Principles and Practice of Knowledge Discovery in Dtabases.*

Zhang, Yu, and Yeung, Dit-Yan. 2013a. Learning high-order task relationships in multi-task learning. Pages 1917–1923 of: *Proceedings of the 23rd International Joint Conference on Artificial Intelligence.*

Zhang, Yu, and Yeung, Dit-Yan. 2013b. Multilabel relationship learning. *ACM Transactions on Knowledge Discovery from Data,* **7**(2), article 7.

Zhang, Yu, and Yeung, Dit-Yan. 2014. A regularization approach to learning task relationships in multitask learning. *ACM Transactions on Knowledge Discovery from Data,* **8**(3), article 12.

Zhang, Yu, Yeung, Dit-Yan, and Xu, Qian. 2010c. Probabilistic multi-task feature selection. Pages 2559–2567 of: *Advances in Neural Information Processing Systems.*

Zhang, Zhanpeng, Luo, Ping, Loy, Chen Change, and Tang, Xiaoou. 2014. Facial landmark detection by deep multi-task learning. Pages 94–108 of: *Proceedings of the 13th European Conference on Computer Vision.*

Zhao, Junbo Jake, Mathieu, Michaël, and LeCun, Yann. 2016. Energy-based generative adversarial network. *CoRR*, abs/1609.03126.

Zhao, Kai, and Huang, Liang. 2017. Joint syntacto-discourse parsing and syntacto-discourse treebank. Pages 2117–2123 of: *Proceedings of the 2017 Conference on Empirical Methods in Natural Language Processing.*

Zhao, Xiangyu, Zhang, Liang, Ding, Zhuoye, et al. 2018. Deep reinforcement learning for list-wise recommendations. *CoRR*, abs/1801.00209.

Zheng, Vincent W., Pan, Sinno J., Yang, Qiang, and Pan, Jeffrey J. 2008a. Transferring multi-device localization models using latent multi-task learning. Pages 1427–1432 of: *Proceedings of the 23rd AAAI Conference on Artificial Intelligence.*

Zheng, Vincent W., Xiang, Evan Wei, Yang, Qiang, and Shen, Dou. 2008b. Transferring localization models over time. Pages 1421–1426 of: *Proceedings of the Twenty-Third AAAI Conference on Artificial Intelligence.*

Zheng, Vincent W., Cao, Hong, Gao, Shenghua, et al. 2016. Cold-start heterogenous-device wireless localization. Pages 1429–1435 of: *Proceedings of the 30th AAAI Conference on Artificial Intelligence.*

Zheng, Vincent Wenchen, Hu, Derek Hao, and Yang, Qiang. 2009. Cross-domain activity recognition. Pages 61–70 of: *Proceedings of the 11th International Conference on Ubiquitous Computing.*

Zhou, Guangyou, Xie, Zhiwen, Huang, Jimmy Xiangji, and He, Tingting. 2016. Bi-transferring deep neural networks for domain adaptation. Pages 322–332 of: *Proceedings of the 54th Annual Meeting of the Association for Computational Linguistics.*

Zhou, Joey Tianyi, Pan, Sinno Jialin, Tsang, Ivor W., and Yan, Yan. 2014a. Hybrid heterogeneous transfer learning through deep learning. Pages 2213–2219 of: *Proceedings of the 28th AAAI Conference on Artificial Intelligence.*

Zhou, Joey Tianyi, Tsang, Ivor W., Pan, Sinno Jialin, and Tan, Mingkui. 2014b. Heterogeneous domain adaptation for multiple classes. Pages 1095–1103 of: *Proceedings of the Seventeenth International Conference on Artificial Intelligence and Statistics.*

Zhu, Fan, Shao, Ling, and Yu, Mengyang. 2014. Cross-modality submodular dictionary learning for information retrieval. Pages 1479–1488 of: *Proceedings of the 23rd ACM International Conference on Information and Knowledge Management.*

Zhu, Feng, Wang, Yan, Chen, Chaochao, et al. 2018. A deep framework for cross-domain and cross-system recommendations. Pages 3711–3717 of: *Proceedings of the 27th International Joint Conference on Artificial Intelligence.*

Zhu, Jun-Yan, Park, Taesung, Isola, Phillip, and Efros, Alexei A. 2017. Unpaired image-to-image translation using cycle-consistent adversarial networks. Pages 2223–2232 of: *Proceedings of the IEEE Conference on Computer Vision and Pattern Recognition.*

Zhu, Xiaojin. 2005. *Semi-supervised Learning Literature Survey*, Tech. Report, Computer Sciences TR 1530, University of Wisconsin-Madison.

Zhu, Yin, Chen, Yuqiang, Lu, Zhongqi, et al. 2011. Heterogeneous transfer learning for image classification. *Proceedings of the 25th AAAI Conference on Artificial Intelligence.*

Zhuang, Yue Ting, Wang, Yan Fei, Wu, Fei, Zhang, Yin, and Lu, Weiming. 2013. Supervised coupled dictionary learning with group structures for multi-modal retrieval. *Proceedings of the 27th AAAI Conference on Artificial Intelligence.*

Zhuo, Hankz Hankui, and Yang, Qiang. 2014. Action-model acquisition for planning via transfer learning. *Artificial Intelligence*, **212**, 80–103.

Zilka, Lukas, and Jurcicek, Filip. 2015. Incremental LSTM-based dialog state tracker. Pages 757–762 of: *Proceedings of IEEE Workshop on Automatic Speech Recognition and Understanding.*

Ziser, Yftah, and Reichart, Roi. 2017. Neural structural correspondence learning for domain adaptation. Pages 400–410 of: *Proceedings of the 21st Conference on Computational Natural Language Learning.*

Ziser, Yftah, and Reichart, Roi. 2018. Pivot based language modeling for improved neural domain adapation. Pages 1241–1251 of: *Proceedings of the 2018 Conference of the North American Chapter of the Association for Computational Linguistics: Human Language Technologies.*

Zoph, Barret, and Knight, Kevin. 2016. Multi-source neural translation. Pages 30–34 of: *Proceedings of The 2016 Conference of the North American Chapter of the Association for Computational Linguistics: Human Language Technologies.*

Zoph, Barret, Yuret, Deniz, May, Jonathan, and Knight, Kevin. 2016. Transfer learning for low-resource neural machine translation. *CoRR*, abs/1604.02201.

Zweig, Alon, and Weinshall, Daphna. 2013. Hierarchical regularization cascade for joint learning. Pages 37–45 of: *Proceedings of the 30th International Conference on Machine Learning.*

Index

Printed in the United States
by Baker & Taylor Publisher Services